Updated Third Edition

THE DISNEYLAND® ENCYCLOPEDIA

THE UNOFFICIAL, UNAUTHORIZED, AND UNPRECEDENTED HISTORY OF EVERY LAND, ATTRACTION, RESTAURANT, SHOP, AND MAJOR EVENT IN THE ORIGINAL MAGIC KINGDOM®

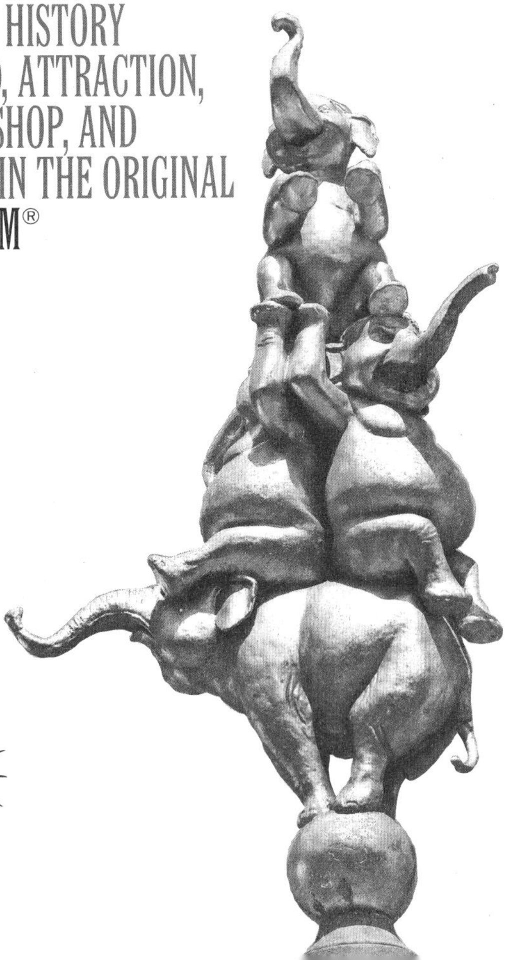

SANTA MONICA PRESS

Published by:

Santa Monica Press LLC
P.O. Box 850
Solana Beach, CA 92075
1-800-784-9553
www.santamonicapress.com
books@santamonicapress.com

MIX
Paper from
responsible sources
FSC® C011935

Printed in the United States

Santa Monica Press books are available at special quantity discounts when purchased in bulk by corporations, organizations, or groups. Please call our Special Sales department at 1-800-784-9553.

This book is intended to provide general information. The publisher, author, distributor, and copyright owner are not engaged in rendering professional advice or services. The publisher, author, distributor, and copyright owner are not liable or responsible to any person or group with respect to any loss, illness, or injury caused or alleged to be caused by the information found in this book.

ISBN-13 978-1-59580-090-9

Library of Congress Cataloging-in-Publication Data

Names: Strodder, Chris, 1956- author.
Title: The Disneyland encyclopedia : the unofficial, unauthorized, and
  unprecedented history of every land, attraction, restaurant, shop, and
  major event in the original magic kingdom / Chris Strodder.
Description: Solana Beach, CA : Santa Monica Press, 2017.
Identifiers: LCCN 2016055735 (print) | LCCN 2017004243 (ebook) | ISBN
  9781595800909 (paperback) | ISBN 9781595807984
Subjects: LCSH: Disneyland (Calif.)--Encyclopedias. | BISAC: TRAVEL /
  Amusement & Theme Parks. | TRAVEL / United States / West / Pacific (AK,
  CA, HI, NV, OR, WA). | TRAVEL / Special Interest / Family. | SOCIAL
  SCIENCE / Popular Culture.
Classification: LCC GV1853.3.C2 S87 2017 (print) | LCC GV1853.3.C2 (ebook) |
  DDC 791.06/879496--dc23
LC record available at https://lccn.loc.gov/2016055735

Cover and interior design and production by Future Studio

THE DISNEYLAND® ENCYCLOPEDIA

Updated Third Edition

THE **UN**OFFICIAL, AUTHORIZED, AND PRECEDENTED HISTORY OF EVERY LAND, ATTRACTION, RESTAURANT, SHOP, AND MAJOR EVENT IN THE ORIGINAL MAGIC KINGDOM®

SANTA MONICA PRESS

CHRIS STRODDER

ILLUSTRATED MAPS BY TRISTAN TANG

CONTENTS

ENTRANCE →

Introduction to
the Third Edition

"There are still plenty of avenues to be explored."
—Walt Disney

P aralleling Disneyland's continuous growth, this new edition of *The Disneyland Encyclopedia* is the largest yet. Since the first edition appeared in 2008 with 502 entries, I've added another hundred. There are fifty-five (now *there's* a nice number!) brand-new entries for this third edition. Among them are new structures that have recently joined or will soon join the park (including Star Wars Land); new exhibits (see Season of the Force); new events and parades (Egg-stravaganza, Paint the Night, etc.); new profiles of Disneyland's Imagineers and performers (like Tony Baxter, Steve Martin, and the Side Street Strutters); new entries for movies and books with scenes set in Disneyland (*Saving Mr. Banks* and *Little Man of Disneyland*); and all-new individual entries for some longtime Disneyland favorites that I'm excited to include for the first time (Big Thunder Trail, Fort Wilderness, Mailboxes, Mouse Ears, Windows of Enchantment, and more).

In addition, I've added some topics that aren't exactly inside Disneyland, but they're still important to its history: entries for Harbor Boulevard, the Heliports, and *run*Disney, for instance, plus new profiles of some influential "outsiders" who helped shape and support the park (such as Arrow Development, Ray Bradbury, and Keith Murdoch). A few new entries might seem a little unusual—I'm looking at you, Happiness—but trust me, they all contribute to this attempt at explicating the complex and fluid history of Disneyland.

If you're new to *The Disneyland Encyclopedia*, here's quick recap of what it is and does. While most Disneyland books group topics together geographically (which means you've got to know where something is if you want to read about it) or chronologically (which means you have to jump from chapter to chapter to find out how something has changed over the decades), this book presents A–Z entries that tell the full story of an attraction, person, or event, self-contained within its own entry. Thus, skipping around isn't necessary—if you know the name of what you're looking for, you can go straight to its alphabetical entry and read all about it. Naturally, you can still skip around if you want to, and the book even helps you do that by bold-facing related entries so you can flip to them easily. In addition, our index of over 4,000 listings should help you find any proper noun in the book.

Readers already familiar with this encyclopedia might notice that the sixty sidebars in the second edition are missing from this one. Actually, they're not missing, they've just been relocated to our sister publication: *The Disneyland Book of Lists*, a photo-laden book published in 2015 that includes 250 lists of information, quotes, rankings, trivia, jokes, celebrities, urban myths, and much more from Disneyland's history. Here in *The Disneyland Encyclopedia*, you'll notice new "Mouscellany" sidebars sprinkled throughout the text—almost 200 of them—that supplement a nearby entry with a bonus fact, a considered opinion, or a little extra pixie dust.

That *The Disneyland Encyclopedia* continues to change is appropriate because the book itself is the product of a lifelong desire to track the changes in Disneyland. I've been visiting and studying this park steadily since 1966 (so long ago that the old Flying Saucers were still hovering in Tomorrowland). Even as a kid walking in for the first time, I already could tell that Disneyland was the world's most influential and famous theme park. I quickly realized that the park wasn't just astonishingly fun, it was also the happiest, cleanest, most courteous, and best-planned public place I'd ever been in. Of course, everyone knows these aspects of Disneyland, even if they've never been there. You don't have to be a genius, or even out of elementary school, to know Disneyland's reputation, and the learning curve for "getting" Disneyland once you're there can be measured in minutes. But once you begin to realize how much and how often the park changes, and you start to see the historic arc of its evolution, the learning curve for truly understanding Disneyland at its most subtle and significant levels can be measured in years, and maybe even decades.

I first got a sense of Disneyland's constant evolution back in the 1960s when, after just a few visits, I realized that some of the things I'd seen in 1966 had disappeared by 1967, and new things had already arisen in their place (especially in Tomorrowland). For the next few years, I perused the park's Fun Maps, pored over its souvenir books, and marked its transitions and tweaks. But Disneyland, ever the ambitious moving target, refused to be pinned down. I continued my informal study of Disneyland's history well into the 1980s and began compiling rudimentary encyclopedia entries and lists in the 1990s. Now, hundreds of visits later, after taking thousands of photographs, measurements, and notes and working incessantly on these three encyclopedia editions for over a decade, I've gained a fuller appreciation of Disneyland's ability to continually reinvent itself.

At times, the park's changes have seemed almost magical. Take, for instance, the 2015-2016 Diamond Celebration for Disneyland's sixtieth anniversary, which featured spectacular new fireworks, a dazzling new parade, and over a year of new events, exhibits, activities, food, and merchandise. The park drew more than 18 million guests and obliterated its annual attendance record by ten percent. Every square inch of Disneyland, it seemed, was fully utilized and decorated. Then, before that celebration was even over, officials announced the single biggest park expansion ever: fourteen acres of Star Wars Land that are sure to send attendance records soarin' over California. This is what I'm talking about. Just when you think Disneyland is about to peak, just when you think there's no room to squeeze in anything else, presto! Another fourteen acres magically appear, and the park prepares to accelerate to an exciting new galaxy.

As Disneyland continues to reach new heights, so will we, in our appreciation. Disneyland is more than beautiful and entertaining; it's wondrous and transportive. Like a magnificent work of art, Disneyland reveals more and more of itself with intense study. The more powerful your mighty microscope, the more details you'll see. Hopefully this book will help you discover those details, understand Disneyland's history, and see for yourself all that Disneyland has to offer, from its simplest fun to its most profound joys. Ultimately, the best lesson of all is that there is always more to learn, especially in dynamic, ever-changing Disneyland.

Chris Strodder
Pismo Beach, CA

62 DISNEYLAND DEBUTS

As of mid-2017, it's been sixty-two years since Disneyland opened. Where were you for these sixty-two debuts?

1955   July 17: Opening Day for special guests and a TV audience, one day before the public is admitted
July 18: Circarama theater
July 22: Rocket to the Moon
July 31: Casey Jr. Circus Train
August 16: Dumbo the Flying Elephant
August 29: Pirate Ship Restaurant
October 11: A-B-C ticket books

1956   March 24: Astro-Jets
June 16: Tom Sawyer Island; Storybook Land Canal Boats
June 23: Skyway to Fantasyland/Tomorrowland
July 2: Mine Train
July 4: Indian War Canoes

1957   April 29: Sleeping Beauty Castle Walk-Through
June 12: House of the Future

1958   June 14: Alice in Wonderland; Sailing Ship *Columbia*
December 31: New Year's Eve Party

1959   June 14: Matterhorn Bobsleds; Monorail; Submarine Voyage

1960   May 28: Nature's Wonderland

1961   June 15: Grad Nite
August 6: Flying Saucers

1962   November 18: Swiss Family Treehouse

1963   June 23: Enchanted Tiki Room

1965   July 18: Great Moments with Mr. Lincoln

1966   May 28: It's a Small World
July 24: New Orleans Square

1967   March 18: Pirates of the Caribbean; Blue Bayou
July 2: PeopleMover; Carousel of Progress; Tomorrowland Terrace; Rocket Jets
August 5: Adventure Thru Inner Space

1969	August 9: Haunted Mansion
1972	March 24: Bear Country June 17: Main Street Electrical Parade
1977	May 4: Space Mountain
1979	September 2: Big Thunder Mountain Railroad
1983	May 25: Remodeled Fantasyland
1986	September 18: *Captain EO*
1987	January 9: Star Tours July 11: Disney Gallery
1989	July 17: Splash Mountain
1992	May 13: Fantasmic!
1993	January 24: Mickey's Toontown
1994	January 26: Roger Rabbit's Car Toon Spin
1995	March 3: Indiana Jones Adventure
1998	May 22: Rocket Rods; *Honey, I Shrunk the Audience*
1999	June 23: Tarzan's Treehouse November 19: FASTPASS tickets
2003	April 11: The Many Adventures of Winnie the Pooh
2005	March 17: Buzz Lightyear Astro Blasters
2006	September 29: Halloween Time
2007	June 11: Finding Nemo Submarine Voyage
2011	June 3: Star Tours: The Adventures Continue
2013	March 12: Fantasy Faire
2015	May 22: Paint the Night November 16: Season of the Force

This way to more happiness!

Notes on the Text

H ere are a few quick things to know about this book before you begin reading. First, many of this encyclopedia's 600 main entries list multiple names for single locations. As any guest who's made repeat visits knows, Disneyland often changes the names of its attractions, stores, restaurants, and services. The main name of each entry is its current title (if the thing being described in the entry still exists); its former names are listed as well, separated by "aka" ("also known as"). For example: Café Orleans, aka Creole Café. When there are more than two former names, they are listed in chronological order, with reasons for the name changes given in the text.

For a few major attractions, the entries begin with the common, well-known names of the attractions, even if technically these were not the original names. For example, look for the Monorail under M, even though it was born in 1959 as the Disneyland-Alweg Monorail System. When in doubt, consult the index, where all the names, current and past, get separate listings and page references.

In each of this encyclopedia's A–Z entries, the descriptive text includes terms that appear in **bold**. This means there's a main entry for that term elsewhere in the encyclopedia.

To make the text more readable, the official names of some entities have been simplified, including Academy Award®, Disneyland Park®, Disney's Animal Kingdom®, Disney California Adventure Park®, and Walt Disney World Resort®. Instead of these formal names, I've used the abbreviated or colloquial forms commonly understood by the general public.

Most encyclopedia entries are marked on one of the maps shown on pages 16–37 (people, films, and a few other non-geographic entries are not marked on maps). These map positions are indicated with a letter (for the map) and a number (for the spot on the map). A = the Adventureland map, Fa = Fantasyland, Fr = Frontierland, and so on. Note that the Hub, Main Street, and Town Square are shown on separate maps.

As for the chronologies, when I couldn't pinpoint an exact date, I occasionally resorted to less precise times like "Ca. 1992." Better to be general and right than specific and wrong.

As you read on, you'll see that my point isn't to glorify Walt Disney and his Disneyland. I'm not saying we shouldn't celebrate Disney as a genius (he was) and his park as a marvel (it is). But while much of the ensuing text praises Disneyland, it also identifies occasional miscues and mishaps. So while I'm obviously a Disneyland fan, I'm not (and never have been) a Disney employee, making this book a completely independent, unbiased production. I always paid my own way into Disneyland, and I did my own research. No foundation grants, no research assistants, no Disney editors, no ghostwriters. Thus any errors in the book are mine and nobody else's.

Errors, incidentally, are what James Joyce called "portals of discovery." Should you run across something you want to question, or if you notice a possible portal of discovery, please do two things: 1) forgive my mistake, and 2) let me know what you found by (politely) writing to me via Encycoolpedia.com. I'll reply with interest and gratitude.

Notes on the Photographs and Maps

Of this book's 300-plus photographs, two were generously loaned to us: the 1985 parade photo on page 369 was taken by Karen Carlson, and the Space Girl photo on page 447 came from Terry Jo Steinberger. I took the rest of the photos, including those on the covers. Virtually all of them were snapped between 2014 and 2016, and all were taken at or around Disneyland during regular park hours. Unlike nearly every other published photo of buildings and attractions ever taken at Disneyland, these photos generally include no people, keeping the focus on the main subject. We haven't appended a caption to each photo because there's usually adjacent descriptive text that provides photo information.

The marvelous maps are the work of Tristan Tang. That's also her 1959-style Monorail that loops across the front cover. I'm still thanking my lucky stars that she so generously agreed to enhance this book with her remarkable talents. I can't imagine a better collaborator.

—C.S.

TERMINOLOGYLAND

Here's a quick primer to some key Disneyland terms you'll come across in this book:

A–E tickets: From 1955 to 1982, guests accessed attractions by paying with tickets from prepaid ticket books. For a full history of tickets and ticket books, please refer to the Ticket Books entry on page 472.

Attraction: What other amusement parks call rides, Disneyland calls attractions. Disneyland has broadened the term to include shows, exhibits, and other activities. Recent guidemaps handed out at the park's turnstiles list the Bibbidi Bobbidi Boutique, Disney Gallery, and Fantasmic! among Disneyland's sixty-two attractions.

Cast Members: Disneyland employees are called cast members, and they are usually seen wearing garments designed to match the theme of the area they

work in. Cast members include ride operators, store cashiers, food servers, security personnel, parade performers, parking attendants, and roving street sweepers. Read more in the Cast Members entry on page 112.

Dark Ride: In the amusement park industry, this is the term for indoor rides with guided vehicles. Pinocchio's Daring Journey (shown) is one example of Disneyland's many dark rides.

Disneyland: *The Disneyland Encyclopedia* focuses exclusively on Anaheim's classic Disneyland Park (shortened to Disneyland in this book). The Disneyland Resort is different—that large area includes Disneyland, Disney California Adventure, Downtown Disney, and Disney's Anaheim hotels. Occasional references are made to these other locations, as well as to Walt Disney World in Florida and Disney parks outside the U.S. This book, however, does not expound on those, nor does it give information about local motels, airport shuttles, and other topics commonly found in travel guides.

Imagineers: This hybrid term is usually attributed to Harrison Price and/or Claude Coats (both of whom are profiled in this book). The word Imagineers merges imagination with engineering to describe the architects, illustrators, sculptors, model makers, set designers, costume designers, musicians, and inventors who work creatively on Disneyland and its attractions; "a combination of artists and scientists" is how Bob Gurr, an acclaimed Imagineer, describes them in the *Sleeping Beauty* DVD's special features. The most important Imagineers have been named Disney Legends, a title the Walt Disney Company has been using since 1987 to recognize key contributors to the Disney legacy.

Main Street, U.S.A.: In *The Disneyland Encyclopedia*, the full name Main Street, U.S.A. is nearly always shortened to just Main Street. Our maps and text delineate Main Street as the commercial blocks running south-to-north *between* Town Square and the Hub (because they're separate areas, Main Street, Town Square, and the Hub have their own maps and encyclopedia entries in this book).

Wienie: This was Walt Disney's term for a vivid landmark with either a visual or sonic pull that entices curious guests and draws them toward it. Sleeping Beauty Castle is an iconic wienie that draws arriving guests into the heart of the park.

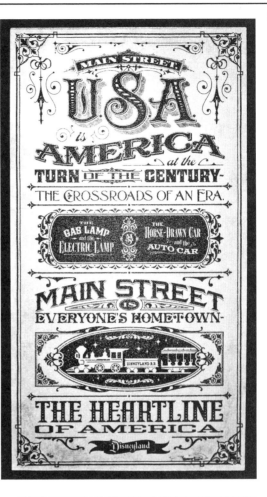

Park
(Map P)

P-1:   Marquee
P-2:   Lost and Found; Parking Lot
P-3:   Main Street Lockers & Storage
P-4:   Newsstand
P-5:   Entrance
P-6:   Stroller Shop
P-7:   Guest Relations; Kennel Club
P-8:   Main Street Vehicles; Town Square
P-9:   Main Street; Main Street Vehicles
P-10: Main Street Vehicles; Hub
P-11: Adventureland
P-12: New Orleans Square
P-13: Holidayland

P-14: Bear Country; Critter Country
P-15: Frontierland
P-16: Fantasyland
P-17: Mickey's Toontown; Pony Farm
P-18: Season of the Force;
         Tomorrowland
P-19: Star Wars Land

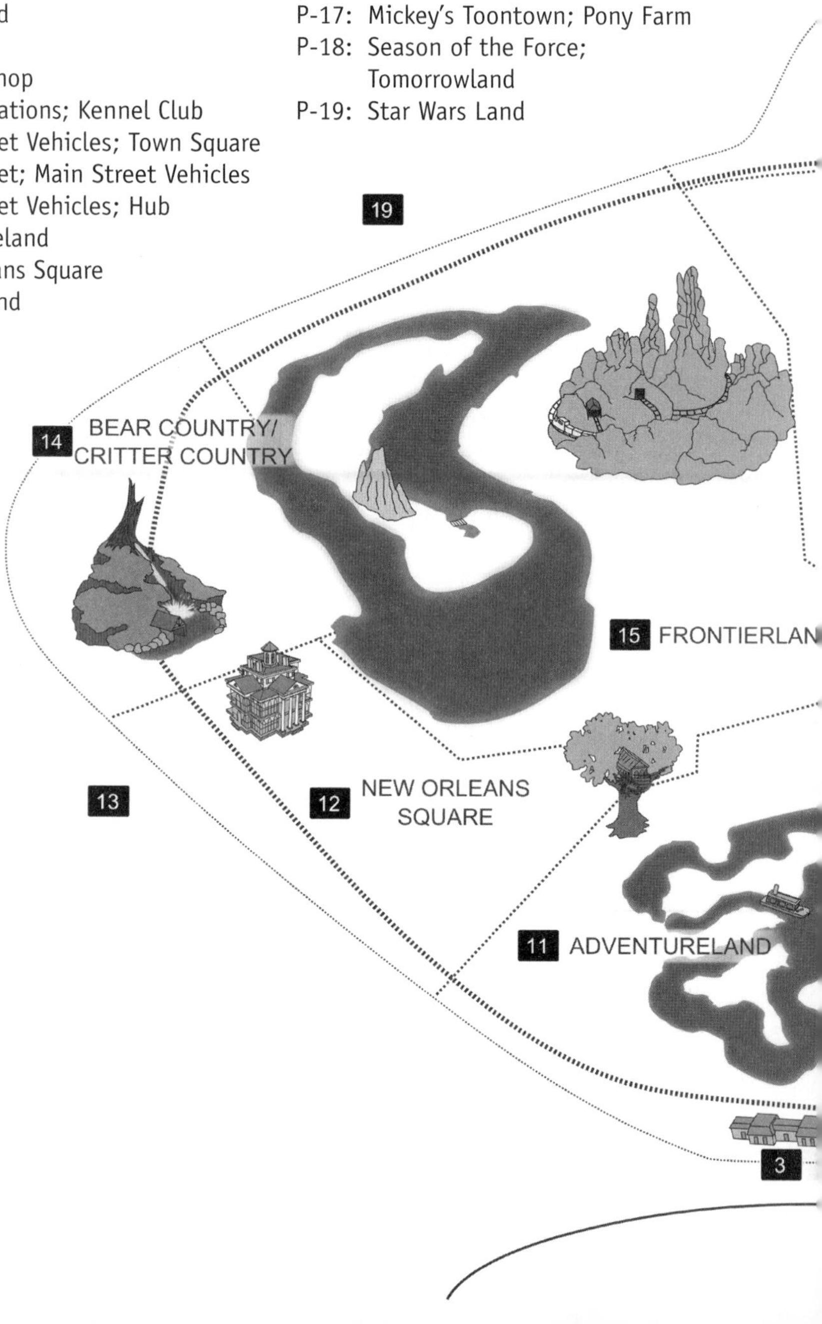

19

14 BEAR COUNTRY/
     CRITTER COUNTRY

15 FRONTIERLAN

13

12 NEW ORLEANS
     SQUARE

11 ADVENTURELAND

3

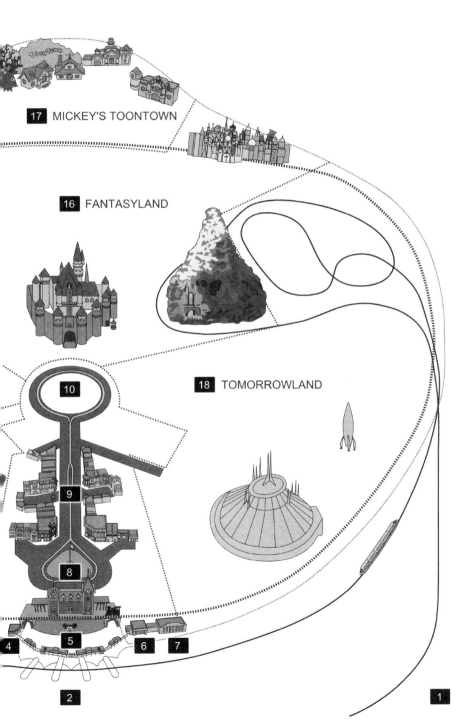

17 MICKEY'S TOONTOWN

16 FANTASYLAND

18 TOMORROWLAND

10

9

8

4

5

6

7

2

1

Town Square
(Map TS)

TS-1: Railroad
TS-2: Tour Guides
TS-3: Police Station
TS-4: City Hall; First Aid and Lost Children; Guest Relations
TS-5: Apartments; Fire Department
TS-6: Flagpole
TS-7: American Egg House; Dalmatian Celebration; Guest Flow Corridors; Hills Bros. Coffee House and Coffee Garden; International Street; Liberty Street; Maxwell House Coffee Shop; Town Square Café
TS-8: Jimmy Starr's Show Business Souvenirs; Mad Hatter of Main Street; Wonderland Music
TS-9: *Babes in Toyland* Exhibit; *Disneyland: The First 50 Magical Years* Film; Great Moments with Mr. Lincoln; Lost and Found; Mickey Mouse Club Headquarters; Opera House; The Walt Disney Story
TS-10: Bank of America; Disneyana; Disney Gallery; Town Square Realty

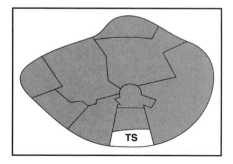

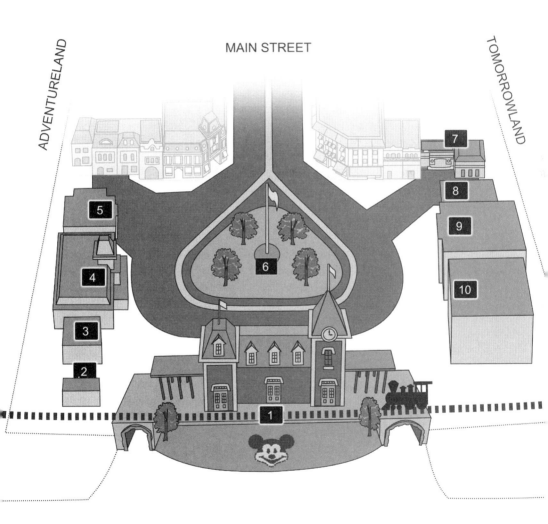

Main Street, U.S.A.
(Map MS)

MS-1: Carriage Place Clothing Co.; Main Street Lockers & Storage; Lost and Found

MS-2: Emporium; Windows of Enchantment

MS-3: Candle Shop; Crystal Arcade; Glass Blower; Jemrock Shop; Story Book Shop

MS-4: Disneyana; Fortuosity Shop; Hurricane Lamp Shop;
New Century Watches & Clocks; Upjohn Pharmacy

MS-5: Center Street; Carnation Café; Flower Mart

MS-6: Blue Ribbon Bakery; Carnation Ice Cream Parlor; Puffin Bakery;
Sunkist Citrus House

MS-7: Gibson Girl Ice Cream Parlor; Sunny-View Farms Jams & Jellies

MS-8: Main Street Shooting Gallery; Penny Arcade

MS-9: Candy Palace

MS-10: Refreshment Corner

MS-11: Cole of California Swimsuits; Guest Flow Corridors;
Mad Hatter of Main Street

MS-12: Carefree Corner; Main Street Photo Supply Co.

MS-13: Blue Bird Shoes for Children; China Closet; Crystal Arts; Ellen's Gift Shop;
Grandma's Baby Shop; Intimate Apparel; Kodak Camera Center;
Ruggles China and Glass Shop; Silhouette Studio; Watches & Clocks;
Wonderland Music

MS-14: Card Corner; Disney Clothiers, Ltd.; Gibson Greeting Cards;
Hallmark Card Shop

MS-15: Coin Shop; Pen Shop

MS-16: Main Street Lockers & Storage; Lost and Found; Main Street Cone Shop

MS-17: Center Street; Chinatown; Flower Mart; Main Street Fruit Cart

MS-18: Market House

MS-19: Disneyana; Fine Tobacco; Jewelry Shop; Main Street Cinema;
Main Street Magic Shop; Patented Pastimes; 20th Century Music Company;
Yale & Towne Lock Shop

MS-20: Disneyland Presents a Preview of Coming Attractions; Disney Showcase;
Egg-stravaganza; Legacy of Walt Disney; Wurlitzer Music Hall

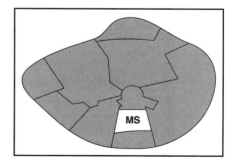

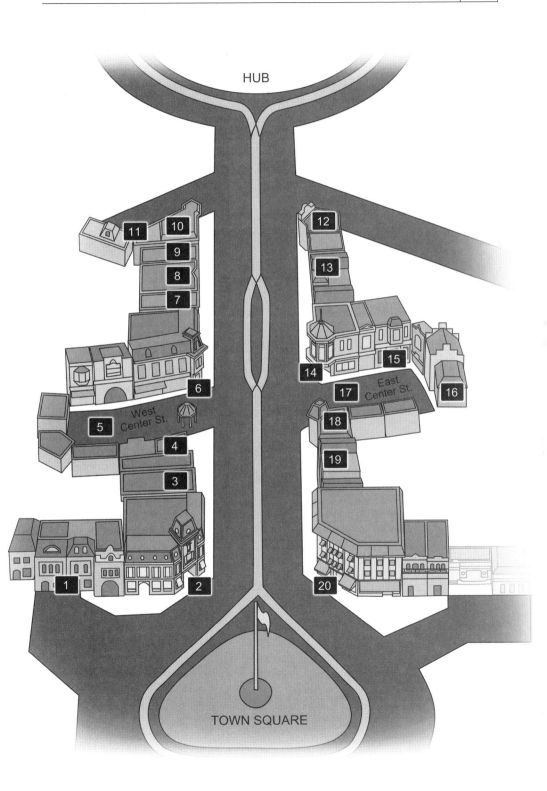

Hub
(Map H)

H-1: Disney Vacation Club Kiosk; Jolly Holiday Bakery Café; Plaza Pavilion
H-2: Bandstand; Date Nite; Fairytale Treasures; Fantasy Faire; Maurice's Treats;
      Plaza Gardens
H-3: Plaza Inn
H-4: Edison Square; First Aid and Lost Children
H-5: Little Red Wagon
H-6: Baby Care Center
H-7: Dream Machine; Gift-Giver Extraordinaire Machine; *Partners*

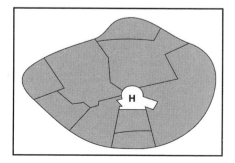

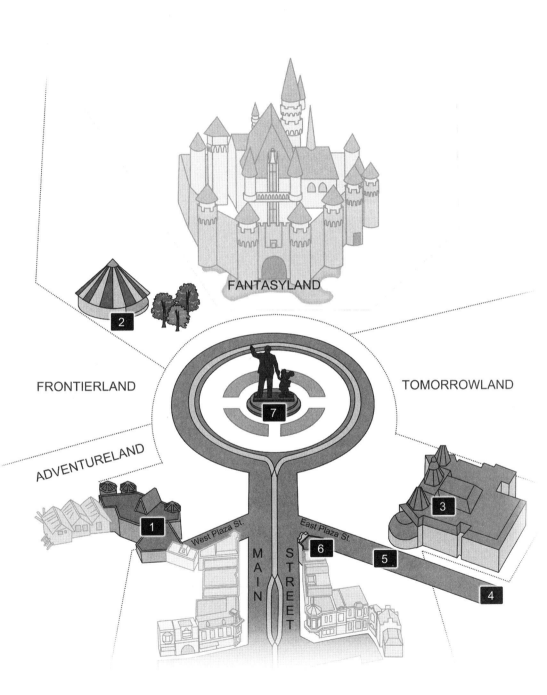

FANTASYLAND

FRONTIERLAND

TOMORROWLAND

ADVENTURELAND

West Plaza St.

East Plaza St.

MAIN STREET

Adventureland
(Map A)

A-1: Adventureland Bazaar
A-2: Big Game Safari Shooting Gallery; Indiana Jones Adventure Outpost;
      Safari Outpost; South Seas Traders
A-3: Bengal Barbecue; Sunkist, I Presume; Tropical Cantina
A-4: Magnolia Park
A-5: Swiss Family Treehouse; Tarzan's Treehouse
A-6: Indiana Jones Adventure; *Little Man of Disneyland*
A-7: Indy Fruit Cart
A-8: Jungle Cruise
A-9: Tropical Imports
A-10: Aladdin's Oasis
A-11: Enchanted Tiki Room; Tiki Juice Bar
A-12: Tahitian Terrace

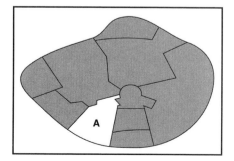

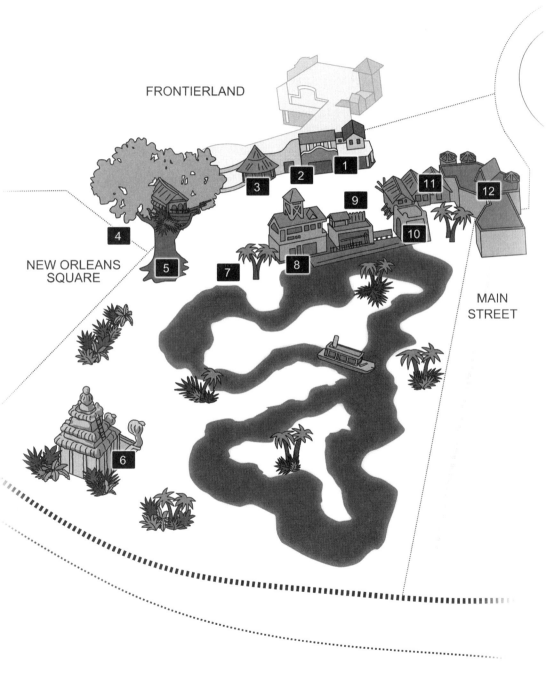

FRONTIERLAND

NEW ORLEANS
SQUARE

MAIN
STREET

New Orleans Square
(Map NOS)

NOS-1:   Apartments; Disney Gallery; Pirates of the Caribbean
NOS-2:   Royal Street Veranda
NOS-3:   Bookstand; Le Bat en Rouge; Le Gourmet; One-of-a-Kind Shop;
          Pieces of Eight; Pirate's Arcade Museum; Port Royal
NOS-4:   Blue Bayou; Club 33
NOS-5:   Chocolate Collection; La Boutique de Noël; La Boutique d'Or; Le Forgeron;
          Le Bat en Rouge; Le Gourmet; L'Ornement Magique, Le Bayou Magique;
          Pirates League; Port d'Orleans; Portrait Artists
NOS-6:   Cristal d'Orleans; Laffite's Silver Shop; Portrait Artists
NOS-7:   Café Orleans; Royal Street Sweets
NOS-8:   La Petite Patisserie
NOS-9:   Jewel of Orléans; La Mascarade d'Orléans; Le Chapeau;
          Marché aux Fleurs, Sacs et Mode; Mlle. Antoinette's Parfumerie
NOS-10: Disney Vacation Club Kiosk; French Market; Parasol Cart
NOS-11: Mint Julep Bar
NOS-12: Haunted Mansion; Holiday Cart; New Orleans Square Lemonade Stand

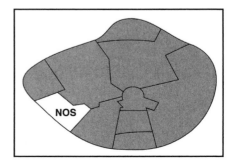

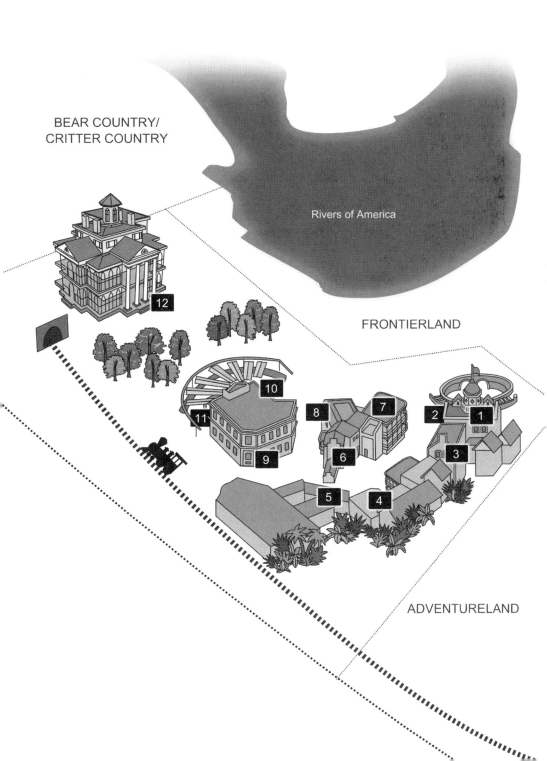

BEAR COUNTRY/
CRITTER COUNTRY

Rivers of America

FRONTIERLAND

ADVENTURELAND

Frontierland
(Map Fr)

Fr-1: Bone Carving Shop; Davy Crockett Arcade; Davy Crockett Frontier Museum; Davy Crockett's Pioneer Mercantile; Frontierland Miniature Museum; Leather Shop; Reel-Ride

Fr-2: Bonanza Outfitters; Pendleton Woolen Mills Dry Goods Store

Fr-3: Silver Spur Supplies

Fr-4: American Rifle Exhibit and Frontier Gun Shop; Golden Horseshoe; *Golden Horseshoe Revue*

Fr-5: Oaks Tavern; Stage Door Café

Fr-6: Don DeFore's Silver Banjo Barbecue; Malt Shop and Cone Shop; Wheelhouse and Delta Banjo

Fr-7: Aunt Jemima's Pancake House; Magnolia Tree Terrace; River Belle Terrace

Fr-8: LB's Extraordinary Elixirs; Petrified Tree

Fr-9: Rivers of America

Fr-10: Chicken Plantation

Fr-11: Rafts to Tom Sawyer Island

Fr-12: Mike Fink Keel Boats

Fr-13: Fowler's Harbor

Fr-14: Davy Crockett's Explorer Canoes

Fr-15: Indian Trading Post; Indian Village

Fr-16: Dixieland at Disneyland; Fantasmic!; Fort Wilderness; Tom Sawyer Island

Fr-17: *Mark Twain* Riverboat; Sailing Ship *Columbia*; Ship to Shore Marketplace

Fr-18: Disney Vacation Club Kiosk; Westward Ho Conestoga Wagon Fries

Fr-19: Big Thunder Ranch; Big Thunder Ranch Jamboree; Big Thunder Trail; Family Fun Weekends; Jingle Jangle Jamboree; Three Kings Day

Fr-20: Big Thunder Ranch Barbecue; Festival Arena; Santa's Reindeer Round-Up

Fr-21: Big Thunder Mountain Railroad; Conestoga Wagons; Mine Train; Mule Pack; Stage Coach

Fr-22: Discovery Bay; Nature's Wonderland; Painted Desert

Fr-23: El Zocalo Park; Three Kings Day

Fr-24: Casa de Fritos; Mineral Hall; Rancho del Zocalo Restaurante

Fr-25: Marshal's Office; Miniature Horse Corral

Fr-26: Frontierland Shooting Exposition

Fr-27: Calico Kate's Pantry Shop; Frontier Trading Post; Westward Ho Trading Co.

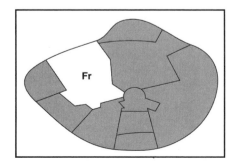

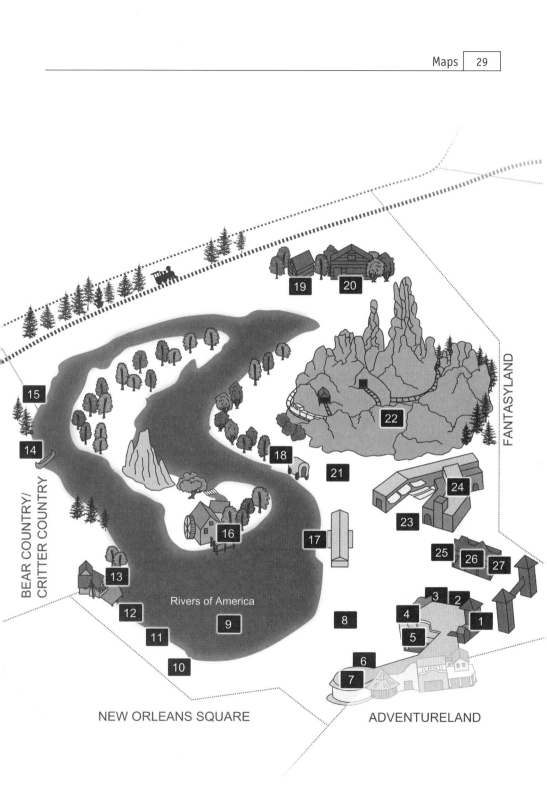

BEAR COUNTRY/
CRITTER COUNTRY

FANTASYLAND

Rivers of America

NEW ORLEANS SQUARE

ADVENTURELAND

Bear Country/Critter Country
(Map B/C)

B/C-1:   Harbour Galley
B/C-2:   Critter Country Fruit Cart
B/C-3:   Hungry Bear Restaurant
B/C-4:   Country Bear Jamboree; The Many Adventures of Winnie the Pooh
B/C-5:   Brer Bar; Mile Long Bar; Pooh Corner
B/C-6:   Teddi Barra's Swingin' Arcade; Ursus H. Bear's Wilderness Outpost
B/C-7:   Crocodile Mercantile
B/C-8:   Professor Barnaby Owl's Photographic Art Studio
B/C-9:   Splash Mountain
B/C-10: Briar Patch; Critter Country Plush

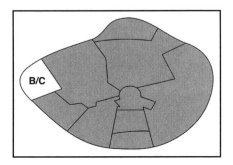

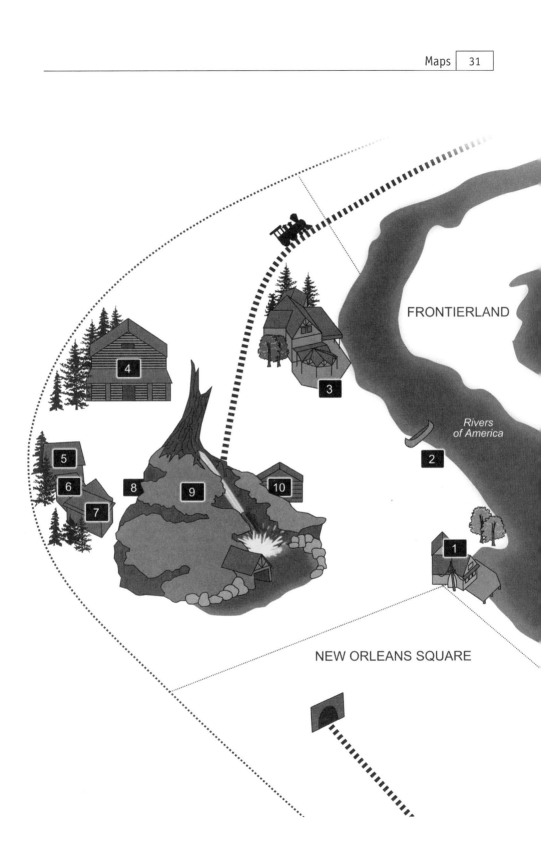

FRONTIERLAND

*Rivers
of America*

NEW ORLEANS SQUARE

Fantasyland
(Map Fa)

Fa-1:   Snow White Wishing Well and Grotto
Fa-2:   Fireworks; Sleeping Beauty Castle; Sleeping Beauty Castle Walk-Through
Fa-3:   Arts and Crafts Shop; Castle Arts; Castle Christmas Shop; Clock Shop;
        Enchanted Chamber; 50th Anniversary Shop; Princess Boutique;
        Tinker Bell & Friends
Fa-4:   Castle Candy Kitchen; Names Unraveled; Three Fairies Magic Crystals
Fa-5:   Carrousel Candies; King Arthur Carrousel; Sword in the Stone Ceremony
Fa-6:   Duck Bumps; King Arthur Carrousel; Mad Hatter's Mad Tea Party;
        Peter Pan Crocodile Aquarium
Fa-7:   Tinker Bell Toy Shoppe; Bibbidi Bobbidi Boutique
Fa-8:   Snow White's Scary Adventures
Fa-9:   Fantasy Faire Gifts; Frozen Royal Reception; Geppetto's Arts & Crafts;
        Geppetto's Candy Shoppe; Mickey Mouse Club Theater; Names Unraveled;
        Pinocchio's Daring Journey; Tangled; Welch's Grape Juice Stand
Fa-10: Character Foods; Stromboli's Wagon; Village Haus
Fa-11: Dumbo the Flying Elephant
Fa-12: Skyway to Fantasyland and Skyway to Tomorrowland
Fa-13: Casey Jr. Circus Train
Fa-14: Dumbo the Flying Elephant; Pirate Ship Restaurant; Skull Rock and
        Pirate's Cove
Fa-15: Canal Boats of the World; Rock Candy Mountain; Storybook Land Canal Boats
Fa-16: Fantasy Faire Gifts; Midget Autopia
Fa-17: Troubadour Tavern
Fa-18: Princess Fantasy Faire; Fantasyland Theatre
Fa-19: Baloo's Dressing Room; Dumbo's Circusland
Fa-20: It's a Small World Toy Shop
Fa-21: Brave: Meet Merida; Happy Lunar New Year Celebration; It's a Small World;
        The Magic, the Memories, and You!; Topiary Garden
Fa-22: Disney Afternoon Avenue; Edelweiss Snacks, Fantasyland Autopia;
        Garden of the Gods; Keller's Jungle Killers; Le Petit Chalet; Lilliputian Land;
        Mickey Mouse Club Circus; Motor Boat Cruise
Fa-23: Fairytale Arts; Fantasia Gardens; Junior Autopia; Names Unraveled
Fa-24: Matterhorn Bobsleds;
        Matterhorn Mountain;
        Peter Pan Crocodile Aquarium
Fa-25: Mad Hatter's Mad Tea Party
Fa-26: Alice in Wonderland
Fa-27: Character Foods;
        Mad Hatter of Fantasyland
Fa-28: Mr. Toad's Wild Ride
Fa-29: Peter Pan's Flight

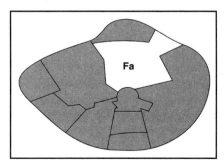

Fa-30: Briar Rose Cottage; Disney Villains; Heraldry Shoppe; Knight Shop; Merlin's Magic Shop; Mickey's Christmas Chalet; Quasimodo's Attic; Villains Lair

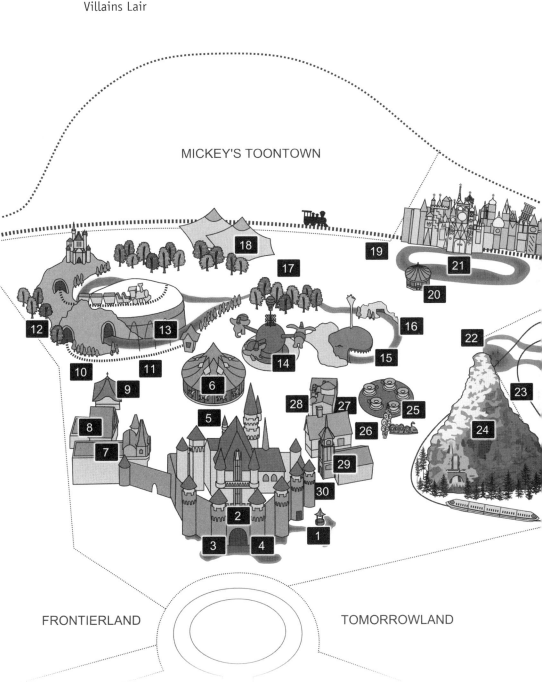

Mickey's Toontown
(Map MT)

MT-1: Goofy's Playhouse
MT-2: Donald's Boat
MT-3: Gadget's Go Coaster
MT-4: Chip 'n Dale Tree House
MT-5: Mickey's House
MT-6: Minnie's House
MT-7: Goofy's Gas Station; Toon Up Treats
MT-8: Clarabelle's Frozen Yogurt; Daisy's Diner; Pluto's Dog House
MT-9: Toontown Five & Dime
MT-10: Gag Factory
MT-11: Roger Rabbit's Car Toon Spin
MT-12: Disney Vacation Club Kiosk; Jolly Trolley

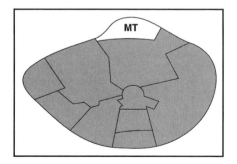

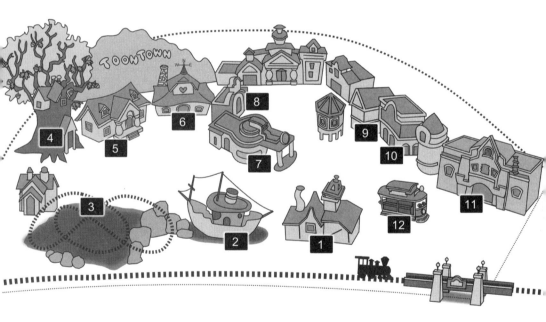

FANTASYLAND

Tomorrowland
(Map T)

T-1: Alpine Gardens; House of the Future; King Triton Gardens; Pixie Hollow; Pixie Hollow Gift Cart

T-2: Avenue of the Flags

T-3: Astro-Orbitor; Clock of the World

T-4: Buzz Lightyear Astro Blasters

T-5: American Space Experience; Art of Animation; Bell Telephone Systems Phone Exhibits; Circarama; Corridor of Murals; Space Station X-1

T-6: Art Corner; Little Green Men Store Command; Our Future in Colors; Premiere Shop; World Beneath Us Exhibit

T-7: Yacht Club

T-8: Astro-Jets; Court of Honor; Disney Vacation Club Kiosk; Lunching Pad; Observatron; PeopleMover; Radio Disney Broadcast Booth; Rocket Jets; Rocket Rods; Space Bar; Tomorrowlanding

T-9: Club Buzz; Galactic Grill

T-10: Autopia Winner's Circle; Monorail; Phantom Boats; Submarine Voyage; Viewliner; Yacht Club

T-11: Mermaids

T-12: Autopia

T-13: Autopia Winner's Circle; Mad Hatter of Tomorrowland; Skyway to Fantasyland and Skyway to Tomorrowland

T-14: America Sings; Carousel of Progress; Innoventions; Tomorrowland Expo Center; Space Bar

T-15: Moonliner; Spirit of Refreshment

T-16: Flight to the Moon; Mission to Mars; Redd Rockett's Pizza Port; Rocket to the Moon; Toy Story Funhouse; Space Place

T-17: Grand Canyon Diorama; Primeval World Diorama

T-18: Adventures in Science; Flying Saucers; Space Mountain

T-19: *Captain EO*; *Honey, I Shrunk the Audience*; Magic Eye Theater; Starcade; Tomorrowland Stage

T-20: Cosmic Waves; Hobbyland

T-21: Flight Circle

T-22: Bathroom of Tomorrow; Character Shop; Fun Fotos; Mad Hatter of Tomorrowland; Star Trader

T-23: American Dairy Association Exhibit; Corridor of Murals; Fashions and Fabrics Through the Ages; New York World's Fair Exhibit; 20,000 Leagues Under the Sea Exhibit

T-24: Adventure Thru Inner Space; Hall of Aluminum Fame; Hall of Chemistry; Omnimover attraction (Inner Space); Star Tours

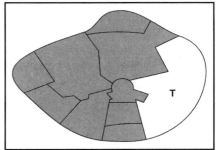

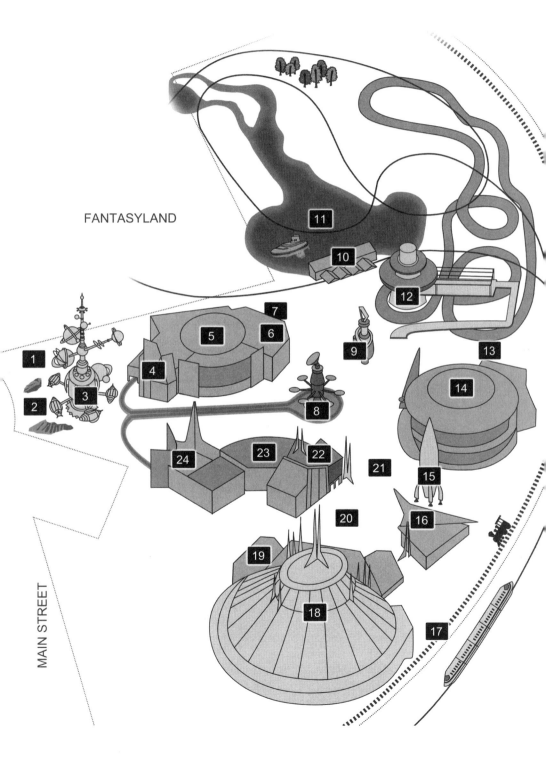

FANTASYLAND

MAIN STREET

Address

Historically, Disneyland's street address has been given as either 1313 **Harbor Boulevard** or 1313 S. Harbor Boulevard, Anaheim, CA 92803. This location is on Disneyland's east side, and we've had both addresses given to us at City Hall at different times. **Cast members** will explain that this address points to Disneyland's main administrative offices, visible from the **Monorail** as it passes along Harbor. Searches online and in books, and even calls to Disneyland's information line (714-781-INFO) occasionally give a *west*-side address for Disneyland at both 1313 Disneyland Drive and 1313 S. Disneyland Drive (in 2016, we easily found all four "1313" addresses while searching and calling around).

It's possible that the street number was intentionally selected and has some special significance. This idea is supported by Stephen Faessel's *Historic Photos of Anaheim*, which says that "Anaheim's civic government took care of . . . arranging the signature address of '1313' South Harbor Boulevard." *Window on Main Street* by Disney Legend **Van France** claims that **Walt Disney** personally selected the numbers because they're part of Donald Duck's license plate (313) and Disney's wedding anniversary (July 13). Some people claim that Disneyland's address makes a reference to Mickey Mouse; "M" is the thirteenth letter of the alphabet, and thus 1313 = MM. Others note that there's a precedent for this street number in the Disney canon: a 1954 Uncle Scrooge comic pinpoints Donald Duck's address as 1313 Webfoot Walk, Duckburg. When all these theories were presented to the Anaheim Planning and Zoning Department in 2013, the amused representative said the numbers are "simply a coincidence."

> **MOUSCELLANY**
>
> At Disney California Adventure, 1313 appears in another form: it's the room number on the souvenir pin and keychain for the Hollywood Tower Hotel. In 2013's *Monsters University*, the school in the film was established in 1313.

Admission

Today's guests are used to seeing Disneyland open every day of the year, but it wasn't always so. From 1955 to 1957, the park was closed on Mondays in the off-season; from 1958 to 1985, it was closed on both Mondays and Tuesdays (in 1985, Disneyland switched to its current 365-day schedule).

The method of payment for a Disneyland ticket has changed, too—credit cards were not accepted for admission until the mid-1980s. And even the policies about *who* can come into the park have been tweaked: in its first decade, Disneyland didn't admit male guests with excessively long hair, and on March 18, 2013, the park announced that anyone *under* the age of fourteen could only enter when accompanied by someone *over* the age of fourteen.

Thankfully, Disneyland has nearly always been able to keep its posted hours, so guests can rely on the entrance gates being open as scheduled (though Disneyland typically stays open for an extra hour past closing time to accommodate late shoppers). However, there have been thirteen unscheduled closures in Disneyland history (as of January 2016). Eleven of these have been the result of extreme winter weather conditions. One death led to a sudden all-day closure—not Walt Disney's passing in 1966, as one might expect, but President Kennedy's assassination in 1963. Park officials also locked the gates on September 11, 2001, in response to that morning's terrorist attacks. Two earthquakes changed the circumstances at Disneyland but did not cause an overall closure: the 6.7-magnitude quake that shook Northridge early on January 17, 1994, delayed the attractions, which were individually inspected before they were opened to guests; a 5.1 earthquake on March 28, 2014, left Disneyland and its guests unscathed, but still compelled a precautionary shut-down of attractions and the cancellation of that night's fireworks. A more unusual situation occurred on March 3, 2012. While the park was open, Disneyland officials called the Orange County bomb squad in response to a "suspicious" (but ultimately benign) package found near the turnstiles, and during the subsequent lockdown no guests could enter or leave the park for three hours.

See **Passports** and **Ticket Books** for specifics about Disneyland admission and attraction pricing.

Adventureland

MAP: Park, P-11

DATES: July 17, 1955–ongoing

Guests are so used to seeing Adventureland on the left side of the **Hub** that they might be surprised to find out that Adventureland was moved around in the early plans for Disneyland. One of the first color overhead illustrations of the park, drawn by **Marvin Davis** two years before **Opening Day**, placed Adventureland on the Hub's east side, making it the first land on the lower-*right* side as guests walked north from **Main Street** toward **Sleeping Beauty Castle**. Adventureland ended up, of course, located to the lower *left* of the Hub (the lower-right area became **Tomorrowland**).

Early on, Adventureland's name also went through several iterations. One cartographer labeled it Adventureland; another used True-Life Adventureland, referencing the popular *True-Life* nature documentaries Disney Studios began to release in 1949. The exotic settings of these short films—especially *The African Lion*, in production as Disneyland was being designed—helped inspire the themes and textures of Adventureland, as did numerous Hollywood classics (think *The African Queen*) and great literary tales of exploration. Ultimately, however, the setting was generalized, with no one specific place pinpointed and no particular era identified. Adventureland was and is an amalgamation of African, Asian, and Polynesian influences that's more cinematic than real, and more mysterious than overt.

Even though the Adventureland location, name, and source material varied, key Adventureland elements—a boat ride on a winding river, rows of stores, and restaurants designed as remote locales—were always shown on the early maps. Artists like **Harper Goff** tried their best to pre-conceive everything (Goff included a hotel and a saloon in some of his early concept sketches), but in truth many of Adventureland's details were made up on the spot during construction. The result is a wonderfully evocative four-acre meeting place between outposts of civilization and untamed nature. From the Hub, the main Adventureland entrance is across a small pond (the same one that spreads beneath the **Frontierland** entrance) and through a tall bamboo gate topped by elephant tusks. The walkway ahead curves for about 300 feet toward **New Orleans Square**, with a two-story row of thatched shops and restaurants lining the right-hand side and the **Jungle Cruise** and **Indiana Jones Adventure** attractions on the left.

Massive in its scale and significance, the Jungle Cruise was Adventureland's only major attraction until the **Tahitian Terrace**, **Swiss Family Treehouse**, and **Big Game Safari Shooting Gallery** were added in 1962, to be followed a year later by the **Enchanted Tiki Room** and then the Indiana Jones Adventure in 1995. Because of the three-decade development gap between the Tiki Room and Indiana Jones, Adventureland is one of Disneyland's least modified sections. However, the always-photogenic Adventureland has also been one of Disneyland's most promotable sections, getting focused attention on various episodes of the ***Disneyland* TV series** and lots of merchandise, such as Adventureland ashtrays, dishes, shirts, and even an official Parker Brothers Adventureland board game.

Though in its infancy it may have had fewer attractions than the other lands, Adventureland has never lacked for verdant abundance. According to Disneyland's **souvenir books**, Adventureland was intended to be a "wonderland of nature's own design." As such, it has always been the most densely planted of the lands, blending thousands of transplanted trees and bushes with old-growth trees saved from the original orchards Disneyland was built on. Even the tiki-style **trash cans** look like they belong in the jungle. Attentive guests will notice that the resplendent natural scenery is supplemented with the sounds of chattering monkeys and chirping birds (all natural-sounding, but all prerecorded).

In 1955, an Adventureland plaque celebrating the spirit of "romance," "mystery," "tropical rivers," and "the eerie sounds of the jungle" was created but never installed. No matter—the Adventureland concept was so exciting, its execution so detailed, and its appeal so universal, it's doubtful that any guests have ever needed an explanation of the area.

Adventureland Bazaar

MAP: Adventureland, A-1

DATES: July 17, 1955–ongoing

A prime location has helped make the Adventureland Bazaar a perennial shopping favorite since **Opening Day**. Sort of like an **Emporium** for **Adventureland**, this big store can be seen from the Adventureland entrance and stands in a high-traffic spot across from the **Enchanted Tiki Room**. Covering approximately 2,800 square feet, the Bazaar operates on the first floor of a two-story structure that has always sported variations on adventure-themed décor, including an arched entryway, thatched awnings, and weathered paint. Disney Legend **Rolly Crump** was the principal designer of the appealing exterior that hasn't changed much over the years.

The interior, on the other hand, has changed substantially. So many different shops selling unique imported merchandise have moved in and out that the building has sometimes been more Bizarre than Bazaar. In its first decades, the building was subdivided into individual businesses that offered non-Disney items from around the world. At various times, these interior shops—as well as several small huts outside—have included the Curio Hut (island-themed gifts), Here & There Imports, Far East Imports, Guatemalan Weavers, the Hawaiian Shop, India Magic Carpet, the Island Trade Store, the Mexican Mart, and Lee Brothers (imported Chinese gifts). The diversity of merchandise was fascinating; back then, Disneyland's **souvenir books** often boasted about the Bazaar's "colorful wares imported from exotic lands," "items from India," "carvings from a Kenyan tribe in Africa," "tropical ceramics," and other "rarities."

In 1994, the store was temporarily closed for a major **Adventureland** remodel that brought extensive changes to the nearby **Jungle Cruise** building. The individual shops inside the Bazaar were absorbed into one all-encompassing store. For the first decade of the twenty-first century, the store was filled with more Disney toys than imported exotica, but in recent years the Bazaar seems to be going more upscale with pricey bags, dresses, dishes, glassware, sunglasses, and big plush toys. Appropriately enough for Adventureland, the store sells towels, shirts, bags, and more with exotic animal prints on them.

One unusual novelty here is Aladdin's Other Lamp, a display along the back wall that dispenses "the wisdom of the genie" for a few coins and a quick rub. The store also features what is perhaps Disneyland's most elaborate coin-press machine, Rajah's Mint, which is topped by a large stone elephant.

Adventures in Science

MAP: Tomorrowland, T-18

DATES: Never built

Page 26 of Disneyland's 1958 **souvenir book** displays a spellbinding painting of a coming **Tomorrowland** attraction called Adventures in Science. In the painting, guests queue up under a large sloping roof and gaze through tall picture windows upon a tantalizing alien night: sharp, lunar-like mountains and a large crater, with what looks like a domed observatory and a giant protruding telescope standing off to the side. An immense ringed planet fills the distant sky, small moons hover over the horizon, and stars spangle the blackness beyond. The view is more than beautiful or tantalizing—it is breathtaking, and it dramatically evokes the inspiring future that Tomorrowland represents.

That same year, Disneyland's poster-size **Fun Map** marked a huge parcel of Tomorrowland real estate for the coming Adventures in Science attraction. Had the attraction been built, its location would have been approximately where **Space Mountain** arose in 1977. Adventures in Science would have begun with a Powercade—a long covering that curved from the open Tomorrowland walkway and back toward a two- or three-story white building. Under the Powercade covering, all kinds of strange-looking futuristic gizmos were to be exhibited. A walk along the length of the Powercade would have brought guests into the Adventures in Science building and onto some sort of transport for a trip through the universe and/or a tour of scientific discoveries through the centuries. Concept sketches, which are included in the **John Hench** book *Designing Disney*, show guests in small rocket-like pods gliding past immense colliding planets and other galactic wonders.

Alas, by 1961, the souvenir books had stopped showing the Adventures in Science attraction. In 1966, planning was already underway for a scientific tour that really would materialize a year later, albeit on a different site—**Adventure Thru Inner Space**.

Adventure Thru Inner Space

MAP: Tomorrowland, T-24

DATES: August 5, 1967–September 2, 1985

Adventure Thru Inner Space was a groundbreaking new attraction when it debuted auspiciously in 1967 as a key part of **Tomorrowland's** extensive remodel. From 1955 to 1966, the Inner Space building had housed, among other things, Monsanto's static **Hall of Chemistry** display, a walk-through exhibit that showed off the wonders of chemical engineering. Similarly science-influenced and sponsored by Monsanto, Adventure Thru Inner Space was also intended to show chemical wonders, but these were to be viewed from a unique vantage point: inside the atom.

Entered from the main walkway just inside Tomorrowland's entrance, the Inner Space **queue** was a bustle of activity orchestrated by **cast members** wearing futuristic yellow-and-black jumpsuits and white boots. As they waited in line, guests walked

past eight TV-sized display terminals that previewed the amazing sights to come. Guests also watched riders up ahead step into Atomobiles, blue pods that slid inside the thirty-seven-foot-long Mighty Microscope (in early 1967, Magic Microscope was one of the names considered for the whole attraction; Micro-World was another). This huge microscope "shrank" the Atomobiles and aimed them (eight-inch-tall replicas, actually) through a glass tube at a colorful, illuminated snowflake. All of this was witnessed not only by guests in the queue, but also by curious passengers on the **PeopleMover**, since its elevated track crossed the back of the room.

Once they were out of view of the queue, "miniaturized" Atomobile riders listened as a scientist, who had already undertaken this journey, informed them that they were now hearing "suspended . . . thought waves" of his experience. To create the illusion that the Atomobiles were, according to the narrator, continuing to shrink "beyond the limits of normal magnification-cation-cation," the approaching snowflakes grew bigger and bigger, until finally the Atomobiles actually entered them. More shrinking took Atomobiles into the domain of the water molecule, and finally into one of the molecule's oxygen atoms, where speedy electrons whipped by on all sides and a red nucleus pulsed.

Before the Atomobiles entered the dangerous realm of the nucleus, they were gradually enlarged back to normal size—but not before more drama ensued. The original snowflakes melted, bringing unexpected motion to the Atomobiles and the surrounding molecules. The final return to normal size was monitored under the watchful blue eye of a scientist peering at riders through a giant microscope. Guests exited into a hallway of Monsanto and Disneyland displays, among them the Fountain of Fashion, a delicate floor-to-ceiling sculpture of oil beads spiraling down thin wires.

When it was introduced in 1967, Adventure Thru Inner Space was one of Disneyland's most advanced attractions. Working closely with Monsanto engineers, Disney's own **Claude Coats** designed much of the journey, which lasted about six minutes and covered some 700 feet of displays. **Paul Frees**, who later spoke the Ghost Host's lines for the **Haunted Mansion**, voiced the narrating scientist; **X. Atencio**, writer of the **Pirates of the Caribbean** and Haunted Mansion ride scripts, also wrote Frees's Inner Space monologue. **Richard and Robert Sherman**, veterans of many other Disney attractions (**It's a Small World**) and movies (*Mary Poppins*), created the exhilarating "Miracles from Molecules" exit song, while **Buddy Baker** (who also co-wrote "Grim Grinning Ghosts") penned the background music. **John Hench** drew up some of the initial concept sketches, which showed guests riding past sofa-size protozoa inside an enlarged water droplet; John Drury did the abstract design for the striking **attraction poster**.

As exciting as the concept, sets, and effects were, the real breakthrough of Adventure Thru Inner Space was the Atomobile itself—it was the first Disneyland iteration of the innovative **Omnimover** ride system. In addition to efficiently convey-ing over 3,000 riders per hour through the attraction (at 1–2 mph) and cueing visual and sonic effects, the partially enclosed Atomobiles gave riders a sense of privacy and made Inner Space a prime rendezvous spot for amorous encounters. Even worse, the privacy seemed to provoke some riders to lean out and damage the sets. Hoping to curtail any in-the-dark intimacies or out-of-the-pod vandalism, supervisors installed closed-circuit TV cameras and sped up the Atomobiles to help limit opportunities for misbehavior.

Thanks to Monsanto's support, Inner Space was a completely free attraction, requiring no A–E ticket for entry; however, children had to use a special coupon from inside the **ticket books**, thus limiting the number of times they could ride unsuper-vised by parents. On December 15, 1972, the coupon system was abandoned, as was the free admission. Subsequently, a C ticket opened up the atom.

In 1985, with its sets aging and its audience disappearing, Adventure Thru In-ner Space closed to make way for the new **Star Tours** attraction that would debut two years later. In tribute to Inner Space's legacy, Star Tours incorporated a small Atomobile replica into its line-area exhibits. A miniature Mighty Microscope was also visible in the hangar scene of the original Star Tours film, snowflakes and molecules adorned an exterior mural on the **Buzz Lightyear** building across the way, and an Inner Space banner (shown) hung on the **Innoventions** building, all reminders of one of Tomorrowland's most revolutionary and wondrous experiences.

Aladdin's Oasis

MAP: Adventureland, A-10

DATES: July 2, 1993–ongoing

Three months after the thirty-one-year-old **Tahitian Terrace** in **Adventureland** closed, Aladdin's Oasis opened. While its location across from the **Adventureland Bazaar** was the same as its predecessor's, the architecture of the 300-square-foot building had drastically changed. Instead of Polynesian stylings, the new façade featured exotic el-ements in the style of *The Arabian Nights*, in keeping with the theme of Disney's 1992 hit movie *Aladdin*. Guests at Aladdin's Oasis enjoyed Middle Eastern delicacies (shish kebabs, tabbouleh, chutney, etc.) and watched an Arabian-themed show featuring belly dancing, magic, and even a lamp and genie inspired by the movie.

In its debut year, Aladdin's Oasis wasn't open every day. After two years, the Arabian show wasn't open at all, and the Oasis was solely a table-service restaurant. It was closed even more frequently in 1996, and the building was often used for private parties. Later that year, the restaurant aspect of Aladdin's Oasis vanished, to be replaced in early 1997 by a new stage show called *Aladdin and Jasmine's Story-Tale Adventures*. The twenty-five-minute presentation featured **cast members** dressed as *Aladdin* characters who (with the audience's help) retold tales from *The Arabian Nights*. This show went on hiatus in 2006 and closed permanently in April of 2008. Excitement briefly returned with a stunt show called *Secrets of the Stone Tiger*, which promoted the latest Indiana Jones movie in mid-2008. Then, with no special show to offer, the area became a simple meet-and-greet location where guests could mingle with costumed characters.

Late in 2014, Aladdin's Oasis became one of the options for the special dining packages offered for **Fantasmic!** That year's new On the Go menu presented full meals (chicken or lasagna entrees, sides, and beverages) for $19.99. In December 2015, special $22.99 packages were added that include seating reservations for **Paint the Night**. These boxed meals could be taken to the show, or they could be ordered and enjoyed during the day, before the evening's performance. Aladdin's Oasis offers a shaded patio area with two-dozen tables, a roped-off stage, and the giant lion's head from the desert scenes in *Aladdin*.

No matter what changes have come to the schedule or menu, today's Oasis still seems seriously underused. One hot summer day in 2016, Disneyland was at almost full capacity and we didn't see a single guest inside the open Oasis at noon. Hopefully this pretty spot can be revived to become a destination as lively and popular as its two next-door neighbors, the **Enchanted Tiki Room** and the **Jungle Cruise**.

Albright, Milt

(1916–2014)

Born in 1916, this Missourian joined Disney Studios in 1947 as a junior accountant. After getting to know **Walt Disney** personally and designing an unused but impressive car for the **Autopia** attraction in **Tomorrowland**, Albright was transferred to the nascent park and made manager of accounting. In this role, one of his duties was to write and deliver paychecks to Disneyland brass, including Walt Disney himself.

In the late 1950s Albright invented and ran Disneyland's **Holidayland** picnic area, making him "the only manager of a land at Disneyland that failed," according to his own description on the 2007 *Disneyland Secrets, Stories & Magic* DVD. Later, while overseeing the Group Sales department, he founded two longtime staples of Disneyland history: the **Magic Kingdom Club** for neighboring businesses and frequent visitors (Albright was also listed as the editor of the club's quarterly magazine) and **Grad Nite** for teens celebrating their high school graduations. Albright eventually headed the Special Projects and Guest Communications departments and mentored many young Disney executives before retiring in 1992. When Milt Albright was named a Disney Legend thirteen years later, he was also acknowledged as being Disneyland's first-ever employee. He died in 2014 at the age of ninety-seven.

Alice in Wonderland

MAP: Fantasyland, Fa-26

DATES: June 14, 1958–ongoing

One of Disneyland's long-standing dark rides, Alice in Wonderland is modeled after the popular Disney animated movie, as is the nearby **Mad Hatter's Mad Tea Party**.

Alice in Wonderland places its guests inside a pastel caterpillar-shaped car and drops them into the bizarre world of Lewis Carroll's famous Victorian novel. Originally, however, the attraction was conceived as a series of displays for guests to stroll past. Among the walk-through scenes were some tilting stairs for guests to climb and a slide to ride down. This version of the attraction was originally meant to be ready for 1955's **Opening Day**. Unfortunately, time and money were too tight for Imagineers to make the mid-July deadline. The delay turned out to be much longer than expected—as the animated Alice says to the White Rabbit in *Alice in Wonderland*, "Oh dear, this is serious."

Three years after it was supposed to open, Alice in Wonderland finally debuted in mid-June of 1958. By then, its location had been moved from the western **Fantasyland** row that held Snow White Adventures (now **Snow White's Scary Adventures**) to the east side of **Sleeping Beauty Castle**, opposite from **Matterhorn Mountain** (today, **Pinocchio's Daring Journey** fills the site that Alice originally would've occupied). Twenty-five years after its late opening, Alice in Wonderland was late to the party once again. When Fantasyland temporarily shut down for a massive renovation before its 1983 unveiling, Alice didn't reopen until April 14, 1984. During this renovation, Disneyland removed the topsy-turvy Upside Down Room and added about a minute of ride time, making it a more impressive four-minute attraction. Something else that has evolved over the years has been the cost: Alice required a D ticket for admission in the late 1950s and a C in the 1960s, but in 1971, it required only a B ticket.

Pre- and post-renovation, the attraction has always been unique when compared to other Fantasyland dark rides in that it takes guests outside its building into the open air—in this case, for a gentle forty-five-second glide across the tops of oversize plants. Most guests probably don't realize that Alice in Wonderland shares its building with **Mr. Toad's Wild Ride**. During the delightful 700-foot trip through Wonderland, the caterpillar cars actually climb up to the second floor above the Mr. Toad layout. Guests

are then lowered from the second floor to the ground floor and taken to a surprise "un-birthday" celebration that was added in 1984. Because of the outdoor stretch of track and the possibility of slippery situations, Alice in Wonderland often closes when there's rain.

Inside the attraction, the displays include familiar Carroll characters—the White Rabbit, Cheshire Cat, Mad Hatter, etc.—and incorporate the surreal styles, kaleidoscopic colors, and buoyant music from the 1951 Disney movie. Kathryn Beaumont, who voiced the movie's Alice character, reprised her vocals for the attraction and even updated them in 1984.

Disney Legend **Claude Coats**, who worked on the *Alice in Wonderland* film, is credited as the main designer of the attraction's original iteration. **Sam McKim** designed the 1958 **attraction poster** that spirals Alice from the rabbit hole down into her "wonderful world." **Tony Baxter**, the Imagineer who spearheaded the **Big Thunder Mountain Railroad** in the 1970s, was in charge of bringing eye-popping new effects to the attraction's 1984 renovation. A four-month closure in 2014 added enhancements to the exterior and clever digital projections inside.

With its large butterflies, flowers, and mushrooms out front, Alice in Wonderland has long presented an inviting view to guests riding on the nearby **Monorail** and **Matterhorn Bobsleds**. Attentive pedestrians will note more nifty design elements along the walkway outside the attraction, where recessed White Rabbit and Cheshire Cat statues are mounted in the walls.

Guests will also find plenty of Alice-themed merchandise on sale in various park stores, including Wonderland Tea, "the official unbirthday tea" that comes in blends such as Mad Tea Party and Topsy-Turvy. But there's one facet of the attraction that nobody can see because it was never realized—a proposed Alice in Wonderland Toy Shop that would have presented its fanciful wares within a Wonderland-style interior.

All-American College Band,
aka Collegiate All-Star Band

Disneyland's All-American College Band (renamed the Collegiate All-Star Band from 1998 to 2002) was born on June 14, 1971, as a part-time work experience program for local college musicians. Dressed in snappy uniforms, and now including players from all across the country, the band still plays themes from Disneyland's attractions and various Disney films from mid-June to mid-August. In 2015, their schedule included performances five days a week along Disneyland's **parade** route before **Paint the Night**, near **Sleeping Beauty Castle**, and at the daily **Town Square** flag retreat, as well as in Disney California Adventure. The band has also performed for special events throughout the park (such as Disneyland's forty-fifth birthday celebration in 2000).

By now, over 2,500 members have graduated from the band, which had twenty-one players in 2014. The band's longest tenured musical director was Dr. Art Bartner, who began leading it in the late 1970s and continued for the next twenty-eight summers; the current director is Dr. Ron McCurdy from USC's Thornton School of Music. In 2005 and 2015, Disneyland threw reunions for its All-American alumni and welcomed back over 150 members for unique afternoon performances in Town Square and at Sleeping Beauty Castle.

Alpine Gardens
MAP: Tomorrowland, T-1
DATES: December 1967–August 25, 1995

When the all-plastic **House of the Future** was demolished in 1967, the all-natural gardens surrounding it were retained. Rather than install another high-profile attraction in the area, Disney designers decided to save the space as a serene, largely undeveloped rest area.

Conveniently located just to the left of the main **Tomorrowland** gates, the Alpine Gardens offered pedestrians a quiet, convenient stop halfway between Tomorrowland and **Fantasyland**. The presence of a conical souvenir stand lessened, but didn't ruin, the bucolic effect. The "Alpine" in the name referred to the view of **Matterhorn Mountain**, which towered only 150 feet away to the northeast.

Walk-around Disney characters would occasionally appear here, but mostly the Alpine Gardens were left for guests to enjoy on their own. After closing in mid-1995, the area reopened in early 1996 as **King Triton Gardens**, with new landscaping and graceful new fountains.

American Dairy Association Exhibit,
aka Dairy Bar

MAP: Tomorrowland, T-23

DATES: January 21, 1956–September 1, 1958

Six months after Disneyland opened, the American Dairy Association brought some of its trade show displays into **Tomorrowland**. The building, second on the right inside Tomorrowland's entrance, already housed the walk-through **20,000 Leagues Under the Sea Exhibit. Souvenir books** from the 1950s describe the ADA location as a not-so-tantalizing presentation of "future techniques in production and distribution of dairy products." Among other things, the room included big plastic cows watching televisions while being milked; the large, sleek gauges and containers of modern milking machines; and a model of a milkman making a delivery in a small, jet-powered flying vehicle.

The interior barn-shaped Dairy Bar offered guests a folksy place to sit at tables and drink obligatory glasses of cold milk in front of a sign that proclaimed milk as "nature's most nearly perfect food." Many people referred to the entire exhibit as the Dairy Bar, but Disneyland's souvenir books listed the exhibit and the Dairy Bar as two separate entities (even though they shared the same sponsor and one naturally led to the other).

In 1958, the ADA was o-u-t when a Tomorrowland remodel preempted the site for **Fun Fotos** displays. All the buildings along this row of Tomorrowland would later undergo massive changes—within a decade, the walk-through exhibits were replaced by major attractions and stores, most notably **Adventure Thru Inner Space** and the **Character Shop**.

American Egg House

MAP: Town Square, TS-7

DATES: July 14, 1978–September 30, 1983

The American Egg House is unusual because it is still one of the only Disneyland attractions, shops, or restaurants to be supplanted by the very same establishment it had replaced earlier.

In 1976, the **Town Square Café** took over for the **Hills Bros. Coffee House and Coffee Garden** on **Main Street**. After two years as the Town Square Café, the American Egg House moved in and quickly became known as a great breakfast spot by virtue of its prime location at the beginning of **Main Street** (part of the Egg House was in the side room now used by the big **Disney Showcase** store). For many guests, it was the first eatery visible as they entered Disneyland and walked past the big **Opera House.** The Egg House also had the ideal morning menu; sponsorship by the American Egg Board led to many egg-themed menu items, especially elaborate omelets. Lunches and dinners would feature salads and sandwiches (some with eggs, naturally).

At the end of September 1983, the American Egg House cracked its last shell and the Town Square Café returned the next day for a nine-year run.

American Rifle Exhibit and Frontier Gun Shop

MAP: Frontierland, Fr-4

DATES: 1956–ca. 1986

Actual weapons in Disneyland? Yessiree, and they were right at home in **Frontierland,** an area described on the *Disneyland* **TV series** in 1958 as "a great place to warm up your six-shooters." Frontierland, remember, was where staged "shoot-outs" once took place between lawmen and villains, where guests could aim realistic rifles mounted atop the **Tom Sawyer Island** fort, where the **Opening Day** celebration featured sixteen Frontierland dancers cavorting with guns while singing about Davy Crockett's rifle, Ol' Betsy, where the **Sailing Ship *Columbia*** still blasts its cannon, and where a shooting gallery has been operating since 1957. With all its firearms, a more fitting name for Frontierland might be Gun-tierland.

The 1956 **souvenir book** lists an American Rifle Exhibit in Frontierland, and the 1957 book lists the exhibit and a Frontier Gun Shop, both located in the **Davy Crockett Arcade** building. The exhibit's glass cases displayed antique weapons from American history, including various muskets, Kentucky rifles, and Colt pistols. The small Gun Shop sold replicas of those weapons—many of them, it's safe to speculate, to spirited, rifle-ready kids wearing the Crockett-style coonskin caps made popular by TV's gun-totin' Fess Parker. Some sundries, such as film and inexpensive gifts, were also available.

The rifle exhibit lasted for three decades, with subtle changes: by the 1970s, the small guidebooks presented by INA (longtime sponsors of the **Carefree Corner**) were calling this exhibit a Gun Collection, not a Gun Shop, with "over fifty rifles, pistols, and swords" on view.

In 1987, the whole Crockett Arcade was remodeled and transformed into a large retail store called Pioneer Mercantile, minus the extensive gun displays. In a nod to tradition, modern Frontierland stores such as **Bonanza Outfitters** have continued to display individual antique rifles on their walls.

American Space Experience

MAP: Tomorrowland, T-5

DATES: May 22, 1998–October 26, 2003

While other **Tomorrowland** exhibits have pointed to the future, the American Space Experience celebrated the recent past, specifically the previous forty years of NASA's achievements in outer space. Opened in 1998 along with new attractions in the remodeled Tomorrowland, this educational walk-through exhibit and **Rocket Rods** shared the large building just inside the Tomorrowland entrance that had housed the **Circarama** theater.

Because the space exhibit was sponsored by NASA, displays included an actual moon rock, Hubble Space Telescope photos, an Apollo spacesuit, and a screen that showed NASA launches. A scale that revealed weights on other planets, models of future rockets, and a look at a bizarre Space Age material called aerogel were among the other displays that made this a fun and fascinating destination. In 2002, the exhibit added mock-ups of the Mars *Odyssey* spacecraft and one of the rovers soon to explore the red planet. A year after the mock-ups arrived, the Space Experience lost its space to a new **FASTPASS** area for **Buzz Lightyear Astro Blasters**.

America on Parade

DATES: June 12, 1975–September 12, 1976

In the mid-1970s, the proud patriotism already displayed throughout Disneyland, especially in such vivid attractions as **America Sings** and **Great Moments with Mr. Lincoln**, blossomed into a memorable bicentennial spectacular. A week after debuting in Walt Disney World, America on Parade began rolling through Disneyland on June 12, 1975. For the next fifteen months, an immense daily cavalcade of American popular music, oversize characters, floats shaped like red, white, and blue hot air balloons, displays of iconic moments from American history, and marching bands celebrated the nation's two-hundredth birthday.

Over 150 performers appeared in the **parade**, some made to look like famous people from history, such as Christopher Columbus and Benjamin Franklin. The variety of characters was impressive: cowboys, Mark Twain characters, old-fashioned aviators, generic modern athletes, and more. Mickey, Goofy, and Donald portrayed the three Spirit of '76 marching musicians. A TV special showed off all the pageantry, and in America's bicentennial year, the parade proved to be a big hit—according to

MOUSCELLANY

Next door to the **Main Street Cinema** is the fictional Casting Agency, which posts humorous Disneyland jobs that are available. Among the dozens they're "now casting" is one that references America on Parade: "NOW CASTING: A TWO-STORY-TALL SANDWICH. Must be able to pass the mustard. American Parade Productions, rooms 1975-76."

Disneyland: The First Thirty Years, 25 million people watched the 1,200 performances. After the finale on September 12, 1976, the **Main Street Electrical Parade**, which had been suspended for the duration of America on Parade, returned for another long run.

America Sings

MAP: Tomorrowland, T-14

DATES: June 29, 1974–April 10, 1988

Located in the back corner of **Tomorrowland** near the **Autopia**, the two-story Carousel Theater opened in 1967 as a three-quarter-acre cornerstone of the area's dramatic remodel. The innovative **Carousel of Progress** was the circular building's first attraction. When its six-year spin ended in 1973, the building was revitalized with a lively new attraction, this one arriving just in time for the bicentennial festivities that would peak in 1976.

Though it revolved in the opposite direction, America Sings utilized the same rotating-theater format the Carousel of Progress had used to slowly wheel the audience around a stationary hub. Whereas the Carousel of Progress had presented mini-plays with dialogue, America Sings was more like a six-part Carousel of Music. Another famous Walt—Whitman—wrote that he could "hear America singing," and sing it would in this new show. Thus, a group of 114 **Audio-Animatronic** characters—Disneyland's largest assembly of robotic figures at the time—saluted America's musical heritage with a show that included a prologue, four lighthearted musical medleys, and an epilogue. At twenty-four minutes, America Sings was one of Disneyland's longest attractions (others that have clocked in at over twenty minutes include the *American Journeys* film, **Fantasmic!**, the **Main Street Electrical Parade**, and the **Disneyland Railroad**).

Overseeing the proceedings was a patriotic pair of Audio-Animatronic birds, an eagle named Sam, and an owl named Ollie. A simple rendition of "Yankee Doodle Dandy" kicked off the show, followed by performances of more than three-dozen classic American songs from, among others, a swamp of bullfrogs, a wailing possum, gospel-singing foxes, an Old West bird quartet known as the Frontier Four, barbershop geese, grim vultures, storks on old-fashioned bicycles, and a long-haired, modern rock band featuring a crane on lead guitar who invited the audience to join in for the rousing "Joy to the World" finale. Classic American costumes—cowboy hats, Gay '90s dresses, Jazz Age suits, etc.—and gentle humor boosted the feel-good tunes.

Some of the characters' voices probably sounded familiar to guests. Sam was performed by the amiable folk singer Burl Ives, and the pig who belted out "Bill Bailey, Won't You Please Come Home" was vocalized by **Betty Taylor**, the singer who starred as Slue-Foot Sue over at the **Golden Horseshoe** in **Frontierland**. Many of the charming anthropomorphic animals were first drawn up by Disney Legend **Marc**

Davis, whose illustrations in the 1960s had added comic flair to **Pirates of the Caribbean** and the **Haunted Mansion**.

The whole production was popular enough to be released in 1974 as a Disneyland Records soundtrack LP with thirty-nine songs. However, once the bicentennial events had passed, so had the audiences for America Sings. With attendance dwindling, the admission ticket was downgraded from an E to a D, and in 1988, the last song was finally sung. After that, offices occupied much of the building and the downstairs theaters were used for in-house presentations until **Innoventions** opened in 1998.

Although the America Sings attraction disappeared, its characters didn't. Most of the musical animals joined the zip-a-dee-doo-dah critters inside **Splash Mountain** (such as the vultures, one of which is shown on page 51), and the armatures of a couple of the geese were transformed into high-tech droids for the **queue** leading into **Star Tours**. In 2010, sharp-eyed Disneyland guests may have spied a new tribute to the old America Sings: a small illustration of the show's bandstand (with two **America Sings** characters inside it) was painted on one of the walls inside **Innoventions**.

Anderson, Ken
(1909–1993)

Like many of the Disney Legends who helped create Disneyland, Ken Anderson worked on Disney's animated films before he started designing park attractions. Born in 1909 in Seattle, Washington, Anderson had been studying architecture and art when he was hired by **Walt Disney** in 1934 to work first on the *Silly Symphonies* cartoons and then on *Snow White and the Seven Dwarfs* (he's credited as the artist who, among other things, added Dopey's wiggling ears).

After contributing story ideas, art, and layouts to many more animated classics of the 1940s and '50s, Anderson sketched the scenes of Norman Rockwell-style Americana that would have formed the miniature Disneylandia sets Walt Disney wanted to take on tour (when the tour idea proved to be unworkable, the park concept coalesced). In the early 1950s, Anderson joined the core Disneyland design team and became a major contributor to **Fantasyland** attractions, especially the Snow White, Peter Pan, and Mr. Toad attractions. Anderson later worked on the **Haunted Mansion**, among other major attractions.

To other Imagineers, Anderson was more than just a brilliant artist. The book *Walt Disney Imagineering*, written by Anderson's peers, calls him "the first Imagineer" because, years before Disneyland opened, he had tried to develop a nine-inch-tall "dancing man"—the earliest attempt at a Disney **Audio-Animatronics** figure.

Anderson was named a Disney Legend in 1991; two years later, he died of a stroke in La Cañada-Flintridge, California. *The Jungle Book* fortieth anniversary DVD (2007) includes in its special features a short profile of Anderson and shows some of his earliest work in animation.

Apartments

MAP: Town Square, TS-5; New Orleans Square, NOS-1

DATES: July 1955–ongoing; ca. 1970–1987

Walt Disney had a private apartment built above the **Fire Department** in **Town Square** so he and his family could have their own secluded nook at Disneyland. This apartment wasn't merely a VIP rest stop—it was an actual residence, a place where Disney and his family could stay overnight inside Disneyland, for days at a time if necessary.

Appropriately enough for this Disneyland neighborhood, the posh apartment was decorated like something out of the early 1900s. **Emile Kuri**, who decorated the sets for dozens of live-action Disney movies, brought in white columns, patterned wallpaper, red drapes, antique Victorian furniture, a working Victrola phonograph, and even an old-fashioned candlestick phone (a big, squat TV was one of the few conspicuous concessions to modern times). The apartment was small, though, just 500 square feet with a changing room, a cozy front room where the couches unfolded into beds, a bathroom, and a tiny kitchen area with a grill, refrigerator, and sink. An outside lounge area stretching toward **City Hall** was decorated with white statues, plants, and wicker chairs.

In the *Disney Parks: Disneyland Resort Behind the Scenes* DVD, Disney Legend **Martin Sklar** says that the apartment "was a place where [Walt Disney] could be close to the action and yet be separated from it. I think Walt really wanted to be able to be close to what was happening here to understand it." From his front windows, Disney could look out on the bustling activity of Town Square, with the train station to his right, the **Opera House** straight across, and the **Emporium** to his left. The public wasn't allowed inside the private residence, of course, and in fact, the fire pole in the **Fire Department** below was blocked off to prevent anyone from shinnying up (supposedly Disney himself used to slide down the pole occasionally). Also, so that the residents upstairs wouldn't be disturbed by people ringing the fire bell downstairs, the outer doors of the Fire Department were usually closed when the apartment was occupied.

No mention of the apartment is made in Disneyland's early **souvenir books**, and no photos of the apartment were released until an exclusive shot of the Disney family relaxing in the main room ran in the August 1963 issue of *National Geographic* (the magazine dubs the apartment "Disney's supersecret hideaway"). One of the few times the general public has seen anyone in the apartment was **Opening Day**, when the TV broadcast of the festivities showed some people watching from the front window. Today, Walt Disney's relatives occasionally use the apartment, and it's sometimes included as a stop on special tours. As a tribute to Disney, a lamp, visible from Town Square, remains lit in the front window. During the holidays,

MOUSCELLANY

Veteran guests may recall another set of apartments briefly marked inside Disneyland—the faux Plaza Apartments, identified from 1955 to 1956 by a sign at the northeast end of **Main Street** (the **Carefree Corner** hospitality center moved here in August 1956).

a lighted Christmas tree sometimes fills the window as well.

In the 1960s, Disney decided that he needed a bigger apartment at the other end of Disneyland for both himself and his brother, **Roy Disney**. This 3,000-square-foot residence would be located above the **Pirates of the Caribbean** entrance in **New Orleans Square**, with bedrooms for grandchildren and a balcony that connected to the private dining rooms at **Club 33**.

Walt Disney died before the second apartment was completed. It was used as offices for the Disneyland staff until 1987, when the whole space was converted into the **Disney Gallery**, with lavish décor to suggest what the finished rooms would have looked like. On the balcony outside the gallery's front door was an ornate iron railing with the initials of the apartment's intended occupants—WD and RD—woven into the design (shown). In late 2007, the rooms were remodeled into a 2,600-square-foot Disneyland Dream Suite for the 2008 Disney Dreams Giveaway. Over five times larger than the tiny Town Square apartment, the new guest quarters include a patio with "fireflies," a living room with French Provincial décor, two master bedrooms, two bathrooms, an electric train, a full-size carousel horse, vintage toys, and unique audio and visual effects. In 2015, guests could win a night in the Dream Suite as one of the prizes in that year's special sweepstakes timed with Disneyland's **Diamond Celebration**.

Aramaki, Hideo
(1915–2005)

In the 1960s and '70s, guests who enjoyed fine meals in Disneyland had Hideo Aramaki to thank. He was the man in charge of food for almost two decades. Born in Hawaii in 1915, Aramaki was of Japanese descent but had gone by his nickname, "Indian," since childhood. A semi-professional baseball player in the 1930s, he began working in restaurant kitchens across the country in the 1940s and moved to Southern California to run a Hawaiian-themed restaurant in the 1950s.

In 1964, Aramaki was hired as the chef at the **Tahitian Terrace** in **Adventureland**. Even though he had no formal culinary training, he was so successful that by 1967, he was the executive chef overseeing all of Disneyland's restaurants, standardizing the food quality, and training the park's chefs, as well as personally preparing special meals for visiting dignitaries. After performing some of these same duties at Walt Disney World, Aramaki retired in 1985. He was named a Disney Legend in 2005, the same year he died at age ninety.

Arrow Development

While most of Disneyland's attractions and vehicles were created from start to finish by Disney designers, engineers, and machinists, some classics came from an outside company. Based in Northern California, Arrow Development built the flying elephants and spinning teacups that most Disneyland guests instantly recognize.

After meeting in the navy, Ed Morgan and Karl Bacon founded a machine shop business in 1946 (later they claimed to have named the company Arrow after a stickpin in Ed's necktie). For seven years, they built playground equipment and simple carnival rides until they caught **Walt Disney's** eye with the *Lil' Belle*, a small, old-fashioned paddlewheeler that cruised on Oakland's Lake Merritt. Disney contracted Arrow in 1953 to work with Disney Legend **Roger Broggie** on some of the earliest **Fantasyland** attractions, starting with a dozen autos for **Mr. Toad's Wild Ride** and soon including everything from the horses on the **King Arthur Carrousel** to the engines and cars of the **Casey Jr. Circus Train**.

The overwhelming success of these Fantasyland attractions led to further Arrow contributions to Disneyland, most notably the revolutionary **Matterhorn Bobsleds**, the ambitious **Flying Saucers**, the complicated **Omnimover** mechanisms for **Adventure Thru Inner Space** and the **Haunted Mansion**, and the water-pumping system and boats for **It's a Small World** and **Pirates of the Caribbean**. Disney bought in as a minority investor in 1960, helped relocate Arrow to a larger space, and then enlisted the company for Walt Disney World attractions.

For non-Disney parks, Arrow's innovations led to imaginative roller coasters and flume rides that have often been credited as being the world's fastest, tallest, or steepest. Arrow was later bought and subsumed within other companies, though the name briefly reappeared as Arrow Dynamics in the 1990s.

Art Corner

MAP: Tomorrowland, T-6

DATES: October 1, 1955–September 6, 1966

During the summer of 1955, a temporary art show operated at the north end of **Main Street** under some canopies and a red-on-blue banner that read, "Disney Artists Exhibit." That October, the exhibit relocated into a corner building about 200 feet inside **Tomorrowland.** The boxy Art Corner adjoined the round **Satellite View of America** building and stuck out toward the **Astro-Jets** some fifty feet away. To help make the gallery fit in with the futuristic Tomorrowland, the Art Corner's exterior was painted with colorful modern art motifs.

Inside was a French-themed setting for art supplies and many Disneyland postcards, among them sets that depicted Disney characters frolicking in the Art Corner itself. Disney artwork was also for sale, including thousands of inexpensive—and now rare—animation cels (one of the frequent buyers of these cels was **Ray Bradbury**, who describes his collection in *Bradbury Speaks*). As mentioned on Bjorn Aronsen's **attraction poster**, guests could "see **Walt Disney** artists at work," and indeed they could: animators were on hand to draw quick portraits of guests for only $1.50, and for convenience the shop offered framing, mailing services, and even a mail-order catalog.

Because of the comprehensive remodel that closed many attractions throughout Tomorrowland in 1966, the art departed from the corner site, and a year later the building reemerged as part of the larger Tomorrowland Terrace (now the **Galactic Grill**). Though the Art Corner's attraction poster listed only one location (the one in Tomorrowland), Disneyland's **souvenir books** of the 1950s and '60s list another Art Corner selling "pictures and art supplies" in **Fantasyland**; early maps put it in a spot approximately where the **Village Haus** stands today.

Art of Animation

MAP: Tomorrowland, T-5

DATES: May 28, 1960–September 5, 1966

Like the **Art Corner**, the Art of Animation seemed slightly out of place in **Tomorrowland**, because both of these art establishments basically celebrated the past, not the future. The Art of Animation sat in the big building next to the **Circarama** theater. Previously, the **Satellite View of America** had spun in this large, round space; however, by the end of the 1950s, the novelty of looking at Earth from high altitude had worn off and audiences had disappeared. So did the attraction, in February of 1960.

Its replacement that spring, the Art of Animation, was an exhibit promoting Disney's own movies and requiring a B ticket from Disneyland's **ticket book**. It was basically the same as several other Art of Animation exhibits that had already been touring the world to build excitement for *Sleeping Beauty*, the 1959 movie that was, at the time, Disney Studios' most expensive production ever. Acknowledging the other touring exhibits, Paul Hartley's large **attraction poster** for the Art of Animation shows Disney characters on a burnt-orange background with text that touts the attraction as the "international exhibit direct from London–Paris–Tokyo."

The inside perimeter of the Art of Animation exhibit was lined with displays showing how animated movies were made. The center of the room presented arrangements of plastic chairs, potted plants, and ashtrays, enabling guests to sit, reflect, and smoke. In the fall of 1966, the Art of Animation vanished when the adjacent theater building expanded to become Circle-Vision 360 for 1967's "new Tomorrowland."

Arts and Crafts Shop

MAP: Fantasyland, Fa-3

DATES: Ca. 1958–ca. 1963; ca. 1970–1982

In the late 1950s, this intimate shop was located in a small spot just inside the entrance to **Sleeping Beauty Castle**. The **Clock Shop** replaced the Arts and Crafts Shop around 1963, but by the beginning of the 1970s, the Arts and Crafts Shop had returned. This reappearance was one of the few times a closed Disneyland business reopened with the same name in the same location (among the other establishments to close "permanently" and reopen later in the same location are **Great Moments with Mr. Lincoln**, **Mlle. Antoinette's Parfumerie**, **Sleeping Beauty Castle Walk-Through**, and the **Town Square Café**).

Delicate, expensive gifts were sold in the Arts and Crafts Shop, including ornate imported clocks and hand-blown glass sculptures. Around 1982, with Fantasyland undergoing a major remodel, the shop closed permanently; a year later, a new glass shop, **Castle Arts**, opened in its place. The old arts-and-crafts theme lived on, however, because another new store, **Geppetto's Arts & Crafts**, also debuted in 1983, its location about 200 feet north, near **Pinocchio's Daring Journey**.

Ask Otto and Official Apps

In the late 1990s, Otto Matic told corny jokes inside Manhattan's Disney Store. That Otto was a small **Audio-Animatronic** figure voiced by Penn Jillette. Disneyland introduced a new Otto in mid-July 2012, and though it's not an A-A robot and no longer has Jillette's voice, it's still entertaining and is definitely more helpful.

By dialing (714) 520-7090, guests can reach Otto, Disneyland's cheerful voice-response information system. Questions about daily schedules, wait-times for attractions, and park basics all get quick answers and are often supplemented with enthusiastic descriptions and rudimentary tips; more complicated questions (menu specifics, for instance) are relayed to a live **cast member**. Occasionally, Otto will pause to whistle or hum such Disney classics as "I've Got No Strings."

Late in 2012, Disneyland followed this phone line with an official Twitter account, @DisneylandToday, to give guests live, up-to-the-minute information. In May of 2013, the park launched @DisneylandAP, another Twitter account just for Annual Passholders. Mobile Magic, Disney's official interactive app with updated wait-times and maps, launched in 2009 with a $9.99 price tag. Within two years, it had transformed into a free app, and by the end of 2013 it had disappeared altogether. Disney Electronic Content, Inc. then created a new and improved official app that it released in August 2015. Called simply Disneyland, the free app for Android and iOS devices enables guests to peruse maps, investigate dining options, check on wait-times, locate **restrooms**, find walk-around characters, and more.

Astro-Jets, aka Tomorrowland Jets

MAP: Tomorrowland, T-8

DATES: March 24, 1956–September 5, 1966

Disney designers didn't invent the basic Astro-Jet idea. Rides with similar vehicles that whirled around a central pivot were already working in amusement parks before Disneyland even opened. The Disneyland spin on the spinners was to upgrade them with better detailing. Disney artist **John Hench** drew up a concept for a whirling rocket attraction in 1955, dubbing it the Saturn Patrol Ride Rocket. The Astro-Jets, however, didn't debut until 1956, making this Disneyland's first major post-**Opening Day** addition.

For the next four decades, some variation of the Astro-Jets stood in the heart of **Tomorrowland**, about fifty feet west of the big circular Carousel Theater building.

From 1956 to 1964, the astro-attraction was known as the Astro-Jets, a dozen stubby cylinders with thin wings, a headlight on the nose, and open cockpits barely big enough for two adults. Named after bright Milky Way stars from A (*Altair*) to V (*Vega*), the jets were white with either red or blue trim and seemed more like contemporary air force aircraft than futuristic astro-craft (indeed, honorary air force personnel were on hand when the attraction opened). Each jet was mounted on an arm extending about twenty feet from an axial column that looked like an air-traffic control tower. Guests paid C, and later B, tickets from their Disneyland **ticket books** and entered the jets at ground level. Once the whirling began, pilots controlled their altitude with a cockpit lever, raising the jets up to a height of thirty-eight feet. Disney's cost to build the attraction: about $200,000.

On August 7, 1964, the name Tomorrowland Jets supplanted Astro-Jets to avoid any unintentional association with American Airlines, which had started painting "Astrojet" on its airliners. Two years later, the countdown to a much bigger change began. On September 5, 1966, the Tomorrowland Jets closed for a renaming/remodeling that reopened in mid-1967 as the dramatic new **Rocket Jets** in a dramatic new location.

Astro-Orbitor

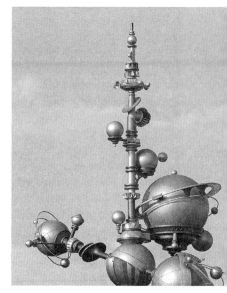

MAP: Tomorrowland, T-3

DATES: May 22, 1998–ongoing

From the **Astro-Jets** to the **Rocket Jets**, variations of a whirling-jet attraction operated in **Tomorrowland** from 1956 to 1997. In 1998, another spinner arrived. For the new Astro-Orbitor, stylings came from both Disneyland Paris, where it had originated as the Orbitron Machine Volantes (Orbitron Flying Machine), and Walt Disney World, where it had opened in 1994 as the Astro-Orbiter (with an "-er" suffix). Designers basically recreated the Parisian and Floridian attractions—one of the few times a Disney design emigrated from east to west, instead of the reverse (other imports from Walt Disney World: **Buzz Lightyear Astro Blasters**, *Captain EO*, the **Country Bear Jamboree**, **FASTPASS**, *Honey, I Shrunk the Audience*, *Magic Journeys*, **Innoventions**, **The Many Adventures of Winnie the Pooh**, the **Mile Long Bar**, **PhotoPass**, **Pirates League**, **Space Mountain**, and *Wonders of China*).

Compared to the uncomplicated Astro-Jets and sleek Rocket Jets, the Astro-Orbitor is a complex conglomeration of moving spheres and fanciful spaceships inspired, as Disneyland's own publications have noted, by the works of Leonardo da Vinci. The color scheme is no longer stark and achromatic—vintage gold and brass tones, punctuated by strong blues, help create the impression that this intricate whirligig with a steampunk spire (shown) is a fascinating antique built in some earlier century (or if not built, at least imagined in one of Jules Verne's nineteenth-century novels).

Not only is the look drastically different, the new location is, too. The Astro-Orbitor stands about 250 feet away from the Astro-Jets' previous site, which was deep inside Tomorrowland. By contrast, today's sixty-four-foot-tall Astro-Orbitor anchors Tomorrowland as the first attraction at the land's entrance (another contrast: instead of standing high above the walkway, as the Rocket Jets did, the Astro-Orbitor's base sits in a depression below the level of the walkway). This new spot is just in front of the PeopleMover tracks and about fifty feet outside Tomorrowland's metallic gates. At night, its gleaming lights and shining metal transform the Astro-Orbitor into a kind of animated lighthouse that guides guests into the future.

As with previous iterations of Disneyland's whirling-jets concept, there are twelve vehicles, the altitude of each vehicle is controlled by the pilot via an inboard handle, and the ride-time is about ninety seconds. One curiosity never explained is the spelling: the "-or" suffix has been said to be the result of a typo in the original plans, or perhaps it was intended to be a quick way to differentiate the Florida and Anaheim attractions. The hyphen in the name appears irregularly in Disneyland's own literature.

Atencio, Francis Xavier
(1920–)

From classic movies to classic rides, Francis Xavier Atencio's Disney career paralleled Disney history from the 1930s to the 1980s. Born in Colorado in 1920, Atencio came to Los Angeles in 1937 and began studying at a local art institute. A year later, he was hired as a Disney animator, and soon he was working on *Fantasia*. Known since he was a teenager as simply "X" (or "X.," as it's punctuated on his **Main Street Tribute Window**), he served in World War II and then returned to Disney to work on some of the studio's most popular productions, including several Oscar-winning shorts and acclaimed features like *The Parent Trap* and *Mary Poppins*.

In the 1960s, Atencio began contributing to projects throughout Disneyland. Some projects were highly technical—the August 1963 issue of *National Geographic* shows him programming an **Audio-Animatronics** bird for the new **Enchanted Tiki Room**. But Atencio was nothing if not versatile: he helped with the **Grand Canyon** and **Primeval World** dioramas, wrote the scripts for **Adventure Thru Inner Space** and **Pirates of the Caribbean**, and penned the pirates' legendary "Yo Ho (A Pirate's Life for Me)" lyrics (Atencio even performed the creepy voice for the talking pirate skull that prefaces the first waterfall). At the end of the decade, Atencio thrilled audiences with his work on the **Haunted Mansion**. Once again, he wrote the narrator's script and the lyrics of the main theme song ("Grim Grinning Ghosts"). The

MOUSCELLANY

It's possible that X. Atencio took inspiration for his Pirates of the Caribbean lyrics from "The Pirate Song," a short tune deleted from Disney's 1953 *Peter Pan* movie. The film's song includes the lines "a pirate's life is just the life for you" and "yo ho ho, buccaneering you must go!"

cemetery outside the mansion honored Atencio's contributions with an honorary tombstone that read: "Requiescat Francis Xavier: No Time Off for Good Behavior RIP."

When Disney expanded its theme parks to Florida, Atencio was right alongside, assisting on such major attractions as **Space Mountain** and EPCOT. He even helped with Tokyo Disneyland in the early 1980s before finally retiring in 1984. A dozen years later, Atencio was named a Disney Legend. Attentive guests in the Pirates of the Caribbean's outdoor **queue** will see the name of this living legend listed first on the elaborate plaque that honors "Walt Disney's Buccaneer Crew" (detail shown).

Attendance

Before Disneyland opened, "the Disney people" anticipated that attendance would be "60,000 a day," according to reporter Bob Thomas's July 16, 1955, preview for the Associated Press. However, those same officials were going to "try to hold the total at one time to 46,000" because they were reluctant "to jeopardize the enjoyment" of those who had paid to get in. To their credit, the prognosticators were right on target with the 46,000 figure, for that has approximately been Disneyland's average daily attendance for the last decade. Annual attendance has hovered around 16 million.

In an era when the park routinely entertains 40,000+ guests a day, it's hard to believe there were days when attendance dipped below a thousand guests, but that did happen on rainy days in Disneyland's early years. In general, though, attendance at the young park steadily accelerated from year to year. After **Roy Disney** bought the first Disneyland admission ticket (#000001) for $1 on July 18, 1955, the millionth ticket was sold only fifty-eight days later. It took sixty-nine months for Disneyland to draw its first 25 million guests, but then only fifty-two months to draw its next 25 million. Almost ten years after **Opening Day**, Disneyland admitted its 50 millionth guest, but then only six more years passed before guest number 100 million clicked through the turnstiles.

Disneyland's attendance milestones quickly piled up by the tens of millions. Guest number 100 million arrived in 1971, sixteen years after Opening Day, but the next 100 million arrived less than a decade later (1981). The park reached its next 100 million eight and a half years after that

MOUSCELLANY

At least two guests have visited Disneyland every single day for an entire year (actually, both visited for two consecutive years starting January 1, 2012. One of these guests continued on and celebrated consecutive visit #1,500 in February of 2016).

(1989), the next 100 million less than eight years after that (1997), and the next 100 million—bringing the total to 500 million—just six and a half years later (2004).

Disneyland's current annual attendance figures would astonish a 1955 guest. The estimated attendance in Disneyland's first year of operation was about 3.6 million people, but by 2015, that number had quintupled to 18 million, with an average of over 49,000 guests every single day of the year, rain or shine. No other entertainment or sports venue in the world has achieved Disneyland's steadily rising attendance figures for over sixty consecutive years. Concert halls and sports stadiums can draw 20,000–50,000 people or more pretty regularly, and they might even draw over 100,000 people on some days, but no entertainment facility has ever drawn Disneyland's daily attendance figures for over 21,000 days in a row (not counting those rare

sudden closures mentioned in the **Admissions** entry).

At times, Disneyland becomes so overwhelmed with crowds that it has to stop letting people in. On the busiest days, when attendance is around 80,000 guests, the park will close its turnstiles completely and redirect late arrivals to Disney California Adventure. These "level 4 closures" happen several times a year, sometimes during the holiday season and often when there are special events, such as the all-night party that led off 2015's **Diamond Celebration**. Various strategies are also enacted within Disneyland itself to ease frustrations on particularly crowded days: additional live entertainment is presented to guests waiting in long **queues**, two **Guest Flow Corridors** are opened up on either side of **Main Street** to make it easier to enter and exit in the evening, and extra **cast members** help direct pedestrian traffic during **parades**.

An informal record of Disneyland's total attendance is kept outside the main train station, where a sign facing the turnstiles announces Disneyland's "official population." In March of 2013, that number jumped from 500 million (the total posted as of 2005) to 650 million. At that rate, guest number 1 billion should enter the park soon after Disneyland's seventy-fifth birthday in 2030.

Attraction Posters

Beautiful attraction posters have adorned Disneyland since 1956. So ubiquitous, recognizable, and important are these posters that they've been analyzed in books, sold as valuable framed artworks, and incorporated into films such as *Up* and *Monsters, Inc.*

Most of today's guests are familiar with the sixteen posters inside the two main tunnels that lead from the turnstiles to **Town Square**, but the posters haven't always been there. In the 1950s and '60s, they were placed along the low metal fence that surrounds the Mickey Mouse flower bed in front of the train station (when **Saving Mr. Banks**, a movie set in the early 1960s, was being filmed in 2012, the posters were temporarily returned to this fence). Additional posters have also appeared elsewhere in Disneyland, such as along the **Avenue of the Flags**, on the walls of the **Plaza Gardens**, on the **Monorail** pylons just outside the main **entrance**, and inside **Redd Rockett's Pizza Port** and the **Penny Arcade**. Often the posters promote attractions far from the location where guests are currently standing, thus inspiring them to seek out something completely different in another land.

No matter where they've been placed over the years, the posters have always offered tantalizing glimpses of Disneyland's highlights. The large size of the posters—three feet wide by four-and-a-half feet tall—means they can be seen from a distance, drawing guests toward them like moths to a thrilling flame. Imagineer **Tony Baxter** describes their long-range appeal in his foreword to *Poster Art of the Disney Parks*; he writes about the "slow crawl" across the busy **parking lot** and how the colorful posters with "oversized images" and "eye-popping graphics" would "trigger kids' imaginations and make this final stretch to the main entrance actually . . . thrilling!" "A great poster," Baxter declares, "sells its story from a distance and needs to be glimpsed just briefly to work its magic."

The Disneyland Book of Lists identifies sixty-one posters, all with bold artwork that captures the spirit of their subjects at the expense of literal renderings. Thus the Jungle River poster magnifies an elephant into a trumpeting goliath towering over the foliage, the **Skyway to Tomorrowland** poster hyperbolically raises its buckets hundreds of feet aloft, the poster for **Fantasyland** puts the flying Dumbo sky-high above tiny people below, and the **Flying Saucers** poster shows saucers that actually work.

Simple designs make the posters easy to understand—a key requirement considering that most of the viewers are distracted, on the move, and perhaps unfamiliar with the attraction that's being illustrated. The text doesn't just name the subject being shown; it also gives a brief, dynamic description and the location (**Adventureland**, **Frontierland**, etc.), so guests will know where to find it. A plaque adjacent to attraction posters at the Walt Disney Family Museum states that **Walt Disney** "insisted on approving all final posters, often meeting with the printer, S. H. Burrows, in the hallway of the studio."

In Disneyland's early decades, the hand-stenciled posters usually presented blocky shapes and a handful of strong colors instead of intricate details and a complex palette of subtle shades. When guests are shown, they're usually either small silhouettes (their diminutive size contrasting with the immensity of something else on the poster) or flat, cartoony caricatures complementing, not distracting from, the main subject.

This blocky style is reminiscent of the classic travel posters that would've been seen in mid-century travel agencies and airports. Starting in the 1970s, however, Disneyland began displaying a new poster style with an ornate "window box" design—

MOUSCELLANY

The land that has had more of its attractions on posters than any other? **Tomorrowland.** The fewest? **Mickey's Toontown** hasn't had a single attraction make it onto a poster.

the later **Jungle Cruise**, **Big Thunder Mountain Railroad**, and **Country Bear Jamboree** posters all have decorative borders, use dozens of colors, and show fine details.

No signatures appear on any of the posters, but several poster artists have been identified over the years. Disney Studios artist Bjorn Aronsen designed most of the early posters between 1955 and 1958, the year he left the company. **Mary Blair**, **Claude Coats**, **Rolly Crump**, Paul Hartley, and **John Hench** are among the other artists who designed posters. A few posters have inside jokes worked into them: according to *Poster Art of the Disney Parks*, artist Drew Struzan showed his wife in the jungle vehicle of his 1995 **Indiana Jones Adventure** poster, and Collin Campbell used his own likeness for the main swashbuckler on his 1966 **Pirates of the Caribbean** poster.

While the majority of the posters have spotlighted major attractions and exhibits, some have also promoted restaurants and businesses. **Casa de Fritos**, the Red Wagon Inn (now the **Plaza Inn**), the **Art Corner**, the **Art of Animation**, and the **Disneyland Hotel** have all had their own posters. Several of the attractions have had two or more separate posters: the Jungle Cruise, Monorail, **PeopleMover**, **Star Tours,** and **Enchanted Tiki Room** are among those that appear in multiple versions. Original posters mounted on fabric are collectors' items that sell for thousands of dollars today. Relatively inexpensive reproductions have been sold in and out of the park for years in various formats and sizes; Disneyland's own Art on Demand service has offered customized presentations.

Audio-Animatronics

Much has been written about Disneyland's innovative Audio-Animatronics. Even as scholarly a commentator as the medievalist Umberto Eco surrendered to the "miraculous efficacy" of the park's A-A figures. They enabled Walt Disney to construct "a fantasy world more real than reality," Eco says in *Travels in Hyperreality*, with "perfect imitation" that has "reached its apex." It took years of focused effort for **Walt Disney** to attain that apex.

The seed for what would later blossom into **Great Moments with Mr. Lincoln** was planted on vacations Walt Disney took in the 1940s. During trips to New Orleans and Europe, Disney was fascinated by small mechanical birds and toys, which he brought home and studied. Inspired to attempt something similar, Disney began dreaming of a traveling exhibit with miniature sets and small mechanical figures. In 1951, he even had several employees, notably **Ken Anderson** and **Roger Broggie**, create a small mechanical man who executed pre-recorded dance moves (film footage of long-limbed song-and-dance-man Buddy Ebsen helped the engineers work out the steps). Once Disneyland was on the drawing board, early plans called for talking Chinese characters and animals in an unrealized **Chinatown** area off of **Main Street**.

The first appearance of early Audio-Animatronic figures came in 1955, with the wild beasts and dancing natives along the **Jungle Cruise**, followed five years later by the varied animals of **Nature's Wonderland** (the **Frontierland** acreage toured by mules and mine trains). On these two attractions, hundreds of mechanical birds, reptiles, bears, hippos, and other wild figures made repeated motions that, though simple compared to later creations, seemed completely realistic from a distance. Walt Disney knew he was on the brink of something truly innovative: "A new door opened," he said about this era's Audio-Animatronics, "a new way of entertainment appeared for us . . . another dimension in our world of animating the inanimate."

The breakthrough came in 1963. That year, the **Enchanted Tiki Room** brought Audio-Animatronics up-close and center stage with its cast of authentic tropical birds and fanciful tiki sculptures that performed a complex show filled with dialogue, song, and movement all choreographed by a primitive computer the size of a closet. It was in those years that Disney Legend **Bill Cottrell** coined the trademarked term Audio-Animatronics, blending sound and animation into a portmanteau word that Disney literature began formally defining as "a unique concept in entertainment which electronically combines and synchronizes voices, music, and sound effects with the movement of animated objects." Walt Disney eagerly appropriated and proudly used the word when he described on TV the ambitious electro-mechanical figures his design team was now steadily producing for Disneyland.

If audiences were delighted by the tiki show, they were startled by the next developments. First unveiled at the 1964–1965 New York World's Fair, **It's a Small World** immediately charmed audiences with its singing mechanical children. Elsewhere at the fair, towering dinosaurs squared off in an exhibit that later became Disneyland's **Primeval World Diorama**; Progressland presented thirty-two realistic Audio-Animatronic family members in what Disneyland guests would come to know as the **Carousel of Progress**; and, most ambitiously, a life-size President Lincoln stood up and delivered a speech to the amazement of nearly everyone in attendance.

With the hydraulics and electronics quickly improving, by the mid-1970s Audio-Animatronic figures populated every corner of Disneyland. There were brainy Mission Control engineers talking to guests in **Flight to the Moon**, personable pirates cavorting in **Pirates of the Caribbean**, guitar-strummin' bears in the **Country Bear Jamboree**,

bike-riding birds in **America Sings**, and so many more for so many years now that it's hard to remember a time when Audio-Animatronic figures *weren't* on display.

"People get more out of [Audio-Animatronics] than if there were a real actor there," says Disney Legend **John Hench** in Thomas and Johnston's *Disney Animation*. According to Hench, advanced A-A characters "actually do a better job—there's something *super* human about them."

By the time Indiana Jones began swinging through the **Indiana Jones Adventure** in 1995, the art and technology of Audio-Animatronics was so advanced that the truly lifelike Indy didn't simply dazzle guests, he fooled some of them into believing he was an actual person. Dazzlement and believability—two words that initially inspired the creation of Disneyland and then came to describe Disney's remarkable achievements with Audio-Animatronics.

> **MOUSCELLANY**
>
> The term "Audio-Animatronics" does get referenced outside of Disney's theme parks. In 1993's *Jurassic Park*, the "blood-sucking lawyer" mistakenly asks if the dinosaurs use "auto-erotic" technology. In 2015's *Tomorrowland*, the two starring girls stutter over "audio-animatronic" and settle on "robot" as a more easily understood name for the artificial beings chasing them.

Aunt Jemima's Pancake House,
aka Aunt Jemima's Kitchen

MAP: Frontierland, Fr-7

DATES: August 9, 1955–1970

Back in the 1950s and '60s, Quaker Oats sponsored a restaurant that brought a "gracious 'Old South' setting" (according to an original place mat) to the western tip of **Frontierland**. Aunt Jemima's Pancake House opened a few weeks after the rest of Disneyland did, its location about seventy-five feet from the nearest bank of the **Rivers of America**. A huge, twenty-two-ton Monterey Bay fig tree, craned into place in front of the restaurant, offered shade for alfresco dining.

The great pancakes, according to an ad in the July 15, 1955, issue of the *Orange County Register*, were served "hot off the griddle—tender and golden brown with the flavor folks all over America say can't be matched," thanks to a "treasured 4-flour recipe." Besides the pancakes and waffles that were topped with Aunt Jemima syrup, the restaurant was known for having Aunt Jemima herself on hand. Aunt Jemima was a Quaker Oats character, of course, first played in public early in the century by a former slave who died in 1923. Seven women assumed the character over the decades, including Aylene Lewis, who portrayed her at Disneyland. As Aunt Jemima, Lewis would greet guests, visit tables, and, as declared on the place mats, "send you on your way with a cheerful 'You all come back!'"

Early in 1962, the restaurant closed temporarily. Expanding into the space next door where **Don DeFore's Silver Banjo Barbecue** had been, it reopened in July as Aunt Jemima's Kitchen. The restaurant had two doorways, since it straddled the

corner between Frontierland and **Adventureland.** The Frontierland entrance incorporated plantation architecture, while the Adventureland entrance featured a thatched,
jungle-themed roof. Quaker Oats ended its participation at Disneyland in 1967, but
the Aunt Jemima theme stayed until 1970, when the restaurant was remodeled and
renamed the **Magnolia Tree Terrace.**

Autopia, aka Tomorrowland Autopia, aka Autopia, Presented by Chevron, aka Autopia, Powered by Honda

MAP: Tomorrowland, T-12

DATES: July 17, 1955–ongoing

Of the four Autopias that have existed at Disneyland, the one in **Tomorrowland** was
the only Autopia up and running on **Opening Day.** This original Autopia track curled
across approximately three unlandscaped acres of Disneyland's eastern edge, with
most of the track design attributed to Disney Legend **Marvin Davis.**

As Ralph Waldo Emerson wrote in 1844, "everything good is on the highway." So
it seemed in the mid-1950s, when the promise of freedom lured millions of drivers to
the nation's rapidly developing interstate highway system. Capitalizing on the excitement, most of the Disneyland **souvenir books** from that decade label Tomorrowland's
driving attraction as Autopia Cars and Freeway. The 1959 book renames it the "Super
Autopia Freeway," differentiating the D-ticket **Tomorrowland** original from the C-ticket **Junior Autopia** (opened in 1956) and the B-ticket **Midget Autopia** (1957). The
large **Fun Maps** of the 1960s and beyond use the site-specific designation Tomorrowland Autopia to avoid confusion with the **Fantasyland Autopia** that debuted in 1959.

From 1955 to 1970, the Richfield Oil Corporation, "the official gasoline of Disneyland," was the Autopia's sponsor, and the Richfield name was prominently displayed
on the signage at the site (in 1970, Richfield would become the R in ARCO). The 1956
souvenir book calls the Autopia "Disneyland's cars of the future," though it's hard
to see how these small, noisy, slow, gas-powered autos driven mostly by kids were
futuristic. Fun, yes; futuristic, no. What really was futuristic was the concept of freeway driving—the Autopia celebrated this vital new freedom as one of the high-profile
symbols of Tomorrowland.

Ironically, what was intended to be a safe, fun tribute to progress was, in its
first decade, almost as dangerous as a drive on a real freeway. As seen in 1956's
Disneyland, U.S.A. featurette, the original track did not have a guide rail running
down its center. A rail-less track meant drivers could veer their cars into each other,
pass each other, and in some cases even go against traffic (according to a persistent
legend, Sammy Davis Jr. was chased off the road into some bushes in 1955). Not until
1963 was a center rail installed down the middle of the Autopia freeway to keep cars
aligned.

In contrast, the cars themselves, which were mostly designed by Disney Legend
Bob Gurr, went through many modifications. The earliest sketches show bulbous,
heavy fenders and running boards on the cars, just like on classic American autos of
the 1940s and '50s, thus making the "cars of the future" more like "cars of the recent

past." Powered by *"years-ahead* New Richfield Ethyl" (according to Richfield's ads), the Mark I cars that hit the Tomorrowland road in 1955 were modeled on foreign sports cars—Porsches and Ferraris in particular—to give them a sleek, low-slung look that anticipated styles of the next decade, if not quite the next century. Unfortunately, with bodies made of fiberglass and bumpers of soft aluminum, the cars couldn't withstand anything more than slight impacts, even though their speeds were under eight miles per hour. Consequently, when drivers decided to ram other vehicles or bounce off the side of the track, the toll was both disastrous and immediate—according to the 2007 *Disneyland Secrets, Stories, & Magic* DVD, ninety-five percent of the cars running at the start of Opening Day were disabled by day's end (thirty-eight out of forty cars were no longer "usable"). If guests were hard on the cars, the cars were hard on the guests, too; in *Window on Main Street*, Disney Legend **Van France** writes that with "no safety belts or protection from the steering wheels . . . giving first aid to the young drivers who had teeth knocked out was a frequent activity." France says that **cast members** had a nickname for the Autopia: Blood Alley. With all the accidents (mostly from drivers rear-ending each other), David Koenig claims in *The People v. Disneyland* that the Autopia "would produce more injuries—and lawsuits—than any other Disneyland attraction."

Before the end of 1955, two more versions of the Autopia cars—the Mark II and Mark III—arrived with sturdier engines and chassis. Yet another update, the Mark IV, appeared midway through 1956, and an even heavier, slower (hence safer) version came in 1959. This iteration, the 1,100-pound Mark V, was the longest-lasting design yet, making it to 1964. With the arrival of 1963's center rail, drivers could no longer sideswipe each other, so the side bumpers were taken off the lighter Mark VI cars. Then, in keeping with the dramatic remodel of "new Tomorrowland," new Mark VII Autopia cars debuted in 1967. They were durable and, at over $5,000 apiece, expensive (by comparison, guests could have bought two brand-new, full-size Ford Mustangs for that price). Designed by **Arrow Development** and looking like little Corvette Stingrays, these 830-pound Autopia cars rode the track until the end of the century.

After temporarily closing in September 1999, a revised version of the attraction opened in June 2000 with a large video screen displaying animations, a grandstand viewing area, new cars that still ran on gas but came in three different styles (Dusty, Suzy, and Sparky, to coincide with the TV ads of Chevron, the new sponsor), and a longer, more exciting, and more humorous driving experience. The new half-mile layout incorporated the extinct Fantasyland Autopia track, pushed the ride time closer to six minutes, and even included a bouncy "off-road" section.

Once Chevron's sponsorship ended in June of 2012, the Chevron name came off the signage. Three years later, Honda took over the sponsorship, and the Autopia was immediately closed for five months. When it reopened on April 29, 2016, the Autopia roadway itself hadn't really changed, but the main building and **queue** area had been updated with vibrant blue colors, revised signs, and a new series of vintage videos. The big **attraction poster** was redesigned, and Honda insignias now adorn the freshly painted cars. The 270-cc Honda engines seem to run a little quieter and cleaner, but they're still limited to about 6.5 mph. Driver's licenses are still available at the attraction's exit, as they have been since the 1950s (Richfield's early "official Autopia Driver's License" made the holder "an active member of the Richfield Autopia Safe Driving Club").

No matter the era, guests of all ages have enjoyed the Autopia experience, and it remains one of Disneyland's most consistently popular attractions (and the only one left from Opening Day in Tomorrowland). This popularity may seem ironic, since most guests have to fight their way through freeway traffic just to get to Disneyland—it seems unrealistic to ask them to wait in line for a chance to get into another car. However, many adults, prominent celebrities (a smiling Frank Sinatra), and even **Walt Disney** himself have happily gone for a spin. Kids, naturally, have always jumped at the chance to take the wheel, especially if they were tall enough to drive alone (the height minimum is currently fifty-four inches).

Decades of nifty enhancements have helped make the Autopia a utopia for trivia fans. Of the original Mark I cars, four were designed to look like patrol cars, with black-and-white color schemes, sirens, and flashing lights. Along the current route, one sign warns of a "Mouse Crossing" near a mouse hole; another designates the road as Disneyland Route 55 (in honor of the inaugural year); and cartoony roadside billboards advertise clever products.

No matter what modifications have been made over the decades, the Autopia remains a nice reminder of nostalgic '50s fun. Those little cars continue to zoom along as pleasantly as ever, and the track still offers a mile of Tomorrowland scenery. For millions of drivers, that's a mile of smiles.

Autopia Winner's Circle,
aka Autopia Winner's Circle, Powered by Honda

MAP: Tomorrowland, T-10, T-13

DATES: June 29, 2000–ongoing

Again tying in a store with a nearby attraction, Disneyland opened the small Autopia Winner's Circle shop next to the **Autopia** in 2000. The new shop's debut was timed to the reopening of the forty-five-year-old Autopia, which had temporarily shut down for a remodel to accommodate its new sponsor, Chevron. With its motoring souvenirs (including models of the cute cars from Chevron's TV commercials) and an actual Autopia car on display, the store was a nice pit stop for automotive fans. Guests could also get the photos for their Autopia Driver's Licenses taken here.

Back in 2000, the Winner's Circle was located close to the lagoon where guests had once lined up for the **Submarine Voyage**, which had closed in 1998. But with the submarines scheduled to resurface in mid-2007 and the Winner's Circle space slated to become the subs' **queue** area once more, in late 2006 the Winner's Circle relocated to its current position next to the **Innoventions** building, a spot in the walkway where the **Mad Hatter of Tomorrowland** had once set up shop.

The merchandise has changed significantly in recent years. In 2015, half the store was dedicated to car-oriented items (such as die-cast cars, chrome license plate frames, and *Cars*-themed sunshades), while the other half offered more generic items (Disney towels, hats, toys, and bagged candy). However, in the spring of 2016, virtually the entire store had been filled with hats and **mouse ears**. By the end of April of that year, the store had added the name of a new sponsor, Honda, to its main sign (Honda also took over sponsorship of the nearby Autopia).

Avenue of the Flags

MAP: Tomorrowland, T-2

DATES: March 1956–September 1966

On **Opening Day**, flags from all the states in the union—there were only forty-eight in 1955—flew on tall aluminum flagpoles in the star-shaped **Court of Honor** deep inside **Tomorrowland**. A year later, the newly created **Astro-Jets** needed a home, so the flagpoles were uprooted, the Court was adjourned, and the Astro-Jets touched down.

The flagpoles, meanwhile, were re-installed in a prominent new location that needed some kind of dramatic statement: the 150-foot-long walkway that connected the **Hub** with Tomorrowland. At one time, a science-inspired sculpture rising up from the middle of a wide fountain had been planned for this walkway, but as construction invoices lengthened and deadlines shortened in the frantic spring of 1955, the sculpture concept was abandoned.

While not as imaginative as the sculpture-fountain combination, the flagpoles were a convenient and patriotic addition to the landscaped walkway, soon dubbed the Avenue of the Flags. When they were installed in 1956, the flags were placed in the numerical order in which their states had been admitted to the Union; three years later, Alaska and Hawaii were added to complete the fifty.

Mounted six feet up each flagpole was a black plaque identifying the state and its date of admission, ordinal number among the states, and motto. Crowning the Avenue of the Flags was Old Glory, flying at the Tomorrowland end of the walkway right in front of the **Clock of the World**; 250 feet behind the clock soared the majestic *Moonliner*, with the Astro-Jets twirling nearby. In September of 1966, the flags were removed as construction began on futuristic new Tomorrowland gates that would debut ten months later.

Babes in Toyland **Exhibit**

MAP: Town Square, TS-9

DATES: December 17, 1961–September 1963

Babes in Toyland, Disney Studios' first big-budget, live-action musical, hit the 1961 **holiday season** accompanied by lots of holiday hoopla. With Annette Funicello, America's sweetheart, starring alongside teen idol Tommy Sands and Disney mainstay Tommy Kirk, the picture was expected to be a winter blockbuster, and so in December a *Babes*-related **parade** began to march down **Main Street**, and a walk-through *Babes in Toyland* Exhibit was installed in the **Opera House** in **Town Square**.

When it opened, the *Babes in Toyland* Exhibit gave guests their first look at the Opera House's interior. From **Opening Day** in 1955 and onward for the next six and a half years, the Opera House doors had been locked because the interior space was being used to store lumber for other construction projects. However, three days after *Babes in Toyland* opened in theaters, the Opera House's doors opened to guests. Inside the building were some of the actual sets and props from the movie, including the Mother Goose Village and the Forest of No Return, plus **cast members** dressed like Bo Peep, anthropomorphic trees, and other movie characters.

The exhibit proved to be only slightly more popular than the movie, which ended up failing at the box office. There is no mention of the exhibit in any of the Disneyland **souvenir books** of the early 1960s, and within a year of its opening, some of the sets were struck down. Segments of *The Mickey Mouse Club* TV show were shot on what remained, but by September of 1963, the *Babes in Toyland* Exhibit was gone and the Opera House had become the **Mickey Mouse Club Headquarters**.

Baby Care Center, aka **Baby Station,** aka **Baby Center**

MAP: Hub, H-6

DATES: July 1957–ongoing

On the **Fourth of July** in 1979, the first baby was born at Disneyland on a bench in the **Hub**. Fortunately, the Baby Station was nearby. The Baby Station has always been located on E. Plaza Street, about twenty-five feet from what was called the Red Wagon Inn back in 1955 and the **Plaza Inn** as of 1965. Anyone trying to find it could just look for all the baby strollers parked outside (a photo in Disneyland's 1959 **souvenir book** even shows a row of small "reserved parking" spots for strollers).

Though Baby Station's frontage is only about ten feet wide, the interior is about fifty feet deep. Inside the room, parents can find all manner of helpful services and purchasable supplies, plus diaper-changing tables and private nursing areas with rocking chairs (no babysitters, however). The Mead Johnson Corporation, maker of Pablum baby cereal, was the establishment's first sponsor, and thus the room was originally called the Pablum Baby Station. However, by 1961 it was called simply the Baby Station, followed later by Baby Center, Gerber Station, Gerber Baby Care Center, and Carnation Baby Care Center. In 2007, the name was Disneyland Baby Care Center, hosted by Nestlé, but by 2016, Huggies had become the new sponsor. No matter the name or sponsor, this facility has always had an adorable baby picture on an interior wall. The baby? None other than a ten-month-old **Walt Disney**.

> **MOUSCELLANY**
>
> At least three babies have been born at Disneyland, making them the park's youngest guests. The oldest guest? That was most likely a 108-year-old woman from New Mexico who visited the park with her great-granddaughter (both were photographed by the *Long Beach Press-Telegram* on December 31, 1965).

Baker, Buddy
(1918–2002)

The rollicking "Grim Grinning Ghosts" theme music in the **Haunted Mansion**? That's the work of prolific composer Buddy Baker, who wrote the music for hundreds of Disney attractions, movies, and TV shows.

Norman Dale Baker was born in Missouri in 1918. After earning his doctorate in music, he played with noted big bands and began composing music. Hired at Disney Studios in 1954, he wrote and/or arranged music for *The Mickey Mouse Club* show, the **Disneyland TV series**, and dozens of Disney films.

At Disneyland, in addition to composing the Haunted Mansion's music, Baker wrote the background music for **Great Moments with Mr. Lincoln**, the **Carousel of Progress**, the **Monorail**, the **PeopleMover**, **Adventure Thru Inner Space**, and **Innoventions**. He also arranged a simple **Sherman Brothers** ditty into a multi-lingual anthem for **It's a Small World**. And it was his "Swisskapolka," a composition he wrote for the film *Swiss Family Robinson*, that played inside the **Swiss Family Treehouse**. His later accomplishments included numerous compositions at Walt Disney World and Tokyo Disneyland.

After receiving an Oscar nomination and numerous prestigious music awards, Buddy Baker was named a Disney Legend in 1998. He died in 2002 in Sherman Oaks, California, at age eighty-four.

Baloo's Dressing Room

MAP: Fantasyland, Fa-19

DATES: March 15, 1991–September 8, 1991

The 1990s TV show *Disney Afternoon* spawned Disney Afternoon Avenue, an area in **Fantasyland** that opened in 1991. Throughout that summer, while walking north from the **Storybook Land Canal Boats** toward **It's a Small World**, guests could interact with popular cartoon characters. One of them was Baloo, co-star of 1967's *The*

Jungle Book and Dhg Room was a popular meet-and-greet site with *TaleSpin*-themed décor. After six months, Baloo and the rest of the Avenue regulars left as bigger plans emerged for the area. Two years later those plans were realized, and Baloo's spot at the train tracks became the tunnel walkway into **Mickey's Toontown**.

Bandstand

MAP: Hub, H-2; Adventureland, A-4

DATES: July 17, 1955–1962

Other than a pretty photo in the 1955 **souvenir book**, the Disneyland bandstand got little mention in the park's early literature. This cozy, open-air gazebo where live music could be performed was, however, a topic of much discussion in mid-1955.

As he re-created small-town Midwestern America on **Main Street**, **Walt Disney** knew that a traditional bandstand was a mandatory accessory for a pastoral park (nine years earlier, he'd placed a sweet little bandstand in the old-fashioned "Casey at the Bat" section of *Make Mine Music*).

For Disneyland's bandstand, location was the issue. Before **Opening Day**, the bandstand sat in **Town Square** as one of the first structures incoming guests would see. Unfortunately, that was the problem—the bandstand obscured the view of **Sleeping Beauty Castle** from the train station. So, before any guests ever saw the bandstand in its original spot, a sixty-five-foot flagpole was installed as the cynosure of Town Square, and the bandstand was moved up near the **Hub**, a new location halfway between the entrances to **Frontierland** and **Fantasyland**. It stood in this spot on Opening Day and for about a year after, a white wooden structure approximately fifteen feet tall with a short staircase, pastel roof, decorative railings and finials, and a flagpole on top.

The **Disneyland Band** played at the bandstand

every day to audiences sitting on nearby park benches. Realizing that the bandstand was becoming increasingly popular, Walt Disney had the area transformed into the **Plaza Gardens** in 1956, featuring a bigger stage and a dance area. Meanwhile, the bandstand was relocated again, this time to a Southern-styled rest area at the far tip of Adventureland called **Magnolia Park**. The bandstand played on for six more years until a 1962 expansion of the **Jungle Cruise** encroached on its section of Magnolia Park. Happily, the bandstand was bought before it was dismantled, and today it lives on at a nursery in nearby Corona Del Mar called Roger's Gardens. Meanwhile, Disneyland continues to incorporate variations of the bandstand in its store displays, such as those inside the **Disney Showcase** (shown on page 72).

Bank of America, aka Bank of Main Street, aka Annual Pass Center, aka Annual Passport Processing Center

MAP: Town Square, TS-10

DATES: July 17, 1955–2009

Walt Disney knew guests would need lots of money to fully enjoy Disneyland, so he wisely installed a bank within the park. But he didn't put it just anywhere—it was conveniently located within one of the very first buildings guests encountered as they walked in. Situated on the first floor of the handsome **Opera House** building, in its early years the thirty-five-foot-long Bank of America had another serious organization, **Town Square Realty**, as its immediate neighbor to the north.

Inside the bank, the main room had the feel of a traditional financial institution, replete with teller windows and conservative décor; however, this particular B of A always functioned a little differently from the other branches scattered across 330 California communities. For instance, it was one of the few in America open on weekends and holidays (and not many other banks required their customers to pay an admission fee to gain access). In 1955, the Disneyland branch sold special $1, $5, and $10 souvenir money orders that could be converted into cash at stores and banks. Also, from **Opening Day** in 1955 until mid-1993, guests could open a genuine B of A account inside and get checks with Disneyland images on them.

After Bank of America terminated its participation at Disneyland (simultaneously ending its sponsorship of **It's a Small World**) in mid-1993, the B of A became the B of MS for eight more years. The Bank of Main Street, however, wasn't a true bank with bank accounts; instead, it was more of an information center that also happened to exchange currency, cash small checks, and offer ATM access.

In 2001, even though the building still looked like a bank with teller windows and still sported the Bank of Main Street name out front, the bank began focusing more on selling Annual Passports. Four years later, the B of MS ceased all bank functions and existed solely as the Annual Pass Center, where guests could buy the various year-long plans that offer frequent admission at discounted prices.

The space closed in 2009 and reopened later that year as the **Disney Gallery**, which had formerly been located in **New Orleans Square** (Annual Pass Center functions, meanwhile, relocated to the **Plaza Pavilion**). Today, an artistic reminder of the old bank's years in Town Square is painted on the building's south wall: a nostalgic bank mural declares that "a penny saved is a penny earned." Unbeknownst to most pedestrians walking by this building toward **Main Street**, the curtained windows on the second floor front the sound rooms that generate Disneyland's public-address announcements.

Bardeau, Renie
(1934–)

Above the **Main Street Photo Supply Co.** is a window identifying Renie Bardeau and his "Kingdom Photo Services." Bardeau began taking photographs at Disneyland in 1959 and was the park's chief photographer for almost forty years. Among the hundreds of thousands of photographs he took at Disneyland are some of the most iconic images ever taken of **Walt Disney** and his park.

Born in 1934 and raised in Tucson, Arizona, Bardeau learned photography when he was in the navy during the Korean War. Returning stateside, he was a college student trying to land a summer job in 1959 when he lucked into an interview with Charlie Nichols, Disneyland's chief photographer at the time. Hired on the spot, Bardeau's first official assignment was to photograph Walt Disney and Vice President Richard Nixon together on the brand-new **Monorail** (Nixon was one of many American politicians to visit Disneyland, including George H. W. Bush, Jimmy Carter, Dwight Eisenhower, Gerald Ford, John Glenn, Hubert Humphrey, John Kennedy, Robert Kennedy, Ted Kennedy, Ronald Reagan, Mitt Romney, Harry Truman, and George Wallace; none of the presidents visited while in office).

As the summer job morphed into full-time employment, Bardeau got to know Walt Disney personally and took two of the most famous photos ever captured of him in Disneyland. *Footsteps* (1964) shows a contemplative Disney strolling alone through **Sleeping Beauty Castle** one morning before Disneyland opened (an image often reproduced on merchandise and posters); two years later, the last official photo of Disney taken in the park shows him smiling next to Mickey as they sit in Disneyland's small fire engine in the **Hub** with the castle behind them (an image later used for a large **photo collage** inside the **Opera House**).

After Charlie Nichols's retirement in 1968, Bardeau became Disneyland's chief photographer. One of his continuing goals was to look for new angles and perspectives, which meant he would stand on top of buildings, walk through the attractions when they were closed, and even shoot from the top of **Matterhorn Mountain**. Over the years, some of his photos included famous celebrities who visited Disneyland: Cary Grant, Ronald Reagan, Elizabeth Taylor, and many more. Even after he retired in 1998, his photos continued to publicize and advertise Disneyland, and they are still used today in magazines, newspapers, and books. Moreover, they have created a permanent record of Disneyland's ever-evolving

MOUSCELLANY

One of Bardeau's successors, Paul Hiffmeyer, became Disneyland's chief photographer in 2005 and continued until he retired in 2016 at age seventy.

history. Now in his eighties, Bardeau lives in Glendale, California.

Bathroom of Tomorrow

MAP: Tomorrowland, T-22

DATES: April 5, 1956–August 31, 1960

One of the more unusual exhibits in Disneyland's history was born nine months after **Opening Day**. The Bathroom of Tomorrow was located at the end of the row of buildings on the right as guests entered **Tomorrowland**. This row already housed the science displays in the **Hall of Chemistry** and the **Hall of Aluminum Fame**, so one more exhibit about life in the near future seemed appropriate.

To show off various features of the modern bathroom, the Crane Plumbing Company installed a twenty-foot-wide bathroom exhibit that looked like something from an industrial trade show. From behind a railing, guests inspected the facilities and fixtures, all designed in a yellow color scheme, with some parts plated with twenty-four-karat gold. Flush with enthusiasm, Crane added to the excitement with separate laundry facilities and a kids' play area called Fun with Water (a colorful mobile, plus guest-controlled fountains and spigots).

While it's easy to joke about an archaic exhibit called the Bathroom of Tomorrow in retrospect, at the time it was a serious attempt at showing how technology would impact the modern world. Disneyland, remember, wasn't built merely to entertain, but also to educate, even when the lessons involved a posture-enhancing toilet seat. At the end of August 1960, the Bathroom of Tomorrow became the Bathroom of Yesterday when it was replaced by uncomplicated **Fun Fotos** displays.

Baxter, Tony
(1947–)

Tony Baxter, one of the most prominent Imagineers of the last thirty years, grew up in Orange County and began visiting Disneyland as an eight-year-old child in 1955, the year the park opened. Ten years later, he got a job scooping ice cream at Disneyland's **Carnation Plaza Gardens**. He then worked as a ride operator on **Adventure Thru Inner Space** and other attractions while he was studying theater design, architecture, and landscape architecture at local colleges.

In 1970, Baxter began his career in Walt Disney Imagineering, building models alongside Disney Legend **Claude Coats**. By decade's end, he had come up with one of Disneyland's most exciting new attractions, the **Big Thunder Mountain Railroad**. Over the next thirty-four years, he spearheaded important developments that energized every corner of Disneyland: **Star Tours**, **Splash Mountain**, the **Indiana Jones Adventure**, **Finding Nemo Submarine Voyage**, **Fantasy Faire**, and more. Baxter also worked on projects at other Disney parks, and fans will recognize him as an articulate spokesperson on numerous Disney documentaries. In one of these documentaries, *Disney Parks: Disneyland Resort Behind the Scenes*, Baxter summarizes the challenge of being an Imagineer: "For us to be successful we have to not only come up with new ideas, but they have to challenge the limits of what everybody sees as entertainment. So we're constantly on the prowl all over the planet, seeing films, seeing new shows and things, to spur us on with ideas to take off and deliver something that no one has ever expected before."

On his birthday in 2013, Tony Baxter stepped down from his position as senior vice president of creative development, opting to stay on as a part-time consultant. He called his Disney career "wondrous." To honor that wondrous career, Baxter was soon given a **Main Street Tribute Window** (detail shown) and recognition as a Disney Legend.

Bear Country

MAP: Park, P-14

DATES: March 24, 1972–November 23, 1988

Bear Country, the seventh major land in Disneyland, was added in 1972 after the plans for a Disney ski resort in California called Mineral King were abandoned. An elaborate show with singing **Audio-Animatronic** bears would've been performed in one of the Mineral King buildings, but when the ski dream ended, so did the bear show, at least for the next five years. In 1971, the **Country Bear Jamboree** opened in Walt Disney World, and that success prompted a new Bear Country back in Anaheim.

Veteran guests recognize Bear Country as a familiar Disneyland name. Starting in 1960, there was a small **Frontierland** site called Bear Country along the route traversed by the **Mine Train**. This early Bear Country, featuring realistic bears fishing in a lake, lasted until 1977, when it was obliterated by **Big Thunder Mountain Railroad** construction.

In March of 1972, the "real" Bear Country opened on the land that had been home to the **Indian Village** from 1956 to 1971. Bear Country, however, extended beyond the area of the Indian Village, which was bordered on the west by Disneyland's **railroad**. Over half of Bear Country's four acres spread *under* the train tracks, pushing westward through Disneyland's perimeter **berm** into what had been an employee parking lot. One of the awkward results of this expansion was Bear Country's entrance and exit—they were in the same location, so there was only one way in and out. Every other existing land—**Adventureland**, **Frontierland**, etc.—had at least two pathways to neighboring areas. Bear Country, however, rounded into a cul-de-sac that didn't lead anywhere else.

Bear Country was built for approximately $8 million—almost half of what it cost to build all of Disneyland back in the mid-1950s. Disneyland's 1972 **souvenir book** plays up Bear Country's arrival with a colorful back cover that reads, "A whole new land . . . a wild new band" and a two-page spread that described the new area as "a lighthearted blend of the authentic with the fanciful." The nineteenth-century Pacific Northwest inspired Bear Country's rustic design: the buildings were made out of wooden planks and exposed timbers, old-fashioned fonts decorated the stores, and transplanted trees grew thick and tall. The entrance to Bear Country was marked by a wooden sign supposedly created by J. Audubon Woodlore, a park ranger from old Disney cartoons who declared this to be "a honey of a place" and then joked about its scratching, hibernating, tree-climbing residents. Also to the left of the entrance was a cave, home to an ever-snoring but never-seen Rufus Bear.

When it opened, Bear Country had only one significant new attraction: the **Country Bear Jamboree**, a musical extravaganza performed by eighteen Audio-Animatronic bears that were accompanied by a variety of other A-A animals. Bear Country's other new establishments were **Teddi Barra's Swingin' Arcade**, **Ursus H. Bear's Wilderness Outpost**, the Golden Bear Lodge (now the **Hungry Bear Restaurant**), and the **Mile Long Bar** (the two holdovers from the Indian Village were the **Indian Trading Post** and the Indian War Canoes (now **Davy Crockett's Explorer Canoes**).

For some line-weary guests, the absence of high-profile attractions was welcome, because it meant rural Bear Country would remain a relatively quiet, relaxing corner of Disneyland. But the attenuating crowds concerned park officials, and after a decade they began working on a major new attraction. The arrival of **Splash Mountain** brought a name change to the whole area—since late 1988, Bear County has been known as **Critter Country**, and the name on the mailbox out front has changed from Rufus Bear to Brer Bear.

Bell Telephone Systems Phone Exhibits

MAP: Tomorrowland, T-5

DATES: 1960–1982

In 1960, Bell Telephone Systems started sponsoring the prominent **Circarama** theater in **Tomorrowland**. Redesigning the pre- and post-show areas of the five-year-old theater, Bell installed interactive phone exhibits that fulfilled the Tomorrowland mission statement printed in Disneyland's **souvenir books**: Tomorrowland would offer a "living blueprint of our future."

For Bell, that blueprint included the wonders of dialing long distance, something Alexander Graham Bell had shown in its embryonic form at the 1904 St. Louis World's Fair. Disneyland's 1960 souvenir book announces a new "demonstration of coast to coast Direct Distance Dialing. . . . Bell Telephone System representatives will dial cross country to local Weather Bureaus as a stop watch records the time necessary to complete the call." Also part of the theater's exhibits was "a dimensional mural" of movie screens that told the story of communications. In 1964, Bell added a Picture-Phone, which guests could observe but not actually try out with their own personal calls (what friends with Picture-Phones could visitors have called, anyway?). The idea of seeing whom you're talking to may have seemed attractive at the time, and it was a moderately interesting spectacle to watch, but obviously the Picture-Phone on display did not make it into every American home.

Around 1967, Bell added devices that guests really could use: small rooms called Chatterboxes. In a Chatterbox, a group sat in a booth in front of a large pay phone, dialed any phone number, paid the charge via coins, and then talked conference-style to the dialee via a microphone mounted on the Chatterbox phone. Having a group conversation in a phone booth with no cumbersome handset to pass around was a fun novelty back then, and the speakerphone idea really did come to fruition. One drawback to the Chatterbox was that the calls could only be made one way—a sign clearly announced that the phones did not accept incoming calls, which meant if one group wanted to tie up a Chatterbox for a long time, they'd be pumping lots of quarters into the slot.

Other options in the Bell exhibits included the Dial a Character wall, where guests could pick up phones and hear recordings of Disney characters talking on the other end, and a phone that enabled listeners to hear what their own voices sounded like. Naturally, actual Bell phones that guests could buy were also displayed. Bell hung up its Phone Exhibits around 1982 when it withdrew from the theater and the airline PSA flew in as the new sponsor.

Bengal Barbecue

MAP: Adventureland, A-3

DATES: June 4, 1990–ongoing

The instantly popular Bengal Barbecue replaced **Sunkist, I Presume** in 1992, taking over a high-traffic location across from the **Indiana Jones Adventure**. While Sunkist offered juices and snacks, the Bengal Barbecue has always provided more substantial fare to hungry guests (the sign, clutched in the jaws of a large tiger's head, helps makes that point). The highlight is the selection of marinated skewers—beef, chicken, and vegetables—that come with various sauces. And they're reasonably priced, too: in a park where a single cupcake can cost $6, it's nice to find a tasty, filling lunch of a barbecued beef skewer for under $5.

Following the **Adventureland** theme, side dishes are called Extra Provisions and have included SSS-innamon Snake Twists, Pomegranate Piranha Lemonade, and Tiger Tails (breadsticks). Also in keeping with the local color is the décor—the counter and tables sit under a thatched jungle roof.

Berm

In order to enhance the illusion that Disneyland is a complete world in itself, a tall earthen barrier, known as the berm, wraps around the park's perimeter. "The terraced embankment which completely encloses Disneyland," explains the 1955 book *The Story of Disneyland*, "was designed to keep the outside world from intruding upon you."

Walt Disney knew how effective a berm could be—he'd already built one around a section of his Disney Studios in Burbank. Later, to shield his Holmby Hills neighbors from the elaborate one-eighth-scale miniature railroad he ran on a half-mile of track behind his house, he surrounded his backyard with another embankment.

Disney included a tall berm in his plans for Disneyland even when it was in the design stages; the famous concept drawing executed by **Herb Ryman** in 1953 shows an un-landscaped dirt wall as Disneyland's boundary. When it came time to build Disneyland's berm, dirt was readily available in **Frontierland**, where 350,000 cubic yards of dirt were being excavated to create the **Rivers of America**. By **Opening Day**, the berm outlined the park and defined its familiar rounded-triangle perimeter. The maximum north-south distance of the 1955 park (from the southern train station to the northern tip of **Fantasyland**) was about 1,900 feet, or just over one-third of a mile; the maximum east-west distance (from the **Frontierland** berm to the eastern berm behind the **Autopia**) was some 2,150 feet—approximately two-fifths of a mile. Over fifty football fields could have fit within the original berm.

Construction over the decades (including the addition of **Bear Country** and **Mickey's Toontown**) has pushed the berm outward, changing its shape and expanding its original 1.3-mile length (the new **Star Wars Land** will redefine the berm's northwest section when it opens). In addition, several major attractions that have entrances within the berm's boundary actually take guests under the berm and out to cleverly concealed "show buildings." The **Haunted Mansion**, for instance, is entered from **New Orleans Square**, but the mansion's descending elevator and long subterranean corridor take guests to a building west of the berm that's explored via Doom Buggies. The **Indiana Jones Adventure**, **It's a Small World**, and **Pirates of the Caribbean** also convey guests from within Disneyland to structures beyond the berm.

Planted along the berm are dense stands of trees and shrubs to help block outside distractions (in 1976, a new tower proposed for the Disneyland Hotel next to Disneyland was limited to thirteen stories as part of the agreement to keep outside buildings from being visible from inside the park). While the foliage and the approximately ten- to twenty-foot-high berm do keep Disneyland guests from seeing the world beyond, the berm has never been high enough to prevent guests on the **Matterhorn**, **Splash Mountain**, **Tarzan's Treehouse**, and other elevated attractions from seeing Anaheim buildings nearby.

While it is a formidable security precaution, the berm hasn't always managed to keep nonpaying guests out. On **Opening Day**, park crashers found sneaky ways to get over the berm; by now, virtually every section of the berm and its supplemental fence has been tested by climbers, fence-cutters, and even tunnelers. But the dirt berm has always successfully fulfilled one other vital function: it's the support for the main train tracks circling Disneyland.

Bibbidi Bobbidi Boutique

Map: Fantasyland, Fa-7

DATES: April 17, 2009–ongoing

Kids needing the full royal treatment can get it at this **Fantasyland** salon. Having debuted in Florida three years earlier, the Bibbidi Bobbidi Boutique came to Anaheim in 2009 and moved into a large retail space inside the **Sleeping Beauty Castle** courtyard. Previously the site of the **Tinker Bell Toy Shoppe**, the location has an imposing column outside to mark its entrance, two separate door-ways for easy access, enticing window displays, and detailed cottage décor (note the small *Peter Pan* carvings out front that acknowledge Tink's for-mer shop). The Bibbidi Bobbidi name is taken from *Cinderella* and the song sung by the Fairy Godmother, who's depicted in stained glass (shown).

Inside, walls of merchandise fit for a princess—formal dresses, tiaras, bags,

MOUSCELLANY

The Bibbidi Bobbidi Boutique isn't the only Disneyland location named after a song: Main Street's Fortuosity Shop gets its name from "Fortuosity" in *The Happiest Millionaire*, and the Hub's Jolly Holiday Bakery Café is named after "Jolly Holiday" in *Mary Poppins*.

gloves, and wands—draw in little girls like mag-nets (as Disney princesses have become more action-oriented lately, the store has also been stocking less delicate items such as swords, shields, and archery sets). Farther back, the sa-lon offers an area with plush chairs where **cast members** provide fairytale makeovers. The pack-age deals, which usually require reservations and are priced from around $60 to $195, include ev-erything from princess hairstyles, makeup, and nail polish to royal gowns, accessories, and shoes. Hidden mirrors magically open up to reveal the enchanting results. For under $15, boys can get transformed into knights with a new hairstyle, a shield, and a sword.

Big Game Safari Shooting Gallery

MAP: Adventureland, A-2

DATES: June 15, 1962–January 1982

There had already been shooting galleries on **Main Street** and in **Frontierland** when another one opened in **Adventureland** in 1962. The Adventureland version was the largest of the three galleries and occupied a prominent space next to the **Adventure-land Bazaar**. The attraction went by several names during its two-decade existence, including Safari Shooting Gallery, Big Game Safari, and Big Game Shooting Gallery. It had a jungle theme, naturally, that included a thatched roof and bamboo decorations.

Elephants, rhinos, hippos, snakes, and jungle cats were among its exotic targets. No tickets were required to pick up an "elephant rifle"—this was a pay-to-play attraction that cost a quarter for a tube full of lead pellets.

Although the gallery's dozen air rifles were limited in their range of motion to keep the barrels away from guests, the use of pellets meant that the target area had to be repainted every night to look fresh for the next day's shooters. Another pellet problem was the toxic lead dust they generated, a gradually accumulating threat to **cast members** breathing the gallery air for long spells. The Big Game Gallery shut down in 1982, when a major remodel filled this stretch of Adventureland with new shops.

Big Thunder Mountain Railroad

MAP: Frontierland, Fr–21

DATES: September 2, 1979–ongoing

For several years in the 1970s, tantalizing concept art for a new railroad attraction was displayed on **Main Street** inside **Disneyland Presents a Preview of Coming Attractions**. In the fall of 1979, the preview became a reality (which, unfortunately, can't be said for all the ideas presented in that Coming Attractions room). Big Thunder Mountain was the third major mountain constructed in Disneyland after **Opening Day** (**Matterhorn Mountain** debuted in 1959, and **Space Mountain** in 1977). The mountain and its attraction, Big Thunder Mountain Railroad, required two years of construction—double the amount of time it took to build all of Disneyland from 1954 to 1955. Big Thunder's $16 million price tag was almost as high as the one for the original park.

Devised by Disney Legend **Tony Baxter**, Big Thunder was heralded as an instant classic among E-ticket attractions. Its two-acre site is located in the large **Frontierland** area formerly known as **Nature's Wonderland**, which the **Mine Train** had once toured. Some of the old rocks, landscaping, and desert props from that area were retained, but the dominant Big Thunder feature was brand-new. Standing 104 feet high, the central  mountain is about three-fourths as tall as Matterhorn Mountain and borrows its dramatic, soaring orange buttes from Utah's Bryce Canyon National Park.

Today's signs at Big Thunder Mountain Railroad describe it as "a high-speed, roller coaster-type ride" with "sharp turns and sudden drops and stops." And how! An exciting thrill ride, Big Thunder was designed to compete with other Southern California theme parks that were wowing 1970s teens with rapidly proliferating variations of kinetic roller coasters. Big Thunder's half-mile-long track is steep, tightly curved, and wet, thanks to a splash area similar to the one at the end of the **Matterhorn**

Bobsleds (Big Thunder's finale, however, is in front of an exposed wall of dinosaur bones). Though they average only about thirty miles per hour during their three-minute trip, the half-dozen runaway trains seem faster and definitely put the wild in Wild West. The rollicking trains are noisy, too: according to *The Imagineering Field Guide to Disneyland*, Steven Spielberg recorded their raucous sounds to accompany the mine-cart chase in *Indiana Jones and the Temple of Doom*.

More than just thrills, though, Big Thunder has always offered humorous details as well. A sign touts Big Thunder as "the biggest little boom town in the West" with a steadily decreasing population. The little train engines have names like *I. B. Hearty*, *I. M. Loco*, and *U. R. Daring*, and a famous goat can be seen holding a stick of dynamite (shown). Frontier flair is everywhere: an old coot narrates the attraction, genuine Old West antiques decorate the **queue**, and up until 2010, a derelict Mine Train engine and some cars could be seen crashed in the woods nearby.

A fourteen-month closure that began in January of 2013 added new track to the ride, a remodeled loading area with new vehicles, improved sound, fiery new effects, and a rebuilt miniature town of Rainbow Ridge (these little structures were holdovers from the days of the old Mine Train).

Several much-publicized accidents over the years have tarnished Big Thunder's legacy. But the "wildest ride in the wilderness" has stayed consistently popular and often moves 2,200 guests per hour along the rails. To make sure the wildest ride doesn't get too wild, cast members communicate with each other using eleven different hand signals for row requests, commands to close the gates, "all clear" announcements, etc.

So iconic is this attraction that variations have been installed in other Disney parks, albeit with Monument Valley-style landscaping. The railroad also gets its share of promotion in ads and on merchandise; during "Show Your Disney Side Week" in April 2015, *Wheel of Fortune* brought one of the engines onto its set, generating praise as "a great ride" from host Pat Sajak; that same year, a thousand-piece jigsaw puzzle devoted to the attraction was on sale in Downtown Disney. Now almost forty years old, Big Thunder is still a big draw.

Big Thunder Ranch, aka Festivals of Fools,
aka Little Patch of Heaven

MAP: Frontierland, Fr-19

DATES: June 22, 1986–January 10, 2016

Two unused **Frontierland** acres behind 1979's **Big Thunder Mountain Railroad** were finally developed in 1986. Built to match the frontier railroad nearby, the serene Big Thunder Ranch looked like a working 1880s ranch, complete with log cabin, stables, and "the happiest horses on Earth," according to nearby signs. The most photographed subject back here was probably Mickey Moo, a white cow with a natural black patch on its hide that resembled Mickey Mouse's head. Late in 1986, the **Big Thunder Ranch Barbecue** opened to provide down-home food in a spacious outdoor dining area.

On June 21, 1996, the ranch got a makeover and a new name based on the Disney movie *The Hunchback of Notre Dame*: the Festival of Fools, an acclaimed twenty-eight-minute pageant of music and effects that retold the *Hunchback* story. The elaborate multi-stage show ran for almost two years. During this time, the little log cabin was turned into a shop called Esmeralda's Cottage.

The Big Thunder Ranch name and theme reappeared on May 30, 1998. Six years later, Little Patch of Heaven was added to the ranch, referencing the 2004 animated movie *Home on the Range*. The log cabin, renamed Pearl's Cottage after one of the movie's characters, began offering "Crafts & Fun!" to visitors. Within two years, however, Little Patch of Heaven had disappeared and Pearl's name had been removed from the cabin.

For the next decade, the area was again referred to as Big Thunder Ranch. The outdoor performance space became the **Festival Arena**, where special events were occasionally held, like 2011's **Family Fun Weekends** and the *Pirates of the Carib-*

bean: On Stranger Tides movie premiere. Lots of all-inclusive entertainment events called "roundups" were also spread between the ranch and its arena. Among them: Woody's Halloween Roundup, the Celebration Roundup, the Cowboy Roundup, Woody's All-American Roundup, and the Springtime Roundup of 2014 and 2015.

The cabin, called Miss Chris' Cabin, was often used for kids' coloring activities (Miss Chris was a musical performer who played the Festival Arena stage until it closed on January 10, 2016). For years, the little log structure transformed into the Scare-dy-Crow Shack at **Halloween Time**, and it hosted Santa Claus during the **holiday season** (Santa relocated to **Critter Country** for the 2015 holidays). Across from the cabin, goats (shown) and lambs were available for petting most of the year; these cute critters would get a winter break when husky, well-antlered reindeer were brought in for **Santa's Reindeer Round-Up**, but the reindeer stopped coming in 2012. That live farm animals had become part of Disneyland fulfilled one of Walt Disney's early park plans: pre-1955, he discussed a pastoral Frontierland project called Granny's Farm that was, according to Karal Ann Marling's *Designing Disney's Theme Parks*, "going to be stocked with a whole menagerie of live, dwarf farm animals."

A range of performers continued to entertain at the ranch right up until its final closing. For example, in January of 2014, the Frontierland Troupe, a mix of live entertainment and meet-and-greets with Disney characters, moved into the ranch temporarily. For 2015's Black History Month, the ranch presented a commemorative show called Celebrate Gospel. Live painters decorated Easter eggs here in the spring, and pumpkin-carvers demonstrated their art in the fall. What didn't change was the long-time sponsor, Georgia-Pacific, whose Washin' Station not only stocked G-P's Brawny Paper Towels, but also gave official directions on washin' up.

After almost three decades of providing old-fashioned fun, festivities, and food, Miss Chris' cabin was locked up in late 2015 and Big Thunder Ranch finally closed in early 2016 as Disneyland got ready to step into its future with the huge new **Star Wars Land** development.

Big Thunder Ranch Barbecue, aka Festival of Foods, aka Celebration Roundup and Barbecue

MAP: Frontierland, Fr–20

DATES: December 14, 1986–January 21, 2001; April 2009–January 11, 2016

Seven years after the **Big Thunder Mountain Railroad** debuted, a rustic, cafeteria-style restaurant called Big Thunder Ranch Barbecue opened directly north of the rowdy railroad. Previously, this section of **Frontierland** had been called the **Painted Desert**, a sun-bleached territory explored by **mule packs** and **mine trains**. The restaurant was within the **Big Thunder Ranch** area and shared the same Wild West theme. Recreating nineteenth-century American frontier life, the Big Thunder Ranch Barbecue offered alfresco dining on picnic tables near old-fashioned chuck wagons and a fire pit. Barbecued ribs, chicken, turkey legs, and a Trail Boss Sampler of meats satisfied even the hungriest trail hand.

After a four-month remodel, Big Thunder Ranch Barbecue reopened on June 20, 1996, as Festival of Foods. The new theme featured gypsy décor to echo the 1996 animated movie *The Hunchback of Notre Dame*. (Exactly why an outdoor barbecue restaurant in Frontierland was suddenly echoing fifteenth-century France was never clear.)

The Festival of Foods closed on April 18, 1998, and reopened a month later. The name and theme had reverted back to the Big Thunder Ranch Barbecue, Georgia-Pacific's Brawny had become the sponsor, and the food was (temporarily) accompanied by the musical stylings of **Billy Hill and the Hillbillies** on a small outdoor stage.

In early 2001, the restaurant closed to the public for what seemed like forever, though it was still occasionally fired up for corporate functions and private picnics. A farewell sign announced that they had "moved down the trail a bit" to a "new hacienda, **Rancho del Zocalo**."

However, the ol' ranch rebounded in April 2009, this time with a new name—Celebration Roundup and Barbecue—and a new *Toy Story* theme, with movie characters circulating and performing in the restaurant. The updated menu included new vegetarian options in addition to the hearty barbecue fare. In 2011, a new all-you-can-eat prix fixe menu boasted $19.99 lunches and $24.99 dinners of barbecue meats, beans, and corn bread. However, in early 2016, the restaurant finally shut down permanently so that Disneyland could replace the entire Big Thunder Ranch development with **Star Wars Land**.

Big Thunder Ranch Jamboree

MAP: Frontierland, Fr-19

DATES: May 3, 2012–Fall 2012

The **Festival Arena** in the rear of **Frontierland** was finally put to regular use in May of 2012. Beforehand, the big open area had been used for special corporate events and occasional movie-themed promotions, but for five months it became home to a popular event called the Big Thunder Ranch Jamboree. Supposedly run by Miss Chris, who is identified as the owner of the nearby cabin, the Jamboree offered a spirited medley of music, pin-trading, Disney characters, and arts and crafts. Veteran entertainers **Billy Hill and the Hillbillies** and a new Cowboy Roundup show added to the old-fashioned fun. Late in 2012, this area was converted into the **Jingle Jangle Jamboree**, a festive event that quickly became a **holiday season** tradition.

Big Thunder Trail

MAP: Frontierland, Fr-19

DATES: September 2, 1979–January 10, 2016

Along with the opening of the **Big Thunder Mountain Railroad** in 1979 came a fascinating new walking area. Wrapping around the back of the tall, sculptured Big Thunder rocks, the 800-foot-long Big Thunder Trail delivered pedestrians from the western edge of **Fantasyland** to the *Mark Twain* Riverboat, the **Golden Horseshoe**, and other main locations at the center of **Frontierland**. The walkway averaged twenty to twenty-five wide, though it could narrow to only fifteen feet and spread to about thirty-five feet. But the Big Thunder Trail offered much more than just a shortcut between the two lands.

Theming was detailed and comprehensive along the trail. Previously blocked off, the new northern end started just west of the **Village Haus** restaurant. Stone pillars and signage announced the trailhead. Here the rockwork subtly transitioned from Fantasyland's smooth pastels to a rougher, darker style anticipating the wilderness landscapes to come. As they walked, guests might have noticed that the path gently sloped downward and that its texture had changed. It also showed the impressions of carts, horseshoes, and boots, effective details that were carried through into the heart of Frontierland.

Heading south from Fantasyland, walkers immediately passed a shaded sitting area on the left that had formerly been reserved for smokers. Behind this area's benches was a mural attempting to recruit horse soldiers with dramatic imagery and words: "Join the Cavalry and have a courageous friend" and "The Horse Is Man's Noblest Companion." The first of three tunnels along the trail came next; the sounds of miners working inside were added in 2014. A little farther down the trail were the entrance to the **Big Thunder Ranch Barbecue** with its stage and **Big Thunder Ranch** with its petting zoo and Miss Chris's Cabin; on the left, behind high strands of real barbed wire, were the towering spires of Big Thunder Mountain. All along this stretch, guests heard the rowdy sounds of Big Thunder's rollicking railroad.

Crossing a footbridge that was twenty-seven feet long and twenty-one feet wide, guests passed under trees that draped almost completely across the trail. On the left (eastern) side, a patch of varied cacti had at least one Hidden Mickey on view (shown). To the right, a large, still pond invited a restful pause. Hooting owls were among the recorded bird sounds heard here on the trail's western side. Two tunnels gaped behind the pond, one that was

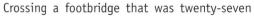

MOUSCELLANY

Many animals are seen along the Big Thunder Trail, especially at the main pond: real ducks, crawdads, turtles, lizards, tiny fish, and big, albeit artificial, leaping fish (shown). Oh, and one more critter, which has often been rumored to exist but is rarely seen by guests: live feral cats, such as this one that the author saw sneaking into the brush near Big Thunder Ranch in 2015 (shown on page 87). Disneyland encourages the feral cats to live in the park to help control the rodent population.

open and moodily lit at night night (shown on page 86), and another that was loosely boarded up. The trail emptied out past Big Thunder's railroad at a small building decorated with a beautiful *Mark Twain* mural and the **Ship to Shore Marketplace** beckoning ahead.

It was possible to explore Fantasyland and Frontierland without ever taking the Big Thunder Trail that connected them at the back. Thus, not everyone traveled this route through the wilderness, and they may never get to, now that most of the trail has been torn up for the **Star Wars Land** construction that began in early 2016.

Billy Hill and the Hillbillies

A legacy over two decades long established Billy Hill and the Hillbillies as one of Disneyland's most popular entertainment groups. Mixing bluegrass tunes with slapstick humor, the nascent band began as the Barley Boys (Barley, Charlie, Farley, Gnarley, Harley, and Ed), who hosted pig races and entertained guests at **Big Thunder Ranch** during the 1987-1988 **State Fair** promotion. Soon the group took a new name—Billy Hill and the Hillbillies (supposedly all brothers named Billy)—and moved their guitars, banjos, fiddles, mandolins, harmonicas, and basses to the outdoor stockade area of **Frontierland**.

After relocating to **Critter Country** in 1989 for the debut of **Splash Mountain**, the Billys moved into the **Golden Horseshoe** in 1992 and alternated appearances with the *Golden Horseshoe Variety Show*. The group temporarily returned to Big Thunder Ranch late in the decade, but after 2003, they became regulars at the Golden Horseshoe. In mid-2012, the Billys shifted to the outdoor **Festival Arena** at the north end of Frontierland as part of the **Big Thunder Ranch Jamboree**. For that year's **Halloween Time**, they became the Haunted Hillbillies at the seasonal Halloween Carnival.

With their daily schedule of five half-hour performances, the Billys played over 20,000 Disneyland shows (leader Kirk Wall played in nearly all of them and told us that, with all the improvisation, no two shows were identical). The full roster of Billys, all of them stellar bluegrass players, included about a dozen members to accommodate all the shows. The repertoire included everything from classic bluegrass favorites to modern songs given the bluegrass treatment. Billy Hill and the Hillbillies recorded a live CD a few years back, and occasionally they would perform as the Billys in other concert venues around Southern California.

After their long Disneyland run ended on January 6, 2014, they changed the group's name to Kirk Wall and the Hillbillies (later Krazy Kirk and the Hillbillies) and moved to Knott's Berry Farm. The initial replacement for the Billys at Big Thunder Ranch was the Frontierland Troupe, a sprawling meet-and-greet with Disney characters, live entertainment, and a themed snack area (the Troupe and its activities were gone by summer, replaced by a promotion for a TV show).

Blair, Mary
(1911–1978)

It's a Small World, one of Disneyland's most popular attractions ever, was given color and style by the prolific artist Mary Blair. Her imaginative art, which is simultaneously childlike and sophisticated, was the perfect match for a fanciful cruise past the children of the world.

Blair was born Mary Robinson in 1911 in McAlester, Oklahoma. She graduated from a Los Angeles area art school in 1933 and soon got a job in the animation department at MGM Studios. She got married in 1934 and in 1940, began working in the Disney Studios animation department.

Over the next two decades, Blair enhanced the color palettes of such films as *Cinderella*, *Alice in Wonderland*, and *Peter Pan*. Her art also greatly influenced Eyvind Earle and the other Disney animators who were creating a new look for *Sleeping Beauty* (Blair and some of her bold illustrations are shown on the film's 2008 DVD). She contributed to Disney movie sets and costume designs before leaving the company in 1953 to become a freelance illustrator for ads and children's books.

At the invitation of **Walt Disney**, Blair styled It's a Small World for the 1964-1965 New York World's Fair before it came to **Fantasyland** in 1966. Blair also had a great influence on Disneyland itself. In 1967, the main buildings in **Tomorrowland** were decorated with huge, beautiful tile murals of Blair's joyous art, giving this walkway the name **Corridor of Murals**. Blair's importance was underscored in 1965, when she became one of the few artists to make an appearance on the TV show *Walt Disney's Wonderful World of Color* (she's shown working on Small World lighting effects). She later created an enormous mural for the Contemporary Resort at Walt Disney World.

Blair died in 1978 at age sixty-six in Soquel, California. Inducted as a Disney Legend in 1991, she was the subject of a biography called *The Art and Flair of Mary Blair* in 2003. Her exuberant work appeared in major exhibitions at the **Disney Gallery** in 2011 and the Walt Disney Family Museum in 2014, where exterior banners displayed her portrait (shown). And a century after her birth, she was represented as a Google Doodle. Today, Disneyland visitors will find a nice little tribute to Blair inside It's a Small World: perched on the Eiffel Tower is a balloon-holding doll that's dressed to look like her.

Blast to the Past Celebration

DATES: Spring 1988–Spring 1989 (seasonal)

To jump-start the 1988 and 1989 summer seasons, Disneyland introduced an elaborate celebration called Blast to the Past. This springtime spectacular followed on the
heels of 1986's **Circus Fantasy** and 1987's **State Fair**. At a time when the 1950s was
a popular decade in the media (*Happy Days* was a TV hit all the way through 1984,
and *Grease* and *Back to the Future* were blockbuster movies in 1978 and 1985, respectively), Blast to the Past featured rockin' music, colorful costumes, special giveaways,
and themed **parades**, all of which evoked the innocent bygone days of poodle skirts
and sock hops. The celebration even extended to Disneyland's décor, which was altered dramatically: Blast to the Past signs were added over the **entrance** tunnels; an
enormous jukebox joined the **Hub**; a scene featuring palm trees and a sandy beach
appeared in front of **It's a Small World**; and a nostalgic name, Rainbow Diner, was
given to Tomorrowland Terrace (now the **Galactic Grill**).

From March to June, daily **parades** of hot rods and classic motorcycles wended
their way from **Fantasyland** to **Main Street**, and on weekends, a Main Street Hop
presented legions of costumed dancers cavorting to a spiffy soundtrack while confetti showered down from above. What's more, hit bands from the 1960s, including
Herman's Hermits and the Turtles, performed at Videopolis (now the **Fantasyland
Theatre**); the venerable **Dapper Dans** transformed into the doo-wop group Danny
and the Dappers; and Disneyland sold a special collection of familiar songs reworked
for Disney characters (Donald Duck's "Quackety Quack" instead of "Yakety Yak," for
instance). There were plenty of prizes—the Guess-o-Rama offered an opportunity to
win a car, and, thanks to a cross-promotion with McDonald's, guests could win discounted Disneyland admission. And there were lots of special events, including world
records for mass hula-hooping and twisting.

The festival peaked on May 20, 1989, when the TV special "Disneyland Blast to
the Past" aired just a month before the celebration itself passed into the past.

Blue Bayou

MAP: New Orleans Square, NOS-4

DATES: March 18, 1967–ongoing

Though **New Orleans Square** was officially dedicated and opened to the public on
July 24, 1966, its showpiece restaurant—indeed, Disneyland's showpiece restaurant—didn't open for another eight months. When it did, it was instantly hailed as a
landmark dining experience. Because it is incorporated within a major attraction, the
Blue Bayou is truly *sui generis*.

That attraction, of course, is **Pirates of the Caribbean**. The revolutionary cruise
and the Blue Bayou debuted on the same day in 1967. The entrance to the Blue
Bayou is adjacent to the Pirates' exit and next door to **Club 33** (the Blue Bayou's
address is 31 Royal Street). Inside the Blue Bayou building—and guests really are
inside a building, despite the al fresco feel—the illusory setting is a terrace along

a quiet, crepuscular riverbank. Here the ambience is always serene and the time is always twilight, no matter what the real weather and time of day are outside. Nearby, crickets chirp, fireflies meander, and shallow boats full of guests drift past; overhead, thin clouds drift slowly across an indigo sky that's punctuated by shooting stars (we clocked a meteor every five seconds in 2015). This is visual spectacle that never bores.

There are other touches that make the Blue Bayou special. For a long time, it was the only restaurant inside Disneyland that took reservations. Its menu is something of a collectible and can usually be taken home upon request. And the candlelit tables are a welcome departure from all the quick-stop food counters elsewhere in the park.

Over a million of the Blue Bayou's Le Spécial de Monte Cristo sandwiches have been sold, making this gently fried turkey/ham/Swiss cheese delight the restaurant's most popular lunchtime entrée. Dinner may include crab cakes, steak Diane, pork loin, prime rib, pan-seared salmon, Cajun gumbo, or jambalaya, plus some lighter side dishes introduced in 2013. For dessert, there's pecan pie or chocolate mousse cake. Unlike the food at many other establishments in Disneyland, these gourmet dishes aren't presented buffet-style. Instead, they're served by well-trained **cast members**.

The Blue Bayou: great scenery, great food, great service, and a recipient of the Four Star award from the Southern California Restaurant Writers in 2014? It's no wonder that the Blue Bayou is still Disneyland's premier restaurant destination.

Blue Bird Shoes for Children

MAP: Main Street, MS-13

DATES: July 17, 1955–1958

Main Street evokes **Walt Disney's** small-town childhood, so naturally it would include an old-fashioned children's shoe store. On Main Street's eastern side, Gallen-Kamp ran Blue Bird Shoes, perching a big circular bird logo on the signage. But guests were most likely far too distracted by Disneyland's many attractions to want to spend time shoe shopping, and the store exited within three years of opening. Chester Drawer's now resides in Blue Bird's former home.

Blue Ribbon Bakery

MAP: Main Street, MS-6

DATES: April 6, 1990–January 5, 2012

Guests who love the smell of sticky buns in the morning used to flock to the Blue Ribbon Bakery. Blue Ribbon was the second bakery on **Main Street**; in the 1950s, **Puffin Bakery** occupied the same west-side stretch next to the **Penny Arcade**, until the **Sunkist Citrus House** replaced it in 1960. When Sunkist closed in 1989, the Blue Ribbon Bakery took over a year later.

In January of 1997, the bakery temporarily closed. When it reopened three months later, it had acquired a new sponsor, Nestlé Toll House. It had also traded places with the **Carnation Ice Cream Parlor**, jumping from the middle of the block to the corner of Main and **Center Street** (the ice creamery switched to the space where the Blue Ribbon Bakery had been and reopened with a new name, the **Gibson Girl Ice Cream Parlor**).

No matter where it was located, the bakery was always a popular breakfast destination specializing in delectable baked temptations like fresh muffins, scones, croissants, biscotti, and humongous cookies. The bakery also whipped up gourmet sandwiches and exotic coffees; for the winter holidays, it offered specialty beverages and seasonal cookies and cupcakes.

After two decades on Main Street, the bakery finally closed in 2012 so the adjacent **Carnation Café** could supplement its outdoor tables with some prime indoor seating.

Boag, Wally
(1920–2011)

Originally signed to a two-week Disneyland contract in 1955, Wally Boag went on to enjoy a record-setting career that lasted almost three decades. What kind of record did he set? The Guinness-verified world-record kind. Boag was one of the stars of the longest-running stage show in history, the **Golden Horseshoe Revue**, which he co-wrote. Boag performed in the revue approximately 40,000 times—from 1955 until his last performance on January 28, 1982.

Comedian **Steve Martin** has consistently singled out Boag as a major inspiration. In his memoir, *Born Standing Up*, Martin writes that Boag "wowed every audience every time" as he "plied a hilarious trade of gags and offbeat skills such as gun twirling and balloon animals" while maintaining an air of "amiable casualness." On the *Steve Martin: The Television Stuff* DVD, he says that Boag's was "a likeable act," adding that "he did exactly the same show every time . . . but you never ever thought he was tired, you always thought it was the first time he was doing the show."

Born in 1920 in Portland, Oregon, Boag learned his trade as a teenage dancer and comedian in vaudeville theaters across the country. MGM Studios gave him small roles in several films, including the Oscar-nominated musical *It's Always Fair Weather* (1955), in which he's one of a dozen athletic dancers in the three-and-a-half-minute "Thanks a Lot, But No Thanks" number. Disneyland, however, was about to beckon.

In 1955, Boag successfully auditioned in front of **Walt Disney** to work at the **Golden Horseshoe**. Instantly popular as the show's versatile Traveling Salesman and Pecos Bill characters, the quick-witted, acrobatic Boag charmed audiences three times a day in the wholesome *Golden Horseshoe Revue*. Disney put him to work on the small screen, too, where he guest-starred on **Disneyland** and The

MOUSCELLANY

Boag appeared in several Disney films, though he was woefully underused. In *The Absent-Minded Professor* (1961), he has two short lines as a bespectacled reporter; in *Son of Flubber* (1963), he steals the ninety-second Flubberoleum commercial with crazy pratfalls; and in *The Love Bug* (1968), he plays an irate driver with a one-line joke in a three-second cameo.

Mickey Mouse Club (on October 4, 1955, he got nine minutes on the latter as a "balloonologist" folding balloons and as a bagpiper screeching the pipes). Veteran guests might recognize Boag as the voice of Jose the parrot in the **Enchanted Tiki Room**. He was also one of the main creative forces working on the **Chinatown** area that was planned for Disneyland in the late 1950s but never built.

Boag and his two Golden Horseshoe costars, **Fulton Burley** and **Betty Taylor**, were inducted as Disney Legends in 1995. Wally Boag died at age ninety in 2011, one day before **Betty Taylor** died.

Bonanza Outfitters

MAP: Frontierland, Fr-2

DATES: June 29, 1990–ongoing

The **Pendleton Woolen Mills Dry Goods Store**, a **Frontierland** fixture since 1955, finally closed after almost thirty-five years of meeting guests' flannel needs. Two months later, just in time for the 1990 summer season, Bonanza Outfitters opened in Pendleton's same large location near the **Golden Horseshoe**.

The store still has the same wooden sidewalk out front and the same kind of rustic interior it had in its Pendleton days, and the clothes are still frontier-friendly. At times, cowboy boots, countrified kitchen supplies, old-fashioned farm dresses, and Western-themed gifts have made it to the shelves and displays, but there are always plenty of the usual Disney shirts, pins, and hats available. In 2014, Bonanza Outfitters seemed to be going a bit more upscale while manifesting a cowgirl theme that brought in non-Disney clothing (such as dresses, belts, blouses, and a $209 fringe leather jacket), blankets, bags, books and Old West displays.

Bone Carving Shop

MAP: Frontierland, Fr-1

DATES: Ca. 1956–ca. 1964

In the 1950s and '60s, Disneyland's **souvenir books** and maps sometimes listed the Bone Carving Shop as either Bone Jewelry or Bone Craft. The shop was inside the **Davy Crockett Arcade**, which was the first main building on the left as guests entered **Frontierland**. Crockett's arcade went through several remodels, and during one of them the Bone Carving Shop got remodeled out of existence as the building evolved into **Davy Crockett's Pioneer Mercantile**.

Bookstand

MAP: New Orleans Square, NOS-3

DATES: Ca. 1966–ca. 1973

Over the years, Disneyland has offered many small establishments that sell books and postcards. One of them, simply called the Bookstand, stood in **New Orleans Square** on Royal Street, near the **Pirates of the Caribbean** exit. The Bookstand has never been mentioned in Disneyland's **souvenir books** (which the Bookstand sold), and only briefly did it turn up on some maps between 1966 (when New Orleans Square opened) and 1973 (when the Bookstand disappeared in a building renovation).

Boyajian, Chuck
(1917–2004)

Guests have always admired and appreciated the immaculate cleanliness of Disneyland, which is known as the world's tidiest, most sanitary park. Early on, **Walt Disney** made cleanliness a part of his Disneyland dream, as noted in *The Quotable Walt Disney*: "When I started on Disneyland, my wife used to say, 'But why do you want to build an amusement park? They're so dirty.' I told her that was the point—mine wouldn't be." Once the park opened, James B. Stewart's *Disney Wars* pointed out that "no tradition was more hallowed than Walt's habit of personally picking up any scrap of paper or refuse that he detected on his frequent visits to Disneyland. Walt was obsessed by cleanliness." There was a motive behind Disney's fastidiousness: he felt that a glistening park would inspire guests to help keep it pristine. Also, with fewer things to slip on or trip over, a debris-free park was a safer park.

One man was in charge of establishing and maintaining Disneyland's spotless reputation—Chuck Boyajian. Born in 1917, Boyajian grew up in Ohio and later served in the navy during World War II. He worked at Disneyland from 1955 until 1981, and as the manager of custodial operations, he created procedures, set standards, and trained **cast members** to believe that, when it came to cleaning, "nobody does it better." The most famous and most photographed member of Boyajian's team was the mustachioed Trinidad Ruiz, who swept the Main Street area in Disneyland's first decade as a conspicuous "white wing" (the term for an old-fashioned, white-clad sanitation worker). Mostly, however, custodians are Disneyland's unsung heroes.

To maintain radiant cleanliness even when Disneyland was packed with guests, Boyajian's crews worked efficiently, unobtrusively, and persistently, with many of the sweepers walking up to fifteen miles a day (distances like that are accumulated because all the streets, plazas, walkways, and **queues** inside Disneyland are visited four times an hour by roaming sweepers, according to Barron and Pellman's *Cleaning the Kingdom*). In the park's early years, Boyajian's crews had extra days for cleaning, because during the off-season Disneyland was closed at least one day a week (Disneyland has been open daily since 1985).

Some cleaning problems were anticipated—Walt Disney decreed that no peanuts would be sold in their shells, because he knew from his visits to other amusement parks that there would be pieces of broken shells everywhere. But other issues quickly presented themselves—chewing gum being one of the toughest, since it is difficult to remove quickly in the hot sun. (Gum joined the list of things not sold in Disneyland; custodians still carry putty knives with them for scraping up gum and other sticky substances.) Diane Disney Miller, Walt Disney's daughter, named other problematical products in *The Story of Walt Disney*: candy with cylindrical sticks ("because people might slip on those discarded sticks") and spun candy ("because children get it all over everything"). Always a concern was the sheer volume of trash—about twenty tons on an average day, and forty on busy days.

Ultimately, Boyajian's methods were so successful that he was brought in to help set and meet the same standards in the Disney areas at the 1964-1965 New York World's Fair, Walt Disney World, and Tokyo Disneyland. Chuck Boyajian died in 2004 at age eighty-six, one year before his induction as a Disney Legend.

Bradbury, Ray
(1920–2012)

When Ray Bradbury died at age ninety-one on June 5, 2012, the world lost one of its great visionary writers, and Disneyland lost one of its biggest advocates.

Bradbury's prolific writing career has been well-chronicled: from his upbringing in Waukegan, Illinois, to his early science fiction stories in pulp magazines of the 1930s and '40s, to his breakthrough 1953 novel, *Fahrenheit 451*, which he typed on a rented computer at the UCLA library. For decades, Bradbury filled bestseller lists with a steady stream of fiction that slipped smoothly from fantasy and sci-fi to horror and mystery. Among his most familiar collections are *The Martian Chronicles*, *The Illustrated Man*, and *Dandelion Wine*. He also wrote plays, essays, and screenplays (such as John Huston's *Moby Dick*). Additionally, many of his works were turned into movies (including *The Beast from 20,000 Fathoms*, *Something Wicked This Way Comes*, *A Sound of Thunder*) and TV shows (*The Ray Bradbury Theater*).

By mid-1958, Bradbury had visited Disneyland seven times (including once on a personal tour given by **Walt Disney**), and he continued to visit up to five times a year until the mid-1960s, according to his book, *Bradbury Speaks*. In fact, he became such a Disneyland fan that he rallied in the park's defense when it was criticized in *The Nation* (in his letter to the magazine, he wrote that when Walt Disney "flies, he really flies" and achieves "true delight and wonder"). In the 1960s, Bradbury and Disney become friends and occasional lunch partners; on the day of Disney's 1966 funeral, Bradbury took his four daughters to Disneyland. Later, Bradbury was shown the **Pirates of the Caribbean** and **Haunted Mansion** before they opened, and these landmarks quickly became two of his favorite attractions.

On the *Walt Disney Treasures: Tomorrow Land, Disney in Space and Beyond* DVD, Bradbury discusses Walt Disney: "Enthusiasm was Walt Disney's middle name," he said. "With Disneyland and . . . the World's Fair in New York in 1964-65, he proved that he was ahead of everyone." Bradbury loved that Disneyland was "full of things we didn't need but really needed." He saw the park as a model of urban planning, "an example of a way of living, not just an entertainment center." "When you enter Disneyland," he said, "you're entering . . . a fabulous time machine with a series of doors you can open and go into the past or into the future."

Bradbury consulted on Florida's EPCOT, and he eventually contributed directly to Disneyland; every autumn since 2007, a Halloween Tree (honoring a Bradbury novel) has been decorated in front of **Silver Spur Supplies** in **Frontierland**.

Brave: Meet Merida

MAP: Fantasyland, Fa-21

DATES: May 21, 2012–December 2014

A month before *Brave* opened in theaters, Brave: Meet Merida opened alongside the walkway in front of **It's a Small World**. Every day, this interactive area enabled guests to safely shoot arrows at targets, play a cake-toss game, and make stone rubbings, all while surrounded by decorations reminiscent of a Scottish tournament. The red-haired heroine, the movie's three bear cubs (shown), and official park photographers were on hand for photo opportunities. For Memorial Day weekend in 2013, Opa! A Celebration of Greece temporarily took over Merida's area. Brave: Meet Merida quickly returned for another fourteen months but was gone by the time 2015 arrived.

Brer Bar

MAP: Bear Country/Critter Country, B/C-5

DATES: July 17, 1989–2002

When **Bear Country** was reinvented as **Critter Country** in 1988, many of the area's establishments got new names. The **Mile Long Bar** was one of them, adopting the name Brer Bar, which echoed the *Song of the South* stylings of nearby **Splash Mountain**. The bar's location (the northern tip of the wide building at the back of Critter Country) didn't change. Nor did the food—like its predecessor, the Brer Bar was a quick-stop food spot for hot dogs, cookies, Mickey Mouse-shaped pretzels, and drinks.

The Brer Bar closed in 2002, and the space was swallowed up in the major remodel that created the big new **Pooh Corner** store.

Briar Patch

MAP: Bear Country/Critter Country, B/C-10

DATES: December 1988–February 1996; October 1996–ongoing

Located in a back corner of **Frontierland**, the rustic **Indian Trading Post** was a longtime holdover from the days of the old **Indian Village**. But in 1988, with **Critter Country** replacing **Bear Country**, the American Indian arts, crafts, and jewelry moved out and Briar Patch moved in.

Like the nearby **Brer Bar**, the Briar Patch took its name from the "Zip-A-Dee-Doo-Dah" theme of **Splash Mountain**, the area's major attraction. The Briar Patch also adopted some of the ride's décor—for instance, Brer Rabbit's carrots grow downward through the roof into the interior. Souvenirs, toys, clothes, sunglasses, and gifts were originally sold on the shelves of the Briar Patch, but changes were made in early 1996, when the store briefly became **Critter Country Plush** and filled up with new merchandise. Eight months later, the Briar Patch name returned, but the plush toys stayed. In 2004, the store temporarily closed for yet another change, one that retained the Briar Patch name but replaced some of the plush with big hats. By 2015, the store was basically just a hat store, with lots of **Mouse Ears** on the racks and even fuzzy raccoon-tailed caps among the varied headgear.

> **MOUSCELLANY**
>
> Inside, the Briar Patch is a wonderfully themed cabin, sporting carved wooden mirrors, thorny briars, shelves filled with miniatures, rustic lamps, and pine cones, and (in 2016) at least one fun **Hidden Mickey**—a three-lobed cabbage on a shelf near the cash register (shown).

Briar Rose Cottage

MAP: Fantasyland, Fa-30

DATES: May 29, 1987–July 15, 1991

In the late 1980s, guests who walked through **Sleeping Beauty Castle** and into the main **Fantasyland** courtyard found an enchanting store on their immediate right. The name, of course, is a reference to the beautiful Briar Rose, who is cursed by wicked Maleficent in Disney's *Sleeping Beauty*. Previously, this choice location next to **Peter Pan's Flight** was the home of **Mickey's Christmas Chalet**, a charming spot selling holiday ornaments. The Briar Rose Cottage was no less charming, and its merchandise (Disney-themed figurines and collectibles) no less ornamental.

In mid-1991, evil conquered good when the **Disney Villains** store took over this spot for about five years.

Broggie, Roger
(1908–1991)

Roger Broggie, the man known throughout Disney Studios as a mechanical genius, was born in Massachusetts in 1908. Broggie grew up in Illinois, learned to work industrial tools and machines, and subsequently headed west to join the burgeoning film industry of the 1930s. In 1939, Broggie landed at Disney Studios, where he developed special cameras and photographic equipment and eventually ran the company's machine shop. Away from the studio, he helped **Walt Disney** create an elaborate miniature train—the famed Carolwood Pacific in Disney's Holmby Hills backyard.

This successful train experience presaged Broggie's long-term involvement with Disneyland. He was instrumental in the development and construction of the original **Santa Fe & Disneyland Railroad** (a plaque on the *E.P. Ripley*, shown, identifies "R.E. Broggie, Gen Mgr."). Broggie's triumph with the trains propelled him to help develop other major attractions, including the groundbreaking **Great**

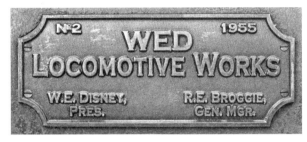

Moments with Mr. Lincoln and the novel 360-degree films for the **Circarama** theater, as well as the classic *Mark Twain* **Riverboat**, sleek **Matterhorn Bobsleds**, charming **Casey Jr. Circus Train**, and futuristic **Monorail**.

Broggie also contributed to the special effects for the film *20,000 Leagues Under the Sea* and to Florida's EPCOT Center before he finally retired in 1975. He was named a Disney Legend in 1990, one year before he died in Los Angeles at age eighty-three. In tribute to Broggie, one of the train engines at Walt Disney World is named after him. *Walt Disney's Railroad Story*, a handsome book about Broggie and Disney trains, was written by his son, Michael, in 1997. Another of Roger Broggie's sons, Roger Jr., was also a mechanical wizard who worked on Disneyland's **Audio-Animatronics** (as well as the trick cars in Disney's *The Love Bug*).

Bruns, George
(1914–1983)

Several of Disney's most famous songs were composed by George Bruns. An Oregonian born in 1914, Bruns took piano lessons as a child, studied brass in high school, and ultimately mastered a dozen different instruments. After playing with big bands and working for Portland radio stations, Bruns traveled to Los Angeles in 1934 to work first for Capitol Records and later for Disney Studios. Bruns was a prolific composer of Disney film scores, including three that earned Oscar nominations: *Sleeping Beauty*, *Babes in Toyland*, and *The Sword in the Stone* (he also shared an Oscar nod for a song in Disney's *Robin Hood*). His most famous screen composition, however, was "The Ballad of Davy Crockett" for the ***Disneyland* TV series**.

At Disneyland, Bruns is celebrated as the composer of "Yo Ho (A Pirate's Life for Me)," one of the park's most famous songs (in the first *Pirates of the Caribbean* movie, Johnny Depp's character sings it and then announces, "I love this song!"). Bruns wasn't just a writer of music *for* Disneyland; he was also a performer *at* Disneyland, playing tuba with the popular **Firehouse Five Plus Two** jazz band.

After retiring in 1975, Bruns returned to Oregon to teach and make more music. He died at age sixty-eight in 1983, and was inducted as a Disney Legend in 2001.

Burley, Fulton
(1922–2007)

Born in 1922 in Ireland but raised in Canada, Fulton Burley was around lucky horseshoes for most of his long showbiz career. In 1943, having already appeared in several MGM films, he auditioned over the phone and got the lead in Broadway's *Diamond Horseshoe Revue*. Burley and actor **Wally Boag** both played airmen in the 1945 movie *Thrill of a Romance*; seventeen years later, Boag invited Burley, who was appearing in Las Vegas, to come to Disneyland's **Golden Horseshoe**, where Boag was already starring in the successful *Golden Horseshoe Revue*.

At the Golden Horseshoe, Burley's rich tenor voice, comedic skills, and Irish accent were a hit for the next two decades. He also appeared at special Disney functions and live shows, and provided vocals for the parrot Michael in the **Enchanted Tiki Room**. In 1995, eight years after he retired, Burley was inducted as a Disney Legend along with the two other stars of the *Golden Horseshoe Revue*, Wally Boag and **Betty Taylor**. In 2007, the eighty-four-year-old Burley died of heart failure in Carlsbad, California.

Burns, Harriet
(1928–2008)

According to *Dream It! Do It!* by **Martin Sklar**, Harriet Burns "was **Walt Disney**'s favorite Imagineer." Born in Texas in 1928, Burns graduated from Southern Methodist University with an art degree and then continued her studies at the University of New Mexico before moving to Southern California in the early 1950s. There, she worked for a company that designed TV show sets and Las Vegas hotels.

In 1955, Burns started working on *The Mickey Mouse Club* TV show for Disney Studios (she's credited as the designer of the Mouse Clubhouse). Switching to Disneyland projects, she was one of the original model makers for the attractions and thus was a key contributor to **Sleeping Beauty Castle**, the **Storybook Land Canal Boats**, the **Enchanted Tiki Room**, **New Orleans Square**, the **Submarine Voyage**, the **Jungle Cruise**, **Great Moments with Mr. Lincoln**, **Pirates of the Caribbean**, and the **Carousel of Progress**. Even while creating pirate hair, mermaid costumes, the Tiki Room birds, and Lincoln's head, Burns still contributed to Disney films like *Babes in Toyland*.

Burns retired in 1986 and lived in Santa Barbara, California, until her death in 2008. Today she is remembered not only as a Disney Legend (inducted in 2000), but also as something of a pioneer—she was Disney's first female Imagineer. Disney even introduced her to national TV audiences on several episodes of *Walt Disney's*

Wonderful World of Color. "His enthusiasm," she says in *Disneyland . . . The Beginning*, "left us all inspired." Her own unique contributions were further acknowledged with an "H. Snrub" gravestone outside the **Haunted Mansion**.

Buzz Lightyear Astro Blasters

MAP: Tomorrowland, T-4

DATES: May 5, 2005–ongoing

Needing a new **Tomorrowland** attraction that would generate some positive buzz after the problematic **Rocket Rods** expired in 2001, Disneyland designers looked to other Disney theme parks for inspiration. Buzz Lightyear's SpaceRanger Spin at Walt Disney World and Buzz Lightyear's Astro Blasters at Tokyo Disneyland were already high-flying hits, so the theme seemed obvious.

Buzz zoomed into the former pre-show and theater rooms of Disneyland's old **Circarama** theater. What was once a **Mary Blair**-designed tile mosaic on the curving exterior became a painted mural showing speeding rockets, floating space mountains,

and fantastic planets. Inside, the attraction features characters and themes from *Toy Story*, intensified by bright neon colors and humorous sci-fi art (Buzz himself appears as a sophisticated **Audio-Animatronics** character). As described on the sign out front, the attraction is "an interactive adventure in which you travel aboard slow-moving spaceships that you can spin while helping Buzz Lightyear battle the evil Emperor Zurg." The "spaceships," a new iteration of the **Omnimover** system first developed in the 1960s, are indeed slow, but guests really can twirl them 360 degrees.

What makes this four-and-a-half-minute ride popular enough to necessitate the **FASTPASS** ticket center outside is its interactive shoot-'em-up element. As passengers wend through the ten different space scenes, they fire "laser cannons" at different targets with various point values. Point totals display inside the cockpit, and rankings from Star Cadet to Galactic Hero are posted at the end. Unsurprisingly, guests then exit directly into an adjacent gift shop, the **Little Green Men Store Command**.

Café Orleans, aka Creole Café

MAP: New Orleans Square, NOS-7

DATES: July 24, 1966–ongoing

From mid-1966 until 1972, the Creole Café was a choice spot for **New Orleans Square** dining. Entered from Royal Street, the café was halfway between the **Pirates of the Caribbean** entrance and the **French Market** restaurant. Since it jutted out toward the **Rivers of America**, it was highly visible to anyone walking the main thoroughfare from **Frontierland** to the **Haunted Mansion**.

In 1972, the Sara Lee Corporation took over sponsorship of the café and changed the name first to Sara Lee's Café Orleans and then to the simpler Café Orleans. Marie Callender's briefly sponsored the restaurant in 1987. Over the years, the relatively inexpensive meals have included sandwiches, crêpes, chicken dishes, gumbo, French onion soup, a plate of thick-sliced Bananas Foster French Toast, and salads. Best of all may be the well-seasoned pommes frites with a spicy Cajun rémoulade.

Though the menu has changed often and the days and hours of operation have varied, the riverside setting has never been anything but picturesque, especially when live music plays nearby. Inside the café, the pretty rooms are decorated with stained glass and sketches of New Orleans Square. Café Orleans is recognized as one of Disneyland's top restaurants—in 2014, the Southern California Restaurant Writers bestowed upon it a Four Stars award.

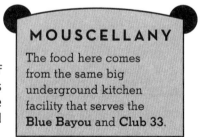

MOUSCELLANY

The food here comes from the same big underground kitchen facility that serves the **Blue Bayou** and **Club 33**.

Calico Kate's Pantry Shop

MAP: Frontierland, Fr-27

DATES: 1965

This sounds like a charming store created by Disney designers, but actually Calico Kate's Pantry Shops had already been established elsewhere before one debuted in

Disneyland. The first Calico Kate's was a countrified gift shop that opened in Colorado in 1959, followed later by an Arizona spin-off. The business was begun and run by a couple whose daughter designed the Calico Kate character. Disneyland's 1965 **souvenir book** lists a Calico Kate's in **Frontierland**, but the shop was closed after just one year.

Canal Boats of the World

MAP: Fantasyland, Fa-15

DATES: July 17, 1955–September 16, 1955

Long before there was a Disneyland, **Walt Disney** collected miniatures. Consequently, one of his first Disneyland ideas was to set a little boat gliding quietly through a setting decorated with adorable miniature buildings. He'd already seen something similar while vacationing in Europe. Unfortunately, the Disneyland version didn't live up to anyone's expectations, at least not at first.

The canal in the title of Disneyland's short-lived Canal Boats of the World referred to a winding river dug into one acre at the back of **Fantasyland**. The "world" was going to be made up of tiny international buildings lining the riverbanks. Early concept drawings also portrayed low-slung canal boats entering a colorful mound of "candy" called **Rock Candy Mountain.** In addition, a 1954 Bruce Bushman drawing positioned Monstro the Whale at the *end* of the ride so boats could slide out of his mouth to a splashdown near the unloading dock. But when the attraction debuted on **Opening Day** in 1955, the miniature buildings, candy mountain, and Monstro slide weren't in place.

Disappointingly, the view from the eight boats as they toured the narrow canals was basically of desolate dirt banks (although guests could watch the **Casey Jr. Circus Train**, which circled the same area). What's more, the boats' primitive outdoor motors were so loud that they preempted the skippers' narration. The boats themselves took their names from an odd mix of sources, including the Wild West (*Annie Oakley*), Scottish literature (*Bold Lochinvar*), Arthurian legend (*Lady of the Lake*), and American journalism (*Nellie Bly*).

Two months after it opened, the original Canal Boats cruise sank into history. Happily, however, Walt Disney's idea survived. Nine months later, the wonderfully remodeled **Storybook Land Canal Boats** opened with quieter boats, lavish landscaping, and the kind of delightful miniatures Disney had originally desired.

Candlelight Procession and Ceremony

DATES: December 1958–ongoing (seasonal)

The event known as the Candlelight Procession (or Processional) and Ceremony has long been one of the inspirational highlights of the **holiday season**. First performed in 1958, the Candlelight Procession sends legions of carolers and candles southward down a garlanded **Main Street** toward the towering Christmas tree. Culminating the procession is the candlelight ceremony in a darkened **Town Square**, where choirs gather in front of the train station and form a Living Christmas Tree. Supporting the singers is an orchestra and a narrator who retells the traditional story of Christmas. Dozens of celebrities have served as the event's narrator, starting with actor Dennis Morgan for the first decade and then diversifying to include such stars as Henry Fonda, Cary Grant, Charlton Heston, Gregory Peck, Mickey Rooney, and John Wayne.

There have been several scheduling changes over the decades. From 1998 to 2002, the show was relocated to the Videopolis/**Fantasyland Theatre** site at the back of **Fantasyland**, a move that was not universally acclaimed. After testing a private $275-per-person Candlelight event exclusively for D23 members in 2009 and then offering a $2,500 Candlelight Experience in 2011, Disneyland dramatically expanded the show from two nights to twenty in 2012, with two performances nightly. The first two nights of 2012 were by invitation only, but the rest of the nights could be reserved by Annual Passholders and guests who booked special dining packages. The long list of celebrity narrators for 2012 included Marcia Gay Harden, Dennis Haysbert, Patricia Heaton, Lou Diamond Phillips, Molly Ringwald, Kurt Russell, and Dick Van Dyke. By 2015, the event had been scaled back to just two nights, December 5 and 6, with two performances each night and two celebrity narrators: actresses Geena Davis and Lana Parrilla. Actress Ginnifer Goodwin did the narration on December 3 and 4 in 2016.

Candle Shop

MAP: Main Street, MS-3

DATES: 1958–ca. 1977

Disneyland's Candle Shop stood in the back of the big **Crystal Arcade** building on the western side of **Main Street**. Starting with the 1958 edition, the **souvenir books** consistently play up the Candle Shop with prominent photos that make the interior look as colorful as a candy store. According to the captions, "a rainbow of color" filled the Candle Shop: colorful candle displays hung from the ceilings, lined the walls, and covered the tables. Among the hundreds of offerings were fun seasonal favorites (October pumpkins, November turkeys, etc.), plus candles shaped like food, spirals, and tiki heads. In the mid-1970s, the Candle Shop's flame flickered out and the store disappeared during a Crystal Arcade remodel.

Candy Palace, aka Candyland, aka Candy Palace and Candy Kitchen

MAP: Main Street, MS-9

DATES: July 22, 1955–ongoing

Five days after **Opening Day**, the Candy Palace opened on the western side of **Main Street**. During its first year, the Candy Palace was also called Candyland (Disneyland's 1956 **souvenir book** lists both names). South of the Palace was the **Penny Arcade** entrance, and to the north was Coke's **Refreshment Corner**. In 1997, the Palace was renovated and renamed as the Candy Palace and Candy Kitchen.

Pedestrians cruising Main Street have always been tempted by the confections on view in the Candy Palace's windows and display kitchen. The space around this kitchen was broadened in 2012 to accommodate all the viewers, especially the crowds that gather during the **holiday season** to watch the creation of big handmade candy canes.

Today, the ever-popular candy counters and shelves serve up lots of nostalgic treats, including caramel apples, which are created with different designs and accelerating prices leading up to incredibly intricate gourmet caramel apples. New seasonal delicacies (such as fudge Easter eggs and new Mickey-shaped treats for 2015's **Diamond Celebration**) are all made on-site. Bulk candy is sold by the bag, and until 2015, fourteen flavors of sour Pucker Powders made by Goofy's Powder Candy Co. were sold by the tube.

But it's not just the Candy Palace's colorful sights and exotic flavors that tempt guests; historians have long surmised that vents in front of the store pump candylicious aromas like vanilla and peppermint out into the Main Street air.

> ## MOUSCELLANY
>
> During the holiday season, the Candy Palace's immense candy canes are the edible version of the Christmas spirit. So popular are these freshly made wintery treats that in 2012, Disneyland started issuing wristbands to limit how many canes guests could buy. Guests now eagerly wait for Disneyland to announce the days (there were eleven in 2016) when batches of fresh candy canes will be available.

Captain EO, aka *Captain EO* Tribute

MAP: Tomorrowland, T-19

DATES: September 18, 1986–April 6, 1997; February 23, 2010–June 17, 2014

Few attractions have left Disneyland and returned later, but *Captain EO* was one of those few.

After successful screenings at Walt Disney World, the *Captain EO* film flew into the **Magic Eye Theater** in **Tomorrowland** in September of 1986. The look of the film and its plot draw on themes from such movies as *Alien*, *Star Wars*, and even *The Wizard of Oz*. But it was the film's remarkable cast that garnered most of the attention: Michael Jackson, the world's biggest recording star at the time, portrays the title astronaut, and Oscar-winner Anjelica Huston plays the galaxy's Supreme Ruler. Both performed under the guidance of Oscar-winning director Francis Ford Coppola. The film was produced by *Star Wars* creator (and Disney Legend) George Lucas.

Jackson's weapons against his wicked space foe were his singing and dancing, aided by a freakish alien crew with cuddly names like Odee, Geex, and Fuzzball. Guests wearing 3-D glasses watched objects jump out at them and laser beams fire over their heads while Jackson's music filled the theater. Estimates place the cost of this effects-laden extravaganza at over $17 million, or approximately $1 million per minute of finished film.

Touting its exciting new attraction, Disney launched the movie with a

star-studded premiere in 1986 and aired a mak-
ing-of TV special called "*Captain EO* Backstage"
in 1988. However, the big crowds of the late
1980s dwindled down in the mid-1990s as the
luster of Jackson's superstardom gradually wore
down. In early 1997, *Captain EO* was sent packing and another 3-D Walt Disney World import,
Honey, I Shrunk the Audience, successfully
jumped to the West Coast.

About eight months after Jackson's death in
June 2009, *Captain EO* (renamed *Captain EO* Tribute) reopened in the same theater it had occupied before, with Kodak taking over as the new
sponsor. Officials termed this tribute a "limited
engagement," but audience enthusiasm kept the
show going into June of 2014. Two weeks after
EO flew out, the theater welcomed 3D previews of a new movie, *Guardians of the
Galaxy*.

Card Corner

MAP: Main Street, MS-14

DATES: June 14, 1985–October 1988

From 1956 until 1985, the prime corner location at the northeastern tip of **Main
Street** was an information center called **Carefree Corner**. In mid-1985, the spot
became a card shop known as Card Corner, and its sponsor was the Gibson Art Company. Gibson had already sponsored one other eponymous greeting card shop on Main
Street from **Opening Day** until 1959—**Gibson Greeting Cards**, located on the corner
of Main and **Center Street**.

Advertisements for the new Card Corner displayed four old-time illustrations of
sample items inside the shop—greeting cards for Thanksgiving, Easter, Valentine's
Day, and the **holiday season**. This second Gibson card shop lasted over three years.
Gibson was later sold to American Greetings, and Card Corner was replaced by Carefree
Corner, back for another run that lasted until the mid-1990s.

Carefree Corner

MAP: Main Street, MS-12

DATES: August 22, 1956–Spring 1985; November 1988–November 1994

For decades, guests have used the name Carefree Corner to refer to the prominent
corner location where the east side of **Main Street** runs into the **Hub**. The signage
on that corner building has supported the cheery reference, but technically this spot
has served a slightly less carefree function as Disneyland's official information center.

When it opened in mid-1956, the site was hosted by Disneyland's insurance carrier, Insurance Companies of North America. According to the 1957 **souvenir book**, the info center offered "road maps, hotel-motel information, places of interest to see." It wasn't until the 1958 souvenir book was published that the location was referred to as Carefree Corner.

The corner remained carefree until 1974, when INA's sponsorship ended and the site became known as the Hospitality Center. In 1985, Gibson Greeting Cards moved in and introduced a new name, **Card Corner**. When Gibson left in 1988, the Carefree Corner sign returned until it was replaced in 1994 by the current resident, the **Main Street Photo Supply Co.** The six-year Carefree Corner revival of the 1980s and '90s marked one of the few times that an extinct Disneyland shop has reopened in its original location with its original name.

Back when the building was INA's Carefree Corner, the interior was an open room that resembled an early-twentieth-century hotel lobby (upstairs, supposedly, were the Plaza Apartments, though these didn't really exist). Guests could relax on a round velvet banquette in the middle of the uncluttered room, get information about Disneyland or the surrounding area from helpful **cast members** in old-fashioned costumes, and sign the official registration book. For years, INA gave away small park maps and brochures that are collectors' items today.

Disney Legend **John Hench** is credited as the designer of the building's impressive exterior, three sides of which angle around the corner to form an inviting entrance set back from the street. For a long time, the upper floor displayed a large circular insignia that read, "Founded 1792"—the year INA issued its first insurance policy.

Carnation Café

MAP: Main Street, MS-5

DATES: March 21, 1997–ongoing

When the venerable **Carnation Ice Cream Parlor** closed in January of 1997, it took three months for Carnation to open a new business on **Main Street**. When it did, the new café was just a few steps south of the Ice Cream Parlor's former location. Situated on the western side of **Center Street** (where the **Flower Mart** had once spread its outdoor floral displays), the Carnation Café's patio tables quickly became a prime people-watching spot.

As the only table-service restaurant on the street, the Carnation Café has the most complete menu in the immediate area. "Serving delicious hometown fare," the sign outside accurately proclaims about the comfort food offered here. Breakfast has featured huge sticky buns, tasty croissants, and Mickey Mouse-shaped waffles; Oscar's Choice is a nod to the cook Oscar Martinez (shown in the **Cast Members** entry), who was hired in 1956 and still greets guests at the café (his signature dish is a reasonably priced breakfast of eggs, potatoes, bacon, or sausage). Lunch and

MOUSCELLANY

Disney fans will love the Carnation Café's menu section called Walt's Favorites, which includes Chicken-Fried Chicken and Walt's Chili.

dinner offerings have included seafood, gourmet burgers, big sandwiches, pasta, soups, and fancy salads, as well as tempting desserts and gourmet coffees.

After a five-month remodel of the place that ended in June 2012, the café also added some unique new menu items (PB & J soda, fried pickles, apple-granola pancakes, etc.), new exterior colors, new awnings, and a significant new feature for the outdoor café: indoor seating. The new tables are in a beautiful room adjacent to the café, the result of an expansion into the choice corner space formerly occupied by the **Blue Ribbon Bakery**. While much is new, the old-fashioned décor and signs (shown) evoke Main Street's nostalgic style.

Carnation Ice Cream Parlor

MAP: Main Street, MS-6

DATES: July 17, 1955–January 4, 1997

Carnation, the dairy company founded in 1899, was one of Disneyland's original sponsors. Its first enterprise at the park, the popular Carnation Ice Cream Parlor was open for business on Disneyland's **Opening Day.** The original site was the corner where **Main Street** meets the western half of **Center Street**, on the same block as the **Penny Arcade.** In those days, the western side of Center Street was filled with the **Flower Mart's** fragrant displays.

Carnation's initial building was the three-story structure that still wraps around the street corner at Main and Center; the exterior has elegant touches like a mansard roof, dormer windows, and a widow's walk. So photogenic was the 1890s-style interior, with its traditional counter and stools, that it was often spotlighted in Disneyland's **souvenir books.** For years, the books re-ran the same photo of a wholesome family sitting happily at the Carnation counter while a female **cast member** in an old-fashioned costume served them.

In 1977, Carnation expanded onto Center Street's western side, pushing the Flower Mart onto the eastern side of the street. The parlor's new outdoor patio area offered a relaxing spot for alfresco dining with tableside service. The menu featured fancy salads, Mickey's Chicken Pot Pie, and various sandwiches with cottage cheese on the side (a nod to the dairy-oriented sponsor). But it's the indulgent dessert list that visitors remember—especially the gigantic sundaes named after Disneyland attractions (The Big Thunder, The Matterhorn, etc.).

Some twenty years later, Carnation closed its Ice Cream Parlor and opened the outdoor **Carnation Café.** Simultaneously, the **Blue Ribbon Bakery** moved into the picturesque corner building where Carnation had served up its memorable ice cream treats for over forty years.

Carousel of Progress

MAP: Tomorrowland, T-14

DATES: July 2, 1967–September 9, 1973

Disneyland's Carousel of Progress was an import from the 1964–1965 New York World's Fair. There, **Walt Disney** had his Imagineers devise an ambitious time machine for General Electric called Progressland, which featured an auditorium that rotated around a stationary circular stage. On the stage were depictions of four different decades of American life populated by thirty-two **Audio-Animatronic** figures demonstrating how electricity (the sponsor was G.E., remember?) had improved domestic life. Progressland had been a crowd-pleasing hit in New York, so after the fair closed, Disney brought it to Anaheim.

In Disneyland, Progressland was originally meant to be a walk-through exhibit in **Edison Square**, a new land intended to go behind the eastern blocks of **Main Street**. When Edison Square failed to materialize, Progressland was installed with a new name, Carousel of Progress, in the new Carousel Theater. Built where the large **Space Bar** had stood on the eastern edge of **Tomorrowland**, the 200-foot-wide, two-story Carousel Theater looked like a stack of immense pancakes wrapped by a swooping ramp and adorned on the side with a thin sculpture that sported—what else?—the G.E. logo.

Inside this free attraction, **cast members** ushered guests into a small, 240-seat theater on the ground floor. The Carousel of Progress show began with an infectious theme song, "There's a Great Big Beautiful Tomorrow" by **Richard and Robert Sherman**. The theater, one of six surrounding the stage, then rotated to the first Audio-Animatronic (A-A) scene featuring a typical family at home. The year was approximately 1890, and in the room were A-A parents, two A-A children, an A-A cousin, A-A grandparents, an A-A dog (named Rover, Buster, and Sport throughout the show), and such turn-of-the-century devices as an early telephone, a gramophone, and gas lamps.

When the brief presentation ended, the theme song began to play as the theater spun and the audience moved ahead in time by three decades. (Meanwhile, the next audience, seated in another 240-seat theater on the building's perimeter, was wheeled into position for the 1890s scene.) The audience watched as presumably the same family, now updated to the 1920s, used electric lights, an electric fan, a radio, and other electric gadgets.

Cue the music, and the theater moved to the 1940s stage and a scene filled with handy appliances (the kitchen had an automatic dishwasher and Grandma now wore a hearing aid). The next stage displayed a late 1960s scene, with a self-cleaning oven, sleek kitchen appliances in matching colors, and a color TV with a "built-in video tape recorder" to record shows for later viewing.

The last scene and the reprised theme music seemed like the show's finale, but there was actually one more act to go. Guests made their way up the Speedramp to the second floor, where they walked past an incredibly detailed model of Progress City, Walt Disney's dream of the ideal city of the future. The model was huge, covering almost one-sixth of an acre and containing over 4,000 buildings, 20,000 miniature trees, thousands of individual vehicles, soaring skyscrapers, a climate-controlled downtown area, an airport, a theme park, and a sports arena, as well as "a welcome neighbor"—a G.E. nuclear power plant. Narration and lighting cues directed guests' attention to various parts of Progress City. (At one time in the planning stage, ride vehicles were considered that would have toured guests around the enormous model, which is how General Motors' acclaimed Futurama ride at the 1939–1940 New York World's Fair showed off its futuristic version of a 1960 city and suburbs.) Visitors left Disneyland's Carousel of Progress building with optimistic theme music playing in their ears and hopeful feelings swelling in their hearts.

Disney Legends **Roger Broggie**, **Marc and Alice Davis**, **Blaine Gibson**, **John Hench**, **Sam McKim**, **Wathel Rogers**, and **Herb Ryman** were the main Carousel contributors. Despite the huge commitment of space and energy required to create it, the attraction wasn't spotlighted in Disneyland's **souvenir books**, which instead focused on Tomorrowland highlights that could be grasped more easily, like the **Submarine Voyage** and **Autopia**. The Carousel did get an **attraction poster**, though, plus a souvenir 45 rpm record: "There's a Great Big Beautiful Tomorrow," issued in 1968 and featuring the theme song on one side backed by "A Medley of Disney Tunes" on the other.

After opening in the remodeled Tomorrowland in mid-1967 and playing to 3,600 guests an hour at its peak, the Carousel stopped turning in September of 1973. For a show so complex, advanced, and confident, it barely lasted six years. Once again, it moved across the country, this time to Walt Disney World, where Walt Disney's dream of Progress City was becoming the reality of EPCOT. Disneyland's Carousel Theater didn't stay dark long, however—**America Sings** opened there the following June.

Carriage Place Clothing Co.

MAP: Main Street, MS-1

DATES: Ca. 1993–ongoing

This handsome little clothing store can be accessed from within the big **Emporium**, which presides over the southwestern corner of **Main Street**. Tucked away near the **Fire Department**, the Carriage Place has its own attractive doorway on the side of the Emporium facing **Town Square**. Self-proclaimed "Clothiers of Distinction," the store is filled with Disney shirts, hats, and small gifts, accompanied in 2016 by a wall of plush characters.

Carrousel Candies

MAP: Fantasyland, Fa-5

DATES: Ca. 1983–ongoing

In addition to its many major edifices, **Fantasyland** also hosts a small candy cart called Carrousel Candies. Operating on a variable schedule, the cart is located in the **Sleeping Beauty Castle** courtyard, between the castle and the **King Arthur Carrousel** (hence the cart's name). The cart originally sold Disney-themed specialty sweets made at Goofy's Candy Factory, but now offers more traditional candy, souvenirs, and royal accessories. The cart's look has changed, too: the original wide, blue wagon is now a tall, compact, pink coach topped with the heads of white horses (shown on page 108) like those on the nearby Carrousel.

Casa de Fritos,
aka Casa Mexicana

MAP: Frontierland, Fr-24

DATES: August 11, 1955–April 1, 2001

Three weeks after **Opening Day**, Casa de Fritos made its **Frontierland** debut on the corner where the big **River Belle Terrace** stands today. In 1955, the River Belle Terrace location was dominated by **Aunt Jemima's Pancake House**, with a small space next door for Casa de Fritos.

Just a year later, however, the thriving little Casa was looking to expand. In mid-1956, it jumped Frontierland's main walkway and replaced the **Marshal's Office**, which was rebuilt to look like a whitewashed adobe structure in Mexico. The exterior was simple, with antlers serving as decorations. Some **cast members** here wore colorful, south-of-the-border-themed clothing, and strolling guitar players added to the ambience. Meanwhile, **Don DeFore's Silver Banjo Barbecue** moved into the old Fritos spot next to Aunt Jemima's.

Fritos, of course, are the crunchy tortilla chips made by Frito-Lay, which guests were reminded of as soon as they entered the restaurant. Inside was a large replica of the Fritos cartoon mascot, the Frito Kid, which stood next to a clever vending machine that dispensed little bags of the crunchy snack. As for the restaurant's original menu, to modern eyes it looks like standard Mexican fare that one would expect at any decent Mexican restaurant—tacos, chili, combo plates, etc. But back in the 1950s, Mexican food wasn't as commonplace as it now,

> **MOUSCELLANY**
>
> Proof that Mexican food wasn't as commonplace in the days of Casa de Fritos comes in the form of a standout line from 1986's *Peggy Sue Got Married*. Thirty-eight minutes into the film, when Peggy Sue has returned to 1960, a student describes "a Mexican food called a burrito" that he had once when his parents took him to Disneyland.

> **MOUSCELLANY**
>
> A fascinating nugget of Disneyland history emerged in 2012 when Gustavo Arellano, author of the book *Taco USA*, credited the old Casa de Fritos with the invention of a famous snack food. When the cooks at Casa de Fritos repackaged broken, discarded tortilla shells as chips, guests grabbed up the snacks so quickly that they were soon added to the menu. Continued popularity led Frito-Lay to roll out a whole new product in 1966 with a now-familiar name— Doritos, the "little golden things" originally created in Frontierland.

and a hacienda-style restaurant with outdoor tables probably seemed fairly exotic at the time, especially to visitors who didn't live in the western U.S. For guests who didn't know what to expect, the original Bjorn Aronsen-designed **attraction poster** depicted the familiar Frito Kid and listed some of the restaurant's menu items, including Taco in a "Tacup" and Frito Chili Pie.

Over the years, the restaurant gradually expanded toward the **Mineral Hall**. Finally, after a brief closure in 1982, it reopened that October with a larger outdoor space, more authentic-looking Mexican architecture, a new name (Casa Mexicana), and a new sponsor, Lawry's. The name, décor, sponsor, and menu were revised again when the restaurant became the **Rancho del Zocalo Restaurante** nineteen years later.

Casey Jr. Circus Train

MAP: Fantasyland, Fa-13

DATES: July 31, 1955–ongoing

The sturdy little train from *Dumbo* was almost derailed before it got going at Disneyland. Initially planned as a slightly faster, roller coaster-style attraction, its early test runs through an acre of hills in the back of **Fantasyland** raised serious safety questions. Although the Casey Jr. Circus Train was shown in TV coverage of Disneyland's **Opening Day** festivities, the train didn't really begin carrying passengers for two more weeks as workers flattened the track layout to make the three-and-a-half-minute trip smoother, slower, and safer.

When it did finally open to the public, Casey Jr. was a whimsical little train headed by a colorful engine that was followed by a line of circus-themed cars (shown). Disney Imagineers Bruce Bushman and **Roger Broggie** are credited with developing the two adorable trains that shared the track. The trip wasn't much, though; that first year, the tracks skimmed the barren dirt banks that lined the waterways of the **Canal Boats of the World**. Once the remodeled **Storybook Land Canal Boats** hit the water in the summer of 1956 with a full complement of miniature buildings along its shores, the views from the Casey Jr. train were as charming as the train itself.

Though never more than a B-ticket attraction, Casey Jr. has always had enough delightful detail to make it a Fantasyland favorite. The trip lasts about three and a half minutes, which is double the amount of screen time the moving train gets in the *Dumbo* movie (we don't actually see it in motion for more than 110 seconds). Once he hits Disneyland's track, Casey Jr. is an automatic mood-lifter. Who isn't cheered up by the passenger car labeled "Monkeys," or the beautiful sleigh-style cars (which were transplanted from the original merry-go-round that became the **King Arthur Carrousel**)? Who wouldn't want to sing along to the swingin' theme song written by Frank Churchill (who worked on *Snow White and the Seven Dwarfs*) and Ned Washington (*Pinocchio*)? Who isn't inspired by the audible "I think I can, I thought I could" mantra (heard just over a minute into the ride)? This isn't just a train ride; it's therapy.

Veteran guests may remember that the whole track was replaced in 1989; careful observers might recognize that the propulsion for the Casey Jr. train is provided by the car *behind* the decorative engine, not the engine itself; and adults may lament that the cramped cages are more suitable for kids. But happy passengers won't mind how the jaunty train came to be, what's driving it, or how tight the seating arrangements are, so jolly is Casey's journey.

Castle Arts

MAP: Fantasyland, Fa-3

DATES: Ca. 1983–ca. 1987

The Arribas Brothers, Tomas and Alfonso, were master glass-cutters who learned their craft in Spain. After meeting **Walt Disney** at the 1964–1965 New York World's Fair, they opened several shops in Disneyland, followed by another one in the Disneyland Hotel called Marina Crystal Arts. They also opened a little shop along the Downtown Disney walkway, and more in Disney parks around the world.

One of their Disneyland shops, Castle Arts, was located inside **Sleeping Beauty Castle**, in a small room along the walkway through the castle to the main **Fantasyland** courtyard. Previously, this spot had been the **Arts and Crafts Shop**, and in the late 1980s it would become the **Castle Christmas Shop** before transforming into the **Princess Boutique** a few years later. Beautiful glassware and cut-glass sculptures of Disney characters have long been an Arribas specialty.

Castle Candy Kitchen, aka Castle Candy Shoppe

MAP: Fantasyland, Fa-4

DATES: 1958–1994

Over the years, many businesses have occupied spots along the well-traveled walkway through **Sleeping Beauty Castle**. From 1958 until the mid-1960s, the Castle Candy Kitchen took up the right-hand side of that walkway, with the **Arts and Crafts Shop** on the opposite side. Kids could stock up on Castle Candy's array of distinctive sweets before hitting the attractions ahead in **Fantasyland**. The name changed to Castle Candy Shoppe around 1967.

Castle Christmas Shop

MAP: Fantasyland, Fa-3

DATES: Ca. 1987–ca. 1996

This choice location along the walkway through **Sleeping Beauty Castle** belonged to the cozy **Castle Arts** store for much of the 1980s. After the nearby **Mickey's Christmas Chalet** closed in 1987, the Castle Christmas Shop replaced Castle Arts to satisfy guests looking for holiday ornaments. A decade later, the shop relocated to **New Orleans Square** as **La Boutique de Noël**. Meanwhile, back at the castle, the **Princess Boutique** filled the vacant space along the interior walkway.

Cast Members

In the park's earliest years, Disneyland employees were called Disneylanders; in the 1960s, they were called (as they are now) cast members. Usually seen wearing clothing that corresponds to the theme of the area they work in, cast members include ride operators, store cashiers, food servers, security personnel, **parade** performers, parking attendants, and roving street sweepers. They have their own unions, parking lots, cafeterias, pharmacy, barber shop (Cast Cutters), First Aid station, locker areas, restrooms, credit union (Partners!), stock-purchase program, park discounts, cast-member-exclusive collectibles, honors (the Walt Disney Legacy Award), newsletter (*Disneyland Line*), competitions (annual canoe races in the **Rivers of America**, a tradition since 1963), and discount store (Company D). Cast members employed for Disneyland's first decade even have their own club, Club 55, founded by Disney Legend **Van France** in 1970.

The number of active Disneyland cast members on the payroll at any one time has swelled dramatically over the years: 600 were employed when the park opened; 3,400 in 1958; 6,000 for the summer of 1972; and 12,000 before Disney California Adventure opened in 2001. Over 28,000 cast members now work throughout the entire Disneyland Resort (including hotels, parks, and Downtown Disney).

Though cast members come from around the world, most are hired from a large pool of local applicants. Many are college-age kids, though older adults and even retirees are also hired. Even though the initial hourly pay starts around minimum wage, the supply of applicants has usually overwhelmed the demand, and thus Disneyland has nearly always been able to be selective, choosing people who are smart, attractive, personable, poised, and available for evening/weekend/holiday hours. Former cast members who worked at Disneyland in their pre-celebrity days include **Steve Martin**, Kevin Costner, Michelle Pfeiffer, Teri Garr, and Debra Winger.

According to John Van Maanen's article "The Smile Factory," there's an "internal status ladder" of Disneyland jobs, with Disneyland Ambassadors and bilingual tour guides at the top. He also places skilled ride operators (such as the "officer-like Monorail operator") in the upper rungs. More recent additions

to the "upper class" are the royals—the prince and princess characters—plus the other famous characters who don't have to wear all-concealing costumes. Guests will wait in long lines to meet these characters and will treat them like favorite celebrities. At the bottom of Van Maanen's social hierarchy are the "proletariat" sweepers and "sub-prole" service personnel who work the shops, restaurants, and concessions. Also on the lower rungs are behind-the-scenes, after-hours employees—all the gardeners, maintenance workers, and clean-up crews whom guests rarely see. Of all the jobs at Disneyland, the one often mentioned as the "coolest" is the wise-cracking, joke-telling **Jungle Cruise** skipper position (on the *Walt Disney Treasures: Disneyland Secrets, Stories & Magic* DVD, Oscar-winning writer/director/producer John Lasseter, himself a former Disneyland skipper, claims that "being a ride operator on the Jungle Cruise is the best job in the whole park").

The most uncomfortable jobs are most likely those inside hot, restrictive, cumbersome costumes ("fuzzies," as cast members have nicknamed them). These character costumes can weigh as much as seventy pounds, and many provide extremely limited vision as the wearers try to navigate curbs and crowds. Bruises and abrasions are the badges frequently worn at the end of the day by these walk-around employees. David Koenig's *Mouse Tales* books describe stabbings and costumes set on fire; Richard Stayton's *Unknown California* tells of frequent attacks on the Seven Dwarfs and the Three Little Pigs; and Trevor Allen's one-man show, *Working for the Mouse* includes anecdotes about kids punching and kicking Allen when he worked as a costumed character.

Many of the costumes, incidentally, are worn by dancers, and often the Mickey and Pinocchio costumes are worn by women for height reasons. Taller characters, such as Roger Rabbit, are usually men. Guests today might struggle to identify some of the retired character costumes from the past, including the albatross Orville from *The Rescuers* and characters from *The Black Hole*. Some of the characters made only brief appearances long ago—an old-fashioned organ grinder with an actual monkey on 1950s **Main Street**, for instance, and the masked Mr. Hyde character who scared patrons of the **Main Street Cinema**. These days, fewer characters seem to be roaming the park, as Disney officials now tend to position characters in specific areas.

In Disneyland's first year, some job functions, especially those taking place in the **parking lot** and in the custodial and security departments, were contracted to outsiders, but performance inconsistencies soon led to extensive Disney-oriented training for everyone. **Walt Disney** wanted one guiding principle to steer his workers: "We train them to be aware that they're there mainly to help the guests," he said. Thus, cast members have long been taught to adhere to a strict code of conduct they learn in a weeklong "traditions" orientation held in the Disney University offices behind **Space Mountain**. The four main principles that every cast member learns are safety, courtesy, show (performance, staying in character), and efficiency (formerly called capacity). Politeness, smiles, and practiced answers to questions ("I'll find out" is preferable to "no") are the traditional tools used to deliver **happiness**, safety, and reassurance to guests.

Van France maintained that "it takes a happy crew to produce a happy show," and cast members do indeed appear to be cheerful in front of guests nearly 100 percent of the time. Happiness isn't a byproduct of the job; it's an essential, expected ingredient. According to a 1967 handbook called *The Walt Disney Traditions at Disneyland*, cast members are "devoted to giving happiness . . . and this requires that you develop a sense of humor to help you over the rough spots." Unfortunately, these "rough spots," occasionally require more from a cast member than humor, smiling, and "giving happiness." As described in Barron and Pellman's *Cleaning the Kingdom*, cast members sometimes have to apprehend vandals and thieves, break up fights between guests, help restrain drug-addled guests, and rescue careless guests who have fallen into a body of water.

Just like any employee, Disneyland cast members *are* capable of exhibiting disgruntlement. The most famous example of cast member discontent came in 1984, the year that some 1,800 Disneyland employees went on strike for twenty-two days to protest low wages. Newspapers across the country printed alarming photos of picket signs outside Disneyland. It was the park's third and largest labor strike since the 1955 opening.

While it doesn't address wage expectations, the 1967 cast member handbook does dedicate considerable space to the importance of having a wholesome, clean-cut image. "It is essential—in fact, mandatory," says the handbook, "that you present to the audience what we call the Disneyland look." The handbook covers "baubles, bangles and beads" (they're out), ornate jewelry (it's "in poor taste"), makeup ("only a natural makeup is permitted"), heavy perfumes (definitely out), a clean shave for men ("just like on TV"), and clothing ("help our continuing inspection plan by checking . . . your spanking fresh outfit"). "The Disneyland look," the handbook summarizes, "is *never* a sloppy look."

The image has gradually changed since 1967. For decades, men weren't allowed to have mustaches (even though Walt Disney had one), and they had to wear black shoes and socks. In 2000, men were finally allowed to wear mustaches; a decade later, they could leave their casual shirts untucked; and in 2012, they were permitted to wear short beards. Women used to have to wear stockings, and eyeshadow, eyeliner, fake eyelashes, and earrings in pierced ears were prohibited. However, as of new guidelines updated in 2010 and again in 2013, most women no longer have to wear hosiery with their skirts (nylons are still required for some costumes), and capri pants and sleeveless tops are acceptable for some positions.

In *The Jungle Book*, Colonel Hathi acknowledges what's important among the troops: "Discipline! Discipline was the thing! Builds character, and all that sort of thing, you know." Despite Disneyland's vigilant attempts at maintaining conformity and implementing stringent procedures, cast members have been able to bend/break/ flout the rules and reveal their individual personalities. Many stories have arisen over the years about cast members playing pranks upon one another, taking impulsive swims in the waterways, rearranging store merchandise into **Hidden Mickeys**, adding humorous garments and accessories to some of the **Audio-Animatronic** characters, and bestowing playful nicknames for various creatures in the attractions (cast members routinely refer to the Jungle Cruise elephant spraying water as Bertha, the **Fantasmic!** dragon as either Bucky or Murphy, and the **Matterhorn** yeti as Harold).

The fact that employees are referred to as cast members illustrates how much the operation of Disneyland resembles a theatrical performance. In the park's vernacular, the term "guest" has always been used in place of "customer." "Costume" is used to refer to uniforms, "backstage" refers to behind-the-scenes areas, "onstage" refers to areas in view of guests, and "protein spill" and "Code V" are euphemisms for vomit.

Starting on Opening Day in 1955, cast members used to wear name tags with

impersonal numbers on them. However, since 1962, those name tags have included the cast members' first names and usually their hometowns, for friendly identification (names are helpful when guests want to leave comments about cast members, which they can do at **City Hall**). To honor their contributions to fifty years of Disneyland success, in 2005 the Walt Disney Company presented each cast member with a memory-filled, sixty-four-page book called *The Magic Begins with Me*. The cast member with the longest memories might be Oscar Martinez (shown), whose record-setting Disneyland career is over sixty years long (he still cooks meals and greets guests at the **Carnation Café**).

The cast members seen during operating hours are not the only employees working at Disneyland, of course. After closing, over 600 horticulturists, painters, welders, electricians, divers, and custodians hit the park to fix/clean/polish/repaint/test everything for the next day's activities. Every inch of Disneyland is walked, all the waters are explored, each vehicle is closely inspected, all surfaces are cleaned, brass is shined up, bathrooms are sanitized, and the streets and sidewalks and patios are hosed down. In addition, store shelves are restocked, restaurant kitchens are replenished, and many light bulbs—even if they're still working—are replaced (about a quarter-million Disneyland light bulbs are changed every year).

Then, before the park opens, an early morning Resort Enhancement team installs special decorations and checks every window and balcony display. All of this work is done in an empty park so it won't have to be performed during the day in view of guests, thus maintaining Disneyland's carefully cultivated reputation of impeccable service, immaculate cleanliness, and undiminished illusion.

Center Street

MAP: Main Street, MS-5, MS-17

DATES: July 17, 1955–ongoing

Center Street is the small east–west lane that separates the two southern blocks of **Main Street** from its two northern blocks. Center Street's dimensions are much smaller than Main Street's. Each side of Center Street extends seventy-five feet away from Main Street and ends (for guests) in a cul-de-sac. Main Street, by comparison, is approximately 350 feet long and runs from **Town Square** at its southern end to the **Hub** at its northern end. From building to building, Center Street is about thirty feet wide, while Main Street is approximately sixty feet wide. Running through the center of Center is a ten-foot-wide paved area; Main Street's paved center is about three times that width. Each sidewalk on Center Street is about ten feet wide, and Main Street's are each fifteen feet wide. There's no curb on the eastern side of Center, and the curb on the street's western side is only about two inches high near Main Street. In general, Main Street's curb is consistently six inches tall.

Despite their diminutive dimensions, the eastern and western sides of Center Street have both seen plenty of activity over the decades. At one time, the

eastern side (shown) was to be filled with a **Chinatown** neighborhood, but those ideas never made it into Disneyland. Instead, various shops and eateries have lined this side of the street, most conspicuously the two big corner buildings: the Market House on the southern corner, and Disney Clothiers, Ltd. on the northern corner (while the Market House has always been there, the cloth-

ing shop's location was first occupied by **Gibson Greeting Cards** and then the **Hallmark Card Shop**). At the back of the eastern side, past today's decorative flower carts, is a Locker Area called **Main Street Lockers & Storage**, plus the site of what was once the **Main Street Cone Shop** (it was closed off in 2012). The eastern side of Center has displayed the blooms of yesteryear's **Flower Mart** and the edibles of the current **Main Street Fruit Cart**.

The western side of Center has had the Fortuosity Shop on its southern corner since 2008; this space was originally used by the **Upjohn Pharmacy** and later by **New Century Watches & Clocks**. The northern corner of this side of the street is now occupied by the **Carnation Café**, but this spot was first taken by the **Carnation Ice Cream Parlor** and then the **Blue Ribbon Bakery**. The street itself has been filled with the Flower Mart and, as of 1997, the tables and umbrellas of the Carnation Café.

Supplementing the genuine commercial interests along Center Street are fake advertising windows on the second floor. The eastern side of the street advertises the faux businesses run by the "Painless Dentist E. S. Bitz, D.D.S." and "Piano Lessons,

Ask for Sarah" (sound effects coming from these businesses can be heard from the street). Also on this side of the street is the real-looking (but inaccessible) Hotel Marceline (a nod to the small town where **Walt Disney** spent part of his childhood). The faux businesses advertised on the western side of Center include Milaly Fashions, Sam the Tailor, Chinese Restaurant, Main Street Gym, Turkish Baths, and Massage Parlor (a massage parlor in Disneyland, who knew?).

Center Street also displays some **Main Street Tribute Windows**, which honor real people. On the eastern side, there are windows for Disney Legends **Bill Cottrell**, **Bob Gurr**, and **Bill Justice**; the western side honors Christopher D. Miller (Walt Disney's grandson) and Disney Legend **Fred Joerger**.

Character Foods, aka Character Food Facilities

MAP: Fantasyland, Fa-10, Fa-27

DATES: 1955–1981

For a quarter of a century, two **Fantasyland** fast-food huts shared the name Character Foods. One hut was in a courtyard on the northern side of the old **Mickey Mouse Club Theater**. This location would eventually open up to become the walkway to **Frontierland**. The second hut was on the other side of Fantasyland, near **Alice in Wonderland** and today's **Mad Hatter of Fantasyland**. Each stand was circular and topped with a striped, circus-style cone. Character Foods referred to the snacky menu items named after animated Disney stars. The Character Foods stand near Frontierland disappeared in 1979; the other location was eaten up by the extensive Fantasyland remodel that ended in 1983.

Character Shop

MAP: Tomorrowland, T-22

DATES: Summer 1967–September 15, 1986

The massive **Tomorrowland** remodel that began in 1966 brought an end to the **20,000 Leagues Under the Sea Exhibit** and the adjacent **Fun Fotos** displays. A year later, one of the largest stores in Disneyland, the Character Shop, opened in their combined spaces. Next door was **Adventure Thru Inner Space** (later **Star Tours**), and outside was the **Tomorrowland Stage** (later the ramp to **Space Mountain)**.

Its size and prime corner location made the Character Shop an instant must-visit for guests searching for clothes, futuristic gifts, and, surprisingly, stuffed animals. Described in 1969's *Walt Disney's Disneyland* as a "Disney-themed toy and merchandise mart," the store featured rows and rows of displays and a ceiling hung with abstract shapes. Adding even more character to the Character Shop was the **PeopleMover**, which slipped quietly through the back of the store about ten feet above the floor.

Just as it had appeared during a major Tomorrowland upheaval, the shop disappeared during another Tomorrowland revamp. Late in 1986, only a few months before the adjacent Star Tours opened, the Character Shop was replaced by the space-themed **Star Trader** store.

Charles Dickens Carolers,
aka Dickens Carolers, aka Holiday Carolers

Since 1956, a singing group called the Charles Dickens Carolers, or simply the Dickens Carolers, has enhanced Disneyland's **holiday season** and winter celebrations. Although its cast of singers continually changes to include new members, the lineup typically consists of four (two men and two women) or eight (four and four) performers at a time, all dressed in elegant nineteenth-century costumes: felt top hats, topcoats, and scarves for men, and long-sleeved hoop dresses, bonnets, and hand muffs for women.

The Dickens Carolers have performed up and down **Main Street** and in front of the Christmas tree in **Town Square**. The a cappella group generally sticks to traditional carols but also occasionally includes more modern favorites, such as "Rockin' Around the Christmas Tree" and special requests. In recent years the group abandoned the Dickens title, and is now known as the Holiday Carolers, making more appearances in Disney's nearby hotels than in Disneyland itself.

Chicken Plantation,
aka Plantation House, aka Chicken Shack

MAP: Frontierland, Fr-10

DATES: July 17, 1955–January 7, 1962

On **Opening Day**, Swift, a meat-packing company established in the 1850s, sponsored three Disneyland locations. Two of them, the **Market House** and the Red Wagon Inn, were on **Main Street**, and the third, the Chicken Plantation or Plantation House, was at the far edge of **Frontierland**.

The Chicken Plantation occupied a distinguished-looking two-story building overlooking the **Rivers of America**. Interestingly, the building was schizophrenic. Viewed from the east, it appeared to be a white mansion, with dormer windows projecting from the roof, a decorative wooden balcony circling the perimeter, and about twenty outdoor tables spreading across an expansive patio. Conversely, when viewed from the Disneyland trains to the west, the restaurant appeared to have rough-timber construction more appropriate to the Frontierland wilderness.

The specialty here was a fried chicken dinner for under two dollars. It was so popular that when the building was demolished in 1962 to make way for the **Haunted Mansion**, take-out meals were offered from a temporary Chicken Shack near the construction site.

China Closet

MAP: Main Street, MS-13

DATES: Spring 1964–ongoing

The eastern side of **Main Street** has always featured some form of a china shop. Formerly the **Ruggles China and Glass Shop**, the store has been called the China

Closet since 1964. Though the name changed, the location didn't—it's still one door south of what is now the **Main Street Photo Supply Co.** Inside, the room opens to both the photo store and **Crystal Arts**.

The China Closet sells Disney-themed glass statues, small picture frames, and so many mugs that this could be one of Disneyland's main mug headquarters. In recent years, cooking and kitchen accessories (Disney flatware, serving sets, and kitchen canisters) have occasionally filled the shelves here. Holiday ornaments are available all year, with all kinds of snow globes and delicate ornaments dominating the main room. There's a short dogleg in the back that leads north to the Main Street Photo Supply Co. In 2015, this little room displayed Disney-style Precious Moments figurines. Guests not interested in the shop's wares will find welcome solace on the cozy porch out front (shown), which offers wooden chairs and a bench for a brief rest from the busy street.

Chinatown

MAP: Main Street, MS-17

DATES: Never built

Center Street, the little lane that divides **Main Street** into separate blocks, would look vastly different if the plans for Chinatown had come to fruition. Unlike the rest of Main Street, which was built to echo turn-of-the-century American architecture, Chinatown was going to look like a real Chinese neighborhood filling Center Street's eastern half. According to concept drawings by Disney Legend **Herb Ryman** in the late 1950s, and as seen in the 1960 Disneyland **souvenir book**, Chinese shops and eateries, plus an arcade, would have lined the cul-de-sac next to the **Market House**. An **Audio-Animatronic** stage show in an elegant Chinese restaurant would have featured a philosophizing Confucius and singing birds.

By the summer of 1960, the Chinatown plan had faded away as attention turned to other Disneyland developments. The idea for singing Audio-Animatronic birds survived, however, and flew to **Adventureland**, landing three years later inside the **Enchanted Tiki Room**.

Chip 'n Dale Tree House

MAP: Mickey's Toontown, MT-4

DATES: January 24, 1993–ongoing

Located in the far corner of **Mickey's Toontown**, the Chip 'n Dale Tree House is a fun mini-playland for young children. The small, cute, and architecturally askew structure is built in a gnarled tree studded with oversize acorns. Kid-size stairs pass the chip-munks' mailbox, enter a charming wooden passageway, and climb to the house and balcony some fifteen feet off the ground.

A Tree Slide originally provided the route down from the tree house, and an Acorn Ball Crawl gave kids under forty-eight inches tall a place to go nuts in a pit filled with acorn-shaped plastic balls. In 1998, the slide (which was more uncomfortable than fun) and the pit (which was hard to keep clean) were closed, and the tree house became a walk-through attraction with stairs as the exit. Though the fun may have been reduced slightly, at least there's no time limit on playing.

Chocolate Collection, aka Chocolate Rue Royale

MAP: New Orleans Square, NOS-5

DATES: Ca. 1980–ca. 1995

Throughout the 1980s, the Chocolate Collection sold imported chocolate confections deep in **New Orleans Square**. Previously **Le Forgeron** and **La Boutique d'Or** had occupied this spot at the back of Royal Street. Nestlé sponsored the Chocolate Collection until the mid-1980s, when the unsponsored business took the name Chocolat Rue Royale.

Circarama, aka Circle-Vision, aka Circle-Vision 360, aka World Premiere Circle-Vision

MAP: Tomorrowland, T-5

DATES: July 18, 1955–September 7, 1997

In 1952, *This Is Cinerama* introduced American audiences to wide, multiple-screen movies. The non-Disney documentary showed footage shot from the front of a roller coaster, the cockpit of a swooping plane, and other dramatic locations, all projected on three connected screens that partially wrapped around the audience. Within a few years, major motion pictures (including the Oscar-nominated *How the West Was Won*) were utilizing Cinerama's three-screen projection system.

After *This Is Cinerama* came out, an impressed **Walt Disney** decided he would go Cinerama one better. Before Disneyland opened, he had Disney Legend **John Hench** draw up a concept illustration for a new theater idea. Hench's art showed Grand Can-yon images being presented, not just on a big screen, but *in the round*.

In 1955, on the first day Disneyland was officially open to the public, Disney's film *A Tour of the West* debuted in the new Circarama building near the **Tomorrowland** entrance. Instead of filming with three forward-facing cameras à la the Cinerama process, Imagineers mounted *eleven* 16mm cameras in a circle on top of an American Motors car (American Motors was a Circarama sponsor). Directed by Disney Legend **Peter Ellenshaw,** the twelve-minute documentary takes viewers from Beverly Hills to Monument Valley 650 miles away. Disneyland's 1956 **souvenir book** boasts that the film is "an exciting travel picture."

A Tour of the West was an instant hit. Despite having to stand the entire time with no rails to lean against, audiences loved being at the center of a 360-degree movie that surrounded them with images. The seemingly unrelated displays lining the inside of the theater—American Motors cars and Kelvinator refrigerators—didn't exactly enhance the experience, but they did establish a tradition of exhibits in the pre- and post-show areas that would be fully developed later. Plus, since this was a free attraction requiring no A-B-C ticket from the Disneyland **ticket book**, and since the building offered a cool respite from the Anaheim heat (the air-conditioning was mentioned on a sign outside), nobody was complaining about the extraneous car and refrigerator decorations, no matter how superfluous they might have looked.

A Tour of the West played until January of 1959. It was followed by a new 360-degree movie, the sixteen-minute *America the Beautiful*, which expands the tour to include aerial footage and shots from across the whole country. This impressive new film was even more popular than its predecessor. Bell Telephone Systems was the sole sponsor, adding fun **Bell Telephone Systems Phone Exhibits** into the pre- and post-show areas. Late in 1964, the name Circle-Vision replaced Circarama as a way to avoid any confusion—and any legal entanglements—with Cinerama.

A major remodel of the theater began in early 1967 and lasted all spring. On June 25, 1967, the attraction's name changed again, this time to Circle-Vision 360. A new, longer version of *America the Beautiful* replaced the previous film, the number of screens dropped from eleven to nine larger screens, and a new pre-show area was created where theater space and exhibit areas had been. Guests now waited in a colorful room filled with upholstered blocks while flags displaying abstract representations of all fifty states hung from the ceiling. Three times per hour, a **cast member** conducted a playful identify-the-flags quiz with guests—a suitable activity for a movie showcasing American landscapes. The female cast members wore patriotic outfits featuring red jackets, white gloves, and blue skirts. Inspired by the fun quiz, guests eagerly stood at the new railings inside the theater and enjoyed a fire truck's crazy careen through San Francisco, a wild ride through the Waikiki surf, and more.

After Bell withdrew its sponsorship in 1982, the theater closed once more in early 1984. For the reopening on July 4, the theater again got a new name, and this time it also got an all-new film. With the airline PSA on board, World Premier Circle-Vision began showing an eight-minute short called *All Because Man Wanted to Fly*, followed by *American Journeys*, a twenty-one-minute documentary offering more slices of American life. Later that year, *American Journeys* started alternating with a Walt Disney World import, *Wonders of China*. *China* played in the mornings and *Journeys* in the afternoons, so for the first time, guests had a choice of movies to see in this theater.

In mid-1989, PSA canceled its flight, but another airline, Delta, immediately took over sponsorship for seven years, with both movies still on the bill. Finally, on New Year's Day in 1996, Delta took off and World Premiere disappeared from the theater's name. *American Journeys* and *Wonders of China* continued until June; the next month, *America the Beautiful* returned for one last glorious sprint to the theater's finish line.

Circle-Vision closed for good on September 7, 1997, to be replaced first by the short-lived **Rocket Rods** and then by **Buzz Lightyear Astro Blasters**. Disney Legend **Roger Broggie** was the main architect of Disney's 360-degree filming process (with assistance from **Ub Iwerks**, Eustace Lycett, and other masters of Disney cinema). Today, Circarama/Circle-Vision is fondly recalled as one of the best theater experiences in Disneyland's history.

Circus Fantasy

DATES: Winter 1986–Spring 1988 (seasonal)

Even before Circus Fantasy debuted in January of 1986, circus themes had already been plentiful in Disneyland's history. **Dumbo's Circusland** and an Interplanetary Circus had been on the drawing boards for a while; **Dumbo the Flying Elephant** and the **Casey Jr. Circus Train** had been operating since mid-1955; the **Mickey Mouse Club Circus** had appeared for about six weeks in late 1955; and that same year, daily circus **parades** had frolicked down **Main Street**.

Like the **State Fair** and **Blast to the Past** promotions that followed it, Circus Fantasy was an attempt to speed up ticket sales during what were traditionally the year's slowest months. For the winter and early spring months of 1986, 1987, and 1988, Circus Fantasy filled Main Street and the **Hub** with real circus acts. There were elephants and professional clowns, a high-wire act across Main Street, stilt-walkers, a motorcycle daredevil, and other attractions expected at an actual circus. Circus on Parade trumpeted daily down Main Street, and a circus-themed show filled the Videopolis stage.

When park **attendance** rose in the summer, the circus acts were put on hold until ticket sales began to drop again in the fall. Some of the circus activities were shown on a TV special called "Disneyland's All-Star Comedy Circus" in 1988, the same year Blast to the Past replaced Circus Fantasy as the new spring promotion.

City Hall

MAP: Town Square, TS-4

DATES: July 17, 1955–ongoing

Since **Opening Day**, City Hall has been a handsome presence along the west side of **Town Square**. About thirty feet south of the building is the **Police Station**, with a closed one-story structure connecting it to City Hall, and about forty feet north is the **Fire Department**, connected to City Hall by a row of **restrooms**. These adjacent buildings differ significantly from those shown in a 1953 **Marvin Davis** concept illustration that placed a fire station and hospital to the south and a Hall of Records to the north.

Disney Legend **Harper Goff** designed Disneyland's

City Hall, basing the look on a similar building in his Colorado hometown. Spreading approximately forty-five feet wide, City Hall has two main stories crowned by a mansard roof and widow's walk, with a central tower rising yet one more story. The row of slender columns out front adds a graceful touch to the entryway, while sturdy red bricks and ornate white trim give the main structure a dignified look. In the evening, decorative white lights attractively define the upper stories. Inside City Hall's lobby are displays of art, historic photos, and laudatory proclamations that all feel right for a room where official business could be conducted.

Fittingly, City Hall really has served as Disneyland's official headquarters. The first **souvenir books**, which label the building as both Town Hall and City Hall, identify it as the place to locate lost children, security officers, and First Aid. City Hall is also home to **Guest Relations**, the information center for guests looking for maps, local phone directories, and entertainment schedules. Also available here are binders that identify Disneyland's flora and provide recipes for the dishes served in Disneyland's restaurants. Rarely noticed by guests are the tall, century-old eucalyptus trees behind the building. These were saved from the original groves that preceded Disneyland, making them perhaps the oldest living things in the park.

MOUSCELLANY

Besides the conspicuous official documents mounted on the walls, several more items are fun to peruse here. One is the collection of safety certificates that are mentioned on small signs posted at Disneyland's attractions. The signs usually say, "Documents related to the Certificate of Compliance for this attraction may be viewed at City Hall in Town Square," and it's true—you can see those annually updated safety certificates in a big binder. Also worth seeking out is the small but required Business Tax Certificate posted by the door ("Type of business: Amusement Park").

Clarabelle's Frozen Yogurt

MAP: Mickey's Toontown, MT-8

DATES: January 24, 1993–ongoing

Clarabelle, Disney's cartoon cow, got her own yogurt stand in 1993. Located in **Mickey's Toontown** next to **Pluto's Dog House**, the little blue building has a white awning speckled with irregular black spots. Clarabelle's counter offers a small menu of "udderly refreshing" yogurts, desserts, and soft drinks.

Clock of the World, aka World Clock

MAP: Tomorrowland, T-3

DATES: July 17, 1955–September 1966

Short on dramatic attractions for **Tomorrowland** in 1955, **Walt Disney** added an inexpensive spectacle: the futuristic Clock of the World. Standing inside a land-scaped circle at Tomorrowland's entrance, the clock was a seventeen-foot-tall cylinder pinched in the middle like an hourglass. A world map wrapped around the upper half of the hourglass, and a blue base formed the bottom half. Around the top of the cylinder were the hours 1 through 24, and attached to the very top was a sphere that showed half the sun facing the crescent moon.

Early Disneyland **souvenir books**, which sometimes refer to the structure as the World Clock, highlight the exhibit with photos of captivated guests pointing and staring at it. Their fascination, supposedly, was in the clock's ability to tell the time, right to the minute, for any location on Earth.

Evidently, guests visiting Disneyland after the mid-1960s no longer needed this information. Time ran out for the Clock of the World in 1966, and it was dismantled for that year's major Tomorrowland remodel. In 2010, one of the murals on the walls of the **Innovations** building displayed a small rendition of the old Clock of the World.

Clock Shop

MAP: Fantasyland, Fa-3

DATES: 1963–ca. 1969

In the 1960s, **Fantasyland** had a shop that offered "the most fantastic clocks you ever laid your eyes on" (a line Jiminy Cricket used in *Pinocchio* to describe Geppetto's shop). Disneyland's 1968 **souvenir book** shows off the Clock Shop with a nice color photo of a family surrounded by ornate cuckoo clocks, plus the caption, "The Castle Clock Shop leaves no doubt about the time, especially at the start of a new hour." Actually, the Clock Shop *did* seem to leave doubt about the time—of the dozen clocks with readable faces in the photo, only two were set for the same time, which means that a cuckoo clock was probably cuckooing every few minutes.

The shop itself was located inside the entrance to **Sleeping Beauty Castle**, a spot formerly taken by the **Arts and Crafts Shop**. A 1970 map of Fantasyland restores the Arts and Crafts Shop to its previous position inside the castle arches.

Club Buzz

MAP: Tomorrowland, T-9

DATES: June 30, 2001–October 2006

In 2001, the *Toy Story*-themed Club Buzz replaced the space-themed **Tomorrowland Terrace**, which had occupied the spot since 1967. Borrowing names from the near-by **Buzz Lightyear Astro Blasters** attraction, the eatery was also called Club Buzz: Lightyear's Above the Rest. Club Buzz combined casual dining and entertainment, just as the Terrace had done in the previous century. The large, curved food counter offered an "out-of-this-world menu" of breakfast plates, sandwiches, fried chicken, salads, and "the best burgers in the galaxy."

As guests ate, a kid-friendly show named *Calling All Space Scouts: A Buzz Light-year Adventure* was performed on the Club Buzz stage. As with the old Tomorrowland

Terrace, this stage rose up from below ground level. However, the stage's sleek white planter boxes had been replaced with an elaborate futuristic sculpture in blue, silver, and purple (the sculpture included models of rockets and the **House of the Future**). The band shell took on starry designs in indigo with green trim. The heroic astronaut Buzz Lightyear hosted the new show, which featured a confrontation with the evil Emperor Zurg.

In 2006, when the new *Jedi Training Academy* moved in, Club Buzz reverted back to a semblance of its original design and returned to its former name, Tomorrowland Terrace.

Club 33

MAP: New Orleans Square, NOS-4

DATES: June 15, 1967–ongoing

One of Disneyland's worst-kept secrets is the presence of a private restaurant in **New Orleans Square**. The name Club 33 has long been the subject of speculation by fans, who have come up with a wide range of guesses—everything from 33 being the number of Disneyland sponsors to 33 somehow representing Mickey Mouse's initials (or Mickey Mouse's ears) when the digits are turned sideways. According to official explanations, the name is derived from the original address, 33 Royal Street, a number that's shown on what used to be the ground-level doorway next to the **Blue Bayou**.

There used to be another private dining room in the back of the Red Wagon Inn (now the **Plaza Inn**) on **Main Street**, but that one was much less elaborate than what now exists in New Orleans Square. Initially Club 33 was intended to be a quiet, luxurious private restaurant for VIP guests. It was built on the second story of the New Orleans Square buildings next to what was going to be **Walt Disney's** private **apartment** above **Pirates of the Caribbean**, but Disney passed away before the club and apartment were completed. When it was finished, Disneyland executives used Club 33 to entertain VIPs and business associates (the apartment next door was eventually opened as the **Disney Gallery**).

Within a few years, Club 33 had transformed from a private restaurant for Disney executives and their guests to a private club for a few hundred people who applied for entry, endured the waiting list, and paid the hefty membership fee. In 2007, Disneyland raised the number of members to 500, but new applicants could still expect to wait a decade for membership. By 2011, that membership cost over $10,000 per individual, plus over $3,500 a year in annual dues. In early 2012, Disneyland expanded its membership again to around 800 people and raised its fees to $25,000 for the initial membership, plus an additional $10,000 for annual dues. By mid-2014, the numbers were $35,000 initially and up to $14,000 annually. New membership does come with perks besides entrance into Club 33. Among the extras are park admission, valet parking, VIP tours, and access to a new private lounge, 1901, opened in June 2012 inside Disney California Adventure.

Club 33's interior, initially designed in part by **Emile Kuri**, is considered to be Disneyland's most fascinating dining space. For decades, members entered through Royal Street's Club 33 door and then took an elevator upstairs. Awaiting them were crystal chandeliers, artifacts from Disney movies, antiques purchased by Walt and Lillian Disney, and a gourmet buffet. The floor plan wrapped around the heart of New Orleans Square, from the Blue Bayou area to the spaces across Royal Street, above Café Orleans and the **French Market**. Two lavishly decorated dining rooms overlooked the **Rivers of America**. At one time, some kind of interactive **Audio-Animatronics** arrangement was going to be installed in the Trophy Room, and microphones were even placed inside chandeliers for instant communication between staff and guests. That plan, however, never evolved past the experimental stage.

A major 2013 expansion resulted in the club shutting down for six months (members were offered alternate dining options during the closure). When it reopened, the restaurant had a new entrance through the room that used to be **L'Ornement Magique**, the interior space had doubled, and a new lounge (literally called La Salon Nouveau) had been added. Club 33 also got a new street address, though the number hasn't changed: according to Disneyland's tour guides, the club is now at 33 Orleans Street, not 33 Royal Street as it had been for almost five decades.

No sooner had this remodel concluded than another one began, with the goal of adding a new ultra-exclusive dining option to Disneyland. Named after its location, 21 Royal Street opened in September 2015 as a sophisticated, special-occasion restaurant that could be booked for small groups. With exquisite wall art and custom menus, 21 Royal Street offers the most elegant dining experience and charges the highest prices ($15,000 for a dozen people) in the park.

Besides its luxurious décor and magnificent views, Club 33 offers unique amenities that no other Disneyland restaurant does: it's the only one to serve alcohol; it indulges guests with gifts to remember their visit by; and it offers the impeccable service of Disneyland's most highly trained food servers.

Even as its secrets have been revealed over the years, Club 33 still retains its mystique. While many people have heard of it and even more have unknowingly walked right by the entrance or under its windows, only a very few will ever be able to say they've been inside.

Coats, Claude
(1913–1992)

A San Franciscan born in 1913, Claude Coats earned a degree in architecture and fine arts at USC and then studied at a local art institute. Hired at Disney Studios in 1935, Coats was one of the company's busiest and most gifted artists, known especially for his sublime background paintings in classic animated films like *Pinocchio*, *Fantasia*, and *Peter Pan* (he's glimpsed in Disney's 1957 film *Our Friend the Atom*).

Switching to Disneyland projects in 1955, Coats was a key contributor to many popular attractions. He helped paint the displays and backgrounds on early **Fantasyland** attractions like **Mr. Toad's Wild Ride** and designed almost everything in the original **Alice in Wonderland**. He created the Rainbow Caverns interiors for the **Mine Train** in **Frontierland**, and painted underwater scenes for the **Submarine Voyage** in **Tomorrowland**. In the mid-1960s, he contributed interior designs to **Adventure Thru Inner Space**, the **Haunted Mansion**, and **Pirates of the Caribbean** (**Walt Disney** called Coats "the Imagineer in charge of the Pirates project" in a 1965 episode of *Walt Disney's Wonderful World of Color*).

Before retiring in 1989, Coats also helped with many attractions at Walt Disney World. He died in 1992, a year after he was honored as a Disney Legend.

Coin Shop, aka Stamp and Coin Shop

MAP: Main Street, MS-15

DATES: Ca. 1957–1960

Starting around 1957, a little Coin Shop operated next to the **Pen Shop** in Center Street's eastern cul-de-sac. Disneyland's 1957 **souvenir book** introduces the Coin Shop, and the 1959 edition renames it the Stamp and Coin Shop, but subsequent souvenir books never mention any kind of coin, stamp, or coin-and-stamp business again. The shop disappeared in the 1960 remodel that brought a big **Hallmark Card** store to the corner of Main and Center.

Cole of California Swimsuits

MAP: Main Street, MS-11

DATES: 1956–1957

Formerly a silent-movie actor, Fred Cole created his fashionable line of swimwear in 1923. After his suits became popular in the Hollywood community, he opened a little shop at the north end of **Main Street** in 1956. With two windows displaying swimwear, the shop was tucked around the west-side corner dominated by Coke's **Refreshment Corner**. But as long-lasting as the Cole line has been (Cole swimsuits are still made today), the Disneyland location was short-lived. By 1958, it had been replaced by the first **Mad Hatter of Main Street** shop.

Conestoga Wagons

MAP: Frontierland, Fr-21

DATES: August 16, 1955–September 13, 1959

The Conestoga Wagons were part of the original **Frontierland**, back when the **Painted Desert** was being explored by the **Mule Pack** and **Mine Train**. The wooden wagons were replicas of the horse-drawn vehicles driven across America in the middle of the previous century. Each Disneyland wagon was pulled by at least two horses, held about a dozen guests, and, true to the pioneer spirit, had "Westward Ho!" or "Oregon or Bust" painted on its canvas top.

From 1955 until 1958, a ride in a Conestoga Wagon cost a B ticket from the Disneyland **ticket book** or twenty-five cents. In 1959, the price rose to a C ticket. Heading north to the **Painted Desert** and back, the trip approximated the route of Disneyland's **Stage Coach**. Ironically, the wagons and the stage expired on the same day and for the same reason—unreliable power plants. The horses, unfortunately, were sometimes startled by unexpected noises; even though this Frontierland area was presented as a desert wilderness, around it were train whistles, blank gunfire, amplified announcements, and other random sounds. Fearful of spooked horses blocking stalled wagons—or galloping off with runaway wagons—officials quietly retired the Conestogas after the summer of 1959. The Mule Pack and Mine Train continued to explore the new and improved **Nature's Wonderland** until everything surrendered to **Big Thunder** in the late 1970s.

Corridor of Murals

MAP: Tomorrowland, T-5, T-23

DATES: 1967–1998

For over three decades, beautiful tile mosaics greeted guests as they passed through the metallic entrance to **Tomorrowland**. The mosaics adorned two large, curving buildings that faced each other—the **Adventure Thru Inner Space** building to the south and the Circle-Vision 360 theater to the north. On each building, hundreds of square feet of wall space were covered with one half of a large artwork called *The Spirit of Creative Energies Among Children*, thus naming this stretch of Tomorrowland the Corridor of Murals.

Mary Blair, the principal designer of **It's a Small World**, created the murals. Her mosaics depicted children in international costumes frolicking in colorful scenes, with a big smiling sun, an ocean, trees, ribbons of color, and various abstract shapes composed in her Small World style. What looked like satellites floated near the top of the north mural, but the overall style was more whimsical than futuristic. Even if their theme and execution seemed better suited to **Fantasyland** than Tomorrowland, the murals did help humanize what were otherwise rather sterile buildings.

Unfortunately, neither section of the Corridor of Murals survived the century. The half on the Inner Space building disappeared when **Star Tours** opened in 1987 with its own dramatic space-flight artwork on the exterior. The Circle-Vision half was lost to the 1998 **Rocket Rods** remodel that included a new transportation-themed painting on the building's wall. Today, these northern walls show murals set in outer space, including one section that seems to show flying Space Mountains (shown).

While portions of Blair's original murals have been destroyed, some large sections may be intact (albeit covered by the current walls and artwork). Even if Blair's designs no longer fit in with Tomorrowland's future, they are still cherished reminders of Tomorrowland's past.

Cosmic Waves

MAP: Tomorrowland, T-20

DATES: June 22, 1998–January 2002

The interactive fountain called Cosmic Waves must have seemed like a good idea when the Disneyland designers first conceived it. Who wouldn't have fun jumping among thin jets of water that intermittently shot up from the ground, especially on a blazing summer day? And who wouldn't want to try to rotate a big wet marble sitting in the middle of all the action? Unfortunately, the reality proved to be less cosmic than expected.

Cosmic Waves opened with the remodeled **Tomorrowland** in mid-1998, its location a sixty-foot-wide circular plaza near the *Moonliner*. The plan was for kids to run between the fountain's five-foot-high water jets without getting wet. Additionally, kids could team up to push on a giant, six-ton granite ball that remained in one place while slowly turning.

Unfortunately, *experiencing* the water was more fun than *avoiding* the water, leaving parents and **cast members** to deal with soaking wet kids who hadn't thought to bring bathing suits. More dismaying were some of the male guests who removed their shirts to play in the water. Even worse were the slips and trips on the wet surface, making injuries and lawsuits real possibilities.

By the end of 2001, as Cosmic Waves became more like Cosmic Problems, Disneyland had turned off the fountain. Though the water no longer flows here, the rotating stone ball can still be taken for a spin.

Cottrell, Bill
(1906–1995)

Bill Cottrell was the first Disney employee to be recognized for fifty years of service. He was born in South Bend, Indiana, in 1906. After graduating from Occidental College in Los Angeles and working briefly for the creator of *Krazy Kat* comics, he became a cameraman at Disney Studios. Within a few years, he was working on Disney's cartoons and animated movies, ultimately making major contributions to *Snow White and the Seven Dwarfs*, *Pinocchio*, and *Peter Pan*, among others.

As a key ally (and brother-in-law) of **Walt Disney**, Cottrell was instrumental in bringing the Disneyland dream to life and was said to be Disney's "right-hand man." Besides planning and overseeing many projects, Cottrell wrote scripts for some of the attractions and added many important details, including naming the individual **Jungle Cruise** boats and helping develop the Disneyland lexicon that renamed "rides" as "attractions" and "customers" as "guests."

Cottrell was later promoted to president of the company's design and development department (today's Imagineers). He was named a Disney Legend in 1994, a year before he died at age eighty-nine.

Country Bear Jamboree,
aka Country Bear Playhouse

MAP: Bear Country/Critter Country, B/C-4

DATES: March 24, 1972–September 9, 2001

Like **Space Mountain**, the Country Bear Jamboree existed in Walt Disney World before it reached Disneyland. Actually, an attraction like the Country Bear Jamboree would have appeared first in California's Sierra Nevada mountains, had Disney's plans for a new resort called Mineral King not been scuttled in 1966.

When the Jamboree did finally open in Anaheim, it was the E-ticket showpiece of the new **Bear Country** area built west of **Frontierland**. While other Disney Legends worked on the attraction, the bears and their distinctive personalities were mainly the creations of artist **Marc Davis**, who drew up the original character designs. Disney artist Al Bertino inspired Davis's taciturn Big Al character (shown).

Dubbed "the wildest show in the wilderness" on its ornate **attraction poster**, the rollicking fifteen-minute Jamboree featured eighteen **Audio-Animatronic** bears singing approximately a dozen short, countrified songs on a gaudy stage. Among the tunes were the familiar "Ballad of Davy Crockett" and the heartbreaking "Tears Will Be the Chaser for My Wine," with comical numbers like "My Woman Ain't Pretty (But She Don't Swear None)" sprinkled in. Henry, an amiable, top-hatted bear with a starched collar and bow tie, was the putative emcee; "Zeke and Zed and Ted and Fred and a bear named Tennessee" formed the Five Bear Rugs; Bunny, Bubbles, and Beulah were the singing Sun Bonnets; and cute Teddi Barra swung down from the ceiling with her feather boa to knock out "Heart, We Did All That We Could." Gomer played an upright piano topped with a honey pot, Sammy the raccoon popped up to join the fun, and Big Al stole the show with his languid rendition of  "Blood on the Saddle." Max, Melvin, and Buff, three talking trophy heads mounted on the wall, added to the vaudeville-style festivities (see the **Mile Long Bar** entry for more on this trio). Vocals were provided by some familiar names from Disney-produced record albums, including Pierre Renoudet (aka Pete Renaday), Bill Lee, Bill Cole, Dal McKennon, and **Thurl Ravenscroft**.

In 1975, Wonder Bread replaced Pepsi-Cola as the Jamboree's sponsor. In November of 1984, the bears performed their first Country Bear Christmas Show, which subsequently reappeared each **holiday season** until January of 2001. (In the show, a bear named Rufus was identified as the dim-witted stage manager—fans recognized him as the owner of the mailbox at Bear Country's entrance.) In February of 1986, the bears starred in the new Country Bear Vacation Hoedown, which introduced new costumes, sets, and vacation-themed songs. Five months later, after Wonder Bread withdrew its sponsorship, the theater was officially renamed the Country Bear Playhouse.

The Hoedown held strong for another fifteen years, but ultimately the crowds began to dwindle and in 2001, park officials put the bears in permanent hibernation. The replacement was **The Many Adventures of Winnie the Pooh**, another bear who was also a Walt Disney World import.

Fans of the original bears got to have one more look at them in theaters when

The Country Bears, a movie based on the Jamboree's characters, debuted in 2002. The bears received a satirical treatment in 2009 when they appeared in an episode of *The Simpsons* in chains, costumes, and bad moods. A few of the bears still turn up as walk-around characters at special events, such as 2011's **Family Fun Weekends** and 2012's **Jingle Jangle Jamboree**.

Disneyland tributes to the old attraction have continued into the present, including Frontierland posters of individual bears (shown). And in 2016, the **Hungry Bear Restaurant** started selling Country Bear Jugs styled like the old ceramic containers used by moonshiners and once played by the bear named Ted in the Country Bear Jamboree.

Court of Honor

MAP: Tomorrowland, T-8

DATES: July 17, 1955–March 1956

The Court of Honor was a short-lived exhibit in the heart of **Tomorrowland**. Its location was in the plaza fifty feet west of what was once **Innoventions**. The "court" was a large, star-shaped flower box; the "honor" was represented by the forty-eight flags of all the states in the union (back then, Alaska and Hawaii had not yet been admitted). The flags waved from atop tall flagpoles planted among the greenery, with six poles for each of the star's eight points and an even taller pole in the center displaying Old Glory.

What any of this had to do with Tomorrowland, which the 1956 **souvenir book** describes as "the realm of the unexplored," was unclear. While **Walt Disney** certainly loved to celebrate patriotism, perhaps this tribute to America's past and present landed where it did only out of a desperate need to fill empty Tomorrowland space for **Opening Day**. In March of 1956, the eight-month-old flags and poles were relocated to the new **Avenue of the Flags** at Tomorrowland's entrance. Within a few weeks, the **Astro-Jets** touched down for a long stay where the Court of Honor had been.

Cristal d'Orleans

MAP: New Orleans Square, NOS-6

DATES: July 24, 1966–ongoing

In the heart of **New Orleans Square** is a beautiful crystal shop that is as old as New Orleans Square itself. The sponsors are the Arribas Brothers, the same master craftsmen behind the current **Crystal Arts** on **Main Street**. Their Cristal d'Orleans has two doorways, one on Orleans Street across from **Mlle. Antoinette's Parfumerie**, and the other on Royal Street across from **Le Bat en Rouge**. Like all Arribas shops, glassware, vases, jewelry, paperweights, and delicate Disney-themed sculptures are among the shimmering creations on display, with an engraving service available for personalization.

Critter Country

MAP: Park, P-14

DATES: November 23, 1988–ongoing

With a dramatic new attraction about to debut, in late 1988 Disney officials changed the name of this corner of Disneyland from **Bear Country** to Critter Country. The new name de-emphasized the bears and threw the spotlight on all the various critters of the imminent **Splash Mountain**.

The Critter Country description in the 2000 Disneyland **souvenir book** inventories the animals: "Here amid shady trees and cool streams is a world where the rabbits, bears, opossums, foxes, alligators, owls, and frogs are just as social and neighborly as they can be." Building on that theme, several of the area's businesses surrendered their old ursine identities to new critter-oriented names—**Ursus H. Bear's Wilderness Outpost** became **Crocodile Mercantile**, for instance.

Despite all the changes, Critter Country continued to host musical bears in the **Country Bear Playhouse** until 2001, when the new **Many Adventures of Winnie the Pooh** attraction arrived. No matter what animals rule this land, the lush vegetation has always made Bear Country/Critter Country a quiet, rural contrast to its jazzy, urbane neighbor, **New Orleans Square**.

Critter Country Fruit Cart

MAP: Bear Country/Critter Country, B/C-2

DATES: Ca. 2000–ongoing

Standing along a bend in the walkway to Critter Country, this may be the most remote of Disneyland's three main fruit carts. But it's the most scenic, giving views of the **Haunted Mansion, Splash Mountain**, and the **Rivers of America**. A sign here marks this spot as Tom Sawyer Island Lookout Point, and the island is indeed just across the river.

Like the **Main Street Fruit Cart** and **Indy Fruit Cart**, the Critter Country Fruit Cart peddles simple, healthy snacks. Besides pieces of fresh fruit and juices, guests can also stock up on muffins, cookies, sodas, and a classic giant pickle. Like those other fruit carts, this one has no seating, so everything is for guests on the go.

Critter Country Plush

MAP: Bear Country/Critter Country, B/C-10

DATES: February 1996–October 1996

Located next to **Splash Mountain**, the rustic **Briar Patch** cabin has been a **Critter Country** fixture from 1988 until the present—with one major interruption. In February of 1996, when modern plush toys replaced the previous gifts and clothes, the cabin became Critter Country Plush. Despite the ongoing popularity of its merchandise, the name barely lasted eight months—by Halloween, a sign announcing the Briar Patch's return was already in place. The plush toys, however, stayed in the shop until 2004, when many of them were removed in favor of souvenir hats.

Crocodile Mercantile

MAP: Bear Country/Critter Country, B/C-7

DATES: November 23, 1988–1995

On the same day that **Bear Country** was renamed **Critter Country**, **Ursus H. Bear's Wilderness Outpost** was renamed Crocodile Mercantile. Its location at the back of Critter Country was the same, as was much of the souvenir, T-shirt, and toy merchandise. Disneyland's free brochures touted this spot as the "**Splash Mountain** souvenir headquarters."

In 1995, the Mercantile closed so it could be transformed into a small shop selling Winnie the Pooh merchandise. In 2003, this space and **Brer Bar** and **Teddi Barra's Swingin' Arcade** were remodeled and merged into one big **Pooh Corner** store.

Crump, Rolly
(1930–)

Born in 1930 near Pasadena, California, Roland Crump began his career at Disney Studios twenty-two years later as a young artist working on such animated films as *Peter*

Pan and *Sleeping Beauty*. During the 1960s, he contributed to numerous structures throughout Disneyland, including the **Enchanted Tiki Room** (he sculpted, painted, and installed most of the tiki gods), the Tomorrowland Terrace (his abstract forms crowned the roof), and the **Adventureland Bazaar** (he created the overall look). "Just about everything we did back then was a challenge, because it had never been done before," he told us.

At the 1964–1965 New York World's Fair, Crump had a hand in practically all of Disney's exhibitions. For the fair's **It's a Small World** building, he designed some of the dolls inside and the twelve-story *Tower of the Four Winds* outside. When It's a Small World moved to Anaheim in 1966, Crump helped design the flamboyant façade, especially the oversized exterior clock that still marks every fifteen-minute period with mechanical marchers. Among his other Disneyland efforts were stages and floats for some of the **parades**, and it was Crump who designed the 1961 **attraction poster** for the **Flying Saucers**. A mid-1960s episode of *Walt Disney's Wonderful World of Color* featured Crump and some of his creations for Disneyland's Museum of the Weird (never built as he intended, but some ideas, such as a séance room, later found expression in the **Haunted Mansion**). In the early 1980s, he helped lead the complex **Fantasyland** renovation.

Outside of Disneyland, Crump was a key designer at Walt Disney World. He also helped develop theme projects for other companies, and eventually formed his own design firm. Returning to Disney in 1992, Crump helped remodel EPCOT before retiring in 1996. Eight years later, Crump was named a Disney Legend. His book recalling his life and work, *It's Kind of a Cute Story*, was published in 2012, followed by a series of audio CDs called *More Cute Stories*.

Crystal Arcade

MAP: Main Street, MS-3

DATES: July 17, 1955–ongoing

Since **Opening Day**, **Main Street** has had two arcades on its western side, but only one—the **Penny Arcade**—has kept generations of kids mesmerized with games. The other, the Crystal Arcade, dominates the middle of Main's first western block. How many kids have walked under the Crystal Arcade's big, bright letters expecting to find the same kind of amusements that are in the Penny Arcade 150 feet to the north? What they've found instead is a collection of shops, which has included the **Candle Shop** and the **Story Book Shop**. An actual **Glass Blower** was also a prominent Crystal Arcade figure.

A 1995 remodel opened up the interior to make it more like an extension of the **Emporium** next door. Filled with plush toys and souvenirs, the room still has glittering crystal chandeliers, justifying the arcade's name. A 2005 renovation revitalized the grand blue-green exterior, and the 2006 **souvenir book** features photos of the Crystal Arcade at its best—in the evening, when the semi-circular entrance glows with golden lights.

Crystal Arts

MAP: Main Street, MS-13

DATES: 1972–ongoing

After meeting and impressing **Walt Disney** at the 1964–1965 New York World's Fair, Tomas and Alfonso Arribas, two Spanish brothers who were master glass cutters, opened several shops in Disneyland. Their first was **Cristal d'Orleans** in **New Orleans Square**, and their second was Crystal Arts on **Main Street**. Later, the brothers would open a third Disneyland shop—**Castle Arts**—plus additional stores in other Disney parks.

On Main Street, Crystal Arts sits next door to the **Silhouette Studio** in a space that was once home to Timex's **Watches & Clocks**. Delicate glassware and Disney character figures, bells, vases, and lamps make the interior of Crystal Arts sparkle. But these days, the racks holding glittering tiaras (shown) seem to get the most attention. From time to time, the shop displays an opulent twenty-inch castle made out of Swarovski crystals, trimmed with twenty-four-karat gold, and priced at $37,500  (**cast members** here claim that one of these was purchased by actor Nicolas Cage). Custom creations and engraving are also available.

Daisy's Diner

MAP: Mickey's Toontown, MT-8

DATES: January 24, 1993–ongoing

Daisy, Donald Duck's girlfriend, has a boat named after her in Toon Lake. She also has her own diner near **Goofy's Gas Station**. "Diner" is a misnomer for guests expecting a Blue Plate Special and old-fashioned banquettes. Daisy's Diner is a simple counter serving two kinds of pizza (pepperoni and cheese), plus basic beverages to go, with outdoor tables nearby.

Dalmatian Celebration

MAP: Town Square, TS-7

DATES: November 28, 1996–January 5, 1997

On November 18, 1996, Disney's new live-action remake of 1961's animated *One Hundred and One Dalmatians* premiered in New York. To help promote the new movie, Disneyland opened Dalmatian Celebration ten days later on Thanksgiving Day, 1996. Disneyland's spot for the spots was adjacent to the prominent **Disney Showcase** store, which still occupies the corner where **Main Street** stretches northward from **Town Square**. Various eateries, including the **Town Square Café**, had previously used the Dalmatian Celebration location.

Guests entering Disneyland through the east tunnel couldn't miss the area modeled after Disney's biggest movie of the year. Inside, they found lots of movie-related activities, including spotted face-painting and photo opportunities with Cruella De Vil. The biggest surprise was that, as the nanny announces in the 1961 animated original, "The puppies are here! The puppies are here!" It's true—there were actual puppies on hand in Disneyland for guests to play with. Once the **holiday season** ended, so did the six-week promotion (as the nanny also laments in the film: "The puppies! They're gone! . . . They took the puppies!"). The internal rooms became off-limits offices, and the external space changed into a character-greeting area.

> **MOUSCELLANY**
>
> Dalmatian Celebration wasn't the first time Disneyland had gone to the dogs. From the late 1950s to the mid-1960s, a one-day Kids Amateur Dog Show fetched a few more guests every spring.

Dapper Dans

To many Disneyland fans, **Main Street** wouldn't be Main Street without the Dapper Dans. This lighthearted, all-male barbershop quartet has been performing up and down the southern end of Disneyland since 1957, though not always with the same members. Over a hundred singers have performed as one of the Dans, some of them rotating to other Disney parks.

The group's formula has changed only slightly since the late 1950s: four smiling gentlemen in colorful striped suits harmonize sentimental songs, usually a cappella, to evoke sweet memories of the early twentieth century. The Dans' extensive repertoire emphasizes barbershop standards, classics from Disney movies, and medleys of songs from Disneyland's attractions. For decades, the group's most requested song—since the park's infancy, reportedly—wasn't a Disney song at all. It was "Lida Rose" from the 1957 musical *The Music Man*.

Sometimes a special event will generate special material. In 2013, the group broke out some contemporary songs when it performed for a week as The Original Boy Band during that year's **Limited Time Magic** program. For the recent **Diamond Celebration**, the Dans sang an updated version of the anniversary song used in the 1965 **Tencennial** celebration. The guys also get into the spirit of seasonal events, as when

they appear as the Cadaver Dans at October's after-hours parties or wear red and green in December. The Dans have also been opening up recent performances to include more comedy (teasing each other throughout the shows), more audience participation ("name that tune" and an occasional invitation for a guest to Dan up for one number), more musicality (the Dans might play chimes through several songs), and even some outrageous dance moves (the Dancin' Dans!).

Popular as they were from the start, the Dans weren't shown in Disneyland's **souvenir books** until 1968. That photo presents them wearing white jackets, carrying straw boater hats, and riding their crowd-pleasing quadcycle (which makes a brief appearance in a 2012 episode of *Modern Family* that was filmed at Disneyland). The Dapper Dans appeared on the *Strike Up the Disneyland Band* vinyl LP in 1969, and their own *Shave and a Haircut* CD came out in 2000. Onscreen, they've appeared in several Disney-produced TV shows and specials, such as a 1962 "Disneyland After Dark" episode that shows the group entertaining a Main Street crowd with a humorous rendition of "Carry Me Back to Old Virginny." Fans of *The Simpsons* may recognize the Dans' vocals in the episode about Homer's a cappella group, the Be Sharps, and movie fans might remember the Dapper Dans' performance as the singing busts in *The Haunted Mansion*.

Date Nite

MAP: Hub, H-2

DATES: June 1957–ca. 1968

In Disneyland's early years, Date Nite was a pleasant summer tradition. This musical event began in June 1957 and would sometimes last until 1:00 AM. In the summer of 1958, Date Nite expanded from a weekend-only occasion to a nightly event.

Management's goals for Date Nite were twofold: to fully utilize Disneyland after dark ("See the Magic Kingdom Under Starlight," touted some of the ads), and to draw young couples to the park by luring them with a sophisticated dance concert. The lovely outdoor **Plaza Gardens** in the northwest corner of the **Hub** provided the main dance location, and the Date Niters (officially the Elliot Bros. Orchestra) provided the main dance music. These ten musicians, all wearing red jackets and white pants, included a half-dozen brass instrumentalists, a stand-up bass player, a pianist, a drummer, and a vocalist. The group's 1958 album, *Date Nite at Disneyland*, shows off their repertoire of Gershwin, Johnny Mercer, and Rodgers and Hart standards, with "Goodnight Sweetheart" as its romantic coda.

From 1958 to 1965, the annual **souvenir books** consistently spotlight the Date Niters with the same photo of well-dressed, happy couples dancing in front of the orchestra and this accompanying caption: "A gay twirl with your best girl to the dance rhythms of Disneyland's popular Date Niters orchestra is a Summertime evening favorite." The event proved to be wildly successful and got positive press in local newspapers.

In a 1962 episode of *Walt Disney's Wonderful World of Color*, the Date Niters are seen knockin' out a swingin' song for a national audience. However, by decade's end, the Date Nite campaign had been abandoned, at least under that name. But the trend of evening entertainment at Disneyland had been set. Later concerts at the Plaza Gardens would feature such shows as the Big Bands at Disneyland series of the 1980s.

Davis, Alice
(1929–)

Alice Davis and her husband, Marc, were instrumental in making Disneyland the beloved park that it is. Born in 1929 in Escalon, California, Alice Estes was an art student when she met her future husband; they were married after she graduated. She was a fashion designer for most of the 1950s and worked on costumes for Disney movies, which eventually led to a job researching and designing hundreds of Velcro-lined costumes for Disneyland's **It's a Small World**. (Davis told a convention audience in 2010 that this was her favorite project because, as a child of the Great Depression, she'd never had dolls to play with, and thanks to Small World she finally had hundreds.)

In 1965, she began creating buccaneer costumes for **Pirates of the Caribbean**, using Marc's drawings for ideas. Later, she worked on costumes for Flight to the Moon and the **Carousel of Progress**. Still affiliated with Disney, she's appeared at special events in recent years and continues to consult. Alice Davis was named a Disney Legend in 2004.

Davis, Marc
(1913–2000)

One half of the husband-and-wife Davis team (he was married to Alice Davis), Marc Davis enjoyed a long Disney career. He was one of the legendary Nine Old Men (a nickname bestowed by an appreciative **Walt Disney**) whose art propelled Disney's classic animated films.

Born in 1913 in Bakersfield, California, Davis studied at several art institutes before settling in at Disney Studios in 1935. For the next twenty-six years, he worked on films from *Snow White and the Seven Dwarfs* to *One Hundred and One Dalmatians*, creating such memorable movie characters as Tinker Bell and Cruella De Vil. In a sixteen-minute Disney short from 1958 called *4 Artists Paint 1 Tree*, Davis is one of the featured artists who presents lengthy commentary while painting his own interpretation of a hillside tree.

Davis joined the Disneyland team in 1961, and his creative talents are still seen and heard throughout the park. He wrote jokes for the **Enchanted Tiki Room**, invented comic scenes for the **Jungle Cruise** and **It's a Small World**, added animals and settings to **Nature's Wonderland** in **Frontierland**, drew up the musical bruins for the **Country Bear Jamboree**, developed characters and scenes for **America Sings**, and painted the humorous "stretching room" portraits in the **Haunted Mansion**.

His finest work may have been **Pirates of the Caribbean**. Davis's original concepts became actual scenes in the attraction: the trio of jailed pirates trying to lure the key-holding dog; the pirate skeleton pinned to the wall by a sword, a seagull nested in his hat; the pirate struggling under a mountain of hats and booty as he steps onto a shaky launch. And that's his painting, *A Portrait of Things to Come*, hanging in the Crew's Quarters scene. In a 1965 episode of *Walt Disney's Wonderful World of Color*, Davis was introduced to a national TV audience, along with highlights of the coming Pirates and Haunted Mansion attractions.

Davis officially retired in 1978 but stayed on to help with EPCOT and Tokyo Disneyland. Named a Disney Legend in 1989, he died in Southern California in 2000.

Davis, Marvin
(1910–1998)

When it came to creating Disneyland's layout and overall design, Marvin Davis probably worked closer with **Walt Disney** than any other Disney employee. Davis was right there in the inner circle as plans for the nascent park began to take shape; he's often credited with drawing up the first overhead view of Disneyland as we now recognize it. His 1953 illustration shows specific building locations, stretches **Main Street** from the **entrance** up to the **Hub**, and branches the lands off into different directions.

Like several other Disney Legends who contributed to Disneyland, Davis got his start in movies. He was born in 1910 in New Mexico, won awards in college as an architecture student, and got a job in 1935 as an art director at 20th Century Fox. He joined the Disneyland design team in 1953 and was working on the park's layout soon after that. Over the next decade, he came up with plans for many areas and attractions: over 100 variations of the main **entrance**, early designs for Main Street buildings and **Sleeping Beauty Castle**, detailed drawings for **Tom Sawyer Island**, and ideas for **New Orleans Square** and the **Haunted Mansion**.

Davis also worked on Disney TV shows, picking up an Emmy in 1962 for art direction and scenic design. In the late 1960s and early '70s, Davis steered the planning and design of Walt Disney World before he retired in 1975. Davis was named a Disney Legend in 1994, four years before he died in Santa Monica at age eighty-seven.

Davy Crockett Arcade,
aka Davy Crockett Frontier Arcade

MAP: Frontierland, Fr-1

DATES: October 1955–1985

Sustaining the momentum of the Davy Crockett craze that was sweeping the nation, the Davy Crockett Arcade replaced the **Davy Crockett Frontier Museum** in October of 1955. The location—just inside the **Frontierland** gates, in the building to the immediate left—didn't change, and for a while not much else inside the arcade did either, since the museum's wax figures remained on display until the following June.

The Davy Crockett Arcade wasn't for game-playing the way a modern arcade is (although Davy's did have a simple coin-operated shooting game). Instead, the building was a collection of subdivided spaces occupied by a changing roster of retailers: the Mexican Village, Squaw Shop, Leather Shop, Frontier Rock Shop, Frontierland Hats, Frontier Print Shop, Western Emporium, and a souvenir stand (according to a small 1970 Frontierland map, these last five shared the arcade that year). Much of the interior space looked like the inside of a nineteenth-century frontier building, utilizing lots of rough stucco and distressed wood.

The whole enterprise was renamed the Davy Crockett Frontier Arcade in 1985. Two years later, it was dubbed **Davy Crockett's Pioneer Mercantile**. This repeated reference to Davy Crockett illustrates his enduring appeal; other than Walt Disney himself, no other real person has been invoked more often in the names of Disneyland's attractions and stores.

Davy Crockett Frontier Museum

MAP: Frontierland, Fr-1

DATES: July 17, 1955–October 1955

To capitalize on the success of the three Davy Crockett episodes that began running on the *Disneyland* **TV series** in late 1954, Imagineers started spreading the Crockett theme throughout **Frontierland**. First up in July of 1955 was the Davy Crockett Frontier Museum, a large building to guests' left as they entered Frontierland's stockade gates. The museum displayed a collection of Crockett-themed exhibits, the highlight being a detailed re-creation of a meeting between Crockett (who resembled Fess Parker, Disney's TV Davy Crockett), his sidekick George Russel (a Buddy Ebsen lookalike), and Andrew Jackson (a dead ringer for Andrew Jackson) inside Jackson's headquarters. The full-size wax figures were dressed in detailed frontier costumes, a row of rifles stood along the wall, historic art lined the rough-timber interior, and a period flag and wax sentry added authenticity. To acknowledge both Davy and Fess, a tribute window (shown) is on today's Pioneer Mercantile building.

Elsewhere in the museum, a coin-guzzling, pistol-shooting game and shops selling Crockett-themed items (coonskin caps, buckskins, and other souvenirs) competed for attention. Three months after opening, the museum was re-billed as the **Davy Crockett Arcade**, and eight months later the wax figures were relocated to **Fort Wilderness** on **Tom Sawyer Island**.

Davy Crockett's Explorer Canoes,
aka Indian War Canoes

MAP: Frontierland, Fr-14

DATES: July 4, 1956–ongoing

Of the many cars, boats, trains, and carts that guests can ride in at Disneyland, only one has required its passengers to provide the actual propulsion. That's what the Indian War Canoes in **Frontierland** asked of its guests, starting on Independence Day in 1956.

Like the *Mark Twain*, the D-ticket canoes made an approximately twelve-minute trip around **Tom Sawyer Island**, but the canoes deferred the right-of-way to bigger, less mobile watercraft. The canoes launched from the northernmost dock along the western bank of the **Rivers of America**, a spot near the **Indian Village**.

The canoes weren't made by Disney, coming instead from a canoe-building company in Maine. Originally, the thirty-five-foot-long, one-ton vehicles had small motors to supplement the paddlers. These, however, were soon eliminated, so all power had to come from the dozen guests and two strong-armed **cast members** in each boat.

On May 19, 1971 the Indian War Canoes got a more politically correct name, though Davy Crockett's Explorer Canoes was basically the same attraction. They've operated irregularly because of weather concerns, and there was some talk that they'd be permanently retired in the late 1990s. However, today the canoes still exist as rustic throwbacks to Disneyland's earlier, simpler years.

Davy Crockett's Pioneer Mercantile,
aka Pioneer Mercantile

MAP: Frontierland, Fr-1

DATES: 1987–ongoing

What was known for three decades as the **Davy Crockett Frontier Museum** and then the **Davy Crockett Arcade** became Davy Crockett's Pioneer Mercantile in 1987. For all three enterprises, the location was the big, rough-timbered building guests encountered as they entered **Frontierland**. The store offered a wide range of toys, polished rocks, videos, souvenirs, books, and hats. Woody from *Toy Story* and Pocahontas from *Pocahontas* have been strong presences among the merchandise over the years; when other Disney figures are sold in the store, they're usually wearing Western duds.

Eventually Davy Crockett was dropped from the store's official name, so it exists today as simply Pioneer Mercantile (though a small wooden sign over the door still

mentions Davy). The modern Mercantile expresses the pioneer spirit with a wood ceiling, rustic
light fixtures, American Indian artifacts, various
antique rifles, and imaginative, wilderness-themed
display cases blended into the décor. At the back of
the room, a big screen shows frontier scenes from
Disney cartoons, and an open doorway connects to
Bonanza Outfitters next door.

These days, most of the store is given to generic Disney merchandise, and not all of it evokes the
Old West (racks of iPhone cases in Frontierland?).
In 2014, the store introduced a cowboy theme
that included non-Disney books, shirts, hats, and
scarves, but by 2015, the authentic cowboy items
and frontier books had been scaled back in favor of toy archery sets, acrylic serapes,
and cool metal Conestoga Wagon lunch pails. Nostalgically, classic 1950s-style coonskin caps "made of all new materials" are available.

> **MOUSCELLANY**
>
> There are several coin-
> operated machines in
> Disneyland that let you
> make a puppet character
> jump and move. The
> **Penny Arcade** has one
> devoted to Pinocchio; the
> Pioneer Mercantile offers
> Woody's Ho-Down, where
> you can pay to "make him
> dance" crazily.

A Day at Disneyland Film

In the tradition of previous Disney-produced documentaries like *Disneyland, U.S.A.*
and *Gala Day at Disneyland*, *A Day at Disneyland* offers a state-of-the-park tour that
celebrates favorite attractions and locations. But unlike the earlier two featurettes,
both of which were paired with Disney films when they were released in theaters, *A
Day at Disneyland* was released on video in June of 1982 and was intended as more
of a souvenir keepsake.

Populating the forty-minute documentary are many Disney characters who frolic
through Disneyland: Goofy floats through the **Jungle Cruise**, Hook and Smee sail
with the **Pirates of the Caribbean**, and more. Footage of now-extinct attractions like
the **20,000 Leagues Under the Sea Exhibit** and **Skyway to Tomorrowland** adds a
touch of nostalgia. A 1994 re-release includes scenes of two 1990s enhancements,
Mickey's Toontown and **Fantasmic!**

Diamond Celebration

DATES: May 22, 2015–September 5, 2016

Disneyland followed up its **Show Your Disney Side** promotion with what was formally
called the Disneyland Resort Diamond Celebration. Announced in January of 2015
and officially begun on May 22 with an all-night pre-Memorial Day party attended by
over 80,000 guests, the long Diamond Celebration honored the sixtieth anniversary
of Disneyland's **Opening Day.** Among the most conspicuous festivities were a dazzling new nighttime spectacular called **Paint the Night** and beautiful new **fireworks**
named Disneyland Forever. Blue-and-white bunting adorned virtually every structure;
many of these additions remained even while orange **Halloween Time** decorations
were added in the fall and Christmas ornamentations were added for the **holiday**

season, leading to a mix of colors and marketing campaigns. Disneyland's most iconic structure, **Sleeping Beauty Castle**, got a sparkly new roof (detail shown) and its own special decorations.

As with most of Disneyland's celebrations, special offerings were added to restaurant menus, such as Pomegranate Silver Sparklers, Longboard Lemonade, and Diamond Celebration Cupcakes. Stores like **Disney Showcase** featured special displays (shown), and over 500 themed items—including sixtieth anniversary plates, pillows, pins, popcorn buckets, and rhinestone-encrusted hats—went on sale (the enormous variety of items filled fifty-five pages of the special merchandise catalog). In addition, a promotion called the Diamond Days Sweepstakes gave away Cinderella-style glass slippers, private parties in **Fantasyland**, nights in the Disneyland Dream Suite, and more.

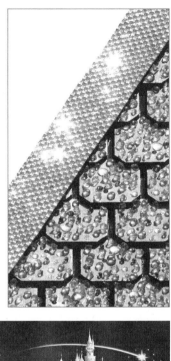

On the actual date of the sixtieth anniversary, July 17, 2015, guests were invited to Show Your 1955 Disney Side by dressing in their finest '50s fashions. Disneyland also handed out commemorative pins, free cupcakes, special guidemaps, and souvenir newspapers. **Walt Disney's** Opening Day dedication speech played over the loudspeakers, Disney Legend Richard Sherman performed live, and crowds joined in on a big "Happy Birthday" singalong to celebrate the momentous day.

Ten years before the Diamond Celebration, the **Happiest Homecoming on Earth** party had honored Disneyland's fiftieth anniversary with

special events from May 2005 to September 2006. Likewise, the Diamond Celebration extended its festivities for sixteen months. Diamonds, however, aren't forever, and the celebration finally concluded on Labor Day in 2016.

Disability Access Service Card

After several 2013 news reports exposed abuse of Disneyland's **Guest Assistance Card**, which gave day-long special access to attractions, the park replaced the GAC with a new Disability Access Service Card later that year. Like the GAC, the DAS Card can be picked up at **City Hall** and helps disabled visitors avoid long lines. Unlike the GAC, the DAS Card includes a photo of each guest and works like a **FASTPASS** ticket, limiting disabled guests to a reservation for one attraction at a time. Once a card is obtained at City Hall, a guest can visit small umbrella-covered kiosks around Disneyland to reserve a time for an attraction.

Discovery Bay

MAP: Frontierland, Fr-22

DATES: Never built

In the 1970s, it seemed like Disneyland was going to build a whole new area in the park. Inside **Disneyland Presents a Preview of Coming Attractions**, a **Main Street** exhibit space that displayed models and art for possible future attractions, guests first discovered Discovery Bay.

Discovery Bay was to be a new body of water located somewhere between **Fantasyland** and **Frontierland**, possibly in the space later filled by Big Thunder's railroad and ranch. The plans included small waterfront buildings evoking the spirit of the nineteenth-century Barbary Coast, while the half-submerged *Nautilus* (which might've been used as a restaurant) echoed a classic Disney movie (*20,000 Leagues Under the Sea*).

Dominating the Discovery Bay imagery was a giant hangar with the sleek airship *Hyperion* (from the 1974 Disney movie *Island at the Top of the World*) emerging for some unexplained purpose. Was it a walk-through exhibit? A balloon-ride attraction? What about the boats taking a Voyage Thru Time—was that into the past or future? And the "looping upside-down on a magnetic roller-coaster" experience mentioned in the book *Walt Disney Imagineering*—where and what was that? Were the rumors of an exotic greenhouse true? And what about the *L.A. Times* articles in 1985 and 1998 claiming that Discovery Bay was going to include a new thrill ride—a geyser shooting an elevator up into the air?

Unfortunately, the public never got answers to any of these questions. The *Island* movie sank at the box office, and Discovery Bay went unrealized, though elements from the unbuilt attraction did turn up later at Disneyland Paris.

Disney Afternoon Avenue

MAP: Fantasyland, Fa-22

DATES: March 15, 1991–November 10, 1991

The success of the *Disney Afternoon* TV series led to a new **Fantasyland** area called, appropriately, Disney Afternoon Avenue. This temporary exhibit was built in early 1991 along 400 feet of walkway between **Matterhorn Mountain** and **It's a Small World**. Afternoon Avenue's cartoony structures represented Duckburg, USA, a brightly colored small town that was a sort of early version of **Mickey's Toontown** (which would open two years later).

As with Toontown, guests could explore cute buildings here and take pictures with Disney characters, including Scrooge McDuck, King Louie, and Baloo (**Baloo's Dressing Room** was at the northern end, near Small World). Several other nearby attractions—**Fantasyland Autopia**, Videopolis (now **Fantasyland Theatre**), and the **Motor Boat Cruise**—joined in on the *Disney Afternoon* theme by adding some temporary décor.

The whole enterprise peaked with the airing of a TV special, "Disney Afternoon

Live! at Disneyland," on September 14, 1991. Never intended to be a long-term presence in Disneyland, Disney Afternoon Avenue closed two months later.

Disneyana

MAP: Main Street, MS-4, MS-19; Town Square, TS-10

DATES: January 9, 1976–April 14, 2013; June 30, 2013–ongoing

Recognizing that Disney collectibles were hot commodities, Disneyland opened its own memorabilia shop in 1976. Originally, Disneyana was located where the **Hurricane Lamp Shop** had once stood, in a small **Main Street** shop next to the **Crystal Arcade**. At first, the Disneyana shop specialized in vintage rarities, but eventually the merchandise expanded to become mostly limited-edition contemporary pieces.

Needing more room, Disneyana switched places with the **Jewelry Shop** on May 30, 1986—the jeweler took Disneyana's westside spot, and Disneyana moved into the east-side space between the **Main Street Cinema** and the **Market House**. After walking through Disneyana's front room, guests might have noticed a small round art gallery at the back; in 1955, this unique space was informally dubbed the Birthday Cake Room because it housed a big birthday cake that celebrated the centennial of Swift, the Market House's sponsor back then.

In the spring of 2013, Disneyana closed to make way for a new Starbucks location. When it reopened in June, Disneyana had moved to the former **Bank of America/** Bank of Main Street building in **Town Square**, a spot that had belonged to the **Disney Gallery**. Within a month, Disneyana had added a new Ink & Paint Department, where artists work in front of guests. Keen-eyed observers might notice a separate sign for an inaccessible Department of Ink & Paint hanging in the back of Mickey's Toontown (shown).

Attentive guests will note that today's Disneyana retains elements of yesteryear's bank building: a vault in the front room displays expensive art, and an old teller booth holds the cash register. These nostalgic touches add to the charm of Disneyana—no matter where it's been located, it's always been a fascinating destination for Disneyphiles interested in animation cels, statues, and other collectibles.

Disney Clothiers, Ltd.

MAP: Main Street, MS-14

DATES: March 23, 1985–ongoing

For a quarter of a century, the **Hallmark Card Shop** occupied one of the large corners where **Center Street** divides **Main Street** into two blocks. In 1985, Disney Clothiers, Ltd.—"where good style is always in fashion"—moved into this prime retail spot across from the **Market House**.

Two signs outside the store identify different retail spaces within Disney Cloth-iers: Castle Brothers ("collegiate fashions") in front and Chester Drawer's ("togs for toddlers") in back. Pretty much everything is adorned with Disney themes. Bath products and linens have also appeared on these shelves, despite the store's proud announcement that it sells "clothing with character—a Main Street tradition since 1905."

By mid-2015, the store's front rooms were tar-geting different groups of customers. The men's side now offers boxer shorts, shirts, and hats in a room with school supplies and antique sports equipment on the walls (manual typewriters, old golf clubs, vintage pennants, a big letterman's sweater, and, behind the register, an actual nine-teenth-century Willshire College diploma for some-one named Louis Elder Brittson). The women's side sells pricey blouses, bags, and jewelry in a room decorated with antique shoes, hats, and other fash-ion accessories.

MOUSCELLANY

In Disney Clothiers, Ltd.'s room for women's fashions, mounted up by the ceiling is a fascinating display of fifty antique bottles for perfume and toilet water (shown). Glassy and classy!

In the back of the store, where Chester Draw-er's sells clothes and accessories for infants and toddlers, the room looks like an adorable nursery, with a five-foot-tall wooden soldier, antique toys, and big Ferris wheel on display. All these rooms inside the store are connected to each other, and the Chester Drawer's area opens into **Crystal Arts** to the north.

Disney Dollars

Scrooge McDuck, motorcycle cops, and news cameras were on hand when Disney Dollars arrived at Disneyland by armored truck on May 5, 1987. Called "currency with character" by Disney, the first series of Disney Dollars came in two denominations: a $1 Mickey bill with **Sleeping Beauty Castle** printed on the back, and a $5 Goofy bill backed with the *Mark Twain* Riverboat. Two years later, a $10 Minnie Mouse bill was added that features several Disneyland attractions on its back.

Created by marketing whiz **Jack Lindquist**, the new currency yielded immediate results—so popular were the bills, they were soon found at Walt Disney World and in Disney Stores across America. After that 1987 debut, guests bought and used the bills just like they were real money—and, in a sense, they were. Available at **City Hall** and other locations, Disney Dollars could be used throughout Disneyland, and they could be exchanged at any time for cash at full monetary value.

The bills themselves underwent many revisions. In 1993, **Mickey's Toontown** imagery was added, and in 1997, Mickey sported his *Fantasia* costume on the $1 bills, Goofy wore a tuxedo on the $5 bills, and Simba (of *The Lion King*) replaced Minnie on the $10 bills. The backs of all the bills feature Walt Disney World imagery (the Florida park was celebrating its silver anniversary at the time).

Redesigns continued into the twenty-first century, too. Donald Duck made his debut on the $10 bill in 2000. That same year, Mickey dressed up for a New Year's millennium party; in 2001, he was joined by Minnie on one of the bills, both wearing aloha shirts and sunglasses, to celebrate the inaugural of Disney California Adventure. A year later, Mickey transformed into the whistling star of *Steamboat Willie*, and in 2005, he was temporarily replaced on the $1 bill by Chicken Little so that Mickey could adorn a new $50 bill to coincide with Disneyland's fiftieth anniversary (Mickey got the spotlight again in 2008 for his eightieth birthday).

In 2007, Disneyland began offering single dollar bills with *Pirates of the Caribbean* movie themes (a skull on the front and a pirate ship on the back), plus singles, fives, and tens featuring Ariel, Aurora, and Cinderella, respectively. Disney Dollars from 2011 show variations on

a party theme with different Disney characters. The 2014 bills feature depictions of three iconic Disneyland mountains—**Splash Mountain** ($1), **Big Thunder Mountain** ($5), and **Space Mountain** ($10), with Mickey on the backs. A small drawing of Tinker Bell always adorns the front of every bill (in 2002, Tink herself got the center spot on the $10 bill).

Playful as they were, the creation of the bills was extremely sophisticated. They were made using complicated engraving and printing processes that rivaled those used for actual U.S. currency. The bills had anti-counterfeiting security symbols worked into their art, and the serial numbers on them were real (numbers beginning with an A are from Disneyland; those with a D are from Walt Disney World). Guests, however, didn't always treat them as currency—they often treated them as collectibles and refused to spend them. Jack Lindquist told us that by 1996, only nine years after they'd been introduced, there was already "over $150 million in unredeemed Disney Dollars in circulation."

Surprisingly, after twenty-nine years, Disney abruptly canceled the Disney Dollars program on May 14, 2016 (Disneyland still honors existing bills, but it no longer sells new ones).

Oh, and the signature on all the Disney Dollars? It's by none other than Treasurer Scrooge McDuck.

Disney Gallery

MAP: New Orleans Square, NOS-1; Town Square, TS-10

DATES: July 11, 1987–August 7, 2007; October 2, 2009–ongoing

What was intended to be a private **apartment** in **New Orleans Square** for **Walt Disney** and his family was finally opened to the public as the Disney Gallery in 1987. Previously the area had been dubbed the Royal Suite due to the discreet entrance on Royal Street intended for the Disney family alone.

The public entered via the outdoor stairways leading up to the second-floor gallery, a dramatic entrance that was added when the walkway to **Pirates of the Caribbean** was remodeled in 1987. Upstairs, the Disney Gallery interior spread through various rooms and short hallways that surrounded a small patio. The luxurious furnishings, elegant moldings, and parquet floors all approximated what the 3,000-square-foot apartment would have looked like, had it been finished for the Disney family in the 1960s. The ornate iron railing outside the art rooms still has the initials WD and RD woven into the filigree as tributes to Walt and **Roy O. Disney**.

But it was the art, not the architecture, that compelled repeat visits. Displays of Disneyland-related paintings and drawings lined the walls, and glass cases held detailed models of Disneyland buildings and attractions. Typically the artwork represented a specific theme, such as the inaugural "The Art of Disneyland 1953–1986" exhibit, 1997's "A Look at the Future—Tomorrowland: 1955–1998" installation, and 2002's showing of Mickey Mouse imagery.

The room to the immediate right of the gallery entrance was called the Disney Gallery Collector's Room and sold Disneyland-inspired books, prints, and note cards. Art on Demand consoles enabled guests to select art that could be picked up later or mailed home. Special events, such as book signings or new releases of limited-edition art, were also occasionally held in the Disney Gallery. **Cast members** here also took evening reservations for the balcony outside, where guests could sample desserts and enjoy an uncrowded view of that night's **Fantasmic!** presentation.

With little notice, the twenty-year-old Disney Gallery closed permanently in mid-2007. That fall, a thorough remodel converted the historic space into a lavish, 2,600-square-foot overnight suite for 2008's **Year of a Million Dreams** promotion. The Disney Gallery, meanwhile, relocated to a prominent space in **Town Square** formerly occupied by the **Bank of America**. Starting in 2009, the gallery operated in this location with its own Town Square doorway and three beautifully appointed rooms inside. An elaborate vault, left over from the building's banking days, stood open in the front room, and the cashier operated out of an old teller cage. Display cases and original art filled the back rooms, and special exhibits included a tribute to **Mary Blair** and a regal display called "Crowning Achievements: Creating Castles for Magical Kingdoms."

In June of 2013, the Disney Gallery moved again, this time relocating to interior rooms within the **Opera House** building so that the retail **Disneyana** store, which used to be on **Main Street**, could have prominent frontage on Town Square. Fortunately, the gallery has continued its tradition of hosting impressive special exhibitions, as with 2014's "Tiki Tiki Tiki Realms" and 2015's "Drawing Disneyland: The Early Years."

Disneyland After Dark

DATES: 1957–ongoing

Disneyland has always been a magical sight at night. Lovely popcorn lights elegantly outline buildings such as the train station above **Town Square** (shown), and the whole park seems to shimmer with new enticements and opportunities. To give guests an additional reason to stay—and dine—after sundown, Disneyland started lighting up the dark Anaheim skies with **fireworks** in 1957.

A few years later, the park further courted nighttime guests by inaugurating special programs called Disneyland After Dark. Early 1960s brochures list "the greatest show in town," presented every summer evening until midnight. The festivities included bands, dancing, "special entertainment," and more, transforming Disneyland into a "date night destination" for teens and a "mecca for adults, too" (according to the 1964 book *Walt Disney's Disneyland*). A 1962 "Disneyland After Dark" episode of *Walt Disney's Wonderful World of Color* showcases all the activity, especially the musical acts.

Despite the attention it was receiving, Disneyland's annual **souvenir books** didn't contain a Disneyland After Dark section until 1965, when a single page shows how "Disneyland becomes a different world after dark." Subsequent books expand the coverage to multiple pages and sometimes include a long quote from Walt Disney about "the new kind of magic and excitement" at night. Decades later, in *Disneyland: The First 50 Magical Years*, narrator **Steve Martin** seconds Disney's sentiment with his own reverie about the lights coming up at dusk.

New nighttime enticements have been added to Disneyland over the years, including the rockin' **Tomorrowland Terrace** in 1967, the **Main Street Electrical Parade** in 1972, Videopolis (now **Fantasyland Theatre**) in 1985, and more. Interestingly, the Disneyland After Dark name has also been used outside of Anaheim. A 1980s Danish rock band called itself Disneyland After Dark until Disney lawyers compelled a name change; the group continued releasing new records as D-A-D into the 2000s.

Disneyland Band

From the moment it debuted on **Opening Day**, the Disneyland Band has helped evoke the feeling of small-town America. Uniformed marching bands have a long tradition in popular culture, of course, and in 1957, they got a boost when *The Music Man*, the nostalgic tale of a small Iowa town starting up its own marching band, became a Broadway hit.

At Disneyland, the 1955 band was sixteen instruments strong, including lots of brass and a big bass drum. The crisp uniforms varied but usually featured bright red or white jackets with ornate trim, pants with gold stripes down the sides, and sturdy, brimmed hats adorned with feathers on the front.

Naturally, the band's musicians have rotated in and out over the years. Usually about twenty are available at a time, and some of the members have occasionally dressed up in costumes to play in combos like the Keystone Cops and the **Strawhatters**. The bandleaders, however, have rarely changed. The very first leader, **Vesey Walker**, stayed for fifteen years. Subsequent leaders have included Jim Barngrover, James Christensen, Art Dragon, Stanford Freese, and the current leader, Kurt Curtis.

Since its inception, the Disneyland Band has been a picturesque target for Disneyland's official photographers. The annual souvenir books have routinely spotlighted the band with big photos and enthusiastic text, and the 1956 featurette *Disneyland, U.S.A.* shows band members playing their instruments while spinning in teacups at the **Mad Hatter's Mad Tea Party**.

According to the "Disneyland Data" section in the 1956 souvenir book, the original band gave 1,460 performances annually (four a day, every day of the year). In the 1950s, the Disneyland Band was also called "the marchingest band in America" (Art Linkletter calls them "the marchingest band in the whole world" on the "Disneyland '59" TV special). Thanks to its familiar appearances in the daily **parades**, the band has probably marched over 4,000 miles total through Disneyland by now. The Disneyland Band also used to perform concerts in the long-gone **bandstand**. What's more, the band has appeared at special events, at the late-afternoon flag-lowering ceremonies in **Town Square**, and even in **Frontierland** in 2016.

Musically, the band has been featured in several albums over the years, among them *Walt Takes You To Disneyland* (1958), *Strike Up the Disneyland Band* (1969), and *I Love a Parade* (1974). Not surprisingly, the "Mickey Mouse March" is the most-performed song, even though the band's 400-song repertoire includes everything from polkas to waltzes to selections from Disney's own movies (such as a medley of tunes from *The Jungle Book* in 2015, for example).

Changes to the band's members came in mid-2015, timed with that year's **Diamond Celebration**. The band has been expanded to eighteen players, and some younger musicians have been integrated into the mix for performances that have become livelier and more comedic.

What has never changed is the Disneyland Band's enduring popularity. Crowds still fill the sidewalks anytime the band marches by, and guests always gather to catch the sit-down performances in Town Square. What they're seeing, hearing, and enjoying is a tradition as old as Disneyland itself.

Disneyland Fun: It's a Small World Video

Like 1982's *A Day at Disneyland*, 1990's *Disneyland Fun: It's a Small World* was released on video, not in theaters, by the Walt Disney Company. Presented by an animated Professor Owl, star of the Oscar-winning cartoon *Toot, Whistle, Plunk and Boom* (see the **Professor Barnaby Owl's Photographic Art Studio** entry), the twenty-nine-minute video features dozens of Disney characters playing in Disneyland. However, because *Disneyland Fun* is part of the Disney SingAlong Songs series, those characters also sing and dance as lyrics show on the screen.

Although the songs target children, the scenery satisfies adults, simply because it includes so many extinct attractions. The **Rocket Jets**, **Swiss Family Treehouse**, **Tahitian Terrace**, **Skyway to Fantasyland**, **PeopleMover**, **Mike Fink Keel Boats**, **Fine Tobacco**, and **Fort Wilderness** are all on view. Additionally, the cameras take prolonged tours of durable landmarks like the **Jungle Cruise**, **Splash Mountain**, and **Matterhorn Bobsleds**. Sharp-eyed viewers will note that, once upon a time, **Sleeping Beauty Castle** had front walls covered in ivy.

Disney timed the *Disneyland Fun* summer video release to coincide with the park's thirty-fifth anniversary. Fifteen years later, the DVD came out in time for the fiftieth.

Disneyland Presents a Preview of Coming Attractions, aka Disneyland Showcase

MAP: Main Street, MS-20

DATES: April 1973–July 22, 1989

Originally the **Wurlitzer Music Hall**, and later the tribute called **Legacy of Walt Disney**, occupied the building where **Town Square** meets the southeastern block of **Main Street**. But from 1973 until 1989, this highly visible corner was filled with the closely studied displays of Disneyland Presents a Preview of Coming Attractions. Here, fascinated guests could linger over detailed models, concept illustrations, and videos depicting proposed Disneyland developments. Among the tantalizing plans were some that were fully realized (**Space Mountain**, **Big Thunder Mountain Railroad**), and some that never materialized at all (**Discovery Bay**, **Dumbo's Circusland**). In 1980, the room spotlighted the park's silver anniversary, and a year later it was renamed the Disneyland Showcase.

The exhibit closed for three months in 1989 while it was converted into the big retail store that also took the name **Disney Showcase**. Some of the Coming Attraction displays appeared later in the **Disney Gallery**.

Disneyland: The First 50 Magical Years Film

MAP: Town Square, TS-9

DATES: May 5, 2005–ongoing

Disney Legend **Steve Martin** stars with Donald Duck in this commemorative film, originally released on May 5, 2005, to coincide with Disneyland's quinquagenary celebration. Martin, who once worked in Disneyland's **Main Street Magic Shop**, delivers humorous, affectionate narration for the seventeen-minute film, which includes footage of **Walt Disney** and Disneyland's construction. According to **cast members**, Martin's scenes were filmed on sound stages made to look like Disneyland locations.

Disneyland: The First 50 Magical Years has been shown in two locations inside the majestic **Opera House**. The first run was in the large theater previously occupied by

Great Moments with Mr. Lincoln. When Lincoln returned in 2009 after a four-year hiatus, the film moved from the Opera House theater to a TV screen in the lobby, where it still plays today amidst historical displays and rare artworks from Disneyland's past.

Disneyland **TV Series**

Television was a great ally to **Walt Disney** as he ramped up work on Disneyland in 1954. Debuting in October of 1954, nine months before Disneyland opened, the weekly *Disneyland* show on the ABC network served as an extended infomercial for Disneyland, making its layout and themes famous even while it was still being built. What's more, the TV show helped finance Disneyland—ABC also presented a loan that went toward construction. For ABC, the benefits were reciprocal—its *Disneyland* show was an instant hit and immediately bolstered the fledgling network, which at the time was floundering far behind its rivals, NBC and CBS.

That Walt Disney, an Oscar-winning movie producer, even deigned to venture into television put him at the vanguard of Hollywood's studio heads. At the time, other major film studios mocked and ignored television disdainfully; although Columbia had been producing television shows since 1951, the studio hid its identity behind the name of its TV division, Screen Gems. But Disney fully embraced the young medium. He put his studio's name, his famous characters and creations, and even himself right up front to celebrate and promote the show. His rapid success on the small screen quickly brought other movie studios aboard—in September of 1955, ABC premiered *Warner Brothers Presents* and *M-G-M Parade* (unlike Disney's long TV run, both shows lasted less than a year). Additionally, Walt Disney's direct involvement with TV presaged the later forays into TV by movie moguls like Irwin Allen, Steven Spielberg, and George Lucas.

Disney launched his first regular prime-time show, *Disneyland*, on Wednesday nights in 1954's fall season. Like the park, the TV series was divided into four main sections called Adventureland, Fantasyland, Frontierland, and Tomorrowland (interestingly, this division points out the same deficiency on TV that there was in Anaheim—just as the **Tomorrowland** area had been the least-developed part of the park in its first year, the Tomorrowland section of the TV show was also the least-developed part in its first year). The interaction between *Disneyland* the show and Disneyland the park is clearly shown in three 1954–1955 TV episodes that detail the progress at the construction site; the park didn't just give the show structure, it gave the show content, too, a relationship that would recur numerous times over the years. Walt Disney notes this synergy when he advises viewers in the first episode that "Disneyland the place and *Disneyland* the TV show are all part of the same."

After only twenty episodes, *Newsweek* labeled *Disneyland* "an American institution." The triumphant series lasted for a record twenty-nine consecutive years, won seven Emmy Awards, and eventually played on all three major networks, switching from Wednesday to Sunday nights. It also changed its name a total of five times: *Walt Disney Presents* (1958–1961); *Walt Disney's Wonderful World of Color* (1961–1969); *The Wonderful World of Disney* (1969–1979); *Disney's Wonderful World* (1979–1981);

and *Walt Disney* (1981–1983). (In 1986, Disney began producing a variation of the original show, trying out different formats and titles that included *The Disney Sunday Movie* and *The Magical World of Disney*.)

Throughout its long history, the show frequently presented episodes devoted to Disneyland. On the premiere episode, "The Disneyland Story," Walt Disney explains the park-to-be by showing maps, models, and illustrations. He also describes his goals for Disneyland: "We hope it'll be unlike anything else on this Earth. A fair, an amusement park, an exhibition, a city from Arabian Nights, a metropolis from the future. In fact, a place of hopes and dreams, facts and fancy, all in one . . . A place of knowledge and **happiness**." Before he died in 1966, there would be eleven more episodes spotlighting Disneyland.

Outside of the weekly show, many Disney-produced TV specials showcased the park. "Dateline: Disneyland," which aired on July 17, 1955, is the most famous, the landmark live presentation of the Opening Day festivities hosted by Bob Cummings, Art Linkletter, and Ronald Reagan for an estimated 90 million viewers. Later specials were often timed to coincide with the debuts of new attractions, such as the **"Disneyland '59"** special that aired on June 15, 1959, that introduces the new **Matterhorn Bobsleds**, **Monorail**, and **Submarine Voyage**; similarly, "Disney's *Captain EO* Grand Opening," which aired on September 20, 1986, shows off Tomorrowland's new movie. Other specials commemorate Disneyland's birthdays divisible by five (the twenty-fifth, thirtieth, thirty-fifth, etc.). Guest hosts for these specials range from movie stars (including Sandy Duncan, Helen Hayes, and Danny Kaye) to comedians (among them George Burns, Jay Leno, and Jerry Seinfeld). Musical guests could be anyone from Glen Campbell to the Moody Blues. (Refer to *The Disneyland Book of Lists* for dates and details about shows and specials.)

> **MOUSCELLANY**
>
> While many park traditions are shown on the *Disneyland* TV series, at least one park tradition was initiated by the series itself. From the premiere episode onward, each show opens with an animated, flying Tinker Bell waving her wand. The public's expectations for that sight at Disneyland led to the appearance of a Tinker Bell character who soared over **Fantasyland** on summer nights beginning in 1961.

Disneyland, U.S.A. Film

Released into movie theaters for the 1956 winter holidays alongside *Westward Ho the Wagons*, this Cinemascope featurette is basically a forty-two-minute Disneyland commercial. It examines the park from the air via spectacular helicopter footage, shows off the new Disneyland Hotel, and presents a walking tour of all the lands.

At the time, the film provided some important national exposure for what had been an exciting year: by the end of 1956, Disneyland had added such vital new attractions as the **Astro-Jets**, the Indian War Canoes, the **Junior Autopia**, the **Mine Train**, the elevated **Skyway**, the **Storybook Land Canal Boats**, and **Tom Sawyer Island**. Anyone who had seen Disneyland on TV in 1955 (which was most of the country) would have been dazzled by the dramatic changes that had already been made in the young park just a year after its debut.

Extensive scenes of extinct attractions (the **Flight Circle**, for instance), plus long looks at areas that have been much-modified over the decades (the **Jungle Cruise** back when the skipper's spiel was serious, and **Fantasyland** with its original medieval decor), make this essential viewing for Disneyland fans. Winston Hibler, who also wrote the words on the dedication plaque in **Town Square**, co-wrote and narrated the film's text. Translated into other languages, the film even got released internationally. In 2007, *Disneyland, U.S.A.* was included on a compilation DVD called *Walt Disney Treasures: Disneyland Secrets, Stories & Magic*. For 2015's **Diamond Celebration**, *Disneyland, U.S.A.* was shown in the **Opera House** on July 18, 2015, honoring the day in 1955 when Disneyland first opened to the public.

Disney, Roy O.
(1893–1971)

Some of the lyrics to "Brothers All," a song that Terry Gilkyson wrote for *The Jungle Book* that wasn't included in that 1967 hit Disney movie, could apply to the relationship between Roy O. Disney and his younger brother, **Walt Disney**: "We are of one mind, you and I . . . We are of one blood, you and I . . . brothers all, brothers all." Without Roy's allegiance, advice, support, and efforts, Walt Disney never would have been able to make his Disneyland dream a reality. "There would be no Disneyland," Disney Legend **Van France** says in *Window on Main Street*, "had it not been for their combination of talents and experience."

Roy Oliver Disney was born in Chicago in 1893, about eight years ahead of Walt. Several years before Walt would hold the same job, teenage Roy worked as a "news butcher," selling inexpensive items on trains. After Roy moved to Hollywood, he invited Walt to join him, and in 1923 the brothers co-founded an animation company. In this partnership, their roles would generally stay the same for the rest of their lives—Roy's financial wizardry supporting Walt's creative genius. Though occasionally distressed by his brother's risky and expensive plans, Roy stayed fiercely loyal to Walt and for over forty years served as CEO of their company (formerly Walt Disney Productions, renamed the Walt Disney Company in 1986).

During his career, Roy supervised the company's lucrative merchandise licensing, negotiated the groundbreaking contract for the *Disneyland TV series* in the 1950s, and, in 1953, successfully wooed the investors who would back Disneyland's construction. Significantly, Roy Disney was also the first person to buy a Disneyland admission ticket, which he purchased in 1955 for $1.

MOUSCELLANY

Not only do the two Disney brothers have stars on the Hollywood Walk of Fame, so does Disneyland, placed in front of the El Capitan Theater (6874 Hollywood Boulevard) in 2005.

After Walt Disney's death in 1966, Roy assumed leadership of the impending Walt Disney World and guided the immensely complex project through the construction stage to its 1971 opening. He died of a cerebral hemorrhage just two months later. Several Disney tributes honor his memory: his initials are curled into the metal balcony above Disneyland's **Pirates of the Caribbean** (shown in the **Apartments** entry), a Disney Studios building and Walt Disney World train engine are named after him, and a statue in Florida's park depicts him sitting on a bench next to Minnie Mouse. And, like his brother Walt, Roy has his own individual star on the Hollywood Walk of Fame. His son, Roy E. Disney (1930–2009), was a top Disney executive who was named a Disney Legend in 1998.

Disney Showcase

MAP: Main Street, MS-20

DATES: October 27, 1989–ongoing

Guests walking north from **Town Square** are welcomed to the eastern side of **Main Street** by the eminent Disney Showcase. There's a lot of history on this busy corner. In 1955, the **Wurlitzer Music Hall** sold instruments here. Later, the space displayed **Legacy of Walt Disney** exhibits, followed by the fascinating displays of **Disneyland Presents a Preview of Coming Attractions**.

Just before the holidays in 1989, the distinguished building became Disney Showcase. Announced by an ornate sign, the retail store has endured as a popular destination for movie- and Disneyland-themed clothes, sportswear, pins, and other gifts. Fun Disneyland-themed displays change seasonally, and the elaborate tin ceiling is always impressive.

The store has two rooms: a main room that opens to Main Street, and a smaller side room closer to the **Opera House**. In 2014, this side room, which formerly held the **American Egg House**, was temporarily filled with stuffed toys plus an array of cookbooks, aprons, oven mitts, and other kitchen accessories until **Haunted Mansion** items moved in for the autumn. By early 2015, the small room had changed again by adding merchandise for little girls—princess figures, dresses, and *Frozen* items as the *Frozen* theme remained hot. At year's end, the room transformed into a glittering display of ornaments, stockings, and hats for the **holiday season**.

In 2015, virtually all of the main Disney Showcase room was given over to sparkly **Diamond Celebration** merchandise. The big displays along the main room's back wall showed **Sleeping Beauty Castle**, Mickey, and Minnie, all of them decked out for the year's park-wide festivities.

Disney Vacation Club Kiosks

MAP: Frontierland, Fr-18; Hub, H-1; Mickey's Toontown, MT-12; New Orleans Square, NOS-10; Tomorrowland, T-8

DATES: Ca. 2006–ongoing

Scattered around Disneyland are kiosks (also labeled Information Desks) designed to entice guests into joining the Disney Vacation Club. The kiosks (at five locations in 2011, three in 2016) correspond to their respective surroundings—the Tomorrowland location, for instance, looks like a spindly flying saucer. After getting basic information on over 500 timeshare properties around the world, guests are then invited to attend an "open house" presentation at the nearby Disneyland Hotel for further details.

Disney Villains

MAP: Fantasyland, Fa-30

DATES: July 16, 1991–May 30, 1996

When the sweet **Fantasyland** store known as **Briar Rose Cottage** departed in July 1991, the sinister Disney Villains store immediately moved in. The location was the same—just through the **Sleeping Beauty Castle** entrance and to the right of the castle's courtyard—but the theme was completely inverted to showcase the wicked characters from Disney films. Images of the jealous queen who torments Snow White, the malevolent Maleficent from *Sleeping Beauty*, the Peter Pan-chasing Captain Hook, and the puppy-chasing Cruella De Vil were all presented for sale on clothing and gifts.

Five years after it opened, the Disney Villains shop was replaced by **Quasimodo's Attic**, following the theme of that year's *The Hunchback of Notre Dame*. Villain merchandise returned when the **Villains Lair** shop opened here in 1998.

Disney, Walt
(1901–1966)

Walt Disney was a man of many contrasts. Born on December 5, 1901, he experienced a peripatetic childhood dominated by a stern father and hard work. Yet he memorialized his youth with Disneyland's sweet, happy **Main Street**. A high school dropout, Disney later aggressively promoted education and drove the development of the California Institute of the Arts. He had a sentimental love of American folklore and history, but he eagerly embraced a utopian future humming with high-tech gadgets and sleek new transportation (just one Disneyland example of this contrast is Disney's nostalgic salute to the revered Mr. Lincoln of the nineteenth century, which brims with some of the most advanced robotics of the twentieth).

Still more contrasts: stridently patriotic, Disney also championed global "small world" unity. He was an extravagant traveler who toured South America, took frequent European vacations, and flew by private jet later in life. But given his choice, his preferred meal might have been chili out of a can, and his preferred activity was riding his miniature train around his backyard. The movies he produced were often about making and keeping friends, but he himself remained distant from longtime associates and rarely socialized. The affable, charismatic exterior Disney displayed in public belied a churlish, impatient, sometimes irascible personality well known to employees who ignited his volatile temper. The same man who demanded intense loyalty also made ruthless business decisions that cut loose some longtime employees.

The kindly, wholesome image Disney cultivated as the world's fairytale-loving uncle was offset by a private man who chain-smoked and enjoyed nightly cocktails. He banned employee mustaches, but wore one himself. Disney is remembered by many as being conservative, square, and old-fashioned ("I'm corny," he freely admitted), but in reality, many of his business and creative decisions were daring, bold, and even radical. In *The Art of Mickey Mouse*, John Updike writes that Disney had a "Napoleonic capacity to marshal men and take risks in the service of an artistic and entrepreneurial vision."

Corny as he may have felt, Disney was a prescient innovator who pushed for progress: cartoons synchronized to sound, the first full-color, three-strip Technicolor cartoon, the revolutionary multi-plane camera, the groundbreaking **Audio-Animatronics** technology, and a Surround Sound forerunner called Fantasound that, according to *Variations on a Theme Park*, made him Hewlett-Packard's first-ever customer.

Though Disney promoted himself as one of the common people with ordinary tastes, during his lifetime this versatile colossus was bestowed with hundreds of major international honors, his name was on one of the world's biggest entertainment companies and the world's most famous theme park, his signature (as others have speculated) might be the world's most recognizable autograph, and upon his death, he was extolled as few people in history have ever been.

Many of these contrasts came into play as Disney invented and built Disneyland. The spark for a "magical realm," historian Dale Samuelson speculates in *The American Amusement Park*, may have been struck by Walt's father, Elias, a carpenter who helped build the fabulous World's Columbian Exposition (Walt wasn't born yet, but profound stories of Chicago's monumental 1893 World's Fair and White City undoubtedly circulated ever after through the Disney household). The Walt Disney Family Museum has stated that Disneyland was conceived as early as Walt's "Kansas City years," which came in the 1920s. Certainly, Walt Disney's visits to San Francisco's Golden Gate International Exposition in 1939, Michigan's charming Greenfield Village in 1940 and 1948, and Chi-

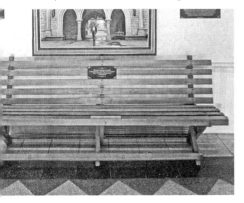

cago's Railroad Fair in 1948 fanned the creative flames. Disney himself said it came from the disappointment he had experienced when he took his daughters to local amusement parks that he considered unattractive, uninspired, unclean, and unfriendly. He said that he first thought about building a park of his own while sitting on a bench at Griffith Park, watching his daughters have fun as he imagined a place where families could have fun together (that actual bench, shown here, is displayed in the Disneyland's **Opera House**).

By the late 1940s, Disney, already famous as a ground-breaking moviemaker, had begun making notes for a small amusement area to be called Mickey Mouse Park or Mickey Mouse Village, taking up several acres of the back lot at his Burbank movie studio. Those first ideas included a section based on a typical small Midwestern town from yesteryear, plus a railroad station, opera house, movie theater, farm, American Indian village, merry-go-round, and ponies. The ideas were still modest, as were his descriptions of "a three-dimensional thing that people could come and visit." At this early stage he was calling it an "amusement enterprise," "some kind of family park," and "a little dream" of a "magical little park." A line he wrote about making the film *Peter Pan* for the April 1953 issue of *Brief Magazine* might just as easily have been about his concept for Disneyland: the goal was "to recreate a children's world, but a children's world in which adults could find a place."

Finances were a pressing concern for an undertaking so experimental and expensive. Millions of dollars would be required—and that was just the seed money to get a firm start. At the time, Disney wasn't exactly flush; his track record at the box office had been dreadful in the early 1940s, when *Fantasia* and *Pinocchio* were costly, labor-intensive flops and World War II sealed off the lucrative European markets. (Although Disney's movie studio was making millions in the 1930s and '40s and had earned thirty Oscar nominations, it never got out of serious debt until the 1950s.) And the Disneyland idea still wasn't something everyone was buying into. "It sounded crazy," said his older brother, **Roy O. Disney**. "We were in the movie business, not the amusement park business. We didn't know a thing in the world about amusement parks. None of us around Walt wanted any part of his amusement park." To many, the park idea would be known, for a while anyway, as "Walt's Folly."

Judith Thurman once wrote, "A mad person sees what isn't there. A visionary sees what isn't there yet." Staying true to a future only he could perceive, the visionary in the Disney family pressed on. Rather than risk his studio, Walt Disney risked himself. "In the end he put his own money into it, not the studio's money," says his daughter, Diane Disney Miller, in *The Story of Walt Disney*. "He hocked his life insurance and raised $100,000 and . . . paid a draftsman out of his own pocket to lay out what he'd planned."

To keep the project advancing, Disney sold his Palm Springs vacation home and borrowed from friends, ultimately pouring about a quarter-million of his own dollars into what was still just an idea. Major corporate sponsors were eventually recruited. Most importantly, Roy Disney negotiated the complex television deal—finalized on April 2, 1954—that brought ABC in as both an investor and a means to promote the un-built park with a Disney-produced TV show. The show debuted 208 days later with the simple title ***Disneyland*** and quickly became ABC's top-rated program.

In the early 1950s, the park moved steadily from vague dream to realistic plan. In 1950, Disney considered including what he called Disneylandia, a series of dioramas and miniatures traveling from town to town by train. Some of these scenes were already being built when he shifted the focus to a permanent park location. After Disney visited Copenhagen's immaculate Tivoli Gardens in 1951 and met art director **Harper Goff** in London later that year, he dispatched Goff to amusement parks throughout Europe to gather ideas. Upon his return, Goff started drawing up detailed illustrations of a park that was possibly going to be called Walt Disney's America. This was to be a much larger Burbank enterprise with double-digit acreage that would include an island in a lake, trains, a stagecoach, canal boats, and a circus. Looking ahead, Disney installed horse trainers Owen and Dolly Pope in a trailer at Disney Studios to gather animals for the coming park and start building Western-style carriages.

In 1952, Disney began calling his park Disneyland and his ideas continued to grow; a rocket and a submarine were added to the plans. On March 27, Burbank's *Daily Review* newspaper broke the story about the Burbank park-in-the-making with this headline: "Walt Disney Make-Believe Land Project Planned Here—$1.5 million dreamland to rise on site in Burbank." But that plan soon changed. Disney realized that the sixteen-acre Burbank plot was far too limited for his ambitious dreams, especially after the near-sighted city council coolly rebuffed his unusual plans for fear of a rowdy, tacky carnival setting up in their city.

In the meantime, Walt started assembling and sequestering his core design team, recruiting as members some of the animators and art directors from his movie studio, including designer **Bill Cottrell**, art directors **Richard Irvine** and **Marvin Davis**, layout artists Goff and **John Hench**, and more. These were the pioneers who would revolutionize amusement parks and amusement park rides. (This group would soon be called Walter Elias Disney Enterprises—or WED—Enterprises and then Walt Disney Imagineering in 1986.)

In October of 1952, *Daily Variety* announced that Walt Disney was "shopping for a big tract of land" for his "playground for kids and grownups," and indeed he was. Formalizing the search, in 1953 Walt Disney paid the Stanford Research Institute $25,000 to pinpoint a site. SRI's **Harrison Price** found the spot thirty-eight miles south of Burbank—Anaheim, where a century earlier, the great Rancho San Juan Cajón de Santa Ana had sprawled across 36,000 Orange County acres. Anaheim's mild weather, convenient freeway access, welcoming politicians and administrators, and cheap land were positive variables in Price's formula for success.

Disney first saw the Disneyland site that fall. He got **Keith Murdoch**, Anaheim's city manager, to close off Cerritos Street, which cut across the land he wanted to buy. One way Walt Disney reciprocated for this and other favors the city granted was to give Anaheim a special gift: he had one of his artists draw up a new Andy Anaheim cartoon character—a cute bug in the shape of a large A—that became the city's official mascot in 1953.

Working quietly so he wouldn't drive up prices, Disney began to purchase Anaheim orchards from seventeen different farmers for around $4,500 an acre. Moving quickly on his now-unified assemblage, in the spring of 1954, Disney hired Los Angeles's sixty-nine-year-old McNeil Construction Company (the builders of many Southern California landmarks) as the prime building contractor. He also had 12,000 orange trees (plus hundreds of eucalyptus and walnut trees) removed from the site, got the telephone poles cleared from the area and their lines buried, designated 100 acres for the **parking lot**, and prepared to build his sixty-acre park. Anaheim's *Bulletin* newspaper officially announced the switch to Orange County on May 1, 1954.

Realizing that his own designers could execute his ideas better than any outsiders, Disney released the architectural firm he had hired to draw up plans and expanded his core design group. Long brainstorming sessions with those designers, who later became known as Imagineers, ensued throughout 1954. To observers, the resilient and resourceful Disney was in his element, happily working off his own nervous energy with an all-consuming new project that demanded tenacious focus.

Before construction began, Disney sent Harper Goff and a team of designers back out to amusement parks, fairs, zoos, museums, and other tourist areas around the country for more ideas and inspiration. Disney himself made additional scouting trips to other parks (among them the nearby Knott's Berry Farm) to watch the crowds and step off measurements of park geography. He also consulted with numerous experts in the amusement industry, several of whom derisively predicted failure and delivered their standard advice: sell alcohol, add a Ferris wheel and simple carnival games, don't waste money on landscaping and non-revenue-producing structures like **Sleeping Beauty Castle**, don't stay open more than four months a year, etc. To

those unimaginative disbelievers who ran gimcrack carnivals, "real" and "ideal" were trains traveling on perpendicular tracks.

Disregarding the unsettling suggestions of the "experts," ignoring the recession of 1953 and '54, and relying on his own intuition and rectitude (as he had often done in his movie-making career), Disney finally broke ground on his Anaheim park in mid-July of 1954. Unlike nearly every subsequent event in Disneyland's history, there was no fanfare, no initial spade-turning ceremony. For this reason, the official groundbreaking date is disputed—many authorities say it was July 12, 1954, while others claim it was July 16. Walt's daughter, Diane Disney Miller, states in *Disneyland . . . the Beginning* that it

was the July 17; architectural historian Karel Ann Marling, Disney Chief Archivist Emeritus Dave Smith, and Disneyland Hotel historian Donald W. Ballard pinpoint July 21 (Smith has written that July 21 was when the first trees were removed from the property); and Michael Broggie (son of **Roger Broggie**) writes that it happened in August of 1954. As shown on the *Walt Disney Treasures: Your Host Walt Disney* DVD, Walt Disney announced to audiences that the Disneyland "dream really started to come to life in July 1954, when the bulldozers moved in and started leveling the site."

No matter what the start date was, the end date is indisputable; TV commitments placed the finish line at July 17, 1955. With the hourglass officially upended and the sands starting to trickle, work progressed for the next year—steadily at first, then hurriedly, and finally frantically, especially in the last weeks when construction stretched around the clock. That final month, over 1,200 construction workers put in long hours, and even Walt Disney's wife, Lillian, picked up a broom to sweep off the decks of the ***Mark Twain* Riverboat** in the final days.

Incredibly, despite spiraling costs that drove the price from over $4 million in mid-1954 to over $17 million in mid-1955, frustrating labor strikes and incessant construction problems that lasted throughout the rainiest spring in two decades, and Walt Disney's own staff telling him that he needed to postpone the opening (especially in **Tomorrowland**), Disney finished his park on time. That is, it was at least finished enough to *look* complete to the masses of guests who were coming, whether the park was ready or not. Some of the attractions, including the **Casey Jr. Circus Train** and **Rocket to the Moon**, were ready only for viewing, not for riding. Tomorrowland had to be swathed in balloons and bunting to camouflage its empty buildings. Still, the remarkable park was open for business right when Walt Disney said it would be, and an instantly seduced America quickly set the turnstiles spinning at a record-setting pace.

Meanwhile, Disney himself was a creative whirlwind stirring multiple pots. During the mid-1950s, when he was so deeply immersed in detailed Disneyland planning and construction that he was actually living in an **apartment** at the park much of the time, he also oversaw the ongoing production of his studio's most ambitious animated film yet, *Sleeping Beauty*. At the same time, he completed the films *Peter Pan* (1953), *20,000 Leagues Under the Sea* (1954), and *Lady and the Tramp* (1955), produced numerous documentaries and dozens of cartoons, and created his new TV show with its landmark Davy Crockett character. "He was like a ringmaster directing a twenty-ring circus," wrote animator Bill Peet, who worked at Disney Studios for thirty years. "There were the live action features, the true-life adventures, the TV shows, and, above all, Disneyland, which had outgrown his most extravagant dreams." Busy as Disney and his company were, there was no drop-off in quality—the Disney productions he made during this time earned thirteen Oscar nominations.

Although Disney didn't do all of this single-handedly, he was extremely (some said obsessively) involved in everything his company did, and he routinely worked all day and late into the evening. His mantra: "Get a good idea and stay with it. Dog it and work at it until it's done, and done right." When Disney neglected something and allowed others to run with it—the 1951 film *Alice in Wonderland*, for instance—it was usually derided by critics as one of the studio's lesser efforts.

With Disneyland, the arc of Walt Disney's life up to that point was finally complete. He had begun his career with unrefined sketches and transitioned to silent black-and-white cartoons, then to singing color cartoons. He'd leapt to full-length animated features, live-action movies, and documentaries. Then he had topped it all off with the real-life world of Disneyland.

When Disneyland opened in mid-1955, it wasn't the first American theme park. Walter Knott had launched his Ghost Town in 1940, Indiana's Santa Claus Land had debuted in 1946, and the ocean-themed Marineland of the Pacific had opened in 1954, to name a few. But Disneyland was the cleanest, safest, most efficient, most scrupulously planned, and most totally immersive park anyone had ever seen—as well as the most imaginative. It wasn't merely a fair, a village, or even a park in any traditional sense—it was a *land*, an entire kingdom of possibilities.

The sixty-acre triangle was bursting with archetypal imagery from Disney movies and kids' dreams—pirates and princesses, cowboys and stage coaches, rockets and rivers, majestic castles and quaint towns, cool cars and fun boats, twirling teacups and flying elephants—and enough exhibits, **parades**, and live music added in to enable everyone to find something to enchant/engage/entertain them no matter their age or disposition.

For a long time, the things Disneyland offered really couldn't be found elsewhere. That singularity was even more conspicuous in Disneyland's first few decades, before the proliferation of Universal Studios, Six Flags, and the other Disney parks, and back when amusement parks were often tacky, dirty, seedy places jammed with cheap rides and random games. Disneyland's special harmony, encompassing its landscaping, architecture, music, signage, and costumes, was magnificently unusual for the industry, and magnificently appealing to the public.

To name just one example of its singularity, Disneyland has routinely offered transportation systems unavailable to most people outside the property. Roller coasters and cars and carousels can be found all over the country, but not the submarines, monorails, PeopleMovers, and Doom Buggies that Disneyland introduced. New as it all was, the conspicuous presence of dozens of respected sponsors like Coca-Cola and TWA eased concerns about quality and helped make the untried park a little more familiar.

Though there were certainly fast, exciting experiences to be had here that held the potential for chaos and terror, everything somehow seemed orderly and family-friendly. Many attractions were related to a noble American heritage or to timeless fairytales, and most espoused traditional values even while celebrating wonderful new technology. Everything was either fun, patriotic, or educational, and sometimes all three. Even the revolutionary switch-back **queues**, cleverly doubling back upon themselves and offering eye candy to sweeten the line-waiting experience, seemed entertaining and even comforting, and were thus another expression of Walt Disney's people-pleasing philosophy. "All I want you to think about," he told his designers, "is that when people walk through or ride through or have access to anything that you design, I want them, when they leave, to have smiles on their faces. Just remember that; it's all I ask of you as a designer."

A smile. Disneyland guests would be confronted with cemeteries, pits, dungeons, demons, oncoming trains, abominable snowmen, headhunters, pirate skeletons, witches, ghosts, and many other villains, but they'd still leave merry. Ultimately, what Disney sought wasn't the most thrilling, or the most terrifying, or the most educational, or even the most fun park in history—his kingdom, he famously declared, would be "the happiest place on Earth." Disneyland's joyous spirit might have reminded guests of a park they'd already seen—in the 1940 Disney classic *Pinocchio*, where Honest John sings about the boisterous Pleasure Isle: "Hi diddle dee dee, it's Pleasure Isle for me. Where every day is a holiday, and kids have nothing to do but play!" (Audiences had also seen another—tamer—Disney amusement park in 1938's *Brave Little Tailor* cartoon. That one featured a Ferris wheel, a carousel, and a flying ride like Disney California Adventure's Silly Symphony Swings, and all of it was wind-powered by a snoring giant.)

What his daughter, Diane Disney Miller, called his "insatiable, omnivorous curiosity" drove Disney to nurture Disneyland for the rest of his days (to "plus" the park, as he called it). Miller quotes Walt: "The way I see it, my park will never be finished. It's something I can keep developing and adding to. A movie is different. Once I've wrapped it up and have turned it over to Technicolor to be processed, I'm through with it. As far as I'm concerned the picture I've finished a few weeks ago is done. There may be things in it I don't like, but if there are I can't do anything about them. I've always wanted to work on something alive, something that keeps growing. I've got that in Disneyland. Even the trees will grow and be more beautiful every year."

True to his word, by the time Disneyland was five years old, Disney had doubled the original $17 million investment with new additions and improvements. By 1965, the year of the tenth anniversary (the **Tencennial**), he'd tripled it, bringing the total investment to around $53 million. (The total investment would cross the $100 million threshold in 1968, and $200 million ten years after that.)

After Walt sold most of WED Enterprises to Walt Disney Productions in 1965, he created a new name, Retlaw, for the remainder that he still owned. Retlaw ("Walter" spelled backwards) controlled the Disneyland Railroad and Monorail until the Disney family sold the company to Walt Disney Productions in 1981.

Walt Disney greets a new arrival at the Walt Disney Studios in 1953.

Disney the perfectionist continued to tinker persistently with every detail in every corner of his endlessly regenerable park, right up to the very end of his life (his last visit to his beloved Disneyland probably came on October 14, 1966, sixty-two days before his death on December 15). In mid-1966, he approved the designs for two of his most ambitious attractions yet, **Pirates of the Caribbean** and **Adventure Thru Inner Space**, while simultaneously working on a redesign for Tomorrowland, pushing forward the **Haunted Mansion**, Walt Disney World, and the CalArts campus, devising a new California ski resort (Mineral King, never built), and overseeing production on his *Wonderful World of Color* television show and his last major films, *The Jungle Book* and *The Happiest Millionaire*. So many projects, so many complex, exhausting projects, even as he lived with constant pain and failing health in the '60s.

Not everyone has accepted Disneyland with equal glee, of course. Condescending detractors continue to use the adjective "Disneyfied" pejoratively; Richard Schickel, one of the park's most widely discussed critics, includes words like "horror," "frustrating," "excessive," "worse than a nightmare," "maniacal," and "peculiar" as he derides some aspects of the 1960s park in *The Disney Version*. Not all aspects of the park are criticized, though. Rarely does anyone disparage Disneyland's incontrovertible craftsmanship or exquisite landscaping. What the carping critics do condemn is what they see as meretricious artifice and saccharine sweetness; others might vilify the rampant merchandising and sky-high prices. Tendentious accusations that Walt Disney was a calculating phony with his ear eagerly cocked to the silvered sirens of the marketplace are often supported by Disneyland as Exhibit A.

Though he was occasionally assailed by anhedonic intellectuals, Disney didn't seem to care. After all, he hadn't created his extraordinary park for them. He was focused on the millions of eager guests streaming through Disneyland's turnstiles who were happily enjoying themselves all day long, scooping up souvenirs to commemorate their experiences, and enthusiastically planning their return visits. "You don't build it for yourself," Disney said. "You know what the people want and you build it for them."

MOUSCELLANY

Urban myth dictates that Walt Disney was cryogenically frozen before he died so he could be revived when there was a cure for the cancer that was killing him. But it was cremation, not freezing, that consumed him after he died on December 15, 1966.

Fortunately, most of the public loved Disneyland from **Opening Day** and made it an instant and lasting financial success. It helped that in 1955, rampant construction across the eighty-square-mile L.A. basin had reduced the amount of parkland to only eight percent, a number noted by David Helvarg in *The Golden Shore* as "one of the lowest ratios of green space to cement in the nation," thus making Disneyland a vital oasis. Further boosts came from the era's propitious surge in both disposable personal income and the number of American children (from 1946 to 1964, almost eighty million babies were born in the U.S.). Plus, low gas prices and a new freeway system put Anaheim within easy driving distance of millions of people. Best-selling futurist Alvin Toffler (*Future Shock*) even pinpointed 1955 as the beginning of society's Third Wave, a post-Industrial Age revolution in lifestyles, information, and wealth. Disneyland, it seemed, had arrived at the perfect historical moment.

Roy Disney summarizes the park's appeal in his personal greeting inside *The Walt Disney Traditions at Disneyland*, the handbook for new **cast members**: "In everything he did my brother had an intuitive way of reaching out and touching the hearts and minds of young and old alike. His entertainment was an international language. In Disneyland he created a revolutionary new concept of outdoor entertainment . . . a world-famous theme park without equal or precedent." Revolutionary, without equal or precedent—Roy was right, because Disneyland wasn't merely ahead of the curve; it *became* the curve.

Walt Disney's teetering pre-Disneyland company was in the black soon after the park opened. In 1956, its first full year of operation, Disneyland generated $10 million in revenue, according to Richard A. Schwartz's *The 1950s*; within a decade, the total was more than twenty times that, which was more than Disney movies were making. Disneyland's "phenomenal success made the Disney organization the most profitable Hollywood studio," according to Rice's *The Elusive Eden*, and "Walt Disney, who had been more or less 'tolerated' by the moguls of the prewar era, sat on the top of the heap in 1965" (Bryman's *Disney and His Worlds* puts those Walt Disney Productions profits at a meager $500,000 in 1952, a surging $3.4 million in 1956, and a robust $11 million in 1965). Mid-1960s Disneyland was, according to Kirse Granat May's *Golden State, Golden Youth*, "the number-one tourist destination in the entire

country" with an "overall park **attendance** equal [to] one-fourth of the total population of the United States." Historian Andrew Rolle called the young park "the largest
tourist attraction in the world." In 2015, sixty years after it opened, Disneyland drew
over 18 million guests (averaging more than 49,000 people every single day of the
year, most of them repeat visitors). And with **Star Wars Land** looming, well, as the
two kings in *Sleeping Beauty* sing, "The outlook is rosy, the future is bright!"

"I'm not interested in pleasing the critics," Walt Disney once said. "I'll take my
chances pleasing the audiences." Yet another contrast, one that worked for him in
movie theaters and again in Anaheim, that has kept Walt Disney in the rarified pantheon of beloved geniuses. Ultimately, the words on the dedication plaque in **Town
Square**—"a source of joy and inspiration to all the world"—apply as much to the
revered man who spoke them as they do to the wondrous park he was describing.

MOUSCELLANY

Today's guests can find Disney's name and likeness everywhere in the park (and
not just at the *Partners* statue in the Hub). Here are twenty Disneyland evoca-
tions of Walt Disney:

1. At the east-side pedestrian entrance on **Harbor Boulevard**, he has a star
   in the Anaheim Walk of Fame.
2. The mural in the queue area for **Mr. Toad's Wild Ride** includes a train in the
   upper-right corner marked WED RAIL (WED = Walt Elias Disney).
3. **Peter Pan's Flight** begins with a flight out of a bedroom window, and occasionally the alphabet blocks on the bedroom floor have been arranged to
   spell Disney.
4. Since the mid-1960s, "the official Disney family crest" has adorned Sleeping
   Beauty Castle's entrance.
5. At the **Storybook Land Canal Boats**, some of the boats have the words Walt
   Disney Limited painted on the side of their cabins.
6. Equestrian-themed photographs of Walt Disney (detail shown) have been
   displayed in **Frontierland**.
7. At Frontierland's train station, a landline telegraph clicks out lines from Walt
   Disney's Disneyland dedication speech (more of the text is displayed at the
   base of the **flagpole** in **Town Square**).
8. The Engineer of the Day commemoration handed out at the **Disneyland Railroad** is signed by longtime engineer Harley Ilgen and Walt Disney ("President").
9. The Pilot's Certificate given upon request at the *Mark Twain* **Riverboat** is
   signed by Commodore Walt Disney (shown on page 313).
10. Walt Disney's baby photo hangs on a wall inside the **Baby Care Center**.
11. Walt Disney's boyhood neighbor (Doc Sherwood M.D.), grandson (Chris-
    topher D. Miller), and father (Elias Disney) all have **Main Street Tribute
    Windows**.

12. Walt Disney's boyhood home of Marceline, Missouri, is memorialized by the Hotel Marceline on **Main Street** and by the nametag on Tilly, the **Main Street Cinema's** ticket taker (shown).

13. Walter Elias Disney is identified as the Founder & Director Emeritus of the Disneyland Casting Agency on the door just north of the Main Street Cinema.

14. The giant penny above Main Street's **Penny Arcade** is dated 1901, Walt Disney's birth year.

15. In **Mickey's Toontown**, a window above the library reads "Laugh-O-Gram Films, Inc., W. E. Disney, Directing Animator" (shown on page 160).

16. Displayed inside **Mickey's House** is a book called *My Pal Walt: A Tribute* by Mickey Mouse, from the Marceline Publishing Company.

17. Ornamental designs of "WD" and "RD" (for Walt and Roy, respectively) are woven into the railing above Pirates of the Caribbean (shown in the Apartments entry).

18. Disneyland's most popular guided tour is called Walk in Walt's Disneyland Footsteps, which includes recordings of his voice.

19. The Disneyland Railroad's lavishly appointed Presidential Parlor Car is named the *Lilly Belle*, after Lillian Disney.

20. Above the **Fire Department** is Walt's private apartment, recognized by the lamp lit in the second-floor window (shown in the **Fire Department** entry).

Dixieland at Disneyland

MAP: Frontierland, Fr-16

DATES: October 1, 1960–1970

One of the most exuberant musical events at Disneyland was a concert series called Dixieland at Disneyland, held every fall from 1960 to 1970. Requiring a special ticket that included park admission and attractions, Dixieland at Disneyland featured live performances by world-renowned jazz musicians. Among the stars were Louis Armstrong, Kid Ory, and Al Hirt, plus Disneyland's own **Firehouse Five Plus Two** and the **Strawhatters.**

For the first five years, the shows were held during the evening at the **Rivers of America** in **Frontierland.** With crowds lining the riverbanks, musicians played either on the southern tip of **Tom Sawyer Island** or out on the water on rafts and **Mike Fink Keel Boats.** The grand finale involved **fireworks** and the *Mark Twain* paddlewheeling past the cheering audience while the musicians and a 200-person choir performed "When the Saints Go Marching In." An ensuing **parade** carried musicians through

Disneyland for more celebrating.

The show was updated in 1963 to include Mardi Gras-style floats, singers, and dancers. For the last half of the 1960s, the show moved to **Main Street**, where the bands performed on wagons and then embarked on a park tour. The undeniable star of any show was Louis Armstrong, who first performed at Disneyland in 1961 and racked up a half-dozen park engagements during the 1960s. The king of jazz's raft was specially designed with a huge crown on top, and Satchmo himself wore a crown while leading the festivities.

Donald's Boat, aka *Miss Daisy*

MAP: Mickey's Toontown, MT-2

DATES: January 24, 1993–ongoing

Maximum play, minimum complexity. That seems to be the philosophy behind several **Mickey's Toontown** attractions, including Donald's Boat. Named for Donald Duck's girlfriend, the *Miss Daisy* sits in little Toon Lake like a big, colorful rubber duck. Guests enter via a walkway, and then the boat reveals itself as a simple walk-through—or, more accurately, a simple play-through—attraction. The interior reminds guests who the owner of this craft is, and the exterior decks offer space for kids to run around.

MOUSCELLANY

The giant speaker inside Donald's Boat projects various voices and sounds—even the pirates' "Yo Ho!" song, as sung by ducks!

Nifty details abound to quack up the young clientele: Donald's sailor suit hanging on the laundry line between the masts, a speaker shaped like a duck's bill, etc. There used to be more to climb on inside the boat, but some of those activities have disappeared for safety reasons. Nevertheless, because there's no minimum height requirement, Donald's Boat is still a good spot for children to burn up excessive energy while parents rest in the nearby shade.

Don DeFore's Silver Banjo Barbecue

MAP: Frontierland, Fr-6

DATES: June 15, 1957–September 1961

Almost two years after Disneyland's **Opening Day**, the self-proclaimed "finest barbecue this side of the Mississippi" opened in **Frontierland** next door to **Aunt Jemima's Pancake House**. Previously, this ground-floor space was the site of **Casa de Fritos**, which had vacated in 1956 in favor of a more prominent Frontierland location.

The Silver Banjo was named after the popular Emmy-nominated actor best known as Thorny, the Nelsons' neighbor on *The Adventures of Ozzie and Harriet*. On the national TV broadcast of Disneyland's Opening Day, DeFore is briefly seen in an **Autopia** car and on the **Casey Jr. Circus Train**. In the restaurant, DeFore himself was the chef, and his brother Verne was the manager. The Silver Banjo referred to one of DeFore's prized personal possessions (a fortunate choice, since another name he considered was Don DeFore's Bean Palace).

Barbecued ribs, chicken, pork, and fish were the restaurant's specialties, all prepared on the premises in a kitchen so small it was chided by fire marshals for code violations. After the Silver Banjo closed in 1961, the interior space was engulfed in an expansion that transformed Aunt Jemima's Pancake House into Aunt Jemima's Kitchen, while the front areas became the **Malt Shop and Cone Shop**.

Dream Machine

MAP: Hub, H-7

DATES: 1990

Always ready to celebrate any anniversary ending in a multiple of five, Disneyland cranked up the Dream Machine in 1990, thirty-five years after **Opening Day**. As they entered, guests received special tickets decorated with smiling Disney characters. Each ticket granted a pull on a lever of the Dream Machine, which waited up at the **Hub**.

Though it looked like a giant, wildly decorated cake, the Dream Machine worked like a slot machine. Usually the winners got free food and beverages, but occasionally they won videos, toys, or watches. Sometimes the prizes were extravagant—flights to any American location, for instance—and once a day, it was a new Chevy. Guests who won the car watched it rise up from inside the cake while Mickey danced around it and confetti rained down. The car, though, was only a duplicate of the actual prize—guests had to go claim theirs from a dealer at a later date.

MOUSCELLANY

Here are some other real people who have had Disneyland locations (in parentheses) named after them: Marie Antoinette (**Mlle. Antoinette's Parfumerie**); Arthur, King of the Britons (**King Arthur Carrousel**); river brawler Mike Fink (**Mike Fink Keel Boats**); Disney Legend Joe Fowler (**Fowler's Harbor**); the Gibson Brothers printers (**Gibson Greeting Cards**); illustrator Charles Dane Gibson (**Gibson Girl Ice Cream Parlor**); entertainer George Keller (**Keller's Jungle Killers**); pirate Jean Laffite (**Laffite's Silver Shop**); Abraham Lincoln (**Great Moments with Mr. Lincoln**); publicist Jimmy Starr (**Jimmy Starr's Show Business Souvenirs**); Mark Twain (**Mark Twain Riverboat**); inventors Linus Yale and Henry Towne (**Yale & Towne Lock Shop**).

Duck Bumps

MAP: Fa-6

DATES: Never built

As shown in **Bill Martin's** 1954 illustration, Duck Bumps was to be a watery attraction located near the **King Arthur Carrousel**. Duck Bumps placed eleven ring-shaped boats in a pool for "bumper-car" maneuvering. A Donald Duck head was mounted on a tall pole attached to each boat. Adjacent to this attraction was a twenty-foot windmill called *The Old Mill*, named after the landmark 1937 cartoon, but neither the Duck Bumps nor the big windmill ever made it past the drawing board.

Dumbo's Circusland

MAP: Fa-19

DATES: Never built

Circus-themed attractions have long been part of Disneyland's history. By the 1970s, guests had already seen the short-lived **Mickey Mouse Club Circus** and the long-running **Casey Jr.** and **Dumbo the Flying Elephant** attractions. In the 1970s, another circus project was being seriously considered for several acres of **Fantasyland** real estate near **It's a Small World**. Imagineers Bruce Bushman and Ward Kimball drew up concept art for various aspects of Dumbo's Circusland, which would have included a thrilling indoor attraction called Mickey's Madhouse and a fountain featuring the wacky firemen from *Dumbo*.

Enthusiasm for Dumbo's Circusland faded, as it did for the adjacent **Discovery Bay** project, toward the end of the decade. As the 1980s began, the focus switched to the huge Fantasyland remodel, which was completed in 1983.

Dumbo the Flying Elephant

MAP: Fantasyland, Fa-11, Fa-14

DATES: August 16, 1955–ongoing

"The world's mightiest midget mastodon—Dumbo!" That's Timothy Mouse's proclamation in *Dumbo*, Disney's 1941 film, and Disneyland's first Imagineers brought that same enthusiasm to their initial plans for a lighthearted Dumbo attraction in **Fanta-**

syland. However, there was a considerable difference between what appeared in the first drawings and what actually materialized in 1955.

Originally, the elephants were pink, representing the pink elephants (not Dumbo himself) that parade through the movie's memorable hallucination sequence, and their ears were going to flap. Timothy Mouse was slated to stand atop a circus-themed column in the middle, and ultimately the whole attraction was supposed to be in operation on **Opening Day**.

Problems with time, budget, and flawed prototypes created an attraction that was both different and delayed. Almost a full month after the rest of Disneyland opened, Dumbo the Flying Elephant finally debuted ten gray elephants, all wearing collars and hats of various colors. There were no flapping ears, and Timothy was nowhere to be found.

For the next twenty-seven years, Dumbo spun as a minute-and-a-half attraction in Fantasyland's far western corner. Back then, there was no connecting walkway to **Frontierland**, making the Dumbo corner more of a Dumbo cul-de-sac. But crowds still found it.

"Hot diggity! You're flyin'! You're flyin'," Timothy declares in the movie. And indeed the guests were. The colorful **attraction poster** even includes this rhyme: "Whirling and twirling way up in the blue . . . elephants fly, and so can you!" Kids loved the aerodynamic elephants because they could control their own altitude with the same kind of cockpit-lever system used to elevate the **Astro-Jets** in **Tomorrowland**. One guest who wouldn't board the ride was former President Truman, a Democrat who happily visited Disneyland in 1957 but refused to be photographed on an attraction that evoked Republican Party symbolism.

Changes started to come two years later, when the price in the **ticket books** rose from B to C. Later, Timothy was added to the attraction, wielding his whip from atop a shiny silver ball. In the 1970s, plans for an expansion called **Dumbo's Circusland** were announced with a display inside **Disneyland Presents a Preview of Coming Attractions** on **Main Street**. Although Circusland never became a reality, Dumbo did undergo a significant modification that relocated the elephants about seventy-five feet to the northeast. This was the extensive 1983 Fantasyland transformation that replaced the **Pirate Ship Restaurant** and **Skull Rock** with Dumbo (Dumbo's former cul-de-sac was opened up as a Frontierland shortcut). Dumbo also got his own vintage band organ—a three-quarter-ton, century-old, refurbished antique that pumped out Disney classics.

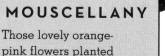

MOUSCELLANY

Those lovely orange-pink flowers planted near Dumbo the Flying Elephant? They're Disneyland's official rose, the delicately scented *Disneyland Floribunda*, which can be seen elsewhere in the park.

Another revision came in 1990, when the entire attraction was beautifully refurbished. Instead of ten elephants, there are now sixteen (originally built for Disneyland Paris, they came to Anaheim instead and Paris got its own elephants later). Additionally, Timothy Mouse lost his silver-ball platform but gained a colorful hot-air balloon to stand on. The whole attraction now sits in a lovely fountain setting where the charming elephants are "whirling and twirling" more gracefully than ever.

"You're a big hit," Timothy says in *Dumbo*, but he might as well be talking about Disneyland's long-running, high-flying pachyderms. "You're terrific! You're colossal! Stupendous!"

Edelweiss Snacks

MAP: Fantasyland, Fa-22

DATES: September 25, 2009–ongoing

Just when there didn't seem to be any more space for new structures inside **Fantasyland**, in 2009 a new A-frame cottage arose along the walkway next to **Fairytale Arts**. Swiss-themed like the nearby **Matterhorn Bobsleds**, the fifteen feet of counters at the front of Edelweiss Snacks serve up take-away chimichangas, corn on the cob, and the giant turkey legs that should come with their own strollers. In 2013, the menu began offering the barbecue-glazed pork shanks popularized at Walt Disney World.

Edgren, Don
(1923–2006)

Don Edgren installed the streaking rockets inside **Space Mountain**, took **Pirates of the Caribbean** underground, and figured out how **Matterhorn Mountain** could carry bobsleds. Whatever the Imagineers dreamed up, Edgren, leader of Disneyland's engineering team, got it built.

Edgren was born in Los Angeles in 1923. Upon graduating high school, he joined the Air Force and flew forty-five combat missions in World War II. Returning to Southern California, he began working at an engineering firm that was readying Disneyland for **Opening Day**. Edgren worked as a field engineer at the busy construction site. A few years later, Edgren helped build **Matterhorn Mountain** and its unique bobsleds tracks.

In 1961, Edgren started working full-time for Disney. His team's biggest challenge may have been Pirates of the Caribbean—what was originally designed as a walk-through exhibit became a subterranean boat ride requiring elaborate waterways and a new "show building" beyond Disneyland's perimeter **berm**.

Away from Anaheim, Edgren supervised Disney exhibits at the 1964–1965 New York World's Fair. Later, he became chief engineer at Walt Disney World and leader of that park's Space Mountain project. Afterwards, he moved to Japan to help build Tokyo Disneyland before finally retiring in 1987.

Don Edgren was named a Disney Legend in 2006, just a few months before he died of a stroke at age eighty-three.

Edison Square

MAP: Hub, H-4

DATES: Never built

The same 1958 **Fun Map** that lays out a detailed plan for **Liberty Street**, an area that was never built, also portrays another **Main Street** spin-off that was intended to open in 1959 but never made it beyond the drafting table. Whereas Liberty Street would have run roughly parallel to Main Street, designers imagined another new side street, this one situated at the north end of Main Street and running eastward for two blocks.

As shown on the 1958 map, **Edison Square** began at the **Hub** as a narrow street and ended behind **Tomorrowland** as a cul-de-sac. The theme of this new area was to be American progress as propelled by Thomas Edison; a statue of the iconic inventor would have graced Edison Square's center, his life story told with a series of dioramas surrounding the figure.

Unlike Main Street, which was a commercial area of colorful shops and eateries, Edison Square was intended to look more like a mature residential neighborhood of attractive two-story homes from the early twentieth century. Inside each building, there was to be a theater that would lead guests through decades of electronic progress. According to the map, the four theaters would have been named American Home: Pre-Electricity, American Home: Advent of Electricity, Contemporary Living, and The Electronic Age. **Audio-Animatronic** figures would have occupied the four stages.

Unfortunately, the technology needed to pull this off wouldn't be perfected until the mid-1960s. By then, Edison Square had vanished from Disneyland's plans. However, visitors may recognize the attraction's planned theme of electronic progress, its sponsor (General Electric), and Audio-Animatronic figures as the cornerstones of the **Carousel of Progress** that started spinning in Tomorrowland in 1967.

Egg-stravaganza

MAP: Main Street, MS-20

DATES: April 10, 2014–April 20, 2014; March 27, 2015–April 5, 2015; March 6, 2016–March 31, 2016

Though only a few years old, Disneyland's Egg-stravaganza (also sometimes spelled without the hyphen) has quickly become a popular Easter-time egg-sperience. First tried in 2013 as a brief **Limited Time Magic** event, it debuted more formally in the spring of 2014, was successfully repeated for two weeks the following spring, and expanded to over three weeks in March 2016.

The Egg-stravaganza is basically an egg hunt throughout Disneyland, Disney California Adventure, and (as of 2016) Downtown Disney. Players begin by purchasing a helpful map that directs them to a dozen hidden eggs. They then collect stickers for their maps to show that they've located the eggs, and later the successful hunters return their completed maps to a redemption center (in Disneyland, it's the **Disney**

Showcase store) to claim their prize of a special character-themed egg. This activity typically generates such long lines that temporary redemption centers are set up to accommodate the egg-cited crowds.

Ellen's Gift Shop

MAP: Main Street, MS-13

DATES: July 17, 1955–May 1957

In the mid-1950s, Ellen's Gift Shop (also sometimes called Ellen's Metal Gifts) stood next to **Gibson Greeting Cards** on **Main Street**. Named after Ellen Wynegar, who had an Orange County company called Wynegar Enterprises, the shop sold "original metal and wood sculptures," according to the book *Disneyland: The Nickel Tour*.

After Ellen left in 1957, art was displayed in the space until the corner **Hallmark Card Shop** engulfed it in 1960. Today, the big **Disney Clothiers, Ltd.** engulfs much of this block.

Ellenshaw, Peter
(1913–2007)

Peter Ellenshaw painted beautiful movie backdrops and extraordinary Disneyland art-works. Born in London in 1913, Ellenshaw developed his love of art as a teenager and soon landed a job painting sets for various English films.

A 1947 meeting with **Walt Disney**, who was in England to start work on *Treasure Island*, earned Ellenshaw an invitation to create detailed background paintings for the movie, as well as for *20,000 Leagues Under the Sea* a few years later. For the former, Ellenshaw painted English coastlines and dock areas seen behind the main action; for the latter, he depicted Vulcania, the submarine's secret island base. In both movies, Ellenshaw's work looks more like realistic photographs than paintings.

Following these early successes, Ellenshaw enjoyed a long Disney career as a matte artist and production designer, eventually contributing to about three-dozen Disney films and winning an Oscar for his memorable cityscapes in *Mary Poppins*. Film expert Leonard Maltin calls him "the undisputed master of the matte painting" in a special-feature documentary about *Mary Poppins*.

Before Disneyland was built, Ellenshaw painted one of the park's most publicized images: a majestic, four-by-eight-foot aerial view as seen from a third of a mile above the property. Ellenshaw showed Disneyland's overall triangular shape and its lands spreading out from the **Hub** (he also included some details that were never realized, such as a hot-air balloon). The iconic work was featured in the ***Disneyland* TV series**, appeared on the first-ever Disneyland postcard, and graced the cover of the 1955 **souvenir book**.

For **Tomorrowland**, Ellenshaw created the detailed backdrop for **Space Station X-1**, an attraction that offered a view of Earth from space. Later, he directed *A Tour of the West*, the **Circarama** theater's first film.

Peter Ellenshaw was elected a Disney Legend in 1993. Three years later, a book of his art, *The Garden Within*, was published, and in 2002 he appeared in the special features on the *Swiss Family Robinson* DVD.

Ellenshaw died in 2007 in Santa Barbara, California, at age ninety-three. His son, Harrison Ellenshaw, is an Oscar-nominated visual effects artist who has worked on several *Star Wars* films.

El Zocalo Park

MAP: Frontierland, Fr-23

DATES: 1958–1963

When Disneyland was in its infancy, Zorro was one of Disney's most popular characters, thanks to the 1957–1959 *Zorro* TV series. El Zocalo Park incorporated some of Zorro's south-of-the-border style.

Zocalo is the traditional Spanish word for "town square." In **Frontierland**, El Zocalo Park covered about a fifth of an acre near the landing for the **Mark Twain Riverboat**. There were no real attractions in El Zocalo Park, but there were certainly some nearby, including the **Mule Pack** and **Stage Coach**. What El Zocalo Park did offer was Mexican atmosphere. Mexican-inspired gifts were sold in the little plaza, the adjacent **Casa de Fritos** offered Mexican food to guests, and music by performers such as the Gonzalez Trio added an air of authenticity.

Though the original El Zocalo Park was gone by 1964, the concept has enjoyed a modest resurgence in the twenty-first century. Casa de Fritos—later Casa Mexicana—reopened in 2001 as the **Rancho del Zocalo Restaurante.** A small stage and some landscaping now fill the old Zocalo site. In the recent years, this area was the center of the first **Three Kings Day** celebration held in 2012; *calacas* (decorated skeletons, detail shown) and colorful displays go up here in the fall to celebrate the Day of the Dead; and mariachis are sometimes here playing lively music.

The flag-decorated sign sometimes displayed above the stage reads, "El Zocalo Park, dedicated 55," an affectionate tribute to Disneyland's own history. More often, though, the little park is unmarked and unused—a sign, perhaps, of changes to come.

Emporium, aka Disneyland Emporium

MAP: Main Street, MS-2

DATES: July 17, 1955–ongoing

Just as a small American town's main street would probably contain a sizeable department store, Disneyland's **Main Street** has its expansive Emporium. Inside this attractive building are over 4,000 square feet of souvenirs, gifts, hats, clothing, jewelry, and more (a sign above a doorway announces the Emporium's slogan: "We carry the best from east to west"). Everything is on view in an open room given even more character by the deep-brown woodwork decorating the walls and the beautiful light fixtures added in a 2011 refurbishment. For added interest, balconies near the ceiling use old-fashioned artifacts and expressive figures to display nostalgic scenes, such as a barber with a

surprised boy and a girl clothes-shopping with her elegant mother (detail shown).

The main Emporium entrance is located 800 feet south of **Sleeping Beauty Castle**, on the corner of Main and **Town Square**. Since this is the last major store guests encounter before exiting Disneyland, it offers a final chance to splurge on whatever they haven't already bought with whatever they haven't already spent. To maximize shopping opportunities, the Emporium is accessible from many areas on the block; guests can reach it from within the **Carriage Place Clothing Co.** to the west and from other shop interiors to the north (in fact, in 2013 an Emporium Directory appeared in the hallways connecting these smaller shops, thus suggesting that the entire block could be considered the Emporium). With so much merchandise available in these other connecting rooms, the main Emporium space has been opened up to be more navigable than ever.

The Emporium's exterior is as impressive as anything inside. A white balcony wraps around its corner, and the handsome, mansard-style upper stories are dotted with decorative circular windows. At night, thousands of lights outline the building with electric splendor. Most memorably, some of the big rectangular windows on the ground floor are filled, not with merchandise and mannequins, but with imaginative animated dioramas depicting characters and settings from classic Disney films. Thanks to these **Windows of Enchantment**, the Emporium offers the best window-shopping in Disneyland.

Enchanted Chamber

MAP: Fantasyland, Fa-3

DATES: 2008–ongoing

In 2008, **Tinker Bell & Friends** moved out of **Sleeping Beauty Castle**, and the Enchanted Chamber moved in. The small L-shaped shop has three entrances—one along the walkway through the castle and two in the castle's courtyard—though often only two doors are open simultaneously. The interior design is worthy of the majestic castle around it—the intimate space has timber beams,

MOUSCELLANY

Big, elaborate displays always catch our eye, but we love the little, often-overlooked details, too, such as the Enchanted Chamber's small, stained-glass birds on the doors along the back wall (shown on page 176).

painted ceilings, beautiful light fixtures, and medieval-style decorations, including wonderful displays behind the counter.

Instead of Tink's fairy themes and merchandise, the Enchanted Chamber's interior now displays an array of accessories, autograph books, dolls, and playsets with themes from Disney movies. From *Frozen* comes a sixteen-inch costumed figure, from *Brave* comes a bow with arrows and quiver, and from princess dreams come glittery princess-inspired blouses.

Enchanted Tiki Room,
aka Walt Disney's Enchanted Tiki Room

MAP: Adventureland, A-11

DATES: June 23, 1963–ongoing

A tidal wave of tiki culture surged onto American shores in the late 1950s as restaurants, cocktails, movies, TV shows, music, and fashion all drew inspiration from the South Seas. In 1963, that tiki wave splashed into **Adventureland** with the debut of the Enchanted Tiki Room.

As fun and timely as the tiki theme was at its opening, the Tiki Room's real significance was its advancement of **Audio-Animatronic** technology. Previously, Disneyland had displayed moving animals on the **Jungle Cruise** and in **Nature's Wonderland**, but those machines offered simple, repetitive motions viewed at a distance. Inside the Tiki Room, the A-A characters sing and move with sophisticated subtlety just a few feet away from over 200 pairs of watchful eyes.

The seventeen-minute show (later tightened to about fifteen minutes) showcases 225 moving birds, drumming tiki figures, chanting tiki masks, and singing blossoms, all within an air-conditioned tropical hut where fountains bubble and an elaborate "birdmobile" descends from the ceiling while a rainstorm rages outside. The songs have included the iconic "Hawaiian War Chant," the sing-along "Let's All Sing Like the Birdies Sing," and Offenbach's operatic "Barcarolle" (played during the "enchanted fountain" sequence, but discontinued in the mid-1990s). Hosting the festivities are Fritz, José, Michael, and Pierre, four wise-cracking A-A macaws of international heritage.

The birds themselves still appear incredibly lifelike, thanks to their varied movements and real feathers. The lively presentation has brought glowing reviews, especially in its first decades of operation. A 1963 issue of *National Geographic* calls the Tiki Room "a tremendous show." Disneyland's own 1963 **souvenir book** proclaims it "a new dimension in entertainment."

The Tiki Room is actually a scaled-down version of what had been originally planned for the attraction. Designers first envisioned a restaurant with an after-dinner bird show, but when the plan proved to be unworkable, the entertainment was expanded into an entire attraction. The Tiki Room **attraction poster** makes a

reference to what might have been: "Tiki talk say, 'Better go! Wondrous food! Wondrous show!'" Another novelty was the initial ticket pricing: instead of spending one of the tickets from their A–E **ticket books**, guests had to buy separate 75-cent tiki tickets (by the mid-1960s, admission to the hut had changed to an E ticket).

The Tiki Room's success inspired **Walt Disney** to sprint ahead with his next Audio-Animatronic attraction—the 1964–1965 New York World's Fair exhibits, which included a realistic Abraham Lincoln. Back at Disneyland, United Airlines took over sponsorship for the Tiki Room from 1964 to 1973, followed by Dole Pineapple from 1976 onward. (Dole added a pre-show video about pineapples and also began sponsoring the **Tiki Juice Bar** next door.) After years of neglect, a 2005 renovation upgraded the Tiki Room's interior and thatch-roofed exterior.

Many Disney Legends contributed to the Tiki Room's legacy. **Rolly Crump** and **Marc Davis** worked on the whole project from its inception; **John Hench** drew up colorful sketches and invented the rising-fountain concept; **Harriet Burns** created the birds' intricate plumage; **Wally Boag** from the **Golden Horseshoe** wrote the script and voiced both José the macaw and the talking bird that used to sit outside the attraction; **Fulton Burley**, also a Golden Horseshoe regular, did the vocals for the Irish macaw, Michael; **Thurl Ravenscroft**, later a prominent **Haunted Mansion** presence, vocalized Fritz, the German macaw; singer Ernie Newton performed Pierre's French voice; and the **Sherman Brothers** wrote the infectious "Tiki Tiki Tiki Room" theme song.

Though the Enchanted Tiki Room may seem tame to twenty-first-century audiences, it is well-loved by veteran guests who recognize its significance, enjoy the classic entertainment it offers, and relax in the statue-filled Enchanted Tiki Garden in front of the attraction (detail shown). As proof of its enduring popularity, fans flocked to the Tiki Room's fiftieth anniversary celebration in June of 2013, when Disneyland handed out free souvenir replicas of 1963 brochures.

Entrance, aka Main Gate

MAP: Park, P-5

DATES: July 17, 1955–ongoing

"Walt understood the function of an entranceway, or threshold," says **John Hench** in the book *Remembering Walt*. "The threshold is supposed to embrace you. It's where you feel like you're entering some very special place." This architectural philosophy wasn't new in 1955, but Disneyland's distinctive entrance sure was.

Against the advice of seasoned operators of fairs and parks around the country, **Walt Disney** opened Disneyland with only one entrance. Whereas many "experts" advocated having a variety of convenient ways to get into the park, Disney thought that multiple entrances might confuse guests. He also reasoned that he'd be better able to control the initial Disneyland experience if he welcomed guests through a single portal.

The result was the wide entrance at Disneyland's southern tip, an area immediately accessible to the thousands of guests who had left their cars in the adjacent **parking lot**. An elevated train station still beckons guests to come to the entrance below the building, just as it always has.

Guests standing in the Esplanade (the open plaza between Disneyland and Disney California Adventure) and looking northward at Disneyland's entrance will see one-story buildings stretching 200 feet to the west. These house, among other things, lockers and **restrooms**. To the east is a shorter row of buildings that includes pet kennels. Freestanding ticket booths are scattered across the Esplanade, and the Monorail still glides twenty-five feet above the turnstiles.

Once they've bought their admission tickets, guests stream into Disneyland through thirty-two covered turnstiles arranged in a slight semicircle bulging outwards from the park (old photos and aerial footage reveal that this semicircle originally curved in the opposite direction and had only ten turnstiles). Guests then find themselves seventy-five feet from a smiling twenty-five-foot wide Mick-

ey Mouse parterre (shown) with the train station above them. Park photographers and characters are often milling about in this picturesque area. For decades, the smooth concrete here was red; many observers have speculated that this was Disney's way of extending an inviting "red carpet" to his guests. Today, guests' feet are greeted by reddish pavers.

Even at this stage, when guests have paid their way into Disneyland and passed through turnstiles, the park is still not clearly visible. The revelation only comes once guests walk through one of the two tunnels on either side of the manicured Mickey garden. Each of these arched tunnels is decorated on the inside with eight beautiful **attraction**

MOUSCELLANY

At the Disneyland entrance, Mickey's face has been carefully formed out of over 10,000 small flowers and plants that are replanted every few months. How different his face has looked here over the years! At times, he's been edged with short hedges, had purple ears and then green ears, and even been given a colorful hat, all done in flora.

posters and topped with plaques that quote Walt Disney's declaration about the wonders just ahead: "Here you leave today and enter the world of yesterday, tomorrow and fantasy." The tunnels lead guests under the train tracks and into **Town Square**, with **Main Street** and all its enticements waiting ahead.

Evans Brothers (Jack and Morgan)
(Unknown–1958) (1910–2002)

Many guests love Disneyland's landscaping and ornamental flower gardens almost as much as they love its attractions. Those guests can thank Morgan "Bill" Evans and his older brother, Jack, the men who first planted the greenery.

Gardening was always a big part of the Evans's lives. Jack and Bill grew up in a Santa Monica home that had a huge garden filled with exotic flora. Upon returning from the Merchant Marine Academy in the late 1920s, Bill studied geology in college. In 1934, the twenty-four-year-old helped turn the family garden into a thriving business that supplied rare plants to the growing Hollywood community, including such luminaries as Clark Gable and Greta Garbo.

In 1952, **Walt Disney** invited the Evans brothers to plan the landscaping around his large home near Beverly Hills (Disney's famous Carolwood Pacific miniature railroad was in the backyard). Impressed with their work, Disney recruited Jack and Bill to be Disneyland's chief landscape architects two years later, with a budget of about a half-million dollars.

Between mid-1954 and mid-1955, Evans and Reeves Landscaping Inc. of West Los Angeles, billed as the "Official Landscape Architects for Disneyland," transformed sixty acres of bulldozed Anaheim fields into a verdant, beautifully manicured park. The challenge, of course, was enormous. Plants had to be brought in for many different uses: to provide shade in sunny locations; to screen off walls and areas not meant to be seen; to define borders and paths; to create entire environments (something like 700 trees were planted in the **Jungle Cruise** area); to add thematic colors and patterns (as in the gardens at **It's a Small World**); to create recognizable shapes (like the Mickey parterre at the **entrance**); and to meet all the special landscaping requirements for Disneyland's unique attractions (imagining the landscaping of the future for **Tomorrowland** was especially difficult, Bill Evans later wrote). To meet the challenge, the brothers sought input from notable landscapers, including Ruth Shellhorn, who did the landscaping for hundreds of private homes, shopping malls, and other commercial sites throughout

MOUSCELLANY

Very early in the Disneyland planning process, Walt Disney considered building a botanical garden in "True-Life Adventureland" on the southeast side of the **Hub**, where **Space Mountain** is located today. Michael Harvey's map inside the 1955 **souvenir book** even shows a southwest-side Arboretum. Though that wasn't built, Disneyland "would later become classified in landscaping circles as a botanical garden," according to the summer 1995 issue of *The Disney Magazine*.

Southern California. The Evans's overriding goal was always to add beauty everywhere; according to Bill's 1965 book *Walt Disney: Disneyland World of Flowers*, ultimately he hoped to create "a perennial welcome mat of flowers" that bloomed all year long.

Among the thousands of plants and flowers brought in were some mature trees Bill Evans rescued after they were uprooted by local freeway construction (acknowledging these replantings, one of the descriptive lines on his **Main Street Tribute Window** reads "Freeway Collections"). According to one story, the Evans brothers intentionally planted trees upside-down along the riverbanks of the Jungle Cruise so their twisted, exotic-looking roots would spread above ground. Another tale, related in the Bob Thomas biography *Walt Disney: An American Original*, recounts the last frantic days before the opening, when the brothers were running out of time, money, and plants. With some of the berm behind **Fantasyland** still bare, Walt Disney requested little signs with long Latin names to disguise the weeds as desirable specimens. Eventually, the brothers filled Disneyland with about 800 varieties and species of plants, of which, they claimed, only five percent were native to California. Some were bought in from as far away as Australia and the Orient.

After suffering a heart attack in 1955, Jack Evans died in 1958. In Bill's *World of Flowers* book, Walt Disney remembers how Jack "worked mightily to create authentic and delightful landscapes" throughout Disneyland. Bill Evans continued to supervise Disney landscaping and to train the company's landscape architects. So valuable was his knowledge that he was asked to consult on other Disney parks even after he retired in 1975. Bill Evans was named a Disney Legend in 1992, ten years before he died at age ninety-two.

Fairytale Arts

MAP: Fantasyland, Fa-23

DATES: December 2006–ongoing

Fairytale Arts is a collection of open booths in **Fantasyland**. They stretch eastward from **Edelweiss Snacks** for about fifty feet alongside the waters formerly toured by the **Motor Boat Cruise**.

Kaman's Art Shoppes (a company that has been providing artists for amusement parks since the 1970s) runs the booths and offers two main services that would fit right into a Renaissance Faire. Fairytale Scripts are decorative signs with personalized calligraphy, and Fairytale Faces are forty-three styles of exotic face-painting, ranging from single-cheek designs to complicated full masks. Nearby is Fantasia Freeze, a cart that cools off guests with tart ice drinks.

Fairytale Treasures

MAP: Hub, H-2

DATES: March 12, 2013–ongoing

Young princesses seeking the latest and greatest in royal fashions will find everything they need inside Fairytale Treasures. Located in **Fantasy Faire** next to the Royal Theatre, this little shop is packed with gowns and accessories from Disney movies.

A girl who enters here with $100 can leave dressed like Jasmine, Snow White, or Cinderella, tiara to toe. In 2015, a wall of *Frozen* items included pricey gowns, plus additional slippers, gloves, wands, and more. Charming fairytale displays and props add to the Disney magic.

Family Fun Weekends

MAP: Frontierland, Fr-19

DATES: January 14, 2011–March 6, 2011

When **Main Street** was blocked off for renovation in early 2011, guests were temporarily denied the daily **parades**. To compensate, Disneyland launched a short-lived program called Family Fun Weekends. Held for eight consecutive three-day weekends, the event was initially staged at **Big Thunder Ranch** in **Frontierland**. There, the outdoor **Festival Arena** was transformed every weekend with a different theme.

First up was Fiesta Disneyland, featuring mariachi music and local artisans presenting their wares. Next came the Kickin' Country Weekend, a celebration of country-and-western costumes, music, food, and crafts. The third weekend, Character Fan Days, welcomed roaming Disney characters, including some that are rarely seen anymore, such as the **Country Bear Jamboree** bears. Lunar New Year was the theme of the last two February weekends. Finally, the revelry shifted to **New Orleans Square** for three weekends of Mardi Gras celebrations.

The success of the Family Fun Weekends in 2011 led to new Disneyland events a year later. Centered in front of **It's a Small World**, the January 2012 **Happy Lunar New Year Celebration** promoted Chinese, Korean, and Vietnamese cultures; soon after, the **New Orleans Bayou Bash** brought five Mardi Gras weekends to New Orleans Square.

Family Reunion

DATES: 1980

In 1980, the Family Reunion theme unified Disneyland's celebration of its silver anniversary. For the event, former **cast members** were invited for a special night of entertainment and festivities on April 11. On TV, Danny Kaye hosted a March special called "Kraft Salutes Disneyland's 25th Anniversary" (Michael Jackson was a guest). A new Family Reunion Parade and twenty-five-hour party that lasted from 12:01 AM on July 17 until 1 AM on July 18 were additional highlights.

Fantasia Gardens

MAP: Fantasyland, Fa-23

DATES: January 1993–2006

Fantasia already had a Disneyland presence with the dinosaur scenes of **Primeval World**, and in 1993, the 1940 classic got further representation along Small World Way in **Fantasyland**. Previously, the **Motor Boat Cruise** had putted around this area north of the **Matterhorn**. Soon after the last motor boat shut down, the lushly planted grounds were renamed Fantasia Gardens. **Fairytale Arts** set up nearby in 2006, and later the section that was formerly the motor boats' loading dock became a designated smoking area.

Fantasmic!

MAP: Frontierland, Fr-16

DATES: May 13, 1992–ongoing

"Some imagination, huh?" So concludes Mickey Mouse at the end of Fantasmic!, and it's doubtful anyone could disagree. Originally intended to be called either *Imagination* or *Phantasmagoria*, Fantasmic! is an elaborate, state-of-the-art outdoor music and pyrotechnic show that almost defies definition.

To install the stage and create the special effects, in 1992 the **Rivers of America** waterway was drained, the southern tip of **Tom Sawyer Island** was rebuilt, and the island's Mill was relocated. After the first year proved to be overwhelmingly successful (but also overwhelmingly crowded), terraced walkways were added near **New Orleans Square** to accommodate the 5,000-plus guests who gather nightly along the riverbanks to witness the mesmerizing twenty-two-minute show.

The Fantasmic! plot follows the hero, sorcerer Mickey, as he battles various Disney villains, resulting in a tour of classic Disney movies from *Snow White and the Seven Dwarfs* to *Beauty and the Beast*. While the story may seem simple, the show is incredibly intricate. The complicated multimedia presentation incorporates many different elements, usually including over fifty **cast members** (most with multiple roles) and featuring thrilling music, thirty-foot-tall spotlight towers, 125 special effects that can generate six-foot flames, eleven floating watercraft, and an assortment of smoke machines, lasers, black lights, and water cannons. The show also utilizes a 100-foot-long snake, a crocodile twenty-five feet wide by seventeen feet tall, a twenty-foot-tall Ursula (from *The Little Mermaid*), an appearance by the *Mark Twain* **Riverboat** and/or the **Sailing Ship** *Columbia*, and, as of 2009, a forty-five-foot-tall, nine-ton mechanical fire-breathing dragon. Full-color animated images are projected on huge water screens that are thirty feet tall by fifty feet wide by four inches thick, requiring thousands of gallons of water.

One drawback of Fantasmic! is that it is canceled in any inclement weather (wind would soak viewers with water from the water screens). Up until a 2007 park remodel, the guests' best views were from a reserved spot on the balcony outside the nearby **Disney Gallery**. Annual Passholders had their own special showings when Disneyland recognized the twentieth anniversary of Fantasmic! with four nights of celebratory events in May of 2012. And to improve the whole experience, in December 2014, Fantasmic! started offering **FASTPASS** reservations and new dining packages with preferred seating.

> **MOUSCELLANY**
>
> In 2012, Fantasmic! introduced Glow with the Show technology that lit up enhanced **mouse ears** during the presentation.

Disneyland's **souvenir books** have justifiably touted the pioneering Fantasmic! experience as "one of the most complex and technically advanced shows ever presented." Just as the **Main Street Electrical Parade** reinvented nighttime entertainment in the 1970s, so too did Fantasmic! reinvent it in the 1990s.

Fantasy Faire

MAP: Hub, H-2

DATES: March 12, 2013–ongoing

For fifty-five years, the **Plaza Gardens** (aka Carnation Plaza Gardens) was a stylish entertainment venue in the **Hub**. This prime location next to **Sleeping Beauty Castle** finally closed in 2011; less than two years later, Fantasy Faire debuted. A medieval village square, a tower inspired by *Tangled*, a character meet-and-greet area, live entertainment, and interactive experiences all combine to make the half-acre Fantasy Faire one of Disneyland's biggest developments in years. **Tony Baxter** is credited as being one of the project leaders.

Five routes take guests to and from Fantasy Faire: from the **Frontierland** stockade; from the **Rancho del Zocalo** hallway; across a twenty-foot bridge from the **Hub**; across a thirty-foot bridge from the Hub that's closer to the castle; and via the **Sleeping Beauty Castle** west-side entrance/exit. Once they're in Fantasy Faire, guests are immersed in abundant activities from the world of fairytales. For live entertainment, Disney royalty meets guests in the Royal Hall, and two Renaissance storytellers present live, twenty-minute reenactments of Disney movies in the Royal Theatre. **Fairytale Treasures** is a well-themed gift shop, and an old-fashioned wagon called **Maurice's Treats** supplies tempting snacks. Especially charming in Fantasy Faire are the little touches, in-

cluding Clopin's Music Box (an interactive mechanical device) and an **Audio-Animatronic** Figaro who wakes up from a nap on a windowsill (shown).

While some Disneyland purists lamented the loss of the old Plaza Gardens, Fantasy Faire was instantly popular and has settled in as a worthy addition to Disneyland. Incidentally, its buildings and activities may be new, but the alliterative Fantasy Faire name isn't, having previously been used for a gift shop and the **Princess Fantasy Faire** area in **Fantasyland**.

Fantasy Faire Gifts,
aka Fantasy Shop, aka Fantasy Emporium, aka Fantasy Gift Faire

MAP: Fantasyland, Fa-9, Fa-16

DATES: Ca. 1955–ca. 1981; ca. 1996–ongoing

In Disneyland's early decades, a little gift shop shared a **Fantasyland** building with the **Mickey Mouse Club Theater**. At various times, park maps called it Fantasy Faire Gifts, the Fantasy Shop, Fantasyland Emporium, and Fantasy Gift Faire. Small and castle-themed, it lasted until the early 1980s, when a major renovation introduced Pinocchio designs and the Village Inn (now the **Village Haus**) restaurant.

After disappearing for over a decade, Fantasy Faire Gifts reopened near **It's a Small World** in the mid-1990s. Today's freestanding, open-air shop offers candy, small toys, and souvenirs.

> **MOUSCELLANY**
>
> Starting in the summer of 2013, the Royal Theatre welcomed the return of swing dancing with the Royal Swing Big Band Ball, a variation of the much-loved Jump, Jive, Boogie Swing Party that used to be held here back when this area was the Carnation Plaza Gardens (in 2015, the swing dancing continued on Saturday nights with music by Stompy Jones).

Fantasyland

MAP: Park, P-16

DATES: July 17, 1955–ongoing

Fantasyland fans may be surprised to know how fortress-like this charming land appeared at its inception. In 1953, ten months before construction began, **Herb Ryman** drew up a detailed sketch of Disneyland as envisioned by **Walt Disney**, who coached Ryman with ideas and instructions.

That landmark drawing depicts Fantasyland atop a high plateau. Imposing walls, turrets, and battlements form a ring around an enormous vertical castle in the center, making Fantasyland look more like a Fantasyempire. A crooked moat winds completely around the plateau's perimeter, isolating it from the rest of Disneyland. Other details are far less formidable, such as the carousel located in front of the castle.

A few months before Disneyland was built, Disney artists created a smaller study of a circular "Fantasy Land" that looks a little closer to what guests see today. The area stretches from a structure much like **Sleeping Beauty Castle** up to a big lagoon with an island in the middle. Some attractions on this revised map (a "Mother Goose Fun Thru," Nemo's submarine from *20,000 Leagues Under the Sea*, and an undefined attraction called Pinocchio Square) were never built. Another Fantasyland proposal that never materialized was Bruce Bushman's concept drawing of a Ferris wheel derived from the 1937 cartoon *The Old Mill*.

Clearly, Fantasyland went through many design changes, but one theme endured through all the revised plans: movies. More than any other Disneyland area, Fantasyland celebrates classic films. Within a few years of its opening, Fantasyland already included two *Dumbo* attractions (the airborne elephants and the **Casey Jr.** train); two *Alice in Wonderland* attractions (the indoor ride and the spinning teacups); **Mr. Toad's Wild Ride** from the 1949 film *The Adventures of Ichabod and Mr. Toad*; attractions echoing *Snow White*, *Peter Pan*, and *Sleeping Beauty*; and a theater that played Disney cartoons.

Walt Disney probably had several strategies in mind as he was infusing Fantasyland with his movies. Certainly the buildings and attractions would be marvelous ways to promote his films, including old favorites like *Snow White* and *Dumbo* and new additions like *Peter Pan* and *Sleeping Beauty*. More importantly, with so many attractions and lands—**Adventureland** and **Tomorrowland**, in particular—that were unfamiliar and overwhelming to 1955 guests who had never been to a theme park before, Walt Disney perhaps sensed that Fantasyland's familiar cartoon faces would be a welcome comfort. This same general strategy—acclimating and comforting guests before introducing them to the unfamiliar—most likely influenced the placement of **Main Street**, which eases guests into Disneyland with a stroll down a gentle, recognizable avenue before they stream off to strange new worlds.

In addition to this connection with Disney films, Fantasyland stirs up idyllic, dreamy memories of childhood fantasies—  including those of Walt Disney himself. "The world of make-believe has always delighted and absorbed me, ever since I was a little boy," he writes in the April 1953 issue of *Brief Magazine*. Disneyland literature emphasizes this collective memory of joyous childhood make-believe—the **souvenir books** have called Fantasyland "the happiest kingdom of them all," "a magic land that takes you back to childhood," and a "carefree kingdom" "where dreams could actually come true." Introducing Fantasyland on the ***Disneyland* TV series**, Disney declares that here you can do "anything your heart desires, because in this land hopes and dreams are all that matter." That's a whole lot of **happiness**, magic, make-believe, fantasy, delight, hope, heart, and nostalgia for a little six-acre area.

Unfortunately, twenty-eight years would pass before the Fantasyland Walt Disney had envisioned would actually be built. With

Opening Day approaching, time pressures and budget restrictions forced Disney to abandon his idea of uniting Fantasyland's attractions with old-fashioned village architecture. Instead, he had his artists create medieval-style façades for the attractions, and had banners and pennants installed along the roofs, an attempt to give Fantasyland the atmosphere of an Old World fair.

The medieval look would last for decades, but within a year of opening, some major changes were already arriving. Delightful **Storybook Land Canal Boats** replaced the dreary old **Canal Boats**, the scenic **Skyway to Fantasyland** drifted above the land, and the **Junior Autopia** cranked up to the east of it. A smaller **Midget Autopia** and the passageway to the **Sleeping Beauty Castle Walk-Through** opened in 1957. Two years later, Disneyland's tallest structure, **Matterhorn Mountain**, was completed, flanking Fantasyland near the new **Fantasyland Autopia**. Fantasyland expanded dramatically northward in 1966 when **It's a Small World** pushed past the train tracks and Disneyland's

> **MOUSCELLANY**
>
> With so much to look at in Fantasyland, it's easy to miss the charming spires and weathervanes atop some of the structures. Look up to see a golden crown (King Arthur Carrousel); a crocodile, a galleon, and a star (**Peter Pan's Flight**); a school of eight fish, a stork with a baby, and a whale (Pinocchio's Daring Journey); a compass (**Motor Boat Cruise** dock); Mr. Toad riding in a car (Mr. Toad's Wild Ride); and a rooster (Village Haus).

perimeter **berm**. What didn't change, however, was the cul-de-sac at Fantasyland's western edge (where the current **Village Haus** is located); in Fantasyland's early decades, **Dumbo the Flying Elephant** spun near here, and there was no open walkway that led to **Frontierland** the way the **Big Thunder Trail** did later.

In 1983, a massive $50 million remodel transformed the heart of Fantasyland into what Disney had originally visualized. Some old attractions were retired (the **Pirate Ship Restaurant**, **Skull Rock**, and the Fantasyland Theatre); others were relocated (Dumbo, the teacups, and the **King Arthur Carrousel**); tired attractions got facelifts and extensions that lengthened the rides (Mr. Toad, Snow White, Peter Pan, and Alice); and a new attraction was added (**Pinocchio's Daring Journey**). In addition, everything within the castle courtyard got a makeover to approximate the movies the attractions were based upon. Consequently, the exterior of Mr. Toad's building now really looks like his English manor, the Pinocchio building evokes Geppetto's alpine village, etc.

Disney's Fantasyland vision had finally come to life. He must have believed it eventually would—after all, according to a Fantasyland dedication plaque he created (but never placed in view), "Fantasyland is dedicated . . . to those who believe that when you wish upon a star, your dreams come true."

Fantasyland Autopia, aka Rescue Rangers Raceway

MAP: Fantasyland, Fa-22

DATES: January 1, 1959–September 7, 1999

An immediate hit when it debuted in 1955, Tomorrowland's **Autopia** remained so popular that three more Autopias soon followed it. After the smaller **Junior Autopia** and **Midget Autopia** were built for children, the Fantasyland Autopia for older drivers opened in 1959. With roadways spread across Disneyland's northeast corner, the new Fantasyland Autopia entrance was located north of **Matterhorn Mountain**.

Disneyland's **souvenir books** sometimes described this attraction as the Super Autopia Freeway with "the latest Mark V cars." Mark V was a reference to the fifth iteration of Autopia car design and matched what was running concurrently in Tomorrowland's Autopia nearby (ten-foot-long cars that weighed over half a ton and had a top speed of under eight miles per hour). In fact, from 1959 until 1991, the Fantasyland and Tomorrowland Autopias were almost identical in many ways, sharing sponsorship (Richfield Oil Corporation), similar layouts (the cars were side-by-side in some places), and prices (usually a C ticket from the Disneyland **ticket book**).

The biggest difference between the two Autopias came in March of 1991, when the Fantasyland version was briefly renamed the Rescue Rangers Raceway in accordance with a temporary re-theming that installed **Disney Afternoon Avenue** in **Fantasyland**. The Fantasyland Autopia name was restored eight months later and lasted until 1999, at which point the attraction was closed so it could be merged into Tomorrowland's heavily remodeled Autopia, Presented by Chevron.

Fantasyland Theatre, aka Videopolis

MAP: Fantasyland, Fa-18

DATES: June 22, 1985–October 2006; May 25, 2013–ongoing

When the indoor **Magic Eye Theater** replaced the outdoor Space Stage in 1986, Disneyland was left without a venue for large open-air concerts. Enter Videopolis, a $3 million, state-of-the-art concert area that opened in **Fantasyland** even before the Magic Eye was completed. Videopolis, the au courant name capitalizing on 1980s videocassette technology, was constructed near **It's a Small World** in under four months, opening in June of 1985. A new depot, the Videopolis Station, made the site accessible to train-traveling guests.

Catering to teenagers in its first decade and billed as "a musical kaleidoscope of sight and sound," Videopolis offered boisterous nighttime concerts by contemporary stars (for instance, Buster Poindexter, the raspy-voiced lounge lizard who had a hit with "Hot Hot Hot," appeared in 1988). Bands performed on a brilliantly lit stage in front of large dance areas totaling 5,000 square feet, a space larger than an NBA basketball court. Perimeter bleacher seats, light shows, special effects, big video screens, and seventy monitors around the dance area all combined to make concerts here as dazzling as those in any rock arena.

MOUSCELLANY

According to Barron and Pellman's *Cleaning the Kingdom*, the Videopolis area was previously called the Small World Meadows Amphitheatre, a little-used name that's barely mentioned in Disneyland's history.

They were just as loud, too, but fortunately the location up at Disneyland's northern boundary kept the noise far from guests in the rest of the park.

By the 1990s, with teens losing interest, the theater got 1,200 new first-come, first-served floor seats and a new purpose: instead of live concerts for dancin' teens, Disneyland tried out live stage shows for seated families. The results were so successful that in 1995, Videopolis received a more traditional theater name. Actually, its new Fantasyland Theatre name wasn't all that new—it had been applied to the **Mickey Mouse Club Theater** from 1964 to 1981 (the 1983 arrival of **Pinocchio's Daring Journey** in that building made the theatrical name available).

The Spirit of Pocahontas was the debut stage show for the revived Fantasyland Theatre. Shows usually lasted one or two years and became increasingly spectacular. *Snow White: An Enchanting Musical* boasted Patrick Stewart as the voice of the Magic Mirror, elaborate sets, and a Broadway production team. Late in 2006, the theater finally closed and was reinvented as a new area called the **Princess Fantasy Faire**. After six years of princesses, the space closed and reopened on May 25, 2013, as the Fantasyland Theatre once again. The new twenty-two-minute show is an energetic,

high-tech musical called *Mickey and the Magical Map* (shown), a crowd-pleaser that has been praised as a triumph in mixed-media presentations.

Fashions and Fabrics Through the Ages

MAP: Tomorrowland, T-23

DATES: March 1965–December 1965

To keep up with the styles of the future, guests need to understand the styles of the past. Or so it seemed in 1965, when **Tomorrowland** welcomed a fashion exhibit, of all things, into its pantheon of unusual displays. Like its neighbors, the **Bathroom of Tomorrow** and the **Hall of Aluminum Fame**, Fashions and Fabrics Through the Ages was an industrial show added to promote a sponsor—in this case, the formidable multibillion-dollar Monsanto chemical company, founded in 1901.

Lasting only nine months in 1965, Fashions and Fabrics was the shortest-lived of Monsanto's four Disneyland attractions and exhibits (the others were the **Hall of Chemistry**, the **House of the Future**, and **Adventure Thru Inner Space**). The new exhibit was adjacent to the Hall of Chemistry in the first right-hand building inside the Tomorrowland entrance. The fashions on view were all women's garments, most of them historical, shown in wall displays or on mannequins. Ragged animal skins worn by cavewomen led to the exotic attire of ancient Egypt and Renaissance Europe and finally to the fine dresses of the eighteenth, nineteenth, and twentieth centuries. The exhibit culminated with synthetic spacewear, which dovetailed nicely with the chemical advances being showcased in the Monsanto hall next door.

At the end of 1965, the Monsanto fashion exhibit was removed in preparation for 1967's **Adventure Thru Inner Space**.

FASTPASS

Already a triumph in Walt Disney World and Disneyland Paris and already tested in Disneyland in July of 1999, the FASTPASS ticketing system officially began in Anaheim on November 19, 1999, just in time for Thanksgiving. The first attraction to get a FASTPASS ticket distribution machine was **It's a Small World**. Soon many of Disneyland's other top attractions—**Space Mountain**, **Splash Mountain**, etc.—had their own FASTPASS machines, and guests happily took advantage of them to avoid standing in lines.

Anyone who has ever waited two hours for a busy attraction can appreciate how advantageous FASTPASS reservations are. All a guest has to do is show up at the popular attraction of his choice and insert his park admission ticket or annual pass into the accompanying FASTPASS machine. He'll then receive a free FASTPASS ticket that will allow him to bypass the regular line and board more quickly when he returns during the one-hour window designated on the ticket.

However, the lineup of FASTPASS attractions changes throughout the year; new attractions are occasionally added to meet demand, and even some of the entertainment (such as **Fantasmic!**) has had its own FASTPASS machines. The system doesn't always work perfectly, especially when overwhelming crowds form a FASTPASS line alongside the regular line. Normally, each guest is allowed to obtain only one ticket at a time and must wait for the designated time to arrive before getting another one (occasionally there are exceptions to this policy—when **Buzz Lightyear Astro Blasters** re-started its FASTPASS distribution in August of 2015, guests could also get FASTPASS tickets for other attractions without waiting to use their Buzz tickets). Disneyland closed a loophole in 2013 by enforcing the times shown on FASTPASS tickets; no longer can a guest show up at a busy attraction hours after her FASTPASS reservation window has opened and expect to jump ahead of the line. Instead, she must now use her FASTPASS ticket only during that one-hour reservation window, or the ticket becomes invalid.

Typically, FASTPASS does enable guests to move rapidly through the crowded queue of a popular attraction. Even more benefits will be available when a new fee-based digital MaxPass service arrives in 2017. For Disney, a big advantage to both FASTPASS and MaxPass is that guests who normally would have spent hours idly waiting in lines now have free time for shopping and dining until their reservation windows open.

The FASTPASS system has been so successful that the amusement park industry lauded it with a Breakthrough Innovation award in 2001. *The Simpsons* even acknowledge the FASTPASS advantage in an April 2015 episode. At the Disneyland-like Itchy &

Scratchy Land, Bart complains that he's only been on two rides and is advised that he "should've used FASTPASS." Bart retorts, "FASTPASS can't solve *everything*," but he's told that his words are "spoken like a kid who's never lived in a non-FASTPASS world."

Festival Arena

MAP: Frontierland, Fr-19

DATES: June 1996–January 10, 2016

For two decades, the stage and outdoor seating area behind **Big Thunder Ranch** hosted various special events. In 1996, the Festival of Fools show coincided with the release of a new Disney movie, *The Hunchback of Notre Dame*. In early 2011, **Family Fun Weekends** filled the space with outdoor activities, and that spring's pre- miere of *Pirates of the Caribbean: On Stranger Tides* inspired pirate-themed celebrations. Only then did the performance area get an official name: Festival Arena.

The closing of the **Plaza Gardens** in April 2012 brought a new rush of diverse activities. Starting on May 3 of that year, the **Big Thunder Ranch Jamboree** presented country-and-western music, dancing, and crafts. Further- more, the school bands and community choirs that used to appear at the Plaza Gar- dens began performing here. Later in 2012, **Halloween Time** brought a new seasonal carnival with the Conjure a Villain sideshow and magic tricks; for the fall seasons of

2013 and 2014, the **Pirates League** sailed in with buccaneer costumes and accessories. Springtime Roundup, a new Easter event with Disney charac- ters (shown), crafts, colorful hand-painted eggs, and a hot dog cart called Chuck Wagon Delights ran daily in 2014 from March 28 to April 20, and again in 2015 from March 20 to April 18 (plus weekends until June 7). In mid-2014, a show called *The Music of Nashville* featuring the Kelly Rae Band celebrated country music.

Spring of 2015 brought in the red, white, and blue All-American Roundup, but no Halloween activities appeared here in September of that year. The Festival Arena was permanently lost when the whole Big Thunder Ranch area was demolished in early 2016 to make way for **Star Wars Land**.

50th Anniversary Shop

MAP: Fantasyland, Fa-3

DATES: May 5, 2005–November 2006

Concurrent with the celebrations planned for Disneyland's fiftieth birthday, in 2005 the **Princess Boutique** in **Fantasyland** transformed into the 50th Anniversary Shop. The location was the same—inside the **Sleeping Beauty Castle** entrance—but the merchandise switched from princess accoutrements to fiftieth anniversary souvenirs, including some collectibles sold here exclusively. Once the partying subsided, the shop reopened as **Tinker Bell & Friends** in 2006.

Fine Tobacco

MAP: Main Street, MS-19

DATES: July 17, 1955–June 1, 1990

For its first thirty-five years, Disneyland squeezed a genuine tobacco shop between the **Main Street Magic Shop** and the **Main Street Cinema**. A tobacco shop would have been a natural component of any small-town street at the turn of the century, so an establishment that sold international brands of cigarettes, cigars, and pipes was an authentic addition to Disneyland's **Main Street**. Just as authentic was the wooden statue of an American Indian out front. In the nineteenth and twentieth centuries, a cigar store Indian was a traditional symbol for smoking and smoke shops (witness the giant Indian-shaped machines dispensing stogies along Tobacco Row in 1940's *Pinocchio*).

Many items in Disneyland's shop had park logos on them, and there was also a special Disney tobacco available (during his last decades **Walt Disney**, a heavy smoker, preferred the Gitanes brand, imported from France). In a nod to tradition, Fine Tobacco handed out complimentary matchbooks with stylish designs, including depictions of the shop's exterior and an old-fashioned lamppost. Cigarettes were sold at other park locations, too, among them **Ursus H. Bear's Wilderness Outpost** in **Bear Country** and the **Character Shop** in **Tomorrowland**.

In the politically correct 1990s, however, tobacco's days were numbered. Fine Tobacco closed at the beginning of the decade, replaced by the **Patented Pastimes** collectibles shop and later the **20th Century Music Company** store. Sale of tobacco elsewhere in Disneyland concluded by century's end, and within a few years the designated smoking areas were dwindling (in mid-2015 there were only two—one near the **Matterhorn** and the other near the **Sailing Ship *Columbia***).

Even though Fine Tobacco is long gone, the memory of it isn't. The shop's location is still noted by the nameless cigar store Indian that continues to stand watch in his usual place along Main Street, just as he has since 1955.

Fire Department, aka Fire Station

MAP: Town Square, TS-5

DATES: July 17, 1955–ongoing

An attractive, two-story brick building trimmed in white stone, the Fire Department (or Fire Station) has stood proudly next to **City Hall** since **Opening Day**. However, though it may look authentic, and though it certainly adds atmosphere to the old-fashioned **Town Square**, the Fire Department has never actually been used to fight fires. Really it's more of a museum, and thus it's filled with displays. Of these, the most conspicuous is the horse-drawn fire engine (Disneyland's **souvenir books** have also dubbed it "an old-time hose and chemical wagon"). This beautifully appointed red wagon was one of the original **Main Street Vehicles** that cost only an A ticket for a ride to the **Hub**.

In mid-1960, this wagon was withdrawn from service and permanently parked inside the Fire Department, where it has stayed on view alongside actual firefighting equipment, a pot-belly stove, and antique fire extinguishers. The horses that once pulled the wagon were moved to Disneyland's **Pony Farm**, but their Fire Department stalls remain intact and are still adorned with the names Bess and Jess—the building's first equine employees.

Upstairs and off-limits to the public is a private **apartment** for **Walt Disney** and his family; the lamp in the window (shown) is kept lit as a tribute to the man Disneyland is named after. Also off-limits is Disneyland's real fire department, located behind the **Opera House** on the opposite side of **Town Square**.

Firehouse Five Plus Two

The rollicking septet known as the Firehouse Five Plus Two was a summertime staple at Disneyland for fifteen years. The group traveled all over the park, playing in **Town Square**, inside the **Golden Horseshoe**, on the streets of **New Orleans Square**, and in **parades**. Their signature look was a fireman's outfit—a bright red shirt, white suspenders, and an authentic fire helmet—and their signature sound was guest-friendly Dixieland jazz punctuated by bells, whistles, and sirens.

As with the **Dapper Dans**, membership varied during the group's career. Among the longtime players were Danny Alguire (cornet), **George Bruns** (tuba), **Harper Goff** (banjo), Ward Kimball (trombone, and the band's leader), Johnny Lucas (trumpet), Clarke Mallery (clarinet), Monte Mountjoy (drums), Erdman Penner (tuba), George Probert (saxophone), Dick Roberts (banjo), and Frank Thomas (piano). Kimball and Thomas were two of the famed Nine Old Men, the legendary animation team nicknamed by **Walt Disney**.

The Firehouse Five Plus Two formed in the late 1940s as a lunchtime, after-work, and weekend hobby for a few Disney animators and technicians. For their early performances at parties, they went by the names Huggajeedy Eight and then the San Gabriel Valley Blue Blowers. In 1949, the group developed its good-time firehouse theme, complete with an old fire engine for photos. In 1950, the guys got major exposure on the *One Hour in Wonderland* TV special hosted by Walt Disney; the introduction identifies them as "the most famous new band in the country," and they're shown working at their drawing boards before they suddenly don their fire hats, pick up their instruments, and break into three rollicking minutes of "Jingle Bells."

During the 1950s, the Firehouse Five Plus Two performed live on TV variety shows, on radio shows, and in nightclubs (the group would arrive at gigs in a fire engine). The FF+2 also got significant airtime when it was featured in the 1955 *Dateline Disneyland* TV special, which introduced the nation to the newly completed park; presented as "probably the most famous little Dixieland band in the world," the group proceeded to put on a lively show in **Frontierland.**

Additionally, the group recorded a dozen albums throughout the 1950s and '60s. One of them, 1962's *At Disneyland*, was recorded live at the Golden Horseshoe. The songs include numerous popular stomps and rags, and the CD cover shows the boys hamming it up while sitting in the **Fantasyland** teacups.

The Firehouse Five Plus Two recorded its last album in 1970 and disbanded a year later. The firehouse-jazz tradition has been taken up by the Hook and Ladder Company, a sextet that often plays in front of the **Fire Department.**

MOUSCELLANY

Disney's *The Great Mouse Detective* (1986) includes a nifty little tribute to the Firehouse Five Plus Two. About twenty-nine minutes into the movie, there's a wind-up toy of a frantic four-piece jazz band all dressed in firehouse gear. Since there are only four musicians, the emblem on the front of the toy reads "5-1." Additionally, the jazz band at the end of *The Princess and the Frog* (2009) is called the Firehouse Five + Lou.

Fireworks

Starting in 1954, episodes of the ***Disneyland* TV series** began with an animation of fireworks exploding over the park. However, Disneyland itself didn't actually have this pyrotechnic ability until the summer of 1957. According to *Disneyland: The Nickel Tour*, the fireworks were the brainstorm of entertainment director **Tommy Walker**, who was trying to entice guests to linger at Disneyland for dinner.

Disneyland's first fireworks show was called Fantasy in the Sky, launched by pyrotechnicians from the northern area, where **Mickey's Toontown** would eventually be built (Toontown now closes early so the fireworks can launch safely). When they debuted, the beautiful bursts of kaleidoscopic color, synchronized to music and visible in some Anaheim neighborhoods, were state of the art. Disneyland's **souvenir books** were quick to show off the fireworks with dazzling photos and text about the "cascade" of effects and "shower of color." The captions also noted how the appearance of **Tinker Bell** drew "the curtain on daytime fun" by "shining the footlights on nighttime magic." Tink, actually a seventy-one-year-old female circus aerialist named Tiny Kline, joined the fireworks show in 1961.

In the twenty-first century, the fireworks show was given a new theme and renamed several times with ever-present ellipses: Believe . . . There's Magic in the Stars (2000); Believe . . . In Holiday Magic (2000); Imagine . . . A Fantasy in the Sky (2004); and Remember . . . Dreams Come True (2005). These later shows added narration, new moves for Tinker Bell, and the most complex, expensive pyrotechnics yet. In a nostalgic nod to past glories, the original Fantasy in the Sky show returned briefly in 2005 and 2006 for several special events, and it came back again on weekends starting in September 2016. Themed fireworks are also presented on Halloween, during the winter holidays, and for Independence Day (Disney's Celebrate America! A Fourth of July Concert in the Sky was introduced in 2008).

New gimmicks are occasionally added to enhance the fireworks. The 2012 winter holiday fireworks incorporated Glow with the Show technology that lighted special wearable **mouse ears** in sync with the presentation (in 2014, the line of "glow" merchandise expanded to include oversize gloves, headbands, and wands). Starting in 2009, the Magical fireworks sent Dumbo and other flying characters aloft as part of the show. The **Diamond Celebration** begun in 2015 introduced a new spectacular called Disneyland Forever that not only exploded incredible fireworks, but also splashed vibrant moving projections onto **Matterhorn Mountain**, **It's a Small World**, and **Main Street** buildings, with a new **Richard Sherman** song called "A Kiss Goodnight" playing as a soothing finale.

Some of the fireworks shows have been memorialized with special tributes. Four shows have gotten their own **attraction posters**: Fantasy in the Sky (shown), Magical, Remember . . . Dreams Come True, and Disneyland Forever. And samples of fireworks music have made it onto Disney recordings. The Fantasy in the Sky music is on *Walt Disney Records: The Official Album* (1997), while the music of the twenty-first-century fireworks shows appears on later CD collections of park-related songs.

The show's schedule has stayed fairly uniform. The total presentation can last about fifteen to thirty minutes (though we watched truncated shows barely five minutes long in 2015). Typically, 200-plus firework shells are launched every night in the summer and on weekend nights year-round, with a total of

Disneyland
FIREWORKS SPECTACULAR

about 250 shows per year (occasionally there are two shows a night). A mural on a **Frontierland** wall reminds viewers all day long what to expect at night: "Laod Bhang."

First Aid and Lost Children

MAP: Town Square, TS-4; Hub, H-4

DATES: 1955–ongoing

Back in 1955, the facilities for First Aid and Lost Children were both headquartered in **City Hall**. An old park map pinpoints the specific location and offers descriptions of the two services: "A doctor and registered nurses are always in attendance" at the former, and "experienced attendants" "maintain a special playground" at the latter.

Starting in 1958, Disneyland's **souvenir books** placed the First Aid and Lost Children rooms on the eastern side of the **Hub**. To alleviate guests' anxieties, an early First Aid sign depicted a cartoon Alice (wearing a nurse's hat) and the White Rabbit attending to guests, with Pluto looking on; the sign for Lost Children showed various Disney characters leading kids to safety.

These days, the First Aid sign offers no cartoon graphics—just sedate text and a red cross. First Aid is in its own building near the **Plaza Inn**. For almost six decades, this one-story building had a spartan exterior, as if to make it inconspicuous. Then, while there was construction nearby from July to October 2014, First Aid temporarily relocated to the **Locker Area** space at the eastern end of **Center Street** formerly occupied by Main Street Lockers & Storage; when First Aid returned to its Hub home, its building had two stories and was beautifully remodeled with an old-fashioned theme consistent with **Main Street**. As always, inside First Aid are registered nurses who treat injuries, dispense aspirin, and offer anti-nausea remedies. There are also rooms with beds for a short rest, and refrigerators for guests to store their medications. Most medical matters are pretty routine; blisters are still the primary malady.

First Aid used to share its building with the Lost Children area, but what was formerly the kids' space is now the Wish Lounge served by the Make-A-Wish Foundation. Disneyland has had a special relationship with the Make-A-Wish Foundation since 1980, the year the first wish—a visit to the park—was granted to a boy with a life-threatening medical condition. Since then, over 100,000 children's Disney-related wishes have been granted. (Not surprisingly, wish #100,000, which was granted in October of 2015, was to visit Disneyland.)

Today's Lost Children room is actually a subsection of the **Baby Care Center** next to the **Main Street Photo Supply Co.** Here children have an attractive waiting area where they are tended to by **cast members** and shown Disney books and movies to pass the time.

Flagpole

MAP: Town Square, TS-6

DATES: July 17, 1955–ongoing

Since **Opening Day**, a flagpole has been located in the center of **Town Square**. But that wasn't the original plan. **Walt Disney** intended to place an old-fashioned **bandstand** in this spot—in fact, one was briefly installed there. However, just days before the park officially opened, Disney realized that the gazebo-like structure blocked guests' views of **Sleeping Beauty Castle** from the train station. Disney relocated the bandstand to the **Hub** and had a stately sixty-five-foot-tall flagpole erected in its place.

Today, the flags of the United States and California fly from the top of the flagpole and are occasionally lowered to half-mast—for September 11 observances, for example. Interesting details add some colorful history to the flagpole area. Surrounded by a twenty-five-foot-wide flower bed, the ornate base was supposedly rescued by **Emile Kuri** from an electric light pole that had been knocked down in a car accident. Two authentic nineteenth-century French army cannons are positioned in the surrounding garden. Seating around the flagpole is provided by old restored park benches from San Francisco. A respectful, patriotic flag-lowering ceremony usually attended by the **Disneyland Band** or the **Dapper Dans** is held daily around dusk (**City Hall** provides the specific times). Disney characters also frequent this area for meet-and-greet visits.

On the flagpole's base is a plaque that quotes Walt Disney's Opening Day dedication speech:

MOUSCELLANY

This isn't the only flagpole erected at Disneyland. In the 1950s, flags for every state decorated the **Court of Honor** and the **Avenue of the Flags**, and for decades a flagpole stood in the center of **Fort Wilderness** on **Tom Sawyer Island**. Today's guests can find additional flagpoles throughout Disneyland, including several in **Frontierland** (inside the entrance, at the *Mark Twain* Riverboat dock, and above the **Golden Horseshoe**), in **New Orleans Square** (such as one on top of **Pirates of the Caribbean**), and more around Town Square (on top of **City Hall**, the **Fire Department**, and the train station).

DISNEYLAND

TO ALL WHO COME TO THIS HAPPY PLACE:

—WELCOME—

DISNEYLAND IS YOUR LAND.

HERE AGE RELIVES FOND MEMORIES

OF THE PAST . . . AND HERE YOUTH MAY SAVOR

THE CHALLENGE AND PROMISE OF THE FUTURE.

DISNEYLAND IS DEDICATED

TO THE IDEALS, THE DREAMS, AND THE HARD

FACTS WHICH HAVE CREATED AMERICA . . . WITH THE

HOPE THAT IT WILL BE A SOURCE OF JOY

AND INSPIRATION TO ALL THE WORLD.

JULY 17, 1955

Flight Circle, aka Thimble Drome Flight Circle

MAP: Tomorrowland, T-21

DATES: September 4, 1955–January 1966

The Flight Circle was a free exhibit that opened about two months after the rest of Disneyland. Located in the plaza area in front of the *Moonliner* rocket, the exhibit's paved circle was about seventy-five feet in diameter, had the four compass points marked in the center, and was surrounded by a chain-link fence. Guests stood behind this fence to watch demonstrations of motorized model planes, cars, and boats. (Most of the planes whirled around in a circle, controlled by an operator holding a long cable.) Model-plane manufacturer Wen-Mac (the original partners were name Wenland and McRoskey) was the first sponsor; Cox Manufacturing, a ten-year-old company that constructed a line of Thimble Drome model vehicles that burned Thimble Drome "glow fuel," assumed sponsorship in 1957 and renamed the exhibit the Thimble Drome Flight Circle (the boats motored around a small pond nearby).

Anyone who heard the loud, droning planes can attest to their annoying noise, but somehow the exhibit proved popular enough to stay in operation for over a decade. An illustrious moment came when the **Rocket Man** took off from this spot in late 1965. A few months later, most of Tomorrowland was closed for major remodeling. Eventually some of the Flight Circle real estate became a walkway, and part of it was transformed into the **PeopleMover's** loading area.

Flight to the Moon

MAP: Tomorrowland, T-16

DATES: August 12, 1967–January 5, 1975

The original **Rocket to the Moon** in **Tomorrowland** took guests on simulated lunar flights from July 1955 to September 1966. After closing for a major refurbishment, the attraction opened the following summer with a new sponsor (McDonnell-Douglas, replacing Douglas Aircraft), a new ticket price (D instead of C), a new neighbor (the **Carousel of Progress**), and a dramatic new presentation.

The updated Flight to the Moon simulator basically worked the same way as its predecessor by showing a receding Earth on one screen and an approaching moon on another. But the new journey was more authentic. In addition to accommodating more guests, the attraction boasted better effects inside the ship (including a brief moment of weightlessness), and offered views of astronauts on the moon.

Even more impressive was a new pre-launch Mission Control area. Previously, the pre-flight area had been confined to a plain room where a short film was shown; now it was a complex, computer-lined area populated with eight **Audio-Animatronic** scientists. This busy team was headed by a sophisticated A-A character named Tom Morrow, Director of Mission Control. Morrow described the ready-to-launch Lunar Transport Flight 92 and directed guests to look at wall monitors and catch humorous footage of a supposed UFO that turned out to be a clumsy incoming bird. As ambitious as the Flight to the Moon update was, it still fell short of the bold concept illustration sketched out by artist Bill Bosche, who had originally depicted the flight heading to Saturn and beyond.

Two years after it debuted, the Flight to the Moon was superseded by the real drama of Apollo 11. As scenes of actual astronauts walking, driving a lunar rover, and even swinging a golf club on the moon became more commonplace in the 1970s, attendance for Disneyland's lunar flight began to dwindle, leading to 1975's new and improved **Mission to Mars.** Flight to the Moon's Tom Morrow became a featured character in **Innoventions**, and **Redd Rockett's Pizza Port** now serves meals in the spot where Flight to the Moon once launched its guests.

Flower Mart, aka Flower Market

MAP: Main Street, MS-5, MS-17.

DATES: 1957–ca. 1995; December 6, 2013–January 2014; June 2015; October 2015–January 2016

If Disneyland had sold fresh-cut flowers, they wouldn't have lasted long in the California sunshine or survived a whirl on the teacups. Fortunately, artificial flowers could do both. In 1957, Disneyland added the beautiful little Flower Mart, or Flower Market, to the **Main Street** neighborhood.

"The world's finest natural flowers not grown by nature" were sold out of open-air, wheeled carts in two different locations. Originally, the Flower Mart was located on the western side of **Center Street**. The plastic posies remained there until the

Carnation Ice Cream Parlor on the corner expanded into the western side of Center Street in 1977, sending the flower carts across the way to the eastern side of the street, where **portrait artists** had once set up their easels. In its heyday, over a dozen different blooms were available for sale, even through the mail.

The Flower Market vanished quietly in the mid-1990s. Surprisingly, lovely carts filled with artificial flowers and seasonal plants reappeared on the eastern side of Center for 2013's winter holidays. Real and artificial flowers then went on display in June of 2015, and again that October. The October flowers introduced a new floral archway leading into the area (shown). A winter update added holiday lights, and by the spring of 2016, there were bright, sunny blooms. Although none of them were for sale, the pretty flowers added festive color and nostalgic memories to this cozy side street.

Flying Saucers

MAP: Tomorrowland, T-18

DATES: August 8, 1961–September 5, 1966

Showing more ambition than practicality, Disneyland debuted a unique, space-age bumper car ride in mid-1961. UFOs had been a hot topic throughout the 1950s, when sightings headlined newspapers and bug-eyed Martians invaded America's drive-in movie screens. Thus the time seemed right for Flying Saucers to invade Disneyland.

Disneyland's promotional literature played up the attraction: "Fly Your Own Flying Saucer" at the "Space Terminal," touts the **attraction poster**; "Each guest pilots his own ship in free flight," announces the 1961 **souvenir book**; "Space travel" at a "space station," captions the 1962 book for its Flying Saucers photo; "Choose a 'flight pattern' . . . and away you go," exhorts the 1965 book. All intriguing descriptions, to be sure. In reality, Disneyland's Flying Saucers probably should have been called the Hovering Saucers. Operating in a circular, open-air platform that covered a third of an acre next to **Rocket to the Moon**, the **Bob Gurr**-designed saucers were small, one-seat hovercraft six feet in diameter.

MOUSCELLANY

In 2012, forty-five years after Disneyland's Flying Saucers closed, Disney executives resurrected the saucer concept when they opened Luigi's Flying Tires in Disney California Adventure. Once again, "flying" felt like a misnomer, and the lumbering attraction closed within three years.

Like disks on a giant air-hockey table, the saucers became airborne when they were lifted up by high-powered jets of air generated by large motors under the platform. When they hovered successfully, the sixty-four saucers (two fleets of thirty-two) could lift several inches off the ground. Though they had no controls—only handles—inside their cockpits, the saucers could be steered independently by guests, who only had to lean to dip their saucers in any direction, and even into other saucers for some bumper-bashing.

Unfortunately, persistent problems with the air jets led to lots of ground time for the E-ticket attraction. Body weight was an issue; lightweight guests couldn't get their saucers to dip, while some heavier guests couldn't get off the ground. Other guests occasionally turned their saucers completely over. Too often, guests couldn't go anywhere because the whole system would shut itself down.

Some 5 million pilots gave the saucers a test flight, but after five years of headaches and extremely loud noise, Disney designers finally grounded the troublesome ride in 1966 and remodeled the whole area as the **Tomorrowland Stage** in 1967.

Fortuosity Shop

MAP: Main Street, MS-4

DATES: October 3, 2008–ongoing

The prime corner location on Main Street that was once the **Upjohn Pharmacy** and then **New Century Watches & Clocks** became the Fortuosity Shop in 2008. Named after a sanguine song from the 1967 Disney movie *The Happiest Millionaire*, the classy space offers "fashion accessories," according to the nearby map of the **Emporium** and its adjacent shops. Actually, the recent merchandise is very similar to what's found in **Le Bat en Rouge**, which means ladies' tops, hats, and bags. A smaller side room presents rings, bracelets, and cameos.

Until October of 2012, the shop offered customized Disney watches hand-painted by artists who sat at the front window; in 2013, the **cast members** here assembled the watches, rather than painting them. For 2015's **Diamond Celebration**, Fortuosity offered special diamond-studded wristwatches for $1,000. The abundant seasonal theming in this store (especially during **Halloween Time**) can be delightful and is definitely worth a look.

Fort Wilderness

MAP: Frontierland, Fr-16

DATES: June 16, 1956–2003

Tom Sawyer Island has had various structures spread across its three acres, from Lafitte's Tavern at the southern end to the burning cabin that stood at the northern end some 800 feet away. The island's biggest building is one that's been closed since 2003: Fort Wilderness, a two-story log structure that evokes the American frontier in the War of 1812, which was the era the fort and its fifteen-star flag were meant to represent. The original wood fort is long gone, demolished in 2007 and rebuilt; it's open now only to **cast members**, many of whom perform in the nightly **Fantasmic!** shows.

The size and exterior shape of the new structure are basically the same as those of the old one. Located north of the island's center, the fort covers about 3,000 square feet; for comparison, two Fort Wildernesses could fit side by side in **Town Square**. According to *Disneyland: The First Quarter Century*, the original fort was constructed "from logs hewed by hand and trucked in from local mountains. The timber was floated across the '**Rivers of America**' and hoisted up to dry land, where it was assembled." Approached today from the south, guests confront two blockhouses bracketing a tall locked gate that's marked by a Fort Wilderness sign. Towering wood walls hide the interior, though a guest **restroom** can be found on the fort's east side.

The fort has a proud, prominent place on the 1957 Tom Sawyer Island map drawn by **Sam McKim**—a large flag flies above the fort, smoking rifles point westward from the blockhouses, gates are swung open invitingly, and the caption identifies the fort as "Regimental Hdqr.'s Maj. Gen. Andr. Jackson & Davy Crockett." On the new map updated in 2007, when the island was recast as Pirate's Lair on Tom Sawyer Island, the closed fort is shrouded in trees, only the very tops of the blockhouses are visible, and the adjacent caption reads, "Uncharted Lands."

In its heyday, Fort Wilderness was a much-visited center of island activity. It usually got the same photo in Disneyland's **souvenir books**—a cast member dressed like a nineteenth-century cavalry soldier helping a young guest take aim from inside a blockhouse, where "rifle practice is the order of the day." Inside the fort was an open, dirt-covered central courtyard marked by a tall flagpole. Along the western wall were a small Canteen and Trading Post for snacks and souvenirs; adding historical interest along the eastern wall

MOUSCELLANY

Guests exiting Fort Wilderness could take a "secret" passageway that led from the fort's northeast corner down to the trails on the island's eastern shore. In case guests couldn't find it, a conspicuous sign marked the passageway as the "Secret Escape Tunnel to the River."

was a frontier-themed room that displayed Davy Crockett and Andrew Jackson mannequins reused from the **Davy Crockett Frontier Museum**. Stairs led to an open walkway on the second floor that circled the fort's interior. Lookout towers on the corners provided views of the river and offered real-looking rifles that delivered bulletless bangs.

The fort has been the site of some unfortunate history. Chanting **Yippie Day** protesters invaded Fort Wilderness in 1970 and briefly replaced the Stars and Stripes with their own flag, forcing Disney officials to suspend raft trips to the island. A 2001 accident in which a young guest was injured while holding one of the blockhouse rifles led to the rifle areas being sealed off. Nevertheless, the inaccessible fort still stands with tantalizing potential as a future destination for new discoveries.

40 Pounds of Trouble Film

The first major movie to be filmed in Disneyland was made not by Disney, but by Universal Pictures. Released in 1962, *40 Pounds of Trouble* is a light family comedy starring Tony Curtis and Suzanne Pleshette. The nineteen minutes of sunny Disneyland scenes include aerial footage, a ride on the **Matterhorn Bobsleds**, and extinct park attractions like the **Skyway**. However, even more notable are the scenes with blatant fabrications. For instance, the film's **Monorail** drops passengers at **Town Square**, and guests who board **Peter Pan's Flight** also get to go through **Mr. Toad's Wild Ride** and **Snow White's Scary Adventures** on the same ride. While it's silly fun, the movie can rightly claim to be one of the few ever filmed inside Disneyland.

40 Years of Adventure

DATES: 1995

Disneyland had a lot to celebrate in 1995, and celebrate it did with its wide-ranging 40 Years of Adventure promotion. Back then, **Mickey's Toontown** still felt new, the 1994 blockbuster *The Lion King* was winning Oscars, the Lion King Celebration was packing **Main Street** by day, and the **Main Street Electrical Parade** was still running

MOUSCELLANY

Here are ten more films that feature Disneyland (minutes of park footage are in parentheses): *The Boys*, a Disney-produced celebration of the **Sherman Brothers'** lives and music, 2009 (three minutes); Disney's *A Day at Disneyland*, in which characters frolic in the park, 1982 (forty minutes); *Disneyland Fun: It's a Small World*, a Disney sing-along video, 1990 (twenty-nine minutes); *Disneyland Resort: Behind the Scenes*, Lightship Entertainment's engaging documentary, 2003 (fifty-two minutes); *Disneyland, U.S.A.*, a Disney featurette, 1956 (forty-two minutes); *Exit Through the Gift Shop*, Banksy's Oscar-nominated documentary, 2010 (six minutes); *Gala Day at Disneyland*, a Disney featurette, 1960 (twenty-seven minutes); *The Magic of Disneyland*, a Disney documentary (twenty-one minutes); Disney's *Saving Mr. Banks* with Tom Hanks as Walt Disney, 2013 (five minutes); and *That Thing You Do!*, Tom Hanks' Oscar-nominated feature film for 20th Century Fox, 1996 (fifteen seconds).

at night. Best of all, 1995 welcomed the debut of the biggest single attraction since 1989's **Splash Mountain**—the landmark **Indiana Jones Adventure**. Indy's exciting arrival was heralded with a TV special in March, bold emblems on the 1995 **Fun Map** and **souvenir book**, and a new gift shop (the **Indiana Jones Adventure Outpost**) showcasing 40 Years of Adventure merchandise. Additionally, a unique "time castle" was buried in front of **Sleeping Beauty Castle** on July 17, the fortieth anniversary of **Opening Day**. Over at the Tomorrowland Terrace, a fun-filled musical show called the Magic Kingdom Kabaret presented a loose retelling of Disneyland's history.

Fourth of July

Some of Disneyland's seasonal events were created to draw crowds to what would otherwise be off-season months with lower **attendance. Halloween Time**, for instance, offers an October full of activities and special décor that attracts guests between Labor Day and Thanksgiving. Since Independence Day falls in the heart of the busy summer season, Disneyland has never had to promote it much—guests will come to the park in July, whether there's a Fourth of July celebration or not.

Many new attractions have debuted at Disneyland in early July. Opening between July 1 and July 4 in various years were the Indian War Canoes and **Rainbow Caverns Mine Train** (1956); the **Primeval World** (1966); the **Carousel of Progress, People-Mover, Rocket Jets**, and **Tomorrowland Terrace** (1967); **Aladdin's Oasis** (1993); The Lion King Celebration **parade** (1994); and **Innoventions** (1998).

But Independence Day itself draws the most attention in July. That Disneyland would celebrate this most patriotic of holidays is no surprise, of course. "Disneyland will be based upon and dedicated to the ideals, the dreams, and hard facts that have created America," says **Walt Disney** in *The Quotable Walt Disney*. "Disneyland will be the essence of America as we know it." Consequently, American history and pageantry have been on display in Disneyland since its inception. A quick scan of just a few events and attractions (**America on Parade, America Sings**, and **Great Moments with Mr. Lincoln**, for example) shows how pervasively patriotic Disneyland has always been.

Typically, red, white, and blue (or blue-and-white) bunting arrives in late spring (and stays up all summer). Also, red, white, and blue blooms are planted in flower beds, and red, white, and blue cupcakes and other treats start appearing in display cases. As the Fourth nears, special holiday **fireworks** are usually set off for several nights (seven nights in 2013 for that year's **Limited Time Magic** program, but only single nights in 2015 and 2016 with the addition of a "patriotic finale" to the usual Disneyland Forever fireworks show). Additionally, Disneyland presents live music performances by different military groups and honor guards in various locations (2016 brought a special one-performance-only concert to the **Fantasyland Theatre** on the Fourth).

Attendance-wise, the results have sometimes been spectacular: one of Disneyland's busiest days ever came on July 4, 1987, when an estimated 85,000 guests visited Disneyland (almost double the daily average). The real surprise is that such extreme numbers aren't achieved more often; after all, as Christopher Finch notes in *The Art of Walt Disney*, Disneyland is "a kind of permanent Fourth of July celebration."

Fowler, Joe
(1894–1993)

Joe Fowler, the man in charge of building Disneyland, was born in Maine in 1894. After graduating from both the Naval Academy and MIT, Fowler worked as a naval architect, designing World War II aircraft carriers and heading two-dozen naval shipyards in the 1940s.

Fowler retired from the navy as a rear admiral in 1948, but an introduction to **Walt Disney** brought him an invitation to oversee construction of Disney's new Anaheim project. He joined the Disneyland team in April of 1954, began construction three months later, and, in a year, had the vast park ready for guests. Significantly, Fowler appeared in the wheelhouse of the *Mark Twain* on the national TV broadcast of Disneyland's **Opening Day**, piloting the grand paddlewheeler's first voyage after it was christened by actress Irene Dunne.

Once Disneyland opened, Fowler supervised its operations into the next decade and had a hand in every building project. Within a few years, he was leading several exceedingly complex Disneyland developments: the **Matterhorn**, the **Submarine Voyage**, and the **Monorail**. In the 1960s, Fowler took on **New Orleans Square**, the **Haunted Mansion**, **Pirates of the Caribbean**, and the heavy remodel of **Tomorrowland**, all built while Disneyland was still open for business.

By the late 1960s, Fowler was in charge of construction at Walt Disney World. As a senior VP, he also ran the entire Imagineering department before he finally retired for good in 1978. Nicknamed Can-Do for his optimism, Fowler was inducted as a Disney Legend in 1990, three years before his death at age ninety-nine. At Disneyland, **Fowler's Harbor** in **Frontierland** is named after him.

Fowler's Harbor,
aka Fowler's Landing

MAP: Frontierland, Fr-13

DATES: June 14, 1958–ongoing

Fowler's Harbor is the name of the dock along the **Rivers of America** where the **Sailing Ship** *Columbia* is often moored. Years ago, the **Mike Fink Keel Boats** launched just south of this dock, and the Indian War Canoes (now **Davy Crockett's Explorer Canoes**) launched just north.

The dock's name honors **Joe Fowler**, the navy admiral who supervised the construction of Disneyland and remained a top Disney executive until 1978. Back in 1955, the little dock area was an informal, unnamed location for servicing the *Mark Twain* (Walt Disney referred to it as "Joe's Ditch," according to Michael Barrier's *The Animated Man*). However, once the *Columbia* began berthing there in 1958, it was christened Fowler's Harbor (aka Fowler's Landing).

Small structures at the harbor are decorated with **Frontierland**-themed façades, including one named Fowler's Inn. For a while, one sign at Fowler's Harbor promoted a nonexistent restaurant called Maurie's Lobster House, named after Fowler's wife. The serene, eighty-foot-long path that winds behind Fowler's Harbor offers picturesque views of **Tom Sawyer Island**.

France, Van Arsdale
(1912–1999)

One of Disneyland's hallmarks is extraordinary customer service. Van Arsdale France was the man who first trained the park's **cast members**, creating many of the training techniques along the way that are still used throughout corporate America.

France was born in Seattle in 1912 and earned a college degree in liberal arts twenty-two years later. He soon established himself as a labor relations expert in the 1940s. Beginning his Disney career four months before Disneyland opened, France and his assistant, **Dick Nunis**, who would later become the president of Walt Disney Attractions, converted an abandoned house near Disneyland's construction site into an early training center called the Personnel Annex (the Disneyland Hotel was later built on the property). France's task was to make cast members the most efficient and congenial employees found anywhere. Just as a clean park would inspire guests to avoid littering, polite employees, **Walt Disney** believed, would inspire guests to be on their best behavior. "You can design, create, and build the most wonderful place in the world," he once said, "but it takes people to make the dream a reality."

To accomplish his ambitious goals, France established Disney University, which convened in small trailers before moving to an office building outside Disneyland's southeast corner. France wrote the manuals that set procedures and attitudes for decades to come. These manuals, with names like "You're On Stage at Disneyland," "The Traditions of Walt Disney at Disneyland," and "The Spirit of Disneyland," taught Disney philosophy first and specific Disneyland job skills second. Cast members learned how to create **happiness** before they learned how to serve food or park cars. France transformed employees into actors and actresses in an elaborate show where all customers, not just the famous ones, were treated as special guests.

Among his other duties, France briefly supervised **Tomorrowland**, helped resolve traffic issues on nearby streets, smoothed relations with the community, put together *Backstage Disneyland* (the first magazine for cast members), and set up the Disneyland Alumni Club. Though he officially retired in 1978, France stayed on as a consultant. His autobiography, *Window on Main Street*, was published in 1991. Named a Disney Legend three years later, France died in Newport Beach in 1999.

Frees, Paul
(1920–1986)

Guests may not know the name, but they certainly know the voice. Born Solomon

Frees in Chicago in 1920, Paul Frees was a D-Day veteran who performed thousands of radio, TV, and movie voices in a career stretching from the 1940s to the mid-1980s. Movie buffs recognize him as the narrator of *War of the Worlds* (1953), the voice of the talking rings in *The Time Machine* (1960), and even as Tony Curtis's "Josephine" voice in *Some Like It Hot* (1959). Disney fans also recall his narration and on-screen appearance in *The Shaggy Dog*, his vocals in *The Absent-Minded Professor*, and more. On TV, he gave voices to many memorable cartoon characters, including Boris Badonov, Ludwig von Drake, and John and George on the Beatles' cartoon show. He also voiced several famous characters in commercials, among them the Pillsbury Doughboy and Froot Loops' Toucan Sam.

Many more movies and cartoons followed, but it was at Disneyland that Frees found his biggest audience. Since the late 1960s, he has been heard by hundreds of millions of visitors in a variety of landmark attractions. Among them, he voiced the Ghost Host in the **Haunted Mansion**, the auctioneer and other rogues in **Pirates of the Caribbean**, and the shrinking scientist in **Adventure thru Inner Space**. The author of Frees's scripts for all three attractions, Disney Legend **X. Atencio**, told D23.com in January 2016 that Frees "was a genius. One take! Other people would try doing it all sorts of ways. Not Paul. He just ran with it and he'd put things in it and ad-lib it at exactly the right place."

The man with the versatile voice died of heart failure in 1986; two decades later, Frees was named a Disney Legend.

French Market

MAP: New Orleans Square, NOS-10

DATES: July 24, 1966–ongoing

The French Market has been an attractive dining destination since **New Orleans Square** opened in 1966. The location—*c'est magnifique!* From its corner near the train depot, the restaurant's patio, with its fifty-plus tables, offers alfresco dining and views of the **Rivers of America**. The patio's small stage regularly offers live jazz from the **Royal Street Bachelors**.

The French Market's menu has changed considerably from the open-face, turkey-on-white-bread sandwiches served in the late 1960s. In recent years, guests can order more sophisticated (and pricier) Creole cuisine. The well-received lunch and dinner offerings feature such New Orleans favorites as red beans and rice with andouille sausage, an elaborate Shrimp Po' Boy sandwich, and jambalaya (a specialty). A decadent Haunted Mansion Cake celebrates the famous structure across the way. Stouffer's, the frozen-food company that also sponsored the **Plaza Pavilion** and the **Tahitian Terrace**, was a longtime host here.

Frontierland

MAP: Park, P-15

DATES: July 17, 1955–ongoing

Covering some twenty acres and about thirty-three percent of Disneyland in the 1950s, the original **Frontierland** was the largest of the park's first five lands. Even after **New Orleans Square** and **Bear Country** were carved into the Frontierland space in the 1960s and '70s, the remaining land was still bigger than either **Tomorrowland** or **Adventureland**. Much of this vast Frontierland acreage was, and still is, accessible only by boat, mule, or train, since the **Rivers of America**, **Tom Sawyer Island**, the **Painted Desert**, and **Nature's Wonderland** have sprawled over large portions of the territory.

Early in the planning stages, **Walt Disney** decreed that one of Disneyland's areas would be inspired by "America's frontiers." The **souvenir books** added temporal boundaries, declaring these to be the frontiers "from Revolutionary days to the great southwest [sic] settlement" (the late 1700s to the late 1800s), where guests would "experience the high adventure of our forefathers who shaped our glorious history."

True to that frontier spirit, the land was positioned in Disneyland's western half. Once guests passed the gateway town, they encountered vast regions that appeared to be undeveloped. This "wilderness" was carefully constructed, of course, and plenty of attractions were added over the decades that have transformed Frontierland into Funtierland.

Like its neighbor Adventureland, Frontierland has an entrance (shown) from the **Hub**. The portal, which spans a shallow pond, was built with real logs to look like the gates of a frontier stockade. Pre-opening concept drawings by both Bruce Bushman and **Herb Ryman** depicted guests passing teepees before they entered the gates of the fort, but ultimately teepees were placed on the far-west edge of Frontierland in the **Indian Village.** As today's guests pass through the gates, on their right they immediately see a cannon with ammo boxes at the ready.

Once they're inside the stockade, guests find themselves forty feet from a flagpole with a plaque that was presented to Walt Disney by the American Humane Association in 1955. Guests then walk toward a small, Western-style "downtown" straight out of the nineteenth century, featuring wooden sidewalks, small shops, an exuberant saloon, and a shooting gallery. Impressions of wagon tracks, cowboy boots, and horseshoes are stamped into the pavement (shown), and country music drifts through the air. Even the brown metal **trash cans**, painted to look as if they were made out of planks, contribute to the theme.

Some 300 feet from the stockade gates roll the Rivers of America, which cover almost a third of Frontierland with 6 million gallons of dyed water. Tom Sawyer

Island appears straight ahead, an expansive wilderness area stretches to the right, and stores and restaurants line the walkway toward New Orleans Square on the left. Plying the river's waters is an array of watercraft—everything from a grand paddlewheeler and magnificent sailing ship (both shown) to simple rafts and canoes. In the 1950s, a **Marshal's Office** stood along the main walkway, a **Miniature Horse Corral** bordered the Frontierland Shooting Gallery, and the wilderness to the north was explored by a horse-drawn **Stage Coach**, a lumbering **Mule Pack**, rustic **Conestoga Wagons**, and an old-fashioned **Mine Train**. More Old West realism materialized every day in the form of a staged "shootout" between Sheriff Lucky and Black Bart in front of the **Golden Horseshoe**.

While the basic building architecture has remained the same over the decades, massive changes have uprooted the low-capacity transportation systems that used to explore the desert wilderness. The biggest modifications began in 1979, when a sweeping renovation added the high-speed, high-capacity, high-tech **Big Thunder Mountain Railroad** to the Nature's Wonderland area, followed later by the **Big Thunder Ranch Barbecue** and **Big Thunder Ranch**. The stockade at the front gate has been remodeled twice, first in 1980 and again in 1992, and the nightly shows have graduated from **Dixieland at Disneyland** jazz concerts to the elaborate **Fantasmic!** presentation.

In addition to its rowdy thrills, majestic ships, and high-tech entertainment, Frontierland has also offered some of Disneyland's loveliest experiences. Best of these might be its rustic walkways—the serene riverfront lane behind **Fowler's Harbor** (shown), the closed but still memorable **Big Thunder Trail**, the dirt footpaths on Tom Sawyer Island—that evoke past centuries and distant places far removed from a

modern theme park in a major metropolitan area.

Disneyland continues to make changes to Frontierland now that **Star Wars Land** is encroaching on its northern border, but it remains faithful to Walt Disney's original vision. His inspirational articulation of that vision would have been shown on the land's 1955 dedication plaque, had it ever been installed: "Frontierland is a tribute to the faith, courage, and ingenuity of the pioneers who blazed the trails across America." Five decades later, the old frontiers of the past are still thrilling and satisfying guests.

Frontierland Miniature Museum

MAP: Frontierland, Fr-1

DATES: Never built

Walt Disney's love of miniatures almost found expression in a rustic museum intended for a spot just inside the **Frontierland** gates. There, guests would have found displays of miniature towns and a small mechanical dancing man that foreshadowed later **Audio-Animatronic** figures. Some of these displays (and the mechanical man) were actually created before a Disneyland plan was even under discussion, and Disney hoped to tour them around the country.

Ultimately, a museum did open in Frontierland, but its theme was something that mid-1950s TV audiences could more easily relate to. In 1955, the **Davy Crockett Frontier Museum** opened in the building now occupied by **Pioneer Mercantile**.

Frontierland Shooting Exposition,
aka Frontierland Shooting Gallery,
aka Frontierland Shootin' Arcade

MAP: Frontierland, Fr-26

DATES: July 12, 1957–ongoing

Two years after Disneyland opened, the success of the **Main Street Shooting Gallery** prompted the addition of a rootin' tootin' rifle range to **Frontierland**.

The Frontierland Shooting Gallery opened in a forty-five-foot-wide spot along the main walkway where the **Miniature Horse Corral** had been. The gallery offered sixteen air rifles that fired lead pellets at frontier-themed metal targets. To keep the guns from being aimed too far from the targets, they were tethered by a cord and were later held in a cradle—although the sheer weight of the rifles was enough to keep kids aiming them forward. As with the later **Big Game Safari Shooting Gallery** in **Adventureland**, the Frontierland Shooting Gallery took quarters, not admission tickets.

The attraction wasn't all fun and games,

MOUSCELLANY

Clever puns are scattered all over Disneyland, and one of our favorites is on view here at the Frontierland Shooting Exposition. Shorty's Hotel (shown), one of the shooting targets, has a distinctive wall mural commanding you to "Drink Mousehead Beer." Would that we could.

though. Ricochets occasionally struck **cast members**, the pellets generated hazardous lead dust, and the gallery was considered high maintenance because the targets had to be laboriously repainted every night. Imagineers solved all these problems in March of 1985, when they installed eighteen electronic rifles that fired infrared beams at new targets with humorous sound effects. The gallery got a new name, too—Frontierland Shootin' Arcade.

The name and effects were updated once more with the 1996 debut of the Frontierland Shootin' (later Shooting) Exposition. The mining town of Boot Hill was the new target, and the effects included a skeleton that popped up when guests hit a graveyard shovel. Today, some of the Boot Hill tombstones have playful epitaphs reminiscent of those at the **Haunted Mansion**: "An arrow shot straight n' true/made its mark on Little Lou," says one. For fifty cents, today's guests can "empty the gun" of its twenty shots at this traditional but expertly executed attraction.

Frontier Trading Post

MAP: Frontierland, Fr-27

DATES: July 17, 1955–1987

From 1955 until the late 1980s, guests walking from the **Hub** through the **Frontierland** stockade gates found the Frontier Trading Post (not to be confused with the similarly named **Indian Trading Post**) on their immediate right. The Frontier Trading Post had a rustic wood-plank design that fit right in with this stretch of walkway near the rowdy Frontierland Shooting Gallery. From its small space, the Trading Post sold frontier souvenirs, many of them related to the Davy Crockett craze that overwhelmed America in the mid-1950s. In 1987, the Trading Post name was traded for the **Westward Ho Trading Co.**

Frozen Royal Reception

MAP: Fantasyland, Fa-9

DATES: November 4, 2013–December 22, 2014

Tangled enjoyed a three-year **Fantasyland** run, but with winter approaching in 2013, it was finally *Frozen* out. The new Frozen Royal Reception moved into this cottage next to **Pinocchio's Daring Journey**, but snow, not Rapunzel's hair, covered the roof. A clever **Audio-Animatronic** snowman (shown) entertained guests who were waiting to meet the Nordic royals from *Frozen*, the 2013 film phenomenon.

So well-liked was this meet-and-greet opportunity (wait-times were often over two hours) that in June of 2014, a special Frozen float was added to Mickey's Soundsational Parade, making the princesses more visible and hopefully shortening the lines back at the cottage. Disneyland even tried using special Frozen Royal Reception tickets as a way to alleviate crowding. Finally, in December the popular characters moved over to Disney California Adventure. Face-painting became the cottage's temporary activity until a new shop arrived in February of 2017. Called Royal Reception, the little cottage is filled with a traditional array of Fantasyland-inspired items, such as themed mugs, shirts, and dolls.

MOUSCELLANY

Ever since the new Frozen Ever After attraction debuted at Walt Disney World in 2016, rumors have been circulating that something similar will eventually make its way to Disneyland, perhaps in areas adjacent to the upcoming **Star Wars Land**.

Fun Fotos

MAP: Tomorrowland, T-22

DATES: 1959–1967

In Disneyland's first decade, whenever vacancies opened inside the exhibit buildings along the right-hand side of **Tomorrowland**, Fun Fotos stations were installed as temporary, inexpensive space fillers. The **American Dairy Association Exhibit**, **Bathroom of Tomorrow**, and **Hall of Aluminum Fame** were all replaced by Fun Fotos at one time or another.

The fun of the fotos was twofold. First, guests got their pictures taken in front of Disneyland-themed backgrounds (such as a small Monstro display where a child could sit in the whale's open mouth). Next, those Polaroids were developed with impressive "while you wait" technology (quick-developing photos were still a novelty back then). The price? One dollar per black-and-white photo.

Fun Fotos disappeared around 1966, when the buildings were completely remodeled for **Adventure Thru Inner Space** and the **Character Shop**.

MOUSCELLANY

Something similar to the old Fun Fotos reappeared in 2015. For that year's **Diamond Celebration**, three photo backdrops were positioned around Disneyland to create fun illusions—that guests were scaling **Matterhorn Mountain**, riding the **Big Thunder Mountain Railroad**, or being memorialized as cemetery busts at the **Haunted Mansion**. These popular new settings proved that guests still love a clever photo opportunity.

Fun Maps

Guests entering the lobby of the Disneyland Hotel's Fantasy Tower will encounter an amazing full-color illustrated map of old Disneyland. Standing ten feet tall and spreading fifteen feet across, the map is enhanced by a dozen simple animations that spotlight the Hippo Pool of the **Jungle Cruise**, a back-scratching bear in **Nature's**

Wonderland, the hotel's own pool, and more. In one corner, a smiling Walt Disney welcomes viewers to 1966 Disneyland.

This beautiful map is a 150-square-foot recreation of one of Disneyland's classic Fun Maps. These visually rich, poster-size paper maps are among the most evocative Disneyland souvenirs. For generations of Disneyland fans, they recreate fond memories and build eager expectations; many guests have happily studied the maps to recall previous visits and plan for the next one.

The first Fun Map sold at Disneyland was drawn by Disney Legend **Sam McKim**, who seemed to specialize in park cartography (he also drew the **Tom Sawyer Island** maps). This 1958 map positions the Disneyland Hotel in one corner ("designed and priced for family fun") and **Walt Disney's** face and text from his **Opening Day** speech in another. It also has a compass featuring **Tinker Bell** and a legend to point out **restrooms**, telephones, "future developments," and more. Best of all, detailed drawings and captions saturate the layout with information. Nearly everything in Disneyland is labeled, even some things that are not usually identified (for example, Swan Lake is the name of the **Sleeping Beauty Castle** moat on the 1958 map, and Glacier Grotto is the hollow interior of **Matterhorn Mountain** on the 1962 map). Early maps also depict **Holidayland** west of **Frontierland**, the **heliport** outside of **Tomorrowland**, and attractions that were never actually built in Disneyland, such as **Adventures in Science**, **Edison Square**, and **Liberty Street**. Surprisingly, the maps even reveal some secrets: in the 1960s, two maps depict the hidden "show buildings" west of the **berm** that housed large portions of the **Pirates of the Caribbean** (the 1966 map) and the **Haunted Mansion** (the 1968 map); the maps even identify areas within the show buildings. Not everything in the park is shown, of course—the crowds, construction walls, and areas blocked-off for **parades** were all left out—but the parts that *are* shown are endlessly enchanting.

By the 1990s, the maps had acquired some significant design changes. For one thing, the size shifted from year to year (Fun Maps have usually been around thirty inches tall by approximately forty inches wide). Several maps include drawings of smiling Disney characters around their perimeters (with Mickey Mouse at the top-center), presenting the park like welcoming hosts. In some years, the maps have had far fewer identifiers, making them much less useful. Also, the scale on the maps is inconsistent—**Jungle Cruise** animals might be as big as buildings, and Sleeping Beauty Castle sometimes looks as tall as the Matterhorn, even though the actual castle reaches only about half the mountain's height.

Attentive guests have probably noticed that sometimes the maps aren't very current. For instance, a Fun Map purchased new in 1994 had actually been drawn in 1989; thus, it doesn't include **Mickey's Toontown**, which opened in 1993, and it still includes the **Mile Long Bar**, which was renamed in 1989. Cartoon heads are still sprinkled around the edges, though many guests would be hard-pressed to identify little-known characters like Horace Horsecollar. A year later, a new 1995 map spotlights Disneyland's fortieth anniversary and the new **Indiana Jones Adventure** attraction, but that map also had problems—before a quick revision and reprint, the 1995 map gave the wrong date for Disneyland's **Opening Day**.

The 2011 Fun Map changed size again, this time to twenty-seven inches tall by

thirty-four inches wide. Walt Disney's face is back, and so are many more captions, exemplified by the nine named sections of the **Grand Canyon Diorama**. Nomenclature continues to be slippery; what most guests call the **Hub** is called the Plaza on the 1958 Fun Map, the Plaza Hub on the 1989 map, and the Central Plaza on the 2011 version. A Fun Map is even the subject of a thousand-piece jigsaw puzzle (shown). But no matter how they've changed over the decades, the maps continue to be beautiful artworks that stir up memories.

Gadget's Go Coaster

MAP: Mickey's Toontown, MT-3

DATES: January 24, 1993–ongoing

Gadget's Go Coaster is a kid-size version of a rowdy outdoor roller coaster. This fun attraction is marked by a twenty-eight-foot-tall hill at the west end of **Mickey's Toontown**.

The star of this coaster is Gadget Hackwrench, the mouse inventor from the *Chip 'n' Dale Rescue Rangers* TV show. The roller coaster is supposed to be one of Gadget's clever inventions, and it's also supposed to represent the world from a mouse-eye view. Guests are placed inside colorful acorns for a trip on what looks like a Tinker Toy track surrounded by oversized displays of gigantic pencils, combs, matchbooks, and more. Part of the track ventures over a small pond.

Lasting just under a minute, the brief, 700-foot-long trip is perhaps Disneyland's shortest ride, but it's a popular one. Unfortunately, with only two trains on the track (one roller coastering at just over twenty miles per hour while new passengers load in the other), and with each train holding a maximum of only sixteen guests at a time, lines can get long here.

Appropriately enough for an attraction targeted to young children, the sponsor, Georgia-Pacific's Sparkle Paper Towels, helps parents clean up messes.

Gag Factory

MAP: Mickey's Toontown, MT-9

DATES: January 24, 1993–ongoing

Comedians might suggest that a place named the Gag Factory probably sells really bad food, but actually this is a clever retailer in the downtown section of **Mickey's Toontown**. The shop's brick interior and gears on the walls evoke a factory theme. The gags include a talking mailbox and bendable jail bars out front, a painted interior wall that reads, "Do not paint on this wall," and the motto "Carpe Gag 'Em" posted above the door.

The shelves here used to be full of crazy toys, practical jokes, and magic tricks, but these days, the merchandise has shifted to less-jokey jewelry, mugs, plush dolls, pins, clothes, and hats. The Gag Factory added the first-ever Disney dime-press machine in 2005, some two decades after the first Disney coin-press machine arrived on **Main Street**. This store connects to the adjacent **Toontown Five & Dime**, making this block a funtastic shopping destination.

MOUSCELLANY

Mickey lends a hand—his giant gloves support the walls and shelves (shown) at the Gag Factory!

Galactic Grill, aka Tomorrowland Terrace

MAP: Tomorrowland, T-9

DATES: July 2, 1967–2001; 2006–ongoing

When "new **Tomorrowland**" debuted in 1967, every addition was conspicuous—except one. Sitting in the open, about 100 feet from the loading area of the **Monorail**, was a futuristic design of some kind. Decorated with **Rolly Crump**-designed pylons and flowing plants, guests could admire the serene, forty-foot-long display without really understanding what it was or how it added to the Tomorrowland atmosphere.

Understanding came when, every few hours, the display ascended to reveal itself as the roof of a small oval stage, where a spirited music group was already in mid-song even as the stage rose up. Sometimes called the Coke Terrace or the Coca-Cola Tomorrowland Terrace in deference to its sponsor, the stage was decorated with the same sleek arcs and Op Art abstractions that adorned the sculptural planter on top of it. Performers included 1960s hit-makers Paul Revere and the Raiders and 1980s new wavers Sparks.

Teens were the target audience, especially at night. During the day, tables in front of the raised stage offered seating for hundreds of guests; at night, the tables were cleared away to open up 3,000 square feet for dancing. Disneyland's old **souvenir books** showcase the Tomorrowland Terrace's youth appeal with energetic photos.

A counter-service eatery nearby offered fast food staples like burgers, sandwiches, fries, and Cokes (naturally). About a decade after the Tomorrowland Terrace opened, this menu was supplemented with the Tomorrowland-themed Moon-burger, and two decades after that (in the late 1990s), the lunch and dinner menus were updated with healthier wraps, fruit, and salads. In 2015, breakfast at the Terrace featured burritos, French toast, and a platter with eggs, bacon, and potatoes.

In 1990 and 1995, two of Disneyland's major anniversaries (the thirty-fifth and fortieth) were commemorated with large displays on top of the terrace. At decade's end, Coca-Cola shifted its sponsorship from the Tomorrowland Terrace to the nearby **Spirit of Refreshment** when another "new Tomorrowland" remodel arrived in 1998. The Tomorrowland Terrace music and fast food continued to operate, but a new sculpture crowned the roof and the colors were updated to the same warm bronzes and golds of the **Astro-Orbitor** and other Tomorrowland attractions. In 2001, **Club Buzz** reinvigorated the stage and dining area with a new name, a vibrant new color scheme dominated by purples, and a new *Toy Story*-themed show.

The name of the original Tomorrowland Terrace, and much of its old familiar look, returned in 2006. Along with the changes came a revised menu called Flight Command Cuisine (mostly sandwiches and burgers) to tie in with the new presentation on the Terrace stage. Sponsored by Hasbro and performed a half-dozen times a day, *Jedi Training Academy* brought *Star Wars* themes and characters to life by training earnest young guests to "master the ways of the Force." Kids learned the art of lightsaber fencing and squared off against Stormtroopers and the two evil Darths, Maul and Vader. The confrontations were more hilarious than terrifying, thanks to the intense kids and fast-paced narration. In December of 2015, this long-running show was replaced by a new one called *Jedi Training: Trials of the Temple*. On summer nights, the Tomorrowland Terrace transformed into the TLT Dance Club, with deejays spinning dance music during the week and live bands often rocking the weekends.

On November 16, 2015, the Tomorrowland Terrace transformed into something inspired by a galaxy far, far away. The **Season of the Force** campaign saturated Tomorrowland with *Star Wars*

> # MOUSCELLANY
>
> It's possible that the whole concept of a rising bandstand, like the one at the Tomorrowland Terrace, derives from something similar at Rio's famed Urca Casino, which **Walt Disney** visited during his 1941 trip to South America.

imagery, and it took firm hold on the new Galactic Grill. *Star Wars* toys now come with many of the food items, and *Star Wars* names pepper the menu. For example, breakfast might be Bantha Blue Milk Bread (basically French toast) or a Moisture Farm Fresh Fruit Platter. Lunchtime offers a spicy Cheese-3PO burger, Wicket's Wicked Veggie Wrap, an indulgent Darth by Chocolate éclair with red-velvet cake, and Light Side/ Dark Side specialty beverages. Some items get two prices: a First Order Burger costs an additional $10 if it's served in a Han Solo Carbonite Bucket.

Gala Day at Disneyland Film

This twenty-seven-minute documentary was released in movie theaters on January 21, 1960. Like an earlier Disney featurette, 1956's *Disneyland, U.S.A.*, *Gala Day at Disneyland* was essentially meant to be an extended commercial for the park's newest attractions. Key among these in 1960 were the **Monorail**, **Matterhorn Bobsleds**, and **Submarine Voyage**, which had all debuted the previous summer as Disneyland's first E-ticket attractions. **Parades**, **fireworks**, **mermaids**, and Richard Nixon also get some screen time.

Garden of the Gods

MAP: Fantasyland, Fa-22

DATES: Never built

Looking for ways to enhance the slow-moving **Motor Boat Cruise** in **Fantasyland**, in the 1960s, Disney designers considered adding pastoral design elements from the movie *Fantasia*. For Garden of the Gods, artist **Marc Davis** designed Olympian sculptures that incorporated peaceful fountains. Boats shaped like swans and rail cars shaped like steeds were considered for transportation. Classical music from the movie would have been the soundtrack.

Unfortunately, before these serene scenes were constructed, reality hit home: the tracks of **Fantasyland Autopia** circled all around these waterways and would have intruded loudly upon the bucolic gardens. However, the *Fantasia* theme did ultimately arrive in 1993; when the Motor Boat Cruise finally sank into the past, the lush landscaping of **Fantasia Gardens** took root.

Geppetto's Arts & Crafts, aka Geppetto's Toys & Gifts, aka Geppetto's Holiday Workshop

MAP: Fantasyland, Fa-9

DATES: May 25, 1983–2004; 2006–2007; 2010

The village-themed architecture that surrounds **Pinocchio's Daring Journey** once embraced a Pinocchio-themed gift shop as well. Next to the attraction's exit was a store named after Pinocchio's toy-making father.

Dense with charming Old World details, Geppetto's Arts & Crafts was designed to look just like the cozy toy shop in the classic movie. In its first incarnation, lots of thimbles, music boxes, marionettes, figurines, and old-fashioned cuckoo clocks dominated Geppetto's place. In the mid-1990s, the shop's name switched to Toys & Gifts and focused more on plush toys and dolls, offering same-day, custom-made dolls as its specialty. Geppetto's was also the site of special toy-related events and frequent appearances by Disney princesses.

Ten years later, the toy maker and his creations moved out and **Names Unraveled**, formerly a cart that operated elsewhere in

 Fantasyland, moved in. In 2006, the sign above the door announced a new name: Geppetto's Holiday Workshop. However, early in 2007, the store closed again. When it reopened in 2010, it did so as **Geppetto's Candy Shoppe**, selling sweets instead of toys.

MOUSCELLANY

A little tribute to the old Geppetto's Arts & Crafts can be seen; next door, in today's **Village Haus**, is a mural (detail shown) in a small corner alcove that reminds guests of the cute shop that used to be nearby.

Geppetto's Candy Shoppe

MAP: Fantasyland, Fa-9

DATES: May 26, 2010–October 2010; Fall 2011–ongoing

Poor Geppetto—his Disneyland stores never seem to last. After starting out in 1983 with **Geppetto's Arts & Crafts**, then moving on to toys, gifts, and holiday items until 2007, the old toymaker tried selling candy in 2010. Pre-packaged sugary sweets filled the adorable little store for a summer, but in October of 2010, the space transformed into **Tangled**, a meet-and-greet area for the stars of the Disney movie of the same name.

Gibson, Blaine
(1918–2015)

Blaine Gibson's childhood hobby was sculpting; eventually, his hobby became his career. Born in Colorado in 1918, Gibson began working in the animation department at Disney Studios in 1939. He's listed in the credits of many classic films and cartoons from the 1940s to the early 1960s, including *Peter Pan* and *Sleeping Beauty*. Even while working at the studio by day, he continued to take sculpting classes at night, and in 1954, **Walt Disney** invited him to start making models for Disneyland attractions.

Over the next three decades, Gibson supervised the sculpture department and created hundreds of works that were transformed into the **Audio-Animatronic** characters of such diverse attractions as the **Enchanted Tiki Room**, **Great Moments with**

Mr. Lincoln, and the **Haunted Mansion**. Today, Gibson's Timothy Mouse creation rides the top of **Dumbo the Flying Elephant**, his fair maiden graces the bow of the **Sailing Ship *Columbia***, and his little demons line the fiery finale of **Mr. Toad's Wild Ride**.

In 1965, Disney introduced Gibson and some of his **Pirates of the Caribbean** figures on *Walt Disney's Wonderful World of Color*. Later, Gibson sculpted representations of all the chief executives for the Hall of Presidents at Walt Disney World. After he retired in 1983, Gibson created *Partners*, the famous bronze statue of Disney and Mickey Mouse installed in Disneyland's **Hub** in 1993. That same year, Gibson was named a Disney Legend in celebration of his four decades as one of the company's master artists. He died in 2015 at age ninety-seven.

Gibson Girl Ice Cream Parlor

MAP: Main Street, MS-7

DATES: March 21, 1997–ongoing

In the 1997 shuffle of ice cream parlors and bakeries along **Main Street**, the new Gibson Girl Ice Cream Parlor landed next to the **Penny Arcade**. The **Blue Ribbon Bakery** had been located there until early 1997; when the bakery moved to the cor-

ner space where the **Carnation Ice Cream Parlor** had been, Gibson Girl took the vacant space in the middle of the block.

Gibson Girls are the curvy pin-ups created by American illustrator Charles Dane Gibson in the early twentieth century. Except for a few discreet drawings (detail shown), the curvy-pin-up element wasn't recreated for the ice cream parlor interior. The parlor does evoke the early twentieth century, though; from the ornate display fonts and striped awning outside to the old-fashioned lighting fixtures and soda fountain inside, this is a place where the time travel is as enticing as the desserts.

An expansion in early 2012 added more space to the interior and a new look that more closely resembles a classic soda fountain (the colors and some of the fixtures subtly suggest ice cream and sherbet). Lost in the remodel was a unique conversation piece: a four-foot-tall glass elephant that had been imported from Disneyland Paris and installed in a rear dining area. This pachyderm has since found a new home in a display area above **Tropical Imports** in **Adventureland**.

"Old-fashioned hand scooped ice cream" and "a perfect treat for someone sweet" have been touted on the signage outside, referring to the sundaes, ice cream cones, floats, sodas, and lemonade

MOUSCELLANY

Disney publicists claim that in one year, the Gibson Girl Ice Cream Parlor sells enough ice cream to build a full-size **Matterhorn Mountain!**

available. New float flavors appeared in 2012, and the latest Specialty Sundaes include a decadent Firehouse Dalmatian Mint Sundae piled with mint chocolate ice cream, hot fudge, and more. The shop doesn't offer many varieties of ice cream (nine flavors in 2016), but what they have is served up generously. Special creations for the holidays are big hits, as are the homemade waffle cones sold year-round. And there's one more cool little feature here: site-specific souvenir cups with a stylish Gibson Girl design. Not surprisingly, two ice cream companies, Nestlé and Dreyer's, have sponsored this location.

Gibson Greeting Cards

MAP: Main Street, MS-14

DATES: July 17, 1955–1959

Gibson Greeting Card stores sold products printed by an Ohio-based company that dated to 1850. At first the Gibsons, four Scottish brothers, printed labels and business cards, but in the 1880s they added a new product, **holiday season** greeting cards, and soon established themselves as one of the country's biggest card companies.

At Disneyland, the Gibson Art Company had two different stores in two **Main Street** locations (neither store was related to the **Gibson Girl Ice Cream Parlor**). The first store, Gibson Greeting Cards, debuted on **Opening Day** and lasted until 1959. This initial location was on the busy Main Street corner where **Disney Clothiers, Ltd.** now sits.

The **Hallmark Card Shop** took over for Gibson in 1960, and Gibson disappeared from Disneyland until mid-1985, when its **Card Corner** filled the spot formerly known as **Carefree Corner**. **John Hench**, the influential designer and Disney Legend, designed the first Gibson location.

Gift-Giver Extraordinaire Machine

MAP: Hub, H-7

DATES: 1985–September 1986

To celebrate its thirtieth anniversary, in 1985 Disneyland displayed a running tally of ticket sales in anticipation of the arrival of guest number 250 million. At the **entrance** stood the "Incredible Countdown Clock," designed with gears shaped like Mickey's ears and a counter with nine digits.

Throughout the year, every thirtieth guest who walked through the turnstiles won an instant prize. For some lucky winners, the prize was a chance to take home a new car, determined by a spin of the Gift-Giver Extraordinaire Machine in the **Hub**. This showy device was a precursor of the **Dream Machine**, the slot machine cake created for Disneyland's thirty-fifth birthday five years later. As it worked out, every thirty-thousandth guest got a new car (which comes out to about a car a day, and sometimes two a day), and every three-millionth guest got a new Cadillac (with over 12 million guests that year, 410 cars and four Caddies were given out). Winners collected their prizes (except for the actual cars) at a Prize Redemption Center next to the **Opera House**.

The idea for the birthday prize giveaways came from Disneyland's longtime marketing chief, Disney Legend **Jack Lindquist**. Lindquist's goal was to spark 1985 **attendance** after a disappointing 1984 (that year's L.A. Olympics had kept many guests away from Disneyland). After a February TV special and months of generous giveaways, park attendance jumped up by twenty-two percent over the previous year's tally, and that 250 millionth guest finally arrived on August 24, 1985.

The Gift-Giver Extraordinaire didn't stop giving, however, until September of 1986. Prizes that year included airline tickets, videocassettes, watches, color TVs, and "the official car of Disneyland '86," a Pontiac Firebird.

Give a Day, Get a Disney Day

DATES: January 1, 2010–March 9, 2010

A short but sweet off-season promotion for 2010, Give a Day, Get a Disney Day enabled guests to earn free Disneyland admission by volunteering. After registering and performing one of the community volunteer options, guests received a voucher they could exchange either for admission or a special **FASTPASS** ticket. Numerous promotions and TV commercials helped spread the word.

The word did indeed spread fast and far: less than ten weeks after it debuted on January 1, the Give a Day program closed abruptly on March 9. Disney officials, touting the program's success, claimed that a million volunteers had taken advantage of this special opportunity.

MOUSCELLANY

In July of 2016, Disney introduced a program similar to 2010's Give a Day, Get a Disney Day campaign. For the next ten years (until 2026), the new Happiest Class on Earth program pledged to give free Disneyland admission tickets to Anaheim sixth-graders who complete community-service projects.

Glass Blower

MAP: Main Street, MS-3

DATES: 1955–1966

For over a decade, a glass blower had his own shop on **Main Street**. His name was Bill Rasmussen, and he leased a space in the rear of the Crystal Arcade. There, Rasmussen created delicate, whimsical glass figurines in full view of guests. He even worked in full view of the whole nation when he appeared on an episode of *The Mickey Mouse Club*.

Rasmussen left Disneyland in 1966 and opened a series of shops in San Francisco, Boston, and other American cities (he called his Honolulu shop the Little Glass Shack). Meanwhile, back in Disneyland, other glass blowers filled Rasmussen's Crystal Arcade spot into the 1970s.

Goff, Harper
(1911–1993)

Movie fans know Harper Goff's *Nautilus* from a memorable Disney film; Disneyland fans know his widespread designs throughout the park; jazz fans might know him as the banjo player in the **Firehouse Five Plus Two.**

The multi-talented Goff was born in 1911. His upbringing in Fort Collins, Colorado, influenced Disneyland—several Goff-designed buildings, including **City Hall**, were based on actual buildings in his hometown. After attending art school in Los Angeles, Goff moved to New York and in the 1930s drew illustrations for *Esquire* and other popular magazines. Back in Hollywood in the 1940s, he became a set designer at Warner Bros. and worked on *Casablanca*, *Captain Blood*, and other films. Moving to Disney Studios in the 1950s, Goff and helped make *20,000 Leagues Under the Sea* an Oscar-winning classic.

Goff was involved with Disneyland even before Anaheim was set as its location. At **Walt Disney's** behest, he took several trips around the country to gather information about other amusement parks, fairs, and museums; it was his research that informed the earliest Disneyland plans.

As one of the project's first designers, in 1951 Goff drew up concept art for a sixteen-acre Burbank park that would have featured boats on a lake, an island, a circus tent, a frontier town, and a train ride. As Anaheim plans came to fruition, Goff oversaw construction on the **Jungle Cruise** and created the interior for the **Golden Horseshoe**, among countless other contributions (some of his art was included in a 2015 **Disney Gallery** exhibition devoted to early Disneyland drawings). Later he helped create EPCOT in Florida and consulted on Disney theme parks into the early 1990s.

Named a Disney Legend in 1993, Goff died that same year in Los Angeles at age eighty-one. He's memorialized at Disneyland with a window above the **Adventureland Bazaar.**

Golden Horseshoe

MAP: Frontierland, Fr-4

DATES: July 17, 1955–ongoing

The beautiful Golden Horseshoe has been delighting guests since **Opening Day**. Situated on a prominent **Frontierland** corner that juts toward the **Rivers of America**, the Golden Horseshoe is an eye-catching, two-story structure. It was particularly radiant when it was painted white with gold trim (in 2010, the colors were softened to yellows and creams). The decorative finials on the roof and the long balcony with a turned balustrade add timeless elegance, while the wooden sidewalk out front grounds the building in frontier history.

Disney Legend **Harper Goff** created the glamorous interior, basing his designs on the Golden Garter saloon set he had already drawn up for the 1953 Doris Day film *Calamity Jane*. The approximately 2,500-square-foot room features a curtained stage flanked by private boxes, a main floor with dining tables, and a horseshoe-shaped balcony. A prominent golden horseshoe is mounted above the stage; **Walt Disney** is said to have personally selected the thirteen displays of large steer horns that ring the room. The bar along the right-hand side of the interior serves up a menu of Main Show entrees (chicken breast nuggets, fish and chips, chili, etc.), sides called Supporting Roles (salads, fries, chili in a bread bowl) and elaborate Grand Finale desserts (including a Golden Horseshoe Ice Cream Float) that guests then take to their tables.

Several shows and sponsors have been involved with the Golden Horseshoe over the decades. Most famously, the lighthearted *Golden Horseshoe Revue* began running on July 17, 1955, and continued for over 50,000 performances until October 12, 1986, with Pepsi-Cola as its sponsor for all but the last four years. Disney would often catch the *Revue* from his preferred box at stage left (the view from that box is shown; seen from the audience, the box is to the lower right of the stage). After Eastman Kodak took over sponsorship from 1982 to 1984, the unsponsored show continued into 1986. On November 1, the *Golden Horseshoe Jamboree* began an eight-year run, the last four sponsored by Wonder Bread.

Since December 1994, various short-term special presentations and long-term acts have appeared on the Golden Horseshoe stage, including *Woody's Roundup* (a 1999 *Toy Story*-themed show), the *Golden Horseshoe Variety Show* (2000), and the durable musical hilarity of **Billy Hill and the Hillbillies** (until January of 2014). A two-month "experience" called **Legends of Frontierland: Gold Rush** opened in July of 2014, followed by the return of the Laughing Stock Company and its well-received audience-participation comedy show. In August of 2015, the Silver Dollar Six, a new group of "desperadoes posing as musicians," started playing several times a day on the outside balcony above the entrance.

The Golden Horseshoe's many shows and entertainers—the *Jamboree*, the *Variety Show*, Billy Hill, a lively jazz revue called *The Class of '27* that occasionally played in the 1970s, etc.—have all been accomplished and popular, but it's unlikely that anything will ever endure like the original *Golden Horseshoe Revue*.

Golden Horseshoe Revue

MAP: Frontierland, Fr-4

DATES: July 17, 1955–October 12, 1986

The original *Golden Horseshoe Revue* established the golden reputation of the **Golden Horseshoe**. It's called "the Grandest Show in the West" and "Dazzlin' Rootin' Tootin' Fun" on the **attraction poster**, "the most scintillating shows in Disneyland" in the 1955 **souvenir book**, and "the world's longest-running live stage show" in the

Guinness Book of World Records.

The show's original stars were singers Judy Marsh and Donald Novis and comedian **Wally Boag**. Marsh played Slue-Foot Sue (noted on the sign out front as the building's owner), but she was soon replaced by the spunky **Betty Taylor**. Irish tenor **Fulton Burley** took over for Novis in 1962. The durable Boag stayed with the show from its inception until 1982, playing a traveling salesman and Pecos Bill (after Boag retired, comedian Dick Hardwick replaced him; Taylor, Burley, and Boag would all be named Disney Legends in 1995). Supporting the actors was a small live band and high-kicking can-can girls wearing gaudy dresses, colorful headwear, and black garters (on the 1955 and 1983 attraction posters, the girls get all the attention).

So popular was the *Golden Horseshoe Revue* that it was recreated one night in the Olympic Village for the 1960 Olympic Games at Squaw Valley. Additionally, a 1962 episode of *Walt Disney's Wonderful World of Color* spotlighted the show to honor its ten-thousandth performance. Reminding modern guests of the show's fabled legacy, for three weeks of 2013, the Golden Horseshoe staged a popular "Salute to the Golden Horseshoe Revue" as part of that year's **Limited Time Magic** program.

Goofy's Gas Station

MAP: Mickey's Toontown, MT-7

DATES: January 24, 1993–ongoing

This toontastic rest stop in the heart of **Mickey's Toontown** offers bathrooms, snacks, water fountains, a playful car to sit in, and occasional opportunities to meet the Goof himself. As with everything else in Toontown, the real fun is spotting all the humorous details worked into the décor—for example, the fish swimming inside the gas pumps, the talking water fountains, and the sign that reads, "Did we goof up your car today?"

> **MOUSCELLANY**
>
> A sign posted outside Goofy's Gas Station identifies the types of Goofy Water available here: Whacky, Screamin', Surfin', Liquid, Wet, Woozy, Rockin', Rollin', Zippy, Loopy, and High.

Goofy's Playhouse,
aka Goofy's Bounce House

MAP: Mickey's Toontown, MT-1

DATES: January 24, 1993–ongoing

No frowns are allowed in this interactive structure. Goofy's Bounce House launched with the rest of **Mickey's Toontown** in January of 1993. Designed to look, uh, goofy, the lopsided Bounce House appears, from the outside, to be a wildly discombobulated residence where all the angles are askew and a car has bashed into Goofy's mailbox (shown).

Inside, the building was originally constructed

as a giant playpen for toddlers. To ensure that it was used by only the youngest kids, there was a height maximum of four feet four inches tall, making this one of the few attractions that put an *upper* limit on a guest's height. A **cast member** supervised the kids, who literally bounced off the walls. And the floor. And the furniture, since everything was inflated and made for play. The charming décor (including a kite flying inside the house and a nutty piano) and the wacky noises added to the silly fun.

After temporarily closing on January 7, 2005, the Bounce House reopened on March 5, 2006, as Goofy's Playhouse with an additional play area outside. Everything out in the yard is screwy, suggesting that the builder is a klutz; however, the garden now grows pre-carved pumpkins, bell peppers that are actual bells, and ears of popcorn, suggesting that the gardener is a genius. Out here, kids enjoy mildly active playtime while their parents enjoy some restful sitting time. Meanwhile, the house's interior has lost its bounce and is now a calmer place more for curious exploration than energetic exercise (which may explain why there's never a line to get in). Afterwards, everyone can cool off with icy beverages from Goofy's Free-Z Time, a trailer with flat tires that is always parked next door but only occasionally open.

Gracey, Yale
(1910–1983)

It's no coincidence that one of the characters in the 2003 film *The Haunted Mansion* is named Master Gracey; in fact, the whole eerie building carries the Gracey name. Yale Gracey created many of the memorable special effects in Disneyland's **Haunted Mansion**.

Born in China in 1910, Gracey grew up in Shanghai before studying art in California. His Disney Studios career began in 1939, and he eventually became an art director and layout artist on films and cartoons ranging from 1940's *Pinocchio* to 1961's *Babes in Toyland*.

Throughout the 1940s and '50s, Gracey supplemented his studio commitments with hours spent devising homemade gadgets and models. An impressed **Walt Disney** invited him to bring his gadget-making talents to new Disneyland attractions. During the 1960s, Gracey added special effects to the **Carousel of Progress** and **Pirates of the Caribbean**, among others (one specific example of his ingenuity is the fiery Pirates finale that seemingly burns down the town).

Though he retired in 1975, Gracey continued to consult on special effects at Walt Disney World. In 1983, he died at age seventy-three in Los Angeles; sixteen years later, he was inducted as a Disney Legend.

Grad Nite

DATES: June 15, 1961–ongoing (seasonal)

The long-running party known as Grad Nite is a marketing concept created in the early 1960s by Disney Legend **Milt Albright**. His idea was to invite graduating high school seniors from the L.A. area to Disneyland, charge them a special fee, keep the park open to them all night long, and sell them special souvenirs.

Obviously, filling a late-night park full of jubilant teenagers was a recipe for disruption, so to ensure proper conduct Disneyland had several strictly enforced rules, in addition to the usual no-drinking and no-bad-behavior rules. Teenage guests had to arrive on school buses with chaperones; shorts and T-shirts weren't allowed (guys had to wear ties in the early years); nobody could leave before dawn; and nobody could nap at the park. However, as Disneyland officials soon discovered, rules are made to be broken.

The inaugural Grad Nite was held on June 15, 1961 for over 8,000 local students. They paid $6 each and got unlimited access to attractions (as shown in *Disney: The First 100 Years*, this ticket also included a free photo). Guests were admitted between 11 PM and 1 AM only, and the party lasted until 5 AM. Within a few years, tens of thousands of students were coming from all over the country to party at Grad Nite. And they were winning some pretty impressive prizes, too—in 1964 and 1965, Disneyland gave away a total of eight new Ford Mustangs at Grad Nite. By the 1990s, over 150,000 grads were being spread over seven or eight different spring nights each year and were being entertained by big-name bands such as No Doubt and Berlin.

Unfortunately, the kids were enjoying the party more than Disneyland's security personnel were. Alcohol consumption, minor vandalism, and overly affectionate couples were persistent problems that kept adults on continual alert.

Walt Disney acknowledged the challenge in a *Walt Disney Conversations* talk about Grad Night with Bill Ballantine: "Over 50,000 young kids—the boys in coat-and-tie, the girls all in party dresses—the park is theirs. *Beautiful!* And of them all, there are only fifty or a hundred characters that we have to take care of." The "characters," Disney was referring to were the more unruly grads in attendance; by "take care of," he was alluding to security keeping those grads in a holding area or removing them from Disneyland altogether. Additional precautions over the years have included a "friendly frisk" at the **entrance**, closure of some dark attractions, periodic sweeps through theaters to clear out sleepers, and the conspicuous presence of the Anaheim police.

Despite the occasional troublemakers, Grad Nite continues on today, usually from mid-May to mid-June, and often on Friday and Saturday nights (there were eighteen dates scheduled for 2017, at $92 per grad). As one might expect, commemorative merchandise is available (shirts, pennants, stuffed characters, and buttons, like the one shown from 1974). The events have expanded to include a Blast Off pre-party before the main party begins,

MOUSCELLANY

The modern list of banned items at Grad Nite includes certain kinds of tattoos, clothing (including wedding dresses), hats, bandannas, bags, toys, and noise-makers. One more thing: no cremated remains are allowed.

special **fireworks** shows, new dance areas, big-name musicians, a new sponsor (Honda), and, starting in 2013, a new Grad Nite location (Disney California Adventure).

What's also expanded is the list of rules for Grad Niters, which is longer than ever and details with great specificity what items and behaviors are banned. Still, the event continues to be a popular tradition, and the five-millionth Grad Niter arrived in 2009. For many teens, high school isn't over until they've graduated from Grad Nite.

Grand Canyon Diorama

MAP: Tomorrowland, T-17

DATES: March 31, 1958–ongoing

While Disneyland's **souvenir books** have always named this a **Main Street** attraction, and while the images and animals in the diorama seem more suited to **Frontierland**, the beautiful Grand Canyon Diorama is actually situated in **Tomorrowland** behind **Space Mountain**. The diorama lines one interior wall of a long tunnel that stretches along the train track just east of Disneyland's **entrance**.

Like many other attractions, the Grand Canyon Diorama was inspired by a Disney movie—in this case, the Oscar-winning 1958 documentary *Grand Canyon*. As in that documentary, the diorama pairs visually stunning images with the clip-clopping of horses to portray the "On the Trail" passage from Ferde Grofé's *Grand Canyon Suite*. The Grand Canyon Diorama presents a ninety-second pass along one rim of the immense canyon, a view that includes a sunrise, cliff-dweller ruins, a storm, a 180-degree rainbow, and a sunset, all separated from the train by a glass wall.

Combining a detailed 306-foot-wide, thirty-four-foot-tall background painting with dozens of foreground animals and hundreds of rocks, bushes, and other props, the diorama was touted for years as the world's longest. With a 1958 price tag of over $400,000, it was also most likely one of the world's most expensive dioramas. Certainly it is still one of the world's most realistic.

Disney Legend **Claude Coats** and Disney Studios artist Delmer Yoakum were its primary painters, while the cougar, eagles, skunks, mule deer, snakes, and other desert animals were the products of a taxidermist (none of them are **Audio-Animatron-**

ic machines). A 1968 issue of *Vacationland* magazine proclaims that creating the Grand Canyon canvas took 4,800 man hours and 300 gallons of paint.

At the official opening, a band, park officials, and American Indians in native dress dedicated the new D-ticket attraction with a blessing-of-the-trains ceremony. The diorama has changed very little since then. However, it got a mighty supplement in 1966 when the new **Primeval World Diorama** and its impressive dinosaurs joined the next section of train track, thus doubling the diorama drama.

Grandma's Baby Shop

MAP: Main Street, MS-13

DATES: July 17, 1955–September 1955

A charming shop for infant clothes was born on **Opening Day**. Unfortunately, Grandma's Baby Shop, still an infant at barely two months old, was the first **Main Street** business to fold. By autumn, the **Silhouette Studio** had taken over Grandma's spot near today's **Disney Clothiers, Ltd.**

Great Moments with Mr. Lincoln,
aka The Disneyland Story Presenting Great Moments with Mr. Lincoln

MAP: Town Square, TS-9

DATES: July 18, 1965–Spring 2005; December 18, 2009–ongoing

A decade of advances in **Audio-Animatronic** technology culminated in 1964 with the creation of a mechanical Abraham Lincoln. Although it was originally planned for the Hall of Presidents in the **Liberty Street** area, it ultimately was never built at Disneyland (Liberty Square and the Hall of Presidents would be built later at Walt Disney World). When the A-A Lincoln did appear for the first time in public, it was being used by the State of Illinois in its pavilion at the 1964–1965 New York World's Fair.

The life-size electronic effigy incorporated everything Disney designers had learned from the mechanical animals they'd made for Disneyland's **Jungle Cruise**, **Nature's Wonderland**, and **Enchanted Tiki Room**. Lincoln, however, was by far the most ambitious Audio-Animatronic project yet. Not only did he look exactly like the very famous, very dignified public figure (Lincoln's life mask was the model for the face), but he also had a wide range of complex motions. Mid-1960s viewers expecting a stiff, seated Lincoln that would merely swivel its head and blink were utterly astonished to see the Great Emancipator stand up, move his arms, and deliver an impassioned speech that utilized hand gestures and remarkably subtle facial movements.

Calling Lincoln's realism "alarming," the August 1963 issue of *National Geographic* details the engineering wonders of the fourteen hydraulic lines running through the figure's body and sixteen air lines working inside its mechanical head to produce fifteen different facial expressions. Some members

MOUSCELLANY

For Liberty Street's Hall of Presidents and then for the Lincoln attraction, Walt Disney considered including Audio-Animatronic critics as part of the show. In the May 1959 issue of *Think*, Disney tells Lee Edson, "I'll have Lincoln standing up and delivering an address. I'll have other speakers and I'll even have hecklers in the audience booing them." Disney also mentions robotic hecklers "sitting in the boxes with the visitors" while describing a new theater idea in the December 31, 1962, issue of *Newsweek*.

of the press were so amazed by the verisimilitude that they invented details about what Lincoln could do, crediting the seemingly sentient figure with walking around and shaking hands with front-row guests.

While the robotic Lincoln couldn't do all that, Disney's Imagineers had enough of a challenge creating the figure's actual movements. Over two years of development went into the project; yet even in the final tests, Lincoln was still capable of flattening a chair when he sat on it. After the public's overwhelmingly positive reception at the fair, Walt Disney had an even more sophisticated Lincoln rushed to Disneyland's **Opera House** for the 1965 **Tencennial**. Presented by Lincoln Savings and Loan, Great Moments with Mr. Lincoln opened as an E-ticket attraction, though anyone under seventeen years old could get in free thanks to a special coupon in the **ticket books**. Billed as a "personal adventure with history," the thirteen-minute show began with a short biographical film, featured a dramatic monologue by the electronic Lincoln that blended excerpts from four of the former president's speeches, and ended with a fifty-foot post-show mural that celebrated American freedom.

Mr. Lincoln temporarily "retired" on New Year's Day in 1973, when a film about Walt Disney's life moved into the Opera House. However, fans were so insistent about bringing him back that Lincoln returned in 1975, generating one of the longest attraction titles ever: The Walt Disney Story Featuring Great Moments with Mr. Lincoln. Updates in 1984 and 2001 improved the presentation with new special effects and better sound (the latter revision also incorporated Lincoln's Gettysburg Address). Starting in 2005, the celebratory movie *Disneyland: The First 50 Magical Years* temporarily replaced the president, but a further-enhanced Lincoln returned late in 2009 with a new title that acknowledged some new exhibits in the Opera House: The Disneyland Story Presenting Great Moments with Mr. Lincoln. From June 15, 2012, to April 7, 2013, an a cappella vocal group called Voices of Liberty performed as a patriotic prelude to Mr. Lincoln.

Lincoln's voice was originally performed by Royal Dano, a character actor with a long career in movies and TV shows. Dano, forty-two when he first recorded the Lincoln vocals, died in 1994 at age seventy-one. New Lincoln vocals were recorded by Warren Burton, an award-winning soap opera star and noted voice actor, for the 2001 update (though Dano's remastered vocals returned in 2009). **Paul Frees** spoke the original narration introducing Lincoln (Dano and Frees can both be heard on the 1964 LP of the original World's Fair attraction). Another Disney Legend, **Buddy Baker,** provided the heart-swelling music for the attraction. As for the mechanical president, Disney Legends **Roger Broggie**, **Harriet Burns**, **Marc Davis**, **Blaine Gibson**, **Bob Gurr**, and **Wathel Rogers** helped make Great Moments great.

MOUSCELLANY

Although most audiences have loved the presentation, some elite academics are scathing in their sardonic criticism of Disney's Lincoln, insisting that the robotic figure diminishes the venerated president. Richard Schickel's much-discussed 1968 book *The Disney Version* unleashes a particularly venomous attack, calling Disney's version of Mr. Lincoln "ridiculous" and a "grotesquery."

Guest Assistance Card

The Walt Disney Company endeavors to accommodate anyone with a disability. Consequently, Disneyland offers disability parking spaces, wheelchairs, Assistive Listening Systems, Braille guidebooks, and much more. Also on that list for nine years was the GAC, or Guest Assistance Card. This small card was available (with no support documentation required) at **City Hall** from 2004 until October 9, 2013. It came with a date and a stamp indicating the special accommodations the guest and the guest's party would be able to utilize, which could include preferential seating and alternate entrances to attractions. After reports of abuse by some guests, the GAC was replaced in 2013 by the **Disability Access Service Card.**

Guest Flow Corridors

MAP: Main Street, MS-11; Town Square, TS-7

DATES: Spring 2015–ongoing

It's rare when a third of an acre inside Disneyland suddenly opens up to guests, but that's what happened in 2015. After almost a year of construction, two new Guest Flow Corridors were unveiled that spring. Their purpose: to give guests more efficient walkways when nightly **parades** and **fireworks** bring huge crowds of spectators to **Main Street**. The need for the corridors was exacerbated by two new evening shows—**Paint the Night** and Disneyland Forever **fireworks**—that arrived with 2015's **Diamond Celebration**. With the new Guest Flow Corridors in place, guests now have wide alternatives to crowded sidewalks as they enter or exit Disneyland at night.

In 2016, the two corridors usually opened up on busy nights before the 8:50 PM performance of Paint the Night. The two corridors run parallel to, and are about the same length as, Main Street. The corridor on the east side, used by guests heading into Disneyland, starts in **Town Square**. This corridor's entrance gates (shown) are between the big **Disney Showcase** store and the **Mad Hatter of Main Street**. During the day, this entrance is blocked off and used as a character meet-and-greet location. Today, signs indicate that behind the walls, there is some kind of Livery Service and Stable offering Carriages for Hire. At night guests walk  northward from here and leave the corridor near the **Little Red Wagon.**

The corridor on the west side, which is used by guests ready to leave Disneyland, starts at the back of the **Refreshment Corner** and continues southwards behind the **Penny Arcade**, **Crystal Arcade**, and **Emporium**, exiting through the gates adorned with a beautiful "Discover the Joy of Motoring" mural. As guests pass through this gate on their way to the exits, they will see the **Carriage Place Clothing Co.** on their left and **Town Square** in front of them.

Both corridors are open-air, but that may be their only similarity. Of the two, the eastern corridor that leads guests to the **Hub** is more completely themed. This walkway is about fifteen feet wide, and the high painted walls that line the corridor are topped with turn-of-the-century gingerbread. Flower boxes, forty-one attraction posters, and a few **outdoor vending carts** might make guests feel that the corridor has been made for them to enjoy, not just rush through on the way to somewhere else.

By comparison, the west-side corridor varies from ten to twenty-five feet in width and looks a lot less polished than its east-side counterpart. There is a little Main Street theming back here, and fifteen **attraction posters** are mounted on the walls, but mostly guests are looking at the backs of buildings. Of special interest are, at the northern end, the 120-foot walk past the pens where the **Jungle Cruise** boats are kept and, at the southern end, the back of the upstairs **apartment** that **Walt Disney** occasionally used. In both corridors, **cast members** are positioned to encourage guests to keep moving as they walk to and from Disneyland's center.

Guest Relations

MAP: Town Square, TS-4; Park, P-7

DATES: 1955–ongoing

Disneyland's 1956 **souvenir book** was the first to note the existence of Guest Relations inside **City Hall**. It's still there, serving as an information center for guests who have questions, want to make reservations, are looking to file a complaint or a compliment about a **cast member**, or require maps of the surrounding area. Disney Legend **Robert Jani** originally headed up Guest Relations, with another Disney Legend, **Cicely Rigdon**, taking over in the 1960s.

For visitors who had not yet walked through the gates, a second Guest Relations office later existed in a small building to the right of Disneyland's main **entrance**; this Guest Relations eventually moved to the left of the main entrance to Disney California Adventure.

Gurr, Bob
(1932–)

Anyone who has ever ridden in an **Autopia** car knows the work of Bob Gurr, the man who created and engineered Disneyland's imaginative transportation.

Born in Los Angeles in 1932, Gurr grew up fascinated with machines and automobiles. After graduating from college in 1952 with a degree in industrial design, he promptly started his own company and found himself consulting on the new Autopia in **Tomorrowland**. Soon Gurr was designing the attraction's cars. From then on, he worked full-time to make a reality of the elaborate vehicles dreamed up by **Walt Disney**, including such diverse devices as the hovering **Flying Saucers** and the old-time **Main Street Vehicles**.

In the 1950s, Gurr transformed an automobile into the **Viewliner** train, redesigned a boxy German monorail train into Disneyland's sleek **Monorail** (and even piloted the first test drive), drew up the original passenger coaches for the **railroad**, made **Mr. Toad's** wild cars, and built the **Matterhorn Bobsleds**. He also came up with some of the mechanical devices needed to pull off the delightful special effects inside the **Sleeping Beauty Castle Walk-Through**. In the 1960s, Gurr designed several old-time electric runabouts for Walt Disney's personal use, worked his wizardry on **Great Moments with Mr. Lincoln**, and assisted on the **Omnimover** pods for **Adventure Thru Inner Space** and the **Haunted Mansion.**

Retiring from Disney in 1981, Gurr worked on creations for other theme parks and special events, among them the King Kong attraction at Universal Studios and the UFO at the 1984 Summer Olympics. Still a consultant on Disney attractions, Gurr was named a Disney Legend in 2004. He published a book of behind-the-scenes stories, *Design: Just for Fun*, in 2012 (this was Gurr's third book—two others about car design were published in the 1950s).

Hallmark Card Shop

MAP: Main Street, MS-14

DATES: June 15, 1960–January 6, 1985

Three businesses have operated out of the attractive, **John Hench**-designed building that sits on the northeast corner where **Center Street** meets **Main Street**. Two of those businesses were card shops, starting with **Gibson Greeting Cards** from 1955 to 1959. When Gibson bid farewell, the Hallmark Card Shop took over in mid-1960.

It was probably only a matter of time before Hallmark showed up at Disneyland. Founded in 1910, the company had been making Disney-themed greeting cards since 1931. Also, its headquarters were in Kansas City, where **Walt Disney** had spent some of his childhood and later started his Laugh-O-Gram animation company. Disneyland's Hallmark Card Shop continued selling cards, stationery, puzzles, diaries, and wrapping paper for almost twenty-five years; it closed in early 1985 to make way for a big new retailer, **Disney Clothiers, Ltd.**

Hall of Aluminum Fame

MAP: Tomorrowland, T-24

DATES: September 16, 1955–July 1960

In Disneyland's first year, **Walt Disney** needed some **Tomorrowland** sponsors who could provide their own exhibits, thus freeing him to concentrate time and money on other aspects of Disneyland. Two months after **Opening Day**, the Kaiser Aluminum & Chemical Company debuted its shiny Hall of Aluminum Fame in the same educational-exhibit building that already housed Monsanto's **Hall of Chemistry**. This building, prime real estate just inside the Tomorrowland entrance, would eventually house **Star Tours**.

Early **souvenir books** describe Kaiser's walk-through Hall as an "entertaining exhibit" of "today's and tomorrow's uses of the vital metal." Guests first encountered a sign announcing "the brightest star in the world of metals" next to a forty-foot slanting aluminum cylinder that looked like a giant telescope, complete with oversize dials and two narrow finder scopes mounted along the top.

The telescope was actually the entrance to the Hall—guests walked through the base and entered a room lined with displays showing the history and uses of aluminum. A six-foot-wide "time sphere" in the center of the room presented images of men using and even wearing aluminum. Above, a cascade of aluminum stars streaked past exposed rafters and beams. Enjoying the proceedings from a pedestal near a wall was a three-foot-tall grinning aluminum pig named Kap. Wearing work clothes and holding a wrench, Kap was a cute mascot, but he was not a Disney character; "Kap" was an acronym for Kaiser Aluminum Pig, "pig" being the term for the impure base alumina that is refined into pure aluminum. Like the Hall itself, Kap was a strained attempt at making science and industry entertaining to kids and laypeople.

Five years after opening, the lights dimmed on the brightest metal's exhibit in favor of the less cerebral **Fun Fotos**.

Hall of Chemistry

Map: Tomorrowland, T-24

DATES: July 17, 1955–September 19, 1966

Of the four Monsanto attractions that existed in **Tomorrowland** in the 1950s and '60s, the Hall of Chemistry was the only one to debut on **Opening Day** (the **House of the Future** opened two years later, followed by **Fashions and Fabrics Through the Ages** in 1965 and **Adventure Thru Inner Space** in 1967).

The Hall of Chemistry's big rectangular building inside Tomorrowland's entrance was adorned on the outside with the red Monsanto logo and Space Age atoms. Inside, the Hall was a free walk-through exhibit that featured informational displays demonstrating how the modern world benefited from chemical engineering. Oversized test tubes, electrified wall displays, and a metaphorical arm reaching across the ceiling all contributed to the educational experience. "Carpet makes it home" was Monsanto's pitch for synthetic floor coverings.

As pedestrian as the Hall of Chemistry sounds today, it lasted for over a decade and educated millions of visitors. The attraction finally closed in 1966 and was replaced by the dramatic Adventure Thru Inner Space attraction the following year. Today's guests will find **Star Tours** where corporate chemistry was once celebrated.

Halloween Time

DATES: September 29, 2006–ongoing (seasonal)

Other Southern California parks began celebrating Halloween with month-long activities as early as 1973, the year Knott's Berry Farm debuted its seasonal Halloween Haunt/Knott's Scary Farm transformation. Surprisingly, Disneyland didn't do much in-park Halloweening during the twentieth century, only offering a free-admission party for costumed guests in 1994 and several nights of Mickey's Halloween Treat in 1995 and 1996 (a relatively low-key event featuring hayrides, costume contests, special merchandise and dozens of "treat stops"). The twenty-first century was a different story, however; Disneyland executives decided to scare up some big off-season crowds of their own. On September 29, 2006, it was finally time for Halloween Time.

The Disney difference was its target audience—while other parks aimed their Halloween attractions at teens and offered intense thrills and chills, Disneyland captured the family audience with gentler activities that were as fun as they were scary. Those activities have included special shows called Woody's Halloween Roundup in **Frontierland**; a seasonal Ghost Galaxy re-theming of **Space Mountain**; special Halloween-themed foods; and a playful Haunted Mansion Holiday overlay (continuing a **Haunted Mansion** tradition that began on October 5, 2001). A Halloween fireworks display (Halloween Screams—A Villainous Surprise in the Skies), a Happiest Haunts tour, and after-hours costume parties have also added to the festivities (those parties were held on seventeen nights in 2016, and cost up to $99 for admission, which included a special Frightfully Fun Parade). A new Halloween Carnival—featuring games, entertainment, magic, a short mask-arade procession, and a fortune-teller—came to the **Festival Arena** in recent years, but disappeared in 2015 once **Star Wars Land** was officially targeted for this **Big Thunder Ranch** area.

No matter the year, hundreds of carved pumpkins are placed in every corner of Disneyland during Halloween Time, including a sixteen-foot-tall, Mickey-shaped

jack-o'-lantern on **Main Street**. In addition, windows and lampposts are adorned with Halloween décor, and stores are stocked with spooky items. In **Frontierland**, a majestic Halloween Tree decorated with hanging pumpkins has stood in front of **Silver Spur Supplies** every October since 2007. The tree celebrates both the season and the 1972 novel The Halloween Tree by **Ray Bradbury**, a noted Disneyland fan (Bradbury himself

attended the dedication).

So popular is Halloween Time that it's been starting earlier and earlier every year (Halloween merchandise begins appearing in mid-August, and in 2016, the event itself began on September 9). Once the season is over and Halloween Time has run out, **cast members** have barely a month to prepare Disneyland for the winter holidays with elaborate new decorations. And that in October **attendance** the park hoped for? It jumps about forty percent compared to pre-Halloween Time years, with comparable spikes in merchandise and food sales.

Happiest Homecoming on Earth

DATES: May 5, 2005–September 30, 2006

In honor of its fiftieth birthday, Disneyland staged the Happiest Homecoming on Earth, a comprehensive celebration that lasted from May of 2005 through September of 2006. Julie Andrews served as the official ambassador for the eighteen-month party. Among the special events and new shows were celebratory decorations appearing on **Sleeping Beauty Castle** and other significant buildings; Walt Disney's Parade of Dreams, held daily; a nightly fireworks spectacular called Remember . . . Dreams Come True; and *Disneyland: The First 50 Magical Years*, a new documentary starring **Steve Martin** and shown all day in the **Opera House**. Disneyland welcomed one new attraction in 2005 (**Buzz Lightyear Astro Blasters**), reopened old favorites with new updates, and launched a plethora of fiftieth anniversary merchandise. Guests were certainly happy to celebrate; 2005 had one of the highest annual attendances in Disneyland history.

On July 16, 2005, fans started lining up for entry the next morning—the actual fiftieth anniversary of **Opening Day**. Elsewhere, Disney parks around the globe honored the Disneyland tradition with Happiest Celebration on Earth festivities of their own. One day after Disneyland's fiftieth birthday party ended, the **Year of a Million Dreams** promotion began.

Happiness

It might seem unusual that an abstract emotional state such as happiness should be an entry in an encyclopedia—unless that encyclopedia is about Disneyland. This park, we'll argue, was *created* to inspire the transcendent feeling of happiness.

Disneyland's raison d'être is spelled out in the 1953 prospectus that summarizes **Walt Disney's** plans. The very first thing stated about the proposed park is that "it will be a place for people to find happiness," an assertion that is repeated at the end. Then, on June 14, 1959, Walt Disney dedicated the latest **Tomorrowland** attractions by stating that Disneyland's "only purpose" is "the pursuit of happiness for all" (his phrasing dovetails nicely with Disneyland's conspicuous patriotic pageantry; "the pursuit of

-Disneyland-
TO ALL WHO COME TO THIS HAPPY PLACE:
— WELCOME —

happiness" is one of the fundamental "inalienable rights" named in the Declaration of Independence).

As noted in this encyclopedia's Walt Disney entry, Disney's intentions for the park can be reduced to basically just one, which is the instruction he gave to all his designers: put smiles on guests' faces. Of all the thousands of Disney quotes that could have been used for the plaque on the *Partners* statue, this is the one that made it: "Most of all what I want Disneyland to be is a happy place." On Disneyland's famous dedication plaque (shown), there's only one adjective directly applied to Disneyland among its seventy words and numbers: "happy." Starting in 1955, the Disney Traditions training given to new cast members emphasized one common objective: "We deliver happiness."

If anything, the happiness theme has only strengthened over time. In 1975, a new advertising slogan reminded everyone that Disneyland is "the happiest part of growing up." In 2005 and 2006, the comprehensive celebration of Disneyland's fiftieth birthday was named the **Happiest Homecoming on Earth.** And a 2014 promotion introduced new signs to remind everyone that Disneyland just "Keeps Getting Happier."

Happiness isn't just something Disney latched onto for his family-friendly ad campaign. It's actually observable. In October 1965, sci-fi legend **Ray Bradbury** wrote an article for *Holiday* magazine called "The Machine-Tooled Happyland." In it, he advises readers to visit Disneyland for themselves: "There you will see the happy faces of people. I don't mean dumb-cluck happy . . . I mean truly happy." Significantly, in 2015 a welcome sign near the Mickey and Friends parking structure didn't read, "This Way to Disneyland"; it read, "This Way to More Happiness" (shown on page 11). After sixty years of reminders, the sign implied, everyone knows that Disneyland and happiness are one and the same.

Thus it's no accident, no mere marketing gimmick, that Disneyland is called "The Happiest Place on Earth" instead of "The Most Entertaining Place on Earth," "The Most Magical Place on Earth," "The Funnest/Friendliest/Greatest place on Earth," etc. Happiness was the designated goal; it is the inner emotion being externalized. For over sixty years, happiness has been the delivered result that helps

MOUSCELLANY

Want to know what "happy" looks like? There's a statue of him standing in the **Snow White Wishing Well and Grotto** next to **Sleeping Beauty Castle** (shown).

explain why the vast majority of Disneyland's guests come back again and again, even when they know high prices and long lines await them.

Coming to Disneyland makes them happy.

Happy Lunar New Year Celebration

MAP: Fa-21

DATES: January 20, 2012–January 29, 2012

After the success of **Three Kings Day** in early January of 2012, Disneyland inaugurated another special event two weeks later. Centered in front of **It's a Small World** from January 20 to January 29, 2012, Lunar New Year festivities celebrated Chinese, Korean, and Vietnamese culture via musical performances, themed foods, and meet-and-greets with Mulan and other Disney characters. The party was held again in 2013, 2014, and 2015, but these celebrations were relocated to Disney California Adventure.

Harbor Boulevard

The busy city street that runs along Disneyland's eastern border is Harbor Boulevard. This is where the giant **marquee** and entrance into the long-gone **parking lot** used to be. About twenty-three miles long, Harbor extends from the Orange County city of Costa Mesa (starting about a mile from the ocean) and continues north through the cities of Santa Ana, Fountain Valley, Garden Grove, Anaheim, and Fullerton as it goes to the L.A. County line. Along the way, Harbor Boulevard's name changes to S. Harbor and N. Harbor. Several major freeways are on Harbor's long route: it goes under the 405, over the 22, under Interstate 5, and under the 91.

Most notably, Harbor Boulevard goes past a half-mile of Disneyland, parallel to a stretch of **Monorail** track (shown). When Disneyland opened in 1955, the rapid proliferation of tacky motels and businesses in this area prompted **Walt Disney** to buy thousands of Florida acres for Walt Disney World. Today, these blocks (at least alongside the Disneyland Resort) are a little more upscale than they were decades ago.

A walk along Harbor Boulevard just outside Disneyland presents some interesting sights. One of them is the Anaheim Walk of Stars. Starting on Harbor at the park's welcoming **marquee** (shown on page 314) and heading south, the west-side sidewalk features a starry tribute that has been saluting notable local names since 2006 (Walt Disney has a prominent star right at Disneyland's pedestrian entrance). Also notable are the large sidewalk maps of the "Anaheim Resort" (detail shown on page 236) that are placed in the intersections where Harbor crosses other streets near Disneyland.

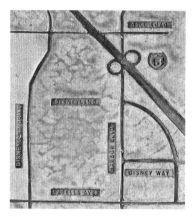

At 1530 S. Harbor Boulevard is the former site of the old Carousel Inn & Suites; Disney bought this property for $32 million in 2015 and a year later announced plans to raze the buildings. In their place will be a new walkway to an east-side, 6,900-car parking structure set to open in late 2018. Pedestrians will cross Harbor via a new fifteen-to-twenty-foot-high bridge.

Besides Harbor Boulevard, several other major streets border Disneyland. Busy Katella Avenue on the south separates the park from the Anaheim Convention Center; S. Disneyland Drive (formerly West Street) separates Disneyland from the Disneyland Hotel property; S. Walnut Street and Anaheim residences are to the west; and W. Ball Road to the north is a key artery that connects guests with Interstate 5.

> **MOUSCELLANY**
>
> In her 2004 song "Cool," Gwen Stefani (whose former band, No Doubt, was from Anaheim) asks her old boyfriend to "remember Harbor Boulevard."

Harbour Galley

MAP: Bear Country/Critter Country, B/C-1

DATES: July 1989–ongoing

In 1989, a small counter-service eatery called the Harbour Galley opened near the **Haunted Mansion**. The riverfront location was on a walkway named Mill View Lane, a reference to both Disney Legend **Joe Fowler** (this was reportedly the name of the Florida street where he lived) and the Old Mill over on **Tom Sawyer Island.**

As the maritime sign out front announced, the Harbour Galley offered "delectable seafood specialties," including Cajun popcorn shrimp, fish and chips, and chowder. Unfortunately, business was often so slow that the Harbour Galley was frequently closed. In mid-2001, while still retaining its name, the restaurant transformed into a McDonald's stand that served fries and beverages (an abbreviated McMenu similar to the one in **Westward Ho Conestoga Wagon Fries**). After closing in September of 2008, the Harbour Galley reopened nine months later, with a menu of soups and salads replacing everything from McDonald's. In 2013, the menu was updated to include a buttery lobster roll and chowder served in sourdough bread bowls.

Haunted Mansion

MAP: New Orleans Square, NOS-12

DATES: August 9, 1969–ongoing

One of the most eagerly awaited days in Disneyland history finally arrived with the

debut of the Haunted Mansion. The public had been hearing about the attraction since 1961 and had been staring at its unfinished exterior in **New Orleans Square** since 1963. When it finally opened at the height of the summer in 1969, the exciting new attraction drew some of Disneyland's largest crowds ever.

Tentative plans for some kind of haunted house had actually preceded Disneyland itself—**Harper Goff's** 1951 concept drawing depicts a haunted mansion on a hill, and **Marvin Davis's** 1953 illustration places a rickety haunted house at the end of **Main Street.**

Two years after Disneyland opened, **Ken Anderson** invented a basic design for the attraction and a story to go with it. He drew up a mansion that was inspired by an early-nineteenth-century house in Baltimore that was approximately the same size as Disneyland's eventual mansion, with the same four stately columns out front and the ornate balcony ironwork later echoed in Anaheim. Anderson also devised a plot that included the Headless Horseman and a murderous sea captain who hanged himself (most of this plot was abandoned in the end, but some individual elements endured, such as the maritime weathervane atop the building and the hanging corpse seen early in the attraction).

As the building's design evolved, **Walt Disney** quickly rejected any sketches that portrayed dilapidated mansions reminiscent of the stereotypical haunted houses in films (and in his own 1937 *Lonesome Ghosts* cartoon). Disneyland structures, he decreed, would not look run-down and neglected.

Excitement for the attraction probably started as early as 1958, when that year's **Fun Map** positioned a large "haunted house" overlooking the **Jungle Cruise.** Announcements in 1961 said that the Haunted Mansion would open within two years, and in fact, an elegant, three-story mansion *was* built in 1963 near **Adventureland.** Guests were tantalized, and all decade long Disneyland's **souvenir books** touted the coming attraction with an eerie painting by **Sam McKim.**

In reality, construction on the mansion had stopped. Instead, Disney put his design team to work on four new attractions for the 1964–1965 New York World's Fair. He stirred up excitement once again when he re-announced the mansion in a 1965 episode of his *Wonderful World of Color* TV show, even mentioning such specific details as a Museum of the Weird (which was never built). But it was not until 1967 that the mansion construction got underway again.

Using ideas approved by Disney before he died in 1966, an all-star team of future Disney Legends ran with the project: **John Hench** was the overall supervisor; **Bill Justice** developed **Audio-Animatronic** ghouls; **Fred Joerger** made plaster models; **Rolly Crump**, **Bill Martin**, and **Yale Gracey** designed scary special effects; **Marc Davis** added whimsical touches; **Claude Coats** designed the spooky interiors; and **Buddy Baker** and **X. Atencio** wrote the "Grim Grinning Ghost" theme song sung by **Thurl Ravenscroft** and the MelloMen (Atencio also penned the Ghost Host's script).

From its genesis to its actual debut, the Haunted Mansion underwent two major revisions. The first came when it gradually transformed from being a seriously scary attraction to a "happy haunt." It would be mildly chilling, yes, but not terrifying, and the ghosts would be "frightfully funny" instead of alarmingly menacing. The

second revision came when the attraction changed from a walk-through exhibit into an **Omnimover** attraction. Omnimovers—basically semi-enclosed pods on a conveyor belt—had already proven themselves as a safe, efficient way to move crowds through **Adventure Thru Inner Space** in **Tomorrowland**. Realizing that pedestrians would move too slowly through the mansion's interiors (especially if those pedestrians were either frightened or fascinated), designers decided to convey up to 2,500 "foolish mortals" through the attraction per hour via Doom Buggy pods that would swivel on pre-programmed command.

Once inside the building and past the foyer, guests step into a "stretching room" of humorous portraits (shown); this room is actually an elevator that lowers guests fifteen feet down to a 120-foot subterranean walkway. The first seventy-foot hallway is the "portrait gallery." While showing off clever intaglio busts (shown) and flickering double-image paintings, the gallery leads guests under Disneyland's train tracks, effectively taking them beyond the perimeter **berm** to a one-acre "show building" next door. There, 131 Doom Buggies carry guests through almost 800 feet of haunted rooms, a haunted attic, a haunted ballroom, a haunted cemetery, and even some final haunted mirrors. It's possible that a few of the ghosts, ghoulies, specters, and skeletons on view were inspired by some of the streaking, swirling shapes seen in the seven-minute *Night on Bald Mountain* sequence in *Fantasia*, which was probably Disney's most demonic display of frights prior to the opening of the Haunted Mansion.

Besides **Pirates of the Caribbean**, the $7 million mansion was the most ambitious and complex attraction of its time. Just before it opened to the public in mid-1969, the anticipation was so intense that stories circulated about viewers who had reportedly died of fright on preview tours. When the attraction finally opened, guests were welcomed by elegantly dressed **cast members** who intensified the suspense with their uniformly somber demeanor (they are encouraged *not* to smile).

The Haunted Mansion quickly became Disneyland's most popular attraction. On August 16, 1969, one week after officially opening, a record 82,516 guests lined up to get scared by eight minutes of haunted horrors (that **attendance** record lasted for almost two decades; though Disneyland stopped giving attendance figures in 1984, it's believed that the Haunted Mansion's record was finally eclipsed in 1987 when **Star Tours** debuted). The busy attraction has also generated a plethora of merchandise, including a jigsaw puzzle, an hourglass with purple sand, a board game, Rest in Peace pillows, candlesticks, a mini-coffin that holds coasters, and record albums (on the 1969 LP *The Story and Song from the Haunted Mansion*, Ronny Howard and his date are given a tour by the Ghost Host).

Over the years, loyal fans have teased out some of the mansion's secrets. For instance, in contrast to the colorful flowers planted elsewhere in the park, many of the plants outside the mansion are dark and foreboding. There's a conspicuous pet cemetery in the front gardens that was enlarged to its current size in 1993 (some new tombstones were added to the hill in mid-2016), and there are also humorous names interred in the wall at the back of the **queue** area (including U. R. Gone, Ray N. Carnation, M. T. Tomb, etc.). There's also a smaller hidden cemetery (detail shown) to the right of the mansion that was installed around 1980. One long-rumored "secret" is that the horse-drawn hearse near the front door is from Brigham Young's funeral. This rumor, however, proved to be false.

There are even more secrets to be found inside the mansion. For example, a black cat, and then a raven, were considered to be guides inside the building before an unseen Ghost Host was invented. Walt Disney himself considered doing the Ghost Host narration that was later performed by **Paul Frees**. (The Ghost Host, by the way, isn't the mansion's owner; he's a servant. The owner is Master Gracey, a name that honors Disney Imagineer Yale Gracey). The Madame Leota head-in-a-crystal-ball

MOUSCELLANY

Before the Haunted Mansion was built, Imagineers proposed so many ideas for the attraction that not all of them could be realized. One unused idea (revealed in 2015 by D23.com) pitched by **Wally Boag** in 1966 was to put a phone outside the building that guests would pick up. They'd then hear a "ghost to ghost hookup," a short vignette about a terrified painter trapped inside the mansion's basement. A creepy voice was to come on the line to deliver scary lines about the ghosts waiting inside the mansion.

illusion shows the face of Leota Toombs, another Imagineer (the voice was provided by veteran actress Eleanor Audley, who also voiced characters in *Cinderella* and *Sleeping Beauty*). The organ in the ballroom is the one used in the film *20,000 Leagues Under the Sea* (it plays "Grim Grinning Ghosts"). The cake on the banquet table has thirteen candles, and the graveyard's singing busts (shown on page 11) have names: Cousin Algernon, Ned Nub, Phineas P. Pock, Uncle Theodore, Rollo Rumkin, and Thurl Ravenscroft (many have believed that it was Walt Disney's visage on Ravenscroft's broken bust). And at one time, live cast members in costume (including a suit of armor) would jump out at guests to enliven the experience for repeat visitors.

As with virtually everything else in Disneyland, the venerable mansion gets revised occasionally. On October 5, 2001, the building was dressed up for the first time with *The Nightmare Before Christmas* décor for a new event called the Haunted Mansion Holiday. This elaborate seasonal tradition still continues today, with new décor on the mansion's exterior, new portraits in the stretching room, new

artworks on the walls (shown), singing pumpkins in the graveyard, and more. In 2006, high-tech updates in the attic added a murderous bride named Constance Hatchaway, along with vanishing portraits of her victims. Additionally, the soundtrack has been revised, Madame Leota's head now floats around the séance room, and in May 2015, the long-awaited Hatbox Ghost character (shown) finally returned. This standalone figure, whose head transitions from his neck to a hatbox he's carrying, had been briefly and ineffectively tried out in 1969, but new technology makes the illusion delightfully convincing.

No matter what changes it goes through, the Haunted Mansion continues to have an irresistible pull on guests. Not that it has been critic-proof: occasionally, some reviewers have insisted upon a linear story and exposition where there is only inscrutability and ambiguity; they've craved clarity where there is only pure sensation shrouded in special effects; and they've demanded answers when the building only provokes questions. Like any supernatural location, the Haunted Mansion is a wonderful place of mystery that is to be enjoyed, not fully explained and exposed (even Albert Einstein once said, "The most beautiful thing we can experience is the mysterious"). Guests continue to enjoy the mansion's compelling experience, glad that "there's no turning back now" (as the Ghost Host warns). Even after multiple visits, they still "hurry ba-ack, hurry ba-ack," just as the Little Leota figure near the exit has encouraged them to do for almost fifty years.

Heliports

DATES: 1955–1972

Ever since the first freeways were built in the 1950s, people have been looking for ways to speed up their commutes. To shorten the travel time between his studio in Burbank and his park in Anaheim thirty-eight miles away, **Walt Disney** constructed his own heliport in 1955. This spartan landing pad was located outside **Tomorrowland**, beyond the southeast corner of Disneyland's berm; today's guests who walk in from **Harbor Boulevard** (with **Space Mountain** on their right) would be crossing the area where the first heliport was located. Los Angeles Airways soon introduced passenger

> **MOUSCELLANY**
>
> In Annie North Bedford's children's book *Little Man of Disneyland* (1955), the characters board a helicopter for the same flight from Disneyland to Disney Studios that Walt Disney might have taken, "over oil wells and city streets and towering brown hills."

service from Los Angeles International Airport to this spot, offering guests a scenic fifteen-minute flight back and forth between LAX and Disneyland. Early **Fun Maps** clearly show a whirlybird hovering over this southeastern heliport, and Disneyland's 1956 **souvenir book** boasts that "five helicopter flights arrive daily."

Five years later, a second heliport was built, this time beyond the western berm. This pad was located across West Street (aka Disneyland Drive) and just north of the burgeoning Disneyland Hotel. Once they'd landed, passengers took trams to the hotel. These flights by Los Angeles Airways were so popular that by decade's end, they had brought over a million guests to Disneyland's doorstep. Tragically, two fatal crashes in 1968 (killing forty-four people) brought the service to a halt. Los Angeles Airways briefly tried to revive the flights but was unsuccessful; Golden West Airlines launched a new helicopter service to this heliport in 1972, but canceled it after five months.

Hench, John
(1908–2004)

Many historians conclude that no person—other than the man Disneyland was named after, of course—had more influence on Disney theme parks, or had a better understanding of them, than John Hench. And no one appreciated Disneyland more than this erudite jack-of-all-trades. "Disneyland is our greatest achievement," Hench writes in *Designing Disney*. "Disneyland was first and set the pattern for others to follow."

An Iowan born in 1908, Hench studied at art institutes in New York, San Francisco, and Los Angeles before joining Disney Studios in 1939. There he worked as an artist and story editor for almost twenty years on classics like *Fantasia*, *Dumbo*, and *Peter Pan*. Hench also helped with the Oscar-winning special effects on *20,000 Leagues Under the Sea*.

In 1954, Hench started designing Disneyland projects and shaping the park's aesthetics,
which meant that everything from attraction layout to garden landscaping to color schemes was
within his purview. He was a crucial contributor
to **Tomorrowland**, the *Moonliner*, the **Carousel of
Progress**, the **Snow White Wishing Well and Grotto**, **New Orleans Square**, the **Haunted Mansion**,
and many **Main Street** buildings. **Cast member**
costumes, **queue** areas, **attraction posters**, and
even **restrooms** were sketched by Hench. The na-

> **MOUSCELLANY**
>
> Today's sharp-eyed
> Disneyland guests can
> find a small tribute to
> John Hench inside **Space
> Mountain**—the Bay 12
> Command Module in
> the attraction's queue
> identifies "Capt. J. Hench."

tion got a glimpse of him working on restaurant interiors on a 1965 episode of *Walt
Disney's Wonderful World of Color* (in 2015, Disneyland guests could see some of his
artwork in a **Disney Gallery** exhibition called "Drawing Disneyland: The Early Years").

Hench, however, was quick to point out that **Walt Disney** was the real designer
of everything in Disneyland. "By the time you got your ideas back from Walt," Hench
says in *Remembering Walt*, "you wouldn't recognize them as your own. . . . In the end,
the production was all his."

Outside Disneyland, Hench was Disney's right-hand man in developing opening
and closing ceremonies for the 1960 Olympic Games. He also helped with new exhibits for the 1964–1965 New York World's Fair and was a key contributor as other
Disney parks opened around the world. As Mickey Mouse's official portrait artist, he
created commemorative paintings for the star's twenty-fifth, fiftieth, sixtieth, and
seventieth birthdays.

Named a Disney Legend in 1990, Hench was long respected as the wise mentor
to young Imagineers. In 1999, Disneyland's great theorist celebrated a sixty-year
Disney career, and in 2003, he eloquently summarized what he'd learned in a retro-
spective book called *Designing Disney*. The following year, Hench died in Burbank at
age ninety-five.

Heraldry Shoppe, aka Castle Heraldry Shoppe

MAP: Fantasyland, Fa-30

DATES: 1994–January 12, 2017

Over the years, **Fantasyland** has offered several resources for genealogical research.
While the now-absent **Names Unraveled** service looked up guests' names, the Heraldry Shoppe enabled them to investigate their family histories. The Heraldry Shoppe
was also called Castle Heraldry, which was appropriate for a business located in, and
then near, **Sleeping Beauty Castle**. After operating for almost fourteen years along
the walkway through the castle's entrance, in 2008 Castle Heraldry moved into a
building in the courtyard next to Peter Pan's busy attraction, a prominent spot that
had formerly housed **Merlin's Magic Shop**. The regal split-level shop was made of the
castle's stone, had a suit of armor in the doorway, and was adorned inside with eerie
gothic statuary.

Heraldry got its start in the Middle Ages as a way for English families to trace their heritage, establish their ruling status, and define their coats of arms. At Disneyland, guests could learn the geographic and historical origins of their family names, check out family crests, and purchase attractive hard copies of all the pertinent information. Also available were souvenir coats of arms, $150 swords, daggers styled after those in *The Lord of the Rings*, personalized plaques, shirts with heraldic symbols, and more. Operated by a lessee (the Historical Research Center), the shop was occasionally closed even when other Fantasyland shops were open.

Hidden Mickeys

The term Hidden Mickey is something of a misnomer, since the Mickeys that are supposedly hidden are actually in plain sight. A Hidden Mickey is a shape made of three circles that is patterned after Mickey Mouse's silhouetted head and round ears. However, simple **mouse ears** placed on a different character, or the appearance of Mickey's oversized gloves or shoes, can also qualify as Hidden Mickeys.

The Hidden Mickey concept probably started at Disneyland in the 1970s, when Disney Imagineers planted a few Mickeys in the park for their own amusement. But as interest in Disneyland trivia intensified over the decades, the Imagineers began incorporating Hidden Mickeys into Disneyland's architecture and attractions with increasing frequency, to be discovered by enthusiastic guests. By now, scores of Hidden Mickeys of varying sizes, shapes, and subtlety are scattered throughout Disneyland. Several fan websites catalogue new Hidden Mickeys as they appear, and field guides help pinpoint them. NASA even released a photo in 2012 that showed a cluster of craters on Mercury that formed the classic Mickey shape.

Hidden Mickeys are distinguished from "actual" Mickeys that have obviously been worked into a design (the large parterre at the **entrance**, for example) or that constitute the shape of a product (a Mickey Mouse-shaped lollipop wouldn't count). Finding a true Hidden Mickey usually requires careful observation and repeat visits for confirmation. The shapes can be small or large, and they can be either distinct markings  or groupings of objects. Sometimes proper perspective is required to turn the abstract into a pattern: seen from water level while paddling a canoe, an arrangement of rocks at the north end of **Tom Sawyer Island** looked totally arbitrary, but when viewed from the upper decks of the *Mark Twain* **Riverboat**, those same rocks formed a deliberate Hidden Mickey (shown).

One scene inside **Pirates of the Caribbean** shows contrasting ways that Hidden Mickeys can be formed. At the end of the scene, as the bateaux are about to rise up the waterfall, they pause in a room where pirates are shooting at each other. To the left, a pirate sprawls across a cannon, and on the wall behind him are three breastplates, one of which has a tiny but conspicuous Hidden Mickey carefully fashioned in the center of the shining metal. Meanwhile, hanging above the guests at that moment is a trio of large barrels that have been roped together into the familiar configuration, turning what might have been a random array of objects into a Hidden Mickey.

For Disneyland's fiftieth golden anniversary in 2005, fifty additional blue-and-gold Hidden Mickeys were incorporated into various locations throughout the park. These temporary Mickeys were much more prominent than their hidden brethren, and in fact, **City Hall** even provided a list of locations to help guests find them all.

Ten years later, Disneyland introduced a new scavenger hunt called the Looking for Mickey Quest. Starting on July 16, 2015, and continuing for two weeks, guests could buy a guide that spilled clues about Hidden Mickey locations. Once all twenty Mickeys were found, guest could redeem their completed guides at the **Disneyana** shop on **Town Square** for a prize. The fun quest was reminiscent of the **Egg-strava-ganza** egg hunt, a popular interactive event that debuted in 2013.

Hills Bros. Coffee House and Coffee Garden

MAP: Town Square, TS-7

DATES: June 13, 1958–December 1976

Eight months after Maxwell House closed its **Town Square** coffee shop, Hills Bros., a San Francisco coffee company founded in the early 1900s, opened one of its own in the same location. Because it had an expanded outdoor area, old **souvenir books** dubbed this the Hills Bros. Coffee House and Coffee Garden. The location was ideal for a morning coffee business, since it faced guests as they entered Disneyland through the east tunnel and headed to **Main Street**.

There was more than just coffee here, though. A small 1972 guidebook presented by INA (the insurance company that sponsored the **Carefree Corner** for eighteen years) touts the "waitress service" and the breakfast served until 11 AM. Sandwiches, soups, and pastries were also offered. What's more, according to Donald Ballard's *The Disneyland Hotel* book, this was one of two spots (Carefree Corner was the other) where guests could "make direct reservations" for the nearby hotel while still inside Disneyland. In 1976, Hills Bros. headed for the **Market House**, and the **Town Square Café** took over this spot as a full-service sit-down restaurant.

Hobbyland

MAP: Tomorrowland, T-20

DATES: September 4, 1955–January 1966

For over ten years, the open area south of the **Flight Circle** in **Tomorrowland** was the site of a freestanding retail area called Hobbyland. If Hobbyland were in place today, it would begin outside the **Star Trader** store and extend to **Cosmic Waves**.

Lackluster in design, Hobbyland was nothing more than about a dozen counter-tops separated by aluminum struts that supported temporary fiberglass roofs. What interested its devotees, however, was the Hobbyland treasure they could mine here. Hobbyland's jewels were its model kits. Guests could sift through a comprehensive collection that included everything from cars and ships to rockets and dinosaurs, plus some of the Flight Circle's motorized vehicles.

In 1966, this whole area was closed off for the extensive Tomorrowland remodeling that would put the **PeopleMover** and new walkways where Hobbyland's simple booths had once dazzled model-makers.

Holiday Cart

MAP: New Orleans Square, NOS-12

DATES: October 2013–ongoing

The Holiday Cart is what **cast members** call this spooky coach near the **Haunted Mansion**. Actually, the coach is closer to the **Harbour Galley**, but there's no mistaking its ghostly connection to the nearby mansion. This retail cart used to be wheeled out before Halloween for the **holiday season** (thus the "Holiday Cart" name, as the cast members will explain), but in 2014, it seemed to become a permanent fixture, and lately it's there all year long.

Black with silver-and-purple trim, the old-fashioned coach has black umbrellas next to it and displays racks filled with Haunted Mansion and *The Nightmare Before Christmas* merchandise: hourglasses, candlesticks, shirts, CDs, and more (even a Haunted Mansion version of The Game of Life—but shouldn't it be The Game of After-Life?).

Holidayland

MAP: Park, P-13

DATES: June 16, 1957–September 1961

One of Disneyland's most unusual areas wasn't actually *in* Disneyland. Holidayland was located outside the perimeter **berm**, in a field west of **Frontierland** where nine acres were devoted to simple, inexpensive, outdoor family fun. Minimally landscaped, the area offered refreshment stands, picnic tables, a baseball field, volleyball nets, a children's playground, and horseshoe pits, as well as square dancing (plans for ice skating and some other seasonal activities never came to fruition). Dominating Holidayland was a traditional red-striped circus tent where special events, ranging from bingo to performances by the Mouseketeers, could be held. This tent was the same one used for the short-lived **Mickey Mouse Club Circus** in **Fantasyland**.

Holidayland was intended to attract big family reunions or, ideally, corporations that could buy up to 7,000 tickets for employees and day-long company picnics. Admission to Holidayland, unfortunately, did not include admission to Disneyland. It did, however, include access to a special Disneyland entrance where a park admission ticket could be purchased and then a path into Frontierland

MOUSCELLANY

Swift, the same company that sponsored the **Market House**, Red Wagon Inn, and **Chicken Plantation**, sold Holidayland picnic baskets that included prepared food and (surprise!) beer.

could be taken under the train tracks. This was the only time in Disneyland's history when guests could enter the park in a location other than the front gates or via the **Monorail** station in **Tomorrowland**.

Disney Legend **Milt Albright**, who would later devise more successful group-sales strategies, supervised Holidayland in its early years. Ticket sales for this isolated area were always a challenge, and so in September of 1961, its circus tent already tattered by a storm, Holidayland closed. Guests still visit the old Holidayland site, though they aren't aware of it; this is where the "show buildings" for **the Haunted Mansion** and **Pirates of the Caribbean** are hidden.

Holiday Season

DATES: November 24, 1955–ongoing (seasonal)

Borrowing some words from *A Christmas Carol*, Disneyland has always managed to "keep Christmas well," making the winter holidays one of the park's best-attended seasons. Since 1955, the centerpiece of the celebration has been a perfectly symmetrical, sixty-foot-tall tree erected in **Town Square**. Up until 2008, the tree was real and flocked in white; today's guests will find an artificial green tree densely decorated with thousands of lights and lavish ornaments.

For its first holiday season, the park held a Christmas at Disneyland Festival from November 24, 1955 until January 8, 1956. The festival featured a special **parade** and a concert held daily in an open space west of **Sleeping Beauty Castle** called the Christmas Bowl. As described on a 1955 promotional flier, this holiday concert featured "leading church and school choral groups from all over the West." When the Christmas Bowl site became home to the **Plaza Gardens** in 1956, the strolling **Charles Dickens Carolers** took their holiday music to **Main Street**.

Disneyland's winter celebration has evolved over the decades with a variety of events and decorations. In 1961, the now-familiar Christmas toy parade (borrowing themes from the Disney movie *Babes in Toyland*) began marching down Main Street. Starting that year, a sparkling twenty-four-foot, 44,000-pound star, helicoptered into position and visible from the Santa Ana Freeway, topped the **Matterhorn** until energy concerns ended its long run in the mid-1970s. The park has also helped spread the cheer far and wide through TV. Just one example is "Disneyland Around the Seasons," a 1966 episode of *Walt Disney's Wonderful World of Color*, which showcases that winter's parade and inspirational **Candlelight Procession**.

Disneyland's holiday parades are among the most popular of all the holiday events. Parades from previous decades include the Christmas in Many Lands Parade (1957–1964) and the Very Merry Christmas Parade (1977–1979 and 1987–1994). The parades have included such familiar favorites as marching toy soldiers, dancing gingerbread cookies, and Disney princesses with their princes.

Nowadays, Christmas comes early. Decorations start to go up in early September and saturate Disneyland shortly after **Halloween Time** ends; holiday merchandise fills some of the stores and windows by mid-October; and the season officially begins at least one week before Thanksgiving (in 2016, it started on November 10 and didn't end until January 8, 2017). Come December, virtually every structure in Disneyland twinkles with beautiful ornaments and lights, there are live celebrations around nearly every corner, and all day long, guests crowd around Town Square's stunning Christmas tree (shown). The sheer variety of joyous events ensures the park's popularity—there's literally something for everybody, no matter what their age or interest. There's even a special holiday tour that helps guest take everything in.

Here's a *partial* list of the daily proceedings in 2016: the Believe . . . In Holiday Magic fireworks spectacular, including "snow" for the finale; a creative Haunted Mansion Holiday at (and around) the **Haunted Mansion**, with Jack Skellington dressed as

Sandy Claws; festive foods, including the highly coveted handmade candy canes in the **Candy Palace**; new holiday gifts and collectibles in the stores; the return of a winter favorite, the Christmas Fantasy Parade; classic holiday songs from the **Dapper Dans** and the Dickens Yuletide Band; the **Jingle Jangle Jamboree** and Mr. and Mrs. Claus in **Critter Country**; dozens of decorated Christmas trees of various sizes scattered throughout Disneyland; **Sleeping Beauty Castle** adorned with "icicles" and special illumination; seasonal Jingle Cruise theming for the **Jungle Cruise**; and 50,000 holiday lights decorating the **It's a Small World** façade. Everything adds up to what the *L.A. Times* has called "the best holiday magic in town," and it all supplements Disneyland's legendary lineup of exhibits, attractions, and live entertainments. Even Scrooge would be impressed.

Honey, I Shrunk the Audience

MAP: Tomorrowland, T-19

DATES: May 22, 1998–January 3, 2010

Replacing the decommissioned *Captain EO* in the **Magic Eye Theater** was *Honey, I Shrunk the Audience*, a Kodak-hosted 3-D movie that debuted with the rest of the remodeled **Tomorrowland** in 1998.

Like *EO*, *Honey* had been shown in Florida before it was brought west to Anaheim. During the film's eighteen minutes, guests wore the obligatory 3-D glasses and met emcee Dr. Nigel Channing (Eric Idle of *Monty Python's Flying Circus*). Channing then welcomes the Imagination Institute's Inventor of the Year, Professor Wayne Szalinski (Rick Moranis, reprising his role from the *Honey, I Shrunk the Kids* and *Honey, I Blew Up the Kid* movies). Soon Szalinski accidentally miniaturizes the theater to lunchbox size, and merriment ensues as the audience views everything in the film—the cast, the props, a dog, a lunging snake—as if it were gigantic. Several special effects were built into the theater itself, such as jets under the seats that blasted air around audience members' feet to simulate scurrying mice.

EO, it turned out, wasn't gone for good. Michael Jackson's death on June 25, 2009, revived interest in the pop star and catalyzed the 2010 return of *Captain EO*. Ironically, by playing once again in the Magic Eye Theater, *EO* replaced the very film that had been its replacement in 1998.

House of the Future

MAP: Tomorrowland, T-1

DATES: June 12, 1957–December 1, 1967

In *The Graduate*, Benjamin Braddock (played by Dustin Hoffman) receives one key word of advice as he considers his prospects: plastics. Anyone who saw Disneyland's House of the Future might have summarized modern living the same way.

The second Monsanto-sponsored attraction at Disneyland (after the **Hall of Chemistry**), the House of the Future was a free walk-through exhibit located outside the entrance to **Tomorrowland**. The attraction stood on a 256-square-foot raised platform surrounded by contemporary gardens and a winding pool that collectively covered about a quarter of an acre. The pool wasn't there just for aesthetics—its water was part of the building's cooling system.

From above, the 1,280-square-foot, three-bedroom, two-bath home was shaped like a graceful plus sign. Its four rectangular modules were each eight feet tall and twice as long, extending from a central core outwards over open air. These smooth, streamlined, compartmentalized modules ("half jet fuselage, half legume," according to writer P. J. O'Rourke) could be supplemented with additional modules to accommodate the expanding family. An optional rotating platform would have enabled inhabitants to spin their house to face any direction.

During its decade-long existence, the House of the Future welcomed some twenty million guests (more than California's entire population at the time). Instead of an amusing, Disney-designed attraction, guests found a serious home designed by

MOUSCELLANY

Not everyone was a fan of the futuristic House of the Future. In *Let's Just Say It Wasn't Pretty* (2014), actress Diane Keaton writes about her disappointment when, at age eleven, she visited "what looked like an enormous wheel of cheese" with her family during the first week it opened in 1957; her brother called it "Plasticland," and Keaton herself, who "didn't care about the zillions of gadgets," thought "it was so sterile I had to be excused."

MIT and Monsanto engineers to show off technological advances from Monsanto's Plastics Division. Not that the house was humorless—during the **holiday season** it was wrapped with ribbon and a big bow like an enormous present.

Though it was made of plastic, one of the strengths of the house was, in fact, its strength: when it came time to dismantle the entire structure in 1967, engineers discovered that the four extending wings of the house had drooped less than a quarter-inch, despite a decade of heavy traffic. The two-week demolition had to be done by hand with crowbars and saws because the wrecking ball they swung at the house merely bounced off its sides.

Pre-recorded narration playing inside the home bragged that nearly everything on view was artificial and adjustable. Fixtures in the bathroom and shelves in the cabinets could be raised or lowered at the push of a button, and the climate-controlled air could be instantly warmed, cooled, purified, or scented. The futuristic communications included an intercom, push-button speaker phones, picture phones, a sound system in the shower, and a large, wall-mounted TV screen. Interior illumination was provided by "panalescent fixtures," "trans-ceiling polarized panels," and mobile lights that could "bathe each room with the glow of natural sunlight." The sleek furniture was made from vinyl and urethane, and the drapes from nylon. Highlights in the "step saver" kitchen included an "ultrasonic dishwasher" and a microwave oven.

Although the House of the Future may seem silly or dated now, at the time it was an ambitious attempt to make the spirit of the Space Age real and practical, which is what **Walt Disney** would later try to do with the **Monorail** and **PeopleMover**. While the **Astro-Jets**, **Autopia**, and other Tomorrowland attractions entertained guests, the House of the Future educated them with a working vision of what the future could be. After the House of the Future closed in 1967, the **Alpine Gardens** were established over the landscaped grounds, and a souvenir stand incorporated part of what had once been the futuristic patio. The seeds planted by the House of the Future later blossomed into the Progress City model inside the **Carousel of Progress**.

Hub, aka Plaza, aka Plaza Hub, aka Central Plaza

MAP: Park, P-10

DATES: July 17, 1955–ongoing

All the earliest concept drawings of the full-size park depict a broad center axis as the organizing principle for the overall layout. **Walt Disney** wanted his guests to walk through a cozy, familiar setting—**Main Street**—before they ventured into his unknown lands. Once past Main Street, guests would arrive at Disneyland's chief terminal, from which all other areas could be accessed. Situated 800 feet north of the Main Street train station, this terminal, the park's nucleus, is called the Hub.

Labeled as the Plaza Hub on 1989's **Fun Map**, identified as the Plaza by the **PeopleMover's** recorded narration, and formally called the Central Plaza today, this location was called "the Plaza, or the Hub," by Walt Disney when he introduced a park model on his *Disneyland* **TV series**. The single word Plaza might confuse twenty-first-century guests who have seen signs for the Main Entry Plaza (located outside Disneyland's turnstiles), the Gateway Plaza, and the Sunshine Plaza (both formerly located inside Disney California Adventure).

Known to most guests as simply the Hub, the area is both a departure point and a meeting point. Radiating out from the Hub like the spokes of a wheel are six main walkways: one takes guests south to Main Street, two head west to **Adventureland** and **Frontierland**, two go north toward **Fantasyland**, and one heads east to **Tomorrowland**. Smaller walkways also lead to a number of main restaurants, including the **Plaza Pavilion** to the southwest, the **Plaza Gardens** to the northwest, and what was once the Red Wagon Inn (now the **Plaza Inn**) to the southeast (there have been no restaurants that incorporate the Hub name into their monikers).

Experience taught Walt Disney that his idea for a central Disneyland area was a good one: "The more I go to other amusement parks in all parts of the world," he says in *The Quotable Walt Disney*, "the more I am convinced of the wisdom of the original concepts of Disneyland. I mean, have a single entrance through which all traffic would flow, then a hub off which the various areas were situated. That gives people a sense of orientation—they know where they are at all times. And it saves a lot of walking."

It's very unlikely that a guest could avoid crossing the Hub circle at least once during a park visit. Few guests, however, *want* to avoid the Hub. Its circular expanse covers about 35,000 square feet (four-fifths of an acre), and it's beautifully landscaped with trees, shrubs, and flowers. The central position of the Hub makes it one of Disneyland's best spots to people-watch, view **fireworks**, and admire transportation (**Main Street Vehicles** round the Hub on their trips to **Town Square**). In addition, **popcorn carts**, cappuccino stands, and character greeting areas are usually positioned along the sidewalks. A helpful Information Board near the Plaza Pavilion offers up-to-the-hour information about **parades**, shows, and wait-times (plus a large Braille map, installed in mid-2011). Along the Hub's southern border are W. Plaza Street and E. Plaza Street, home to the **Baby Station**, and other sites.

Since 1993, the ***Partners*** statue of Walt Disney and Mickey Mouse has stood on a pedestal in the Hub's center. The placement is significant. This dignified tribute to Disneyland's origins wasn't installed in Town Square, or outside the highly visible **entrance**, or in Fantasyland (reputed to be Disney's favorite area), or in any of the other key locations around the park. *Partners* is at the heart of the Hub, and thus at the very heart of Disneyland itself.

Hungry Bear Restaurant, aka Golden Bear Lodge

MAP: Bear Country/Critter Country, B/C-3

DATES: September 24, 1972–ongoing

One of Disneyland's most serene dining experiences debuted in 1972: the Golden Bear Lodge. It was located just inside the entrance to **Bear Country** on a large plot adjacent to the **Country Bear Jamboree**. Since this big two-story building sits along the **Rivers of America**, its upper and lower terraces have always offered scenic views of riparian life (shown).

By 1977, the lodge had a new name, the Hungry Bear Restaurant. The eatery has always been a counter-service establishment, serving burgers, hearty sandwiches, salads, and desserts. A 2011 menu update added some new items, including an acclaimed vegetarian fried-green-tomato sandwich, followed in 2015 by a deluxe turkey wrap. Disneyland's best burger might be the Hungry Bear's Pioneer Chili Cheeseburger (a 1/3-pounder crowned with a "hand-battered onion ring") and its best summertime beverage might be the refreshing Honey Bee Frozen Lemonade. The Pulled Pork Hot Dog with citrus slaw, fried jalapeños, and fresh cilantro is another favorite, and it illustrates how Disneyland has always tried to upgrade traditional amusement park fare into distinctive modern classics.

Hurricane Lamp Shop

MAP: Main Street, MS-4

DATES: 1972–1975

In 1972, a **Main Street** room that was formerly part of the **Upjohn Pharmacy** became home to the Hurricane Lamp Shop. Victorian hurricane lamps with glass chimneys and oil-burning wicks might have seemed like appealing items for turn-of-the-century Main Street, but guests would soon glow out of them. In 1976, the **Disneyana** shop replaced the non-Disney lamps with Disney collectibles.

Indiana Jones Adventure

MAP: Adventureland, A-6

DATES: March 3, 1995–ongoing

Debuting in 1995, the Indiana Jones Adventure was the first major new attraction in **Adventureland** since 1963's **Enchanted Tiki Room**. As with *Captain EO* and **Star**

Tours, Indy's adventure was the result of a fruitful pairing of Disney and George Lucas.

Plans for the attraction actually began in the mid-1980s, back when the second Lucas-produced Indiana Jones movie, *Indiana Jones and the Temple of Doom*, was pulling crowds into theaters. Various Disney designers took a crack at incorporating elements from the Indy films into some kind of Disneyland adventure. Some of the early concept drawings show battered vehicles careening along a cliff above a lava-filled ravine; others include a roller-coaster-style mine-car chase. Nearly all the early ideas incorporated the rolling boulder sequence from *Raiders of the Lost Ark*.

When the Indiana Jones Adventure finally opened, it had accumulated the highest price tag for any Disneyland attraction ever (most estimates are over $100 million, about six times the total cost to build the entire park in the mid-1950s). Before construction began in 1993, designers first reshaped the adjacent **Jungle Cruise** river to make room for the tall temple structure and its elaborately themed **queue**

area. Winding a half-mile with lots of turns and tunnels, this would be the longest line in Disneyland history.

The real achievement, however, wasn't the construction of the building as much as the engineering of the cars, the "Enhanced-Motion Vehicles." The EMVs are Disneyland's most complex vehicles. Created to look like well-used jungle jeeps from 1935, the sixteen vehicles are basically split in half horizontally: the bottom half accelerates and brakes while rolling along the ground, and the upper half has hydraulics that create dips, swerves, shakes, and tilts all along the 2,500-foot track. The multiple motions make for a crazy and unpredictable ride (and a somewhat dangerous ride, too—in its first year, the vehicles generated so many minor injuries that designers quickly added several safety modifications). What's more, each six-ton vehicle carries its own computer that instigates sudden bumps, fire flashes, and other effects to create 160,000 possible variations of the Indy experience.

Once they leave the "archaeological dig" at the boarding area, the trucks speed up to thirteen miles per hour and whip about 1,800 guests per hour through a perilous three-and-a-half-minute journey inside the Temple of the Forbidden Eye. Snakes, rats, bugs, fire, blow guns, a collapsing bridge, that famous rolling boulder, and sophisticated **Audio-Animatronic** Indiana Jones figures await (an Indy at the end, updated in September 2010, is one of the most lifelike A-A machines ever made). Pumping through the on-board audio systems are realistic sound effects, Indy's voice, screaming mummies, and the familiar movie music, all propelling the excitement to unprecedented heights.

Just like the first Indiana Jones film, Disneyland's Indy ride was an instant hit. Publicized on a 1995 TV special called "40 Years of Adventure," the new attraction drew the biggest crowds since 1987's Star Tours debut. Fans have always loved the delightful little details that add to its authenticity and fun. Among them: Sallah, one of Indy's movie sidekicks, delivers the pre-boarding instructions; the **queue** area displays coded symbols (Maraglyphics) that guests could decipher via special decoder cards; one of the crates in the queue area is addressed to Obi Wan, a character from another Lucas movie; the jungle trucks don't really go in reverse, even though an illusion suggests they do; and, in the finest **Hidden Mickey** tradition, one of the skeletons often sports **mouse ears**. A three-month renovation in 2012 resulted in enhanced effects to make the journey even more thrilling.

> **MOUSCELLANY**
>
> In August 2015, a tiny, delightful detail appeared at this location. The Indiana Jones Adventure sign out front is mounted on a realistic (but fake) tree; at the bottom of that tree is now a small, discreet home for Patrick Begorra, the diminutive leprechaun in a classic children's book. See the *Little Man of Disneyland* entry for more info and a photo.

These and many, many other surprises make this attraction one of the most exhilarating and inventive Disneyland additions in a generation. To paraphrase one of the original movie ads—if adventure has a name, it must be the Indiana Jones Adventure.

Indiana Jones Adventure Outpost

MAP: Adventureland, A-2

DATES: Spring 1995–ongoing

Capitalizing on the massive attention brought to **Adventureland** by the **Indiana Jones Adventure**, the Indiana Jones Adventure Outpost debuted across from the new attraction's entrance in 1995. The Outpost's interior is about forty-five feet wide and twenty feet deep, and it opens to **South Seas Traders** next door. Indy's Outpost replaced the **Safari Outpost**, which had been selling khaki safari gear.

Once the Indy name was on it, the Outpost began stocking merchandise designed in the style of the Indy movies, such as classic felt fedoras, whips, maps, rubber snakes and spiders, a gun-and-holster set, a $50 Indy bag, and archaeological artifacts. Displays of movie posters and old maps adorn the walls, and a fabulous Indiana Jones: The Pinball Adventure machine with a pistol grip stands in one corner (four balls for a quarter). For one summer month in 2014, the store turned into the headquarters for the Adventure Trading Company, a new interactive role-playing game similar to the **Legends of Frontierland: Gold Rush** game that guests were already playing in **Frontierland**.

Indian Trading Post

MAP: Frontierland, Fr-15

DATES: July 4, 1962–December 1, 1988

The rustic little store known as the Indian Trading Post joined the seven-year-old **Indian Village** in **Frontierland** on 1962's Independence Day. The picturesque location near the **Rivers of America** offered guests swell views of boats on the water and kids on **Tom Sawyer Island**. Inside the Trading Post were authentic American Indian crafts, such as turquoise jewelry, clothing, and pottery.

Despite the 1972 remodeling that replaced the Indian Village with **Bear Country**, the Indian Trading Post was left untouched, its American Indian theme still appropriate for the new land set in the Pacific Northwest woods of the 1800s. However, the Indian Trading Post didn't survive the 1988 remodel that replaced Bear Country with **Critter Country**; a week after the critters arrived, the Trading Post became the more Disney-esque **Briar Patch**.

Indian Village

MAP: Frontierland, Fr-15

DATES: July 1955–October 1971

American Indian villages had participated in world's fairs for decades: fifty-one tribes, an assortment of authentic villages, and an autograph-signing Geronimo were all on view at the 1904 St. Louis World's Fair. So it wasn't unusual to find a realistic Indian Village in Disneyland, this one opening in 1955 near the **Chicken Plantation** restaurant at the western edge of **Frontierland**.

For the first few months, the Indian Village consisted of a small collection of teepees and simple wooden structures that recreated the dwellings of various nineteenth-century Plains Indians. Unlike most of Disneyland, the village had dusty dirt paths winding through it instead of paved sidewalks.

Inside the Indian Village, American Indians brought realism to Frontierland by demonstrating their customs and performing genuine ceremonial dances like the Eagle and the Mountain Spirit. Disneyland's 1985 hardcover souvenir book proudly notes that the "authentic dances from such tribes as the Apache, Navajo, Comanche, and Pawnee" were "performed with the permission of the respective tribal councils and the U.S. Bureau of Indian Affairs."

Within a year, the Indian Village was relocated farther north along the river's west bank, a spot opposite the center of the brand-new **Tom Sawyer Island**. This was a larger space with more development, including an ornate dance circle, additional teepees, lodges, a burial ground, and Indian War Canoes. Demonstrations of archery and displays of arts and crafts added to the fun. A 1962 remodel of the village expanded the location and brought in the **Indian Trading Post**.

Disneyland's **souvenir books** often showed photos of "full-blooded Indians" performing "tribal dances," Chief Shooting Star in his elaborate native garb, and canoes paddling past painted teepees. In one happy photo, a smiling **Walt Disney** poses in front of a tribal drum, wearing a ceremonial headdress with his gray suit. The Indian Village was showcased on a 1970 episode of *The Wonderful World of Disney*, but dwindling interest and mounting labor problems numbered the village's days. In October 1971, the Indian Village was dismantled so the area could be transformed into **Bear Country**.

However, a nostalgic reminder of the old village continued for decades (until construction began on **Star Wars Land** in 2016). At the northern bend in the **Rivers of America**, realistic props and Audio-Animatronic figures (shown) presented a fascinating display that could be studied from the decks of the passing *Mark Twain* **Riverboat** and **Sailing Ship** *Columbia*.

Indy Fruit Cart

Map: Adventureland, A-7

DATES: Ca. 1995–2006

Of the various fruit carts that have been stationed throughout Disneyland, one of the most memorable was the Indy Fruit Cart parked at the western end of **Adventureland**. Designed to match the theme of the nearby **Indiana Jones Adventure**, the cart was shaped like a battered World War II jeep, complete with dings and faded paint. The menus lodged in the steering wheel and chained to the body announced various fresh fruit selections, supplemented with nuts, chips, and juices. This healthy haven was towed away around 2006.

Innoventions

MAP: Tomorrowland, T-14

DATES: July 3, 1998–March 31, 2015

A quarter of a century after the **Carousel of Progress** show stopped spinning, and a decade after **America Sings** sang its last song, Innoventions opened in the big, round Carousel Theater at the back of **Tomorrowland.**

Innoventions wasn't a daring risk for Disneyland—it had already been a success at Walt Disney World before it came to Anaheim. At Disneyland, the attraction was an ever-changing, multi-faceted presentation of innovative edutainment. Innoventions focused on the future—not the distant future, but a future that sometimes seemed like it was only ten minutes away.

In its early years, Innoventions spread displays of gadgets and games, many of which were already on the market, across its 30,000 square feet and two big floors. Subdivided zones pertaining to modern living—entertainment, home, transportation, information, and sports/recreation—grouped exhibits together thematically, with each zone sponsored by major companies like Yamaha and Pioneer. Displays were frequently updated, making each Innoventions visit a new experience. Typically there was a ring of exhibits circling the slowly rotating perimeter that were demonstrated by **cast members** (one complete revolution took about eighteen minutes). In the central hub were hands-on games, quizzes, gadgets, and computers for guests to linger over. The upstairs floor offered more exhibits, corporate displays, and the building's exits.

Throughout the building, guests may have seen voice-activated appliances, the latest PlayStation games, an imaging program that aged a photograph that was just taken, a tree made out of circuit boards, a futuristic car, and virtual-reality exercycles. From 2008 to February of 2015, the interior space was dominated by the 5,000-square-foot Innoventions Dream Home, a variation of Tomorrowland's old **House of the Future**. Sponsored by Microsoft and other companies, the new Dream Home displayed high-tech, well-furnished rooms used by the fictional Elias family (Elias was Walt Disney's middle name and his father's first name).

> **MOUSCELLANY**
>
> Though aimed at the future, Innoventions did give nostalgic nods to Disneyland's past. The **Sherman Brothers'** familiar "There's a Great, Big, Beautiful Tomorrow" tune could be heard here, bolstered with new lyrics. Outside, the theater's exterior often saluted old Tomorrowland attractions with colorful banners—nice reminders that innovation is nothing new at Disneyland.

Elsewhere in the Innoventions building, guests could hear long spiels about next-generation cars coming from a major sponsor, Honda. What guests couldn't find inside Innoventions were **restrooms**—evidently those hadn't been innovented yet.

Back in the day, the Carousel Theater was usually filled with **Audio-Animatronic** figures—there were over 100 for America Sings—but this century, only one prominent A-A character was on view. He was a doozy, though. Up until about 2013, the host of the Innoventions proceedings was a wise-cracking robot with transparent skin, a see-through lab coat, and Nathan Lane's voice. Called Tom Morrow, he recalled the similarly named flight director in the **Flight to the Moon** attraction, but now both Toms are gone.

The building got Marvel-ous in 2013, when Marvel Comics characters and their Disney-made movies started to arrive. On April 13 of that year, a major new exhibit—Iron Man Tech Presented by Stark Industries—filled much of Innoventions' second floor with displays and costumes that reminded guests of the new *Iron Man 3* movie opening soon. On November 6, 2013, a meet-and-greet and weapons display called Thor: Treasures of Asgard opened in Innoventions to promote *Thor: The Dark World*. Finally, on March 7, 2014, another Marvel-inspired exhibit debuted, this one called *Captain America: The Living Legend and Symbol of Courage*.

Everything shut down in March of 2015, and Innoventions was completed re-innovented. When it reopened eight months later, the building had a prosaic new name, **Tomorrowland Expo Center**, and a dominant new theme, *Star Wars*.

International Street

MAP: Town Square, TS-7

DATES: Never built

From 1956 to 1958, a sign on a tall wooden fence near the **Opera House** announced that a new International Street area was under construction. Behind the fence, visible to curious guests through small viewing holes, were photographs of what the street would look like when finished. According to the photos, International Street was to run parallel to the eastern row of buildings along **Main Street**, and it would be lined with architecture and shops inspired by a half-dozen countries.

What guests were seeing through the viewing holes was a scaled-down version of something called International Land, which had been intended for Disneyland's northeast corner beyond **Tomorrowland**. Roughly triangular in shape, International Land, as depicted in the book *Disneyland: Then, Now, and Forever*, would have been surrounded by water and connected to the rest of Disneyland by three bridges. Some kind of transportation system curled through the five-acre triangle, and several large buildings graced the interior.

Although neither International Street nor International Land was built, similar concepts did find expression two decades later in Walt Disney World. At Disneyland, announcements for the upcoming International Street were replaced in 1958 by plans for **Liberty Street**, but those, too, would soon pass.

Intimate Apparel, aka Corset Shop

MAP: Main Street, MS-13

DATES: 1955–December 1956

Ever since Disneyland opened, one of the most peaceful places along **Main Street** has been an elevated porch (shown on page 119) along the street's eastern side. Today, guests who take a rest on the bench and chairs here probably don't realize that this little porch, only about eighteen feet wide and five feet deep, originally belonged to the Intimate Apparel shop (aka the Corset Shop in Disneyland's 1956 **souvenir book**).

In case the euphemistic Intimate Apparel name didn't register with 1950s guests, the sign above the porch clearly spelled out what was available inside: "Brassieres" and "Torsolettes." The sponsor was the twenty-five-year-old, Los Angeles-based Hollywood-Maxwell Brassiere Company, aka the H-M Company, better known at the time as "the Wizard of Bras." H-M had created, and was selling at Disneyland, the "strapless Whirlpool bra" that "makes the most of you." Not only that, Intimate Apparel even told the history of women's undergarments via a small in-store exhibit that compared old-fashioned and modern styles (while pushing H-M's latest designs, the recorded narration said: "This is how it was . . . this is how it is").

Some experts speculate that the porch was built as a buffer to keep the window displays a few feet back from young pedestrians; others suggest that the porch was intended as a seating area for gentlemen while their ladies shopped for unmentionables inside. It's also possible that the porch was simply provided as an inviting rest stop on a busy commercial street.

In any case, H-M abandoned the porch and closed up shop in Disneyland in late 1956, at which point the **Ruggles China and Glass** shop next door spread into the vacant room.

Irvine, Richard
(1910–1976)

Imagineers have led the way to new Disneyland attractions, and Richard Irvine led the Imagineers. Born in 1910 in Salt Lake City, his family moved to California twelve years later. Irvine attended Stanford University, USC, and an art institute before getting a job in the budding film industry. Working as an art director for the next two decades, he contributed to such notable films as *Miracle on 34th Street*, Disney's *The Three Caballeros*, and *Sundown*, the latter earning him an Oscar nomination.

Joining the Disneyland designers in 1952, Irvine worked with outside architects to create the park. However, Irvine soon realized that the best people to translate themes from the silver screen into Disneyland were those who were already working on Disney films. Accordingly, **Walt Disney** gathered many of his top animators, artists, set designers, and craftspeople from his movie studio into a newly formed design department, which would eventually be called Imagineering.

For the next twenty years, Irvine headed this team in the creation of every Disneyland attraction, including sophisticated classics like **Pirates of the Caribbean**. After Walt Disney died in 1966, Irvine became the master planner for Walt Disney World, where an old-fashioned steamboat is now named after him.

Irvine retired in 1973 and died three years later in Los Angeles. He was named a Disney Legend in 1990. His daughter-in-law, Kim Irvine, is now an acclaimed Disneyland art director who has worked on everything from the **Rivers of America** to the **Disney Gallery**.

It's a Small World

MAP: Fantasyland, Fa-21

DATES: May 28, 1966–ongoing

It's a Small World was launched on a very large stage: the 1964–1965 New York World's Fair, where over 10 million visitors joined "the happiest cruise that ever sailed 'round the world."

Ideas for It's a Small World, however, pre-dated the World's Fair. In his book *Walt: Backstage Adventures with Walt Disney*, Charles Shows claims that the inspiration for It's a Small World was a 1950s TV series that Shows produced, wrote, and directed for Disney called *Children of the World* (the series used actual footage of international customs and traditions). The attraction's title definitely wasn't new—it had already been used for two non-Disney movies (one in 1935, the other 1950), both called *It's a Small World*. And "Small World" had already been a song title in the 1959 Broadway hit *Gypsy*. (While

Disney prefers to spell this attraction's name with all lower-case letters, It's a Small World has often appeared capitalized, even in Disneyland's own official souvenir books. We've retained the capitalized spelling to be consistent with other attractions in our encyclopedia.)

Wherever the theme came from, Disney's World's Fair attraction was still unique. It saluted UNICEF by presenting a charismatic boat ride past singing **Audio-Animatronic** dolls and stylized representations of countries around the world. The boats were especially significant: as the first Disney attraction with this kind of high-capacity vessel, It's a Small World dramatically increased hourly ridership into the thousands (a year later, **Pirates of the Caribbean** would open with similar boats).

The happy cruise went through major changes before it ever launched in Disneyland. At the World's Fair, the international dolls were initially going to sing the various national anthems from all their different countries. This would have resulted in a disharmonious jumble as guests listened to one anthem while approaching the next. Instead of a multitude of overlapping melodies, a single anthem was written by **Richard and Robert Sherman** to fill the fifteen-minute trip with a catchy reminder that it was indeed a small world after all. The Shermans originally intended their song to be played as a slow ballad, but the playful spirit of the cruise demanded a bouncier tempo. The song, one of the most recognizable in history, is now played about 1,200 times a day inside Disneyland's attraction (that's over 21 million times since 1966).

The building in New York was vastly different from what was constructed in Anaheim. For the World's Fair, It's a Small World was in the Pepsi-Cola pavilion, where the relatively bland exterior was dressed up with signage and an elaborate 120-foot-tall, 100-ton artwork in front. This structure, called the *Tower of the Four Winds*, had mobile elements that expressed "the boundless energy of youth," according to its designer, Disney Legend **Rolly Crump**. At Disneyland, that structure is now echoed with an artistic sign out front made of curving metal tubes.

Anaheim's acre-and-a-half It's a Small World building supplanted the old train depot at the back of **Fantasyland** and extends well beyond the perimeter **berm**. Almost as long as a football field, the multifarious façade is an intricate, smile-inducing collage of moving shapes that evokes grand monuments—the Taj Mahal, the Eiffel Tower, etc.—from around the world. Wonderful and whimsical, this isn't architecture—it's *lark*-itecture.

Designed by several Disney Legends, most prominently **Mary Blair**, the structure's exterior has undergone several paint revisions that have taken it from white-and-gold and white-and-blue color schemes to a sweet rainbow of candy pastels. The gold trim is made of actual twenty-two-karat gold leaf, and some of the fancy decorations are enlarged duplicates of personal jewelry owned by the designers. A lavish **Topiary Garden**, a complex thirty-foot-tall cuckoo clock that chimes with marching toy soldiers every fifteen minutes, and the Disneyland trains (which pass across the building's layered frontage) all add to the fanciful fun. As charming as the cruise is inside, the trip itself is almost unnecessary because there's so much to see outside.

Inside the building, the winding, 1,400-foot river, laid out by Disney Legend **Claude Coats**, meanders past over 300 singing dolls and about 250 kinetic toys and effects. Everything is scattered across dozens of **Marc Davis**-created scenarios to

illustrate how **happiness** is a global emotion, whether it's experienced by island kids on surfboards, Dutch girls clacking their wooden shoes, giggling hyenas in Africa, skating Scandinavians, or a Chilean flautist. **Alice Davis**'s adorable doll costumes put the fun in functional—they're fastened with Velcro for easy access whenever the mechanisms need repair.

Veteran guests may remember the sponsor's cheery reminder at the exit that no matter where in the world they went, Bank of America would be there. B of A, which helped fund Disney film projects dating back to *Snow White* in 1937, sponsored It's a Small World until 1993, when Mattel took over (in recent years, two new sponsors displayed signage inside the attraction—Sylvania displayed a slogan about "making our Small World brighter" and, later, Siemens announced that it's "looking to the future").

Since 1997, merry holiday decorations and yuletide songs have been incorporated into the attraction for It's a Small World Holiday, a winter favorite that beautifully transforms the building's exterior walls and interior spaces. Outside, the building displays lavish lights; inside, bouncy Christmas songs mix with the traditional Small World theme, and all-new effects, sounds, and décor fill the rooms. So popular was the debut of this spectacular display that in its first year, it was held over for an additional three weeks into late January, even though other holiday decorations throughout Disneyland had already been removed. Another major change came in 2008, when a long refurbishment brought updated boats and over two-dozen new dolls to the festivities (the dolls are characters from Disney and Pixar movies, and they're placed in appropriate settings—Pinocchio in Italy, Alice in England, etc.).

After debuting in New York in 1964, It's a Small World got two big pages in Disneyland's 1965 **souvenir book** a year *before* the attraction opened in Anaheim. At its Disneyland premiere in 1966, international children ceremoniously poured water from each of the world's oceans into It's a Small World's river while press photographers snapped away. The E-ticket attraction even had its own soundtrack album, complete with a colorful ten-page booklet. It's a Small World was also the first Disneyland attraction to get the new **FASTPASS** ticket-distribution system

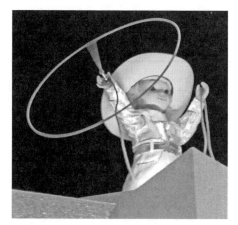

(1999), and by now, the combined trips taken by the hundreds of millions of passengers would total something like 5 million miles (that's about 1,800 trips from Anaheim to the New York World's Fair site). The whole thing may eventually come to a theater near you: in 2014, plans were announced for a new big-budget movie to be based on It's a Small World.

In 2014, the Themed Entertainment Association gave its Thea Classic Award to It's a Small World, praising the "pure charm" and "profound message" that make this attraction "the very definition of a classic." The "happiest cruise" is still as adored and adorable as ever.

It's a Small World Toy Shop

MAP: Fantasyland, Fa-20

DATES: December 18, 1992–ongoing

To cash in on the high volume of pedestrian traffic emerging from **It's a Small World**, two stores sit near the exit of the famous attraction. The smaller store slightly farther away is **Fantasy Faire Gifts**, and the larger one right in the path of departing guests is the It's a Small World Toy Shop. For most of its history, the toy shop was sponsored by Mattel, which also sponsored It's a Small World. This meant that the store has sold lots of Mattel toys, not all of them Disney-related. Hot Wheels cars, games, and Barbie dolls have occasionally populated the shelves.

Today, plenty of Disney dolls, statues, plush toys, and princess figures fill the store (*Brave* archery sets and swords arrived in 2012 with the **Brave: Meet Merida** location nearby, and surprisingly, some *Star Wars* toys arrived in 2015 with **Season of the Force** in **Tomorrowland**). The building's open design brings in lots of air and light; the fanciful decor echoes the playful scenes displayed throughout the Small World cruise.

Iwerks, Ub
(1901–1971)

One of the great Disney animators was also a key creative force behind several major Disneyland attractions. Ubbe "Ub" Iwerks was born in Missouri in 1901, the same year as **Walt Disney**. Employees in a Kansas City art studio, the two teens soon started their own commercial art business. The short-lived company soon led to a bigger one called Laugh-O-Gram Films in 1922, with Iwerks as the chief animator. A few years later, the two friends reunited in Hollywood at the new Disney Brothers Cartoon Studio, where Iwerks worked on the "Alice Comedies" and single-handedly animated Mickey Mouse's first cartoon, *Plane Crazy*.

After pioneering the "Silly Symphonies" of the late 1920s, Iwerks left the company during the 1930s to create his own cartoons. However, his Flip the Frog and other characters weren't as successful as his Disney creations, so he returned to Disney in the early 1940s. Heading Disney Studio's research and development team, Iwerks devised new cinematic advances that propelled imaginative live-action/animation combinations. These special effects would memorably flourish in *Mary Poppins* and win him two Oscars for technical achievements. Iwerks is listed in the credits of dozens of Disney classics, plus Alfred Hitchcock's *The Birds*.

At Disneyland, Iwerks brought his technological wizardry to three of the biggest attractions of the 1960s: the **Circle-Vision 360** theater, **Great Moments with Mr. Lincoln**, and **It's a Small World**. In **the Haunted Mansion**, the illuminated floating head in the séance room and the singing busts in the graveyard are based on projection systems that Iwerks devised.

After working on Walt Disney World's Hall of Presidents, Iwerks died in 1971 at age seventy. He was inducted as a Disney Legend, along with the first fleet of great Disney animators, eighteen years later. His achievements are recalled in the documentary film *The Hand Behind the Mouse: The Ub Iwerks Story*.

Jani, Robert
(1934–1989)

Robert Jani, Disneyland's longtime entertainment specialist, invented imaginative productions that redefined **parades**. Jani was born in Los Angeles in 1934 and graduated from USC two decades later. In 1955, he started working at Disneyland as the first person to lead **Guest Relations** in **City Hall**. Jani then served two years in the army. Upon his return, he eventually rejoined Disneyland in 1967 as its director of entertainment.

At Disneyland, Jani's two most famous creations were **America on Parade**, the patriotic spectacular of the mid-1970s, and the legendary **Main Street Electrical Parade**, which ran for over two decades. The Electrical Parade has probably been the most popular parade in Disneyland's history. However, the unique nighttime concept was initially a tough sell to Disney execs, as Jani explains on the 2007 DVD *Disneyland Secrets, Stories & Magic*.

In addition to these productions, Jani produced several prominent non-Disney events, including Super Bowl halftime shows, New York's 1976 Bicentennial Celebration, massive holiday shows at Radio City Music Hall, and numerous TV specials. Though he retired in 1978, Jani consulted on Disneyland Paris and Disney-MGM Studios.

After fighting Lou Gehrig's disease, Jani died in Los Angeles in 1989 at age fifty-five. He was named a Disney Legend in 2005.

Jemrock Shop, aka Jemrocks and Gem Shop

MAP: Main Street, MS-3

DATES: 1956–1957

Listed among the earliest stores on **Main Street** is the small Jemrock Shop (also called the Jemrocks and Gem Shop). Its location inside the **Crystal Arcade** should have been ideal for a lapidary business, but by the time the 1958 Disneyland **souvenir book** came out, all mention of Jemrocks was gone.

Jewel of Orléans

MAP: New Orleans Square, NOS-9

DATES: 1997–May 2011

A list of the prettiest shops in Disneyland's history would have to include Jewel of Orléans in **New Orleans Square**. The shop featured a decorative ceiling, ornate wall details, embellished mirrors, lace curtains, and an exquisite chandelier found in the Crescent City by Walt and Lillian Disney. All of this combined to evoke a Parisian setting—an appropriate reference, given that the former longtime occupant of this space was the French-themed **Mlle. Antoinette's Parfumerie**, and the **French Market** is next door.

For the first dozen years of its operation, the shop was run by the Jacobs family, owners of an antique jewelry business called Dianne's Estate Jewelry. Their Disneyland shop sold glittering Victorian bangles and cameos, vintage pocket watches, Edwardian pendants and necklaces, Art Deco trinkets, Tahitian pearls, and even some Disneyland-related pieces. Due to its dazzling displays, the Jewel of Orléans sometimes felt more like a museum than a shop, especially since some of its items cost tens of thousands of dollars.

A sluggish economy began to take its toll, however, and in early 2010, the Jewel of Orléans closed for six weeks. Upon reopening, the French name and beautiful décor were the same, but the Jacobs family had departed. Disney was now running things, and the merchandise was completely different. Instead of antiques, the shop sold new jewelry and handbags from high-profile designers, as well as chic Ray-Ban sunglasses. When this shop closed in 2011, Mlle. Antoinette's returned with her perfumes.

Jewelry Shop, aka Rings & Things

MAP: Main Street, MS-19

DATES: 1955–1986

Starting in 1955, a small space near the **Market House** was occupied by the Jewelry Shop. In 1970, the Jewelry Shop absorbed the adjacent space that had been the **Yale & Towne Lock Shop**. New signs were posted announcing the slightly more specific Rings & Things.

In 1986, Rings & Things switched locations with the

Disneyana shop across **Main Street**. The new location was the corner building that had once been the **Upjohn Pharmacy**, and the new name was **New Century**, an umbrella title applied to both New Century Jewelry and New Century Timepieces next door. Today's **Fortuosity Shop** on this corner has a vertical sign outside announcing the Jewelry Shop (shown), identifying what's sold in the Fortuosity Shop and offering a nod to the store that used to be in this vicinity.

Jimmy Starr's Show Business Souvenirs

MAP: Town Square, TS-8

DATES: March 23, 1956–September 20, 1959

Nicknamed Stage Door Jimmy, Jimmy Starr was a longtime Hollywood insider who started working in movies in the 1920s. Starr eventually held many different jobs: actor, screenwriter, newspaper gossip columnist, publicist, and novelist.

In 1956, a collection of Starr's Hollywood memorabilia filled a leased space just north of the **Opera House**. Disneyland's **souvenir books**, evidently figuring that guests might not know who Starr was, listed his shop as Show Business, Show Business Souvenirs, and Motion Picture Souvenirs. Inside, guests could view movie props and buy photos, autographs, and other collectibles. The shop closed after three years and later reopened as **Wonderland Music**. Starr died in 1990 at age eighty-four.

Jingle Jangle Jamboree

MAP: Frontierland, Fr-19

DATES: November 12, 2012–January 6, 2013; November 4, 2013–January 5, 2014; November 13, 2014–January 4, 2015

The summer success of the **Big Thunder Ranch Jamboree** in 2012 led to the creation of a new winter event at the back of **Frontierland**. Decorated for the **holiday season** (from mid-November to early January), the Jingle Jangle Jamboree offered visits with Santa and Disney characters, coloring and decorating activities, Reindeer Games, and live holiday music from **Billy Hill and the Hillbillies** (renamed the Holiday Hillbillies for this event). Jingle Jangle returned the following November, but the Billys left after the show closed in January of 2014. For the 2014–2015 Jamboree, a humorous new musical show called *The Plight Before Christmas* replaced the Billys.

After closing in early 2015, Jingle Jangle never returned to this **Big Thunder Ranch** location because plans were already underway for **Star Wars Land** to land here. The seasonal meet-and-greet with Santa still happened though, but for 2015 and 2016, he and the Mrs. relocated to **Critter Country**.

Joerger, Fred

(1913–2005)

Disneyland's designers and architects make two-dimensional drawings of new attractions and buildings; during his time working for Disney, Fred Joerger turned those drawings into intricate three-dimensional models.

Born in 1913, Joerger graduated in 1937 with a fine arts degree from the University of Illinois. After moving to Los Angeles, Joerger started building models at Warner Bros. Studios. In 1953, he joined Disneyland's model-making team, which included Disney Legends **Wathel Rogers** and **Harriet Burns**. Among Joerger's first creations was a model of the *Mark Twain* **Riverboat**, followed quickly by elaborate miniatures of the **Jungle Cruise**, **Sleeping Beauty Castle**, **Main Street** buildings, villages for the **Storybook Land Canal Boats**, and many more early attractions, all before any of them were constructed. His 3-D **Matterhorn** rendering led to the construction of Disneyland's tallest structure, and his **Haunted Mansion** model

> **MOUSCELLANY**
>
> In addition to building models, Joerger was an expert at sculpting the faux rocks that add realistic atmosphere to such attractions as **Tom Sawyer Island** and **Pirates of the Caribbean**. His rock work was acknowledged on a Haunted Mansion tombstone that read, "Here lies Good Old Fred, a great big rock fell on his head."

preceded one of Disneyland's most iconic attractions. Joerger also contributed models of movie sets to Disney Studios, among them detailed miniatures of the *20,000 Leagues Under the Sea* submarine.

After working on Walt Disney World, Joerger retired in 1979, though he later consulted on EPCOT and Tokyo Disneyland. He was named a Disney Legend in 2001, four years before he died in L.A. at age ninety-one.

Jolley, Stan
(1926–2012)

It's well-known that many of Disneyland's original designers came from movie studios, and Stan Jolley was one of them. Born in New York City in 1926, Jolley came to Hollywood with his family in the '30s. After a navy stint in World War II, Jolley became a set designer at Warner Bros. and later at 20th Century Fox.

In 1953, artist **Herb Ryman** invited Jolley to look into the budding Disneyland project that Ryman was helping conceive. Jolley jumped to Disney and worked on the park for the next couple of years. His artistic talents were spread across several different lands and attractions, including **Sleeping Beauty Castle** in **Fantasyland**, the **Golden Horseshoe** in **Frontierland**, and the **Autopia** in **Tomorrowland**. Once Disneyland was up and running, Jolley transferred to Walt Disney Studios and began designing TV and movie sets, including the "office" that Walt Disney stood in during the long-running *Disneyland* **TV series**.

Leaving Disney in the 1960s, Jolley served as an art director/production designer for TV shows (*Voyage to the Bottom of the Sea* and *Get Smart*) and movies (*Caddyshack* and *Witness*, the latter earning him an Oscar nomination). Retired in Rancho Mirage, California, Stan Jolley succumbed to cancer in 2012.

Jolly Holiday Bakery Café

MAP: Hub, H-1

DATES: January 5, 2012–ongoing

In *Mary Poppins*, Bert says, "What she's probably got in mind is a jolly holiday somewheres or other." The somewheres that Mary had in mind turned out to be on the west side of Disneyland's **Hub**. The venerable **Plaza Pavilion** had been a prominent restaurant here, but for part of the 2000s it had served as the more mundane Annual Passport Processing Center. With Passport functions relocated to the ticket booths in August of 2011, the building was reborn in early 2012 as a new *Mary Poppins*-themed dining experience called the Jolly Holiday Bakery Café.

Touting "practically perfect pastries," the café offers treats like its tall, toasted-coconut macaroon

shaped like **Matterhorn Mountain** (shown) and other delights with spoonfuls of sugar. But there's heartier fare here, too, including quiche, salads, and sandwiches that come with fresh, homemade House Chips. The Specialty of the House is a toasted cheese sandwich paired with tomato basil soup. The movie's penguin waiters are reprised in the restaurant's stained-glass windows, Mary herself balances on the café's weather vane (shown), and the spirit throughout the place is "Poppins Positive."

The presence of this big new bakery signaled the end of the **Blue Ribbon Bakery** on **Main Street**; that prime corner location became indoor seating for the adjacent **Carnation Café**.

Jolly Trolley

MAP: Mickey's Toontown, MT-12

DATES: January 24, 1993–2006

In **Mickey's Toontown**, public transportation was once provided by the wacky Jolly Trolley. "It's clean! It's fun! It bounces a lot!" read the sign for this attraction, and few guests would have disagreed.

A Jolly Trolly had already been operating in Children's Fairyland in Oakland since 1954, but that colorful little train looked nothing like Toontown's wacky 1993 vehicles, which resembled toy versions of the beautiful horse-drawn streetcars that still serve **Main Street**. Toontown's happy trolleys were built with soft curves, painted bright red with gold trim, and given cartoon-ish wind-up keys on top. About ten guests at a time could fit inside for the scenic fountain-to-fountain ramble across Toontown. What put the jolly in the trolley was the series of gentle jiggles, dips, and bumps as it drove along its 800-foot track.

Appropriately enough for this cheery ride, **cast members** wore bright blue conductor uniforms with big yellow buttons, red bow ties, and snappy multi-colored hats. **Souvenir books** of the 1990s nearly always showcase the photogenic Jolly Trolley, which seemed incapable of taking a bad picture.

The trolleys fell out of favor in the mid-2000s as concerns for guest safety increased (though there were no serious accidents, the slow-to-stop trolleys seemed destined for pedestrian entanglements). Thus the Jolly Trolleys went from having two cars, to single cars, to no cars as the ride was quietly chained up at the station, which eventually became a photo op and a **Disney Vacation Club** site.

Jones, Mary
(1915–2008)

Mary Jones was born in 1915 and started working at Disneyland as a secretary in 1962. Within a few months of being hired for her clerical skills, Jones was leading Community Relations, a department that worked with local leaders to assure Disneyland's happy coexistence with its neighbors. She began by administering awards for community service; later, she established the Community Action Team to support nonprofit organizations, followed by Operation Christmas to bring holiday celebrations into children's hospitals. Jones also served as the liaison with consulates and the State Department when foreign dignitaries and royals wanted to visit the park, leading to many impressive photo opportunities that broadened Disneyland's international appeal.

Jones retired from Disneyland in 1986 but continued working with the local government to set up and run the Orange County Office of Protocol, continuing the community work she'd pioneered at the county's most-visited destination. Jones was inducted as a Disney Legend in 2005, three years before she passed away.

MOUSCELLANY

Disneyland's community service and support has expanded impressively over the decades, extending to everything from the Make-A-Wish Foundation (a Disneyland visit was the Foundation's first official wish, granted in 1980) and VoluntEARS (a **cast member** organization dedicated to helping non-profits since 1983) to the annual CHOC Walk (a fundraiser started in 1991 to benefit the Children's Hospital of Orange County) and the highway beautification campaign of recent years (shown).

Jungle Cruise

MAP: Adventureland, A-8

DATES: July 17, 1955–ongoing

The Jungle Cruise was arguably Disneyland's most important early attraction. Until the 1962 arrival of the nearby **Swiss Family Treehouse**, the cruise was the only major attraction in all of **Adventureland**. What's more, since it covers approximately five acres and is about a third of a mile in length, the Jungle Cruise has always been one of Disneyland's largest attractions—and one of the most heavily promoted. Before any construction began, **Walt Disney** was boldly describing an explorer's boat ride down a lush "river of romance." Months before the park opened, the *Disneyland* TV series previewed the coming cruise with footage of Disney taking a car through the dry riverbed while touting the wonders to come.

Once Disneyland opened, the official **souvenir books** devoted more space and photos to the nine-minute Jungle Cruise than to any other attraction. Calling it the Explorer Boat Ride, River Boat Ride, Jungle River Boat Ride, Jungle River Boat Safari, and finally (in 1959) the Jungle Cruise, the early souvenir books liberally mix colorful photos with enthusiastic text that describes how "adventure lurks at every bend" of this "jungle wonder world." In 1969's *Walt Disney's Disneyland*, writer **Martin Sklar** names it "Disneyland's finest achievement." If **Sleeping Beauty Castle** was Disneyland's most iconic structure, for years the Jungle Cruise was its signature attraction.

As with the **Painted Desert** in **Frontierland**, the Jungle Cruise incorporated themes and images from Disney's *True-Life Adventures* films of the 1950s—in this case, the seventy-five-minute documentary *The African Lion*. The original **attraction poster** for the Jungle Cruise emphasized the connection: "For true life *adventure*, ride the Jungle River." However, what the poster's imaginative artwork depicts—a colossal elephant towering over guests who were standing in a boat—wasn't exactly "true life."

Disney Legend **Harper Goff** laid out the four-to-six-foot-deep river and drew some of the first concept sketches of the scenery that would appear along its teeming banks, taking some of his ideas from another 1950s movie, the Oscar-winning *The African Queen*. Africa, however, isn't the only setting of the Jungle Cruise. In addition to the Congo and Nile, scenes along the waterway suggest other exotic rivers like the Amazon and the Mekong (tellingly, Jungle Rivers of the World and Tropical Rivers of the World were two early names considered for the attraction). To reflect the international intentions of the design, the boats themselves were named for rivers around the world, including the *Amazon Belle*, *Mekong Maiden*, *Nile Princess*, *Orinoco Adventuress*, and *Yangtze Lotus*.

Landscapers **Morgan "Bill" Evans and Jack Evans** made creative use of unusual greenery as they planted the dense foliage that soon filled the area to resemble a real jungle. Today, there are more than 700 trees and over forty different kinds of plants (representing six continents) along the banks. As an example of the variety, there are seven kinds of bamboo on view.

Initial plans called for real animals to populate this wilderness, but that idea was quickly scotched when designers realized that jungle wildlife usually sleeps all day, and even those beasts not sleeping would probably be hiding from noisy, intrusive boats. Dozens of realistic mechanical animals and natives eventually went on display, among them majestic elephants (shown), writhing snakes, charging hippos, statuesque giraffes, half-submerged crocodiles, and dancing headhunters. Though their motions were relatively simple and repetitive, these machines were considered advanced special effects in the 1950s, and they gave the Jungle Cruise its unique thrills.

The Jungle Cruise has been updated at least ten times since 1955. Veteran jungle cruisers may also recall that at one time live alligators were briefly penned up near the entrance to add atmo-sphere. Also, the jungle river and Frontierland's **Rivers of America** were linked by a small canal, and the old one-story boathouse had a square lookout tower on the roof so **cast members** could survey the river.

In 1957, Trader Sam, who deals in shrunken heads, joined the waterway; five years later, playful elephants started hosing off in their own bathing pool. The African Veldt and **Marc Davis**'s "lost safari" climbing away from a rhino all joined the fun by 1964. A dozen years later, gorillas started playing in an abandoned camp and a tiger began lurking in the Cambodian ruins. What's surprising is that there was never a scene related to *The Jungle Book*; featuring some of Disney's best songs and most-loved characters, the 1967 hit movie seems like a natural addition, but somehow Mowgli, Baloo, and the rest of the gang never made it into the attraction.

In 1994, with the **Indiana Jones Adventure** under construction next door, Imagineers re-routed part of the river and built a new two-story **queue** area at the dock. This wooden structure, made to look old and abandoned, intentionally sags to suggest that nature is reclaiming what man has encroached upon. Guests waiting inside will hear old-time music and see period artifacts from the 1930s.

The gas-powered, twenty-seven-foot boats have always held about thirty-two passengers each and have always been guided by rails hidden under the river water, which is dyed to look green and cloudy. But the boats have also undergone several revisions. Early on, spotlights were added to allow night cruises. The boats' gleaming white exteriors and red-and-white striped roofs were later replaced with more drab-looking paint and canvas coverings to give them a weathered look, evoking the

Indiana Jones aesthetic. In 2012, the boats got some new bumpers and mesh netting along the sides as added safety features; four years later, the docks were improved to help stabilize the process of getting passengers on and off the boats. During the Jingle Cruise transformation that adds Christmas decorations along the river, the boats are rechristened for the **holiday season**: the *Congo Queen* becomes the *Candy Cane Queen,* the *Ganges Gal* becomes the *Ginger-Bread Gal,* etc.

One key aspect of the Jungle Cruise that separates it from other Disneyland attractions is its unique narration. As Bagheera says in *The Jungle Book,* "It all began when the silence of the jungle was broken by an unfamiliar sound." That would be the sound of comedy, the now-famous patter spoken by the wisecracking skippers. Initially these cast members, wearing safari garb and brandishing blank-loaded pistols, delivered serious narration about the cruise and its dangerous inhabitants, with a few off-script wisecracks thrown in by inventive skippers. However, starting in 1962 with Walt Disney's blessing, the narration officially began to incorporate jokes. The purpose, perhaps, was to interject bursts of humor to deflate the menace of the realistic jungle beasts and savages; the jokes also gave repeat visitors an excuse to come back, just to hear fresh material. Eventually the cruise became a nonstop comedy-fest that begins before guests are even in their seats.

By now, most guests can recite one or two of the corny gags that have been repeated thousands of times: the crocs looking for a handout; the rare view of the back side of water (shown); Trader Sam, the attraction's mascot, who will trade two shrunken heads for yours; and the most dangerous part of the trip, the return to civilization. Fortunately, supplementing the old jokes are clever new gems, as with this beaut from a female skipper in 2015: "Don't worry, I'm going to scare off that charging hippo the same way I scared off my last boyfriend—I love you!" Much of the script is rehearsed, but skippers have a long tradition of ad-libbing new material, especially on the last run of the night. Kevin Costner, Robin Williams, and Nixon's press secretary, Ron Ziegler, are all said to have been Jungle Cruise skippers in their youth. Guests got a chance to try their hands at Jungle Cruise comedy via a special $300 Safari Breakfast in 2015; in addition to enjoying a unique dining experience inside the attraction, guests could take over the microphones and deliver jokes just like real skippers.

Along with the laughs are plenty of fanciful legends and entertaining stories of boats that have sunk and skippers who have swung from ropes in the trees, all helping to make this beloved classic even more fascinating. As Baloo says in *The Jungle Book,* "Ha ha! Man that's what I call a swinging party."

Junior Autopia

MAP: Fantasyland, Fa-23

DATES: July 23, 1956–September 15, 1958

Of the four Autopias that have chugged through Disneyland's history (the first **Autopia**, **Fantasyland Autopia**, and **Midget Autopia** are the others), the Junior Autopia came and went the quickest. Capitalizing on the popularity of the 1955 **Tomorrowland** original, Disneyland opened a second version, the Junior Autopia, in 1956 to accommodate younger, smaller drivers who couldn't handle the bigger Tomorrowland cars.

Located in the **Fantasyland** area where the **Mickey Mouse Club Circus** had briefly operated, the Junior Autopia site was a little farther north of Tomorrowland's Autopia. The Junior Autopia track layout was not as elaborate as Tomorrowland's layout, and it was safer, too—to help guide novice drivers, the Junior track had a center rail, a feature not included in Tomorrowland's Autopia back then. The cars of the Junior and Tomorrowland Autopias were basically identical (sleek, **Bob Gurr**-designed sports cars with fiberglass bodies), except for extended gas pedals and higher seats to make the Junior cars more child-friendly.

About twenty-six months after opening, the Junior Autopia closed for a major remodel. The site reopened in 1959 as the larger Fantasyland Autopia, with some of the land taken over by the waters of the **Motor Boat Cruise**.

Justice, Bill
(1914–2011)

Animator, programmer, Imagineer, artist—Bill Justice wore many hats as a key Disney employee for over four decades. Born in Ohio in 1914, Justice was raised in Indiana and graduated from an Indiana art institute in 1935. Two years later, he was living in Southern California and starting a long Disney Studios career.

Beginning with animated films, Justice contributed memorable scenes and characters to such classics as *Fantasia*, *Bambi* (Thumper is his creation), and *Peter Pan*. Along the way, he directed the opening animation for *The Mickey Mouse Club* TV show, co-created the special opening titles for Disney's *The Shaggy Dog* and *The Parent Trap*, and designed the nursery sequence in *Mary Poppins*.

In 1965, Justice began working on Disneyland and its attractions, especially those involving sophisticated **Audio-Animatronic** figures like **Great Moments with Mr. Lincoln**, **Pirates of the Caribbean**, the **Haunted Mansion**, **Mission to Mars**, **America Sings**, and the **Country Bear Jamboree**. Justice also designed costumes for the walk-around characters, devised floats for the elaborate **parades**, and painted murals for some of the attractions in **Fantasyland**.

After working on Walt Disney World and Tokyo Disneyland, Justice finally retired in 1979. His 1992 autobiography, *Justice for Disney*, recounts his forty-two-year Disney career. Justice was inducted as a Disney Legend in 1996; he died in 2011, one day after celebrating his ninety-seventh birthday.

Keller's Jungle Killers

MAP: Fantasyland, Fa-22

DATES: February 19, 1956–September 7, 1956

Killers in **Fantasyland**? Well, sure. If real guns could be fired in the **Main Street Shooting Gallery**, why not showcase some dangerous animals east of the **Storybook Land Canal Boats**? The surprise is that Keller's Jungle Killers weren't located in the jungle-themed **Adventureland**.

When the short-lived **Mickey Mouse Club Circus** bailed from Fantasyland in early 1956, one of the circus's attractions, Professor George Keller and His Feline Fantastics, stayed on through the following summer. Renamed Keller's Jungle Killers, George Keller's B-ticket attraction featured, not mechanical replicas, but actual jungle cats in a cage. The beasts may have been killers at one time, but they weren't once they'd been declawed and sedated. As **Jack Lindquist** notes in his book *In Service to the Mouse*, the real danger was a sleepy cat slumping onto Keller and crushing him.

Wearing sparkly outfits, Keller, an actual college professor, interacted with the leopards, lions, and tigers. His most famous stunt, which he often performed in fairs around the country, was placing his head inside a lion's mouth. After departing from Disneyland, Keller briefly joined the Ringling Bros. Barnum & Bailey show in 1959 before suffering a heart attack a year later.

Back in Fantasyland, meanwhile, Keller's former site was extensively remodeled. The **Junior Autopia** took over as the area's first new attraction.

Kennel Club,
aka Ken-L Land Pet Motel, aka Pet Care Kennel

MAP: Park, P-7

DATES: January 18, 1958–ongoing

To accommodate pet owners who might otherwise leave their animals sitting in sun-baked cars, Disneyland added a pet care facility in 1958. Conveniently accessible directly from the **parking lot**, the kennel was located in a small building east of the turnstiles. Pets couldn't be left overnight, but they could stay for an entire day in "airy, individual enclosures" under the supervision of an experienced handler. Fees were modest: in 1965, the daily charge was just a quarter per pet; years later, the charge was still under $1, including food. But by 2002 the fee had jumped to $10, and a decade later, it was up to $20. Over the years, lizards, goldfish, pigs, and more have stayed in one of the 100-plus enclosures.

When the kennel first opened, it was called the Ken-L Land Pet Motel. Five different pet food companies have hosted and remodeled the kennel over the decades. Ken-L Ration sponsored its Pet Motel from 1958 to 1967, and Kal Kan created the Kennel Club from 1968 to 1977. After an unsponsored period, Gaines renamed it the Pet Care Kennel from 1986 to 1991 before Friskies restored the Kennel Club name in 1993. Finally, Purina took over in 2002 and kept the Kennel Club signage. In 2010, no sponsor was named, and it was called simply the Disneyland Kennel Club.

Khrushchev in Disneyland Film

Many presidents and royals have toured Disneyland over the decades, but possibly the most famous visit by a dignitary was one that never actually happened. Before embarking on an eleven-day tour of America in 1959, Soviet Premier Nikita Khrushchev requested that he be taken to "the fairytale park," as he called it. Mid-tour, government officials (not park officials) denied the request, saying they couldn't assure security on the busy Saturday set for his visit.

The incident drew international attention when an irate Khrushchev complained loudly about the rejection. On September 19, the afternoon when he would have been at Disneyland, he threw a temper tantrum in front of journalists and celebrities. What, he wondered aloud, did Disneyland have to hide? His wild guesses included "cholera," "rocket-launching pads," and "gangsters." Denied Disneyland, was he now supposed to "commit suicide"?

Walt Disney later said he'd been looking forward to showing off his new submarine fleet to the Communist leader. In the 1960s, Disney briefly considered developing a movie about the whole affair, a comedy to be called *Khrushchev in Disneyland*. Peter Ustinov was to play the petulant premier, who would have been shown inventing his own plan to dodge security and sneak into the park.

Kids of the Kingdom

Kids of the Kingdom was an energetic Disney ensemble put together in the late '60s to perform in Disneyland. The Kids weren't exactly kids the way the pre-teen Mouseketeers were; these Kids were college-age singers and dancers. They usually performed on the large **Tomorrowland Stage** and at special events in other park locations.

Wearing colorful matching outfits, the co-ed Kids belted out upbeat, choreographed versions of Disney classics, show tunes, and popular songs. The cover of *Young Singing Stars of Disneyland*, their 1968 album on Vista Records, shows fourteen well-groomed, white-sweatered performers, half of them holding Mickey balloons and all of them smiling in front of **Sleeping Beauty Castle**.

Two years later, the Kids were introduced to a national audience on a 1970 episode of *The Wonderful World of Disney*. In that "Disneyland Showtime" episode, the Kids, actor Kurt Russell, the **Dapper Dans**, and the Osmond Brothers celebrate the new **Haunted Mansion**. In the 1980s, the Kids performed in a powerhouse musical show called *Disneyland Is Your Land* on Tomorrowland's renamed Space Stage. Although the Kids' Disneyland run had ended by the time their stage became the **Magic Eye Theater** in 1986, a Florida version of the group continued to perform at Walt Disney World.

King Arthur Carrousel

MAP: Fantasyland, Fa-5, Fa-6

DATES: July 17, 1955–ongoing

The carousel near the center of Disneyland is also central to the park's history. **Walt Disney** always maintained that some of his ideas for a new kind of amusement park came while he was waiting near a Griffith Park merry-go-round that his daughters were riding. In 2010, the **Opera House** debuted a display of the actual bench he had been sitting on at the time (shown in the Walt Disney entry).

When it finally came time to build his own park, Disney placed his carousel in a most telling place. Not only is it in the middle of the castle courtyard, where it pumps out gaiety, music, and color as if it were **Fantasyland's** beating heart, but it is in a conspicuous location where it can be seen from hundreds of feet away. Guests on **Main Street** can look across the **Hub** to see the glittering lights of the King Arthur Carrousel through the castle's archway, an alluring sight that draws them into Disneyland's fairytale fantasy.

Regarding the carousel's name, several points need clarification. While King Arthur refers to the same legend that was the basis of Disney's *The Sword in the Stone*, the main imagery decorating the carousel isn't from that 1963 movie—it's from 1959's *Sleeping Beauty*, represented by nine hand-painted scenes circling the carousel's core (a king's crown is, however, part of the spire, as shown). Also, while the attraction uses a traditional English spelling variation of the more familiar "carousel," the meaning—a whirling ride with moving horses—is identical. Carousels differ from merry-go-rounds, which are similar but usually include a variety of animals and benches, some of which don't move up and down.

Ironically, Disneyland's carousel was originally a merry-go-round. It was built in 1875 and was in Toronto, Canada, when Walt Disney bought it and shipped it to California. Disneyland designers took off the non-equine animals and seats and added over two-dozen horses purchased from other carousels, including one on Coney Island (during the renovation, some of the removed seats were added onto the cars of the **Casey Jr. Circus Train**). Disneyland's carousel now has sixty-eight hand-carved, hand-painted, antique wooden horses arrayed in seventeen rows of four each; there were seventy-two horses until one row of four was replaced by a bench in 2003. Most of the horses seem to be leaping, an effect created when designers attached new legs to some of the horses that previously had all four on the floor. All the prancing steeds are now a gleaming white, thanks to new paint applied in 1975 over the previous shades of black, grey, tan, cream, and brown.

For its first three decades, the carousel's rollicking music came from a calliope, and it only cost an A ticket from Disneyland's **ticket book** for a two-minute, four-miles-per-hour spin. Then, in the early 1980s, the King Arthur Carrousel was remodeled along with the rest of Fantasyland. First, Imagineers relocated the carousel north by about sixty feet to open up the congested area near the castle. This move put the carousel closer to **Mr. Toad's Wild Ride** and pushed the twirling teacups next to **Alice in Wonderland**. Next, the music transformed when the Disney classics playing next door at **Dumbo the Flying Elephant** became the same soundtrack for the carousel. A 2003 restoration completely overhauled the carousel, reinforced it, and added new technology.

What hasn't changed in over fifty years is the affection guests have for the King Arthur Carrousel (especially one famous guest, Julie Andrews, whose initials and Mary Poppins silhouette adorn the saddle on Jingles). The carousel is still shown off in modern **souvenir books** as prominently as it was in the books of the 1950s. It is also well-taken care of: the brass poles are polished every night and the horses are touched up frequently. And it still warms hearts with its traditional pleasures, royal style, and timeless beauty, making it the perfect centerpiece for Fantasyland's rich buffet.

> **MOUSCELLANY**
>
> All of the horses on the King Arthur Carrousel have individual names and unique accessories (brightly colored saddles, jewels, and other details) that help distinguish each one. Surprisingly, Samson, the prince's white charger in Disney's *Sleeping Beauty* movie, is not one of the horses.

King Triton Gardens, aka Triton Gardens

MAP: Tomorrowland, T-1

DATES: February 1996–August 17, 2008

The former grounds of the **House of the Future** and the **Alpine Gardens** were re-landscaped into the splashy King Triton Gardens in 1996. Also called simply Triton Gardens, this beautiful water area was named after the ocean monarch from the 1989 Disney movie *The Little Mermaid*. The site sported several statues of the character to establish whose gardens these were, including one water-spouting representation of the king that stood in the pond, and one of his smiling daughter, Ariel, perched on a rock.

> **MOUSCELLANY**
>
> Though Triton's fountain was removed, his statue still exists; it's over at Disney California Adventure, crowning the entrance to the Little Mermaid attraction.

Kids loved the fountain jets that shot playful streams of water over the walkway, and parents appreciated the quiet, 300-foot walkway that circled the pond. At night, iridescent lights made the gardens and waters look especially lovely. In a rocky alcove called Ariel's Grotto, the lovely, red-haired mermaid herself often sat on her shell-shaped throne to sign autographs.

In August 2008, the King was deposed and his gentle gardens were soon revamped into the new **Pixie Hollow** meet-and-greet area.

Knight Shop

MAP: Fantasyland, Fa-30

DATES: August 16, 1997–October 3, 1998

This Middle Ages-themed shop replaced **Quasimodo's Attic** after the excitement over 1996's *Hunchback of Notre Dame* movie subsided. The shop's location was the same as Quasimodo's, greeting guests in the castle courtyard just before they took flight with Peter Pan. The new merchandise included daggers, swords, and armor accoutrements. Disneyland planners must have thought that knight supplies matched nicely with the **Princess Boutique** nearby. A year later, however, the Knight went to the dark side when it was transformed into the **Villains Lair**, a return of the bad guys formerly in the **Disney Villains** store.

Kodak Camera Center,
aka GAF Photo Salon, aka Polaroid Camera Center

MAP: Main Street, MS-13

DATES: July 17, 1955–November 1994

From Day One, guests have loved to snap photos during their Disneyland visits. In pre-digital days, those insatiable cameras gulped film that had to be replenished frequently (Disneyland used to be one of the world's biggest film sellers). Additionally, guests who had either forgotten to bring a camera or had lost theirs at the park had the opportunity to buy one at the Kodak Camera Center, located in the **Main Street** space where Castle Brothers now resides. Not only did the store sell both still and movie cameras, it rented them out, too. To inspire even more picture-taking and film-buying, Kodak posted helpful signs around Disneyland to point out especially scenic locations.

In 1970, the General Analine Film Corporation replaced Kodak as the shop's sponsor and operated as the GAF Photo Salon until 1977. Polaroid got into the picture at the end of the decade and renamed it the Polaroid Camera Center, adding a photo studio where guests could sit for quick portraits while wearing old-fashioned costumes.

Finally, in a development that yanked the camera saga back to its origins, Kodak reappeared as the sponsor in 1984. Ten years later, the whole operation got a new name—**Main Street Photo Supply Co.**—and a new location in the building formerly known as **Carefree Corner**.

Kuri, Emile
(1907–2000)

Anyone who watches movies made between the 1930s and 1970s has probably seen the work of Emile Kuri, one of Hollywood's most prolific set directors. Among the 100-plus films he contributed to are the classics *It's a Wonderful Life* and *Shane*, plus three Hitchcock movies. As the main decorator for Disney Studios, Kuri also designed the sets and décor for dozens of live-action Disney films and TV shows. His long

Hollywood career brought him an Emmy and eight Academy Award nominations for Art Direction/Set Direction (his work on both *The Absent-Minded Professor* and *Mary Poppins* was nominated, and his imaginative *Nautilus* sets for *20,000 Leagues Under the Sea* won an Oscar).

Kuri was born in Mexico in 1907. When his family moved to Los Angeles, he found work as a duster in a Hollywood furniture store, which led to chance meetings with filmmakers and ultimately helped launch his film career. In the 1950s, Kuri began working on Disneyland projects. He's responsible for the **Plaza Inn**'s elegant interior, the old-fashioned lampposts on **Main Street**, the flagpole in **Town Square**, and the antique furnishings on the **Sailing Ship *Columbia***, to name just a few prominent contributions. Others are rarely seen by guests, including the interiors of **Club 33** and **Walt Disney's** Town Square **apartment**. Kuri also assisted on the Disney attractions at the 1964–1965 New York World's Fair, consulted on Walt Disney World, and even decorated Walt Disney's own homes. Kuri died in 2000 at age ninety-three.

La Boutique de Noël

MAP: New Orleans Square, NOS-5

DATES: Ca. 1998–March 2006

The larger of the two Christmas shops that existed simultaneously in **New Orleans Square** (**L'Ornement Magique** was the other), La Boutique de Noël was in the spot where **Le Gourmet** was once located. Filled with colored lights, stocking holders, and ornaments, La Boutique offered Noël all year long. For guests who couldn't visit during the winter season, it provided a nice sampling of Disneyland's holiday cheer. Discounts were available in the off-season, but unfortunately the shop entered its own permanent off-season in 2006. **Le Bat en Rouge** moved from the other end of Royal Street into this space.

La Boutique d'Or

MAP: New Orleans Square, NOS-5

DATES: Ca. 1974–ca. 1980

After **Le Forgeron** withdrew its metal merchandise from the back of **New Orleans Square** in the mid-1970s, La Boutique d'Or brought in its bold gold. Jewelry, home décor, and other golden goods made this a glittering stop across from **Le Gourmet** on Royal Street. A different indulgence followed when the **Chocolate Collection** moved in around 1980.

Laffite's Silver Shop

MAP: New Orleans Square, NOS-6

DATES: Ca. 1966–1988

Jean Laffite has a presence inside the **Pirates of the Caribbean** attraction, where Laffite's Landing is the boats' launching dock. He is also remembered out on **Tom Sawyer Island**, though there his name is spelled Lafitte. Additionally, for about two decades the early nineteenth-century privateer had his own namesake shop in **New Orleans Square**. Tucked in behind what was then the Creole Café, Laffite's Silver Shop offered a wide array of silver items, all of them engravable right on the premises. Laffite la-left when the Creole Café expanded into its space in 1988.

La Mascarade d'Orléans, aka Mascarades d'Orleans

MAP: New Orleans Square, NOS-9

DATES: Ca. 1985–ongoing

From its corner at the back of **New Orleans Square**, La Mascarade d'Orléans beckoned like a fanciful Parisian confection. After it replaced **Marché aux Fleurs, Sacs et Mode** in the mid-1980s, La Mascarade (also sometimes called Mascarades d'Orleans in Disneyland's free brochures) introduced elaborate Mardi Gras masks as the shop's specialty. A 1999 makeover transformed La Mascarade into a vintage shop with artistic items, including beautiful candles and regal princess hats. Later the room became a center for pin traders, and in 2011 there was also a display of Vinylmation, "the new Disney collectible."

In 2014, the store closed as New Orleans Square went through major changes. When it reopened that fall, La Mascarade was no longer primarily a pin store; in a refreshing change from typical Disneyland shops, this one was filled with non-Disney items that were designed to match the theme of the actual land where the shop sits, which meant lots of New Orleans- and French-themed books, dresses, cups, lotions, and CDs. To honor **Le Chapeau**, a shop that used to exist in this spot, hats were also on display.

By March of 2015, La Mascarade had transformed again. A remodel brought in all new décor (which was light, bright, pretty, and pastel, as opposed to the previous dark rich woods) and a new merchandise theme: as noted on the new jeweled sign on the door, Pandora jewelry is inside. Pandora, a Danish company founded in 1982, is known for its distinctive bracelets, some of which are on view here, along with delicate necklaces. Disney themes include a silver Sleeping Beauty Castle charm on a silver necklace (shown).

Despite the room's changes, there's still a longtime reminder of the history here in the form of a lovely mural outside with the name Sacs et Mode included. And in keeping with the trick mirrors in other Disneyland locations (we see you, **Mad Hatter of Fantasyland**), this shop has a special mirror behind the counter that flashes with fireworks every few seconds.

La Petite Patisserie

MAP: New Orleans Square, NOS-8

DATES: 1988–ca. 2004

One of the hidden jewels in **New Orleans Square** was La Petite Patisserie, a hard-to-find spot that wasn't always open but was always satisfying when it was. More walk-up window than true dining location, "the little pastry shop" was located behind Café Orleans and faced the **Jewel of Orléans**.

The patisserie was famous for four different kinds of waffles, which it served on a stick. Waffle variations ranged from the simple Royal (sprinkled with powdered sugar) to the decadent Mascarade (coated in dark and white chocolate). Non-alcoholic daiquiri slushies and delectable cappuccinos made this an indulgent stop for guests lucky enough to find it (and to find it open). With the Patisserie gone, this section of Orleans Street now offers a small outdoor seating area.

LB's Extraordinary Elixirs

MAP: Frontierland, Fr-8

DATES: July 18, 2014–September 28, 2014

Two weeks after **Legends of Frontierland: Gold Rush** debuted in the streets of **Frontierland**, this wooden cart opened near the **Petrified Tree**. Though small, the cart was actually playing a helpful role in the Legends interactive game going on around it. The cart's three "powerful cold beverages," variations of flavored tea and lemonade, supposedly conveyed Luck, Charm, and Knowledge powers to players (**cast members** extended extra cooperation during the game to anyone holding the special $3 drink glasses). The LB in the cart's name referred to a character who had supposedly discovered his extraordinary elixirs over at Big Thunder Mountain's Rainbow Caverns.

Leather Shop

MAP: Frontierland, Fr-1

DATES: Ca. 2000–ongoing

The two separate rooms of the Leather Shop flank the doorway of the big **Pioneer Mercantile** building just inside the **Frontierland** gates. Often only one of the Leather Shop's rooms is open at a time. Both offer small leather items, especially keychains and bracelets, plus some pewter and silver objects (the room on the left also sells cowboy hats and hat bands). **Cast members** here quickly personalize guests' purchases with names and decorative rivets.

Le Bat en Rouge

MAP: New Orleans Square, NOS-3, NOS-5

DATES: October 2002–ongoing

Le Bat en Rouge is a retail spin-off of the popular Haunted Mansion Holiday, which brings *The Nightmare Before Christmas* theme to **the Haunted Mansion.** In 2001, the first year of that holiday celebration, a cart outside the Haunted Mansion sold *Nightmare* souvenirs. A year later, the cart disappeared and the souvenirs relocated to a scary-looking shop near the **Royal Street Veranda.** Formerly the **One-of-a-Kind Shop** and **Le Gourmet** had occupied this space. In 2006, Le Bat flew away again, this time to the spot near the **Blue Bayou** where **La Boutique de Noël** had been. The cart, meanwhile, has reappeared as the nearby **Holiday Cart.**

Le Bat en Rouge, of course, is a playful take on Baton Rouge, the Louisiana capital within 100 miles of New Orleans, making it suitable for a space in New Orleans Square. Jack Skellington is often the store's star, but there have been lots of other creepy, Halloween-appropriate books, posters, clothes, and figurines available. By 2014, however, as a trend toward more upscale items moved through Disneyland's stores (see the **South Seas Traders** and **Bonanza Outfitters** entries for examples), Le Bat started stocking more expensive clothes, such as princess blouses. A year later, the store became something of a cheery Minnie Mouse headquarters, with lots of shirts, bags, small totes, and jewelry spotlighting Mickey's beloved.

Le Chapeau

MAP: New Orleans Square, NOS-9

DATES: 1966–ca. 1974

Disneyland has never lacked hat shops. Most have been dominated by the usual Disney souvenir hats and **mouse ears**, but not the elegant Le Chapeau in **New Orleans Square.** The women's hats formerly on display here on the corner behind the **French Market** were mostly fine, feathered, frilly creations suitable for Mardi Gras. For men, there were derbies, top hats, and other handsome styles. Some Disney hats were also sold, but they weren't as prominent as the more expensive merchandise.

In the mid-1970s Le Chapeau became a different kind of store with a different French name: **Marché aux Fleurs, Sacs et Mode.**

Le Forgeron

MAP: New Orleans Square, NOS-5

DATES: 1966–ca. 1974

Early in the history of **New Orleans Square**, Le Forgeron (the French term for "blacksmith") occupied a spot at the end of Royal Street. The shop offered old-fashioned metal and leaded-glass objects for the home. Paired with **Le Gourmet** across the street, Le Forgeron made it possible for guests' homes to be decorated with authentic-looking styles evoking the French countryside. **La Boutique d'Or** replaced Le Forgeron in the mid-1970s.

Legacy of Walt Disney

MAP: Main Street, MS-20

DATES: January 15, 1970–February 11, 1973

In 1970, the prominent **Main Street** corner formerly occupied by the **Wurlitzer Music Hall** started celebrating the life and achievements of the man behind the mouse. Legacy of Walt Disney offered biographical information and displays of some of the awards, tributes, and honors Disney received in his lifetime.

After three years, the displays were moved to the **Opera House** for a new presentation called **The Walt Disney Story**. Back on Main Street, the Legacy corner became **Disneyland Presents a Preview of Coming Attractions** and, later, the high-profile **Disney Showcase** store.

Legends of Frontierland: Gold Rush

In July of 2014, a new "experience" opened in and around the **Golden Horseshoe**—an interactive role-playing game called Legends of Frontierland: Gold Rush. **Cast members** helped host the game, which featured Western characters invented spontaneously by the guests who played them. Maps were posted around Frontierland's streets, an outdoor jail cell occasionally held guests, and a new **outdoor vending cart** called **LB's Extraordinary Elixirs** was a strategic ally. The two-month-long Legends game was "a fun dose of wacky live action" according to an article in the *Los Angeles Times*. After Legends left in September, the Laughing Stock Company brought its comedy show back to the Golden Horseshoe.

Le Gourmet, aka Le Gourmet Shop

MAP: New Orleans Square, NOS-5, NOS-3

DATES: 1966–ca. 2002

Le Gourmet, or Le Gourmet Shop, filled a large space at the end of Royal Street near the **Blue Bayou**. A photo in Disneyland's 1968 **souvenir book** shows studious shoppers here examining "rare culinary items," which included fine kitchen accessories for connoisseurs. Everything from copper pots, potholders, and chef hats to cookie cutters, recipe books, and Aunt Sally's Creole Pralines was available, much of it adorned with Disneyland or New Orleans Square logos.

After about three decades, part of this space ceased to be a mecca for gourmands and instead became a mecca for holiday decorators when **La Boutique de Noël** moved in; **Port d'Orleans** also filled some of the space with gourmet sauces and coffees. Le Gourmet, meanwhile, moved to the other end of Royal Street next to the **Royal St. Veranda**. There it stayed until **Le Bat en Rouge** started haunting this spot in 2002.

Le Petit Chalet

MAP: Fantasyland, Fa-22

DATES: 1997–ongoing

Matching the theme of the nearby **Matterhorn**, the Swiss-styled, alpine-roofed Le Petit Chalet shop is not all that petite—not with counters that angle around a bend in Small World Way for about sixty feet. Gifts and sundries here have included disposable cameras, autograph books, Disneyland-themed dolls (including a yeti from the mountain next door), and lots of wearable souvenirs—**mouse ears**, princess hats, and big Mickey gloves perfect for wearing on a happy stroll through **Fantasyland**.

Let the Memories Begin

DATES: January 28, 2011–September 2013

Let the Memories Begin was a park-wide marketing promotion that replaced 2010's **What Will You Celebrate?** Cynics could point out that the public's Disneyland memories really began in 1955, not 2011. Still, the Memories campaign did present some new interactive opportunities: guests could share photos and stories on Disney websites, and a new nighttime show called **The Magic, the Memories, and You!** splashed photos of guests across the **It's a Small World** façade.

From January 28, 2011, to mid-January 2012, a colorful Memories signboard with smiling photos dominated the open Esplanade between Disneyland and Disney California Adventure. A temporary new promotion called **One More Disney Day** supplemented the Memories campaign in 2012 and drew overnight capacity crowds on Leap Day. Another temporary promotion, the **Monstrous Summer All-Nighter**, arrived in May of 2013. When Let the Memories Begin finally ended in September of that year, **Show Your Disney Side** followed as Disneyland's new campaign.

Liberty Street

MAP: Town Square, TS-7

DATES: Never built

First announced in 1958 with a sign in **Town Square**, Liberty Street was a coming attraction that would have expressed Walt Disney's unabashed patriotism. Previously the sign had announced **International Street**, but when enthusiasm for that idea cooled off, the Liberty Street concept heated up. According to 1958's **Fun Map**, Liberty Street would have started at the **Hills Bros. Coffee House** on Town Square's northeast corner and run northward behind **Main Street** toward **Edison Square**, another area that was never built.

The 1958 map shows Liberty Street laid out as a quaint small-town avenue that dog-legged to the right. There are no spinning rides on this street, no little cars or cute boats—just a dignified, historically accurate presentation of an American colony in the late 1700s. Listed on the map are these Liberty Street structures: U.S. Capitol in Miniature, Colonial Shoppes, Hall of Presidents, Declaration of Independence

Diorama, Boston Observer Print Shoppe, Paul Revere's Silver Shop, Griffin's Wharf, Glass Shoppe, and Blacksmith. Griffin's Wharf appears to be a small dock where several sailing ships are tied up. What looks like a prominent church steeple stands at the entrance to Liberty Street, and an even more imposing building called Liberty Hall towers over the cobblestone cul-de-sac at the back end (supposedly a Liberty Bell would have rung from the top of Liberty Hall). A color illustration in the 1958, '59, and '60 **souvenir books** labels that cul-de-sac as Liberty Square, with a Liberty Tree and Liberty Hall as the two dominant features.

Although the full Liberty Street area never blossomed as intended, some of its seeds were scattered elsewhere into Disneyland. A large U.S. Capitol model, purchased in 1955, has long been featured inside the **Opera House** lobby. The **Audio-Animatronic** technology needed to create the Hall of Presidents didn't exist in the late 1950s, but by 1965, a solitary Abraham Lincoln figure was up and talking in **Great Moments with Mr. Lincoln**. The full Hall would later be built in Walt Disney World.

Light Magic

DATES: May 23, 1997–September 1, 1997

The 1997 replacement for the long-running **Main Street Electrical Parade** was the short-lived Light Magic. Unlike its venerated predecessor, Light Magic is remembered today as a summer debacle, though in some ways it was a precursor to modern street extravaganzas like 2010's Celebrate! A Street Party.

Promoted as "a spectacular journey," Light Magic moved four big portable stages—each covering 900 square feet and standing twenty-five feet tall—through **Main Street** and presented almost a hundred performers who danced and interacted with the nighttime crowd. The "light magic" was supplied by fiber optics and strobe lights. Screens for movie clips and confetti cannons added to the fourteen-minute spectacle, but many guests left disappointed (and many kids left frightened by the bizarre costumes).

On September 1, 1997, less than four months after its May 23 debut, Light Magic's plug was pulled (a new *Mulan*-themed **parade** followed in 1998). A worthy Main Street Electrical Parade successor finally arrived in 2015, when **Paint the Night** debuted.

Lilliputian Land

MAP: Fantasyland, Fa-22

DATES: Never built

Long before the **Storybook Land Canal Boats** cruised past tiny buildings, **Walt Disney** wanted to build an entire land devoted to miniatures. Named after Lilliput, the tiny kingdom in *Gulliver's Travels*, Disney's Lilliputian Land appears on a map drawn by **Marvin Davis** in September of 1953, some twenty-two months before Disneyland opened. Davis's rendering shows Lilliputian Land as a two-and-a-half-acre rounded triangle sandwiched between **Fantasyland** and **Tomorrowland**. The area has its own entrance from the **Hub**, as well as a curving track for a small railroad, a winding river for canal boats, and plenty of small hills and trees.

Later that month, **Herb Ryman** drew his famous Disneyland map under Disney's watchful eye. His map also features a Lilliputian Land east of Fantasyland. However, once Disney decided to include small mechanical figures, he realized that the **Audio-Animatronic** technology he needed was years away, so the Lilliputian Land idea was scrapped. Instead, a less ambitious attraction, the **Canal Boats of the World**, debuted inside Fantasyland on **Opening Day**. Within five years, some of the acreage originally reserved for Lilliputian Land would be partially occupied by the **Matterhorn,** the **Submarine Voyage**, and the **Fantasyland Autopia.**

> **MOUSCELLANY**
>
> Long before Disneyland's Lilliputian Land was being considered, Coney Island's Dreamland park had already presented something similar in the early 1900s. Midget City was a small-scale community built on a third of an acre and populated by 300 little people who lived and worked in front of fascinated spectators.

Limited Time Magic

DATES: January 4, 2013–December 31, 2013

Announced at a flashy press conference in New York's Times Square in October of 2012, Limited Time Magic brought an inelegant name to an ambitious program of over two-dozen 2013 events. "Surprise" was the theme of Disneyland's year-long lineup, as some of the special events were announced via social media with little advance notice.

Limited Time Magic events usually lasted a long weekend or two and were often timed with seasonal festivities. For instance, kicking off the schedule on January 4, 2013, was **Three Kings Day**, a three-day weekend devoted to the traditional Latin American celebration of the Christmas story. The four weekends given to the **New Orleans Bayou Bash** were modeled after Mardi Gras, True Love Week intersected Valentine's Day, March welcomed a Spring Fling with the Easter Bunny, a Disney Villains dance coincided with September's Friday the 13, and November included a Bite into a Magical Thanksgiving Celebration. A few of the special events, such as

> **MOUSCELLANY**
>
> Running concurrently with 2013's Limited Time Magic was the Year of the Ear promotion, which introduced a steady stream of creative **mouse ears**.

April's Disney Fairies Week, summer's Christmas in July, and September's Celebrate Pirates Week, weren't really connected to traditional holidays and seemed a little more random (though no less fun).

Lindquist, Jack
(1927–2016)

According to his **Main Street Tribute Window** (shown on page 285), Jack Lindquist was Disneyland's Honorary Mayor and Master of Fun. Before earning those titles, Lindquist, born in Chicago in 1927, was a child actor with roles in the *Our Gang* comedies of the 1930s. Two decades later, he was serving in the Air Force and then attending USC.

After starting work at Disneyland in 1955 as an advertising manager, Lindquist later headed the marketing department and eventually became the park's first president. He championed some of Disneyland's signature promotions, concepts, and expansions, among them **Disney Dollars**, **Skyfest**, **Blast to the Past**, the **Tencennial**, and **Mickey's Toontown**. During Lindquist's tenure, virtually every corner of Disneyland was improved or promoted by one of his ideas or decisions. As a testament to Lindquist's significance, Charles Ridgway's book *Spinning Disney's World* identifies him as a passenger in the inaugural boat that cruised through **It's a Small World** in 1966. In the 1970s and '80s, Lindquist was a key contributor to the marketing and promotional plans for other Disney parks.

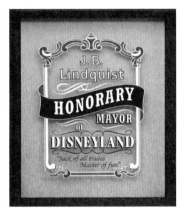

A year after his 1993 retirement, Lindquist was named a Disney Legend. His fascinating memoir, *In Service to the Mouse*, was published in 2010, and he later contributed several long Disneyland anecdotes to *The Disneyland Book of Lists*. When Lindquist died in February of 2016 at age eighty-eight, Robert Iger (the Walt Disney Company's Chairman and CEO) said he was "a true Disney original" who "made sure Disneyland was the Happiest Place on Earth for each guest who walked through the gates, setting the standard for every leader that followed."

Little Green Men Store Command

MAP: Tomorrowland, T-6

DATES: March 2005–ongoing

Aliens have arrived, and they've got their own store. The Little Green Men Store Command is located next to the exit from the **Buzz Lightyear Astro Blasters** attraction—an appropriate (and lucrative) location for a store sharing Buzz's *Toy Story* theme. The store's name, of course, is a take-off on the movie's Star Command. A large photo collage of Buzz hung outside the shop during Disneyland's golden anniversary.

Formerly the **Premiere Shop** had filled this

space, and like its predecessor, Little Green Men Store Command still uses spaceships from the extinct **Rocket Jets** as display cases. Light fixtures are shaped like Saturn, and wall murals depict legions of smiling, three-eyed aliens (detail shown). Pin traders will find a large selection of pins and accessories, while Buzz Lightyear fans will find plenty of toys and clothes that celebrate their galactic hero. Merchandise for other Pixar movies, such as *Planes* and *Cars*, also fill the shelves here.

Little Man of Disneyland

MAP: Adventureland, A-6

DATES: August 2015–ongoing

Many books have been written about Disneyland, but the only one with its own entry in this encyclopedia is *Little Man of Disneyland*. This engaging children's story merits inclusion because it actually has a display inside Disneyland itself.

> **MOUSCELLANY**
>
> Here are eight current Disneyland stores located near similarly themed attractions, thus enabling guests to *Exit Through the Gift Shop* (the title of Banksy's 2010 film): **Autopia Winner's Circle; Carrousel Candies;** the **Indiana Jones Adventure Outpost; It's a Small World Toy Shop; Mad Hatter of Fantasyland; Pieces of Eight; Pooh Corner; Star Trader.**

Published in 1955 under Simon and Schuster's Little Golden Books imprint, the book tells the story of Patrick Begorra, a leprechaun living in the Anaheim orchards where Disneyland is about to be built. With construction imminent, Disney characters take him on a helicopter flight to Disney Studios to see some drawings of "a wonderful place called Disneyland . . . with all sorts of marvelous things for fun." Even-

tually Patrick is given his own residence "out of sight, hidden away" in **Adventureland**. When the book was rereleased in mid-2015, that tiny home, complete with a wee welcome mat, finally appeared at the base of a tree in front of the **Indiana Jones Adventure** (shown).

The author of the book is Little Golden Books editor Jane Werner, who wrote the book under the pen name Annie North Bedford (North Bedford has a geographical connection—it's the Beverly Hills street where the publishing offices were located). Werner wrote several other Disney-themed children's books, including 1954's *Donald Duck in Disneyland* and 1955's *Disneyland on the Air*. The charming *Little Man* illustrations are by Richmond Kelsey, a Disney animator who worked on several classic films.

For young readers in 1955, Werner and Kelsey's enchanting story and artwork helped build excitement about Disneyland; for many adults in this century, the delightful little book evokes cherished childhood memories.

Little Red Wagon

MAP: Hub, H-5

DATES: Ca. 1995–ongoing

This Little Red Wagon isn't the kind that is towed around by a horse or a child—it's a food wagon. More specifically, it's an old-fashioned catering truck that's usually parked in the southeast corner of the **Hub**, a location that has some historical significance. Originally, the adjacent **Plaza Inn** was called the Red Wagon Inn, sponsored by Swift, the meat-packing company with a logo that incorporated a red wagon.

Today, the Little Red Wagon specializes in corn dogs while offering other snacks. To ease the crowding around this popular spot, in June of 2012 a new ordering procedure was put in place that enabled guests to place orders with a **cast member** stationed a few yards away from the Little Red Wagon. The crowds form because this is one of the main corn dog headquarters in the Disneyland Resort, which may not seem like much of an accomplishment at first. *Au contraire, mon ami gastronomique*—over a million of these acclaimed, hand-dipped golden corn dogs are enjoyed by Disneyland Resort guests and gourmands every year.

L'Ornement Magique,
aka Le Bayou Magique

MAP: New Orleans Square, NOS-5

DATES: October 10, 1998–February 2012; November 2012–October 6, 2013

For over a decade, L'Ornement Magique filled a charming little location at the back of **New Orleans Square** with holiday cheer. No matter what season it was, guests could always buy elaborate handcrafted ornaments created by New York-based artist Christopher Radko.

Radko is famous for his delicate glasswork—the *New York Times* dubbed him the "Czar of Christmas Present." At Disneyland, much of his work featured Disney characters, and many of his ornaments were created exclusively for the park. After Radko departed in 2009, the shop was renamed Le Bayou Magique to tie into a new Disney film, *The Princess and the Frog*, with beautiful ornaments by an array of designers. The shop closed in early 2012 and reopened for a few autumn months as the **Pirates League**, but the ornaments returned in time for the **holiday season**. The shop closed for good in October of 2013, and was eventually turned into a private entrance for **Club 33**.

Lost and Found

MAP: Town Square, TS-9; Main Street, MS-16, MS-1; Park, P-2

DATES: July 17, 1955–ongoing

Lost and Found might be Disneyland's most peripatetic office. The 1956 **souvenir book** lists Lost and Found as "above **Opera House**," an upstairs location guests couldn't actually access. The 1957 book instructs guests looking for Lost and Found to "Inquire Security Office" but doesn't identify that office's location (the **Police Station** in **Town Square** would have been a good guess, but old **Fun Maps** show Lost and Found just off of **Main Street**, near the **Market House**). For the decade that followed, there was not a single mention of the Lost and Found in Disneyland's souvenir books.

In the early 1960s, a sign in the park announced that Lost and Found had relocated to the Global Van Lines locker area in Town Square's northwest corner (the 1968 souvenir book finally acknowledges this location). In the 1990s, Lost and Found relocated once again, moving back to the eastern side of **Center Street**; guests could find it by using the small, free maps they got at the turnstiles. For the twenty-first century, Lost & Found (with an ampersand) then moved outside of Disneyland into the Esplanade area near Disney California Adventure; in 2011, it moved once more, this time to a spot west of Disneyland's turnstiles (current guidemaps point guests to this building).

No matter where it's been located, the Lost and Found office has stayed busy. Over 400 items a day are brought to Lost and Found—everything from umbrellas, sunglasses, and wallets to medication, jewelry, and cameras (on average, a cell phone is turned in every twenty minutes).

> **MOUSCELLANY**
>
> Besides returning lost items to their owners, the Lost and Found office matches up items with their *finders*, too. A guest who finds a lost item can bring it to Lost and Found, fill out a form, and claim the item if it isn't picked up within two months.

Love Bug Day

DATES: March 23, 1969; June 30, 1974

The 2003 DVD of Disney's *The Love Bug* includes a twelve-minute documentary about an unusual day in Disneyland history. Love Bug Day was first held on March 23, 1969, to celebrate the box office triumph of *The Love Bug*, which had debuted late in 1968 but had gone into wide release in March of 1969.

As shown in the DVD's documentary (which is as fascinating for the groovy 1960s fashions as it is for the event itself), Love Bug Day had two main parts. The first, held out in Disneyland's **parking lot**, involved a contest whereby guests decorated their own VW Beetles in order to win a new one. Some of these vehicles were so heavily laden with giant ears, noses, legs, eyes, signs, and paint that they looked more like alien creatures or psychedelic hallucinations than familiar cars.

The second part of Love Bug Day was a fun **parade** featuring all the wildly disguised Beetles, with music provided by the **Disneyland Band**. With the cars coming in from the parking lot, this parade began in **Town Square**, cruised northward up **Main Street**, and ended at **It's a Small World**. There, the star of *The Love Bug*, Dean Jones, presented the winning Beetle-decorator with the keys to a new car.

Five years later, with *Herbie Rides Again* in theaters, Disneyland held a second Love Bug Day on June 30, 1974, again with a contest and a parade. Two weeks later, it turned up on a TV special called "Herbie Day at Disneyland," featuring lots of Volkswagens and one of the film's stars, Helen Hayes.

While there were no more Love Bug Days, there were more *Love Bug* movies, plus a 1982 TV series. In the mid-1970s, there was even talk of putting some kind of attraction in **Fantasyland** with vehicles taking wild, Herbie-inspired rides, but those plans never made it off the drawing board.

> ## MOUSCELLANY
>
> Love Bug Day wasn't the first time cars had overrun Main Street—in 1956, the Antique Automobile Parade sent old Ford Model T cars chugging from the **Hub** to Town Square.

Lunching Pad

MAP: Tomorrowland, T-8

DATES: 1977–1998

The year **Space Mountain** opened, a small snack bar with a Space Age theme settled in beneath the **PeopleMover's** second-story loading area. Though it wasn't always open, the Lunching Pad was a handy hot dog/popcorn/soda spot for guests on the go. Previously, a snack stand called the **Space Bar** had been here.

The Lunching Pad lasted two decades, but it blasted off for good in the extensive 1998 remodel of **Tomorrowland** and was replaced by the **Radio Disney** broadcast station.

Mad Hatter of Fantasyland

MAP: Fantasyland, Fa-27

DATES: 1956–ongoing

Four separate Disneyland areas—**Fantasyland**, **Main Street**, **Tomorrowland**, and **Town Square**—have featured Mad Hatter hat shops. The first Mad Hatter opened in 1956 in Fantasyland's castle courtyard. The shop was tucked into a corner of the building that held **Mr. Toad's Wild Ride**, putting the Mad Hatter's hats about seventy-five feet

from the **Mad Hatter's Mad Tea Party**.

Two years later, another related attraction, **Alice in Wonderland**, opened nearby, putting three Alice-related establishments within easy walking distance of each other. In 1983, the three attractions were moved even closer together to form a cozy Alice corner. The twirling teacups were positioned nearer to Alice in Wonderland, and the Mad Hatter's hat shop was relocated from the castle courtyard to an adjacent cottage, where it still operates. Underscoring the connection is one of the teacups in the cottage's front garden (shown).

Hats, of course, are the Mad Hatter's specialty, including everything from princess hats and baseball caps to the famous **mouse ears** that are sold in dozens of different styles. And yes, the shop carries the signature Mad Hatter hat with the "10/6" shillings/pence price on the outside. The fun interior of the shop displays lots of antique hats, an elaborate rabbit display in one corner, and a grinning Cheshire Cat that magically appears inside a wall mirror.

Mad Hatter of Main Street

MAP: Main Street, MS-11; Town Square, TS-8

DATES: June 1958–ongoing

Two years after the **Mad Hatter of Fantasyland** opened, another Mad Hatter debuted at the north end of **Main Street**. Also called Mad Hatter Hats, the shop was around the bend from Coke's **Refreshment Corner** on little W. Plaza Street. Like its older sibling, this Mad Hatter offered classic Disney-themed headgear—Peter Pan hats, Donald Duck caps, **mouse**

ears, etc. But soon this Mad Hatter would be singing the same tune as its namesake character in the *Alice in Wonderland* movie: "No room! No room! No room!"

In 1963, a remodel of this Main Street building meant that the hat shop had to go—and go it did, to a prominent **Town Square** location by the **Opera House**. It's still there today, presenting guests with their first chance inside Disneyland to try on a zany Goofy-eared hat.

Mad Hatter of Tomorrowland,
aka Mod Hatter, aka Hatmosphere

MAP: Tomorrowland, T-22, T-13

DATES: 1958–December 2006

A 1958 **Fun Map** places a Mad Hatter hat shop in the **Tomorrowland** building that held the **Bathroom of Tomorrow** and other exhibits. This was Disneyland's third Mad Hatter shop, and it sold the same kind of merchandise as the **Fantasyland** and **Main Street** versions. When Tomorrowland underwent extensive remodeling in 1966 and 1967, the Mad Hatter re-emerged in a showy location and with a hip name. The new freestanding building was next to the massive **Carousel of Progress** structure, and the new name, appropriately enough for the psychedelic '60s, was the Mod Hatter. As cool as the shop sounded, the merchandise was basically unchanged.

In the 1980s, the name went less mod and more space-y when it changed to Hatmosphere. Mickey's sorcerer hats, whimsical sun hats, and the ubiquitous **mouse ears** were among the many hats 'n caps available here until 2006. That's when the **Autopia Winner's Circle** relocated here, displacing almost fifty years of Mad/Mod/Hatmosphere history.

Mad Hatter's Mad Tea Party

MAP: Fantasyland, Fa-6, Fa-25

DATES: July 17, 1955–ongoing

One of the original **Fantasyland** attractions that debuted in 1955, the Mad Hatter's Mad Tea Party has gone through several changes. Preliminary concept drawings show

basically what guests see now: a whirl of teacups with an *Alice in Wonderland* theme that echoes the 1951 Disney film. The most conspicuous stylistic differences between what was drawn and what was built concerned the track layout and the attraction's centerpiece. One early illustration shows twenty teacups circling around a central hub, as if they are on a racetrack with banked curves.

When it opened, the Mad Tea Party and its colorful teacups were positioned in the **Sleeping Beauty Castle** courtyard to the west of **Mr. Toad's Wild Ride**, a location now occupied by the **King Arthur Carrousel**. Back then, the attraction was out in the open, a big circle of activity surrounded by a waist-high metal fence with a control booth at one end. There were no trees around the circle or lights strung above the teacups as there are today. Originally, the main platform upon which the cups spun was gray; later it was painted with a red-and-orange psychedelic spiral.

Guests instantly took to the crazy cups, enthusiastic about the price (initially only a B ticket from Disneyland's **ticket book**) and the control wheel in the center of each cup, which makes this seemingly simple ride surprisingly complex. As the animated Mad Hatter announces at his *Alice in Wonderland* tea party: "I shall eluci-date!" Each teacup's wheel enables riders to spin the cup faster or slower, clockwise or counterclockwise, giving guests *three* simultaneous spins: the turns served up by the big platter holding all the cups; the rotation of the three smaller dishes holding six cups each; and the independent spins of the individual cups themselves. So fre-netic is the action that many guests don't realize the ninety-second Mad Tea Party is one of Disneyland's shortest rides.

Promoting the Mad Tea Party has always been pretty easy for publicists—the attraction is easily understood and basically sells itself. An early **attraction poster** depicts Mickey, Minnie, and Alice in the teacups, with a tagline about spinning "into the fun-filled world of Wonderland." Old **souvenir books** show off the teacups with large, colorful photos of twirling, laughing people, telling readers that they would "whirl and spin at a dizzy pace." Interestingly, the souvenir books couldn't settle on the attraction's name, listing it in different places as the Mad Tea Party, Mad Hatter's Tea Party, Mad Hatter Tea Party Ride, and Mad Hatter Tea Cup Ride.

A legend that's grown over the years is that the "dizzy pace" of the ride is dizzier in some cups than it is in others; guests are constantly testing out spin rates to de-termine which cups are the fastest (of today's eighteen cups, the purple-and-orange ones seem to get the most votes). Something that isn't a legend is the frequency with which guests stumble out and get sick after a vertiginous reel—Disneyland's website warns riders that it's "best to eat after you spin" and "guests who are prone to motion sickness should not ride." As a precaution, the Mad Tea Party shuts down in the rain so guests won't slip as they stagger away from their cups (even after a light sprinkle, the cups are temporarily stopped so they can be wiped down and dried by hand). The cups themselves have also gotten safer over the years—initially they didn't have doors, like the modern teacups do to seal guests in; instead, each one had just a single fabric strap across the open space that guests stepped through.

In early 1982, the Imagineers shut down the teacups for over a year so they could be re-located near the **Alice in Wonderland** attraction about 150 feet to the east. The carousel, which was already in the castle courtyard, moved north to fill the Mad Tea Party's former location, and the teacups filled what had once been an empty walk-way. New party lights were strung above the cups, and the "Very Merry Un-Birthday" song from the *Alice* film was piped in to enhance the connection. One thing the attraction doesn't have that is found at other Disney parks is a teapot at the center of the whirling platform. Most guests, though, either don't notice or don't care.

While it may seem nauseating and perplexing to some older guests, millions of fans still enjoy this party that has been going for over five decades.

MOUSCELLANY

Classic as it may be, the Mad Hatter's Mad Tea Party got skewered by *Mad* magazine in October 2015. According to a list in the magazine of "7 Ways That Disneyland Is Celebrating Its 60th Anniversary," Disneyland is "finally getting around to fixing that loose bolt that's led to all those decapitations on the teacup ride."

Magic Eye Theater

MAP: Tomorrowland, T-19

DATES: May 2, 1986–ongoing

The big outdoor site that had hosted the **Flying Saucers** and the **Tomorrowland Stage** finally went indoors in 1986 when the 575-seat Magic Eye Theater opened. This new building, located to the right of **Space Mountain**, was one of the first major Disneyland projects completed under the Michael Eisner regime that began in 1984.

Most guests know the biggest attractions that have played inside the Magic Eye, but few can name its initial offering. *Magic Journeys* was a Kodak-sponsored 3-D movie imported from Walt Disney World in June of 1984 for a two-year run, first on the **Space Stage** and then for four months at the Magic Eye. Billed as "a 3-D Film Fantasy" on the **attraction poster**, the sixteen-minute film enabled guests, especially children, to "soar on the wings of imagination."

Magic Journeys, though, was just a placeholder until the star attraction was ready for its 3-D close-up. *Captain EO*, another Florida import, debuted in September of 1986 with a whirlwind of publicity, thanks to the superstar talent involved—singer Michael Jackson, producer George Lucas, and director Francis Ford Coppola.

A decade later, with audiences dwindling, *EO* was replaced with another popular film, **Honey, I Shrunk the Audience**, that jetted in from Orlando. *EO* turned the tables, however, when it replaced *Honey I Shrunk the Audience* on February 23, 2010. After a four-run year, *EO* was replaced once again, this time by a series of promotional "sneak peeks" of upcoming Disney films: *Guardians of the Galaxy* in mid-2014, *Big Hero 6* in late 2014, *Tomorrowland* in April 2015, and *Path of the Jedi* in November 2015.

This last offering presented a ten-minute montage of clips from the seven *Star*

Wars movies to build excitement for the following month's *Star Wars: The Force Awakens*. The clips jumped through the series non-chronologically but managed to introduce key moments and main characters. While it was not the bold new film that *Captain EO* was, *Path of the Jedi* still drew huge audiences eager to fly with the *Star Wars* stories once again.

Magic Kingdom Club

In the 1950s, many businesses implemented marketing programs that offered corporate discounts to their biggest customers. None of these programs, however, was as successful as Disney's Magic Kingdom Club. Founded in 1958 by **Milt Albright** of the Group Sales department, the MKC offered discounts—around fifteen percent—similar to what theaters and other parks were offering, but Disneyland's club seemed more stylish and significant. When companies signed up for the MKC, their employees submitted formal applications to join, a process that enhanced the value of the free membership card they eventually received.

Besides cheaper admission tickets, members also got hotel discounts and received a free quarterly magazine. So successful was the MKC that within five years, it had over a million card holders from dozens of major companies. Before the program ended in 2000, it had spread to other Disney parks, expanded its discounts to a long list of vacation services, and counted over 5 million members.

The Magic of Disneyland Film

Released in October of 1969, this 16mm color documentary gives a general overview of Disneyland. During its twenty-one minutes, all the expected attractions are shown, including some that are extinct, such as the **PeopleMover**, **Skyway**, **Flight to the Moon**, and more. Climbers on the **Matterhorn**, park entertainers, and a live **Tinker Bell** in flight are additional highlights. Some of the aerial shots and other scenes are included among the special features on *The Love Bug* DVD.

The Magic, the Memories, and You!

MAP: Fantasyland, Fa-21

DATES: January 28, 2011–September 2012

Disneyland began a new marketing campaign called **Let the Memories Begin** in January 2011. The showpiece of the new promotion was a nightly multimedia event entitled The Magic, the Memories, and You! During this eye-popping ten-minute presentation, images of happy guests were projected onto the façade of **It's a Small World** for all to see, with background music and synchronized special effects evoking magic and memories. Before the show ended in September of 2012, several updates introduced new imagery, such as a romantic segment added near Valentine's Day in 2012 and a summertime sequence added three months later.

Magnolia Park

MAP: Adventureland, A-4

DATES: May 31, 1956–1962

In Disneyland's early years, a small, serene rest area known as Magnolia Park existed on the far western edge of **Adventureland**. Guests strolling through Magnolia Park were flanked by the **Rivers of America** to the north and the **Jungle Cruise** to the south.

Initially, trees, benches, and quiet paths were all that Magnolia Park offered. The closest thing to a permanent attraction Magnolia Park ever had was the decorative **bandstand** that landed here after it was removed from the **Hub**. Then, in 1958, several outdoor promotions for Disney's *Zorro* TV show were performed in Magnolia Park.

> **MOUSCELLANY**
>
> Today's **cast members** will tell you that the scenic fountain area between the **Haunted Mansion** and the **French Market** is informally called Magnolia Park (though no official signage announces it).

Four years later, Magnolia Park began to disappear as redevelopments supplanted its valuable real estate. First, a Jungle Cruise expansion pushed a new elephant bathing pool into what had been the southern part of the park. By the end of 1962, the new **Swiss Family Treehouse** was dominating the area. **New Orleans Square** construction and its major excavations soon followed. In what might be seen as a tribute to the long-lost little park, **Aunt Jemima's** Adventureland restaurant became the **Magnolia Tree Terrace** in 1970.

Magnolia Tree Terrace

MAP: Frontierland, Fr-7

DATES: 1970–1971

As the 1960s progressed into the 1970s, one prominent **Frontierland** restaurant underwent a quick succession of name changes. Quaker Oats had sponsored **Aunt Jemima's Pancake House** in the 1950s and '60s, and Oscar Meyer began sponsoring the same site with the new name **River Belle Terrace** in 1971. But between these two eras, the building spent a year as the unsponsored Magnolia Tree Terrace. This pretty name referred to **Magnolia Park**, which is what the area off the tip of **Adventureland** had been called before **New Orleans Square** arrived. The restaurant's corner location has always been conspicuous and attractive, offering views of the river only seventy-five feet away.

Mailboxes

Disneyland has dozens of mailboxes, both fake and real. Among the fake ones are those in front of the **Mickey's Toontown** houses owned by Mickey, Minnie, Donald, Chip 'n Dale, and, most humorously, Goofy (whose car has crashed into his mailbox pole). Talking mailboxes can be found near **Toontown Five & Dime,** several of the diminutive houses viewed by the **Storybook Land Canal Boats** have tiny mailboxes out front, and the old **Bear Country** used to have a mailbox at its entrance marked Rufus.

In addition to these mailboxes that add design details, Disneyland also has about twenty actual working mailboxes on display. They've been in the park a long time, too—*Disneyland: The Nickel Tour* clearly shows a **Main Street** mailbox on a 1950s postcard. Today's guests walking from the turnstiles to **Town Square** might notice small mailboxes at the tunnel entrances. Nearby, individual mailboxes are mounted on posts in front of **City Hall**, along Main Street, and at the **Hub**. Other locations include the **Adventureland Bazaar, Autopia, Briar Patch, Heraldry Shoppe, Frontierland Shooting**

MOUSCELLANY

Disneyland's old-fashioned mailboxes are a nice, nostalgic touch, especially since another traditional communication method— the pay phone—no longer exists in the park. Thanks to the proliferation of cell phones, pay phones at Disneyland became superfluous; the last one was removed in 2015.

Exposition, Pioneer Mercantile, Pooh Corner, and **Silver Spur Supplies.**

As with the park's **trash cans**, the mailboxes are often designed to match the themes of their specific locations—for instance, the one at the Briar Patch (shown) has a rustic design appropriate for **Critter Country**. Some of the boxes are oriented vertically, others horizontally; some have lids that lift up, others that pull down. All of them, however, have their mail collected the same way, as noted on some of the boxes themselves: "This Collection Box is Served by Disneyland Personnel, and Taken to Anaheim Post Office." Disneyland itself doesn't stamp or postmark the mail, though an official "Disneyland U.S. Post Office" mailing items with an official "Disneyland, California" postmark was mentioned in the 1953 prospectus that pitched the park to potential investors.

Main Street Cinema

MAP: Main Street, MS-19

DATES: July 17, 1955–ongoing

Since 1955, the Main Street Cinema has presented short films in a stylish brick building along the southeastern block of **Main Street**. Just to the north is a locked doorway that's supposedly the home of the Disneyland Casting Agency, where, according to a sign on the door, "It takes People to Make the Dream a Reality." A prominent marquee projecting from the building announces the theater's program; long ago, there was a sign here announcing this location as "the biggest show on Main Str." Sitting serenely in her ticket booth is the beguiling mannequin Tilly, whose name tag notes that she's from Marceline (the boyhood home of **Walt Disney**).

One of the nice features here has always been the absence of any line—guests can walk in at any time during the day and check out the flicks, which play continuously to sparse crowds. Inside the theater, short movies and cartoons have been run on six small screens in one wood-paneled room, with an oval riser in the center to help kids get a clear view. Like the Circle-Vision 360 theater that once existed in **Tomorrowland**, the Main Street Cinema doesn't have seats, only railings that standing guests can lean on. Back when Disneyland used **ticket books**, admission to the Main Street Cinema initially cost only an A ticket (rising to a B ticket in 1960).

For the first three decades, the program offered black-and-white silent movies, each lasting around ten minutes, and each dating to the earliest years of film history (on **Opening Day**, the marquee above the Main Street Cinema's entrance announced "Gloria Swanson" and "Wm S Hart Western and Keystone Kops"). Some of these old selections included Mack Sennett's *A Dash Through the Clouds* (1912), William S. Hart's *Dealing for Daisy* (1915) and *Tumbleweeds* (1925), Winsor McCay's *Gertie the Dinosaur* cartoon (1915), Thomas Edison's *The Great Train Robbery* (1903), the Keystone

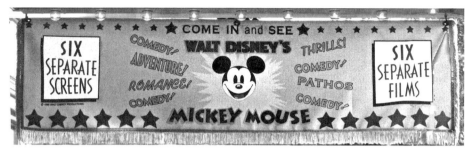

Kops' *The Noise of Bombs* (1914), Gloria Swanson's *Shifting Sands* (1918), and Harold Lloyd's *Spring Fever* (1919). Vintage newsreels also added interest and authenticity. For some of these shows, there would be extra added surprises—during *Dr. Jekyll and Mr. Hyde*, for instance, an actual Mr. Hyde character startled guests in front of the theater in the mid-1960s.

In the mid-1980s, the movie selection changed to early Disney animation. Over the next decades, *Steamboat Willie*, the 1928 cartoon that made Mickey Mouse a star, was a staple in the cinema, joined by such Disney favorites as *The Dognapper* (1934), *Mickey's Polo Team* (1936), *The Moose Hunt* (1931), *Plane Crazy* (1928), and *Traffic Troubles* (1931).

In July 2010, five of the theater's six screens were devoted to a rare eight-minute color film that depicted Disneyland in its earliest years; the sixth screen looped **Opening Day** footage from the national TV broadcast. Today's guests will find a selection of six old Disney cartoons, all offering a few minutes of nostalgic fun.

Main Street Cone Shop

MAP: Main Street, MS-16

DATES: Ca. 2000–Summer 2012

In the **Main Street** area, the eastern side of **Center Street** ended at this little hot-weather delight. Sponsored by Dreyer's, the Main Street Cone Shop wasn't always open, but when it was it served up cold, tempting summertime treats. The ice cream bars were shaped like Mickey, sundaes came with assorted toppings, and root beer floats were served in souvenir cups. Umbrellas offered shade for the outdoor seating amidst humorous sound effects emanating from the upstairs offices of E. S. Bitz, D.D.S., the "painless dentist." Though the Cone Shop stopped serving in mid-2012, its signage didn't come down until June 2013.

Main Street Electrical Parade

DATES: June 17, 1972–November 25, 1996; January 20, 2017–June 18, 2017

These days, it's hard to appreciate just how revolutionary the Main Street Electrical Parade was, now that **Paint the Night** has reinvented the concept of a glowing nighttime parade. But when it debuted in 1972, the Main Street Electrical Parade truly was revolutionary, presenting a wonderful, innovative entertainment totally unlike traditional **parades** that starred marching bands and sunny floral floats. Yes, the MSEP included moving structures and Disney characters and music, but its elements came together in a way never seen before. The recorded narration enthusiastically described it as a "spectacular festival pageant of nighttime magic and imagination in thousands of sparkling lights and electro-syntho-magnetic musical sounds." Close, but still not enough.

> **MOUSCELLANY**
>
> The late-1970s Electrical Parade introduced the amazing, smoke-breathing, thirty-eight-foot-long title character from the film *Pete's Dragon* and a big fiftieth-birthday float for Mickey.

The Electrical Parade was the brainchild of **Robert Jani**, Disneyland's longtime director of entertainment. Though Jani produced other events that are now treasured memories for millions of guests, the Electrical Parade was his signature creation. His inspiration was a display of electrified scenes that had helped inaugurate Walt Disney World in 1971. For Disneyland, Jani put elaborate scenes on a dozen unseen motorized carts, outlined everything with a total of a half-million lights, and had hidden drivers steer the glittering vehicles down a darkened **Main Street** toward **Town Square**.

Another Disney Legend, **Bill Justice**, designed many of the mechanical floats. These included a train and scenes from Disney classics like *Cinderella*, *Dumbo*, and *Pinocchio*. The bouncy electronic music frolicking from loudspeakers was a 1967 non-Disney composition called "Baroque Hoedown," supplemented with snippets of other songs, all played on the futuristic Moog synthesizer.

The twenty-minute Main Street Electrical Parade debuted on Disneyland's twenty-seventh birthday, ended two-dozen years later, and came back in 2017. Its early career was twice interrupted—in 1975 and '76, a special **America on Parade** celebration commemorated the bicentennial; when the Electrical Parade returned, it was longer, had flashy new displays, and ended with a rousing patriotic climax. The second interruption came in 1983, when the Flights of Fantasy Parade landed for a short stay. During the Electrical Parade's main twenty-four-year run, several floats were retired, among them those for **It's a Small World** and the movie *Return to Oz*.

When Disneyland officials announced that the Main Street Electrical Parade's last performance would come in mid-October 1996, the fan response was so strong and the surge in **attendance** so great that the parade's final run was extended to November 25. Afterward, some of the bulbs from the floats were sold for charity.

Replacing the Electrical Parade the following spring was **Light Magic**, a hugely promoted but hugely disappointing street spectacle. In 2001, a modified version of the Electrical Parade reappeared in Anaheim, but not at Disneyland (hence the name change). Disney's Electrical Parade cruised through Disney California Adventure to help spark attendance at the new park. Until 2017, the closest a modern Disneyland guest could get to re-living the Main Street Electrical Parade was to take in the new Paint the Night extravaganza, which debuted in 2015 as part of the sixtieth anniversary **Diamond Celebration**. However, the classic Electrical Parade (with a few small modifications) did return for a "limited-time encore engagement" starting January 20, 2017, and ending six months later on June 18.

Main Street Fruit Cart

MAP: Main Street, MS-17

DATES: Ca. 2000–ongoing

Parked at the busy intersection of **Main Street** and **Center Street** is the highly visible, highly tempting Main Street Fruit Cart. Here, guests can get healthy snacks to go, including fresh fruit and fruit juice. Up until mid-2012, behind the Fruit Cart were the slightly more sinful temptations of the **Main Street Cone Shop**.

Main Street Lockers & Storage, aka Locker Area

MAP: Main Street, MS-1; Park, P-3; Main Street, MS-16

DATES: July 17, 1955–ongoing

A locker area has been available at Disneyland since **Opening Day**, but it's changed locations and names several times. The first location was a small building in **Town Square** to the right of (but not attached to) the **Fire Department**. Early **souvenir books** label this original locker area the Bekins Van & Storage Locker Area and the Bekins Locker Service.

In May of 1963, another moving company moved in and the site became known as both the Global Van Lines Locker Area and the Global Locker Service (though the signs on the building read Lost & Found and Parcels). To promote its presence, Global parked one of its old trucks right out front. Global lasted until 1979, to be followed on June 1, 1980, by the National Car Rental Locker Area until January 2, 1990. During these years, a second locker area appeared about 150 feet west of Disneyland's turnstiles; guests still use this handy storage facility, which offers 513 lockers (including eighteen oversize lockers, twelve of which are large and six extra large) to guests before they even buy admission tickets.

In 1990, when the **Emporium** was remodeled and expanded to include the **Carriage Place Clothing Co.**, the Town Square locker area moved

MOUSCELLANY

Outside the **Center Street** locker area is a subtle but entertaining feature—according to signs, some of the upstairs rooms belong to a dentist, and the realistic sounds of a dental office can be heard from below. Here are nine more Disneyland locations that produce specialized sound effects: someone gargling and shaving inside Hotel Marceline on Center Street; Aladdin's Other Lamp cracking jokes in the back of the Adventureland Bazaar; subterranean voices emanating from the manhole cover outside Toontown Five & Dime; the tick-tock of the fanciful clock in front of It's a Small World; the sounds of exotic birds and animals anywhere near the Jungle Cruise; chatty seagulls at Tomorrowland's lagoon; eerie moans and voodoo sounds drifting down from upstairs windows near the Mint Julep Bar; a landline telegraph tapping out several lines from Walt Disney's Opening Day dedication speech at the New Orleans Square/Frontierland train station; and rattling chains halfway through the Sleeping Beauty Castle Walk-Through, warning of a sudden appearance by a malevolent guard.

to **Center Street** over by the **Market House**. The current Main Street Lockers & Storage has a big gold key planted in a lock above the door and displays of antique luggage on the shelves inside. Lockers are available on a first-come, first-serve basis, with modest daily fees for different size lockers. The room's walls are lined with lockers (shown), plus there are four long islands of extra compartments, yielding a total of 2,055 lockers (a dozen of these are jumbo lockers) in 2015. Phones, phone card machines, postcard machines, and charging lockers for electronic devices have also been available

(none of these could be used for three months of 2014 when **First Aid** temporarily moved in due to construction in its area).

Main Street Magic Shop

MAP: Main Street, MS-19

DATES: 1957–ongoing

The Magic Kingdom's most enduring magic store is tucked into a cozy spot along the southeastern block of **Main Street**. When Main Street Magic opened, it had **Fine Tobacco** as its neighbor to the north. It also had an older sibling in **Fantasyland—Merlin's Magic Shop**, but Merlin pulled the disappearing-store trick in 1983.

At night, the Magic Shop's sign still stands out on Main Street; while nearly every other sign is outlined in pretty white lights, this one is bright blue and yellow. And though the sign announces MAGIC, there's more here than meets the eye—scar makeup, disguises, toys, and gag gifts offer additional amusements.

Still, it's the display of magic tricks that offers a genuinely magical experience. Right before guests' very eyes, skillful **cast members** will demonstrate card tricks, coin tricks, and other sleight-of-hand illusions. Although they won't explain the tricks, the magicians will point out the how-to books that will. As shown in the movie

MOUSCELLANY

What with the Houdini posters, antique magic devices, fascinating books, wall of captivating tricks, and talented magicians drawing guests' attention in this little shop, few visitors notice what the author did in April of 2015–a playing-card **Hidden Mickey** (shown) on the ceiling just inside the doorway. After we relayed this discovery to author Steve M. Barrett, he confirmed that it had yet to be reported and so added it to his authoritative *Disneyland's Hidden Mickeys* book (page 68, hint 176) and included us in the acknowledgements.

Disneyland: The First 50 Magical Years, Disney Legend **Steve Martin** worked the Main Street Magic Shop's counter in the 1960s, developing a rudimentary magic act that would lead to his professional career (Martin's memoir *Born Standing Up* has him working in both of Disneyland's magic shops; his autographed photo is displayed inside Main Street's shop).

A decade ago, the Main Street Magic Shop began to lose some of its luster as it started selling generic Disney merchandise. However, a retailer called Houdini's Magic Shop, already established in Las Vegas, New York, San Francisco, and Downtown Disney, took over shop operations in 2009 to restore the magic that guests had enjoyed for over fifty years.

Main Street Photo Supply Co.

MAP: Main Street, MS-12

DATES: November 19, 1994–ongoing

At the northeast end of **Main Street**, the prominent building formerly known as Carefree Corner has been the Main Street Photo Supply Co. since 1994. As the sign above the door announces, "a picture is worth a thousand words." Whether guests are shooting still photos or making movies, this is Disneyland's best-developed photography center.

"Photo Supply" doesn't begin to suggest the wide range of photo-related products that have been available here—everything from disposable cameras, rentable cameras, film, and various batteries to View-Master reels, Disney picture frames, photo books, and battery chargers. This

MOUSCELLANY

Guests who love antiques should peruse the dozens of old cameras on display in the windows and behind the counter here. There's even what looks to be a giant nineteenth-century studio camera—the kind that stands on a tripod and covers the photographer with a hood.

is also where the photos taken of guests by park photographers—such as the portraits taken with the mouse himself inside **Mickey's House**—can be picked up.

Kodak was the sponsor here until financial problems caused the company to depart in late 2012, which resulted in the Kodak name being taken off the store's signage, off the "picture spot" signs positioned at photogenic locations, and off the free brochures handed out at Disneyland's **entrance**. The new sponsor, Nikon, posted its own logo at the Main Street shop and on some new "picture spot" signs in 2014.

Main Street Shooting Gallery

MAP: Main Street, MS-8

DATES: July 24, 1955–January 1962

Walt Disney wanted to keep traditional (and traditionally tacky) midway amusements out of his magnificent park, but at least one midway perennial—the shooting gallery—found its way in. The first and shortest-lived of Disneyland's three major shooting galleries, the Main Street Shooting Gallery debuted just after **Opening Day** (the Frontierland Shooting Gallery opened in 1957, and the **Big Game Safari** version five years after that).

On **Main Street**, the shooting gallery was located inside (and toward the back of) the **Penny Arcade**. Today, that seems like an odd place to put a rifle range—after all, most of Disneyland's **souvenir books** have included Walt Disney's quote about Main Street representing "carefree times." Evidently, those carefree times involved actual .22-caliber weapons, which are what guests fired at the gallery. As seen in old photos, the rifles were untethered and so were easily picked up and moved around. Even kids got to handle the eight guns—souvenir books from 1959 to 1962 include back-cover illustrations of a smiling adult handing a rifle to a child.

By early 1962, with another shooting gallery already established in **Frontierland** and another one due in **Adventureland**, the live ammo was discharged from Main Street and replaced by the more urbane pleasures of the remodeled Penny Arcade and its associated shops. Though it was gone, somehow the Main Street Shooting Gallery was still shown on the 1964 **Fun Map**.

Main Street Tribute Windows

Many guests know that the hand-painted names on the upper-story windows along **Main Street** pay tribute to real people, most of them former Disney employees who contributed to Disneyland in some significant way. Who originally chose the names? According to Martin Sklar's *Dream It! Do It!*, **Walt Disney** "personally selected the names that would be placed on the windows."

Typically, the windows identify a "proprietor," add some customized graphics, and then give a brief description of a fictional business supposedly operating behind the window. That descriptive text is usually a clue as to what the real-life Disney employee did at Disneyland. For instance, the window for **Wally Boag**, the longtime comedian at the **Golden Horseshoe**, states that his business is "Golden Vaudeville Routines"; for **X. Atencio**, "The Musical Quill—Lyrics and Librettos" references his musical contributions to **the Haunted Mansion** and other attractions. Some tribute windows are not on Main

MOUSCELLANY

Not all tribute windows are on display in Disneyland: upon retiring, longtime **cast members** sometimes receive personalized windows as gifts to be displayed in their homes. For example, Beverly Butrum was given one when she left in 2003 after working in **New Orleans Square** for thirty-seven years.

Street at all: actor Fess Parker (shown on page 140) and designer **Harper Goff** are honored in **Frontierland** and **Adventureland**, respectively.

Not every tribute window has an identifiable name and descriptive text—some on Main Street present names with no descriptive text at all (such as the names above the **Fortuosity Shop**), and some identify a fictional business (Piano Lessons, Massage Parlor) without naming a specific proprietor.

On Main Street, two of the windows represent Disney's relatives: his father, Elias, who died fourteen years before Disneyland opened, and his grandson, Christopher Miller, who was born in 1954 while Disneyland was being built. Walt Disney himself does not have a Main Street Tribute Window, but he does have a window at the **Mickey's Toontown** library: "Laugh-O-Gram Films, Inc. W. E. Disney, Directing Animator."

MOUSCELLANY

Since the release of the 2012 edition of this encyclopedia, new windows have been created for Disney Legend **Tony Baxter**, consultant **Harrison Price**, and Walt Disney's boyhood neighbor, Doc Sherwood M.D. (shown). The complete 2015 list of eighty-nine names can be found in *The Disneyland Book of Lists*.

Main Street, U.S.A., aka Main Street

MAP: Park, P-9

DATES: July 17, 1955–ongoing

Main Street, U.S.A. (shortened here to Main Street) is often used as an all-inclusive heading for three identifiable areas in Disneyland's southern half. Many people assume that Main Street stretches 1,000 feet from the train station at Town Square to Sleeping Beauty Castle just north of the Hub. Disneyland's own souvenir books support this notion, as the photos and descriptions for Town Square, Main Street, and the Hub are usually gathered together into a single Main Street category. However, to throw a fuller spotlight on each separate area, we've defined Main Street as the business district between the rectangular **Town Square** and the circular **Hub**. This smaller, more manageable Main Street begins at the **Emporium** and ends at the **Refreshment Corner** 350 feet away.

Within this concentrated Main Street area are two distinct intersecting streets. The iconic Main Street, about thirty-two feet from curb to curb and lined with candy-colored buildings, is divided in half by the narrower **Center Street**. In addition to Main and Center, a third street, Plaza, runs from west to east across the north end of Main. Plaza Street divides the Main Street district from the Hub and is within the latter's domain.

The four blocks of Main Street (two on each side of the street) constitute the most densely developed acreage in Disneyland. With no large attractions filling up the space, there are far more doorways and businesses here than anywhere else. And, visually at least, this is one of Disneyland's least-changed areas. Dozens of businesses here have opened and closed, yet the exterior architecture remains basically as it's been since 1955. The same can't be said of **Adventureland**, **Fantasyland**, **Frontierland**, or **Tomorrowland**—all original lands that have undergone major remodeling and expansion.

Even in the first planning stages, **Walt Disney** knew that he wanted a long entranceway that funneled guests through a charming recreation of a turn-of-the-century small American town. This strategy, he felt, would help orient guests to Disneyland and ease them into the stranger lands that lay ahead. If the guests themselves didn't live in a small town, thought Disney, surely their relatives did, or their ancestors had, or they'd seen one in popular movies or TV shows. Thus they'd feel comfortable walking into one at Disneyland, especially if there were signs and symbols that greeted them as familiar friends. Theoretically, the same small-town sweetness that had made Andy Hardy one of the most enduring film characters of the 1940s would work in Anaheim in the 1950s and beyond.

Consequently, the early concept drawings for Disneyland had always included a picturesque area like Main Street. But back then, the actual plans of the Main Street area varied considerably from one drawing to the next. Some proposals called for residential homes and a little red schoolhouse. The famous **Herb Ryman** drawing of the forty-five-acre park as Walt Disney had envisioned it in 1953 places an enormous church with a tall steeple on Main Street. A **Marvin Davis** sketch made that same year shows open-air courtyards inside some of Main Street's buildings, and one 1956 con-

cept drawing puts a Disneyland Dog Pound on Main Street, which would have provided a comical photo opportunity echoing a *Lady and the Tramp* scene. What's more, two additional major streets, **International Street** and **Liberty Street**, were almost built in the immediate area, but designers had moved on from that idea by the early 1960s.

Unlike other lands in the park that were inspired by Disney movies and TV shows (the Davy Crockett TV character shaped **Frontierland**; Disney's animated movies spread across all of **Fantasyland**; the *True-Life* nature documentaries informed **Adventureland**; etc.), Main Street takes inspiration from Walt Disney's own life. The Main Street we see today is loosely based on Marceline, Missouri, the small Missouri town Disney grew up in. The Disneyland version, however, is a delightful reimagining of Disney's experience, a much more idealized and generic representation than a specific reproduction of Marceline or any other particular location. It's not Main Street, Marceline; it's Main Street, U.S.A., a place that everybody, not just Missourians, can

identify with. "Here is the America of 1890–1910," reads the introductory text in Disneyland's early souvenir books, not "Here is Marceline."

Disneyland's Main Street has included most of the features that would have been found in any small town's commercial center in the years bracketing the fin de siècle—an apothecary, tobacconist, movie theater, candy stores, bakeries, jewelers, hotel (shown on page 304), horseless carriages, etc. The buildings have actual addresses, too (odd numbers are on the west side, and even on the east). But Disney didn't merely reproduce traditional small towns—he improved upon them. Diane Disney Miller, writing in *The Story of Walt Disney*, calls Main Street her father's "dreamlike re-creation" of what he had known long ago. Thus everything in Main Street is typically sparkling, running perfectly, fresh, and garbage-free. In fact, the street is so perfect and pretty that it's more like a gentle Disney movie representation of what a turn-of-the-century town would have been like, had all the defects and blemishes of the real world been expunged. Like a detailed movie set, the impeccable façades and varied color schemes suggest individual buildings and store fronts, but in reality the interiors of the buildings are all connected and open to each other, making it possible to walk north to south for hundreds of feet from one shop to the next without venturing outside.

On Main Street, the buildings feel safer and cozier than real buildings because the architects designed them that way. The original Imagineers, remember, were art directors from Disney Studios, so they employed visual tricks from the movies as they planned out Main Street. Just as Disneyland's **railroad** is 5/8 the size of a real train, and just as Sleeping Beauty Castle has larger blocks of concrete at the bottom than at the top to give the illusion of towering height, so too do the multi-story buildings on Main Street play with perspective. All along the street, the ground floors are approximately ninety percent of full size, to make doorways slightly less intimidating and shops a little more inviting to anxious guests (especially kids). The second floors are all about ninety percent the size of the ground floors, making them about eighty percent of normal height. Finally, the third floors are about eighty percent the size of the second floors, making them about sixty percent of "normal" size and giving the whole Main Street area a snug, comfortable atmosphere. A small town? Yes, in more ways than one.

Adding to the warm feeling along Main Street is the bright paint on the buildings, which are all multicolored and frequently touched up to keep everything looking fresh (a major repainting project in the mid-1990s introduced even more vivid colors). Every building boasts splendid architectural elements—beautifully adorned upper-story windows, decorative mansard roofs, striped awnings, turned finials, and ornate iron railings. Designers studied old books and historic sites to get the details of the idyllic past just right. The result, according to cultural analyst Margaret J. King in *Disneyland and Culture*, is "possibly the most important 4D artwork ever created . . . a streetscape instantly recognizable by its stylized and distilled iconography."

Main Street is full of intriguing sights, smells, and sensations. Rounded trees add greenery, but they aren't so big that they block the view. Century-old gas lamps sourced from St. Louis and Baltimore light the sidewalks, and vehicles evoking vintage buggies and trolleys drive by frequently. There are old-time musicians, the fragrant scents of baked goods, and the joyous feeling of slow, unhurried exploration (no whirling rides here). Studious guests can try to decipher the proprietors identified on upper-story **Main Street Tribute Windows**, or they can linger over the Emporium's wonderful **Windows of Enchantment**. At dusk, the white trim lights that have been outlining all of Main Street's buildings since 1956 create a warm ambience. (Disney declared that one of his favorite times of day at Disneyland was early evening, as the skies were darkening and the lights were coming up. Steve Martin, in the short film *Disneyland: The First 50 Magical Years*, agrees, saying, "Disneyland's best magic trick happens at dusk." Anyone who has seen Main Street by twilight would find it hard to disagree.) At night, new **Guest Flow Corridors** constructed in 2014 are now often opened up on the east and west sides of Main Street to give less-crowded alternatives for walks to and from Town Square.

As if all that weren't enough, Main Street is usually filled several times a day with buoyant **parades**. In addition, special events occasionally fill the street with unique fun. For example, starting in March of 1957 and repeating every spring until 1964, Main Street has hosted the California State Pancake Races. This multi-day friendly competition was an inexpensive event that supported Quaker Oats, sponsor of **Aunt Jemima's Pancake House** in Frontierland. For the pancake race, two-dozen housewives sprinted from the Hub to Town Square while flipping pancakes over ribbons draped across the street. The winner won $100, a plaque, and a gift basket. So popular were these races that celebrity judges, marching bands, and Disney characters eventually joined the festivities. Other special events have included ice skating on a synthetic Main Street pond for a 1974 TV audience and a swimming demonstration by Olympic athletes in a full-length Main Street pool in 2002.

Although some of these activities may sound corny, they're typical of the old-fashioned fun that has distinguished this timeless area. Main Street may be just a nostalgic fantasy, but for many guests, it's the best one in Disneyland.

MOUSCELLANY

While Walt Disney borrowed ideas from his home town of Marceline for Disneyland's Main Street, Marceline itself also borrowed some name recognition from its most famous former resident. In 1956, the town built a new recreation complex and pool that it named after Disney. Walt Disney Elementary opened in 1960. Disneyland's **Midget Autopia** was given to the town in 1966 and ran until 1977. Disney characters were on hand in 1998 for Marceline's first annual Toonfest animation festival, which is still held on the third Saturday in September. The Walt Disney Hometown Museum was dedicated in 2001, and the local post office was rechristened the Walt Disney United States Post Office Building in 2004.

Main Street Vehicles

MAP: Park, P-8, P-9, P-10

DATES: July 17, 1955–ongoing

Adding immeasurably to the atmosphere on **Main Street** are its various old-time vehicles. Since 1955, seven varieties of public transportation have traveled up and down Main Street from **Town Square** to the **Hub**. They've all made one-way trips to and from designated pick-up/drop-off stations with no stops in between, and they've all traveled at approximately the same speed (three to four miles per hour). Back in the days of **ticket books**, the Main Street Vehicles were considered A-ticket attractions.

Only three types of conveyances were in service on **Opening Day**: the horse-drawn fire wagon, the surrey, and the streetcar. All of them were towed by horses, and all of them charged a dime for a ride. The gleaming, red fire wagon—or fire engine, as it was also called—was "an old-time hose and chemical wagon" pulled by two horses. There was only one fire wagon, and of all the Main Street Vehicles, it had the shortest career, retiring in August of 1960 after only five years of service (it's been on display inside the **Fire Department** ever since). The second Opening Day vehicle was the horse-drawn surrey, which lasted until January of 1971. This horse-drawn cart with tall wooden wheels carried eight to ten passengers spread out over three bench seats. The third vehicle, dating to 1955, is the beautiful streetcar, which still runs today. Two streetcars can operate on Main Street simultaneously; their wheels fit into metal tracks on the street, and the two sets of tracks enable two streetcars to pass each other unscathed. As big as these vehicles are—and they are big, each holding up to thirty passengers and weighing up to two tons—each one can be pulled by just a single horse, usually a Percheron, Belgian, or Clydesdale that sometimes weighs 2,000 pounds or more. Observant guests will find the names of these friendly behemoths on their bridles.

Horsepower of a different kind was introduced to Main Street on May 12, 1956, when a shiny, red horseless carriage, the first of two, hit the street. Seven months later, a second horseless carriage with bright yellow paint was also chugging along the Town Square–Hub route. Although both motorcars were put together meticulously to look like antiques from about 1903, underneath their exteriors are modern cars built by Disney Legend **Bob Gurr**. Still running today, each car has a fringed canopy, toots a bulbous "ah-oo-gah" horn, and can carry a half-dozen passengers on its two bench seats.

On August 24, 1956 a huge, green double-decker bus called the omnibus was added to the roster

MOUSCELLANY

Making a special ride even more special is the honorary "Jr. Firefighter" badge (shown) that kids receive as they disembark from Disneyland's fire truck.

of Main Street Vehicles. It was supplemented by a special second omnibus on Christmas Day in 1957. Also built by Gurr, the Disneyland omnibus looks old but contains modern machinery (power steering, power brakes, etc.); in fact, the only true antique on it is its old-fashioned horn. Modeled after the big buses that toured Manhattan in the 1930s, the omnibus is fully capable of today's freeway speeds. This gentle giant isn't always in service, but when it is it offers a matchless view of the Main Street area for up to forty-five passengers at a time.

The next vintage vehicle to appear at the park was another Gurr creation—the motorized fire truck that began carrying small groups of guests on August 16, 1958. To deliver his creation from Disney Studios (where it was built) to Anaheim, Gurr actually drove the truck down the freeway for almost an hour. Inspired by turn-of-the-century fire engines, the fire truck carries lengths of hose along its sides and has a bell mounted on its rear (the siren has been replaced by a horn).

In 1960, a seventh public vehicle, a diminutive electric car with a surrey-style fringed top, made a brief appearance on Main Street. There were two of these cars, and they were somewhat similar to the horseless carriages (the ones with the bench seats). However the two electric cars had room for only a couple of passengers and barely lasted one summer before they were retired.

Despite all the modernization elsewhere in Disneyland, slow, old-fashioned vehicles still putt-putt along Main Street every day. While these aren't the most thrilling vehicles guests will ride in at the park, they are among the most charming and historically significant.

Malt Shop and Cone Shop

MAP: Frontierland, Fr-6

DATES: Ca. 1958–ca. 1970

A Malt Shop and Cone Shop tandem seems like a natural for **Main Street**, but actually this pair existed for about a decade in **Frontierland**. The location was next door to **Aunt Jemima's Pancake House**, a space previously occupied by **Don DeFore's Silver Banjo Barbecue**. Both the Malt Shop and Cone Shop were quick-serve counters run by a fast-food service called UPT Concessions (which ran several fast-food counters in Disneyland). The first served up hot dogs and burgers along with the malts, and the second served up ice cream to go. A 1970 remodel replaced these two eateries with another pair, the equally small and fast **Wheelhouse and Delta Banjo**.

The Many Adventures of Winnie the Pooh

MAP: Bear Country/Critter Country, B/C-4

DATES: April 11, 2003–ongoing

After almost thirty years, the ursine entertainers of the **Country Bear Jamboree** finally retired in 2001. Replacing them was another bear, this one the rotund star of A. A. Milne's whimsical stories and Disney's animated films. Like the Country Bear Jamboree, The Many Adventures of Winnie the Pooh originated in Florida, where it

had replaced **Mr. Toad's Wild Ride**. When Toad fans protested his possible removal from Disneyland, Pooh found a home in **Critter Country**. There the attraction was built as an indoor ride with an outdoor line.

To experience the Many Adventures, guests sit in adorable beehive-shaped "beehicles"—each with its own character name—and venture for three and a half minutes into the verdant Hundred-Acre Wood. Along the way are visits with Pooh's animal friends, including Tigger, Rabbit, and Eeyore, plus an inevitable search for "hunny," a Heffalump-and-Woozle dream, and a party (Christopher Robin was not invited, it seems, as he appears only as a small silhouette on a balloon at the very end).

A visual treat for children, the attraction is filled with bright colors, friendly faces, heartwarming sentiments, and delightful **Sherman Brothers** music. Happily, it's also an attraction that doesn't require a tedious wait in a long **queue** (wait-times are usually counted in single-digit minutes). Fans of Disneyland history will also enjoy a reminder of a classic attraction: mounted on a darkened wall just past the Woozles are the heads of Max the deer, Melvin the moose, and Buff the buffalo, three Country Bear Jamboree characters (shown in the **Mile Long Bar** entry).

MOUSCELLANY

Pooh's balloon ride is accomplished via the same kind of mechanism that once carried Teddi Barra, one of the singing Country Bears, aloft on her swing.

Marché aux Fleurs, Sacs et Mode

MAP: New Orleans Square, NOS-9

DATES: 1975–ca. 1985

Marché aux Fleurs, Sacs et Mode (which translates to "Flower Market, Stylish Bags") was a shop located in the back of **New Orleans Square** for over a decade. Previously **Le Chapeau** had been on this corner behind the **French Market**. The new merchandise was just as French and frilly as the hats that had been previously been available. Fancy handbags, accessories, and some hats were offered, plus film and a few other supplies. **La Mascarade d'Orléans** brought Mardi Gras masks here in the mid-1980s.

Market House

MAP: Main Street, MS-18

DATES: July 17, 1955–ongoing

The nostalgic Market House has been a **Main Street** favorite since **Opening Day**. Wrapping around the southeast corner of Main and down the eastern side of **Center**

Street, the Market House exterior has three street-facing sides, two of brick, and one of wood. The building's four stories are topped with a mansard roof and a widow's walk, making it one of the most imposing structures on Main Street. A 1954 concept drawing labeled it a combination "grocery store" and "meat market." Ultimately, it was designed as a handsome 1890s general store.

Always a fascinating room to explore, the ground-floor interior has sometimes felt more like a museum than a retail space. An ornate potbellied stove used to dominate the front room and invited guests to relax over a game of checkers. Swirling candy sticks stood in decorative jars, pickle barrels have been displayed on the hardwood floors, and kitchen supplies, gourmet foods, and a huge selection of mugs have lined the shelves. For years, cocoa and coffee drinks were served to guests by costumed women in long, old-fashioned dresses. One delightful touch added in 1974: the antique phones here conveying gossipy party-line conversations.

Swift & Company, the meat packager, was the original sponsor (Swift also sponsored two early Disneyland restaurants, the Red Wagon Inn and **Chicken Plantation**). The 1956 and '57 **souvenir books** call the building Swift's Market House, with the added description "meats and groceries" (just how many groceries were purchased and lugged around is debatable). Later, the Hills Bros. name was established out front, and Del Monte and Sun Giant have also been sponsors, but in recent years the Market House had no corporate names on its exterior until a famous name took over the interior on September 25, 2013. Starbucks brought with it the expensive specialty beverages it's known for, plus baked goods, fresh fruit, breakfast sandwiches, and an intimate new sitting room called the Book Rest that opened in the adjacent room formerly occupied by **Disneyana**. One wonders what **Walt Disney** would think about today's extravagant $6 coffee drinks (*The Man Behind the Magic* quotes him: "Coffee is only worth a dime. As long as I run this park it's only a dime"). He also might question what Starbucks did to the old Market House policy of offering free coffee refills (Starbucks quietly terminated that policy). Starbucks does offer its own merchandise, including **holiday season** ornaments shaped like little Starbucks mugs.

Though much has changed at the

Market House, it has retained its party-line phones (shown), checkerboard, stove, and folksy charm. Thanks to the absence of Disney-themed T-shirts, hats, and modern souvenirs, it's still a favorite old-time location in Disneyland.

Mark Twain **Riverboat**

MAP: Frontierland, Fr-17

DATES: July 17, 1955–ongoing

Nearly every description of the *Mark Twain* includes the words "stately" and "majestic." The graceful white ship certainly is both. At 105 feet long, 28 feet high, and 150 tons (stats listed on a wooden sign in the waiting area), the *Mark Twain* rivals the magnificent **Sailing Ship *Columbia*** as Disneyland's most imposing watercraft.

Walt Disney wanted a resplendent riverboat in his park long before Disneyland

was built—early concept drawings always include something
that looks like the *Mark Twain*
floating in what appeared to
be the **Rivers of America**.
Tellingly, when the ship's landing was built, it was placed in
a highly visible location at the
end of the main **Frontierland**
walkway so that guests would
be able to see the docked, dazzling *Mark Twain* from the **Hub**.
Many a diffident newcomer has

been drawn deep into the wild frontier not only by the riverboat's tempting vision, but also by its iconic whistle—a sonic wienie that can be heard down **Harbor Boulevard** almost three-quarters of a mile away.

The ship's illustrious history began with the steel hull, built at shipyards in nearby Long Beach. Meanwhile, elements of the three wooden decks (Main, Promenade, and Texas) and the ornate pilot house were constructed at Disney Studios in Burbank, trucked down to Anaheim, and then added to the hull inside Disneyland. (According to oft-repeated Disney lore and Bright's *Disneyland: Inside Story*, the *Mark Twain* was the first paddlewheeler built in the United States in fifty years. However, at least two famous paddlewheelers, the *Belle of Louisville* (1914) and the *Delta Queen* (1927), were built in America after 1905.)

The total cost to build the *Mark Twain*? Just $150,000, half the cost of the *Columbia* three years later. The name, of course, was originally the pseudonym of Samuel Clemens, "America's own author, humorist, and occasional riverboat pilot," according to the waiting-area sign.

While the twin-smoke-stacked *Mark Twain* is an authentic-looking replica of the larger sternwheelers that plied the Mississippi in the nineteenth century, it isn't architecturally perfect—some parts were built proportionally to a smaller scale than other parts, in accordance with Disneyland's specific safety and maritime needs. The ship can hold at least 350 passengers (plus freight, according to the waiting-area sign that also identifies the vessel as a Sternwheel Packet Steamboat); however, when it debuted there was no official loading capacity. Thus there are old tales of **cast members** accidentally overloading the boat until it almost capsized when all the guests shifted to one side to view the riverbank. Today, seventeen hand signals exchanged between the crew help monitor the river traffic and keep the trip safe.

On July 13, 1955 the *S.S. Mark Twain* (its name displayed on a beautiful dock-side mural) made a prominent trial voyage at a party thrown by Walt Disney and his wife to celebrate their thirtieth wedding anniversary. Four days later, actress Irene Dunne christened the ship during televised **Opening Day** ceremonies. From then on, it has endured as one of Disneyland's iconic attractions. Strangely, in its first three decades the *Mark Twain* swung back and forth from being a C, D, and even briefly an E-ticket attraction. The views have also changed dramatically over the decades, but the lovely, serene trip hasn't varied significantly. Powered by steam and propelled by its nine-ton stern paddlewheel, the ship travels on a submerged track around, appropriately enough, the island named after one of Mark Twain's greatest characters, Tom Sawyer. On its twelve-to-fourteen-minute journey, the ship travels about a half-mile and takes in panoramic views of island wilderness and attractions in Frontierland, **New Orleans Square**, and **Critter Country**. **Audio-Animatronic** animals and a parked **Mike Fink Keel Boat** are among the additional sights along the water's edge. In decades past, the ship also sold non-alcoholic mint juleps on board as part of the relaxing trip.

Naturally, the *Mark Twain* has often been a star attraction for special events in the park. In its sixty-plus years and 260,000-plus miles traveled, the ship has been specially decorated for holidays, has presented jazz combos to shoreline guests, and has been incorporated into **Fantasmic!** From November 2009 to January 2010, the *Mark Twain* hosted Tiana's Showboat Jubilee!, a spirited Mardi Gras-style musical celebration coinciding with the release of *The Princess and the Frog*. In 2012, with the **Refreshment Corner** on **Main Street** closed for a remodel, the pianist there temporarily moved on

> **MOUSCELLANY**
>
> As they travel on the *Mark Twain*, guests may not realize that their ship is riding a rail. Other watercraft that travel on submerged tracks are the **Storybook Land Canal Boats**, **Jungle Cruise**, **Motor Boat Cruise** (1957–1993), Sailing Ship *Columbia*, and **Submarine Voyage**/Finding Nemo Submarine Voyage. Other boats, like the canoes, the **Rafts to Tom Sawyer Island**, and flume rides like those in **It's a Small World**, are free-floating.

> **MOUSCELLANY**
>
> The *Mark Twain* Riverboat's biggest fan? Walt Disney. "One of the biggest joys of my life," he said, as quoted in *Disneyland and Culture*, "is sitting on the levee in the Frontierland section of our park . . . watching the steamboat *Mark Twain* belching smoke and skirting along toward the tip of Tom Sawyer Island."

board the *Mark Twain* to play live ragtime music. And with the ship docked
in 2016 during the prolonged **Star Wars
Land** construction, the **Strawhatters**
performed lively jazz on the decks.

When the ship is sailing, the trip
can be even more memorable for the
few lucky guests invited to visit the
wheelhouse, where they can ring the
bell and receive an official Pilot's Certif-
icate (shown) signed by Commodore Walt Disney. Back in the day, guests could commemorate their visit by purchasing a box with an official Steamboat Captain Outfit in
it. But most guests have never needed anything special to enliven or memorialize the
experience—on a hot day, a quiet voyage on cool waters aboard the stately, majestic
Mark Twain is plenty special enough.

Marquee

MAP: Park, P-1

DATES: 1958–ongoing

For over forty years, a magnificent marquee graced the automobile entrance to the
Disneyland **parking lot**. Surprisingly, there was no big sign there on **Opening Day**,
and in fact the first true marquee wasn't installed along **Harbor Boulevard** until
1958. When it did go up, the marquee offered a friendly and memorable welcome to
drivers.

For decades, the forty-two-foot-tall sign was in three parts. The top section
spelled out the Disneyland name, with the letters mounted separately in different-size
rectangles and spelled out in a fantasy-style font. A replica of this display now grac-

es the top of the slide over at the Disneyland
Hotel's pool (shown). On the original marquee,
a wide horizontal section below the letters read
"Park & Hotel Entrance" until those words were
replaced with "The Happiest Place on Earth" in
the 1970s. Underneath that section was a board
with manually placed letters listing that day's
hours and special events (this board went electric in 1971). Stretching skyward from the sign
was a row of seven flagpoles festooned with
stiff banners. It wasn't the biggest park marquee ever built (that honor probably goes to
New Jersey's Palisades Amusement Park, which
had a 400-foot-wide electrified sign that could
be read fifty miles away), but the Disneyland
marquee might have been the most beloved.

After some thirty years, a new marquee went up in the same spot on October 6, 1989. At sixty-seven feet tall, this one was considerably bigger than the original, and it had some dazzling new components. Crowning the marquee were small pink, yellow, and blue banners and, in the center, an eighteen-foot-tall gold castle within a blue circle. The Disneyland name was now spelled out in white letters on a blue background. While the letters were still written in the same fantasy font, and while they were still mounted in separate rectangles, those rectangles were now all approximately fourteen feet high for a more uniform look. Underneath the first line, a white-on-pink sign reprised the "Happiest Place on Earth" tag line, and below that, a new computerized billboard flashed special announcements in decorative fonts. For a few years in the 1990s, customers could temporarily rent the electronic billboard through the Disney catalog and have a private message photographed as a keepsake.

On June 14, 1999, this large marquee welcomed its last guest; the whole thing was removed the next day in anticipation of construction for Disney California Adventure. After the sign was dismantled into separate pieces, the Disneyland letters, the "happiest place" section, and the gold castle were auctioned off on eBay, with actor John Stamos placing one of the winning bids.

A less imposing marquee now greets pedestrians along Harbor Boulevard (the style of this modest entrance is similar to a cast-member-only entrance on Katella

Boulevard, about 600 feet west of Harbor and opposite from the Anaheim Convention Center). The eastern walkway into Disneyland is marked by a twenty-foot-wide, fifteen-foot-tall aluminum banner, with a "thank you for visiting" sign on the back and occasional decorations related to different marketing campaigns, such as the special design for 2015-2016's **Diamond Celebration** (shown). In the sidewalk at this entrance is **Walt Disney's** star, a tribute placed in 2006 as the inaugural marker on a new Anaheim/Orange County Walk of Stars.

Marshal's Office

MAP: Frontierland, Fr-25

DATES: July 1955–July 1956

Adding authenticity to **Frontierland** was a small, one-story Marshal's Office standing at the far end of the row that holds today's shooting gallery. Decorated with small flags, the office was primarily used as a backdrop for photos. The sign on top of its slanted roof read, "Willard P. Bounds, Blacksmith and U.S. Marshal." In *Disneyland: The Nickel Tour*, Bounds is identified as a real-life frontier marshal **Walt Disney** actually knew—his father-in-law.

After a year, the nearby Mexican restaurant **Casa de Fritos** relocated to this spot with a newer, bigger building.

Martin, Bill
(1917–2010)

Many of the original Disneyland designers were moviemakers recruited from Disney Studios, but Bill Martin was a moviemaker recruited from 20th Century Fox, where he'd worked as a set designer.

Martin was an Iowan born in 1917. When his family moved to Southern California, he studied architecture and design at local colleges and art institutes until he was hired as a Hollywood art director. After serving in the air force, Martin continued his career at Fox until he joined the Disneyland planning team in 1953.

It's said that Martin had a hand in everything at Disneyland. As seen by the display of his artwork in the **Disney Gallery's** 2015 exhibition called "Drawing Disneyland: The Early Years," one of Martin's tasks was to create the original **Fantasyland**—its layout, its look, and its attractions. Working with other Disney Legends like **Ken Anderson**, Martin designed most of the indoor dark rides that are still favorites today, including **Peter Pan's Flight** and **Mr. Toad's Wild Ride**. A few years later, he was in on the creation of the **Nature's Wonderland** area, the **Fantasyland Autopia**, and the **Submarine Voyage** while also laying out the long looping path of the **Monorail**.

In the 1960s, Martin was a key architect of **New Orleans Square** and its two landmark attractions, **the Haunted Mansion** and **Pirates of the Caribbean**. He also helped design **Walt Disney's** New Orleans Square **apartment**, a decorous space that later became the **Disney Gallery**. Martin rose to the position of vice president of design in 1971, supervising plans and contributing ideas for Walt Disney World. Formally retired as of 1977, he stayed on as a consultant and was eventually named a Disney Legend in 1994. Martin died in 2010 at age ninety-three.

Martin, Steve
(1945–)

Steve Martin has been one of the celebrities seen most often at Disneyland (though not in person). Since 2005, Martin has hosted the seventeen-minute film *Disneyland: The First 50 Magical Years*, which is still shown dozens of times a day in the **Opera House**. Martin's presence at Disneyland, however, actually dates back to the early 1960s; as he notes in his memoir, *Born Standing Up*, at age ten Martin wore a gay-nineties costume and sold twenty-five-cent **souvenir books** at the park; at thirteen, he was demonstrating rope tricks in **Frontierland**; he then spent a year working in the storage room of Tiki Tropical Traders (now **Tropical Imports**) in **Adventureland**; finally, from 1960 to 1963, he began his "show business career" by performing and selling magic tricks at both **Merlin's Magic Shop** and the **Main Street Magic Shop.** In an *Inside Comedy* interview televised in 2013, Martin calls this latter gig "an oasis" because "you could be a little more daring."

During these formative years, Martin frequently attended shows at the **Golden Horseshoe** and carefully studied comedian **Wally Boag** (Martin writes that he had memorized Boag's delivery and timing so well that he fantasized about being called upon to replace Boag, had the star ever gotten sick). Martin's memoir also recalls that, while at Disneyland, he learned how to juggle "passably" by watching Christopher Fair, Fantasyland's juggling court jester. He also made friends with a co-worker, John McEuen, who would later found the Nitty Gritty Dirt Band. John's older brother, William E. McEuen, would become Steve Martin's manager and go on to produce his early record albums and movies.

> **MOUSCELLANY**
>
> According to his memoir, *Born Standing Up*, Steve Martin happened to be present (on his last day working at Disneyland, no less) when Diane Arbus snapped *A Castle in California*, her famous black-and-white photo of **Sleeping Beauty Castle**.

Born in 1945 in Waco, Texas, Martin grew up in Southern California. During his early Disneyland years, Martin's family lived in Garden Grove, just two miles from the park. A cheerleader in high school, Martin developed original stand-up comedy routines in college while studying philosophy and theater. Early club performances were followed by a writing stint on *The Smothers Brothers Comedy Hour*, and in 1969, he was part of the writing team that won an Emmy Award. Later TV writing jobs and TV appearances led to his "wild and crazy guy" years of best-selling comedy albums, a hit song ("King Tut"), and well-known catchphrases (such as "Excuuuuuuusssse meeeeeee," a saying he picked up from a Disneyland co-worker). In 1979, Martin co-wrote and starred in *The Jerk*, which was a smash hit. Dozens of successful films followed over the next couple of decades, including *Roxanne*, *L.A. Story*, and Disney's *Father of the Bride* (he is also one of the hosts shown in the Disney film *Fantasia 2000*).

Meanwhile, this Renaissance man was establishing himself as a master of all media: he wrote popular novels and plays, collected notable artworks, recorded Grammy Award-winning music on the banjo, hosted the Oscars several times, and was awarded honors by the Kennedy Center. Martin was named a Disney Legend in 2005.

Matterhorn Bobsleds

MAP: Fantasyland, Fa-24

DATES: June 14, 1959–ongoing

Nowadays, guests appreciate the fun and aesthetics of this thrilling ride, but few people realize how innovative the Matterhorn Bobsleds were when they debuted in 1959. Before then, all roller coaster-type rides placed long trains on wooden tracks with wide curves. In contrast, Disneyland's first true thrill ride used small, sleek vehicles—not on wooden tracks, but on hollow metal tubes that made the ride both quieter and smoother.

It was wilder, too. Since the metal tubes could be bent easily, the ride had tighter curves. Furthermore, the Imagineers placed more than one bobsled on the track at a time, an important strategy for shortening wait-times (when the single bobsleds were later doubled up into pairs, the Swiss-costumed **cast members** could fill them with over 1,500 guests per hour). Disney Legend **Bob Gurr** is credited as the main designer of the original two-toned bobsleds, while another Disney Legend, **Fred Joerger**, made numerous models of **Matterhorn Mountain** with various track layouts. The result of their efforts was a revolution in ride design and the very definition of an E-ticket attraction.

The bobsleds run on two tracks that climb through the inside of the Matterhorn to a point about two-thirds of the way up. They then glide down quickly around and through the mountain for a total distance of about 2,100 feet. For decades, guests have tested theories that one track is faster than the other, but ultimately the speed has more to do with the load inside the sleds than with the tracks (the track on the Fantasyland side is slightly longer and has tighter curves). During the two-and-a-quarter-minute trip, the sleds on both tracks travel at an average speed of barely twenty miles per hour. The speed certainly *seems* faster, though, and riders can grab only quick glimpses of the spectacular scenery.

When the Matterhorn opened, its bobsleds quickly became known as Disneyland's hottest vehicles, and they kept that reputation until **Space Mountain** arrived in 1977. They are also fondly remembered by many as their first thrill ride because initially, everyone had access, no matter how young or short they were (height minimums were added years later). So special were the bobsleds that on the day they debuted, **Walt Disney**, his family, and Vice President Richard Nixon took the first trip; what's more, two of the old bobsleds now sit in Texas's National Roller Coaster Museum and Archives.

Over the years, various changes have been made to the bobsled experience. Most famously, starting in 1978, an effective Abominable Snowman appeared several times during the ride (he was remade into an even scarier character in 2015). Less conspicuously, in 1978, the ride's controls were computerized and the sleds were modified to make the ride safer. One of the most controversial changes was a 2012 redesign of the actual bobsleds themselves. Previously, two pairs of guests (four passengers total) could sit in a single bobsled, but in 2012, those two long seats were replaced by three shorter, cushionless, bone-jarring seats holding three passengers per bobsled. "Not enough leg room and not enough padding—we hear that all the time," said a cast member helping to load the bobsleds in mid-2015. The following March, small cushions were finally added, to the relief of spinal columns everywhere.

One of the special touches that has made the Matterhorn's downhill sprint distinctive is its climax—a sudden swoop through a "glacier lake" (as described in Disneyland's **souvenir books**). Not only does the splashdown decelerate the speeding sleds, it also provides a great visual effect for riders and pedestrians. Before the lake was in place,

MOUSCELLANY

For decades the pre-recorded voice of **Jack Wagner** has cautioned riders to "remain seated, please"—fans of the band No Doubt will recognize Wagner's request as the ten-second introduction to the song "Tragic Kingdom."

test rides culminated in sandbags and bales of hay, but once the downhill run ended with water, it was instantly recognized as one of Disneyland's finest finishes.

Matterhorn Mountain

MAP: Fantasyland, Fa-24

DATES: June 14, 1959–ongoing

For many guests arriving via the Santa Ana Freeway, their first view of Disneyland has often been a quick glimpse of the Matterhorn. The memorable mountain has been a local icon since 1959, when it opened after less than a year of construction. Along with the **Monorail** and **Submarine Voyage**, it was one of the year's three major additions.

Like dozens of other Disneyland attractions, the mountain was inspired by Disney movies—*Switzerland* (a 1955 documentary) and *Third Man on the Mountain* (a 1958 feature). In addition, **Walt Disney** had already made several trips to the actual

Matterhorn and been enchanted by it, so when the idea for a snow-capped hill with a toboggan ride occurred to him in late 1956, by 1957 that idea had evolved into a taller snow-capped mountain with a roller coaster ride, and by late 1958 it had grown into the majestic Matterhorn with its revolutionary **Matterhorn Bobsleds**. The name evolved along with the plan—as noted in *Disneyland: The Nickel Tour*, what began as Snow Hill became Snow Mountain, then Mount Disneyland, Disneyland Mountain, Sorcerer's Mountain, Magic Mountain, Fantasy Mountain, Echo Mountain, the Valterhorn (adapting Walt's name), and finally Matterhorn Mountain.

The Matterhorn was created on a barely used, roughly landscaped picnic mound called Holiday Hill. Straddling the Fantasyland/Tomorrowland border, this twenty-foot-tall knoll was built up with dirt excavated from the **Sleeping Beauty Castle** moat (in *Roller Coasters, Flumes & Flying Saucers*, Disney Legend **Bob Gurr** claims that, before the hill came down and the Matterhorn went up, a gardener was surreptitiously "growing marijuana up on top," so this area "started out as a marijuana farm").

Because of the Matterhorn's height and location, the "European" mountain is clearly visible from the all-American **Main Street**—a potentially jarring sight that bothered some designers, but not Walt Disney. The location also places the mountain in the middle of lots of park traffic. Not including the bobsleds, five other kinds of vehicles have passed close by over the years—the **Motor Boat Cruise**, the **Fantasyland Autopia**, the Submarine Voyage, the **Alice in Wonderland** caterpillars, and the looping Monorail. Additionally, the old **Skyway** trams actually passed through, not around, the mountain.

During the planning phase, Disney Legend **Fred Joerger** made many models to get the mountain's shape correct from all perspectives. As it grew, the construction project gobbled up over 2,000 steel girders for the frame, with no two girders identical in size and shape. Four acres of cement, smoothed by hand, covered the construction like gray skin, with 2,500 gallons of white resin adding permanent "snow" to the upper third. The finished mountain, its landscaped grounds, and its alpine-themed **queue** area created a circular park footprint of about one and a half acres.

The mountain stands precisely 147 feet tall, which is 1.00054% the height of Europe's actual 14,692-foot Matterhorn. Not only is it still Disneyland's tallest structure, but for a while it was the tallest structure in the entire county until a building boom in the 1960s built up the surrounding skyline. Forced perspective, the same movie-making technique that makes Sleeping Beauty Castle look taller than it really is, also makes the Matterhorn seem to stretch higher than it really does. Here, the trick is in the trees, which are shorter at upper altitudes.

The mountain has many unique features. For one thing, because of its placement between two lands, Disneyland's **souvenir books** originally listed it in Tomorrowland (for its first nine years) and then in Fantasyland. Also, the mountain has been frequently ascended by trained alpine climbers. There are thirty routes to the summit, with views revealing Catalina Island and, on the clearest days, the Hollywood sign some forty miles away. According to a 1963 *National Geographic*, climbers back then scaled the Matterhorn eight times a day. More recently, they've even occasionally made their ascents dressed as Disney characters, though climbs came infrequently. Starting on June 15, 2012, and again exactly a year later, a new team of climbers ascended the Matterhorn daily throughout the summer to celebrate its reopening after a five-month closure for a major remodel; this new summer-climbing tradition continued, adding a nice atmospheric detail to the majestic mountain.

One no-longer-hidden fact about the climbers is that they have had their own small basketball "court" about 100 feet up inside the Matterhorn. It's not a full-size court, just a flat surface with a mounted hoop so that climbers and workers can take a break without having to leave the mountain. At least one local radio station has broadcast its show from this space inside the Matterhorn. The basketball court is identified on the "Now Casting" sheet posted next door to the **Main Street Cinema**; the Announcements section of that sheet reads, "Basketball Club sign-ups tomorrow. No. 5 Matterhorn Court."

Another distinctive feature of the Matterhorn is its interior elevator. Besides carrying maintenance workers, this elevator lifts **Tinker Bell** to a platform for her glide above Fantasyland. Tink's flight isn't the only nighttime event to feature the Matterhorn. From 1961 until the late 1970s, a twenty-two-ton sparkling star, twenty-four feet tall

MOUSCELLANY

On the list of Disneyland's tallest structures, the Matterhorn is still #1, followed by three more mountains: **Space Mountain** (118 feet), **Big Thunder Mountain** (104 feet), and **Splash Mountain** (87 feet). **Sleeping Beauty Castle** comes in at 77 feet, and the original *Moonliner* rocket at 76 feet.

and visible from the nearby freeway and neighborhoods, adorned the mountain's apex over the winter holidays.

Today's bobsled riders may not realize that in the 1960s and '70s, riders could clearly see the support beams inside the Matterhorn. A 1978 remodel added new "ice cave" features that blocked off the exposed beams and introduced an eight-foot-tall Abominable Snowman creature as a scary presence throughout the ride. Another aesthetic improvement came when the Skyway trams were shut down and their mountain openings were sealed off in 1994. At some point, two slender spires were also added to the summit to serve as a lightning rod and an aircraft beacon. A 2012 update enhanced the lighting and sound effects inside the attraction, added a fresh coat of paint and more snow to the mountain's exterior, remodeled the loading areas with a quick-loading single-rider line, and placed new three-seat bobsleds on the tracks. In 2015, an even more ferocious Abominable Snowman and some new displays were added to the mountain's interior.

The Matterhorn is unique in the history of Disney parks. Unlike other Disneyland mountains—**Splash Mountain**, **Space Mountain**, and **Big Thunder Mountain**, which all exist in other Disney parks around the world—the mighty Matterhorn has never been duplicated, an appropriate tribute to the first, and maybe the most beautiful, Disney pinnacle.

Maurice's Treats

MAP: Hub, H-2

DATES: March 12, 2013–ongoing

To get a snack inside **Fantasy Faire**, guests head to the old-fashioned, fifteen-foot-long wagon parked across from the Royal Theatre. Named after Belle's father in *Beauty and the Beast*, Maurice's Treats serves a small selection of flavored bread twists (cheddar-garlic, strawberry-almond, and chocolate), plus a signature Boysen Apple Freeze drink with an optional souvenir goblet. Maurice has treats but no seats, so all orders are to-go.

Maxwell House Coffee Shop

MAP: Town Square, TS-7

DATES: December 1, 1955–October 8, 1957

Almost five months after Disneyland opened, the Maxwell House Coffee Shop brought coffee, sandwiches, and outdoor seating to the **Town Square** spot between the corner **Wurlitzer Music Hall** and the **Opera House**. A charming coffee house facing guests as they approached **Main Street** must have seemed like the perfect blend of location and timing. So perfect that, after Maxwell House left in 1957, **Hills Bros.** stepped in eight months later.

McGinnis, George
(1929–)

Futuristic vehicles may have been George McGinnis's specialty, but he also contributed to some of Disneyland's old-style attractions. Born in Pennsylvania in 1929, McGinnis later spent a year in the navy and then studied engineering and design in the early 1960s. He joined Disney's Imagineers in 1966 and began working on the **Tomorrowland** remodel that arrived in 1967. Among other projects, McGinnis designed the whirling vehicles that updated the old **Astro-Jets** into the new **Rocket Jets**, and he created the Mighty Microscope that greeted guests inside **Adventure Thru Inner Space**.

Moving to Walt Disney World projects, McGinnis designed that park's PeopleMover in the late 1960s. Back at Disneyland, he was one of the key designers of **Space Mountain**'s special effects, and a decade later he redesigned the **Monorail** with sleek and luxurious Mark V trains. During this time, McGinnis also joined Disney moviemakers on *The Black Hole*; his four robot characters were included in the sci-fi production.

Throughout the 1980s and '90s, McGinnis continued to help with a wide variety of significant vehicles and attractions at Disney parks throughout the world, including Disneyland's new **Snow White's Scary Adventures** cars and the jungle trucks in the **Indiana Jones Adventure**. McGinnis was elected to the National Inventors Hall of Fame in 2001. His autobiography, *From Horizons to Space Mountain: The Life of a Disney Imagineer*, was published in 2016.

McKim, Sam
(1924–2004)

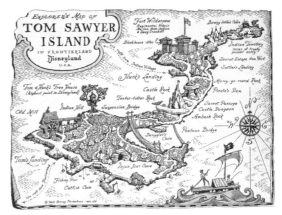

One of the best souvenirs a guest can take home from Disneyland is a large, beautifully illustrated **Fun Map**. Artist Sam McKim drew the first of these in the 1950s; veteran guests may also recall his smaller **Tom Sawyer Island** map (shown), drawn in 1957 and given away for free until 1976. Over the decades, McKim also drew many detailed concept drawings for attractions and buildings that eventually made it into Disneyland (some of his artwork for Frontierland was included in the **Disney Gallery**'s 2015 exhibition "Drawing Disneyland: The Early Years").

A Canadian born in 1924, McKim and his family moved to Southern California in 1935. Related to an MGM casting agent, he was soon getting jobs as a child actor in numerous Westerns. After serving in World War II, studying at Los Angeles art colleges, and winning medals during the Korean War, McKim became an artist in Hollywood. In the mid-1950s he drew set sketches for 20th Century Fox until a layoff sent him over to Disney Studios, where he was hired temporarily to sketch upcoming Disneyland attractions. McKim ended up staying with the company for the next three decades, often working closely with **Walt Disney** himself. Today, McKim's drawings of Frontierland, the **Golden Horseshoe**, **Main Street**, the **Monorail**, **New Orleans Square**, and more still inspire Disney Imagineers.

Outside of Disneyland, McKim sketched storyboards for live-action Disney films of the 1950s and '60s. He also drew concept illustrations for the 1964–1965 New York World's Fair and several Walt Disney World attractions. Though he retired in 1987, he created a lavish park map five years later for the debut of Disneyland Paris.

McKim was elected a Disney Legend in 1996, eight years before he died of heart failure at age seventy-nine.

Meck, Edward
(1899–1973)

Eddie Meck was working in promotions long before he became Disneyland's publicist. Born in Wisconsin in 1899, Meck began his career with Pathé Frères, an early film company that made Harold Lloyd comedies. After publicizing those movies in the 1920s, Meck jumped to Columbia Pictures in the 1930s and pushed Frank Capra's films to Oscar-winning success.

Meck joined the Disneyland team in early 1955 and helped build the **Opening Day** excitement to a fever pitch. Rather than pulling the fantastic stunts and publicity gimmicks that heralded other big premieres and events of that era, Meck used a simple approach, letting Disneyland's beauty and diversity speak for themselves. Meck's idea was to invite the global press to the park (flying them in when necessary) and let them each find their own topics to focus on. After all, there were plenty of unique ways to enjoy Disneyland—why not let the writers discover those pleasures for themselves? Meck did accompany the media at times; while escorting a *National Geographic* reporter on a **Monorail** tour in 1962, Meck quipped that "people ask us when Walt is going to build a Disneyland for kids" (Disneyland had a 3.5-to-1 ratio of adults-to-children).

Buoyed by a flood of gushing travel articles in national newspapers and magazines, Disneyland quickly rose to its longstanding position as a top tourist attraction. Working out of **City Hall**, Meck also invited lots of celebrities to come share in the fun, leading to plenty of well-publicized photos. In 1971, he introduced the media to Walt Disney World, where Meck himself set up the new publicity department.

Meck died in 1973, at age seventy-four. He was inducted as a Disney Legend twenty-two years later.

Meet Me at Disneyland TV Series

During the summer of 1962, KTTV, an independent TV station in Los Angeles, aired a one-hour show on Saturday nights called *Meet Me at Disneyland*. Thirteen episodes ran from June 9 to September 8, all of them shot live in the park with TV announcer/actor Johnny Jacobs as the host.

Filled with attractions and entertainment, the episodes feature performances by such Disneyland standouts as the **Dapper Dans** and the **Firehouse Five Plus Two**. Non-Disney acts like the Osmond Brothers and special guests like astronaut John Glenn also made appearances.

Merlin's Magic Shop

MAP: Fantasyland, Fa-30

DATES: July 17, 1955–January 16, 1983

Merlin's Magic Shop in **Fantasyland**, the first of Disneyland's two magic shops, was ready for its debut on **Opening Day**, about two years before the **Main Street Magic Shop** opened. Although the shop on **Main Street** has never permanently closed, the one in Fantasyland was replaced after twenty-seven years.

Merlin's occupied a great location in the **Sleeping Beauty Castle** courtyard, right next to Peter Pan Flight. The building is still there, featuring a half-timbered, peak-roofed, European-village exterior, like something out of an old fairytale—a suitable look for a magic shop named after the wizard in *The Sword in the Stone*. Inside the shop were magic tricks, how-to books, and practical joke kits, with enthusiastic **cast members** ready to demonstrate sleight-of-hand illusions to guests.

As fun as Merlin's was, it didn't survive the huge Fantasyland renovation of the early 1980s and was replaced by **Mickey's Christmas Chalet**.

Mermaids

Sam McKim's beautiful **attraction poster** for the **Submarine Voyage** depicted a looming sub with lithe, long-haired mermaids swimming underneath it. For three summers in the mid-1960s, mermaids really did splash around in the submarines' lagoon.

Eight of these sirens—attractive local swimmers wearing ocean-themed halter tops and svelte neoprene mermaid tails—joined the celebratory festivities promoting the new submarine attraction when it launched in 1959. On that June day, the mermaids rode on a float in Disneyland's nationally televised **parade** (as seen in the "Disneyland '59" TV special). Minutes later, eight mermaids performed an aqua ballet in the lagoon as **Walt Disney** and special guests looked on.

After the submarines' debut, the mermaids vanished from the pool. But they returned six years later, this time as regular summer performers. In 1965, after conducting auditions for three days in the Disneyland Hotel pool with hundreds of applicants, Disneyland brought the chosen mermaids back to frolic in the **Tomorrowland** waters and

MOUSCELLANY

Just north of the **Main Street Cinema** is the Casting Agency. The witty "Now Casting" sheet posted there lists dozens of available Disneyland jobs, including this one: "ARE YOU A MERMAID? Mermaids needed for exotic location shoot. Swimming ability suggested. Must bring own sunscreen."

lounge on the surrounding rocks.

Entertainment specialist **Tommy Walker** is usually credited with developing the mermaid idea, though its provenance probably dates to 1947, when Florida's Weeki Wachee Springs began presenting underwater shows with live mermaids. In the late 1940s and '50s, mermaids became popular; they were featured in movies such as *Mr. Peabody and the Mermaid*, *Miranda*, and *Mad About Men*. One of the era's top film stars, Esther Williams, was also nicknamed the Million Dollar Mermaid.

At Disneyland, the Tomorrowland mermaids were a popular feature, but extensive exposure to the lagoon's chlorine eventually became a concern. When some male guests felt compelled to jump into the water after the alluring mermaids, park officials whistled everyone out of the pool in 1967.

Mickey Mouse Club Circus

MAP: Fantasyland, Fa-22

DATES: November 24, 1955–January 8, 1956

Many Disneyland attractions that debuted in 1955 thrived for decades, but a few early ideas were utter flops. One of these was the Mickey Mouse Club Circus. On paper, this must have seemed like an appealing attraction to **Walt Disney**, who was a longtime circus lover (tellingly, Circus Day was a weekly feature on *The Mickey Mouse Club* TV show). Four months after Disneyland opened, two striped circus tents went up in the northeast corner of **Fantasyland**, a space that would later be filled by the **Junior Autopia**. The larger tent had bleacher seats for up to 2,500 guests and three rings for circus acts; the smaller tent featured animals that guests could visit. The official circus opened on Thanksgiving Day with a **parade** down **Main Street** and a live hour-and-a-quarter show in heated tents.

Theoretically, fans of *The Mickey Mouse Club* TV show should have been fans of the circus acts: Jimmie Dodd, the TV host, was the ringmaster; Roy Williams, his TV sidekick, was the circus strongman; and Mouseketeers were among the stars (according to a promotional flyer, the young performers were "clowning, riding elephants, and in an Aerial Ballet," though the *L.A. Times* described it as more of a "musical variety act"). Additionally, a dozen professional acts presented a total of 150 animals and top circus performers, including camels, llamas, baby elephants, jungle cats, trained seals, trapeze artists, equestrians, "Serenado,

MOUSCELLANY

Besides the Mickey Mouse Club Circus, here are eight other attractions that closed within one year of debuting: **Canal Boats of the World** (July–September 1955); **Davy Crockett Frontier Museum** (July–October 1955); **Court of Honor** (July 1955–March 1956); **Marshal's Office** (July 1955–July 1956); **Keller's Jungle Killers** (February–September 1956); **Fashions and Fabrics Through the Ages** (March–December 1965); **Disney Afternoon Avenue** (March–September 1991); **Toy Story Funhouse** (January–May 1996); and **Dalmatian Celebration** (November 1996–January 1997).

the Musical Horse," and "Bob-O, the Disneyland Clown."

Unfortunately, several of the animal acts were problematic (some animals actually escaped at one point), and some of the circus professionals weren't exactly consistent with the wholesome Disney image. Disappointingly, the bleachers rarely reached half or even quarter capacity, and occasionally they were barely occupied at all. Disneyland guests, it turned out, wanted to explore the unique park, not pay an extra fifty cents to sit and watch typical circus acts they'd already seen in their hometown. Walt Disney acknowledged this in 1956, when he announced at a merchant's meeting that the failure of the circus proved that Disneyland required "things that are unique—things that are 'Disneylandish.'"

After only six weeks and $375,000 in losses (according to **Van France**'s *Window on Main Street*), the Mickey Mouse Club Circus was dismantled, though some of its elements lingered. The big cats stayed on as **Keller's Jungle Killers**, and the main tent moved to the picnic grounds of **Holidayland**, just outside of **Frontierland**.

Mickey Mouse Club Headquarters,
aka Mickey Mouse Club Shop

MAP: Town Square, TS-9

DATES: September 1963–September 1964

After the **Babes in Toyland** Exhibit left the **Opera House**, the Mickey Mouse Club Headquarters set up shop there, offering membership cards to new members while selling Mouseketeer photos and souvenirs. **Ginny Tyler**, a recording artist with Disneyland Records, was installed as Head Mouseketeer; from the headquarters, she hosted a live, fifteen-minute broadcast that ran with old episodes of *The Mickey Mouse Club* TV series.

The timing for installing a Mickey Mouse Club Headquarters might have seemed off to many guests—after all, *The Mickey Mouse Club* had been canceled in 1959, so what was being shown on TV in 1963 were reruns (except for Tyler's new segment). The headquarters itself was sometimes open only four hours a day. Disneyland finally pulled the plug in 1964 and, a year later, opened an attraction at the Opera House with staying power: the durable **Great Moments with Mr. Lincoln**.

Mickey Mouse Club Theater,
aka Fantasyland Theatre

MAP: Fantasyland, Fa-9

DATES: August 27, 1955–December 20, 1981

The Mickey Mouse Club TV show was still ten weeks away from airing when the Mickey Mouse Club Theater opened in **Fantasyland**. The theater covered about 5,000 square feet in the **Sleeping Beauty Castle** wing where **Pinocchio's Daring Journey** is today. On **Opening Day**, the theater made it into the national TV coverage—not for anything having to do with the theater itself, but for the debut of the Mouseketeers outside.

The theater's exterior carried the same medieval festival theme that the castle courtyard had back then. By late August, the 400-seat, air-conditioned, B-ticket theater was showing half-hour blocks of cartoons from 11 AM to closing, but no live Mouseketeers. Starting on June 16, 1956, a half-hour show called the *3D Jamboree* offered a 3-D Mouseketeer movie, 3-D cartoons, and 3-D glasses. According to the promo poster, the show was "all in color~all in music~all in fun." Behind the scenes, the theater was also used for official meetings and training sessions.

With no new episodes of the original *Mickey Mouse Club* being made, the Mickey Mouse Club Theater finally got a new name in January of 1964. Rechristened the Fantasyland Theatre, it continued to show cartoons on a varying schedule until December 20, 1981, when it was closed permanently for construction that would produce Pinocchio's Daring Journey. The **Fantasyland Theatre** name would live on, however—in mid-1995, it became the new name of Videopolis.

Mickey's Christmas Chalet

MAP: Fantasyland, Fa-30

DATES: May 25, 1983–May 17, 1987

When **Fantasyland** was remodeled extensively in the early 1980s, several venerable attractions and shops disappeared. Among them was Merlin's Magic Shop, which had been purveying magic tricks since 1955. Replacing the magic of Merlin with the magic of Christmas, Mickey's Christmas Chalet opened as a year-round, holiday-themed store filled with decorations and ornaments (including some non-Disney-themed items). Located in the same old world-style building next to **Peter Pan's Flight**, the chalet was freshened up with new paint and flower boxes.

Four years later, the holiday merchandise relocated to the **Castle Christmas Shop** (a nearby room within the castle's entryway), and the charming **Briar Rose Cottage** replaced the chalet.

Mickey's House

MAP: Mickey's Toontown, MT-5

DATES: January 24, 1993–ongoing

For decades, many guests wondered where Mickey Mouse lived in Disneyland and where they could meet him. They found out in early 1993, when the mouse who started it all got his own fascinating home at 1 Neighborhood Lane in **Mickey's Toontown**.

It turns out that Mickey lives in a bright yellow, cartoon-themed bungalow with bulbous columns, white-and-green trim, peaked dormer windows, curved walls, and sloping roof lines. Outside, his garden is exquisitely maintained and outlined by a white picket fence. Inside, Mickey has splurged on beautiful hardwood floors. The mouse's house contains a comfy living room with a handsome fireplace (shown), famous books revamped with mouse-related titles (*Random Mouse Dictionary*, *Mice Station Zebra*, etc.), a "Mouseway" player piano complete with **Hidden Mickeys**,

a smiling old-time radio, a TV that plays cartoons, a passport with Disney-related stamps, and Pluto's bed and water bowl. Throughout the house are clever architectural flourishes and design details that leave no doubt as to whose home this is (the Imagineers must have been laughing constantly as they came up with all the delightful gags and puns). A garage outside holds the star's sports equipment, tools, and garbage cans.

The walk-through house is actually a lead-in to the momentous event. Out back is the Movie Barn, a rustic, prop-filled building where cartoons are supposedly still being made. A small stand-up theater plays Mickey's highlights, and old posters line the walls. Then, it's mouse time. Mickey (shown on page 326), often dressed in his natty tuxedo or bandleader's costume, is available in his dressing room all day long to greet guests and pose for photos.

Fun for kids and adults, Mickey's House is a wonderfully imaginative, amazingly detailed museum worthy of careful study.

MOUSCELLANY

Walking to the Movie Barn, guests pass a magic mirror that operates like the one inside the **Mad Hatter of Fantasyland**. While the Mad Hatter mirror brings forth the image of the Cheshire Cat, this one reveals the image of Sorcerer Mickey.

Mickey's Toontown

MAP: Park, P-17

DATES: January 24, 1993–ongoing

Since the early 1990s, annual **souvenir books** have spent many colorful pages enticing guests to explore the land to the far north. How far? Mickey's Toontown exists completely outside the **berm** that defines Disneyland's original perimeter. This area beyond **Fantasyland** is the former site of a narrow road that led to Disneyland's **Pony Farm** and storage facilities. A tunnel through the berm now provides the gateway into Toontown. A population counter above the tunnel pretends to tally incoming guests, but the wacky digits also include blanks, question marks, and random spinning.

Toontown was the first entirely new land added to Disneyland after 1972's **Bear**

Country. It's also the smallest of the lands, measuring only 200 feet from the back of Toon Park to the door of the Third Little Piggy Bank, and 500 feet from the **Chip 'n Dale Tree House** in the west to Roger's Fountain in the east, an area totaling just over three acres. Though it's served by a nearby train depot, this acreage is so far from the main **entrance** and Disneyland's central **Hub** that it is sometimes overlooked and unappreciated by guests. In fact, the October 2015 issue of *Mad* magazine even took a poke at Toontown's remoteness; in its list of "7 Ways that Disneyland Is Celebrating Its 60th Anniversary," it claimed that Disneyland was "moving that homeless encampment out of Mickey's Toontown."

Originally called Mickeyland in the early plans, Toontown derives from a small character-greeting area that debuted at Walt Disney World in 1988 (some Knott's Berry Farm fans might say that Toontown derives from the Camp Snoopy children's area that debuted in 1983). The concept was then greatly expanded upon at Disneyland to include themes, designs, and gags from Disney's 1988 blockbuster movie, *Who Framed Roger Rabbit*.

Toontown debuted in 1993 with a special ceremony attended by Disney CEO Michael Eisner and comedian Harry Anderson. At the opening, guests were informed that the hilarious little Toontown village had supposedly existed for over fifty years but was only now being unveiled. As an animation destination, everything in Mickey's Toontown is designed primarily for kids (like most cartoons), but can also be appreciated by adults (like the best cartoons). The brightly colored buildings here don't have right angles or straight lines and instead appear cartoonishly swollen or inflatable.

Many of the locations in Toontown are scaled-down versions of places that exist elsewhere in Disneyland. For instance, Toontown has its own City Hall and Fire Department, a walk-through tree house, a roller coaster-style attraction, a car-driving attraction, and a large boat, plus inexpensive snack stands and souvenir stores. Like other small towns, Toontown is divided into a downtown district (to the east) and a residential neighborhood (to the west), with mass transit (the now-defunct **Jolly Trolley**) connecting the two and a food area (Toontown Square) in-between. Downtown includes stores and kid-friendly attractions like **Roger Rabbit's Car Toon Spin**, while the star-studded neighborhood boasts the wacky homes of Mickey, Minnie, Goofy, and Chip 'n Dale, all of them appearing appropriate for their owners but none of them copied from specific Disney cartoons. Two fountains provide centerpieces for the plazas, and rolling hills (adorned with a four-story Hollywood-style sign) provide the backdrop.

Throughout Toontown, random objects produce silly sounds and effects. Stand on a manhole cover near the Five & Dime, and weasel voices will call out to you. Drink from a water fountain, and it will utter wisecracks. Try the Fireworks Factory's plunger, the Electric Company's doorbells, and the town's interactive mailboxes; look for a Dalmatian pup occasionally peering out of the firehouse, a street sign announcing, "Wrong Turn O.K.," and a

MOUSCELLANY

Today, Toontown is Disneyland's least-changed area—while stores have moved in and out of **Main Street** and attractions have come and gone in the other lands, Toontown exists today almost exactly as it did when it opened.

blank sign announcing that it's merely a "Blank Sign." Like the rest of Disneyland, Toontown rewards deliberate exploration with delightful surprises.

Midget Autopia

MAP: Fantasyland, Fa-16

DATES: April 23, 1957–April 3, 1966

Following in the slipstreams of Tomorrowland's popular **Autopia** (opened in 1955) and **Junior Autopia** (1956), the Midget Autopia debuted in 1957 as a destination for the youngest drivers of all—preschoolers. The Midget track was laid out near the **Storybook Land Canal Boats** in **Fantasyland**, in a relatively undeveloped eating area that would later be eliminated in favor of wide walkways leading to **It's a Small World**.

MOUSCELLANY

In 2015, Marceline's Walt Disney Hometown Museum announced plans to bring the Midget Autopia back to life. The museum hopes to raise enough funds to pull the cars out of storage, rebuild them, and run them on a 630-foot track.

Whereas the other two Autopias banned Disneyland's smallest guests from driving the cars, the Midget Autopia actually invited them to take the wheel (adults weren't even allowed in the cars). Since the attraction was just for young kids, it was open only on weekends and in the summer.

In contrast to the sleek Tomorrowland and Junior Autopia sports cars, the Midget Autopia bodies were rounder and friendlier-looking, like cartoon cars with two steering wheels side-by-side. The Midget cars didn't run on internal combustion like their bigger, noisier siblings did; the tiny cars were electric and controlled by ride operators (like the cars on **Mr. Toad's Wild Ride**). And unlike the other Autopias, whose tracks were touted as freeways, the Midget Autopia track was a gentle, winding road that at one point crept through a little building.

After the attraction was dismantled in 1966, the cars and displays were donated to Marceline, the Missouri town where **Walt Disney** spent part of his childhood. The Midget Autopia thus became the first and only attraction to be relocated away from Disneyland. In Marceline's Walt Disney Municipal Park, the cars ran as a kiddie ride until rising costs forced its removal eleven years later.

Today, Disneyland guests can still see one of the Midget Autopia cars on display, mounted on a pedestal alongside the current Autopia track in Tomorrowland and giving twenty-first-century guests a glimpse at 1950s fun.

Mike Fink Keel Boats

MAP: Frontierland, Fr-12

DATES: December 25, 1955–May 17, 1997

For over forty years, keel boats operated in **Frontierland** waters. Many guests today wouldn't even know what a keel boat was unless they'd seen the "Davy Crockett's Keel Boat Race" episode of the old ***Disneyland* TV series**. In the late 1950s, however, everyone would have recognized a keel boat as a small, old-fashioned wooden houseboat, since that popular TV episode helped propel the nation's Crockett craze. On the show, tough guy Mike Fink raced his ramshackle *Gullywhumper* against Davy's *Bertha Mae*. To the loser went the spoils—Mike lost the fictional race but won a long-running Disneyland attraction.

The *Gullywhumper* began operating in Disneyland on Christmas Day, 1955, and was followed three months later by the *Bertha Mae*. Both boats were the actual vessels from the TV show, and both were powered by modern diesel engines and cruised freely without submerged guide rails. With seating on the inside and out, each boat held a total of thirty-two guests (the majority sat on the roof) for an eleven-minute, C-ticket tour of the **Rivers of America.** By 1958, the original wooden boats had been replaced by fiberglass replicas that could better stand the constant wear and tear (the boats also got two open windows).

The boats' route around **Tom Sawyer Island** was basically the same one taken by the *Mark Twain*, but the keel boats launched from the opposite side of Frontierland. For the keel boats, home was a rugged dock on the southwestern riverbank by **Fowler's Harbor**. The boats kept an irregular schedule, operating mostly on the busiest days during the summer. Things became really irregular when the two boats were temporarily pulled from service in the fall of 1994. Then, after returning the following spring, a near-disaster led to their abrupt demise. In May 1997, the (possibly overloaded) *Gullywhumper* suddenly capsized, dumping frightened guests into the water and sending several to the hospital with minor injuries. Both boats were immediately shut down, and eventually the attraction was permanently closed.

In 2001, Disney auctioned off the *Bertha Mae* for $15,000, and two years later, the *Gullywhumper* appeared in the river as a piece of stationary scenery (shown). In 2010, the boat was moved to the northern end of Tom Sawyer Island, where Mike Fink had retired to what was formerly the island's burning cabin.

Mile Long Bar

MAP: Bear Country/Critter Country, B/C-5

DATES: March 24, 1972–July 17, 1989

Debuting in 1972 with the rest of **Bear Country** was the Mile Long Bar, a place where guests could buy cider, ice cream, frozen bananas, and other snacks. Like some of the other Bear Country attractions, the Mile Long Bar had already

thrived at Walt Disney World before it opened a location at Disneyland right next to **Teddi Barra's Swingin' Arcade**.

The bar's brown, two-story exterior looked appropriately countrified; inside, an arrangement of mirrors at either end of the bar created the "mile long" illusion in the name. Also on display were the heads of Max the deer, Melvin the moose, and Buff the buffalo, three smaller versions of the characters that performed inside the nearby **Country Bear Jamboree** (the heads in the Mile Long Bar, shown, are still on view inside **The Many Adventures of Winnie the Pooh**). In 1989, the Mile Long Bar's name was changed to **Brer Bar** to match the theme of its new neighbor, **Splash Mountain**.

> **MOUSCELLANY**
>
> Despite its squeaky clean image, Disneyland has had seven "bars" open to the public within the park, though none of them served alcohol. Here are six more besides the Mile Long Bar: **Brer Bar** (1989–2003); Dairy Bar (1956–1958); **Mint Julep Bar** (1966–ongoing); **Space Bar** (1955–1966); **Tiki Juice Bar** (1976–ongoing); and Yacht Bar (1957–1966).

Mineral Hall

MAP: Frontierland, Fr-24

DATES: July 30, 1956–December 1962

In the late 1950s, guests exploring the little **Frontierland** area called **El Zocalo Park** would have discovered a dignified, two-story white building at the back of the square. Mineral Hall both displayed and sold exotic rocks and minerals, highlighting the merchandise with black lights to draw out their spectacular colors. So impressive was this display that dazzled guests could even buy the lights along with their mineralogical wonders so they could recreate the show at home.

After Mineral Hall closed at the end of 1962, the restaurant next door, **Casa de Fritos**, expanded into the space. Eventually, part of the old building was converted into private offices.

> **MOUSCELLANY**
>
> Nostalgic guests can still find a Mineral Hall window (shown on page 289) at the back of today's **Rancho del Zocalo Restaurante**.

Mine Train, aka Rainbow Caverns Mine Train, aka Western Mine Train Through Nature's Wonderland

MAP: Frontierland, Fr-21

DATES: July 2, 1956–January 2, 1977

Almost one year after 1955's **Opening Day**, the first of several railroad attractions began chugging through **Frontierland's** wilderness. Eventually this land would be traversed by the high-speed **Big Thunder Mountain Railroad**, but back in the 1950s, it was explored at the more sedate speeds by the Mine Train—a common nickname for the Rainbow Caverns Mine Train.

Built for under a half-million dollars, the little Mine Train was closer in size and spirit to **Fantasyland's** cozy **Casey Jr. Circus Train** than it was to a full-size train. At thirty inches wide, the track was six inches narrower than the thirty-six-gauge track of the train that circled the park. After paying with their D tickets (this was Disneyland's first D attraction), guests sat on bench seats in open cargo cars—ten guests per car—behind a small, old-fashioned engine run by an electric motor. They departed from the miniature town of Rainbow Ridge, a collection of small buildings that served as an Old West backdrop, and made a quarter-mile journey along the Mine Train's track, taking in sights that included the **Conestoga Wagons**, **Stage Coach**, and **Mule Pack**, all of which served this same dusty territory.

> **MOUSCELLANY**
>
> Today's Big Thunder Mountain Railroad includes a colorful reminder of the beautiful Rainbow Caverns pools. Thirty seconds into the three-minute trip, look to the left as your train climbs up a hill.

The highlight of the seven-minute trip—and the feature that gave the Rainbow Caverns Mine Train its name—could only be seen by the train's passengers. Rainbow Caverns was a resplendent cave with black lights installed to illuminate neon-colored waterfalls and glowing pools of luminescent water. **Claude Coats** and **John Hench** are acknowledged as the Imagineers behind the caverns. According to the Disneyland Data page in the 1957 **souvenir book**, approximately 270,000 gallons of water were circulated every hour to create the seven multi-colored waterfalls.

The complex visual effects inside the caverns, accompanied by choral mood music, were impressive enough to survive the makeover that hit the rest of the attraction at the turn of the decade. After closing down on October 11, 1959, the railroad reopened on May 28, 1960, as the Western Mine Train Through Nature's Wonderland (sometimes just called the Mine Train Through Nature's Wonderland), which boasted a trip that was two minutes and 600 feet longer. **Nature's Wonderland** was the result of an extensive re-landscaping of the arid terrain to accommodate over 200 new **Audio-Animatronic** animals in river and mountain settings. As with other Disneyland railroads, **Walt Disney** was actively involved in the design of this one, in both of its iterations. **Roger Broggie** was in charge of building the train sets, and the **Sherman Brothers** composed a new theme song for the attraction, "All Aboard the Mine Train." The recorded narration by an amiable ol' coot pointed out scenic highlights along the way.

In early 1977, the Mine Train was finally pulled from service to make way for the Big Thunder Mountain Railroad. For years, a relic of the old days could be seen from the **Rivers of America**—a buckled Mine Train locomotive and a couple of crumpled cars appeared to have crashed into the Frontierland brush. Like the original attraction, that display is now gone. Today, the town of Rainbow Ridge has been rebuilt along Big Thunder's **queue**.

Miniature Horse Corral

MAP: Frontierland, Fr-25

DATES: July 1955–July 1957

The Miniature Horse Corral was an early **Frontierland** exhibit. Behind its rough-hewn wooden fences were ponies, donkeys, and miniature horses (some standing only two and a half feet high). With animals meant for viewing and petting, not for riding, this area was a precursor of the petting zoo that later appeared in **Big Thunder Ranch**.

The quiet corral closed in July of 1957 and was quickly replaced by the noisy Frontierland Shooting Gallery.

Minnie's House

MAP: Mickey's Toontown, MT-6

DATES: January 24, 1993–ongoing

Appropriately enough, Mickey Mouse's girlfriend has her own adorable (but smaller) walk-through house right next to his residence in **Mickey's Toontown**. Like the other homes in the neighborhood, Minnie's House is a bungalow-style structure with a curved roof, stone chimney, rounded columns, and white picket fence. But whereas **Mickey's House** is a sunny yellow, Minnie's is painted a romantic lavender, with hearts and frills decorating the walls and furnishings.

As with other attractions in Toontown, Minnie's place invites interactivity by

offering an array of gizmos to touch and gags to discover. Knock out a tune on the pans on the stove, explore a variety of cheeses in the Cheese-more fridge, view Minnie's e-mails on her heart-shaped computer (with an eight-key keyboard), play at her makeup table, relax in her cozy living room (shown), and check out her magazines (including *Mademouselle*). Outside is a special wishing well that generates a familiar giggly voice (this well used to be behind the house on the west side, but now that area is given to a gazebo with a small sitting area, the well has moved to the house's east side). Minnie herself is usually on the premises for photos and autographs.

Mint Julep Bar

MAP: New Orleans Square, NOS-11

DATES: July 24, 1966–ongoing

Guests may come to the Mint Julep Bar for the mint juleps, but they'll probably stay for the legendary beignets. This little snack counter, tucked away in the back of the **French Market** restaurant in **New Orleans Square**, has been offering some of Disneyland's tastiest baked goods for over fifty years. Chief among these is the beignet, a pillowy,

BEIGNETS DELICIEUX

Mickey-shaped fritter topped with powdered sugar that is famous enough to be promoted on signs (shown). Pairing an order of six beignets with one of the fancy coffee drinks is a morning snack made in heaven.

As the bar's name suggests, the mint julep is its other famous specialty. It is indeed a cool, tasty concoction with "a hint of lime flavor," though purists will decry the absence of bourbon (only one restaurant in Disneyland serves alcohol, and it's not open to the public—the nearby **Club 33**). It's possible, though, that the Mint Julep Bar's virgin version of the drink is more historically accurate, anyway. After all, the name derives from *julab*, the Persian word for "rose water," not "hard liquor."

Miss Disneyland, aka Disneyland Ambassador to the World, aka Ambassador Team

During Disneyland's first decade, **Walt Disney** tried to handle all park-related media events and public appearances himself. But by the mid-1960s, the increasing demands on his time (especially in the serious planning stages of Walt Disney World) necessitated additional official Disneyland representatives to meet the media and the public.

Starting in 1965, Disneyland established a position that was called, for the first few years, Miss Disneyland; later, the title was changed to Disneyland Ambassador to the World. Up until 1994, the position was only held by female **cast members** who were selected on the basis of their appearance, personality, and poise. Every year, a new Miss Disneyland/Ambassador to the World would represent the park in **parades**, on TV shows, and at special events.

The first Miss Disneyland, selected in 1964 but serving in 1965 to help promote the **Tencennial**, was **Julie Reihm**, who had been a Disneyland **Tour Guide** for two years. Connie Swanson, another Tour Guide, was Miss Disneyland in 1966, followed by Marcia Miner in 1967. Miner appeared on a 1968 episode of *Walt Disney's Wonderful World of Color* that showcases the "new **Tomorrowland**," **Pirates of the Caribbean**, and other new attractions. Melissa Taylor, 1985's Ambassador, circled the globe on a thirty-day flight with Mickey Mouse to celebrate Disneyland's thirtieth anniversary.

Since 1995, a two-person Ambassador Team has been selected to be "emissaries of good will" for two-year terms. Actress Julie Andrews was named Honorary Ambassador in 2005 as part of Disneyland's fiftieth anniversary celebration.

Mission to Mars

MAP: Tomorrowland, T-16

DATES: March 21, 1975–November 2, 1992

Once man landed on the moon in 1969, Disneyland's **Flight to the Moon** attraction might as well have been called Flight to the Mundane. So the Imagineers did what NASA would eventually do—they got a new target. In 1975, an upgraded, enlarged flight-simulation attraction called Mission to Mars debuted in Flight to the Moon's space next to **Tomorrowland's** big Carousel Theater.

While the heavenly bodies were different, the two flights were fairly similar. The sponsor, the McDonnell-Douglas aerospace company, hadn't changed, and neither had the price—both rides required a D-ticket from Disneyland's **ticket book**. The pre-show Mission Control area for the Mars mission looked and operated the same way it had for the moon flight. In fact, Disneyland's **souvenir books** of the late 1970s present the same photo for the Mars mission they'd used for the earlier lunar expedition: a picture showing banks of computers attended by **Audio-Animatronic** figures. Overseeing these mission controllers was Mr. Johnson (no longer Tom Morrow from the lunar mission), a dignified mechanical scientist with a headset, glasses, lab coat, and clipboard. Johnson discussed space travel and the Mars vehicle, played the incoming-bird gag that Tom Morrow had sprung before the moon flight, and then excused everyone for boarding.

MOUSCELLANY

Though Mission to Mars closed in 1992, its spirit continued on the big screen with Disney's sci-fi film, *Mission to Mars*. While the movie, made in 2000, doesn't duplicate the attraction literally, there are enough thematic similarities—its setting, name, adventurous vitality, and realistic approach to space travel—to believe that director Brian De Palma's screen version could have been inspired by Disneyland's original Mars mission.

As with Flight to the Moon, about 100 guests sat in a circular theater and watched two screens, one on the floor and one on the ceiling, that showed them where they'd been and where they were going. Small screens positioned around the edge of the theater provided additional views of the fifteen-minute journey. After liftoff (which guests felt through a lowering-raising effect in their seats), the moon came into view on the overhead screen, followed by a speedy jump through hyperspace that brought the Red Planet into range. Camera probes beamed back surface details of the Martian canyons and mountains until a sudden meteor shower compelled the main ship to dash back to Earth.

Although the visuals were still exciting and the synchronized seats simulated G-forces nicely, by the mid-1970s, guests were underwhelmed by the whole space-travel experience. They'd been watching real Gemini and Apollo missions on TV since the early 1960s, and the TV audiences for those broadcasts had become so small and disinterested that some of the later flights weren't even televised.

Tomorrowland's last Mars mission returned home for good in 1992. A dramatic attraction called Alien Encounter was considered for the space, but it was deemed too big for the location and ended up in Walt Disney World instead. In early 1996, the **Toy Story Funhouse** was temporarily installed at the Mission site, but that spring fling was taken down by summer. Finally, along with the big remodel of Tomorrowland in 1998, the old Mission to Mars building reopened, this time serving up lunch instead of interstellar space flights. **Redd Rockett's Pizza Port** still operates here in the shadow of the *Moonliner*.

Mlle. Antoinette's Parfumerie

MAP: New Orleans Square, NOS-9

DATES: 1967–1997; May 28, 2011–ongoing

As shown in Disneyland's 1968 **souvenir book**, this elegant little shop has always had a beautiful, heavily French interior, boasting such features as a sparkling chandelier, ornate mirrors, and display cases lined with delicate perfume bottles. Located in **New Orleans Square**, the original shop fit right in with its neighbors—especially the stylish **Le Chapeau** next door.

As the souvenir book notes, at Mlle. Antoinette's, "ladies blend their own exclusive perfumes." Trained perfumers helped guests mix customized fragrances and filed the formulas for return visits. Dozens of brand-name perfumes were also sold in the shop.

Some thirty years after it opened, the Parfumerie was replaced by the equally sumptuous **Jewel of Orléans**. When the Jewel closed abruptly in 2011, Mlle. Antoinette's quickly stepped back in. The shop's sponsor is the LVMH Group, a conglomerate behind many luxury items (the initials stand for Louis Vuitton Moët Hennessy). Although the Parfumerie doesn't offer custom blends like it used to, many exalted perfumes are still sold here.

Monorail,
aka Disneyland-Alweg Monorail System, aka Disneyland Monorail

MAP: Tomorrowland, T-10

DATES: June 14, 1959–ongoing

The debut of the magnificent Monorail in June of 1959 was an auspicious moment in Disneyland history. Of the three new E-ticket vehicles that began running in **Tomorrowland** that month (the **Matterhorn Bobsleds** and **Submarine Voyage** were the others), the Monorail was the only one intended to be a serious advance in American transportation.

The other two attractions were wonderful, but the Monorail was especially significant. So significant, in fact, that Vice President Nixon was on hand for the ribbon-cutting honors. So significant that it was awarded a special plaque by the American Society of Mechanical Engineers in 1986. So significant that, unlike other Disneyland vehicles that either stayed on their original courses or were eventually closed, the Monorail's service was actually *expanded* to cover more than three times its original length. So significant that it got its own cool board game (which zoomed the Monorail in a figure-eight route to all the corners of Disneyland). While other attractions made memories, the Monorail made history.

Walt Disney and his staff didn't invent the concept of a monorail on an elevated track. Various monorails had been built and demonstrated in America since 1876, the year a steam-powered monorail debuted at Philadelphia's Centennial Exposition. Some eighty years later, Alweg, a design company named for the initials of its Swedish founder, Dr. Axel Lennart Wenner-Gren, began testing advanced monorail train and track designs in Germany. When a vacationing Walt Disney saw a boxy monorail train run on a rural test track near Cologne in 1957, he quickly partnered with Alweg to construct a new, streamlined Disneyland version.

"I think monorail is going to be the rapid transit of the future, and we'll be giving a prevue of it," Disney said in *Walt Disney Conversations*. He wasn't the only one enamored of monorails for mass transportation (Kevin Starr's *Golden Dreams* describes how various Los Angeles urban planning committees were formally recommending monorail development as early as 1950) but Walt Disney was their most famous fan.

Disney Legend **Bob Gurr**, who designed most of Disneyland's vehicles, created a tapered, futuristic train that would be as exhilarating to watch as it would be to ride. **John Hench** enhanced Gurr's pencil drawings with color and effects to make the Monorail look like a horizontal rocket ship. **Roger Broggie** and his engineering team built the first Monorail at Disney Studios, and **Bill Martin** laid out the track approximately where the **Viewliner** had been. For all of these Imagineers, the goal wasn't merely to create an attraction for fun, stylish sightseeing; it was to create a meaningful, pollution-free alternative to public transportation, an all-electric train

that would glide smoothly and silently along an elevated "highway in the sky" and convey guests in and out of Disneyland.

But that's not how the Monorail first operated. When it opened as the Disneyland-Alweg Monorail System (with a price tag of about $1.4 million), it only had one three-car train, called *Monorail Red* (the trains have usually been identified by their colors), and there was only one stop, next to Tomorrowland's submarines. This meant that only eighty-two passengers, not hundreds at a time, were starting and stopping at the same point. From the Tomorrowland station, guests looped for eight-tenths of a mile around the lagoon, **Autopia**, and **Matterhorn Mountain**. It was a scenic journey (the view even included some of Anaheim) but not a vital one.

The Monorail's operation was splendid. Speeds were usually in the twenty to thirty-five miles per hour range, though the Monorail could have approached fifty miles per hour if its drivers had really cut loose. Just as impressive as the quiet, smooth train was the clean, elevated track, which dipped to only about nine feet above the back of **Fantasyland** (by today's Agrifuture billboard). And everybody loved the train's low, booming horn.

With crowds quickly filling the *Monorail Red* to capacity, a second train, the *Monorail Blue*, joined the route three weeks after the *Red*'s debut. Still, the world's first daily public monorail remained a Tomorrowland-only ride. Expansion plans, however, were in the works. On April 10, 1961, the Monorail was temporarily shut down so the track could be dramatically extended outside Disneyland to the Disneyland Hotel (this extension cost $1.9 million, which exceeded the cost of the original Monorail line by a half-million dollars).

Reopening on June 1, the Monorail now traveled on a 2.3-mile-long track that left Tomorrowland, ventured south along **Harbor Boulevard**, zoomed west about twenty feet above Disneyland's **parking lot**, crossed a public street (West Avenue), and reached a new Monorail station at the hotel, where the train dropped off and picked up guests for a return journey past the turnstiles and back into Disneyland. Each one-way trip (park to hotel, hotel to park) took about two and a half minutes. The new route increased the Monorail's significance; by delivering guests from one station to another, it had finally become the mass transit system Walt Disney had always wanted it to be.

> **MOUSCELLANY**
>
> Debuting on national TV in the "Disneyland '59" special, the Monorail's official introduction is preceded by a short documentary about urban traffic problems. Then, in a startling sequence that blends animation with real footage, Monorail trains are shown zipping above and through downtown Los Angeles as the narrator describes their smooth efficiency.

Along with the new route, the vehicles were upgraded, too. Another passenger car was added to the train, upping its capacity to 108 guests, and a new train, the *Monorail Gold*, joined the line. These Mark II trains also included a nifty new design feature: little bubble canopies over the first cars. More revisions ensued—the first Mark III Monorail debuted in 1968 with a fifth passenger car (holding 127 riders total), larger windows, and bucket seats instead of benches. The new *Monorail Green* also joined the group. Not all of the trains operated simultaneously; instead, they subbed for each other during maintenance periods. Most days, two trains shared the track.

Everything about the Monorail was appealing. **Cast members** on the attraction dressed like cool pilots. Paul Hartley's breathtaking **attraction poster** depicts the *Monorail Red*, the lagoon, the *Moonliner*, and the Matterhorn all at once, adding up to one of Disneyland's best promotional images ever. For years, the **souvenir books** featured colorful photos of the Monorail and bold text about "the future in city mass transportation."

New advances kept coming. Although the Mark IV Monorail never made it to Disneyland, debuting in Orlando instead, by 1987 the Mark V was running in Anaheim with a new shape created by **George McGinnis**. The four Mark V models—in

purple, blue, red, and orange—featured automatic sliding doors, air conditioning, and a new
Alweg-less name—it was now called simply the
Disneyland Monorail (Alweg had encountered financial problems in the 1960s and had been taken
over by another company).

In 2001, concurrent with the arrival of Disney
California Adventure, an updated Monorail station
in Downtown Disney replaced the one formerly at
the Disneyland Hotel. Riders boarding at the Downtown Disney station can take a one-way trip into
Disneyland, while riders boarding in Tomorrowland
can take the train round-trip if they want.

On August 21, 2006, the entire Monorail line
ceased operations for four months to accommodate
the construction of the new Finding Nemo Submarine Voyage. Once the subs resurfaced in 2007, one
of the Monorail trains was painted bright yellow
and decorated with portholes and text to help publicize the attraction. All-new Mark VII Monorails

MOUSCELLANY

We've always loved the
view from the Monorail's
front cabin (ask at the
station if these seats for
up to four guests are
available). While the
trailing cars give you views
out the windows as the
scenery slides past, from
the front the panoramic
views come toward you.
The ride is noticeably
bumpier up front,
however—an observation
confirmed by the pilot,
who sits behind you in a
tight cockpit.

hearkening back to earlier, sleeker designs went into service in February 2008. These
Rhode Island-built/Vancouver-assembled trains sport new colors, tinted windows,
and window-facing bench seats that offer panoramic views. The 2012 debut of the
massively remodeled Disney California Adventure brought a temporary change to the
Monorail's styling: the smiling faces of the *Cars* characters on the front of the trains.
Then, for a few spring months in 2015, the trains carried some tasteful advertisements for the new *Tomorrowland* movie.

Unfortunately, the urban revolution that Walt Disney had hoped his 1959 Monorail would begin never arrived. While a few monorails went into service elsewhere
(most notably in Seattle), other major cities never adopted them, making the one in
Disneyland all the more special. The first of its kind built in America, and always a
majestic sight anytime it streams into view, Disneyland's Monorail is still the grand
symbol of an optimistic future.

Monstrous Summer All-Nighter

DATES: May 24, 2013–May 25, 2013

After the overwhelming success of 2012's **One More Disney Day**, Disneyland threw
itself another twenty-four-hour party on 2013's Memorial Day weekend. The Monstrous Summer All-Nighter kicked off a new summertime promotion called Monstrous
Summer, which celebrated Disney-Pixar's new *Monsters University* movie. Disneyland
opened at 6 AM on May 24 and closed at 6 AM on the May 25, with unique merchandise
and food and special entertainment, including live music and dancing in the new
Fantasy Faire area. Guests who stayed for the entire night saw fireworks at the beginning of the event and Disney characters in pajamas at the end. Similar Monstrous

Summer events were held concurrently at Disney California Adventure and Walt Disney World. Another overnight event was held in 2014 with the **Show Your Disney Side** promotion.

Moonliner

MAP: Tomorrowland, T-15

DATES: July 17, 1955–1966; 1998–ongoing

The statuesque *Moonliner* rocket is still remembered as perhaps the most identifiable symbol of classic **Tomorrowland**. Modern tributes to Disneyland's long history justify such a claim: for the fortieth anniversary celebration in 1995 and the fiftieth in 2005, tall models and numerous photos of the *Moonliner* dominated the historical displays. More recently, *Moonliner* imagery still turns up in numerous posters around Disneyland. The *Moonliner* wasn't just a rocket; it was an icon.

Just as the *Mark Twain* draws guests westward into **Frontierland**, so too did the original *Moonliner*, visible from the **Hub**, compel pedestrians to venture eastward as Tomorrowland's primary wienie. The *Moonliner* wasn't a ticketed attraction, and guests couldn't go inside it, but its very design and placement was a dramatic invitation to come explore the world of the future. Most of the early concept drawings that render aerial views of the proposed park show a rocket standing tall in the eastern section of Disneyland.

In 1954, **Herb Ryman** sketched a spindly rocket that looks a lot like the elegant design **John Hench** eventually drew up. When the fuselage was finally lowered into place with a crane on July 13, 1955 (just four days before **Opening Day**), the *Moonliner* towered an imposing seventy-six feet high. It stood right in front of the low-slung **Rocket to the Moon** attraction and was instantly recognized as one of Disneyland's main landmarks.

Unlike the actual moon rockets that fired off from the Florida coast in the 1960s and '70s, the *Moonliner* didn't have separate stages, a capsule, a cluster of engines at the bottom, or an adjacent support gantry. What it did have were three legs, a slender, tapered shape, a cockpit near the top, two rings of portholes, horizontal red stripes on its white hull, and a corporate sponsor, TWA ("the Official Airline to Disneyland"). While the *Moonliner* wasn't exactly what moon rockets turned out to be, it sure was what everyone in the 1950s imagined a cool rocket *should* look like.

Theoretically, the *Moonliner* represented a more permanent space vehicle than the actual rockets of the 1960s. It wasn't supposed to be just a one-time disposable vehicle that visited the moon for a quick scientific visit and returned as a single tiny capsule on parachutes. This was a *liner*, a futuristic ship that conveyed travelers back and forth between the earth and the moon, with lunar bases waiting at one end, reusable launch pads at the other, and the ultimate frequent flyer miles in between. Something so sleek and optimistic perfectly symbolized Tomorrowland; it was often featured in Disneyland's **souvenir books**, and on the Rocket to the Moon **attraction poster**, the *Moonliner* rises proud and tall in the foreground, its needle nose already in the stars.

Somehow, such an important symbol barely lasted a decade. In mid-1962, Douglas Aircraft took over sponsorship, painted its name on the side, and replaced the horizontal red stripes with vertical blue ones. Incredibly, four years later the beautiful *Moonliner* was deemed expendable and was dismantled during Tomorrowland's major remodel. The rocket's site was consumed by the sprawling Carousel Theater. (Douglas, meanwhile, was acquired by McDonnell to become McDonnell-Douglas, which sponsored 1967's **Flight to the Moon**.)

Thirty-two years later, Disneyland welcomed back a *Moonliner* replica. At fifty-three feet tall, this 1998 version was only about two-thirds the size of its classic predecessor. However, the small stature of the new rocket isn't readily apparent because of its new position. Relocated about twenty yards from its previous spot, the rocket now stands on top of the roof covering the **Spirit of Refreshment**. Since this snack stand is sponsored by Coca-Cola, the red stripes have returned to the *Moonliner* to echo the red-and-white livery of Coke cans. On hot days, the rocket's base sprays a cooling mist down on guests.

While it's not the awe-inspiring spectacle it once was, most fans will agree that a stunted *Moonliner* that advertises cola is better than no *Moonliner* at all.

Motor Boat Cruise,
aka Motor Boat Cruise to Gummi Glen

MAP: Fantasyland, Fa-22

DATES: June 1957–January 11, 1993

After never-ending maintenance problems finally sank the infamous **Phantom Boats** in 1956, a new boat ride opened in their former location in June of 1957. Whereas the Phantom Boats had toured the big lagoon in **Tomorrowland**, the Motor Boat Cruise crept along a new **Fantasyland** waterway carved into the land where the **Mickey Mouse Club Circus** had formerly operated. When the new **Monorail** and **Fantasyland Autopia** opened in 1959, their pylons and overpasses carried them right over the motorboats. Walls of oleander along the banks shielded external views, keeping this a cozy cruise.

Even though the boats looked like sleek little speedsters with aerodynamic shapes, open cockpits, brightly colored hulls, and white decks, the Motor Boat Cruise was to boating what the Autopia was to driving. The boats operated on a submerged guide rail that offered limited movement no matter how much effort was put into cranking the wheel. In addition, the gas pedal had little effect on the whole experience (some have suggested that all it did was increase engine volume). Kids probably enjoyed the illusion of control as they perused the rocky river, giving adults the opportunity to relax (and take comfort in knowing that they'd only spent a B ticket for this attraction). Photos of this attraction in Disneyland's old **souvenir books** show boats easing past big boulders in mild waters. In the accompanying caption—"Steering through rapids is fun on the Motor Boat Cruise"—"rapids" is undoubtedly a technical term meaning "gentle ripples."

Though Disneyland added new high-tech, high-speed, high-profile roller coaster attractions in the 1970s and '80s, the mild motorboats lasted into the '90s. In 1991, just before they were shut down for good, the boats underwent a major change. From March to November of that year, the Motor Boat Cruise got a new name—Motor Boat Cruise to Gummi Glen—with new scenery consisting of plywood Gummi Bear images in support of the Gummi's TV show, *Adventures of the Gummi Bears*. By Thanksgiving, the name had reverted back to the Motor Boat Cruise, and by February of 1993, the boats and the waterway had been replaced by the landscaped **Fantasia Gardens**. At thirty-six years old when it closed, the Motor Boat Cruise was one of the oldest attractions to be retired (the thirty-eight-year-old **Skyway to Fantasyland/Tomorrowland** and the forty-year-old **Fantasyland Autopia** are among the park's other older closed attractions).

Mouse Ears, aka Ears Hat

For decades, the famous hats designed to look like Mickey Mouse ears have been among Disneyland's most ubiquitous souvenirs. How ubiquitous? Over 78 million ear hats were sold in Disneyland's first fifty years, according to *Life* magazine in April 2005. A 2006 issue of *The New Yorker* called them "the most recognizable corporate headgear after that of the Playboy Bunnies." According to a 2014 Disneyland press release of "fun facts," mouse ears are "the most popular Disneyland Resort souvenirs of all time, with more than 84 million 'ears' sold since 1955."

Introduced by the TV Mouseketeers in 1955, the ears were initially designed by artist Roy Williams, one of the adults on the show. It's possible that he was inspired by the traditional *montera*, a hat worn by Spanish bullfighters with a somewhat similar shape dating to the mid-1800s. Manufactured for Disneyland by the Benay-Albee Novelty Co. (makers of the pinwheel beanie), they were made with hard-cotton felt and came in basic black. Once purchased, the owner could have his or her name stitched into the back.

These ear hats first appeared in one of Disneyland's **souvenir books** in 1958, the same year the **Mad Hatter** opened on **Main Street**. Since then, the ears have been modified into hundreds of styles, changed into different colors (gold for the fiftieth anniversary in 2005), and had new features added such as "glow" technology that en-

ables them to light up. The simple, basic hats sold for $14.99 in 2016.

In celebration of the ears' long history, Disneyland declared 2013 the Year of the Ear and introduced new limited-edition collectible hats every month of the year. The wild selection included pirate themes, feathers, flowers, veils, embroidery, sequins, and more. For 2015's **Diamond Celebration**, a special "jeweled ear hat" created by the Arribas Brothers could be purchased for $625; another set, a glittery Minnie Mouse style with a pendant, cost $24.95 and quickly became the biggest seller of all the 500+ new items introduced for that year's sixtieth anniversary.

The ubiquitous ears also continue to be represented in popular culture. They've been worn on TV shows (such as "The Spaghetti Catalyst," a 2010 episode of *The Big Bang Theory*) and even in artworks; *Vincent Van Goghs to Disneyland*, Bob Buccella's 1987 painting, depicts Van Gogh wearing a one-eared hat.

> **MOUSCELLANY**
>
> The most expensive mouse ears ever created? Probably the crystal-studded hat created by Swarovski, a dazzling $25,000 prize given away in a 2016 Share Your Ears promotion to benefit the Make-A-Wish Foundation.

Mr. Toad's Wild Ride

MAP: Fantasyland, Fa-28

DATES: July 17, 1955–ongoing

While the other two original **Fantasyland** dark rides either enchant guests with wondrous airborne views (**Peter Pan's Flight**) or effectively reduce a classic story to its most emotional elements (**Snow White's Scary Adventures**), Mr. Toad's Wild Ride has one simple goal: to make guests giggle. The early **souvenir books** emphasize this intention with its photos of the Wild Ride—everyone shown in the pictures is laughing. According to the jaunty captions, "the hilarious misadventures . . . bring fun and laughter to everyone," it's "a hilarious adventure for the young in heart," and it offers "a hilarious race through . . . Old London Town." Back then, the Wild Ride only cost a C ticket, but it was Disneyland's jolliest attraction.

The Wild Ride is housed in a rectangular building that's shared with **Alice in Wonderland**. In fact, Alice's caterpillar vehicles crawl up onto the second floor above Toad's tracks. A whirling ride has always been in the nearby courtyard—first the **Mad Hatter's Mad Tea Party**, and then the **King Arthur Carrousel** beginning in 1983.

Mr. Toad's theme came from Disney's thirty-six-minute animated movie *The Wind in the Willows* (1949), which is based on the classic Kenneth Grahame book. Toad, "the most fabulous character in English literature," according to the film's narrator, is an "incurable adventurer, mad, reckless." There's plenty of excitement in the film, but the attraction doesn't mimic the movie's plot. In the movie, for instance, we never see Toad in a moving car; he steals a train and rides on a horse and in a boat, plane, and cart, but all we see of Toad the motorist is a newspaper photograph of him in a car. Some film elements, however, are reprised throughout the attraction. The cars are named after key characters (MacBadger, Winky, Cyril, etc.), and most of the movie's main characters appear during the two-minute trip. J. Thaddeus Toad's own home is the ride's preliminary race track, and Toad's madcap movie energy propels the whole Disneyland adventure.

A colorful mural in the loading area heralds the hijinks to come. After boarding a stylish but uncontrollable little antique car, riders crash through the hallways and then careen across the English countryside. Their destination: Nowhere in Particular. Their goal: unbridled merriment. The most astonishing portion of the rollicking joyride is its fiery ending. After a police chase, courtroom trial, and prison getaway, the whole frantic caper is brought to a sudden crashing halt by the scary approach of a noisy train. Guests then find themselves . . . in hell. Literally, a blazing, demon-populated Hell.

No other Disneyland attraction veers so far from the movie that inspired it (the film ends with Toad happily soaring off in a flying machine) or ends so calamitously (**the Haunted Mansion** sends guests home with a hitchhiking ghost, but that's nothing compared to the eternal burning and poking that culminates the Wild Ride). Perhaps the finale is a warning—drive like Toad, suffer dire consequences—but it's so unexpected that it probably evokes more laughter than fear, especially as guests burst through the doors back to Disneyland. Whether it's caution or comedy, the ending epitomizes the unpredictable nuttiness that makes Toad's attraction such a fan favorite.

> **MOUSCELLANY**
>
> Fans of Mr. Toad's Wild Ride must be excited about Disney's upcoming feature film, *Mr. Toad's Wild Ride*, which was announced in 2012 as being in development (no release date was given).

When it was first being planned, the attraction was meant to be more roller coaster-ish, but that idea was reined in to make the Wild Ride essentially a simple, glorious gambol. Disney Legends were at the core of its creation: **Claude Coats** drew the interiors, **Ken Anderson** designed the sets, **Bob Gurr** built the vehicles, and **Bill Martin** laid out the basic ride. A 1961 update improved some of the interior that had been hastily painted for **Opening Day**. More significantly, a major renovation in 1983 brought new effects to both the interior and exterior. Inside, new areas and gags filled out the escapade. Outside, a stunning new mansion design replaced the medieval-tournament façade that existed throughout Fantasyland but seemed out of step with Toad's Edwardian-era automobile adventures. Toad Hall is now one of the area's architectural highlights, a wonderful multi-chimneyed structure that is as fun as it is fascinating (a miniature version can be viewed from the **Storybook Land Canal Boats**).

As beloved as this attraction is, Imagineers almost eliminated Mr. Toad's Wild Ride in the 1990s when they considered bringing **The Many Adventures of Winnie the Pooh** to Fantasyland. Fortunately, Mr. Toad was saved, and Pooh moved into **Critter Country**. Mr. Toad's survival brought a sigh of relief to fans and gave generations of newcomers a chance to decipher the fractured Latin of Toad's family motto (*Toadi Acceleratio Semper Absurda*, which the official Disney Parks website translates as "A Speeding Toad is Always Absurd"), smile at all the ride's cleverly titled books (*Rumple Toadskin, Ivantoad*, etc.) on its bookshelves, watch for the Sherlock Holmes silhouette in the upstairs window, take the Toadster's roadster on a rowdy road trip, and experience the surprise of Infernoland for themselves.

Walt Disney himself acknowledged the importance of the Mr. Toad attraction. According to the book *Remembering Walt*, when a park waitress addressed him as Mr. Disney, he reminded her that he was simply Walt, adding that "there's only one 'mister' in Disneyland, and that's *Mr.* Toad."

Mule Pack, aka Rainbow Ridge Pack Mules, aka Pack Mules Through Nature's Wonderland

MAP: Frontierland, Fr-21

DATES: July 17, 1955–October 1973

The Mule Pack debuted on **Opening Day** and enjoyed a surprisingly long run—er, walk. While it's easy to dismiss this attraction as an unsophisticated leftover from the 1950s, it actually persevered well into the '70s. Maybe it was the interactivity that guests enjoyed; although live animals could be seen in everything from the **Miniature Horse Corral** to the **Dalmatian Celebration**, the Mule Pack offered the only opportunity for guests to actually *ride* them.

The attraction operated out of a **Frontierland** loading area that sent guests and their little mules clomping along dusty wilderness trails, with the rowdier **Stage Coach** and **Conestoga Wagons** often in sight. Usually nine mules at a time were strung together in a long line, headed by a cowboy-costumed **cast member** on a lead horse. Kids were the target audience; younger, lighter children were belted into their saddles. Originally purchased for $50 apiece, the mules were kept in Disneyland's **Pony Farm** at night.

In February of 1956, the attraction temporarily closed so the wilderness area could be re-invigorated with more landscaping, simple mechanical creatures, and the new train tracks of the **Mine Train**. When the mules returned on June 26, they had graduated from a C-ticket to a D-ticket attraction and had acquired a new name: the Rainbow Ridge Pack Mules. This lasted until October 2, 1959, when the attraction temporarily shut down again for a desert remodel. On June 10, 1960, the new Pack Mules Through Nature's Wonderland attraction was part of the **Nature's Wonderland** grand opening, a ceremony attended by **Walt Disney** and hundreds of invited guests. The updated mule attraction cost an E ticket, and the tour through the seven-acre Nature's Wonderland ventured past over 200 animated animals and a cool display of dinosaur fossils.

The Pack Mules finally packed up in October of 1973. By then, there were stories circulating of problems along the trail. Mules had been startled by the sudden train noises, boat whistles, and other surrounding Frontierland sounds. The recalcitrant animals had sometimes nipped guests, and occasionally they'd stopped in their tracks altogether, turning a ten-minute ride into a frustrating ordeal. Indeed, when they were shown in Disneyland's **souvenir books**, the mules never look happy. Six years after closing, the trails where the mules had once ambled reopened as the thrilling **Big Thunder Mountain Railroad**.

Murdoch, Keith
(1918–2011)

Once **Harrison Price** pinpointed Anaheim as the best location for Disneyland, someone in the city had to broker the agreements that would make the giant park possible in an agricultural town with fewer than 15,000 residents. That someone was Keith Murdoch, Anaheim's city manager.

Born and raised in Michigan, Murdoch earned a civil engineering degree and studied municipal management. When Disneyland negotiations began in 1953, Murdoch had been on the job for three years. Teaming up with Mayor Charles Pearson, Murdoch "worked personally with **Walt Disney** to bring Disneyland to Anaheim," according to Stephen Faessel's *Images of America: Anaheim 1940–2007*. Murdoch's vision extended beyond Disneyland, however; he was also instrumental in bringing the California Angels baseball team to a modern new stadium ("the Big A" opened in 1966) and building the dynamic Anaheim Convention Center a year later. Within ten years of Disneyland's opening, Orange County had become, as *Disneyland Hotel* author Donald W. Ballard puts it, "the tourist hub of America, producing tourist income greater than any other county in the United States and more than the combined tourist income of all the other fifty-seven counties of California."

> **MOUSCELLANY**
>
> Two enterprises with which Murdoch was closely involved, Disneyland and Anaheim's "Big A" baseball stadium, teamed up for some co-promotion in the late 1960s and early '70s. Angels-Disneyland Fun Day offered a unique double-header: with a special ticket, guests could go to a game and the park (with unlimited attractions) on the same day.

By the time Murdoch retired in 1976, his city had become one of the *world's* leading tourist destinations, its population had multiplied by a factor of fourteen to 210,000, and its physical size (through his annexation of surrounding areas) had increased tenfold, from four square miles to over forty. Pre-Disneyland, Anaheim had fewer than 100 motel and hotel rooms; by the end of 2015, Visit Anaheim (formerly the Anaheim/Orange County Visitor & Convention Bureau) claimed that there were 11,000 hotel and motel rooms within a mile of Disneyland (22,000 rooms total in Anaheim's resort district), and that Anaheim's population had grown to over 300,000.

Murdoch died in 2011 at age ninety-two, an Anaheim resident to the end.

Names Unraveled

MAP: Fantasyland, Fa-23, Fa-4, Fa-9

DATES: Ca. 1995–ca. 2005

Names Unraveled could also be called Names Well-Traveled, since this little specialty service had three locations in its decade-long existence. It started as a **Fantasyland** cart parked in the walkway north of **Matterhorn Mountain**. In the late 1990s, it moved to a room inside the **Sleeping Beauty Castle** entrance. Names Unraveled then relocated to a spot over by **Pinocchio's Daring Journey**, filling a space previously

used by **Geppetto's Toys & Gifts**.

No matter where it went, Names Unraveled always provided the same service: investigating the derivations of guests' names, and then offering ways to take that information home in keepsake form. Hard copy, stationery, plaques, glasses, and more were available, until Names Unraveled became Names Unavailable around 2005.

Nature's Wonderland

MAP: Frontierland, Fr-22

DATES: May 28, 1960–January 2, 1977

The biggest change to hit **Frontierland** during the 1960s arrived in the decade's very first year. Nature's Wonderland was a huge, $2.5 million remodel of a barren area that was mostly unnamed, except for a one-and-a-half-acre northern section called the **Painted Desert**. Beginning in 1955, three old-fashioned modes of transportation had left tracks there: the **Mule Pack**, **Stage Coach**, and **Conestoga Wagons**. As of 1956, the **Mine Train** was chugging through on its way to the luminous Rainbow Caverns. All four of these attractions were shut down in 1959 so the desert could be transformed into Nature's Wonderland.

When the Mine Train resumed service on May 28, 1960, Nature's Wonderland presented guests with a seven-acre area that mixed unspoiled American backcountry with **Audio-Animatronic** technology. To the west, overlooking the **Rivers of America** and **Tom Sawyer Island**, was a new seven-story mountain called Cascade Peak. Across the center of Nature's Wonderland was a T-shaped body of water: the upper horizontal part was Bear Country (not to be confused with 1972's **Bear Country**), and the stem was Beaver Valley. To the northeast was the Living (formerly the Painted) Desert. Gone were the Stage Coach and Conestoga Wagons, but back were the mules and train, both of which would survive into the 1970s.

Like the **Jungle Cruise** and the original Painted Desert, Nature's Wonderland took its imagery from Disney Studios' *True-Life Adventures*. Here, the four inspirations were four half-hour documentaries: *Bear Country*, *Beaver Valley*, *The Living Desert*, and *The Olympic Elk* (the first three won Oscars for Best Short Subject). Populating Nature's Wonderland were over 200 new Audio-Animatronic animals, including everything from snakes and birds to beavers and bobcats. The landscape offered stunning new views of the Big Thunder and Three Sisters waterfalls flowing down Cascade Peak, wildlife splashing in the water, and Old Unfaithful Geyser splashing seventy feet above the desert.

Walt Disney was so proud of this new area he himself had sketched out that he gave it a special wraparound cover on the outside of Disneyland's 1960 **souvenir book**. Called "The Story of Nature's Wonderland," this unique outsert details the new developments: "Here, in a primitive setting that duplicates the remote wilderness country, you may watch beavers, busy as always, on home-building and tree-cutting chores; coyotes and mountain lions; clown-like bears, romping without a care in the world; Olympic Elk engaged in a battle for survival, just as it is enacted daily in the natural wilderness." A colorful, full-page map lays out the entire Nature's Wonderland acreage and spotlights "exciting wilderness scenes" such as a bear scratching its back on a tree and a moose drinking from a river. In addition, Nature's Wonderland even had its own rustic **attraction poster**. Divided into four sections circumnavigated by train tracks, the poster reinforces the movie connection by labeling its quadrants Bear Country, Beaver Valley, Living Desert, and Olympic Elk (shown on page 347).

Despite all the hullabaloo, by the early 1970s work was already underway to undo Nature's Wonderland. The mules were led away in 1973, the train was taken out in 1977, and **Big Thunder Mountain Railroad** was roaring across the dramatically rede-signed landscape by 1979. However, some of the old Nature's Wonderland elements endured. Hollow Cascade Peak, gradually deteriorating from within, didn't give way to demolition until 1998, and a few of the mechanical animals can still be glimpsed from Big Thunder's speeding trains.

New Century Watches & Clocks,
aka New Century Timepieces and New Century Jewelry

MAP: Main Street, MS-4

DATES: January 1972–July 2008

The **Main Street** corner that had been the **Upjohn Pharmacy** since 1955 became a clock shop called New Century in 1972. Sponsored by the watch-making company Elgin, it was first called New Century Watches & Clocks. When Lorus took over spon-sorship in 1986, the store was renamed New Century Timepieces. That same year, the Rings & Things store across the street moved in next door to New Century Timepieces, where a small space had been vacated by the **Disneyana** shop. The Rings name dis-appeared and new vertical signage anointed the entire space as New Century Jewelry, even though New Century Jewelry and New Century Timepieces both operated inside.

From the outside, the businesses looked separate and had different paint jobs. Inside, however, were two rooms wide open to each other, like two halves of one big store. The main corner room offered "Disney traditions in time," meaning vin-tage-style Disney character watches and Disney-themed clocks from prominent man-ufacturers. The jewelry cases in the room to the south showed off sparkling rings, bracelets, and gold charms. One unique specialty was on the timepiece side, where an artisan often sat painting customized watch faces (which sold for $300–$500) in view of guests.

New Century's time ran out in July of 2008, when the store closed permanently. It reopened as the **Fortuosity Shop** just in time for Halloween.

New Orleans Bayou Bash

MAP: Park, P-12

DATES: February 10, 2012–March 11, 2012; January 18, 2013–February 12, 2013

Perfectly styled for Mardi Gras celebrations, **New Orleans Square** didn't really have any major stand-alone Mardi Gras events until three 2011 parties were held on **Family Fun Weekends**. Building on that success, and boosted by the momentum of **Three Kings Day** and the **Happy Lunar New Year Celebration** in January of 2012, the first official New Orleans Bayou Bash kicked off a month later with a full slate of lively entertainment. Meet-and-greets with Disney characters in colorful costumes, energetic music by the **Royal Street Bachelors** and Jambalaya Jazz Band, Tiana's Mardi Gras Procession, face-painting, and beads, beads, beads all combined to fill New Orleans Square with festive fun.

The seven-hour Bayou Bash was held on seventeen different days in 2012: February 10–12, 17–21, and 24–26, and March 2–4 and 9–11. The popularity of the 2012 event led to four more Bayou Bash weekends from mid-January to mid-February in 2013, in conjunction with a new **Limited Time Magic** program.

New Orleans Square

MAP: Park, P-12

DATES: July 24, 1966–ongoing

Walt Disney had long been a fan of New Orleans, and in the late 1950s, he believed that a small, graceful replica of its famous French Quarter would fit in nicely at Disneyland. It would be historic and pretty, like **Main Street**, presenting lots of sophisticated French-themed shops and restaurants. Disney's New Orleans vision wouldn't become a reality until 1966, and it would be the last large-scale Disneyland project dedicated during his lifetime.

Years before New Orleans Square opened, designers had already infused some of Frontierland and its surroundings with Southern themes. The *Mark Twain* had been steaming along the **Rivers of America** since **Opening Day**; **Magnolia Park** and the **Chicken Plantation** restaurant were both operating in the 1950s; until the early 1960s, live Dixieland music was played in a waterfront gazebo; and the mesmerizing, antebellum-style **Haunted Mansion** was erected in 1963. New Orleans Square would consolidate Disney's Delta dreams into one marvelous neighborhood. Those dreams wouldn't be cheap—the price for New Orleans Square, according to *Disney: The First 100 Years*, was $18 million, more than what it had cost to build all of Disneyland a decade earlier.

Disney artists began sketching ideas for a New Orleans area in 1957, just two years after Disneyland opened. The annual **souvenir books** began showing preview illustrations of "Old New Orleans" in 1961. Early construction began that same year, but in 1963, the work stopped to refocus Disneyland's resources on creating new attractions for the 1964–1965 New York World's Fair. In 1965, a full year before New Orleans Square debuted, public excitement began to surge in anticipation of the new land. That year's souvenir book devotes a page of drawings and descriptions to

the coming area, showing off its ambitious streets and buildings.

When New Orleans Square finally opened in mid-1966 with a special ceremony attended by Walt Disney and the mayor of New Orleans, it was the first permanent new land added to Disneyland's original roster of Main Street, **Adventureland**, Frontierland, **Fantasyland**, and **Tomorrowland**. It was also the only land at the time not directly connected to the **Hub**. Three days after Walt Disney's death and a week before Christmas, a 1966 episode of *Walt Disney's Wonderful World of Color* put Disneyland's version of New Orleans in front of a national TV audience.

That audience saw a compressed idealization of what everyone still imagines a few perfect blocks of New Orleans should look like. But there's far more going on here than meets the eye, because the geography of New Orleans Square isn't as readily apparent as, say, the south-to-north Main Street or wide-open **Town Square**. Unlike the actual New Orleans, which has streets crisscrossing in a grid pattern, New Orleans Square isn't really square. Three separate blocks angle through the main neighborhood: to the south, a large east–west block houses **Pirates of the Caribbean** and the **Blue Bayou**; north of that, a smaller diagonal block extends southwest to northeast and juts Café Orleans toward the Rivers of America; and on the west side, a third block containing the **French Market** aims at the Haunted Mansion about 150 feet away. Between the three blocks are two narrow, asymmetrical streets, each only about fifteen feet wide. Royal Street separates the Pirates block from the diagonal Café Orleans block, and Orleans Street separates the Café Orleans block from the French Market block. Bordering New Orleans Square to the west and south is the seventy-five-foot-long Front Street and the train track; on the east side are the Esplanade and views of the river traffic.

Covering only about three acres, New Orleans Square's diminutive scale creates an intimate atmosphere. Not only are the blocks compact, they're short, too, reaching only two and three stories high. To make the buildings seem bigger than they are, Imagineers incorporated the same "forced perspective" strategy they first used on Main Street (where upper stories are built on a smaller scale than lower stories). Compressed as they may be, the buildings *feel* right. Appreciated more by adults than their fast-moving kids, the French-themed shops and cafés are adorned with authentic design details such as hanging plants, French doors, cozy verandas, and lacy wrought-iron railings. Appropriately, there are no noisy, whirling rides in New Orleans Square, no huge **Emporium**-style stores, and no towering mountains to rival

Big Thunder Mountain or the **Matterhorn**. Instead, the emphasis here is on architecture, ambience, shopping, and dining. With Disneyland's best restaurant (**Blue Bayou**), an eatery named after a cocktail (**Mint Julep Bar**), the only in-park restaurant that serves alcohol (**Club 33**), and expensive antique stores (**One-of-a-Kind Shop**), adults, not children, are the true audience of New Orleans Square.

Guests still marvel at the wonderful variety of sights and sounds here that evoke the New Orleans spirit. Because the Crescent City itself was named after French royalty (Philippe II, Duke of Orléans) and was once a French colony, many of the businesses in New Orleans Square have either had French names (**La Petite Patisserie**, **Le Chapeau**, etc.) or been named after famous French figures (**Mlle. Antoinette's Parfumerie**, **Laffite's Silver Shop**). And since New Orleans, the birthplace of Dixieland, is a world-renowned jazz capital, the air in New Orleans Square is often sweetened with the sounds of jazz combos, either playing on the streets or at the French Market.

Among the performers who have enjoyed extensive New Orleans Square stays are the **Royal Street Bachelors** and **Side Street Strutters**.

More pleasing than the authentic New Orleans touches are the nice surprises here that are pure Disney. Until 2013, one of these was the lovely Court des Anges, a serene spot with a winding staircase (shown), small fountain, and abundant plants. Today's guests can still turn a corner and find a quiet alcove with **portrait artists** practicing their craft; tucked behind a building, a hidden counter sells delicious baked goods; stained-glass windows are on the second story and a mysterious doorway marked with the number 33 is on the first. Realistic pre-recorded sounds drift down from the upper windows, just as they do on Main Street—although here, those sounds include a voodoo priestess preparing spells. Above the buildings, some of the roofs are topped with maritime sails, put there both to hide searchlights and to imply where a romantic waterfront awaits. Below the buildings are store rooms, restaurant kitchens, offices, an employees-only cafeteria, and a subterranean honeycomb of tunnels. As famous, familiar, and photographed as it is, New Orleans Square is still a place for discovery.

New Orleans Square Lemonade Stand

MAP: New Orleans Square, NOS-12

DATES: 2009–ongoing

Some **cast members** refer to this outdoor vendor as the NOS Lemonade Stand. It's been sitting in the walkway outside the **Haunted Mansion** entrance since 2009, serving up frozen lemonade and other cool beverages from a colorful, New Orleans-themed counter. Hours of operation vary and are usually limited to weekends and holidays in the off-season.

New Year's Eve Party

DATES: December 31, 1957–ongoing (seasonal)

Disneyland's winter holidays have almost always included an all-park New Year's Eve Party that lasts until 2 AM. The New Year's tradition was inaugurated on the last night of 1957 with relatively modest festivities (this was also the night that Disneyland reached an **attendance** milestone, when guest number 10 million arrived). This first New Year's event required the purchase of a separate $3.95 ticket for a six-hour party that started at 8 PM; in addition to getting unlimited access to all attractions, guests enjoyed "special New Year's Eve dancing parties" and received a "fun package."

Since that first New Year's Eve, the annual event has been expanded to include free hats and horns, unique menu items in restaurants, special **parades** (often a preview of bands from the next day's Rose Parade in Pasadena), creative light shows projected onto **Sleeping Beauty Castle**, a dramatic countdown, unique **fireworks**, a midnight **Fantasmic!** performance, and late-night dances (for the 2014–2015 and 2015–2016 parties, these dances were held near **It's a Small World**, at the **Galactic Grill**, and in **Fantasy Faire**, even as temperatures edged toward forty degrees). Another change has been with the TV coverage: the Univision network began broadcasting Disneyland's New Year's Eve live in 2011.

Crowds have increased steadily; what began with about 7,500 partygoers in 1957–1958 has gradually swelled to about ten times that number (the holiday week from December 24 to January 1 is the year's busiest). Disneyland's all-time biggest New Year's Eve gathering was probably the one at the end of 1999, when well over 80,000 guests came to the huge, once-in-a-lifetime millennium celebration. That night, attendees got free "Happy New Year 2000" glow sticks to help light up the special event.

New York World's Fair Exhibit

MAP: Tomorrowland, T-23

DATES: 1963–1964

In 1963, **Walt Disney** suddenly pulled his Imagineers off their uncompleted Disneyland projects, including **Pirates of the Caribbean** and the **Haunted Mansion**, to create four new attractions for the 1964–1965 New York World's Fair. For Disney, the

WORLD'S FAIR NEW YORK 1964-1965

fair provided an inexpensive way to explore expensive new ideas, since each attraction was being sponsored by a major corporation and was being installed in a building that Disney himself didn't have to construct. Additionally, once they had proved themselves to New York audiences, the attractions (or at least some of their features) would travel to Disneyland. In a sense, then, the two-year New York World's Fair was like a free Disneyland research laboratory.

With all four New York attractions on the drawing board, in 1963 a free preview called the New York World's Fair Exhibit opened in Disneyland. It was installed in **Tomorrowland**, in the spot where the Dairy Bar had once stood. The first new development the exhibit displayed was the Wonder Rotunda's Magic Skyway, sponsored by the Ford Motor Co. This attraction's dinosaurs would later appear in Disneyland's **Primeval World Diorama**, and the vehicles would be modified into the **PeopleMover**. The next attraction was General Electric's Progressland, which would become Tomorrowland's **Carousel of Progress**. Third was **It's a Small World** for Pepsi-Cola, the cruise that came to **Fantasyland** in 1966. The final attraction was the Illinois pavilion's **Great Moments with Mr. Lincoln**, which would develop into 1965's **Opera House** attraction.

Disneyland's New York World's Fair Exhibit served two purposes: it helped gauge the public's interest in upcoming attractions, and it stirred up excitement for Disneyland's immediate future. As usual, Walt Disney's instincts were right on target; his four attractions were among the most visited in New York, and when they moved west, they were quickly among the most visited in Anaheim. In 1965, with the New York attractions either already installed at Disneyland or coming soon, the Tomorrowland exhibit was torn down and replaced by the **Character Shop** after a lengthy remodel. Back in New York, the fair organizers invited Walt Disney to build an East Coast version of Disneyland. Disney declined; his sights were already set on Florida for his next park location.

Fifty years after it ended, the 1964–1965 New York World's

Fair got another exhibit, albeit a temporary one, in Tomorrowland. This one was a room-size display outside the **Magic Eye Theater**, where *Tomorrowland*, a much-anticipated 2015 Disney movie starring George Clooney, was being previewed before its May release. The film has several key scenes set at New York's World's Fair, so at Disneyland, colorful graphics (detail shown on page 353) and informative text briefly revived that important mid-'60s event for modern audiences.

Newsstand

MAP: Park, P-4

DATES: July 17, 1955–ongoing

Back when Disneyland was closed on some Mondays and Tuesdays, the Newsstand stayed open during the day for some quick shopping close to the **parking lot**. Today, guests still get a pre-turnstile look at Disneyland souvenirs and small gifts here on the western side of the main **entrance**.

The sign above the little freestanding building reads both Newsstand and Information because, in addition to selling their wares, **cast members** here can answer questions and hold Package Express items purchased inside Disneyland for convenient pick-up on the way out. Additional newsstand structures selling similar merchandise can be found nearby at the two entrance tunnels leading to **Town Square**.

Nunis, Dick
(1932–)

Born in 1932 in Cedartown, Georgia, Dick Nunis was an Academic All-American football player at USC in the early 1950s. After graduating in 1955, he applied to work at Disneyland two months before **Opening Day**. Hired by **Van Arsdale France**, who was in charge of training new employees, Nunis began his career at Disneyland as an orientation trainer for the first class of **cast members**.

Later, he served as head of the mailroom, supervisor of **Adventureland** and **Frontierland**, and, ironically, Van France's boss in 1962 (he and France developed Disneyland's employee manuals). According to the book *Remembering Walt*, after **Walt Disney** died in 1966, France and Nunis decided to shift the theme of the employee manuals to a "traditions" concept, "so that Walt's words, traditions, and philosophies would go on forever."

Later promotions elevated Nunis to positions as Disneyland's director of operations (he championed a new water ride that became **Splash Mountain**) and executive vice president for both Disneyland and Walt Disney World. He oversaw EPCOT in the 1980s, and Disney-MGM Studios in the '90s.

After exactly forty-four years of helping shape the philosophy, growth, and legacy of Disney theme parks, Nunis retired in 1999 as one of the company's top executives. He was named a Disney Legend that same year.

Oaks Tavern

MAP: Frontierland, Fr-5

DATES: 1956–September 1978

The **Golden Horseshoe** saloon and Oaks Tavern a little farther down the row . . . in the 1950s, these were the kind of businesses that put the wild in Wild West, right?

In **Frontierland**, not so much. The Oaks Tavern was merely a fast-food operation that cooked up chili, burgers, sandwiches, and snacks. Its patio tables overlooked the **Rivers of America** for some scenic dining. Last call came to the Oaks Tavern in 1978 when the space was re-cast as the **Stage Door Café**. The "tavern" name, though, was resurrected in 2009 when the **Troubadour Tavern** opened in **Fantasyland**.

Observatron

MAP: Tomorrowland, T-8

DATES: May 22, 1998–ongoing

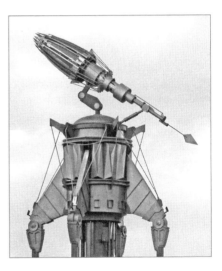

The Observatron was added during 1998's major **Tomorrowland** remodel. While it was new to Disneyland, the Obervatron wasn't new to the Disney canon—a similar device had already been operating at Disneyland Paris.

A futuristic kinetic sculpture with a screwdriver-like top (shown) mounted above dish antennas, the Observatron sits above the old **PeopleMover** loading area. Disneyland's 2000 **souvenir book** includes a full-page Observatron photo and text declaring that it "signals the quarter hour with an impressive array of movements, lights, and vibrant music." As an elaborate timepiece, the Observatron is like the **It's a Small World** mechanical clock that activates every fifteen minutes. Exactly how observers can divine the current time from the whirling Observatron isn't quite clear (especially since it rarely operates at all anymore), but the device does make for a curious sight. For 2015's **holiday season**, the still-inert Observatron displayed nightly light effects.

Olsen, Jack
(1923–1980)

Many of the decades-old Disneyland souvenirs that are now valuable collectibles were first brought into stores by Jack Olsen. Olsen enjoyed a two-decade career as a key Disneyland executive.

Olsen was born in 1923 in Salt Lake City but raised in California. In the early 1940s, he attended Penn State before becoming a medal-winning G.I. in World War II. Returning stateside, he pursued his artistic hobbies while working in L.A. art galleries.

Olsen began working for the Disney Company in 1955, first as a Disney Studios artist and then as a Disneyland store manager. From 1960 until 1970, Olsen supervised the company's merchandising division, bringing cool new T-shirts, hats, toys, gifts, novelties, and more to store shelves. It was also his idea to bring in **portrait artists** to draw caricatures of guests. During the 1970s, Olsen helped with the merchandising at Walt Disney World, where one of the **Main Street Tribute Windows** still identifies him as "the Merchant Prince."

In his book *Window on Main Street*, **Van Arsdale France**, whom Olsen mentored, calls Olsen "a brilliant artist" with a "brilliant mind." Olsen retired in 1977 and, after several years of ill health, died in 1980 at age fifty-six. He was named a Disney Legend in 2005.

Omnimover

Disneyland's most sophisticated attractions from the 1960s era are well-known and much-celebrated, especially **Pirates of the Caribbean** and the **Haunted Mansion**. What's less conspicuous now is the significance of the new Omnimover vehicle system that debuted at the park in 1967.

Before the Omnimover system was implemented, ride vehicles were variations on little miniature cars, trains, boats, and whirling enclosures. As fun as these were, they were limiting. Sitting in open vehicles, guests could look ahead to see other attraction scenes before they were meant to see them, or they could look back to view structural elements they weren't supposed to see at all. Music and narration blared through loudspeakers positioned at different stages of the attraction, causing confusion as guests passed from one stage to the next. What's more, some of these attractions took a while to load, since the entire ride had to stop in order for new guests to board the vehicles (think of the **Mad Hatter's Mad Tea Party**). In the 1960s, the Imagineers realized that their upcoming Disneyland attractions would soon be handling thousands of guests per hour, so they had to invent a new way to both improve the experience and move large numbers of guests through the ride efficiently.

Their solution was the Omnimover, which was actually derived from the vehicles that were first tried out at the 1964–1965 New York World's Fair. There, the General Motors pavilion and Disney-designed Ford Magic Skyway both incorporated long trains of vehicles that formed continuous loops, like a closed necklace of cars. Guests boarded the vehicles from a moving platform, which meant the rides didn't have to stop to load and unload their passengers. The Disney vehicles were otherwise fairly primitive—they didn't move independently, nor did they have their own individual sound systems. But they soon would.

After a year of development, Disneyland's first iteration of the Omnimover ride system was the Atomobile in **Adventure Thru Inner Space**, a major new **Tomorrowland** attraction that debuted in 1967. As with the New York vehicles, the continuous chain of blue, pod-like Atomobiles had a moving conveyor belt next to it for guests in the loading and unloading areas, and each pod had a self-closing metal bar that secured its passengers. To the delight of waiting guests, over 3,000 passengers per hour could now be transported through the world of the molecule.

What's more, Disney Imagineers—particularly

MOUSCELLANY

Just as Adventure Thru Inner Space had a cool closing joke enhanced by the Omnimover's motions, so too does the Haunted Mansion. At the finale, the Doom Buggies swivel toward a mirror as the onboard speaker cautions guests to "beware of hitchhiking ghosts!"

Bob Gurr, **Roger Broggie**, and **John Hench**—added important new possibilities to the Omnimover's movement (*omni*, the Latin word for "all," suggests the vehicle's range of motion). First, the Atomobiles could spin in any direction on computer command, thus directing the rider's attention to particular sights. In addition, the pods could tilt backward or forward, keeping riders level as the pods went up and down hills. The tilting effect also meant that riders could relax back into their seats when the pods leaned backwards to reveal something up near the ceiling. Plus, with an onboard speaker delivering the narration and music, sound did not have to be blasted through an entire room; instead, it could be played within each Omnimover vehicle at the appropriate moments.

A memorable example of how these options all came together occurred at the end of the Inner Space journey, when the pods sprung a nifty joke. While moving forward, one at a time each pod swiveled and bent back to direct attention up at a microscope, where a giant eye was peering at riders. Simultaneously, the narrator's voice inside each Atomobile in turn announced, "We have you on visual."

The next Disneyland attraction to use the Omnimover system was the Haunted Mansion two years later. The mansion's black Doom Buggies (shown on page 356) successfully create an effect often described as cinematic. In *The Art of Walt Disney*, Christopher Finch explains how the Doom Buggy "is used exactly like a movie camera. The rider is traveling through a programmed show which unfolds in time. The choice of where to look is not his to make—it has already been made by the designer, who determines what will be seen, just as a director determines what the movie patron will see." Like audience members watching the same movie, all Doom Buggy riders see the same scenes in the attraction and have the same experience (unless they lean out of the Omnimover pods to sneak looks when they aren't supposed to).

Another Omnimover attraction opened at Disneyland in 2005. **Buzz Lightyear Astro Blasters** added yet one more dimension—rider control. Guests could now point their vehicles in different directions as they tried to shoot at dozens of different targets during their trip. It was the latest improvement to what was a great technological advancement, one so important that it was awarded its own patent in 1971.

One More Disney Day

DATES: February 29, 2012–March 1, 2012

Long before there was such a thing as One More Disney Day, Walt Disney declared that "Disneyland looks forward to Christmas and all of the other traditional holidays, but between these dates we create our own holidays and special events." Some five decades after he said that, One More Disney Day was added to the list of Disneyland's between-holiday events, helping to fill the gap between New Year's Eve and Easter.

The park had hosted all-night parties before (in mid-July of 1985, for instance, Disneyland offered special $30 tickets to celebrate the park's thirtieth birthday). But 2012 welcomed the park's first twenty-four-hour celebration, in honor of Leap Day. Officially announced on December 31, 2011, One More Disney Day gave guests a chance to stay in Disneyland from 6 AM on February 29 until 6 AM on March 1, with no additional admission charge required.

Thousands of guests lined up in advance and tens of thousands more arrived the evening of the February 29, clogging local streets and ultimately bringing the park's total **attendance** to full capacity (some estimate that Disneyland's total attendance for this twenty-four-hour period was almost 90,000). The park offered special foods prepared just for the event, a 1 AM showing of **Fantasmic!**, even later music performances, unique commemorative merchandise, and the rare sight of dawn breaking over **Sleeping Beauty Castle**. Simultaneously, a comparable event was being held in Walt Disney World, marking the first time both parks had been open overnight on the same date.

A special all-night event, massive crowds, tons of new merchandise . . . As the narrator says at the beginning of *Peter Pan*, "All this has happened before, and it will all happen again." As expected, the success of 2012's all-night slumber party led to similar overnighters in 2013 (the **Monstrous Summer All-Nighter**), 2014 (Rock Your Disney Side Party), and 2015 (kicking off Disneyland's **Diamond Celebration**).

One-of-a-Kind Shop

MAP: New Orleans Square, NOS-3

DATES: July 24, 1966–May 13, 1996

The fascinating One-of-a-Kind Shop opened with the rest of **New Orleans Square** in 1966. Located on Royal Street near the **Royal Street Veranda**, the shop was the first retail space guests encountered in this new Disneyland area. Unlike other stores that sold replicas of antiques, the One-of-a-Kind Shop sold the real deal—actual antiques that cost thousands of dollars. The 1968 **souvenir book** confirms the shop's serious intent: a photo shows, not smiling kids, but a mature, well-dressed couple standing underneath ornate chandeliers.

It's said that the shop was suggested, or at least inspired, by **Walt Disney's** wife, Lillian, whose love of antiques had already led to the old-fashioned décor inside their **apartment** in **Town Square**. Inside the One-of-a-Kind Shop were items that were, if not truly unique to Southern California, certainly unique to Disneyland, including large spinning wheels, Victorian music boxes, vintage dolls, objets d'art, and old clocks, all of them authentic antiques. There were also actual movie props for sale.

The number of people walking into Disneyland hoping to walk out with a valuable spinning wheel is debatable, but the store did thrive for three decades. In 1995, the merchandise expanded to include reproductions and more generic gift items. A year later, the One-of-a-Kind Shop was the gone-of-a-kind shop, to be replaced in 1998 by **Le Gourmet**.

Opening Day

DATE: July 17, 1955

In *Sleeping Beauty*, the introductory narration and illustrated book open with this auspicious statement: "Our story begins on that most joyful day." Similarly, Disneyland's own story was meant to start on a joyful July day when the park welcomed its first invited guests and a national TV audience. Unfortunately, Disneyland's Opening Day has nearly always been declared a failure. That's certainly how it was subsequently reported by some of the press, and **Walt Disney** himself, ever the demanding perfectionist, even nicknamed it Black Sunday.

For decades, the many small crises that occurred in Disneyland on Sunday, July 17, 1955, have been well-chronicled, the park's early flaws and deficiencies well-documented, and the disappointments of Opening Day generally accepted. Reading today's retellings of Opening Day, one encounters such hyperbolic pronouncements as "anything that could go wrong did," "nothing was working," and "a disaster from start to finish"—none of which is actually true.

Looking back, Opening Day seems more like a day filled with minor inconveniences than major traumas. Glitches are not catastrophes; there was no riot, no natural disaster, no park-emptying pandemonium, and not a single significant injury. Crowds shown in ABC's TV coverage are generally smiling, excited, and unaware of any problems. There were certainly issues with the TV broadcast—at times, viewers saw fuzzy images and errant camera cues, or they heard no sound at all—but these were mostly ABC's problems, not Disneyland's, and the guests in attendance seemed oblivious to them.

Nearly all of the day's difficulties resulted from an overwhelming number of uninvited guests who came to the infant park even though they were told not to. This may be viewed as success—the success Walt Disney had in building something so alluring that the public had to see it sooner rather than later. Too few visitors, not too many, would have been the real failure, as proven by the ignored advertisements for thousands of embarrassing Broadway openings, forgotten film premieres, and other dead-on-arrival events that litter the fast-moving highway of entertainment history.

The pre-opening promotion had officially started in 1954, when the **Disneyland TV series** gave Disneyland national exposure. Three episodes (aired on October 27, 1954, February 9, 1955, and July 13, 1955) described the park and chronicled its progress at the construction site. Print articles and ads then built up the public's excitement right to the end. On July 15, 1955, the *Orange County Register* reported: "Probably never in history has any attraction, including World Fairs, ever received as much advance publicity."

At the site, early July had seen a frantic sprint to get everything functioning, or if not functioning, at least disguised enough to *appear* to be functioning. And it barely was. Workers were still applying paint to some of the buildings just hours before the first guests were due to arrive. **Tomorrowland's** glaring incompletion had to be hidden behind a distraction of bunting and balloons. Several attractions (**Rocket to the Moon, Casey Jr. Circus Train**) were viewable but not usable. Walt Disney himself helped paint the **20,000 Leagues Under the Sea Exhibit** on the night of July 16 and stayed at the park until 3 AM the next day. At dawn on Opening Day, the efficient Disneyland entertainment machine that guests see today was still an unfinished, unrehearsed idea.

On July 17, guests arrived early and eager. The park's attendees on that first sunny Sunday were supposed to include 10,000 dignitaries, celebrities, reporters, Disney employees, and Disneyland sponsors. All of them supposedly held special invitations with different entrance times in the afternoon so that admissions would be staggered (closing time was set for 8 PM). Alerts had even been posted in the newspapers that the general public would not be admitted on Opening Day, July 17, but evidently some 20,000 additional fans didn't get the message. Excitement trumped patience, and traffic was snarled on all the streets around the park (one of the main thoroughfares, **Harbor Boulevard**, was backed up for seven miles). Between 28,154 (the official count) and 33,000 (the unofficial tally) people got into Disneyland, including many unsolicited guests who presented counterfeit invitations or snuck over the **berm**. By 3:00 PM, the crowd trying to squeeze across **Sleeping Beauty Castle**'s bridge was jammed shoulder to shoulder.

With **attendance** suddenly triple what was expected, the inexperienced **cast members** were immediately confronted with food and beverage shortages and an inadequate number of **restrooms** and **trash cans**. With no tickets or fees required to enjoy the attractions, lines quickly bunched up. Although few people probably knew it at the time, at least one of the watercraft came close to calamity—the *Mark Twain* was so overloaded with guests that water splashed onto its decks.

What predicaments the high attendance didn't cause, bad luck did. The intense summer heat caused some of the newly poured asphalt to soften and trap ladies' high heels. With impatient crowds waiting in line, a few of the indoor ride vehicles stopped working altogether. **Van France** writes in *Window on Main Street* that the doors to Sleeping Beauty Castle were inadvertently left unlocked, allowing inquisitive guests to roam unchecked through the incomplete interior. Walt Disney was even locked into his **apartment** overlooking **Town Square** by mistake.

Dilemmas like these were all new for the dewy employees trying to solve problems they'd never been trained for. Also remember that, back then, not a single person in the world had any familiarity with the practical workings of a huge theme park. Walt Disney was opening his unique, untried vision without the benefit of the "spring training" or "out-of-town tryouts" that sports stadiums and Broadway theaters employ when they want to experiment with something new before the public sees it.

Compounding the naiveté of the cast members was the inexperience of the TV crews on hand to film the opening. According to *Operation Disneyland*, ABC's behind-the-scenes documentary, twenty-nine TV cameras were scattered around the park to film a live coast-to-coast show, the most ambitious live broadcast ever attempted. Nobody had ever televised anything so big, so spread out, and so complex before, and it showed. Cues were missed, stars were in the wrong places, and cameras caught activity they weren't supposed to (like actor Bob Cummings spontaneously smooching a dancer, though this conspicuous indiscretion may have been staged to promote the actor's TV show, on which he played a bachelor photographer). At a time when the total U.S. population was only about 165 million, 90 million Americans tuned in to see what was a humorous, confusing, spontaneous, but ultimately triumphant TV spectacle of unprecedented proportions.

Celebrities were everywhere that day, either being interviewed, walking in **parades**, or enjoying the attractions. Walt Disney's pals Art Linkletter, Ronald Reagan, and Bob Cummings served as jovial TV hosts, and many others celebrities were on hand to celebrate, including Alan Young, Jerry Colonna, Danny Thomas, Frank Sinatra, Sammy Davis Jr., Kirk Douglas, Charlton Heston, Maureen O'Hara, Jerry Lewis, Debbie Reynolds, Eddie Fisher, Fess Parker, Buddy Ebsen, Irene Dunne, Roy Rogers, Dale Evans, Hedda Hopper, California's Governor Goodwin Knight, and Annette Funicello with the rest of the Mouseketeers. A laughing Sammy Davis Jr. chased Frank Sinatra on the **Autopia**; Fess Parker and Buddy Ebsen wore frontier costumes and sang; Irene Dunne christened the *Mark Twain*; Jerry Colonna was the highballin' engineer on Casey Jr.; and Walt Disney roamed the park to make televised speeches.

Interestingly, three VIPs *not* in attendance that day were Walt Disney's own wife and two daughters. On the *Walt Disney Treasures: Your Host Walt Disney* DVD, Diane Disney Miller says that her father "asked us not to come. He said to my mother, 'I don't want any of you women coming out there tomorrow. I've got enough to worry about. It's going to be a mess, I don't want to have to worry about you too'."

Just like every subsequent day at Disneyland, free entertainment was abundant on Opening Day. During a solemn dedication ceremony, various religious speakers spoke and offered a silent prayer, military representatives conducted a flag-raising ceremony, a squadron of planes flew overhead, and doves were sent flying into the sky (the next day's *New York Times* would comment, "For some brief periods, the ceremonies took on the aspect of the

MOUSCELLANY

Los Angeles Dodgers owner Walter O'Malley "was influenced greatly by Disneyland," according to Andy McCue's *Mover & Shaker*. Impressed by his visits there, O'Malley added some Disneyland-like innovations as he built his new Dodger Stadium, in hopes of making the downtown ballpark a clean, friendly, safe place for families. Ironically, the stadium's opening day (April 10, 1962) was plagued by glitches similar to those that had marred Disneyland's debut seven years before. One frequent complaint common to both locations was that there were not enough drinking fountains, which some critics suggested was O'Malley's and Disney's deliberate strategy to boost beverage sales.

dedication of a national shrine"). Later, Disneyland's first parade wound northward from **Town Square** toward the **Hub**. The procession included soldiers wearing Revolutionary War uniforms, horse-drawn buckboards, a stage coach, Cinderella's pumpkin coach, Autopia cars, Disney characters, the **Disneyland Band**, the Mouseketeers wearing cowboy gear and hobby-horse costumes, and, bringing up the rear, a Carnation milk truck. During the day, the **Firehouse Five Plus Two** jazz band played at the **Fire Department**. That night's **fireworks** rocketed above Sleeping Beauty Castle while a jubilant Walt Disney watched from his Town Square apartment. Neal Gabler's *Walt Disney* biography summarizes the day as "the longest and quite possibly the best of Walt Disney's life."

The next day, July 18, Disneyland officially opened to the public. Thousands of guests began lining up before dawn, an enormous traffic jam soon clogged the nearby freeway, and by the time the turnstiles began revolving at 10 AM, the **parking lot** was already full. The first guest to buy a ticket was Dave MacPherson, a twenty-two-year-old college student who had been waiting in front of the park since 2 AM. Walt Disney took photos with two photogenic children who were hanging around near the front of the line: cousins Michael Schwartner, seven, and Christine Vess, five, who only that morning had persuaded their parents to take them to Disneyland—both kids received lifetime park passes). However, for all the high spirits and éclat that day, bad luck continued to plague the park when a gas leak forced **Fantasyland** to close early (as described in Van France's *Window on Main Street*, this problem occurred on the July 18, not the July 17 as others have reported).

On that first Monday morning, several major newspapers published rave reviews of Sunday's special Opening Day events. "Dream Realized—Disneyland Opens," reads the July 18 headline in the *L.A. Times*, supplemented with lots of big photos and enthusiastic text that calls the park "once-upon-a-time land," a "land of magical fantasy," and a "dream come true." However, when several columnists published severe critiques that called Disneyland's debut a "fiasco," a "disappointment," and a "confused mess," Walt Disney immediately assembled his top lieutenants to address the writers' issues. Here he was, only one day into Disneyland's history, and already Disney was changing his park. This was the first of thousands of attempts to improve

---

MOUSCELLANY

Disneyland's Opening Day Attractions (July 17, 1955)

Adventureland
Jungle Cruise*

Fantasyland
Canal Boats of the World
King Arthur Carrousel*
Mad Hatter's Mad Tea Party*
Mr. Toad's Wild Ride*
Peter Pan Flight*
Snow White Adventures*

Frontierland
Golden Horseshoe Revue
Mark Twain Riverboat*
Mule Pack
Stage Coach

Main Street
Main Street Cinema*
Main Street Vehicles*
Santa Fe & Disneyland Railroad*

Tomorrowland
Autopia*
Hall of Chemistry
Space Station X-1

*Still in operation.

Disneyland after it opened. "Disneyland is like a piece of clay," Disney declared. "If there is something I don't like, I'm not stuck with it. I can reshape and revamp."

Revamp his team did, working feverishly to solve the traffic problems on the streets and in the park. Workers quickly attended to the construction and landscaping that had been left unfinished. And over the next few weeks, Disney himself courted the press with special invitations and personal apologies.

Nobody could miss the Opening Day sign above the Main Street train station that optimistically announced Disneyland's population as 5 million people. Skeptics would have wagered that "Walt's Folly" would never draw even a tenth of that number and would close by Christmas. But Disneyland didn't merely survive; it thrived. Attendance in the following months was higher than anyone had expected, just like on Opening Day. According to a press release issued on July 18, 1956, Disneyland's attendance in its first full year was over 3.6 million guests coming from sixty-four different countries (with a ratio of four adults for every child). According to the Disneyland Data page in the 1957 **souvenir book**, guest number 5 million entered the park on October 4, 1956, less than fifteen months after the first fervent guests had rushed in.

Ever since then, the remarkable events of Opening Day have been remembered on various TV specials, with **Opera House** exhibits of memorabilia (detail shown), and in countless books, articles, websites, anecdotes, and legends. Every year, Disneyland itself commemorates July 17 with varying degrees of revelry, most recently with a small Town Square parade and short sing-along for the park's sixty-first birthday in 2016.

These modest celebrations honor one of the most challenging and inimitable days in Disneyland history.

Opera House

MAP: Town Square, TS-9

DATES: July 17, 1955–ongoing

Like **Adventureland**, the Opera House jumped from one side of Disneyland to the other while it was in the planning stages. On **Herb Ryman's** large, detailed map, drawn in 1953 before construction began, the Opera House is clearly shown and labeled on the western side of

Town Square. The imposing two-story building, of course, ended up on the eastern

side, making it one of the first structures guests meet as they walk into Disneyland through the east tunnel. Today, guests still encounter a long, square block that spreads ahead of them for about 180 feet from south to north. The Opera House dominates this block and extends about 125 feet back, giving the Opera House a total area of about a third of an acre. The main entrance to the Opera House is in the center of the block and stretches about thirty-five feet along Town Square; several ground-floor businesses and window displays surround the entrance.

> **MOUSCELLANY**
>
> Town Square's Opera House is not the only Opera House to be built in Disneyland. In the early 1960s a smaller, inaccessible version was installed in Rainbow Ridge, the miniature **Frontierland** town next to what is now **Big Thunder Mountain Railroad**.

Of all the buildings going up in the months leading to **Opening Day**, the Opera House was the first one finished. Perhaps the main reason it needed to be completed so quickly was because of the way it was going to be utilized, at least in its early years. Although **Walt Disney** originally intended it to be a large, opulent theater, from 1955 until mid-1961, the Opera House was really a working lumber mill; its spacious interior was filled with wood and carpentry projects destined for other Disneyland locations.

Starting in 1961 and continuing throughout the 1960s, the Opera House was put to a variety of uses, none of them relating to opera. It served first as the location for the *Babes in Toyland* **Exhibit**; next, as a temporary TV studio for *The Mickey Mouse Club* scenes; then as the site of the **Mickey Mouse Club Headquarters**; and finally, as the home of **Great Moments with Mr. Lincoln**. Lincoln arrived in mid-1965, at which point the 400-seat Opera House really was functioning like the theater it was meant to be.

Lincoln remained until early 1973, when **The Walt Disney Story** temporarily replaced him. Two years later, the Great Emancipator returned for the joint Disney/Lincoln exhibit that continued for the next thirty years. In 2005, the Opera House hosted special exhibits honoring Disneyland's golden anniversary and showed the tribute film *Disneyland: The First 50 Magical Years*. Today, visitors will find ever-changing displays of park models and artwork in the Opera House, an enormous hand-carved model of the U.S. Capitol (originally purchased in 1955 to be displayed on **Liberty Street**), a flat-screen version of the fiftieth anniversary movie, and a special bench that, according to the accompanying plaque, is "the actual park bench from the Griffith Park Merry-Go-Round in Los Angeles, where Walt Disney first dreamed of Disneyland."

A new movie program launched in the summer of 2012 for Annual Passholders, showing classic Disney movies on a big screen. These films usually corresponded to calendar events; the romantic *Lady and the Tramp* was shown during the week of Valentine's Day in 2013, for instance. A new ten-month program called Wednesdays with Walt (featuring highlights from the classic **Disneyland TV series**) began running on November 5, 2014, and ended the following July.

No matter what has filled the interior, the Opera House's exterior has remained dignified, its roof crowned with curling classical ornamentation that makes the structure appear one full story taller than it is. That regal façade was admired often by one significant fan; the Opera House is the building directly across from the front windows of Walt Disney's private **apartment**.

Our Future in Colors, aka Color Gallery

MAP: Tomorrowland, T-6

DATES: March 1956–January 1963

For the first two years of its existence, this exhibit appeared in Disneyland's **souvenir books** as Our Future in Colors. Then, from 1958 to 1963, the books call it simply the Color Gallery. Both iterations were located in the back of the rectangular **Tomorrowland** building that housed the **Art Corner**.

The exhibit's sponsor, the National Lead Company (now known as NL Industries), manufactured Dutch Boy paint. Consequently, throughout the summer and fall of 1955, a Dutch Boy statue marked the exhibit's future site. Construction began that winter for a spring opening. What finally appeared in 1956 was pretty docile: surrounded by color swatches, guests could spin color wheels into new shades. Accompanying musical tones encouraged or discouraged possible color combinations.

In 1963, this spot was absorbed into the **Circarama** remodel that would produce a newer, bigger Circle-Vision 360 theater.

Outdoor Vending Carts

Since 1955, millions of guests each year have stopped at Disneyland's outdoor vending carts (OVCs) to pick up quick snacks, beverages, and souvenirs. The carts have always been colorfully designed, though in the olden days they were often much smaller and simpler. A vintage peanut cart on display in the **Opera House** in 2015 and 2016 was so diminutive that it looked like something a little girl would push a doll in. By comparison, there are *automobiles* smaller than some of the big outdoor vending carts parked in Disneyland today.

Popcorn carts are among the most heavily themed OVCs, thanks to their stylish Roastie Toasties that crank the inner cogs of the carts. But guests will find all sorts of carts throughout Disneyland, especially in open areas that get a lot of pedestrian traffic. One spring day in 2015, we paused along Small World Way, which leads from the **Storybook Land Canal Boats** to **It's a Small World**. Lining this wide walkway were six carts spaced about fifty feet apart, selling churros, pretzels, frozen treats,

MOUSCELLANY

Here are Disneyland's outdoor vending carts with individual entries in this encyclopedia: **Carrousel Candies, Critter Country Fruit Cart, Indy Fruit Cart, Holiday Cart, LB's Extraordinary Elixirs, Little Red Wagon, Main Street Fruit Cart, Maurice's Treats, New Orleans Square Lemonade Stand, Parasol Cart, Pixie Hollow Gift Cart,** Popcorn Carts, **Royal Street Sweets, Ship to Shore Marketplace, Stromboli's Wagon,** and **Westward Ho Conestoga Wagon Fries.**

MOUSCELLANY

The best warm snack treat from an OVC? Churros, a foot-long favorite since they debuted in 1985 at an OVC near Videopolis. Cinnamony and delicious, easy to walk with, and inexpensive at under $5, they can be found in a half-dozen Disneyland locations. (At one time, dipping sauces and fruit-flavored churros were tried out briefly, but purists know that a classic churro doesn't need any extra adornment.) We're not alone in our estimation—about 3 million churros are sold at the Disneyland Resort every year. They even have their own Facebook page.

beverages, toys, and popcorn. Similarly, a June walk in front of the **Haunted Mansion** revealed seven carts selling souvenirs, frozen treats, toys, lemonade, glow toys, popcorn, and churros. That year's Springtime Roundup presented an elaborate hot dog/pretzel cart called Chuck Wagon Delights, designed just right for **Big Thunder Ranch**. Not to be outdone, for the 2015 **holiday season** the OVC options outside the **Village Haus** included fifty feet of barrels, wagons, tubs, and carts, with another set just thirty-five feet to the east.

The carts don't always sell food and toys, however. In 2015, the **Big Thunder Trail** welcomed three purple carts dispensing FASTPASS tickets for **Fantasmic!** The carts were temporary, but they were still well-designed for the event, with slogans coaxing guests to enjoy "Mysteries and Magic," to see "Visions Fantastic," and to "Dream a Fantastic Dream" (shown).

Painted Desert, aka Rainbow Desert

MAP: Frontierland, Fr-22

DATES: July 17, 1955–October 11, 1959

In the 1950s, just as **Adventureland** had a **Jungle Cruise** inspired by Disney's *True-Life Adventures* films, so too did **Frontierland** have its own *True-Life* area. Loosely modeled after the Oscar-winning 1953 documentary *The Living Desert*, the Painted Desert was styled after Arizona's rocky, cactus-studded landscape and spread for an acre and a half across the northeast corner of Frontierland. Disneyland's old **souvenir**

books also call this acreage the Rainbow Desert, noting its panoply of colors.

Previewing what the **Big Thunder Mountain Railroad** would speed through in 1979, the Painted Desert had pale orange rock formations crowned with balancing boulders and rough fields of sagebrush. Colorful, bubbling "desert pools" added bright hues to the landscape, and anthropomorphic saguaro cacti added humor. **Audio-Animatronic** animals weren't displayed yet—any moving creatures in the attraction were actual birds and lizards that had stopped by to visit.

From 1956 until 1959, the **Mine Train** slowly traversed the Painted Desert on its way to the spectacular Rainbow Caverns. The Painted Desert and the train both closed in 1959, but both reopened the following summer. The desert was reborn as the more animated Living Desert section of the bigger, more sophisticated **Nature's Wonderland**, and the train returned as the Western Mine Train Through Nature's Wonderland.

Paint the Night

DATES: May 22, 2015–September 5, 2016

Debuting in 1972, Disneyland's beloved **Main Street Electrical Parade** had spanned three decades in the park, revolutionized the nighttime-parade concept, and proved to be a tough show to follow. Its successor, 1997's **Light Magic**, barely made it from spring to the end of one summer before its lights went out.

Arriving with 2015's **Diamond Celebration** was a worthy successor to the iconic MSEP. Paint the Night came to Anaheim as **parade** that had already proven itself; the original version had been running successfully in Hong Kong's Disneyland for over seven months. At the Disneyland in Anaheim, the show was expanded to include eight major floats (the Hong Kong show used seven; Disneyland's eight were designed to match the themes of *Peter Pan, Monsters, Inc., Cars, The Little Mermaid, Toy Story, Frozen,* Sorcerer Mickey, and the Disney princesses). Over 1.5 million lights and more than eighty vibrant performers made it one of the most stunning shows in recent memory. After regular nightly performances ended on Labor Day weekend in 2016, the parade soon returned for occasional "limited engagement" performances through the winter holidays.

MOUSCELLANY

In a nice touch, Paint the Night gave several nods to the classic Main Street Electrical Parade, including a remix of its opening narration, snippets of "Baroque Hoedown" (the MSEP's theme song), a large electrified drum that mentioned the Electrical Parade, and the small, rotating spheres that roamed between the MSEP's floats.

Parades

As discussed in Bob Thomas's *Walt Disney: An American Original,* **Walt Disney** had to convince his own staff that parades would be a vital part of the Disneyland experience. Disney wanted elaborate, expensive parades to be offered for free every day (not just on holidays or for special events). "We can't be satisfied," said Disney. "We've always got to give 'em a little more. It'll be worth the investment. If they ever stop coming, it'll cost ten times that much to get 'em back."

But it was more than just a financial concern that drove Walt Disney's passion for parades: he'd loved them since boyhood, and had closely observed them whenever one had passed through his hometown of Marceline, Missouri. He transferred that love to Disneyland, where extravagant parades have been a daily ritual ever since **Opening Day**. The parades are so popular that the rest of Disneyland often empties out as guests crowd the parade route, making parade-time also a no-line-time at some attractions.

Disneyland parades typically (but not always) begin deep in **Fantasyland**, proceed southward to the **Hub**, pass through **Main Street**, and circle **Town Square**, finally leaving the public's view through an exit near the **Opera House**. The parades usually last about a half hour and often culminate with an appearance by Mickey Mouse.

In addition to the regular daily parades, the park's special parades have celebrated everything from Olympic athletes and national holidays to Disneyland anniversaries and new Disney movies. In any given parade, you might see automobiles, horses, circus acts, elaborate floats, Disney characters, live music, street performers who interact with the crowd, celebrities, and anything else the Imagineers dream up. The **Main Street Electrical Parade**, the only parade identified on a **Main Street Tribute Window**, is probably the most famous of Disneyland's parades; the **Candlelight Procession**, which debuted in 1958 and still runs every **holiday season**, is the longest-lasting. **Robert Jani**, **Bill Justice**, and **Tommy Walker** are usually named as the parade pioneers.

Parasol Cart

MAP: New Orleans Square, NOS-10

DATES: 1990–ongoing

Parked near the **French Market** in **New Orleans Square** is a pretty, two-wheeled cart selling parasols. Though it might not be the sturdiest thing to carry while riding fast-paced attractions, a parasol provides lightweight, sophisticated shelter from the blazing summer sun (and makes a frilly gift for a Disney princess). The cart is operated by Rubio Arts, a company that places artists in different art-related concessions around Disneyland (the nearby **portrait artists** are also from Rubio). For around $20, the artists at the parasol cart hand-paint flowers, animals, and other happy patterns (names as well) onto the colorful fabric panels of the parasols. Guests who order customized parasols can pick them up later, after the paint has dried.

48 DISNEYLAND PARADES

1955: Opening Day Parade; Mickey Mouse Club Circus Parade; Christmas Show Parade

1956: Antique Automobile Parade (aka Old Fashioned Automobile Parade)

1957–1960, 1962–1964: Christmas in Many Lands Parade

1958-ongoing: Candlelight Procession

1958–1959: Zorro Days Parade

1960–1964: Mickey at the Movies Parade

1961–1962: Parade of Toys; Parade of All Nations

1965–1976, 1980–1985: Fantasy on Parade

1965: Tencennial Parade

1967: Easter Parade

1968: Valentine's Day Party; St. Patrick's Day Parade; Cinco de Mayo Fiesta

1969, 1974: Love Bug Day

1972–1975, 1977–1983, 1985–1996, 2017: Main Street Electrical Parade

1974: Viva Mexico Parade

1975–1976: America on Parade

1977–1979, 1987–1994: Very Merry Christmas Parade

1980–1981: Family Reunion Parade

1983: Flights of Fantasy Parade

1984: Donald Duck's 50th Birthday Parade

1985: Disneyland's 30th Anniversary Parade (shown)

1986: Totally Minnie Parade

1986–1988: Circus on Parade

1987: *Snow White and the Seven Dwarfs* Golden Anniversary Celebration Parade

1987–1988: Come to the Fair Parade

1990: Party Gras Parade

1991: Celebration USA Parade

1992: World According to Goofy Parade

1993–1994: Aladdin's Royal Caravan Parade

1994–1997: Lion King Celebration

1995: Christmas Fantasy Parade

1997: Hercules Victory Parade

1997: Light Magic

1998–1999: Mulan Parade

2000–2005: 45 Years of Magic Parade; Parade of the Stars

2005: Mickey's Shining Star Cavalcade; Sleeping Beauty's Royal Celebration; Mickey's Magic Kingdom Celebration

2005–2008: Walt Disney's Parade of Dreams

2009–2010: Celebrate! A Street Party

2011-ongoing: Mickey's Soundsational Parade

2015–2016: Paint the Night

2016: Frightfully Fun Parade

Parking Lot

MAP: Park, P-2

DATES: July 17, 1955–January 21, 1998

If Disneyland's original parking lot seemed big, that's because it was—in fact, with an area of over 100 acres, it was about forty acres bigger than Disneyland itself in 1955. When it was first built, the lot's capacity was officially announced as 12,175 cars. The main auto entrance was on **Harbor Boulevard** along Disneyland's east side, with the main exit 2,000 feet to the west on West Street. Most of the original lot wasn't paved, which explains why parking cost only twenty-five cents back in 1955. Other than a couple of areas closest to the **entrance**, the dirt spaces were marked with chalk.

After a complete paving, the lot was divided into over 15,000 marked spaces. To help guests remember where they'd left their cars, the parking lot was divided into smaller sections that were labeled with character names and pictures. The names were arranged alphabetically, with Alice designating the first parking area in the northeast corner (near Harbor Blvd.) and Winnie the Pooh marking the last in the southwest corner (near the West Street/Katella Avenue intersection). The Bambi section was closest to the ticket booths; motor homes parked in Eeyore; and Donald had a ten-minute handicapped zone. **Walt Disney** himself didn't park his car in any of these sections—he had a private spot west of **Town Square**, close to his **apartment** above the **Fire Department**.

For four decades, the tantalizing views of Disneyland from the parking lot—especially of the elevated **railroad** and **Monorail**, both of which pass by the **entrance**—incited quick dashes from cars to turnstiles. Guests had the choice of walking across the parking lot to Disneyland or taking the convenient trams that continually circulated to scoop up pedestrians. Requiring no ticket for boarding, these trams were the only free vehicles on the entire property. For the first fourteen years, the trams had bench seating that faced sideways, but in 1969, a redesign introduced rows of forward-facing seats (a 2010 update added doors that kept guests from falling out). Guests who rode the trams from the parking lot to the ticket booths may have saved on footwear, but they didn't always save on time, since the trams took a circuitous route through the parking lot and their top speed was only eleven miles per hour.

One big drawback to the uncovered, unlandscaped parking lot was its lack of shade. Some experts have speculated that the parking lot was intentionally designed to be drab and treeless to throw the color and excitement of Disneyland into high contrast (a flat, unadorned parking lot also made Disneyland's entrance visible from all sections). These thoughts were a small consolation to those who returned to their vehicles during the day to discover that it wasn't a car parked under the searing Southern California sun, but actually a metal furnace on wheels.

The importance of the immense parking lot to car-driving guests, and to Disneyland's image, is not to be underestimated. According to James B. Stewart's *Disney Wars*, in the mid-1980s, retired chairman of the board Card Walker vetoed higher parking fees. "The parking lot is the first thing the guest sees. . . . Walt wanted them to think that this is the greatest place on earth." By implication, no park could be considered "the greatest place on earth" without a huge, convenient, inexpensive parking lot nearby (and it was indeed inexpensive, only fifty cents per vehicle from 1968 to 1982).

Even so, after forty-three years of service, the parking lot was demolished in 1998 to accommodate Disney California Adventure, the Grand California Hotel, and Downtown Disney. During the new construction, the ominous towers that carried high-tension power cables across the parking lot were relocated and made less conspicuous.

These days, most drivers avail themselves of the twenty-two-acre Mickey and Friends parking structure to Disneyland's northwest (the Vacationland campgrounds were on this land for about twenty-five years). This massive concrete edifice is five minutes away by tram and cost $20 a day in 2017 for a car or motorcycle. The parking structure features six levels (named for Chip 'n Dale, Daisy, Mickey, Goofy, Donald, and Minnie) and contains spaces for over 10,000 cars, making it one of the largest of its kind in the world. As of January 2014, Mickey and Friends also boasts charging stations for electric cars.

Supplementing the main parking structure are smaller lots that are readily accessible to hotel guests and Downtown Disney visitors. In total, the Disneyland Resort can now accommodate over 29,000 cars.

> **MOUSCELLANY**
>
> The Mickey and Friends parking structure offers something that others don't—a rooftop view of Disneyland's **fireworks**. Some visitors favor this viewing location because it puts them near their cars for a quick getaway ahead of the exiting crowds.

Partners

MAP: Hub, H-7

DATES: November 18, 1993–ongoing

Disney artist **Blaine Gibson** came out of retirement to sculpt the heralded *Partners* statue that now serves as the centerpiece of the **Hub**. The inspiring bronze statue was installed in a special ceremony overseen by two future Disney Legends,

Roy Disney and Jack Lindquist. The date of the installation—November 18, 1993—wasn't chosen capriciously. Exactly sixty-five years earlier, Mickey Mouse had made his debut in *Steamboat Willie*, making it the superstar's birthday. Eight years later, a re-dedication ceremony was held on December 5, which would have been the one-hundredth birthday of the company's founder.

From the moment it was unveiled, *Partners* instantly became one of Disneyland's most photographed features, due in part to its location in front of **Sleeping Beauty Castle**, but also because of the figures it depicts. Designed by Disney Legend **John Hench**, the statue presents two subjects: a smiling **Walt Disney**, who stands about six feet tall, and Mickey Mouse, who is presented as half Disney's size. Disney's left hand holds Mickey's right, and Disney's raised right arm points southward toward **Main Street** as if he's directing Mickey's attention to something in the distance. While Disney wears his readily identifiable business suit, playful Mickey sports his trademark short pants with big front buttons, shoes, and gloves.

The pair stands on a three-foot-tall cylindrical pedestal that's surrounded by a thirty-foot-wide circular planter bursting with flowers (pre-statue, this circle was filled entirely with blooms). On the southern side of the pedestal is a plaque with a Walt Disney quote: "I think most of all what I want Disneyland to be is a happy place . . . where parents and children can have fun, together." After *Partners* went up at Disneyland, similar statues were installed at other Disney theme parks.

> **MOUSCELLANY**
>
> On the *Partners* statue, the letters STR are visible on Walt Disney's tie. These are the initials for Smoke Tree Ranch, a gated Palm Springs community where Disney had a cherished vacation home, which he sold in 1954 to help pay for Disneyland's construction. Three years later, with Disneyland's success exceeding everyone's expectations, he bought a second STR home.

Passports

From Opening Day until mid-1982, the full Disneyland experience required at least two purchases: park admission, and supplemental tickets for attractions. In most of these early years, attraction tickets were sold in convenient **ticket books**. But because these ticket books were optional, for twenty-seven years it was possible for guests to walk around Disneyland just for the modest admission price, which started out at $1 and for decades was only a few dollars. Reporting from Disneyland the day before it opened, the Associated Press noted that there was so much to do that guests weren't required to spend more than the admission price to have fun: "You probably could have a good time without spending more. There are many arresting sights to see, and many industrial firms have fascinating exhibits for free."

In the 1970s, another theme park about sixty miles away, Magic Mountain, revived a POP (Pay One Price) plan that had been tried elsewhere on a limited basis. One of the earliest big amusement parks, New York's Steeplechase Park, had implemented a POP admission of twenty-five cents; later, Los Angeles's Pacific Ocean Park had tried out a POP plan from 1960 until it closed in 1967. Starting that year, Six Flags Over Georgia offered POP admission for $4.50, followed by Magic Mountain's one-price, $5 admission ticket that included entry and unlimited rides.

The advantages of a POP plan were instantly apparent to Disneyland's guests: everyone paid a higher price to get in, but there were no expensive single-ride tickets that had to be carefully monitored during the day. The only guests left out of this equation were those who wanted to pay for admission only, not tickets for rides.

Those guests must have been few and far between, because by the end of the 1970s, Disneyland was experimenting with its own all-inclusive, unlimited-attraction admission policy patterned after the one at Magic Mountain.

Originally, the only Disneyland guests to be offered all-inclusive admission tickets were **Magic Kingdom Club** members. Then, starting on June 16, 1982, all adult guests found themselves paying a single price, $12, for a Passport—a one-day, unlimited-attraction admission. (The shooting galleries were not included for unlimited use, however. Also, young children were free, as they are now.) During the transition from ticket books to daily Passports, guests could turn in their unused A–E tickets for up to $5 in credit toward a new Passport.

Since 1982, the adult price for a daily admission ticket has risen steadily, sometimes jumping twice in the same year. The price stayed in the teens through most of the 1980s, and then rose to $21.50 in 1987. Since then, it has surged past significant price points every few years—$31 in 1994, $41 in 2000, $53 in 2005, $63 in 2006, $87 in 2012, and $92 in 2013. From 2010 to 2014, the adult price jumped five times, rising a total of 33 percent ($72 to $96). The 2015 increase to $99 for a single-day adult admission nearly doubled the 2005 price.

Daily prices changed dramatically on February 28, 2016, with a new Seasonal Pricing structure. Disneyland now divides the year into three "seasons," with these prices updated in 2017: $97 Value days (about 30 percent of the year—mostly weekdays from September to June); $110 Regular days (about 44 percent of the year—mostly summer days and weekends); and $124 Peak days (about 26 percent of the year—high-demand days around holidays). Dividing those fees proportionately throughout the year, the average daily price rounds up to $110.

The swelling prices noted above have far outstripped the rise in wages. According to the Social Security Administration's wage index, between 1955 and 2014 the average American salary increased by a factor of 14 (from $3,300 a year to $46,500 a year). During those same 59 years, Disneyland's single adult admission charge increased by a factor of 96 (from $1 to $96 in 2014). Or, to limit the comparison just to the Passport era, American salaries between 1982 and 2014 rose by a factor of 3.2 ($14,500 to $46,500), while Disneyland's adult

---

MOUSCELLANY

Everyone takes jabs at Disneyland's high admission prices. *Mad* magazine has done it twice, fifty-nine years apart: "Walt Dizzy Presents Dizzyland" in the December 1956 issue gave the park an overriding "Moneyland" theme; in the October 2015 issue, one of the "7 Ways That Disneyland Is Celebrating Its 60th Anniversary" was by "adding one free small diet root beer to the $999 family pass (weekdays only; no refills)." In the 2014 Disney movie *Saving Mr. Banks*, the P. L. Travers character calls Disneyland a "dollar-printing machine."

fee rose by a factor of 8 ($12 to $96). Guests can take solace in the fact that much of the admission price does go back to improving the park, and the modern prices include unlimited attractions and other entertainment that wasn't offered six decades ago. Besides, the special place they are visiting is steadily increasing in historic significance and remains, as always, unlike every other park ("There will only be one Disneyland," Walt Disney said).

Thankfully, Disneyland offers other ways to reduce the cost of daily admission. Discounts are available via multi-day tickets, various "park hopper" options that combine Disneyland and Disney California Adventure admissions, and lower prices for seniors and local residents. And then there are Annual Passports.

For over thirty years, Disneyland has been selling Annual Passports "for those of you who can never have too much fun!" (as the old ads proclaimed). These plans provide a year's worth of admission for a single price. Plans and prices have evolved over the decades: in 1986, guests paid $114.95 for unlimited admission anytime; $49.95 for admission in May, September, and January ("when crowds are down and special events and entertainment are still going strong"); $49.95 for summer nights after 5 PM; or $13.95 for seniors sixty and over to visit on non-summer weekdays. Today, over a million guests take advantage of Annual Passports, choosing from several tiers with different blackout options that limit the number of days guests can visit. As of February 12, 2017, the least expensive Annual Passport, which gives local residents 174 days of visits per year, costs $339; the Disney Signature Plus option, which allows unlimited visits, costs $1,049. Depending on which Annual Passport is purchased, additional benefits could include extra gifts (like a free magnet, shown on page 373), admission to unique shows, parking privileges, **PhotoPass** downloads, and discounts for merchandise, dining, and tours. In February of 2016, Disneyland even held a month of special events called AP Days, featuring complimentary buttons, **Opera House** screenings of Disney cartoons, and other activities just for those holding Annual Passports.

Not only have prices changed, but so has terminology—"Passport" has gradually been replaced by "Pass" and now applies only to the different annual admission plans (Deluxe Annual Pass, Signature Annual Pass, etc.). An Annual Passport owner is now usually referred to as an Annual Passholder.

Patented Pastimes, aka Great American Pastimes

MAP: Main Street, MS-19

DATES: June 15, 1990–1999

Since **Opening Day**, the **Fine Tobacco** shop had been wedged between the **Main Street Cinema** and the **Main Street Magic Shop**. That changed in 1990, when Patented Pastimes, specializing in crafts, vintage toys, and other collectibles, opened in this small space. Nine months later, the store's name changed to Great American Pastimes and its merchandise expanded to include baseball cards and other nostalgic sports items ("the great American pastime" is one of baseball's nicknames). The approach of a new millennium saw the arrival of a new replacement, the **20th Century Music Company**, in 1999.

Pendleton Woolen Mills Dry Goods Store

MAP: Frontierland, Fr-2

DATES: July 18, 1955–April 29, 1990

Missing **Opening Day** by just twenty-four hours, Pendleton stood for the next thirty-five years as one of the longest-lasting sponsored stores in Disneyland. The location was about fifty feet within the **Frontierland** gates—guests heading to the **Golden Horseshoe** would have walked past Pendleton's door. The exterior featured a wooden sidewalk and a rustic design, as if guests were going to hitch up their horses before shopping inside. The interior continued the Old West theme with frontier décor.

When it debuted in Frontierland, the Pendleton brand was already over forty years old. A respected manufacturer of woolen fabrics and blankets in Oregon, Pendleton had supplemented its line with men's and women's clothes in the mid-century.

In 1990, Pendleton finally left Disneyland and the store became **Bonanza Outfitters**, another retailer of Frontierland fashions.

MOUSCELLANY

In its Disneyland store, Pendleton sold flannel shirts, a style popular with 1960s surfers. In fact, the young L.A. pop group known as the Pendletones named themselves after the shirts, but they had a new name by the time their first album was released in 1962—the Beach Boys.

Penny Arcade

MAP: Main Street, MS-8

DATES: July 17, 1955–ongoing

Staying true to his desire to recreate what would have existed in small American towns in the early 1900s, **Walt Disney** put a classic Penny Arcade on **Main Street**. Mounted above the doorway is an oversized Indian-head penny (shown), dated with Walt Disney's birth year. Below the penny, the arcade's big entrance gapes with tantalizing sights

and sounds that invite curious pedestrians to step inside.

Disneyland's 1957 **souvenir book** lists the Penny Arcade in the "rides" category, but the closest thing the building ever had to a major attraction was the **Main Street Shooting Gallery** from 1955 to 1962. Most of the Penny Arcade has always been devoted to old-fashioned family fun—simple games, hand-cranked silent pictures viewed on Mutoscopes for only a penny, and bizarre gizmos that were neither games nor movies. These latter devices have included Massage-O-Matic chairs, an Electricity Is Life machine that hooked guests up to a shocking battery, and souvenir coin-pressers.

A 1998 remodel replaced some of the old machines with new video games and space for a candy counter; a 2012 remodel revamped the arcade's interior to subtract

most of the old-fashioned arcade games (the Kiss-O-Meter and True Grip Challenge remained) and the Mutoscopes (there were eight left in 2015, and just six a year later). A Pinocchio "Make Him Dance" machine (a movable puppet that guests can manipulate) still stands and still costs twenty-five cents.

Also accepting quarters is the beautiful Esmeralda's enduring fortune-telling machine at the entrance; Esmeralda (shown) has been at the arcade since 1955, though back then she was much plainer and had much shorter hair than today's seductive siren. While she may seem like an inconsequential figure in Disneyland's grand scheme, Esmeralda is popular enough to have her own cloisonné tribute pin.

In exchange for all the machines that were removed, the back area has been opened up and brightened. Elegant chandeliers light the back walls, where racks display all manner of candy, from lollipops and candy apples to candies in tins, bags, and boxes (to signal the switch from entertainment to sweets, a sign announcing, "Candy" now appears above the Penny Arcade's entrance). Additionally, today's guests watching the candy-making artists at the adjacent **Candy Palace** have more elbow room as they admire the fresh creations.

Even if today's Penny Arcade is no longer what it was for decades, there's still a wonderful old-fashioned feeling here, and the main room still has its antique Concert Orchestrion, a century-old mechanical music-maker from Germany that Walt Disney bought before Disneyland opened. Also unchanged is the Penny Arcade's glittering appeal at night, when it seems to burst forth onto the street with bright lights and exuberant activity. That's a lovely sight worth a pretty penny.

MOUSCELLANY

An April 2015 episode of *The Simpsons* points out that a penny doesn't go far in modern penny arcades. When Homer's family visits the Disneyland-like Itchy & Scratchy Land, the Penny Arcade's sign announces, "All games 75 cents."

Pen Shop

MAP: Main Street, MS-15

DATES: July 17, 1955–1960

For the second half of the 1950s, a pen-selling business operated along the eastern side of **Center Street**, the small lane that bisects **Main Street**. The Pen Shop was next to the corner **Gibson Greeting Cards** store and faced the cul-de-sac on the eastern side of Center Street. Writing instruments were the main items for sale, but there was more here than retail—the shop also displayed replicas of historical documents and offered handwriting analyses.

The Pen Shop was written off in the 1960 expansion that transformed the Gibson store into the **Hallmark Card Shop**.

PeopleMover, aka PeopleMover, Presented by Goodyear

MAP: Tomorrowland, T-8

DATES: July 2, 1967–August 21, 1995

"Tomorrow's transportation . . . today!" the PeopleMover's **attraction poster** declares. For forty years, that optimistic description seemed prophetic. The popular PeopleMover is fondly remembered as one of the coolest vehicles in Disneyland history.

Debuting in 1967 with the newly remodeled **Tomorrowland**, the PeopleMover was one of the most visible new attractions. Backed by the smooth music of Disney Legend **Buddy Baker**, the little blue, red, green, and yellow cars slid leisurely along a winding, elevated track that took them across the Tomorrowland entrance, into the **Adventure Thru Inner Space** building (where they could be seen by guests standing in line), past the shoppers in the **Character Shop**, in and out of the Carousel Theater, past the submarine lagoon, through the waiting area of the **Circle-Vision 360** theater, and, as of the late 1970s, inside **Space Mountain**. For the price of a D ticket, guests got a scenic, sixteen-minute Tomorrowland tour.

The PeopleMover was truly different from any other futuristic transportation in Disneyland. The book *Walt Disney's Disneyland* points out that while the Monorail was "an old idea in a new showcase, the PeopleMover was a new concept developed by Disney engineers and introduced for the first time, anywhere, in Tomorrowland." Those engineers had first experimented with PeopleMover technology in their Magic Skyway ride at the 1964–1965 New York World's Fair. There, a new propulsion concept pushed unpowered vehicles along a track like factory cars being moved down an assembly line. According to his book *Designing Disney*, Imagineer **John Hench** actually got the idea from a Ford plant, where he watched steel being moved on tracks from area to area.

Two years later, a similar system propelled Disneyland's PeopleMover. Unlike the Monorail and other trains, the PeopleMover cars themselves weren't motorized—the track was. Rubber tires, mounted every nine feet along the three-quarter-mile "glideway" and powered by electric motors, gently pushed the PeopleMover from walking speeds of under two miles per hour up to running speeds of almost seven miles an hour. Usually four people at a time could fit comfortably on the bench seats inside one of the cars, which had white canopies to shield them from the sun. With sixty-two four-car trains running nonstop, and with guests stepping directly into their seats from a moving walkway, almost 4,900 passengers could be moved through the attraction every hour. Surprisingly, the Goodyear Tire & Rubber Company, the nation's top producer of car tires at the time, sponsored this mass-transit system from 1967 to the end of 1981.

Regretable events marred the PeopleMover's three decades at Disneyland. Tragically, reckless guests trying to move from car to car caused two fatalities in 1967 and 1980. In addition, the attraction got what many people considered to be unnecessary cosmetic makeovers in 1977 and 1982, when a distracting "superspeed tunnel" and futuristic *Tron* movie effects were incorporated into what was an otherwise relaxing trip. The slow-moving trains were finally derailed in the late 1990s, to be replaced by the ill-fated **Rocket Rods**.

A ride similar to the PeopleMover still exists at Walt Disney World. Even better, in recent years there's been talk of the PeopleMover revival at Disneyland, espe-

cially since the unused tracks (detail shown) still arc gracefully across Tomorrowland. **Walt Disney** hoped his PeopleMover would be adopted by cities for urban transit, and the system was indeed studied by city planners. However, nobody wanted it except for a single airport, so the PeopleMover exists today as a memory of an ambitious era in Disneyland history.

Peter Pan Crocodile Aquarium

MAP: Fantasyland, Fa-6, Fa-24

DATES: Never built

Had Bruce Bushman's 1953 color concept art become a reality, a large aquarium with a *Peter Pan* theme would have been built in **Fantasyland**. The location might have been the courtyard where the **King Arthur Carrousel** was installed, or perhaps the open area where the **Matterhorn** eventually arose. A Pan-themed aquarium would have brought the total number of Peter Pan attractions in Fantasyland to three (Peter Pan Flight and the **Pirate Ship Restaurant** both debuted in 1955).

Bushman's art for the Peter Pan Crocodile Aquarium depicts a giant crocodile stretched out in a pool, with the croc's head and tail above the surface. After walking through its gaping jaws and down below the waterline, guests would have entered an aquarium area where live fish swam behind large windows. Bushman's illustration was included in the 2006 *Behind the Magic: 50 Years of Disneyland* exhibit held at the Oakland Museum of California.

MOUSCELLANY

The closest thing Disneyland has to a big, tourable aquarium is the lagoon filled with mechanical marine life in the **Submarine Voyage** attraction. Large fishbowls decorate **Gadget's Go Coaster** and **Goofy's Gas Station**, and Cleo's bowl can be seen at the end of **Pinocchio's Daring Journey** (also in a mural). A ghostly aquarium was also considered for the **Haunted Mansion**.

Peter Pan's Flight, aka Peter Pan Flight

MAP: Fantasyland, Fa-29

DATES: July 17, 1955–ongoing

Many guests count Peter Pan's Flight among their most beloved attractions. **Walt Disney** would undoubtedly be delighted to hear that, because the story of Peter Pan was one of his favorites. As a boy, Disney attended a live performance featuring the Peter Pan character in 1913, and eleven years later he saw a silent-film version. He even played Peter Pan in a school production. After eagerly acquiring the screen rights in 1939, Disney and his staff worked on an animated film version throughout the 1940s. In the April 1953 issue of *Brief Magazine*, Disney expressed his hope that his *Peter Pan* film would be "the same Peter, the same Never Land, and the same Tinker Bell . . . that we have always loved." Happily, the 1953 movie was well-received.

When it came time to plan Disneyland, a Peter Pan attraction was a given. Peter Pan Flight (as it was called from 1955 to 1982) was one of **Fantasyland's** three original indoor rides. Like **Mr. Toad's Wild Ride** and **Snow White's Scary Adventures**, it transports guests into scenes from the film, riding on small vehicles attached

to a track. The Pan innovation is the track's position—rather than winding along the ground, the track hangs from the ceiling to give guests the sensation of flying. The experience is delightful. Bjorn Aronsen's purple **attraction poster** from 1955 shows the magical flight over Big Ben; in the **queue** area, a lovely mural (detail shown) piques interest in the Peter Pan story; and the gilded galleons, flying in for boarding and then soaring out of sight, beckon riders to join the adventure.

Peter's famous cry—"C'mon everybody, here we go!"—sends guests swooping out of the Darlings' nursery window. They're soon floating seven feet above a London cityscape so detailed that it has lighted traffic moving along its streets. At the "second star on the right," the soundtrack encourages guests to "think of a wonderful thought," before the ships soar to Never Land. Flying in the dark above the paradisiacal island, guests get bird's-eye views of **Skull Rock**, Captain Hook's ship anchored in the lagoon, and teepees on a bluff. After ninety wondrous seconds, the attraction's final minute features an action-packed encounter between Peter Pan and Hook, followed by Tiger Lily's rescue.

Much of the attraction was enhanced in 1961, and the second section with Captain Hook was dramatically remodeled in 1983. The 1983 improvements included the addition of three-dimensional figures, brighter colors, some pieces off the old **Pirate Ship Restaurant**, and Peter himself, previously represented only by his shadow. Outside, a majestic new clock tower marked the entrance, and a new sign declared this as Peter Pan's Flight (the sign's new "apostrophe s" was the result of a fundamental change in the attraction—guests were no longer *playing* Peter and taking a Peter Pan Flight, they were now *witnessing* the flight Peter takes). An appealing 2015 update added video projections, brighter colors, and new effects (for instance, guests now see Peter, Wendy, and the Darling boys moving across the clock's face in the London sequence).

The enchanting flight over Victorian London to a fantasy island has always been one of Disneyland's prettiest views, and for most of its years it could be seen for only the cost of a C ticket. However, many guests still count Peter Pan's Flight among Disneyland's most frustrating attractions; even when park **attendance** is low, the attraction always seems to have long, slow-moving lines. Then, after waiting so long to board the ride, guests are quickly whisked away from the scenic Never Land vistas before they can really study them. Displeased Pan fans are like sleepers roused prematurely from a sublime dream.

MOUSCELLANY

Though it's sometimes spelled "Neverland," J. M. Barrie's original play calls it "Never Land." In the *Peter Pan* movie, the island is labeled "Never Never Island" on Hook's map.

Nevertheless, fun details are sprinkled like pixie dust throughout this attraction, including bubbling "lava" inside a volcano, gorgeous mermaids, and a thematic weathervane on top of the tower outside the attraction. A dream it may be, but it's a divine dream—one in which you can fly, you can fly, you can fly!

Petrified Tree

MAP: Frontierland, Fr-8

DATES: September 1957–ongoing

Guests love finding new surprises, but those visiting in 1957 found an *old* surprise in **Frontierland**—a 70-million-year-old surprise, to be exact. That September, Disneyland began displaying an authentic petrified tree along the southern tip of the **Rivers of America.**

Before the tree was placed here, **Walt Disney** had given it to his wife, Lillian, in 1956. They had found the mineralized sequoia stump together while vacationing in the Pike's Peak area of Colorado. Disney bought it on the spot from a private seller for $1,650 and had it sent to California as a gift for Lillian on their thirty-first wedding anniversary. Realizing that Disneyland could exhibit it better than she could, Mrs. Disney donated the petrified tree to the park, where it has been an imposing presence ever since. Surrounded by a low metal fence and supported by a metal brace, the white, stony-looking tree stump stands ten feet tall and weighs five tons. A plaque explains the ancient history of the stump and names Lillian as the donor.

Phantom Boats

MAP: Tomorrowland, T-10

DATES: August 16, 1955–October 1956

The Phantom Boats have two interesting distinctions: they were one of the first attractions removed from Disneyland, and they're one of the only attractions (**Great**

Moments with Mr. Lincoln is another) ever revived from total extinction.

In mid-August 1955, the Phantom Boats replaced the temporary Tomorrowland Boats that had been cruising through the Tomorrowland lagoon since July 30. The odd-looking, nine-foot-long Phantom Boats were slightly futuristic fiberglass vessels with pointy noses, inboard motors, and huge fins (fins being the decade's fab design feature on rockets and cars). Although the boats looked fast, they drove slow. The fourteen boats came in two great 1950s colors, pink and aqua. The "phantom" in the attraction's name didn't have a backstory—apparently, the name just sounded alluring.

Amazingly, guests were allowed to pilot the boats around the lagoon themselves, sans an on-board **cast member** and with no guide rails or tracks. Unfortunately, the boats were so problematic that they often stalled mid-cruise, which perhaps explains why they only cost a B ticket. Park officials became so frustrated with the boats' performance (or lack thereof) and their maintenance requirements (almost nightly) that they added a cast member to each boat to ensure guests would return safely.

The following January, only five months after their debut, the Phantom Boats were pulled from the lagoon permanently—or so it seemed. Their successors, shallow-draft "airboats" pushed by large airplane props mounted above the water, never made it past the test stages. So, in July 1956, with the lagoon still empty of watercraft and the submarines still three years away, the Phantom Boats were resurrected for one last troublesome summer.

By Halloween, the Phantom Boats were phantoms once again. In mid-1957, the nearby **Motor Boat Cruise** debuted as Tomorrowland's new boat attraction.

Photo Collages, aka Photomosaics

DATES: May 2005–September 2006

To help personalize Disneyland's mammoth golden anniversary celebration, in 2005 and 2006 the park prominently displayed unique artworks that required guest participation. These pieces were large photo collages (aka photomosaics) comprised of thousands of guest photos.

The collage concept was announced on Disneyland's forty-ninth anniversary: from July 17 to December 31 of 2004, anyone could submit their Disney vacation photos, which would be integrated with thousands of others into oversize collages depicting Disney-related scenes. The collages were then installed at Disneyland from May 2005 to September 2006. Guests whose photos were accepted even received e-mail notifications with the location of the collage that incorporated their photos. Park kiosks also identified photo and collage locations.

Dubbed "The Happiest Faces on Earth . . . A Disney Family Album," the collages were enormously successful. Over 180,000 photos were sent in, and the completed collages were constantly surrounded by groups looking for recognizable faces. The collages varied from enormous wall-size murals (including a glorious *20,000 Leagues Under the Sea* display featuring the squid and submarine) to smaller poster-size works. The *Steamboat Willie* scene even included smaller collages within the main collage.

The collages included characters from eighteen different Disney movies (*Sleeping*

Beauty was represented three times, and *Toy Story* twice), two different Mickey Mouse cartoons, and four different Disneyland attractions. Typically, the collages were posted in areas with thematic connections: *The Lion King* piece was mounted outside the **Jungle Cruise**, a collage featuring three hitchhiking ghosts was put up at **the Haunted Mansion**, etc. Their frames, strikingly beautiful in some cases (as with the *Snow White* scene near **Mickey's Toontown**), enhanced the collages.

In all, twenty-eight photo collages went up at Disneyland for about eighteen months, with another six collages posted within and outside of Disney California Adventure. Afterward, guests could still see a reminder of the collages inside the **Opera House** lobby, where a single ten-foot-wide, eight-foot-tall collage of **Walt Disney** and Mickey Mouse, based on **Renie Bardeau's** 1966 photograph, was created from tiny photos of Disneyland.

PhotoPass

Guests needing professional-quality vacation photos can get them from one of Disney's PhotoPass photographers. These **cast members** operate in two ways: some are stationed in photogenic Disneyland locations (such as the *Partners* statue), and others roam a half-dozen areas within the park (such as **New Orleans Square**). The photographers will snap expert photos and issue PhotoPass cards so guests can access and purchase the photos later as customized prints, calendars, magnets, etc.

Additional options include PhotoPass+ One Day (a new $39 service introduced in January 2016 that gathers all the photos taken of you in a single day); PhotoPass+ One Week (a new $69 service, same as the One Day plan but lasting seven days); and PhotoPass+ Collection packages at various price points (deluxe compilations that include hundreds of stock photos on CD, and more). Also available are "magic shots" that involve photographic tricks (making it look like a Disney character is sitting in a guest's palm, for example). PhotoPass shutterbugs will even take pictures using a guest's own camera. Like another famous pass (**FASTPASS**), the PhotoPass service was brought to Disneyland from Walt Disney World, where it was first introduced in the mid-1990s.

Pieces of Eight

MAP: New Orleans Square, NOS-3

DATES: 1980–ongoing

Exhilarated guests still humming "Yo Ho (A Pirate's Life for Me)" can walk straight out of **Pirates of the Caribbean** and say "ahoy matey" to Pieces of Eight, a well-decorated shop that has been filled with pirate treasure since 1980. Well, if not exactly pirate treasure, at least there are pirate skulls, weapons, hats, shirts, and other bone-adorned merchandise ready for plundering. There are no buried pirate chests to dig up, but there are open bins filled with glittering gems to scoop out. Some of the shirts here have slogans inspired by the Pirates of the Caribbean attraction ("We wants the redhead," "Dead Men Tell No Tales," etc.). Guests can even dress like buccaneers if they purchase the inexpensive eyepatch-earring set and the long striped pirate socks offered here.

Named after the Spanish coin of the 1700s, Pieces of Eight is in the same space as the former **Pirate's Arcade Museum**. As a tribute to that **New Orleans Square** favorite, the newer store still has some of the museum's old machines. Notable among these are the metal-stamper, which cranks out personalized coins, and Fortune Red, a fortune-telling pirate who delivers small cards with advice written in pirate lingo.

Pinocchio's Daring Journey

MAP: Fantasyland, Fa-9

DATES: May 25, 1983–ongoing

The major 1982–1983 remodel of **Fantasyland** brought extensive changes to existing attractions and also added a new one—Pinocchio's Daring Journey. Imagineers had been dreaming of a Pinocchio attraction since the mid-1970s, and they finally built one in the spot where the Fantasyland Theatre had once been. Pinocchio's Daring Journey was new to Disneyland but not to Disney theme parks—the original version had opened a month earlier at Tokyo Disneyland.

Outside, the Pinocchio structure presents a captivating Tyrolean exterior complete with cobblestone walkways,

a steeply sloping alpine roof, and a half-timbered façade with a puppet show above the doorway. Inside, guests ride in old-fashioned vehicles through a richly colored, three-minute adventure that retells the story of the wooden boy, Geppetto, Jiminy Cricket, and the Blue Fairy. The attraction incorporates meticulously crafted three-dimensional figures and state-of-the-art ride elements to deliver the animated movie's key plot points, including the dramatic encounter with Monstro (shown).

Some of the special effects were derived from other attractions (the effect for the Blue Fairy is the same one that produces the **Haunted Mansion** ghosts), and some of the charming architectural details are borrowed from other buildings (the weathervane and colorful mural are reminiscent of others nearby). At least one new technical achievement debuted inside: the first appearance of a hologram in a Disneyland attraction, used here to transform boys into donkeys. As Jiminy Cricket declares in *Pinocchio*, "Whew! What they can't do these days!"

While not a major technological breakthrough, Pinocchio's Daring Journey is a pleasant trip worthy of the classic film. **Bill Justice**'s lovely **attraction poster** gets it right: "Wish Upon a Star and Relive Fantastic Adventures!"

Pin Trading Stations

DATES: April 2000–ongoing

To support fans who were already buying and trading souvenir pins, Pin Trading Stations—colorful carts in walkways or display cases in existing shops—started appearing throughout Disneyland in 2000. For the next decade, the conspicuous headquarters for pin traders was at the **Hub** in front of the **Plaza Pavilion**. Here, knowledgeable **cast members** made trades with pin pals, offered encouragement and suggestions, and sold accessories like pin cases and lanyards. Special promotions, such as Mickey's Pin Festival of Dreams in 2007 and the PinQuest scavenger hunt in 2016, brought with them some new limited-edition pins. While the Hub headquarters is no longer there, pins and accessories are still sold in many Disneyland shops.

Pirate's Arcade Museum

MAP: New Orleans Square, NOS-3

DATES: February 14, 1967–ca. 1980

The Pirate's Arcade Museum debuted in **New Orleans Square** a few weeks before its famous neighbor, **Pirates of the Caribbean**, was unveiled. Once both were open, dazzled guests leaving the landmark attraction found themselves next to the tempting pirate-themed Arcade Museum, which was much more an arcade than a museum. Most of the arcade games that filled the Pirate's Arcade Museum had pirate imagery worked into their theme and exterior design. Freebooter Shooter, for instance, required guests to blast away at tipsy pirates—a one-dimensional challenge, but all arcade games were simpler back then and only cost a dime to play. Elsewhere in the room, fans of Disney art could feed coins into a postcard machine that sold **Marc Davis**'s concept illustrations for Pirates of the Caribbean. Also available was a metal-stamping machine that created personalized, antique-looking coins.

Fortune Red, a pirate who dispensed fortune-telling cards, became one of the arcade's most enduring amusements. As shown in 2006's *Behind the Magic: 50 Years of Disneyland* exhibit at the Oakland Museum of California, Fortune Red was originally intended to be a full-size, full-body buccaneer with one leg and a parrot, just like Long John Silver from *Treasure Island*, but he ended up as just the upper half of a parrotless pirate. Along with the metal-stamper, Red is now at **Pieces of Eight**, the pirate-themed store that took over this space in 1980.

Pirate Ship Restaurant, aka Chicken of the Sea
Pirate Ship and Restaurant, aka Captain Hook's Galley

MAP: Fantasyland, Fa-14

DATES: August 29, 1955–August 29, 1982

Fans of pirates have always been able to find buccaneers inside Disneyland. The Peter Pan Flight attraction brought Captain Hook and the Pan clan into Disneyland in 1955; **Pirates of the Caribbean** added dozens of colorful swashbucklers in 1967; and

Tom Sawyer Island received Pirate's Lair modifications in 2007. Veteran parkgoers will recall another major pirate-themed destination, this one a restaurant that no longer exists. This nautical eatery is usually called the Pirate Ship Restaurant in early **souvenir books**, but because of its sponsor it was also known as the Chicken of the Sea Pirate Ship and Restaurant. Movie fans who recall Captain Hook from *Peter Pan* have to smile at a restaurant named Chicken of the Sea, seemingly referring to the spineless captain who quivers at the sound of ticking clocks.

The actual Chicken of the Sea, of course, is Starkist Tuna, the staple of the "light meals and snacks" menu that was presented here. Virtually everything—burgers, sandwiches, pot pies—had tuna in it (*"Tender* Tuna Cuts . . . served to you in delicious, different, tempting ways," according to an ad in the *Orange County Register* on July 15, 1955). Food was ordered at a counter within the ship's hull, and guests ate on benches facing a plain pond until 1960, when wooden-keg tables were added and the creepy **Skull Rock and Pirate's Cove** were built.

The real fun, though, was the big ship itself, which was built to look like an elegant, fully rigged frigate with a black hull, red-striped sails, and well-appointed decks that guests could tour. From the waterline to the tip of the main mast, the colorful ship towered approximately eighty feet, a height almost equal to the **Sailing Ship *Columbia*** in **Frontierland**. The Pirate Ship Restaurant was a **Fantasyland** landmark from 1955 until 1982, though it was rechristened as Captain Hook's Galley in 1969. In the early 1980s, there was talk of moving the Galley, Skull Rock, and Pirate's Cove over to the **Storybook Land Canal Boats** area. Unfortunately, water damage had eroded the ship's wooden hull, so it was finally dismantled during the Fantasyland remodel of 1982–1983.

The place where the ship, rock, and cove had been was filled in and given to the relocated **Dumbo** attraction. But the Pirate's Ship Restaurant has never really left Fantasyland; pieces of the old ship, and Captain Hook himself, can be seen inside **Peter Pan's Flight** nearby.

Pirates League

MAP: New Orleans Square, NOS-5; Frontierland, Fr-19

DATES: September 1, 2012–November 1, 2012; September 13, 2013–November 1, 2013; September 12, 2014–October 31, 2014

When the little **L'Ornement Magique** shop in **New Orleans Square** shuttered its doors in early 2012, it took eight months for something new to arrive in its place. What did they choose to replace the shop's delicate holiday decorations?

Pirates.

Starting on Labor Day weekend in 2012, Pirates League began offering pirate makeovers—an idea similar to the princess makeovers offered at the **Bibbidi Bobbidi**

Boutique in **Fantasyland**, but geared toward boys. Girls weren't excluded, however; after taking the pirate oath, anyone could be transformed into a swashbuckler with makeup, pirate accoutrements, and a new pirate name. Packages ran from $30 to $35 and celebrated not only the three *Pirates of the Caribbean* movies but also an animated TV series called *Jake and the Never Land Pirates*.

Having launched in 2009 in Orlando, Anaheim's Pirates League lasted only until November, when the shop reverted to seasonal holiday themes. Pirates League sailed back into the **Festival Arena** for another couple of autumn months in 2013 and 2014.

Pirates of the Caribbean

MAP: New Orleans Square, NOS-1

DATES: March 18, 1967–ongoing

Often regarded as Disneyland's best attraction, Pirates of the Caribbean was one of the last attractions **Walt Disney** worked on. It was also the first major attraction to open after he died at the end of 1966.

In the late 1950s, the **Imagineers** began to discuss opening a pirate museum in the park. In fact, Disneyland's 1958 **Fun Map** even depicts a Wax Museum approximately where the pirate boat ride would later be built. According to Charles Ridgway's book *Spinning Disney's World*, Walt Disney made his first public announcement about the pirate attraction at the opening ceremonies for **Nature's Wonderland** in 1960. A year later, the name Pirates of the Caribbean appeared with a preview in Disneyland's **souvenir book**. These early hints suggested that the attraction would be a walk-through "rogues gallery" displaying "famous pirates of the Spanish Main" and drunken buccaneers in a tavern.

Construction on something pirate-ish began in 1961, but the work was interrupted for at least two years so the company could concentrate on new exhibits for the 1964–1965 New York World's Fair. The 1963 souvenir book mentions an upgraded Pirates of the Caribbean presentation featuring a "Bayou voyage," but the book's moody painting of cutthroats studying a treasure map conveys nothing about the actual ride experience. The 1965 souvenir book describes how **Audio-Animatronic** pirates would "come to life" and "attack, burn and loot a city" in what "promises to be Disneyland's longest and most action-packed attraction." That same year, Walt Disney added more fuel to the fire

MOUSCELLANY

In *The Disneyland Book of Lists*, one of the lists is devoted to our unanswered questions about Pirates of the Caribbean. Here's one of those questions we've been pondering since we first rode in a Pirates of the Caribbean bateau in 1967: Why do some of the skeletons move as if they're alive, while others remain motionless? The talking skull at the first waterfall moves, and the skeleton steering a ship through a storm moves, but between them is a skeleton pinned to the wall by a sword, and he doesn't move. Shouldn't all the skeletons be dead— as in, motionless? Or, conversely, shouldn't they all move? Just wondering.

by showing off models of the coming attraction to a national TV audience on *Walt Disney's Wonderful World of Color*. While guests were excited for the opening of **New Orleans Square** in mid-1966, everyone was especially primed for the Pirates attraction, due the following spring. And they weren't disappointed.

Heralded by an official opening that featured the nearby **Sailing Ship** *Columbia* decked out with a Jolly Roger, the E-ticket Pirates of the Caribbean attraction was the culmination of creative and technological achievement in ride design. No other park in the world had anything nearly as sophisticated, and neither did Disneyland, for that matter. For the first time, Imagineers had implemented Audio-Animatronic humans on a grand scale. Previously, their A-A figures had been either relatively primitive mechanical animals (as in the **Jungle Cruise**) or a single person viewed from a distance (**Great Moments with Mr. Lincoln**). The Pirates cruise, however, presented seventy-five A-A humans and another fifty or so A-A pigs, donkeys, chickens, and dogs cavorting through realistic settings, all viewed from only a few yards away. The ride also included a trip through the bayou, two six-second drops down waterfalls, a raging storm, a fort and a life-size pirate ship lobbing cannonballs at each other, a town engulfed in flames, jailed pirates trying to entice a key away from a dog (shown on page 64), and a forty-five-second trip back *up* a waterfall. All of this was viewed from only a few yards away, and, even more incredibly, all of it was indoors.

The attraction was a tour de force of imagination and engineering. Park rides no longer had to be short and compact: this one is slow (about sixteen minutes long) and covers 1,800 feet of canals that hold 630,000 gallons of water only a couple feet deep. Plunging down two short waterfalls, the forty-six shallow boats traverse three levels. The route courses through two big buildings, one of them constructed across what was formerly **Magnolia Park**, and the other built outside Disneyland's perimeter **berm**, with both structures covering a total of over 2.5 acres. The cost to create what was the world's longest and most elaborate "dark ride"? Some $8 million in the mid-1960s, almost half of what it had cost to build the entire park a decade earlier.

The press and public immediately recognized the magnitude of Disney's monumental achievement. Souvenir books played up the revolutionary pirates with lavish photos and descriptive text. It was also one of only two attractions (**It's a Small World** was the other) to get its own lengthy souvenir booklet in the 1960s. TV audiences watched highlights from the attraction in 1968, which lured future guests and made those who had already seen the motley crew eager to experience the ride again. The attraction quickly became—and has remained—a perennial favorite for hundreds of

MOUSCELLANY

Before boarding their Pirates of the Caribbean bateaux, guests walk by seven murals featuring pirates both fictional and nonfictional. The seven: Anne Bonny with Mary Read (Irish, 1702–1782; English, 1685–1721); Captain Barbossa (fictional); Captain Jack Sparrow (fictional); Ned Low (English, 1690–1724); Captain Charles Gibbs (American, 1798–1831); Sir Henry Mainwaring (English, 1587–1653); and Sir Francis Verney (English, 1584–1615).

millions of guests of all ages, backgrounds, and tastes (Walt Disney Company chairman and CEO Robert Iger named it his favorite ride in an interview with the *L.A. Times* published on June 6, 2015).

Designed with scrupulous attention to detail, the attraction rewards repeat visitors. Precise detail was born out of necessity, of course, since about eighteen guests per bateau—over 2,800 guests per hour—are drifting, not racing, along the river, carefully analyzing everything they see: the moving clouds in the bayou section; the artwork on the scenery walls; the woodwork on the *Wicked Wench*; the pirates' bloodshot eyes; and on and on, until their arrival back at Laffite's Landing. On the *Disney Parks: Disneyland Resort Behind the Scenes* DVD, Disney Legend **Martin Sklar** calls it "the quintessential theme park show anywhere in the world; it has spectacle, it has story, it has great characters."

Even though the behavior on view has always seemed un-Disneylike—what with all the reckless pillaging, bride auctioning (shown), and heavy drinking—the attraction's rollicking spirit has negated any serious complaints about the pirates' debauchery. That spirit was created by a roster of designers and artists that now reads like a who's who of Disney's fabled Imagineers: artist **Marc Davis** generated hundreds of whimsical ideas and concept drawings for the ride; his wife, **Alice Davis,** made the costumes; **Richard Irvine** and **Claude Coats** oversaw the art direction and general design; sculptor **Blaine Gibson** made the models; **Roger Broggie**, **Fred Joerger**, and **Wathel Rogers** were the mechanical wizards behind the moving swashbucklers; **Bill**  **Martin** and **Yale Gracey** invented many of the special effects; **George Bruns** and **X. Atencio** created the instantly hummable "Yo Ho (A Pirate's Life for Me)" theme song (Atencio also wrote the attraction's script); and **Thurl Ravenscroft** and **Paul Frees** were among the vocal performers.

So revered is the attraction that longtime fans have been wary of even the smallest changes. The entrance was modified in 1987, and the attraction was closed for two months in 1997 to replace the pirates-chasing-women scenes with pirates-chasing-food scenes (Atencio, the writer mentioned above, joked that these changes made the attraction more like "Boy Scouts of the Caribbean"). This 1990s remodel also added a re-dedication plaque honoring "the original" in the outside **queue** area. Everything was shut down again in early 2006 for a June reopening that revealed a remixed soundtrack and new characters from the blockbuster *Pirates of the Caribbean* movies.

Celebrated over the years in books, films, merchandise, and exhibits, the cherished Pirates of the Caribbean ride has been duplicated in other Disney parks and enjoyed by hundreds of millions of people. It is still thriving as a supreme example of what intelligent theme park entertainment can be.

Pixie Hollow

MAP: Tomorrowland, T-1

DATES: October 28, 2008–ongoing

The same year she got her own movie, Tinker Bell got her own outdoor area in **Fantasyland**. The adorable Pixie Hollow stands approximately where the imposing **House of the Future and** bucolic **Alpine Gardens** used to be, between the entrance to **Tomorrowland** and **Sleeping Beauty Castle**.

Borrowing an idea from Tomorrowland's old **Adventure Thru Inner Space** attraction, Tink's cozy enchanted glen is filled with oversize objects to make guests feel that they themselves have shrunk in size. A giant teapot, for instance, serves as the fairy's home, surrounded by huge one-story flowers and mushrooms as big as chairs. Tinker Bell herself is regularly on hand for photos and autographs—the chance to meet Tink is a unique opportunity that had never been possible in any Disney Park before (according to the *Disney Parks: Disneyland Resort Behind the Scenes* DVD).

Pixie Hollow got a special winter overlay in 2012 when it welcomed a new fairy, Periwinkle.

> **MOUSCELLANY**
>
> When did Tinker Bell get so tiny? In the movie *Peter Pan*, she flies up to Peter and is as tall as his whole face—a height of maybe seven inches. She also barely fits inside Hook's lantern, again suggesting that she's six to eight inches tall. But in Pixie Hollow, she and the guests are dwarfed by blades of grass, reducing everybody to, what—half an inch tall?

Pixie Hollow Gift Cart

MAP: Tomorrowland, T-1

DATES: October 2008–Summer 2011

Young girls leaving **Pixie Hollow** were primed to buy sparkly merchandise, but alas, there was no gift shop located in the immediate area. To fill the void, the Pixie Hollow Gift Cart (as **cast members** called it) was wheeled in. Parked for almost three years at Pixie Hollow's exit, this elaborate, fairy-themed **outdoor vending cart** and its adjacent display sold dolls, wings, wands, wigs, towels, and gifts inspired by Tink and her fairy friends. A small face-painting enterprise took over this spot in mid-2011 and continues today under leafy umbrellas.

Plaza Gardens, aka Carnation Plaza Gardens

MAP: Hub, H-2

DATES: August 18, 1956–April 30, 2012

Dining and dancing were at their swingin'est at the Plaza Gardens. Located in the northwest corner of the **Hub**, this spacious half-acre site was also called the Carnation Plaza Gardens in deference to its sponsor.

Though it had a long history, the Plaza Gardens didn't date all the way back to **Opening Day**. That honor went to the old **bandstand**, which had occupied the spot from July 1955 until the following summer. As the bandstand's concerts became popular, **Walt Disney** decided to relocate it to **Frontierland** and build a new dance pavilion in its place to keep guests staying and playing after dark.

The result was an old-fashioned wooden building with outdoor tables and a red-striped canopy above the stage and dance area. Guests entered from the Hub by crossing a footbridge spanning a small pond. Passersby could see and hear the live entertainment, making the events here more inviting. A side counter offered cheeseburgers, fries, and ice cream desserts. Occasionally the menu offered items for special events, such as 1969's I Scream Sundaes that celebrated the new **Haunted Mansion**.

More memorable than the menu, however, was the entertainment. Classic swing bands were the traditional performers ("tried and true favorites for Mom and Dad," boasts Disneyland's 1965 **souvenir book**). Walt Disney himself was photographed dancing out on the floor. Other shows included **Date Nite** concerts with the Date Niters in the late 1950s and early '60s, the Cavalcade of Bands concerts beginning in 1962, and the televised Big Bands at Disneyland shows of 1984 with, among others, the Glenn Miller and Count Basie orchestras. The Donny-less Osmond Brothers also appeared here in 1961.

> **MOUSCELLANY**
>
> Fantasy Faire offers a nod to the former Plaza Gardens location: conspicuously displayed on one of its steeples are the gilded initials "CPG" (shown).

In the 1990s, the Plaza Gardens began hosting small stage shows, including *The Enchanted Book Shoppe* (1991–1992) and *The Little Mermaid and Her Secret Grotto* (1997–1998). After the summer of 1998, the Plaza Gardens closed for a remodeling, reopening a year later with a wall of **attraction posters** in the back and a new Jump, Jive, Boogie Swing Party that was sometimes held four times a night. Small live concerts, often featuring school bands and choirs, were held here some afternoons, but the under-utilized venue seemed like a relic of a stylish past. Food service stopped with the turn of the century, and a wide doorway at the back was opened up for quick access to Frontierland.

Disneyland's future, it turned out, didn't include the Plaza Gardens. In 2011, plans were announced to transform the site into a new fairytale village. After some nostalgic last nights, the Plaza Gardens finally closed on April 30, 2012, to make way for **Fantasy Faire**, which arrived in March of 2013.

Plaza Inn, aka Red Wagon Inn

MAP: Hub, H-3

DATES: July 17, 1955–ongoing

Supposedly, **Walt Disney** preferred the posh Red Wagon Inn over any other Disneyland restaurant. In the 1950s, it offered the park's priciest dining experience and was so elegant that it even got its own **attraction poster**, which mentions the restaurant's air conditioning and its adult dinners starting at $2.35. Photos of the Red Wagon Inn's white-trimmed Edwardian exterior made it into all of Disneyland's early **souvenir books**, their captions touting "tempting meals in the beautiful surroundings of Grandfather's day."

The Red Wagon's name derived from the logo of its sponsor, Swift & Company, which also debuted two other Disneyland locations, the **Market House** and the **Chicken Plantation**, in 1955. The full-service Red Wagon offered full-course breakfasts, lunches, and dinners in glitzy, antique-filled rooms lit by crystal chandeliers. It also had a terrace for alfresco dining. Inside the Red Wagon, various furnishings (such as the gingerbread woodwork and marble foyer) were salvaged from an opulent Victorian mansion located in the St. James Park area near downtown Los Angeles.

When Swift ended its sponsorship in July of 1965, the restaurant got a new name, the Plaza Inn, and a new sponsor, the Columbian Coffee Growers. A 1998 renovation kept the plush Victorian interior but introduced some new menu items, including a prix fixe breakfast with omelets, Mickey-shaped waffles, and the company of Disney characters. Special birthday celebrations were also held here until March of 2013. Today, the hearty fare includes pasta, gourmet salads, and fancy desserts, but what the Plaza Inn is really known for is its acclaimed chicken dinner; this house specialty presents three pieces of golden-fried chicken, mashed potatoes, a vegetable medley, and a biscuit in one big $17 meal. More expensive are the slow-roasted pot roast and the Fresh Catch of the Day. All of these can be enjoyed at the two-dozen indoor tables and the 100-plus tables outside, a total seating capacity of over 500 guests.

The Plaza Inn, incidentally, is the third Plaza-named restaurant in the immediate area—across the way are the **Plaza Pavilion** and the **Plaza Gardens**. Of this trio, the Plaza Inn is the only one on the **Tomorrowland** side of the **Hub**.

MOUSCELLANY

Unbeknownst to most guests in the 1950s and early '60s, the Red Wagon had a private room with its own entrance for Walt Disney and his VIP guests. This alcohol-serving area was a precursor to the exclusive **Club 33** in **New Orleans Square**.

Plaza Pavilion Restaurant,
aka Stouffer's in Disneyland Plaza Pavillion

MAP: Hub, H-1

DATES: July 17, 1955–July 1998

The lovely, Victorian-style Plaza Pavilion was an architectural gem in the southwest corner of the **Hub**. In the 1950s, the structure was linked to **Adventureland** more than the Hub; it is listed in the early **souvenir books** as the Pavillion in the Adventureland section. Although guests entered the eatery from the side facing the Hub, they carried their pasta, gourmet sandwiches, fried chicken, and salads on cafeteria-style trays through the restaurant and out the other side to a patio situated above

the banks of the **Jungle Cruise**. Interestingly, the two exterior décor styles still meet in the middle of the building's roof; depending on the angle they're facing, guests see either the Hub's turn-of-the-century cut shingles or Adventureland's tropical thatch.

In 1962, the restaurant got an unwieldy new name, Stouffer's in Disneyland Plaza Pavillion, and that back patio became the Stouffer's in Disneyland Tahitian Terrace. By 1965, the Stouffer's reference had been dropped and the Plaza Pavilion had reverted back to its original name (Stouffer's began sponsoring the **French Market** instead). By 1995, the Plaza Pavilion's sponsor was Contadina, makers of Italian sauces, so the menu emphasized Italian dishes.

Even in its heyday, the Plaza Pavilion was only open on weekends, holidays, and days when Disneyland had high **attendance**. The building closed as a restaurant in 1997, though it was still marked as the Plaza Pavilion outside. For the first decade of the 2000s, it served as the Annual Passport Processing Center where guests received their year-long **Passports**. The building also occasionally hosted the Junior Chef Baking Experience (during which kids donned toques and baked cookies). Outside, the porch facing the Hub frequently featured a ragtime piano player borrowed from Coke's **Refreshment Corner** next door, and the patio dining area hosted a large **Pin Trading Station** from 2000 to 2010. The walkway in front of the building still hosts the information board where guests can find **parade** schedules, attraction wait-times, and more.

None of these functions, unfortunately, tapped into the full potential of what used to be a memorable dining experience. In 2012, dining finally returned to the building when it was transformed into the new **Jolly Holiday Bakery Café**.

Pluto's Dog House

MAP: Mickey's Toontown, MT-8

DATES: January 24, 1993–ongoing

Several restaurants in Disneyland history have been given humorous names (**Lunching Pad**, for instance). The niftiest word play might be Pluto's Dog House, a little snack counter in the heart of **Mickey's Toontown** that, naturally, serves up hot dogs. The Dog House offers foot-long dogs for adults and smaller versions for kids, supplemented by extras like chili, chips, and sodas. Dog-shaped desserts and alfresco dining tables help on-the-go guests develop a case of puppy love.

Police Station

MAP: Town Square, TS-3

DATES: July 17, 1955–ongoing

The first brick building guests walk past when they enter the park through Disneyland's west tunnel and the last one they'll see before they go, the Police Station is one of three "official city buildings" lined up along the western side of **Town Square**. The one-story structure is the smallest of the three (**City Hall** is the big building next door), but it's just as handsome as the others, constructed of red brick and decorated with a yellow balustrade and cream-colored columns. Immediately to the south is the flower-filled Guided Tour Garden, where **Tour Guides** gather their guests.

Despite its name, the Police Station has never been the headquarters for Disneyland's security personnel. A free map handed out to guests in 1955 shows Security Headquarters in City Hall. Similarly, the 1956 **souvenir book** identifies City Hall as home base to "45 Security Officers" who were "employed on a full-time basis at Disneyland with eight others on call to protect the Park and its guests." Within a few years, the security officers were moved to another building behind Town Square, out of public view (guests with security concerns are still directed to City Hall). Often Disneyland's security staff, working undercover to catch shoplifters and vandals, is as invisible to guests as the security building is.

The Police Station, meanwhile, was actually home to the publicity department, which needed to be near the **entrance** to greet the media. At one time, the front of the building also served as the designated rendezvous for lost guests. A 2001 brochure handed out at Disneyland identifies a kiosk outside the Police Station as the American Automobile Association's Touring & Travel Services Center, where guests could pick up AAA maps, arrange flat-tire repair, and more. A big Guided Tours sign came off the Police Station in November 2012, and lately there's been no official designation on the building.

Pony Farm, aka Circle D Corral

MAP: Park, P-17

DATES: July 17, 1955–January 10, 2016

For over sixty years, all the horses, mules, and ponies that were worked, ridden, petted, and paraded in Disneyland were trained at the park's Pony Farm, originally located on about ten acres beyond the **berm** at the back of **Frontierland**. In addition to stables for the horses, the Pony Farm also had a barn and a carpentry shop. In 1980, the Pony Farm was renamed the Circle D Corral. A decade later, the acreage was cut in half and the corral was also relocated farther west to make room for **Mickey's Toontown**.

There was far more equine activity in Disneyland's first decade than there is now. Back then, horses pulled **Conestoga Wagons**, the **Stage Coach**, and several **Main Street Vehicles**. Shetland ponies stood in the **Miniature Horse Corral**, and a **Mule Pack** trekked the Frontierland trails. Most of these attractions closed within a few years, but several horses can still be seen every day on **Main Street** pulling old-fash-ioned streetcars.

Even when there were many attractions at Disneyland that required horses, none of the animals ever had more than part-time employment. According to the 1956 **souvenir book**, "Disneyland horses punch time cards. No horse is allowed to work over four hours per day or six days a week." These days, that six-day workweek has most likely been reduced to four days (the horses, evidently, have a pretty strong union). Some of the horses are rarely used at all—the Lipizzans, for instance, are presented mainly during the **holiday season** and for special wedding events.

Horses were not the only residents at the Pony Farm/Circle D Corral—their train-ers lived there, too. The horses were originally raised by two people who were Dis-neyland's only full-time live-in residents: horse trainers Owen and Dolly Pope, who began working for **Walt Disney** in the early 1950s. Back then, they were building Western-style carriages and acquiring the horses Disney would need for the small park he was originally planning to build next to his Burbank movie studio. Later, the Popes settled into a 1,300-square-foot bungalow on the Anaheim property, and moved their 200+ animals into the Pony Farm's corrals.

The Popes found that one of their main challenges was to get their charges used to distractions. Sudden noises—**Jungle Cruise** gunfire, the *Mark Twain* whis-tle, etc.—are heard all day without warning. To acclimate the animals to Disney-land, the Popes played tapes of shouting voices, a shooting gallery, and other loud sounds. Furthermore, they trained the horses to handle the over-friendly crowds that still rush up close to them for photographs (veteran guests know that polite photo requests made to the operators are almost always accommodated). The Popes also took care of the swans that glided through the water in front of **Sleeping Beauty Castle**.

After getting the Pony Farm up and running successfully, the Popes later left to perform the same function at Walt Disney World before they both retired in 1975. Back in Anaheim, the job of caring for Disney-land's animals was covered by a group of han-dlers, who also took on the farm animals for the petting zoo at **Big Thunder Ranch**. The handlers have become experts in another area, too: recy-cling. In April 2015, the Environmental Protection Agency gave the Disneyland Resort an award for its recycling and donation efforts. One of its noted accomplishments was recycling 99.8 percent of the waste generated by the Circle D's animals.

In early 2016, with the **Star Wars Land** proj-ect underway, the Circle D Corral was closed per-manently. Most of the animals were moved away to Southern California ranches; the horses, still used on **Main Street**, are now being cared for at a near-by off-site location, with trailers bringing them to Disneyland every day.

MOUSCELLANY

With Star Wars Land moving in, Disneyland horse trainers Owen and Dolly Pope's former home at the park (which had been transformed into office space) has now been moved to a parking lot north of Disneyland, which is still on Disney property. The structure is now used for administrative purposes.

Pooh Corner

MAP: Bear Country/Critter Country, B/C-5

DATES: April 11, 2003–ongoing

Guests eager to buy bear necessities should head straight to Pooh Corner, Disneyland's Winnie the Pooh headquarters. A smaller Pooh shop operated in this big building in the late 1990s, and its success let to a massive remodeling that was fully realized in 2003. Pooh Corner fills the large **Critter Country** building where the **Brer Bar**, **Crocodile Mercantile**, and **Teddi Barra's Swingin' Arcade** all used to be.

For over a decade, the 120-foot-long building has had three entrances, and has been divided into thirds. The end closest to **Splash Mountain** offers all the stuffed toys, mugs, cookie jars, and infant clothes any Pooh fan could ever want. The middle room is flush with plush, and the far-right room is filled with enticing candy. Like the **Candy Palace** on **Main Street**, there's a big window looking into this room where guests can watch candymakers shape, swirl, frost, drizzle, sugar, and creatively decorate indulgent Pooh-themed treats, including a Hunny Pot Candy Apple and an orange-and-black Tigger Tail Marshmallow Wand.

With its adorable Pooh-filled interior, detailed corner displays, and all the fun things floating from the ceiling, the store is decorated like something out of the Hundred-Acre Wood. Just outside the shop is Pooh's Thotful Spot, a character-greeting area where guests can take photos with the bear himself.

Popcorn Carts

Disneyland's early **souvenir books** usually feature photos of an old-fashioned red popcorn wagon parked in **Town Square**. Instantly nostalgia-inducing and inviting,

the unmissable carts have always been irresistible. These days, around ten carts selling popcorn and sodas are scattered throughout Disneyland (the number varies with **attendance**). In 2016, a box of popcorn cost $4.25.

Like the **trash cans** and **restrooms** throughout the park, the popcorn carts are often decorated with themes that match their respective areas. These themes apply both to the carts' colorful exteriors and to their glass display cases. A new cart introduced to **Tomorrowland** in the summer of 2015, for instance, sells its Terrestrial Treats from a white wagon topped with sculptures evoking the crown on **Space Mountain** (shown on page 395).

Additional theming continues inside each cart's glass case, where a small mechanical figure turns a hand crank. In the 1950s, these figures were all clowns, but now they wear about a dozen different costumes. Depending on what attractions are nearby, one of the figures might be a creepy **Haunted Mansion** butler, an explorer, a train conductor, or another costumed character. Officially called Popcorn Animation Dolls, these figures are affectionately nicknamed Roastie Toasties.

So familiar and fun are the popcorn carts that even their popcorn boxes have been celebrated. Ceramic versions of Disneyland's classic blue-and-white-striped popcorn boxes went on sale in the **Disney Gallery** in 2010. The popcorn itself was formerly Orville Redenbacher's, but has been Pop Secret as of mid-2015.

> **MOUSCELLANY**
>
> The 2015 Tomorrowland popcorn cart debuted a new Roastie Toastie: a blond **Space Girl** in a shiny astronaut costume (shown).

Port d'Orleans

MAP: New Orleans Square, NOS-5

DATES: Ca. 1995–2002

Part of what used to be the old **Le Gourmet** shop at the back of **New Orleans Square** became a smaller, cooking-related shop in the mid-1990s. Disneyland's 2000 **souvenir book** calls Port d'Orleans "a lively mart that features items imported directly from Louisiana, such as a variety of spicy Cajun sauces, beignet mixes, and coffees with chicory." A remodel in 1999 supplemented the coffees and sauces with lots of souvenirs from **the Haunted Mansion** and other nearby attractions. **Le Bat en Rouge** flew into this space in 2002.

Portrait Artists

MAP: New Orleans Square, NOS-5, NOS-6

DATES: Ca. 1986–ongoing

At different times, portrait artists have graced the **Opera House** in **Town Square**, the **Art Corner** in **Tomorrowland**, and the eastern side of **Center Street**. In *Window on Main Street*, **Van France** writes that **Jack Olsen** had the original idea to bring artists into Disneyland to draw quick, lucrative caricatures of the guests.

Today, portrait artists add a graceful touch to several Disneyland locations. In **New Orleans Square**, the artists often sit with their easels behind the **French Market**, though they can also be found opposite the **Blue Bayou** on Royal Street. On **Main Street**, artists set up shop by the **Market House**, usually lining the north side of Center Street with **Disney Clothiers, Ltd.** at their backs. Rubio Arts manages all of these artists, as well as the illustrators at the nearby **Parasol Cart**.

Depending on the artist, guests may sit for an individual profile or a face-on rendering. They can pick pastels or watercolors, and choose whether they want representational art or a caricature. Scenes from New Orleans Square are usually included in the backgrounds of portraits created at that location.

Port Royal

MAP: New Orleans Square, NOS-3

DATES: 2006–ongoing

In 2006, the spot next to the **Royal Street Veranda** that had been **Le Bat en Rouge** became Port Royal, a name referring to both the street outside and the location popularized in the *Pirates of the Caribbean* movies. Historically, Port Royal was the Jamaican home of many seventeenth-century buccaneers and became known as the world's wickedest town.

At Disneyland, Port Royal's merchandise, advertised above the doorway as "curios and curiosities," was at first piratical and souvenir-ish, with a working doubloon-pressing machine on display. However, by mid-2014, merchandise from **the Haunted Mansion** was encroaching on the pirate clothes, hats, and jewelry sold here. Timed with that 1969 attraction's forty-fifth anniversary, the new items matched Port Royal's new décor, which included cobwebs, a funeral cart, display racks shaped like tombstones, and a wall display devoted to the magnificent mansion.

> **MOUSCELLANY**
>
> Disneyland's portrait artists have been so popular and durable that they were affectionately parodied in 2015 by the artist Banksy when he opened Dismaland, his Disneyland-inspired "bemusement park" in England. His portrait artists sketched accurate likenesses of the *backs* of people's heads.

Premiere Shop

MAP: Tomorrowland, T-6

DATES: 1963–2005

The Premiere Shop spent four busy decades in the center of all the **Tomorrowland** action. While not as big as the **Character Shop** (now **Star Trader**) nearby, the Premiere Shop was still an appealing shopping destination. It sold California- and sports-themed merchandise into the 1990s, but eventually its shelves were restocked with Disneyland-related clothes and gifts.

In the twenty-first century, the Premiere Shop focused more on pin and lanyard sales. The shop was also supplemented by several cool kiosks. The Disneyland Forever kiosks offered stations where guests could burn their own ten-track CDs with a broad selection of Disney songs, sounds from Disneyland attractions, and other auditory gems. At the Art on Demand kiosks, guests could buy Disney artwork.

Little Green Men Store Command replaced the Premiere Shop in 2005, the same year that **Buzz Lightyear Astro Blasters** landed next door.

Price, Harrison
(1921–2010)

Harrison "Buzz" Price was born in 1921 in Oregon, raised in San Diego, and educated at Pasadena's California Institute of Technology. After serving in the air force and working in Peru for three years in the late 1940s, Price returned to California to get his graduate degree from Stanford. In 1952, he joined the Stanford Research Institute, and soon he was consulting on Disneyland.

Back then, Disneyland was just a drawing on paper, and **Walt Disney** was scouring the Greater Los Angeles area for a suitable construction site. He knew the region was perfect—it boasted warm weather, its five-county population was immense, and his movie studio was already located there—but exactly where he should build his park in those 4,000 square miles was still unclear.

Price, a top business consultant whom Disney treated with "paternal affection" (according to the book *Remembering Walt*), is the man who found Anaheim for him. He spent three months studying potential Disneyland locations, among them the west San Fernando Valley (deemed too hot), downtown L.A. (too expensive), and Palos Verdes and the beach communities (too inaccessible). Price narrowed his search to 150 square miles between L.A. and Orange County, and he then identified the ten best available parcels of land in that area. In his report, finalized on August 28, 1953, a 160-acre spread in Anaheim got the top ranking over three other nearby towns—Buena Park, La Mirada, and Santa Ana.

It was not an obvious choice. Anaheim, Orange County's oldest incorporated city, was at the time a sleepy agricultural area—nothing like what it is now, a crowded city among Orange County's endless conurbations. Anaheim also seemed unreasonably far from glamorous Hollywood and other familiar tourist areas. What's more, back then most West Coast amusement parks were built along scenic Pacific Ocean beaches, including eight between San Diego and Santa Monica. So Price was bucking tradition with his inland selection.

After careful consideration, Price declared that within a few decades, a map of Southern California's spreading population would show Anaheim at the center (an amazing prediction—the actual center ended up being in Fullerton, just one town over and only four miles away). Growth in Orange County, Price felt, would continue as it had in the 1940s and early '50s, when its population had almost doubled. He was right again—Orange County's population surged upwards by a third from 1955 to 1956, and Anaheim's population of 14,000 multiplied by seven (to 104,000) during the 1950s (in 2011, it had reached 300,000). Price also recognized that an unfinished north–south freeway project, Interstate 5, would soon pass right through Anaheim, putting the city within easy reach of millions of drivers. He learned that with an annual rainfall averaging only an inch a month, Anaheim stayed drier than L.A. County,

MOUSCELLANY

Harrison Price was so influential that, in 1994, he won the Themed Entertainment Association's first-ever Lifetime Achievement Award (an award now named after him).

and its Mediterranean climate offered milder year-round temperatures (winter highs average in the mid-60s with lows in the upper 40s, while summer highs average in the mid-80s with lows in the mid-60s). Plus, there was plenty of flat, undeveloped, and relatively cheap land available at under $5,000 per acre. For all these reasons, Harrison Price recommended that Walt Disney build Disneyland in freeway-close, financially friendly Anaheim. History, of course, soon proved that this was the right choice.

Three years later, with Disneyland a stunning success, Price formed his own consulting company, Economics Research Associates (ERA), and continued doing research for various Disney projects. In the 1960s, he studied various locations for a "second Disneyland" that would be more convenient to the eastern half of the country. Among the locations he and Walt Disney visited and seriously considered were New Jersey, St. Louis, and the Florida site that ultimately became Walt Disney World. Price also evaluated the Mineral King ski resort in California that was eventually abandoned (the "number-one disappointment" of his career, he said), made recommendations for one of Disney's pet projects, the CalArts campus in Southern California, and even advised Disney to buy a company plane to expedite his many travels.

After selling ERA, Price formed another company in 1978, Harrison Price Company (HPC). For the next two decades, he continued to research new business developments; among the many clients he served over his long career were the Six Flags parks, Knott's Berry Farm, Universal Studios, IMAX theaters, the World's Fairs in Seattle and New York, NASA, famous restaurant chains, major aquariums, and Las Vegas mega-hotels. Price's autobiography, *Walt's Revolution! By the Numbers*, came out in 2003, the same year he was inducted as a Disney Legend.

Price died in 2010 at age eighty-nine, and three years later he was posthumously awarded a **Main Street Tribute Window**.

Primeval World Diorama

MAP: Tomorrowland, T-17

DATES: July 1, 1966–ongoing

About eight years after the **Grand Canyon Diorama** was added along the **Santa Fe & Disneyland Railroad** track, the Primeval World Diorama joined the line. As the train circles Disneyland and rounds the perimeter of **Tomorrowland**, it enters a tunnel (shown) where guests first see the Grand Canyon diorama, followed by one for the Primeval World. This second diorama extends about 500 feet (a little longer than the Grand Canyon's diorama) and ends about 300 feet from the **Main Street** station. The combined tunnel experience lasts approximately three and a half minutes.

While the Grand Canyon Diorama transports train guests to another location, the Primeval World Diorama transports them to another time—the age of dinosaurs, as it's depicted in the dramatic *Rite of Spring* sequence in *Fantasia*. That film's narrator, Deems Taylor, introduces this twenty-two-minute section as "a pageant . . . the story of the growth of life on Earth. It's a coldly accurate reproduction" featuring dinosaurs of "all shapes and sizes, from little crawling horrors . . . to hundred-ton nightmares."

Disneyland delivers on those same precepts with its own "coldly accurate reproduction" that presents dinosaurs of various shapes and sizes, dinosaur bones, and a savage fight to the death. At slow speed, the train crawls past over two-dozen extinct creatures, some fifteen feet tall, and all depicted in a prehistoric world. Gigantic brontosaurus necks rise out of a swamp, mouths munching on vegetation. A pterodactyl gazes down from atop a rock. Raptor-esque reptiles sip from a pond. Triceratops babies wriggle out of their eggs. The most memorable encounter (which is shown on the **Claude Coats**-designed

> **MOUSCELLANY**
>
> Savvy guests who are short on time know they can catch the Primeval World Diorama attraction by boarding a train in nearby Tomorrowland for a quick jaunt back to the primeval past. Invigorated by the time travel and dazzled by the dinosaurs, guests emerge ready to hit Disneyland's exit and brave the modern world beyond the turnstiles.

attraction poster and in photos in Disneyland's **souvenir books**) comes when the towering twenty-two-foot-tall tyrannosaurus—"the worst of the lot, a brute . . . probably the meanest killer that ever roamed the Earth," according to *Fantasia*—attacks a formidable stegosaurus, a powerful scene straight out of the movie. Interestingly, although Disneyland's Primeval World is based on the Stravinsky section of the movie, the stirring music in the background isn't Stravinsky's—it's Bernard Herrmann's, from his score for *Mysterious Island*, a 1961 adventure film made by Columbia Pictures.

Cavemen, who didn't appear in *Fantasia*, are not included in the diorama. However, they were originally part of the attraction when Disney designers first created it for the Ford pavilion at the 1964–1965 New York World's Fair. **Walt Disney** deemed the fair's **Audio-Animatronic** humanoids too rudimentary in their design and execution for inclusion at Disneyland, especially when compared to his much more sophisticated **Great Moments with Mr. Lincoln** figure (cavemen wouldn't have been historically accurate in this diorama, since they followed the dinosaurs' extinction by tens of millions of years).

Princess Boutique

MAP: Fantasyland, Fa-3
DATES: Ca. 1997–2005

Guests have had many chances at Disneyland to buy gifts for the princesses in their lives. For about eight years, one of these shops was located on the western side of the entrance to **Sleeping Beauty Castle**. Like most of the young clientele shopping giddily there, the Princess Boutique was small and pretty, with lots of pink, lots of irresistible dresses, and lots of costume jewelry on display. In 2005, the room was turned into the **50th Anniversary Shop** for Disneyland's golden anniversary celebration.

Princess Fantasy Faire

MAP: Fantasyland, Fa-18

DATES: November 2006–August 12, 2012

After *Snow White: An Enchanting Musical* closed at the Videopolis/**Fantasyland Theatre** in 2006, the large performance space at the back of **Fantasyland** was transformed into a Nestlé-sponsored character greeting area "where happily ever after happens every day." Under a tent roof displaying a starry "sky," and on a stage decorated as a castle, throne, and forest, Disney royalty began making frequent appearances.

Many different activities were held on the grounds. In the Royal Crafts area, guests could have their hair braided and faces painted, as well as shop for Princess merchandise. A Royal Coronation Ceremony and Storytelling with Disney Princesses were also offered. The most popular activity of all was the Disney Princess Royal Walk, where guests lingered with movie characters "along an enchanted pathway." The photo opportunities generated long lines of pint-sized princesses and their camera-clicking parents. In 2009, some Faire activities were curtailed to make room for even more close-ups with the princesses.

To make way for a remodeled Fantasyland Theatre, on August 12, 2012, the Princess Fantasy Faire closed, and the next day the princesses relocated their meet-and-greets to the terraced viewing area in front of **It's a Small World**. This temporary area closed with the opening of a new meet-and-greet village, **Fantasy Faire**, in March of 2013.

Professor Barnaby Owl's Photographic Art Studio

MAP: Bear Country/Critter Country, B/C-8

DATES: January 31, 1992–ongoing

Many guests stop to look at the photos on view here at the back of **Critter Country**, but few guests know Professor Barnaby Owl's legacy. The knowledgeable character appears in two classic *Adventures in Music* cartoons of the 1950s: *Melody* and the Oscar-winning *Toot, Whistle, Plunk and Boom* (he's also in Disney SingAlong Songs videos from the 1980s and '90s).

The photos displayed in the good professor's Art Studio are action shots snapped as guests began their plunge down the **Splash Mountain** log flume. The sudden realization of what's about to happen—a fifty-two-foot drop, presumably into a briar patch—usually brings interesting expressions to guests' faces. The Art Studio displays all the photos captured in the last few minutes and offers printed versions for immediate sale in a cardboard frame (when this service debuted at Disneyland, it was the first time in any Disney park that on-the-attraction action shots were sold at the at-

traction's exit). As of September 2014, guests could also pay to download the images to their smart phones.

Puffin Bakery, aka Puffin Bake Shop

MAP: Main Street, MS-6

DATES: July 18, 1955–June 3, 1960

Had it been ready one day earlier, the Puffin Bakery would have been one of the charter businesses to debut on **Opening Day.** Even though it did miss out on this opportunity, the Puffin Bakery (also called the Puffin Bake Shop in old **souvenir books**) enjoyed nearly a five-year run near the **Penny Arcade** on the western side of **Main Street**. When the baked goods shop finally went flat in 1960, the **Sunkist Citrus House** moved in. The spot was reverted back to a bake shop when the **Blue Ribbon Bakery** took over for most of the '90s. Today, the **Gibson Girl Ice Cream Parlor** serves up tasty treats here.

Quasimodo's Attic, aka Sanctuary of Quasimodo

MAP: Fantasyland, Fa-30

DATES: June 13, 1996–February 9, 1997

In mid-1996, Quasimodo's Attic replaced the five-year-old **Disney Villains** shop in **Fantasyland**. This prominent location in the **Sleeping Beauty Castle** courtyard presented Quasimodo merchandise to help promote that year's *The Hunchback of Notre Dame* film. (Simultaneously, two other *Hunchback*-themed locations opened over in **Frontierland**—**Big Thunder Ranch Barbecue** became the Festival of Foods, and **Big Thunder Ranch** became the Festival of Fools.)

By summer's end, Quasimodo's Attic had changed its name to Sanctuary of Quasi-modo. And by winter's end, with the *Hunchback* juggernaut subsiding, the Quasimodo shop closed permanently, its location to be filled six months later by another medieval store, the **Knight Shop**.

Queues

Imagine first-time visitors seeing young Disneyland in the 1950s and '60s. Back then, queues at fairs, amusement parks, sporting events, and movie theaters always seemed to stretch inefficiently and unimaginatively in one long, boring straight line that blocked walkways and entrances to other rides and restaurants. One of the features these novice visitors would have instantly appreciated at Disneyland was its clever management of long lines. Today's guests take for granted the park's distinctive queues because they are now so widely used in myriad industries. But in Disneyland's early years, switchback queues were more than just a novelty—they were a great innovation.

In his book *Designing Disney*, **John Hench** calls poorly designed queues "a major design problem" resulting in "irritable, disappointed guests." To fight pedestrian traffic jams and wait-line fatigue, Imagineers created unique switchback queues. Waiting in a line that doubles back upon itself, guests are usually in slow, steady motion, so they don't get completely bored or sore from standing still for long durations. When the queue winds around corners (as in the **Indiana Jones Adventure**), guests don't always know how far they are from the head of the line, and thus they aren't immediately discouraged by the sight of a distant boarding area. Also, as the lines snake back and forth, guests are presented with an ever-changing parade of approaching faces. Some queues also ameliorate a waiting guest's discomfort by providing shade, drinking fountains, entertaining videos (as with the modern **Autopia**), and helpful signs that display wait-times.

Most of Disneyland's queues actually amplify guests' anticipation for an attraction. Because guests are kept in the vicinity of the attraction they're waiting for, the close proximity offers abundant opportunities for themed decorations tied to the attraction. For instance, the fascinating façade and elaborate clock in front of **It's a Small World** are brilliant extensions of the cruise experience. The comical garage interior that precedes **Roger Rabbit's Car Toon Spin** introduces various characters and terms but also entertains with a riot of gags. The elaborate queue for the **Jungle Cruise** includes historical material that helps put guests in the mood for some old-fashioned adventure. At **Snow White's Scary Adventures**, the creepy queue readies guests for the scares to come and serves as a test for kids—if they can handle the queue, they can handle the ride. The opposite strategy is used at the **Haunted Mansion** where, instead of preparing guests for upcoming frights, the queue allays apprehensions with displays of humorous tombstones, as if to say that the mansion's interior won't be nearly as terrifying as it could be. These are just a few examples of what the best queues do: work creatively as integral parts of the attractions themselves.

Radio Disney Broadcast Booth

MAP: Tomorrowland, T-8

DATES: March 1, 1999–December 2002

The first radio station near Disneyland was KEZY, an AM station for easy-listening music. Back in the late 1950s, KEZY was run out of a small studio in the Disneyland Hotel. Some forty years later, the station was transformed into the local Radio Disney station, which began operating out of a small, glass-walled booth in the middle of **Tomorrowland**. Disney deejays and broadcast electronics occupied a room underneath the old **PeopleMover** loading platform, a space formerly used for the **Lunching Pad**. As Disneyland's 2000 **souvenir book** explained, "Through soundproof glass, guests can view Radio Disney's state-of-the-art radio studio and watch daily live broadcasts carried across the nation on 'the radio network just for kids'."

Begun in 1996, the Radio Disney Network is still on the air, but Disneyland's own Radio Disney Broadcast Booth went silent in late 2002. In 2006, **Tomorrowlanding** landed where the booth had been.

Rafts to Tom Sawyer Island

MAP: Frontierland, Fr-11

DATES: June 16, 1956–ongoing

Guests could see **Tom Sawyer Island** in 1955, but they couldn't access it until mid-1956. That's when the D-ticket Rafts to Tom Sawyer Island began operating their regular service between a dock on **Frontierland's** riverbank and another one on the island's southern tip about 100 feet away. The following summer, a second Frontierland dock close to the **Indian Village** opened up to accommodate more guests; rafts from that northerly dock delivered passengers to the island's midsection until 1971.

No matter which location guests used, the service was about the same, with some forty or so passengers at a time making the one-minute trip at about four miles per hour. Since the island closes at sundown, the crossing is still only made during daylight hours. The rafts do not run on underwater tracks and are instead controlled by **cast members** carefully working the vessels' throttles and tillers.

The old-fashioned rafts and their promotional materials are designed to appear roughly made. For instance, the hand-painted dock sign that announces rules about strollers and smoking has some of its letters printed backwards. The rustic Tom Sawyer Island **attraction poster** depicts a log raft reminiscent of the one used for the Mississippi River escape in *Adventures of Huckleberry Finn* (the poster shows an unfurled, breeze-filled sail, but at Disneyland the sails are kept wrapped up and the rafts are powered by diesel engines).

The raft names once alluded to Mark Twain's literary heroes and heroines—*Huck Finn*, *Injun Joe*, *Becky Thatcher*, and *Tom Sawyer*. In 2007, the old rafts were replaced by slightly bigger versions, and the *Huck*, *Joe*, and *Becky* rafts were renamed *Blackbeard*, *Anne Bonny*, and *Captain Kidd* to echo the island's new pirate theme.

Railroad, aka Santa Fe & Disneyland Railroad, aka Disneyland Railroad

MAP: Town Square, TS-1

DATES: July 17, 1955–ongoing

Before there was a railroad at Disneyland, there was the little Carolwood Pacific in **Walt Disney's** backyard. With the help of Disney Legends **Roger Broggie** and **Wathel Rogers**, Walt Disney built the one-eighth-scale train behind his house in Holmby Hills, an upscale neighborhood near Beverly Hills. (How upscale? Hugh Hefner's Playboy Mansion is also in Holmby Hills.) That little train, named after Disney's street address, ran on a half-mile-long track that included a tunnel, trestle, switches, and other realistic features sometimes crafted by Disney himself.

Disney's love of railroads dated back to his childhood years growing up in Marceline, a small Missouri town between Kansas City and Chicago with its own Santa Fe train depot (his uncle was a train conductor on the line). In his teen years, Disney had a part-time job selling items on trains in the Midwest. Railroading became one of the driving passions that inspired him to create a theme park: he wanted to ride, display, and just be around trains. "For him," says animator Ollie Johnson in *Walt Dis-*

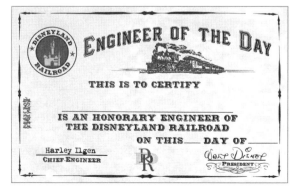

ney's Railroad Story, "the main attraction at Disneyland was the steam trains."

Hence, every concept illustration for the unbuilt Disneyland, whether the acreage was a small sixteen-acre rectangle in Burbank or a sixty-acre triangle in Anaheim, includes an old-fashioned train circling the perimeter. Naturally, when it came time to design, construct, and operate Disneyland's railroad line, Disney was closely involved every step of the way. Most of the early **souvenir books** include a photo of him in an engineer's hat and red neckerchief, waving happily from a train.

The Scenic Wonder Route That Completely Circles Disneyland

LEAVES REGULARLY FROM MAIN ST. DEPOT

Like much of Disneyland, the railroad was built slightly smaller than full-size. Both the train and its track are about five-eighths scale; its cars are three feet narrower than standard train cars, its doorways are closer to six feet tall than seven, and its track is about 36 inches wide instead of the standard 56.5. This makes Disneyland's trains less intimidating and more welcoming.

The trains travel approximately 6,700 feet in a clockwise loop around Disneyland. One engineer told us that the trains can go seventeen feet per second between stations, or around twelve miles per hour (with the capability to go twenty-five to thirty miles per hour). Today, with stops at three other stations along the line, each round trip begun from the **Main Street** station takes about twenty-five minutes, making this Disneyland's longest ride.

On **Opening Day**, the train had a sponsor: the historic, ninety-six-year-old Santa Fe Railroad (aka the Atchison, Topeka, and Santa Fe Railroad). The Santa Fe & Disneyland Railroad also had only two stops—the high-profile station above the **entrance**, and a rustic depot in **Frontierland**. Like the tracks themselves, both stations are perched on the **berm** that surrounds Disneyland. Designed by **Bill Martin** and spreading 270 feet from end to end, the Main Street station can hold 300 guests. Its interior displays have included old photographs, as well as the Carolwood Pacific's miniature engine and caboose. Veteran riders may recall that trains used a siding to pass each other at this station and at the one in Frontierland, back when there were only two stations (a section of the second track still exists at Main Street's station).

That diminutive Frontierland station, renamed the New Orleans Square/Frontierland station in 1996, is based on a design used in the Disney film *So Dear to My Heart*. Guests can watch for the real working water tower just outside this station and listen for quiet, telegraph-coded passages from Walt Disney's Opening Day speech. Note that this station and Main Street's station are at different elevations; a sign at the former claims the elevation is 144 feet above sea level, while a sign at the latter says it's 138 feet (indicating a gradual downward slope from the back of Disneyland to the front).

The history of Disneyland's railroad is a story of change. A new medieval-looking station joined the line in **Fantasyland** in 1956, but the fanciful little building was removed when the **It's a Small World** construction started in 1965. Fantasyland then got a new Videopolis station in 1985, its location a little farther westward from where the earlier station had been; in 1992, this Videopolis station became **Mickey's Toontown** depot. In 1958, an uncomplicated platform was added to **Tomorrowland**. Further additions arrived in 1958 and 1966, the years when the tunnels containing the

Grand Canyon Diorama and the **Primeval Canyon Diorama** opened along the track between Tomorrowland and **Town Square** (the trains slow down noticeably during this portion of the trip for sightseeing purposes). The name of the entire line was simplified to the Disneyland Railroad in 1974 when the Santa Fe Railroad, which had started carrying only freight instead of passengers, ceased its sponsorship.

Periodically, the entire attraction is shut down during construction elsewhere in Disneyland—notably when **Splash Mountain**, the **Indiana Jones Adventure**, and most recently **Star Wars Land** were

all being built. But even when it's closed, the railroad is still worth visiting for its special educational displays. For instance, in 2016, with the trains not running, the New Orleans Square/Frontierland station held a special exhibit featuring a parked train, a handcar, and some cool free giveaways, including a telegram form with the Morse Code courtesy of the Disneyland Resort Telegraph Company and an Engineer of the Day certificate courtesy of the Disneyland Railroad (shown on page 405).

Today, the trains are pulled by one of five brightly painted steam engines. Four of these five "iron horses" are named after the Santa Fe Railroad's former presidents—the *C. K. Holliday* (the company's founder), the *E. P. Ripley*, the *Fred G. Gurley*, and the *Ernest S. Marsh*. The fifth engine, the *Ward Kimball*, is named after a Disney Legend who was a train enthusiast and Disney's close friend. Details differ on the locomotives, but they all sport red wheels and burn biodiesel fuel. To see the engineers in action, guests can request a seat on the tender right behind the engine.

In 1955, machinists headed by Roger Broggie built the first two thirty-five-foot-long engines, the *C. K. Holliday* and *E. P. Ripley*, at Burbank's Disney Studios for about $100,000. These were the only locomotives operating on Opening Day. The *Fred G. Gurley*, which was bought rather than built, dates to 1894 and had been used in Louisiana and sold for scrap before Disney purchased it for $1,200. He spent thirty times that amount for the major overhaul needed before it could go into Disneyland service on March 28, 1958. Built in 1925, the *Ernest S. Marsh* was still chugging along in New Jersey when Disney paid $2,000 for it and had it refurbished. It began circling Disneyland on July 25, 1959. The *Ward Kimball* is another refurbished engine that first began running in 1902; renamed and put into Disneyland service on June 25, 2005, it was the first engine added to the railroad in forty-six years.

In 2005, the park welcomed the *Ward Kimball* and a freshly refurbished *Lilly Belle*. Named after Walt Disney's wife, the latter was a lavishly appointed parlor car that had originally appeared at Disneyland in the 1970s. Redecorated several times, the *Lilly Belle* typically includes potted plants, stained glass, elegant mahogany woodwork with intricate stencils, plush carpets, and furniture upholstered with red velvet. The beautiful red car isn't always on view, but when it is, the *Lilly Belle* is always a special sight to see. In recent years, Disneyland has even allowed guests to ride in it. There's some Disneyland history behind the name—one of the tiny Shetlands in the **Miniature**

Horse Corral was also called Lilly Belle.

In 1955, up to 300 guests per trip around Disneyland sat in traditional forward-facing, bench-seat passenger coaches with windows, or they stood up in wooden "cattle cars," glimpsing the views from openings or through the horizontal slats (these seatless cars were later retrofitted with benches to make the long trip more comfortable). By the time the Primeval World Diorama opened in 1966, some of the cars had been converted to an open-walled design with side-facing seats that afforded better starboard views (side-facing cars are used most frequently today). All guests can ride the trains as long as they want without disembarking; many use the train not as a full-circuit journey, but as a relaxing way to move to different lands. As they ride, guests listen to pre-recorded, deep-voiced narration that was originally spoken by **Thurl Ravenscroft** (actor Pierre Renoudet, aka Pete Renaday, recorded the announcements heard at the Main Street station). The narration and background music sound better than ever now, thanks to upgrades to the sound system in 2013 and 2014.

Guests boarding the trains in 1955 bought old-fashioned-looking tickets that had stubs for each leg of the 1.3-mile journey. When A–E **ticket books** went into effect, a ride on the railroad usually cost a D ticket. By now, the number of riders on the well-traveled Disneyland trains tops 300 million, and the sixty-plus years of train trips total over 5 million miles (equaling ten round-trip flights to the moon). Many souvenirs have commemorated the great trains, including a 1950s official Chief Engineer Disneyland RR Outfit.

What began as Disney's youthful passion and backyard hobby continues to thrive as one of the most venerated, visited, and beloved attractions in Disneyland history.

MOUSCELLANY

Several flags fly above Main Street's train station. One depicts Mickey, but our favorite is the pale blue Disneyland flag (shown), which we've also seen fluttering on the **Mark Twain** Riverboat. This flag is also shown in the back of the Imagineering offices on 1965's "Disneyland's Tenth Anniversary" episode of *Walt Disney's Wonderful World of Color.*

Rancho del Zocalo Restaurante

MAP: Frontierland, Fr-24

DATES: November 2001–ongoing

Casa Mexicana, the Mexican restaurant born in **Frontierland** in 1982, underwent *cambios grandes* in 2001. Ortega, the chili and salsa company, was the new sponsor, and Rancho del Zocalo was the new name, though an old sign reading "mi casa es su casa" still honors the previous establishment. Zocalo refers to the name applied in the 1950s to this section of Frontierland, **El Zocalo Park**. Though the restaurant mainly served standard cafeteria-style Mexican cuisine, the 2001 menu also included tasty specialties like smoked ribs and barbecued chicken.

In recent years, with La Victoria as the restaurant's sponsor, the menu has changed again, this time reverting to mostly Mexican dishes supplemented by a few fire-grilled specialties. A 2013 menu update added some well-received variations (Citrus Fire-Grilled Chicken), and more recently the Street Taco Trio has been a popular favorite. A bigger change came on February 2, 2016, when *el restaurante* began serving breakfast, including the classic Mickey-shaped pancakes once made famous at the **River Belle Terrace**. Design-wise, today's Rancho is bigger and fancier than the old Casa, with exotic tiles, fountains, an exterior Zorro mural, and elaborate ironwork enhancing the Spanish architecture.

Ravenscroft, Thurl
(1914–2005)

Like **Paul Frees**, Thurl Ravenscroft had one of those resonant voices everyone has heard for decades in movies, TV commercials, and Disneyland attractions. A Nebraskan born in 1914, Ravenscroft served in World War II and then established a Hollywood career as a singer. He was part of several different vocal groups, including the MelloMen (aka Mellomen, aka Mello Men) and the Johnny Mann Singers ("You're a Mean One, Mister Grinch" for *How the Grinch Stole Christmas* is still one of his most loved performances). As a successful voice actor, Ravenscroft's single most famous line was Tony the Tiger's enthusiastic "They're grrrrrreat!"

MOUSCELLANY

Southern California residents also knew Thurl Ravenscroft as the narrator of both *The Pageant of the Masters* (a living tableau of artworks held every summer in Laguna Beach) and *The Glory of Christmas* (a holiday spectacular held every winter at Garden Grove's Crystal Cathedral).

Ravenscroft sang and voiced characters for numerous Disney movies, among them *Cinderella, Mary Poppins*, and *The Jungle Book*. At Disneyland, he provided voices for the **Country Bear Jamboree** (he was the mounted buffalo head), the **Mark Twain** (narrator), and the **Enchanted Tiki Room** (Fritz). He also did lengthy narration on 1968's record album recreating the Enchanted Tiki Room and the **Jungle Cruise**. Most famously, he sang the **Haunted Mansion's** theme song, "Grim Grinning Ghosts." He also narrated that attraction's popular record album, and he's even visible during the graveyard scene: in the quartet of singing busts, Ravenscroft's face is on Uncle Theodore, the second bust from the left.

Ravenscroft was inducted as a Disney Legend in 1995. He died of cancer ten years later at age ninety-one.

Redd Rockett's Pizza Port

MAP: Tomorrowland, T-16
DATES: May 22, 1998–ongoing

After **Mission to Mars** stopped flying in 1992, its large **Tomorrowland** building sat empty for four years. The **Toy Story Funhouse** set up here for a brief run in 1996, but two more years would pass before something permanent settled in. Surprisingly, the new arrival wasn't an attraction, but a restaurant serving big portions of fast food.

Redd Rockett's Pizza Port and its new neighbor, *Honey, I Shrunk the Audience*, both debuted in 1998 in conjunction with a major Tomorrowland remodel. The restaurant's name alludes to both the famous *Moonliner* rocket on the roof and the Space Port that was considered for Tomorrowland in the 1960s (**Space Mountain** arose instead in the 1970s).

Redd's features cafeteria-style counters where guests can roam and pick up their meals. Buitoni, a Tuscan pasta and sauce company that is now a Nestlé brand, is the sponsor here, so it's no surprise that Italian food dominates Redd's menu. The selections have had space-themed names like Lunar Cheese Pizza and Planetary Pizza Salad.

In early 2015, Redd's tried a short-lived line-up of Marvel-inspired Heroic Treats. Guests assembled their custom meals from a roster of Marvel-ous items, such as a Black Widow Chocolate Parfait and a Captain America Shield Cookie (if they hit the requisite $20 price point, guests could then opt to buy an *Avengers: Age of Ultron* print for an additional $10).

Then, coinciding with the **Season of the Force** campaign that inundated Tomorrowland with *Star Wars* imagery, new themed items appeared in November of 2015, among them a Forest of Endor pasta entree and Dark Side Chicken Curry Pizza. For a while the stacks of *Star Wars* toys and popcorn buckets on display threatened to turn Redd Rockett's into more of a gift shop than a pizza place, but by 2016, the merchandise was mostly gone and the focus was back on the food.

Proximity to the popular **Starcade** made this a favorite spot for arcade-happy kids (back when the arcade was open). The ten classic **attraction posters** on the walls, evoking images from Tomorrowland's glory days, made it a favorite for nostalgic adults (those posters were replaced by Season of the Force art in 2015). What hasn't changed is the ample seating—the scores of tables on the indoor Flight Deck still make Redd's a favorite for anyone looking to sit in cool comfort.

Redmond, Dorothea
(1910–2009)

Dorothea Redmond was a significant contributor to several different entertainment fields. Born in 1910 in Los Angeles, Redmond studied fine arts at USC and was later hired by David O. Selznick's movie studio to be its first female production designer. After helping create the look for *Gone With the Wind*, Redmond worked closely with Alfred Hitchcock and contributed masterful design illustrations for seven of his films, including *Rebecca* and *Rear Window*.

In the 1950s and early '60s, Redmond worked for a prominent architectural firm until her Disney career began in 1964. Her first job as an Imagineer was to paint designs that would help transform the Red Wagon Inn into the elegant **Plaza Inn**. One of her next big projects was to help create the large private living area that was to be built in **New Orleans Square** for **Walt Disney**. When Disney died before it was completed, this opulent **apartment** above **Pirates of the Caribbean** later became the **Disney Gallery**. In 2008, these rooms were restored according to Redmond's original illustrations and were converted into the Disneyland Dream Suite for the **Year of a Million Dreams** promotion. She also helped design the posh **Club 33** next door and several other New Orleans Square spaces. For Walt Disney World, she drew up concept sketches for various sites, and the enormous mosaic murals she designed are still on display in Cinderella Castle.

Redmond retired in 1974 and was named a Disney Legend in 2008. She died at age ninety-eight in 2009.

Reel-Ride

MAP: Frontierland, Fr-1

DATES: Never built

If the intriguing legend is accurate, Willis O'Brien, the wizard behind the stop-motion special effects for *King Kong* and other movie classics, drew concept art for an attraction intended for **Frontierland**. Unfortunately, his Reel-Ride was never built. As shown in a 2006 museum exhibition called *Behind the Magic: 50 Years of Disneyland*, a color illustration (purportedly O'Brien's) depicted ten children on mechanical horses facing a movie screen. In this attraction-to-be, young buckaroos would have ridden their horses as a rollicking movie of a cowboy star on his horse rolled in front of them. An ungrammatical caption described how the horses were synchronized with "a back-projection on a translucent screen, giving effect of actually traveling through the country. When chase is ended—horses stop."

Had it been constructed and implemented, the three-to-five-minute Reel-Ride might have been the world's first melding of film, motion-simulation, and an amusement park attraction (making it a precursor of **Star Tours**). O'Brien, who was about sixty-eight years old when the 1954 drawing was executed, died in 1962.

Refreshment Corner, aka Coke Corner, aka Coca-Cola Refreshment Corner

MAP: Main Street, MS-10

DATES: July 17, 1955–ongoing

Since **Opening Day**, Disneyland's most enduring fast-food location has thrived on the western corner where **Main Street** meets the **Hub**. The Refreshment Corner, also known as Coke Corner and the Coca-Cola Refreshment Corner, bends around the intersection of Main and W. Plaza Street toward the **Jolly Holiday Bakery Café**.

Inside, the Refreshment Corner opens into the **Candy Palace**; the outside area with alfresco tables is called the Corner Café (the cozy indoor seating inside the Refreshment Corner was lost to a 2012 remodel). The basic menu initially listed just sodas but was supplemented later by hot dogs, chili, Mickey Mouse-shaped pretzels, and other snacks. Introduced in 2014 was a big new dispenser in the back corner that served four flavors of Goofy's Glaciers. By 2016, the most expensive menu item was chili with cheddar cheese in a sourdough bread bowl. And a Coke Corner small Coke with ice? $3.29.

Three features have secured the lasting popularity of this otherwise simple eatery: its long hours (longer than most food establishments in Disneyland); its charming interior with its red-and-white color scheme and ornate turn-of-the-century embellishments; and the presence of an affable piano player. Starting in 1969, Rod Miller, wearing turn-of-the-century clothes and a consistent smile, played exuberant ragtime piano favorites for thirty-six years and chatted with guests on the patio. With Miller now retired, a handful of other pianists currently share the entertainment schedule.

As perky as the Refreshment Corner is in the daylight, it's even brighter after sundown, when the lovely lights and lively music combine to make this one of Disneyland's cheeriest spots. Success here led Coca-Cola to sponsor additional park locations over the decades, including 1967's Tomorrowland Terrace and 1998's **Spirit of Refreshment**.

> **MOUSCELLANY**
>
> At the doorway to the Refreshment Corner, the light bulbs near the ceiling alternate colors (red bulb, white bulb, red bulb, etc.). Notice that one in the middle (shown) is half-red and half-white to keep the color scheme consistent. Now *that's* attention to detail!

Reihm, Julie
(1944–)

Disneyland's **Miss Disneyland** program kicked off in 1965 with a female **cast member** who would be named a Disney Legend fifty years later. The title (eventually changed to Disneyland Ambassador to the World) was created so someone could stand in for a busy **Walt Disney** and represent Disneyland in **parades**, on TV shows, and at special events. Selections were based on appearance, personality, and poise.

Julie Reihm, a twenty-one-year-old Texan and local college student, was the very first Miss Disneyland. After working as a Disneyland **Tour Guide** for two years, she was selected in 1964 and then immediately called on to help promote Disneyland's big **Tencennial** anniversary events throughout 1965. On January 3, 1965, she co-starred in the *Walt Disney's Wonderful World of Color* TV series; wearing her Tour Guide uniform, Reihm examined displays of the coming **Pirates of the Caribbean** and **Haunted Mansion** attractions, contributing comments alongside Walt Disney. That year, she also traveled over 50,000 miles around the world promoting Disneyland (included was a trip to the 1964–1965 New York World's Fair with Walt Disney to open **Great Moments with Mr. Lincoln**). After her year as Miss Disneyland, Reihm returned to college, eventually marrying and settling down in Virginia.

Disney Legend **Jack Lindquist** says in his memoirs that Reihm was "perhaps the best Disneyland ambassador ever," and points out that she is still the only one who was given a new car along with her title. According to Lindquist, she "set the standard that still stands" (introducing her at the D23 convention in 2015, Walt Disney Co. Chairman and CEO Robert Iger reiterated Lindquist's remark that Reihm had "set the standard"). When Julie Reihm Casaletto was named a Disney Legend in 2015, the official Disney announcement described her "as a personification of Disneyland's world-famous spirit of friendliness and happiness," and "the template upon which decades of Ambassadors would pattern themselves." In her acceptance speech, she said that every day on the job was fun, that being an ambassador for Disneyland was "like an E-ticket ride," and that "the greatest honor was to get to know the man, Walt Disney."

Restrooms

On **Opening Day**, Disneyland almost had no working restrooms. A strike by local plumbers forced last-minute negotiations that got the restrooms, but not the water fountains, into operation (**Walt Disney** made this agonizing choice by acknowledging that guests could forgo the latter, but not the former). A free map handed out to guests that day pinpoints only five pairs of public restrooms (five men's and five women's) in the entire park that were open. The maps in Disneyland's 1956 **souvenir book** show just a dozen (six and six): two pairs of restrooms were located on **Main Street**, and the other four main lands had one pair each. Also, by 1956, the coin-operated stalls in some of the restrooms had been converted to free stalls.

Today, Disneyland has over twenty-five pairs of restrooms. Six pairs are located in the stretch from the **entrance** up to the **Hub** restaurants. The lands all have at least three pairs each, except for **Critter Country** and **Mickey's Toontown**, which have only one pair each. The size of the restrooms varies from spacious (like those on the lower floor of the **Hungry Bear Restaurant**, shown) to cramped (such as those on **Tom Sawyer Island**).

What never varies is the cleanliness. Even on the busiest days, every restroom is lightly cleaned every hour and given a thorough sanitization every night. Restroom custodians work from a nineteen-point checklist that covers everything from restocking soap and diaper machines to cleaning mirrors and mopping floors. Disney Legend **Chuck Boyajian**, the original manager of custodial operations, is the one who raised the cleanliness bar to a height that became the industry standard.

Not only are Disneyland's facilities spotless, they're also convenient for parents—most restrooms include baby-changing stations, and some even sell baby-changing kits (diapers, wipes, etc.). A few "companion restrooms" are scattered around Disneyland, and at the **Hub**, special restroom needs are accommodated inside the **Baby Care Center** and **First Aid**.

The door signs, which are designed to match the themes of their respective lands, are delightful enhancements to the restrooms. Aliens, for instance, adorn restroom doors in **Tomorrowland**. What's more, the themes occasionally even extend inside the restrooms; some **Frontierland** restroom interiors feature wooden walls and antique hurricane lamps. The most opulent restrooms are inside **Club 33**, where the ladies' room features gilded seating arrangements that have rightfully earned the nickname "thrones."

Rigdon, Cicely
(1923–2013)

Working her way up from a ticket seller in 1957 to a Disney Legend inductee in 2005, Cicely Rigdon enjoyed a distinguished Disneyland career that lasted over three decades. In 1959, just two years after being hired at Disneyland, the thirty-six-year-old Rigdon headed the new **Tour Guide** program; a 1961 article in *Parade* magazine praises the "attractive, wholesome, friendly girl guides" (called "Disneyettes" in the magazine) she had hired and trained (the article also says Rigdon was from Yorkshire, England). Later Rigdon was promoted to **Guest Relations**, which she supervised in the 1960s and '70s while also overseeing the ticket sellers out front. Additionally, Rigdon supervised the maintenance of **Walt Disney's apartment** above the **Fire Department**, helped launch the new Disney attractions at the 1964–1965 New York World's Fair, and worked closely with Disneyland's Honorary Mayor, **Jack Lindquist**.

In the 1970s, Rigdon took on training responsibilities at Walt Disney World, and a decade later she was updating the **Miss Disneyland** program into the Disneyland Ambassador to the World program. After thirty-seven years of working at Disneyland, Rigdon retired in 1994. She passed away on the last day of 2013 at age ninety.

River Belle Terrace

MAP: Frontierland, Fr-7

DATES: 1971–ongoing

What had been **Aunt Jemima's** restaurant for over a decade and the **Magnolia Tree Terrace** for over a year became the stately, white-trimmed River Belle Terrace in 1971. Its location on the corner where **Frontierland** rounds into **Adventureland** has dictated the style of the two restaurant entrances: cream-colored on the Frontierland side, and pale blue on the Adventureland side. Its unusual roof also has two separate themes to match each land. After a 2007 remodel, the River Belle on the Frontierland side now stretches toward the **Stage Door Café**, usurping spaces previously occupied by smaller eateries. The interior décor remains as pretty as always, and the umbrella-shaded patio out front, with its seventy-plus tables, still affords hundreds of guests attractive views of the **Rivers of America** only seventy-five feet away.

Oscar Meyer, Hormel, and Sunkist have all been sponsors of the terrace over the years. No matter which company is participating, the cuisine has maintained a down-home flavor, offering lots of basic American food that has sometimes followed the Mark Twain theme—Aunt Polly's Chicken, Becky Thatcher's Fresh Fruit Plate, etc. In recent years, tangy Southern barbecue specialties (such as Messy Mississippi BBQ Pork), signature sandwiches, and special selections for kids have joined the menu.

The highlights of the restaurant usually came at breakfast, which included its awesome cinnamon roll and famous Mickey-shaped pancakes "for the child in all of us" that supposedly originated here. Breakfast was discontinued in February of 2016, but the pancakes were quickly moved to the nearby **Rancho del Zocalo Restaurante**, where the price immediately bumped up by $1.

Rivers of America

MAP: Frontierland, Fr-9

DATES: July 17, 1955–ongoing

The man-made Rivers of America area is a highly visible, much-traveled section of Disneyland that debuted on **Opening Day**. The waterway originally might have been more accurately called the Rivers of the Midwest, since the Missouri and Mississippi Rivers seem to have been the main inspirations for the initial design and landscaping.

Though the river area is technically located in **Frontierland**, it is visible from, and bordered by, **New Orleans Square** and **Critter Country** as well. Some of Disneyland's most popular attractions, including the **Big Thunder Mountain Railroad**, the **Haunted Mansion**, and **Splash Mountain** surround the river's perimeter. The river section most often viewed by pedestrians is the southern portion, where **Fantasmic!** is presented. A walk from **Fowler's Harbor** in the southwest corner to the dock for the *Mark Twain* **Riverboat** spans about 650 feet of pavement.

Prior to 2016, when the river was closed for the construction of the nearby **Star Wars Land**, the overall surface area of the Rivers of America, including the island in the middle, covered about 325,000 square feet. These eight acres represented roughly thirteen percent of the total area of the original sixty-acre park. Shaped vaguely like a kidney bean around **Tom Sawyer Island**, the waters stretched almost 1,000 feet from the northernmost to the southernmost shore. Measuring across the water from the mainland to the island, the river ranged from about 80 to 100 feet wide. According to legend, the rivers flow from the hill on Tom Sawyer Island where Tom & Huck's Treehouse was built.

Five watercraft have sailed regularly upon the river (though not all simultaneously): the *Mark Twain* (shown), the *Columbia*, the **Mike Fink Keel Boats**,

Davy Crockett's Explorer Canoes, and the **Rafts to Tom Sawyer Island**. Boats that circumnavigate the island travel about a half-mile through approximately 6 million gallons of water, ranging from four to eight feet deep. Despite its general shallowness, the river has been the site of two accidental drowning, the tragic results of guests entering the waters after dark.

Disneyland: The First Quarter Century describes the main problem with the river's construction. The first time water was pumped into the bulldozed trenches, the water immediately seeped away into the soil. After different types of riverbeds were tried, the river was eventually given a hard clay bottom. These days, the river is drained every few years for cleaning and maintenance. The turbid water that's used to refill the river would be clear if not for a chemical additive that makes it appear a murky greenish-brown, thus concealing the submerged tracks that guide the *Mark Twain* and the *Columbia* (and also covering up the hundreds of cameras, pacifiers, sunglasses, and other items that have been accidentally dropped overboard).

One of the misconceptions about the waterway is that it is stocked with fish. It isn't. Occasionally tiny fish can be seen in the river, but they weren't placed there intentionally. The only time park officials introduced fish to the river was in the early years, when a small sealed area at Tom Sawyer Island's southern tip was abundantly stocked and fishing poles were provided so guests could fish. The practice was soon abandoned, however, when their odoriferous catches began to stink up the lockers or were abandoned in bushes (when the Disneyland Hotel started its own Fishing Pool in

the early 1970s, management knew to provide anglers with cleaning, packing, and shipping services for their catches).

Disneyland's 1956 **souvenir book** identifies additional fauna along the river: "Flocks of wild geese, mallards, and other birds have found Frontierland's River a safe retreat in their pilgrimages south. The birds pause to rest here, and in some cases stay on for several months." Thus, the desultory ducks that are often seen drifting in the waterway aren't **Audio-Animatronic** mechanicals, as some guests might suppose, but are in fact migratory waterfowl passing through. The American Indians and large animals glimpsed around the river—moose, deer, skunks, etc.—are either statues or A-A machines.

A 2010 update to the Rivers of America added details, animals, and landscaping in-

spired by the Potomac, Rio Grande, and Columbia Rivers. The long closure that started in early 2016 will bring more changes, as the Star Wars Land construction to the north has altered the backwoods area where the river drifted past Mike Fink's isolated cabin. However it looks when it reopens, the river's serene waters should still provide a cooling respite from the busy excitement found on the mainland.

Rock Candy Mountain, aka Candy Mountain

MAP: Fantasyland, Fa-15

DATES: Never built

One of the more sugary ideas considered for young Disneyland was something called Rock Candy Mountain (or just Candy Mountain). The Burl Ives ballad "Big Rock Candy Mountain" had been a hit in 1949, so the image of an abundantly sweet wonderland was still fresh when Disney designers began drawing concept illustrations in the early 1950s. Although the project gathered momentum late in the decade and was worked on by such Disney Legends as **Claude Coats**, **Harriet Burns**, and **Rolly Crump**, ultimately no mountain of candy ever materialized.

Had it been built, Candy Mountain would have been incorporated into the **Storybook Land Canal Boats** attraction. Sightseers in the boats would have glided into caverns in Rock Candy Mountain and found scenes inspired by a new Disney movie based on one of L. Frank Baum's many *Wizard of Oz* sequels.

Even more colorful than the plans for the interior were those for the mountain's exterior, which at one time was going to be transparent but was later revised to carry a thick coating of artificial candy. Oversized candy canes, gumballs, lollipops, and more would have covered the six-story mountain, with the **Casey Jr. Circus Train** wrapping around the base. Unfortunately, when plans for Disney's *Oz* movie collapsed, so did plans for the mountain. As related in *Disneyland: The Nickel Tour*, the miniature model—which had been made with real candy—was taken outside, where birds put a quick end to any Candy Mountain dreams.

> **MOUSCELLANY**
>
> Candy Mountain wouldn't have been the only site in Disneyland's first decade to incorporate props and costumes from a Disney movie—the **20,000 Leagues Under the Sea Exhibit** and *Babes in Toyland* **Exhibit** were both walk-through movie displays.

Rocket Jets

MAP: Tomorrowland, T-8

DATES: July 2, 1967–January 6, 1997

For four decades, some variation of a whirling-rocket attraction stood in the heart of **Tomorrowland**. After debuting as the **Astro-Jets** in 1956 and then being renamed the Tomorrowland Jets in 1964, the attraction closed in September of 1966 while a major remodel redefined all of Tomorrowland. When it reopened just before Independence Day in 1967, the attraction had a new name and dramatic new look.

With America's space program in full swing, the Astro-Jets' winged cylinders were jettisoned in favor of the Apollo-style Rocket Jets. Designed by **George McGinnis**, the sleek, bullet-like tubes had sharper noses, prominent yellow headlights, and white and black livery reminiscent of NASA's latest spaceships. The redesigned central tower itself looked like one of the imposing Saturn launchers that thrust astronauts into space.

Even more impressively, the whole attraction had been lifted three stories off the ground to sit atop the main **PeopleMover** platform. With the center rocket topping out at about eighty-five feet, guests now rode an elevator (designed to look like the gantry alongside a NASA rocket) to reach the loading area. The fun factor zoomed higher when pilots pushed their vehicles to maximum altitude, soaring some seventy feet above Tomorrowland's pavement. Guests paid a D ticket to fly in the Anaheim sky.

> **MOUSCELLANY**
>
> To revisit the extinct Rocket Jets, take a look in today's **Little Green Men Store Command**, where two of the attraction's old spaceships, formerly black and white but now colorfully repainted, are being used as display cases.

And fly they did until early 1997, when the rockets were finally grounded and replaced a year later by a spinning sculpture called the **Observatron**. Opening at the same time was a very different expression of the original Astro-Jets idea—the **Astro-Orbitor**, with a new location about 250 feet away at Tomorrowland's entrance.

Rocket Man

In December of 1965, jetpacks were all the rage. In theaters, James Bond used one to soar out of harm's way in the opening sequence of *Thunderball,* winter's blockbuster movie. And at Disneyland, the Rocket Man was soaring high above the **Flight Circle** in **Tomorrowland** for short flights during the holidays. Both Bond and the Rocket Man were using Bell-designed rocket-powered backpacks (also called rocketpacks and rocketbelts) intended for the air force. Though they both wore helmets, that's where any similarities in their attire ended; Disneyland's Rocket Man wore a white flight suit, while Bond wore a natty suit and tie. *Disneyland: The Nickel Tour* identifies Disneyland's rocketeer as William Suitor, the same man who actually did Bond's flight in *Thunderball* and who later wore a jetpack to fly at the 1984 Summer Olympics in Los Angeles.

Rocket Rods

MAP: Tomorrowland, T-8

DATES: May 22, 1998–September 28, 2000

"The Rocket Rods zoom above, through, and around Tomorrowland in the fastest and longest attraction in Disneyland Park. This thrilling experience puts guests behind the wheels of high-speed vehicles of the future as they tear along an elevated highway above Tomorrowland."

So reads the ambitious description of the Rocket Rods in Disneyland's 2000 **souvenir book**. "Ride the road to tomorrow" was the confident boast at the attraction's entrance, and "Magic Highways of Tomorrow" was the proud title of its theme song. Unfortunately, the Rocket Rods' disappointing reality never matched the printed hyperbole or the original ambitious concept. What should have been an exciting, new thirty-five-mile-per-hour thrill ride for the twenty-first century barely sputtered through the last year of the twentieth. Even more embarrassingly, the Rocket Rods were built to be a high-profile showpiece attraction at **Tomorrowland's** entrance, making their failure all the more glaring.

In May of 1998, what had once been the **Circarama** theater opened as the Rocket Rods' spiraling **queue** area. Waiting guests learned about the history of transportation from numerous displays, which included blueprints and vehicles from other Disneyland attractions. Guests also watched an animated film and listened to car-themed music, including a reworked version of "Detroit" from Disney's *The Happiest Millionaire*. The displays and music were fine, but the long, hour-plus wait wasn't.

When they finally arrived at the old **PeopleMover** boarding area, guests found sleek, five-passenger hot rods that looked suitably futuristic and were surprisingly loud. Originally called Rocket Rods XPR (Experimental Prototype Rocket), the initials were dropped before guests could start inventing their own acronyms (Extremely Problematic Ride, Exceptional Patience Required, etc.). Once they headed off along the PeopleMover's elevated tracks, the cars lurched from acceleration on the straightaways to sudden deceleration on the curves, amounting to a spastic three-minute trip that was as hard on the vehicles as it was on the passengers.

While some people liked the experience, nobody liked the frequent breakdowns. After struggling through three trouble-plagued summers, the attraction "temporarily" closed for repairs in September of 2000. The following April, however, the Rocket Rods moved from Disneyland's future to its past and were permanently retired. Four years later, the successful **Buzz Lightyear Astro Blasters** attraction moved into the building; outside, the elevated tracks still stand in mute testament to the fully realized PeopleMover dream of the 1960s and the unfulfilled Rocket Rods dream of the 1990s.

Rocket to the Moon

MAP: Tomorrowland, T-16

DATES: July 22, 1955–September 5, 1966

Visible on **Opening Day**, Rocket to the Moon in **Tomorrowland** didn't truly open until July 22, five days later. When it did debut, the attraction was sponsored by TWA, but Douglas Aircraft took over sponsorship from 1962 to 1966. Rocket to the Moon was located behind the imposing *Moonliner* rocket; guests boarded inside hemispherical buildings that looked something like observatories.

Early **souvenir books** list the attraction as a "round trip to the moon." Something similar had operated five decades earlier, at Coney Island's Steeplechase Park. There, a ride called A Trip to the Moon used projections of a receding Earth and an approaching Moon to simulate a space voyage that

MOUSCELLANY

In Rocket to the Moon's early years, guests received a free commemorative certificate at the end of the ride, signed by the fictitious Captain P. J. Collins.

included a landing, views of lunar creatures, and an appearance by a royal Man on the Moon. At Disneyland, the trip was indeed to the moon—but only into lunar orbit, not to the lunar surface itself. Disney Legends **Claude Coats**, **Peter Ellenshaw**, and **John Hench** helped create Disneyland's memorable space experience.

The attraction operated like a low-tech flight simulator. Guests sat in one of two steeply raked, 104-seat theaters named Diana and Luna. Inside each cylindrical theater, a large circular screen lay flat on the floor, and another was mounted on the ceiling, in the center of the room. For fifteen minutes, the screens displayed views of the ship's previous location (the bottom screen began with footage of the launch pad and morphed into a receding Earth) and its approaching target (the top

screen showed the oncoming moon), all described by an informative narrator. Simple special effects (such as the raising and lowering of seats), views of a glowing comet and the far side of the moon, and a noisy trip through a meteor shower made the trip even more exciting.

In 1966, the C-ticket Rocket to the Moon flights were scrapped so the more elaborate missions of the D-ticket **Flight to the Moon** could launch a year later. Although the original attraction is gone, what remains is one of the most compelling of Disneyland's **attraction posters** (shown): a Bjorn Aronsen design that depicts the majestic *Moonliner*, futuristic Tomorrowland buildings, a star-spangled sky, and tantalizing text that invites guests to "blast off" for "a thrilling trip to the moon."

Roger Rabbit's Car Toon Spin

MAP: Mickey's Toontown, MT-11

DATES: January 26, 1994–ongoing

Roger Rabbit's Car Toon Spin is the signature attraction in **Mickey's Toontown**. After

opening in 1994, one year after Toontown's debut, it became popular enough to warrant **FASTPASS** ticket distribution.

The Car Toon Spin is similar to the **Fantasyland** dark rides, which feature little vehicles moving through decorated sets with animated movie themes. Roger's ride, however, offers something that the **Mr. Toad**, **Snow White**, **Alice**, **Peter Pan**, and **Pinocchio** attractions don't—guest-controlled vehicles. Roger's cars can be spun around a full 360 degrees, like the teacups in the **Mad Hatter's Mad Tea Party**.

After entering a garage and climbing into smiling

cars designed to resemble the cabs in *Who Framed Roger Rabbit*, guests begin a colorful excursion through the movie's Toontown. The trip gets spinny as soon as the cabs slide through the deadly "Dip" slick the weasels have poured onto the road. From this point on, guests can whirl their cars in a circle, pointing them at anything they pass. Some five minutes and a dozen **Audio-Animatronic** characters later, Roger extricates guests by opening a portable hole (shown on page 420) that leads back to the garage.

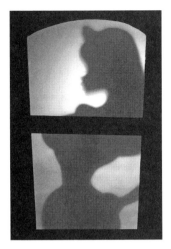

From the entrance to the exit, the attraction's frenetic energy, zany imagination, and madcap gags enliven the whole experience. The **queue** area overflows with clever details: a wise-cracking gorilla, a pin-up calendar, a "Dip" recipe, a wall of Disney-themed license plates (2N TOWN, CAP 10 HK, etc.), a glimpse of Jessica Rabbit sashaying past a window (shown), and many more, making the wait an attraction in itself. During the cab ride, the scenery is more detailed than it is in most attractions because of the freedom of movement enjoyed by the spinning guests—Imagineers had to create fronts, sides, and backs to everything, since guests would be observing from all directions.

Guests may come for the twirl, but they'll return for the barrage of jokes. Any attraction that culminates with a backwards journey through the Gag Warehouse has just got to be ridden again and again.

Rogers, Wathel
(1919–2000)

"Here rests Wathel R. Bender, He Rode to Glory on a Fender, Peaceful Rest."

This tombstone outside the **Haunted Mansion** was a nifty tribute to Wathel Rogers, a Disney Legend who worked for the company for forty-eight years. Born in Colorado in 1919, Rogers studied art in the 1930s and joined Disney Studios in 1939. There he started working as a film animator on such classics as *Pinocchio* and *Bambi*.

After a World War II stint with the Marines, Rogers returned to Disney to help animate *Cinderella*, *Peter Pan*, *Sleeping Beauty*, and more. Meanwhile, his expertise as a model-maker qualified him to help **Walt Disney** construct the miniature Carolwood Pacific train on Disney's Holmby Hills property in the early 1950s. Rogers then became one of Disneyland's main model-makers, creating small-scale 3-D buildings that would be previewed on the *Disneyland* **TV series** and then constructed full-size in the park.

During the 1950s, Rogers took on a special

MOUSCELLANY

While developing new mechanicals for what would become Disneyland's **Carousel of Progress**, Rogers was shown on national TV to demonstrate how an elaborate programming harness could manipulate a robotic character nearby.

task at Walt Disney's request—helping create a mechanical man. Inspired by the lanky Buddy Ebsen, Rogers and several others built a nine-inch dancing man who was the prototypical **Audio-Animatronic** figure, setting the stage for the remarkable achievements ahead. In the 1960s, with technology becoming more sophisticated, Rogers helped make A-A birds for the **Enchanted Tiki Room**, realistic **Jungle Cruise** animals, personable buccaneers for **Pirates of the Caribbean**, and Honest Abe for **Great Moments with Mr. Lincoln**.

There were still more achievements to come. In the 1970s, Rogers built an A-A Ben Franklin figure for EPCOT, and in the 1980s, he organized a team to help solve technical problems in Disney parks. After retiring in 1987, Rogers was inducted as a Disney Legend in 1995, five years before his death in Arizona at age eighty-one.

Royal Street Bachelors

Disneyland's **souvenir books** have often boasted photos, some at full-page size, of an authentic jazz combo that "recreates the sounds of old New Orleans" in **New Orleans Square**. This group is the Royal Street Bachelors, who are among the most enduring entertainers in Disneyland history. The Bachelors still play most days of the week, usually at the intersection of Orleans and Royal Streets, or near the **Royal Street Veranda**, or at the **French Market**. The men are typically dressed in classy outfits that have included matching red or green vests, plaid sports jackets, chalk-stripe suits, bow ties, and festive skimmers.

Generally there are three Bachelors who currently play at Disneyland (occasionally the group is supplemented by an extra musician or two, and sometimes even a vocalist). The main three aren't the same trio who started with the group in 1966. That original trio was comprised of Jack McVea (co-composer of the 1947 hit "Open the Door Richard"), Harold Grant, and Herb Gordy (a relative of Motown Records founder Berry Gordy). McVea was the group's leader, who played the clarinet and the saxophone; Grant strummed a banjo and guitar; and Gordy plucked an upright bass. McVea finally retired in 1992. A 1991 CD called *The Official Album of Disneyland and Walt Disney World* includes eighty-six seconds of the Bachelors' "Swanee River." This number typifies their set, which relies on smooth arrangements of jazz and R & B standards.

> **MOUSCELLANY**
>
> Of all the lands in Disneyland, New Orleans Square is probably the most musical. Other performers who have enjoyed extensive stays here include the Bayou Brass Band, Bilge Rats & Bootstrappers, Delta Ramblers, Gloryland Brass Band, Jambalaya Jazz Band, Jolly Roger, New Orleans Traditional Jazz Band, Orleans Street Band, River Rascals, and **Side Street Strutters**.

In recent years, saxophonist Kenny Treseder has headed the Bachelors, supported by guitarist Terry Evens and bassist Jeffery Littleton. Another longtime guitarist, Ernie McLean, died in 2012.

Royal Street Sweets

Map: New Orleans Square, NOS-7

DATES: 1995–ongoing

Starting in 1966, an anonymous little candy cart stood in **New Orleans Square** near the Creole Café (as it was called before it became **Café Orleans**). In the mid-1990s, the cart got an official name, Royal Street Sweets, and an expanded list of merchandise. There's candy of all kinds, including many with Disney designs, but the sparkly beads, necklaces, and masks promote the area's Mardi Gras spirit. The cart itself occasionally changes its look, sometimes appearing as a nostalgic **Main Street** flower cart, and other times like a black coach delivering ghouls to **the Haunted Mansion**.

Royal Street Veranda

MAP: New Orleans Square, NOS-2

DATES: Ca. 1966–ongoing

The "Royal St Veranda" (as the sign above the door spells it, with no period after "St") is the first dining option for guests entering **New Orleans Square** from **Adventureland**. Located on Royal Street around the corner from the **Pirates of the Caribbean** entrance, the little eatery presents an easily accessible counter. These are quick meals with Cajun flavor—"pot foods" served in sourdough bread bowls (hearty steak gumbo and vegetarian gumbo), as well as clam chowder, fritters, and specialty coffees. The outdoor seating offers scenic views of this riverfront area.

Ruggles China and Glass Shop

MAP: Main Street, MS-13

DATES: July 17, 1955–March 1964

A gift retailer named Phil Papel debuted the Ruggles China and Glass Shop on **Opening Day**. Filling the small store with imported ceramics and gifts, Papel was successful enough to establish nineteen other Southern California locations. The derivation of the Ruggles name isn't clear; it's possible that it refers to New Hampshire's Ruggles Mine, a major producer of the feldspar used in fine ceramics.

Disneyland's early **souvenir books** list the Ruggles store as the China Shop, Ceramics & China, the China & Glass Shop, and China & Glass (even though a photo of the shop with Ruggles signage is in the 1956 souvenir book). The shop's location was one door south of what is today's **Main Street Photo Supply Co**. A year after opening, Ruggles expanded into the adjacent room that became available when **Intimate Apparel** left.

In 1964, the Ruggles China and Glass Shop closed and was quickly replaced by a similar store that's still there today, the **China Closet**.

*run*Disney

DATES: March 26, 1995; September 16, 2006–ongoing (seasonal)

The tradition of holding long-distance races at Disneyland ended almost as soon as it started. On March 26, 1995, the first-ever Disneyland Marathon set off from the park in the morning but quickly ran into trouble: after just a mile of running through Anaheim streets, the racers veered off course and created a spontaneous shortcut. The marathon's organizers immediately calculated the lost distance and barely managed to tack it onto the end in time, thus maintaining the race's official 26.2-mile distance. No other Disneyland marathon has ever been held.

However, eleven years later, Disney created a 13.1-mile Disneyland Half Marathon that was supplemented by a 5K event. Held in mid-September, both races went through Disneyland, Disney California Adventure, and neighboring city streets, with lots of giveaways for the 12,000 contestants.

Now held over Labor Day weekend, these races have become so successful (over 15,000 runners registered for 2016's Disneyland Half Marathon, dubbed "the happiest race on Earth") that additional races have joined the year's line-up, all under the umbrella term *run*Disney. Among the new events: a Disneyland 5K and 10K (also on Labor Day weekend); the Dumbo Double Dare (completing the 10K and Half Marathon on consecutive days); the Star Wars Half Marathon (held in January with its own Rebel Challenge); the Tinker Bell Half Marathon and Pixie Dust Challenge (May); and the Super Heroes Half Marathon (November). Similar *run*Disney events, including a marathon, are held in Walt Disney World throughout the year.

Ryman, Herb
(1910–1989)

"I look upon Walt as a conductor of one of the world's greatest symphonies," Herb Ryman says in the book *Remembering Walt*, "and I was part of the orchestra."

Humble though he was, the truth is that few artists who contributed to Disneyland were as important as Ryman. On September 26–27, 1953, Ryman spent an entire weekend with **Walt Disney**, drawing a detailed aerial view of the unbuilt park as Disney described it to him. That landmark sketch—which took up about eighteen square feet—includes a recognizable **Main Street**, a **Hub** with various lands radiating outward from it, a castle, a **berm** with a train, a river with a riverboat, and a **Jungle Cruise**-style attraction. It became the key component of the successful presentations **Roy Disney** made to potential investors.

Once Disneyland plans were underway, Ryman became one of the key designers of **Sleeping Beauty Castle**, the Jungle Cruise, some of the Main Street buildings, and, later, **New Orleans Square**. On the *Disneyland Secrets, Stories & Magic* DVD, Ryman claims that he proposed one of the castle's distinctive design features—he's the one who spun the top around because he thought it looked better that way. Afterward, **Walt Disney** agreed that the castle should be built with its original "back" facing the Hub (see the Sleeping Beauty Castle entry for more of this story).

Ryman's Disneyland creations were the crowning achievements of his long career.

Born in Illinois in 1910, he studied art before heading West to work in the movies. MGM hired him as an illustrator for some of its great 1930s films, including *Mutiny on the Bounty*. In 1938, Ryman joined Disney Studios, where he worked as an art director on *Fantasia*, *Dumbo*, and other animated films. He then moved to 20th Century Fox and later traveled extensively with the Ringling Bros. Circus before taking on Disneyland projects. Ryman was photographed for a story about Disneyland in a 1963 issue of *National Geographic*; the accompanying photo shows him drawing a New Orleans Square concept illustration.

Ryman formally retired from the Disney Company in 1971, but he stayed on as a consultant for projects at other Disney parks. He also created art for the 1977 Disney film *Pete's Dragon*. He died in Los Angeles in 1989 and, a year later, was inducted posthumously as a Disney Legend. A tree near Sleeping Beauty Castle was planted in his honor, and his art is still frequently displayed in Disneyland.

Safari Outpost

MAP: Adventureland, A-2

DATES: March 1, 1986–January 1995

Starting in 1956, one of the shops at the **Adventureland Bazaar** was a fabric-and-fashions shop called Guatemalan Weavers, sellers of colorful products from Central and South America. Two weeks after that shop closed in 1986, the Safari Outpost opened in its place. The location was at the far west end of the Bazaar, next to the eatery now called the **Bengal Barbecue**. Wacky for khaki, the Safari Outpost's main merchandise was safari clothing (which is to be expected for a retailer across from the **Jungle Cruise**), but there were also plush animals and toys available for young explorers. In 1995, with Indy's major attraction opening nearby, the store became the **Indiana Jones Adventure Outpost**.

Sailing Ship *Columbia*

MAP: Frontierland, Fr-17

DATES: June 14, 1958–ongoing

While most guests think that the **Frontierland** theme is focused on America's nineteenth-century Wild West decades, this area actually gives a prominent nod to America's eighteenth-century Revolutionary War era. The last major addition to Frontierland's roster of varied vessels, the majestic *Columbia*, is a "full rigged 3 masted sailing ship" that takes "a voyage of discoveries on the **Rivers of America**," as described on Bjorn Aronsen's original **attraction poster**. That voyage began in 1958, the year the ship was dedicated under the super-vision of **Walt Disney** and naval officials. For most of the 1950s, '60s, and '70s, the *Columbia* was a D-ticket attraction, occasionally upgraded to an E.

The ship's design was inspired by the original *Columbia Rediviva* ("Columbia reborn"), a private-ly owned, eighty-three-foot sloop that, in 1790, became the first American windjammer to circum-navigate the globe. The actual design, however, may remind viewers of a *Columbia* contemporary— the *Bounty*, the infamous ninety-foot-long ship captained by William Bligh and commandeered by the mutinous Fletcher Christian in 1789. Disney's *The Imagineering Field Guide to Disneyland* asserts that the designs for Bligh's *Bounty* were referenced during the construction of Disneyland's *Columbia*, so it's possible that the park's ship is a blend of both classic vessels.

Whatever its backstory, the *Columbia* is a wonderfully appointed, full-size replica accurately capturing the spirit of the great age of sail, even if it doesn't accurately replicate that era's propulsion (despite appearances, engine power, not wind power, drives the ship along the same half-mile of submerged track used by the **Mark Twain**). The ship's main mast towers eighty-four feet, the decks hold 275–300 guests, and the 110-foot-long hull displays ten cannons, one of which is fired occasionally during the twelve-to-fourteen-minute tour around **Tom Sawyer Island**.

To accommodate the addition of such a large vessel on the Frontierland water-ways, Disneyland added a new dock and landing, **Fowler's Harbor**, to the southwest corner of the Rivers of America. To show off the ship's meticulously detailed interior, a fascinating walk-through exhibit known as the Below-Decks Museum opened on February 12, 1964. Guests who "mind thy head" (as signs warn) can tour the cramped quarters endured by ancient mariners.

For decades now, the *Columbia* has sailed in daylight hours with narration and sailing music as accompaniment; at night, it has a prominent role as the pirate ship in **Fantasmic!** It has also been transformed into a ghost ship for Halloween-related special events. When construction began on the new **Star Wars Land** north of Fron-tierland in January of 2016, the ship stopped sailing for over a year, but it was often made available for guests to come aboard and explore it.

Despite a dockside tragedy in 2001 that precipitated new safety regulations, the *Columbia* is still rightfully considered one of the proud flagships of Disneyland's diverse fleet.

Santa's Reindeer Round-Up

MAP: Frontierland, Fr-20

DATES: November 2005–January 2006; ongoing (seasonal) to January 2012

From 2005 to 2012, Santa's Reindeer Round-Up helped celebrate the **holiday season** in **Frontierland**. Held from early November to early January, this annual event brought Mr. and Mrs. Claus, live reindeer, and Yuletide festivities to **Big Thunder Ranch**. Holiday arts and crafts, sing-alongs, and Disney character meet-and-greets were among the daily events, but the reindeer (usually eight each year) were the most unusual attractions. Additionally, two live turkeys, pardoned by America's president, were occasionally exhibited. While seasonal events here continued, the turkeys weren't displayed as of 2009, and the reindeer stopped coming after the 2012 holidays.

Saving Mr. Banks Film

Five decades after *40 Pounds of Trouble* was released in 1962, Disneyland once again became the setting for extended scenes in a major feature film (the park appears in *That Thing You Do!* for fifteen seconds, but not for any prolonged scenes). Released for the 2013 holidays, *Saving Mr. Banks* presents Tom Hanks as **Walt Disney** and tells the story of Disney's efforts to make *Mary Poppins*.

A year earlier, when Disney's *Saving Mr. Banks* was being shot in Disneyland on November 6–7, 2012, the park stayed open to the public, though a few sections were roped off for filming. Some areas were decorated to look like as they had in the 1960s: at the **entrance**, large **attraction posters** were added to the long fence in front of the Mickey parterre, and the walkway in front of **Sleeping Beauty Castle** was lined with old-fashioned banners. Disney **cast members** were recruited (and dressed in 1960s costumes) as extras. Ultimately, five minutes of Disneyland footage (most of it on **Main Street** and in **Fantasyland**) made it into the final film.

> **MOUSCELLANY**
>
> According to *Saving Mr. Banks*, Walt Disney himself escorted author P. L. Travers through Disneyland in hopes of warming her to his interpretation of her story. This never actually happened—a studio employee took Travers through the park.

Season of the Force

MAP: Park, P-18

DATES: November 16, 2015–ongoing

When Disney executives announced in August of 2015 that a huge new **Star Wars Land** was eventually coming to Disneyland, they also introduced a series of preliminary *Star Wars*-related upgrades to **Tomorrowland**. Debuting on November 16, 2015, and given the umbrella title Season of the Force, this new thematic overlay served several important functions. First, Season of the Force built immediate excitement for *Star Wars: The Force Awakens*, the new movie about to debut the following month (it quickly became one of the top-grossing films in history). Next, the new theme re-energized Tomorrowland by adding new *Star Wars* characters and imagery to numerous attractions, stores, and restaurants. Finally, Season of the Force helped guests keep their eyes on the Star Wars Land prize so they wouldn't become frustrated by the major construction that ensued, blocking off formerly accessible areas and closing familiar attractions.

Guests arriving for that year's **holiday season** saw banners throughout Tomorrowland reminding them that they had arrived during the Season of the Force. They found specific manifestations of the theme in these locations (among others): **Space Mountain** was re-dubbed Hyperspace Mountain and incorporated *Star Wars* sights and sounds into the attraction; **Star Tours** got new scenes that reference *The Force Awakens*; the **Innoventions** building was renamed the **Tomorrowland Expo Center** and its ground floor was re-designed as the Star Wars Launch Bay; *Path of the Jedi* flew into the **Magic Eye Theater**; **Redd Rockett's Pizza Port** and the Tomorrowland Terrace started serving new menu items derived from the *Star Wars* universe (the latter restaurant even took the name **Galactic Grill**); and the **Star Trader** store, which formerly included items showing off Marvel's superheroes, completely shifted to *Star Wars* merchandise. *Star Wars* may be set a long time ago in a galaxy far, far away, but in 2015, Season of the Force started bringing those worlds to Tomorrowland right here, right now.

Sherman Brothers (Robert and Richard)
(1925–2012) (1928–)

The two men behind dozens of familiar Disney songs are the Sherman Brothers. Born in 1925 and 1928, respectively, Robert and Richard first lived in Manhattan, where their father worked as a Tin Pan Alley composer. After several cross-country trips, the family settled in Beverly Hills and began learning various musical instruments. Richard attended New York's Bard College, where he majored in music, while Robert joined the army and received the Purple Heart in World War II. After the war, Robert also studied at Bard College, and when both brothers graduated they teamed up to begin writing songs together.

Their partnership would endure as one of the most prolific, successful pairings in music history. Their "Tall Paul" and "Pineapple Princess" tunes were early hits for Annette Funicello. In 1960, the Shermans joined Disney Studios as staff songwriters, and soon they were cranking out popular songs and soundtracks for such Disney movies as *The Parent Trap*. They also wrote a notable non-Disney hit, Johnny Burnette's "You're Sixteen." In the mid-1960s, the Shermans started getting Oscar recognition—their score for *Mary Poppins* and the movie's "Chim Chim Cher-ee" both won Academy Awards. The brothers also wrote songs for *The Jungle Book*,

MOUSCELLANY

One of the things Walt Disney must have liked about the Sherman brothers was their use of "nonsense words," since several are featured as prominent songs in Disney's movies, including "Higitus Figitus" (*The Sword in the Stone*, 1963), "Supercalifragilisticexpialidocious" (*Mary Poppins*, 1964), and "Fortuosity" (*The Happiest Millionaire*, 1967).

as well as Oscar-nominated music for a non-Disney movie, *Chitty Chitty Bang Bang*. Later Oscar-nominated film projects included *Bedknobs and Broomsticks* and *Tom Sawyer* (for which they also wrote the screenplay).

On the fortieth-anniversary DVD of *The Jungle Book*, the Shermans discuss their goals for writing Disney movie songs: their idea was "to progress the story," says Robert, and "tell the story through the songs. Walt liked that." "The boss," adds Richard, "knew that we didn't care about anything but the story. If we could make the story develop and push forward, he was very happy."

Disneyland would benefit from several key Sherman compositions. Who doesn't know their familiar theme songs for the **Enchanted Tiki Room** and **It's a Small World**? Interestingly, the Shermans originally composed the latter as a slow ballad, not as the peppy romp it became later. Other attractions showcasing their music have included **Adventure Thru Inner Space** ("Miracles from Molecules"), the **Carousel of Progress** ("There's a Great Big Beautiful Tomorrow"), and **The Many Adventures of Winnie the Pooh** ("Heffalumps and Woozles").

By now, Richard and Robert Sherman have been awarded several Grammy Awards, accumulated about two dozen gold albums, had blockbuster shows on Broadway, been named to the Songwriters Hall of Fame, and been inducted as Disney Legends. Richard currently lives in Beverly Hills. Until his death in March of 2012, Robert lived in London, where a popular exhibition of his paintings was held in 2002. The brothers' autobiography, *Walt's Time: From Before to Beyond*, was published in 1998; *The Boys*, a documentary that celebrates their lives while also discussing their long estrangement, was released in 2009.

Ship to Shore Marketplace

MAP: Frontierland, Fr-17

DATES: May 2011–ongoing

The Ship to Shore Marketplace appeared in 2011 next to the dock for the ***Mark Twain* Riverboat** and **Sailing Ship *Columbia***, which explains the stand's maritime theme (decorations include canvas "sails," masts, and shipping crates). Its arrival came almost three years after **Westward Ho Conestoga Wagon Fries** left its spot just up the walkway in 2008. The menu is similar to the one at **Edelweiss Snacks** in **Fantasyland**: jumbo turkey legs, chimichangas, corn on the cob, frozen lemonade, and other take-away snacks. A nearby seating area offers views of the river traffic.

Show Your Disney Side

DATES: September 30, 2013–May 2015

Replacing the long-term **Let the Memories Begin** marketing campaign and the short-term **Monstrous Summer**, Show Your Disney Side arrived on September 30, 2013. The new promotion invited guests to submit photos and videos to social networks, thus illustrating how Disney parks liberate everyone from the work-a-day world. Over Memorial Day weekend in 2014, guests were invited to dress as Disney characters for the Rock Your Disney Side Party, a twenty-four-hour event that included special foods, dances, a movie marathon, a *Frozen*-themed sand sculpture near the turnstiles, and a Disney Side of Summer Sweepstakes. In May of 2015, Disneyland's **Diamond Celebration** replaced Show Your Disney Side as the park's new promotion.

Side Street Strutters

Lively jazz ensembles have a long history in Disneyland, starting with the original **Firehouse Five Plus Two**. The Side Street Strutters brought that tradition into the twenty-first century. Formed at Arizona State University in 1983 by students with a love of early New Orleans jazz, the Strutters starting appearing at Disneyland in 1985 and could often be found in colorful costumes onstage at the **French Market** in **New Orleans Square**. In the fall of 2006, the group ended its successful run of almost twenty-two years as regular Disneyland performers.

Clarinet, sax, tuba, and trombone are among the instruments played by the current seven members, who still tour today. The Side Street Strutters' combination of first-rate musicianship, energy, and humor make them ideal, crowd-friendly performers at Disneyland. The group has also appeared on national TV shows, played at the White House, and performed all across the United States and Europe. In addition, the group has recorded numerous albums, most recently with vocalist Meloney Collins. A sassy vocalist who echoes the great jazz songstresses of the past, Collins has performed for various Disney projects and has appeared at Disneyland with both the Jambalaya Jazz Band and the **Royal Street Bachelors**.

Silhouette Studio

MAP: Main Street, MS-13

DATES: January 19, 1956–ongoing

Just a few months after **Opening Day**, **Grandma's Baby Shop** suddenly departed from its tiny 100-square-foot spot on the northeastern side of **Main Street**. The business that replaced it has lasted much longer than its predecessor; the Silhouette Studio has been operating in Grandma's old location for over sixty years.

The Silhouette Studio does primarily one thing: it hand-cuts black paper silhouettes of guests' profiles. Originating in Europe in the mid-1800s, this silhouette art was revived in America in the early 1900s and transplanted to Disneyland as an interesting souvenir appropriate to Main Street's turn-of-the-century atmosphere. It's an affordable souvenir, too, since the only added expense is the frame, which can be purchased to enhance and preserve the delicate paper silhouette. What's more, the subject doesn't even have to be in the room, since the artists can work from only a photograph (which is how they're able to cut silhouettes of pets). If the subjects have passed away, the artists can add halos above them. Amazingly, each customized cut-out is usually created in under a minute, with slightly more time needed for group portraits.

Although this enterprise may seem like a minor novelty, millions of these silhouettes have been cut at Disneyland by now, and the little shop has gotten more exposure in the annual **souvenir books** than many other Main Street businesses.

Silver Spur Supplies

MAP: Frontierland, Fr-3

DATES: Ca. 2001–ongoing

When **Bonanza Outfitters** replaced the **Pendleton Woolen Mills Dry Goods Store** in 1990, the single Bonanza Outfitters space actually had two additional businesses operating inside it: the American Buffalo Hat Company and Silver Spur Supplies. After a decade, American Buffalo left and Silver Spur expanded into its empty space, thus establishing itself as its own distinct, two-room store—"The Greatest Roundup of Wares in the West," as one sign proclaims.

> **MOUSCELLANY**
>
> To commemorate the store's ongoing success, a new Silver Spur Supplies pin was issued in 2005 featuring a cowboy Mickey.

The Silver Spur interior still connects to Bonanza Outfitters, and the store's back wall is still dominated by the large wooden buffalo sculpture left by American Buffalo Hats. A large, upside-down canoe hangs from the ceiling, a carved eagle, authentic buckskin outfits, and various frontier artifacts stand on shelves, and historic photos of famous frontier figures adorn one wall. Today, the Silver Spur is light on the silver and spurs and heavy on the Disney shirts, hats, and Western-style clothes. By 2014, the shop was definitely aiming at a more luxury-minded clientele, selling beautiful $175 suede jackets and—surprise!—expensive long-sleeve Pendleton shirts, Pendleton mugs, and other nods to the building's Pendleton past, which has made a comeback at the store. Ornaments, Christmas clothes, and edible gifts usually move in for the **holiday season**.

Sklar, Martin

(1934–)

Marty Sklar has been involved in Disneyland since 1955, and he's the only **cast member** to have attended every Disney park opening (including Shanghai Disneyland in 2016). Born in New Jersey in 1934, he attended UCLA and became the editor of the school's *Daily Bruin* newspaper. When he was twenty-one, Disney hired Sklar to create an old-fashioned newspaper called the *Disneyland News* for the park's debut. While this paper was being sold on **Main Street**, Sklar returned to school, graduated, and then joined Disneyland's publicity team in 1956.

Working out of offices in **Town Square**, Sklar became the "chief ghostwriter at Disney," according to his 2013 memoir, *Dream It! Do It!* He wrote speeches for **Walt**

Disney, scripts for Disney TV shows, and "most of the publicity and marketing materials for Disneyland," among them the annual **souvenir books** (he's listed as the sole author of the 1964 and 1969 hardcover editions). Sklar also worked with Disney on new exhibits for the 1964–1965 New York World's Fair, and a decade later, he was named vice president, helping to steer EPCOT and Walt Disney World. Later he was promoted to president and then vice-chairman at Walt Disney Imagineering, roles that placed him in charge of the designers who create new attractions and concepts for Disney theme parks, hotels, and cruise ships.

Now formally retired after a fifty-four-year career, Sklar is widely recognized as an eloquent authority on everything Disney, and is frequently interviewed for documentaries about Disneyland (he makes a long appearance on the *Walt Disney Treasures: Tomorrow Land* DVD). His decades of leadership brought him recognition as a Disney Legend in 2001, as well as a **Main Street Tribute Window** on July 17, 2009, the fifty-fourth anniversary of Disneyland's **Opening Day** (that tribute window is located outside the **City Hall** office where he once worked). Sklar's 2015 book, *One Little Spark! Mickey's Ten Commandments and The Road to Imagineering*, is an insightful examination of the Imagineering profession.

Skull Rock and Pirate's Cove, aka Skull Rock Cove

MAP: Fantasyland, Fa-14

DATES: December 1960–January 1982

Five years after the **Pirate Ship Restaurant** opened in **Fantasyland**, a fully realized lagoon was finally built around the ship. Called both Skull Rock Cove and Pirate's Cove in Disneyland's **souvenir books**, the shallow turquoise pond was shaped like a lopsided rectangle and covered about a quarter-acre. The lagoon and ship were surrounded by prominent attractions, including the **Mad Hatter's Mad Tea Party** and the **Storybook Land Canal Boats**. A **Skyway** tower on the western bank carried gondolas of passengers directly over a corner of the lagoon (but not over the ship). A narrow walkway connected the southern shore to the ship sitting out in the middle of the lagoon, and dining terraces lined the northern shore.

Besides the beautiful pirate ship, the most famous feature of Pirate's Cove was Skull Rock. This thirty-foot-tall, rock-like construction rose on the lagoon's northeastern shore, where it shared the same rock formation that holds the head of Monstro the Whale. Skull Rock had what looked like an open mouth, craggy teeth, large eye sockets, and a wide crack down its forehead. Waterfalls poured from the

MOUSCELLANY

Skull Rock was a Disney invention for the 1953 *Peter Pan* movie; J. M. Barrie's original play didn't mention a Skull Rock (the only named rock in Barrie's 1904 *Peter Pan* is Marooners' Rock, a boulder in a lagoon that got swamped at high tide). Disney's Skull Rock probably owes its design inspiration to *King Kong*, the 1933 classic in which Skull Island was topped by a prominent skull-shaped mountain.

mouth and from either side of the skull. Memorably, the eyes lit up at night with an unearthly green color. Abstract volcanic rock sculptures and palm trees surrounded Skull Rock, and trails seemed to wind through the area; all of this landscaping would have made for great climbing, if guests had been allowed to explore it. Unfortunately, this wasn't **Tom Sawyer Island**, so Skull Rock and its rugged terrain were off limits to adventurers.

Skull Rock, Pirate's Cove, and the Pirate Ship Restaurant were all removed in 1982 during the massive Fantasyland remodel. Dumbo's elephants now fly on the site where the glorious pirate ship once sat in its exotic lagoon. A more elaborate Skull Rock can still be found, however, in Adventureland—the Adventureland in Disneyland Paris, that is.

Skyfest

DATE: December 5, 1985

Culminating the celebrations for Disneyland's thirtieth birthday, and timed to land on **Walt Disney's** birthdate, Skyfest was an ambitious one-day publicity stunt created by Disney Legend **Jack Lindquist**. His goal: to set a new world record by releasing a million balloons simultaneously (the previous record was a third of that total). The launch was arranged by the Glasshouse Balloon Company, a Costa Mesa outfit owned by Treb Heining. Sixteen years earlier, fifteen-year-old Heining had started selling balloons at Disneyland, and he later came up with the combination of Mickey-shaped helium balloons inside larger clear balloons (an effect called a "glasshouse"). Heining's company, meanwhile, has provided balloons for dozens of major events including Super Bowls, national political conventions, and the Olympics.

Held on December 5, 1985, Disneyland's Skyfest began in the **parking lot**, where over 3,000 volunteers filled colored balloons with a total of 70,000 pounds of helium. The balloons were released from locations along nearby Katella Avenue; later reports had them landing as far away as Australia.

Skyway to Fantasyland and Skyway to Tomorrowland

MAP: Tomorrowland, T-13; Fantasyland, Fa-12
DATES: June 23, 1956–November 10, 1994

MOUSCELLANY

Disneyland has plenty of regular-size balloons, but it's also hosted its share of giant hot-air balloons as well. On Easter Sunday, April 22, 1962, the balloon from the 1956 film *Around the World in 80 Days* lifted off from the Hub and rose thousands of feet into the air, landing miles away from the park. A huge Ear Force One balloon resembling Mickey Mouse's head visited the park in 1988 (for Mickey's sixtieth birthday) and 2006 (for Disneyland's fiftieth). Lastly, on February 17, 2013, a colorful blue balloon that promoted a new Disney movie, *Oz: The Great and Powerful*, was inflated and tethered in the Esplanade in front of Disneyland's **entrance**.

For almost twenty-two years, most guests wandering near the **Casey Jr. Circus Train** in **Fantasyland** were oblivious to the alpine chalet on a little hill, half-hidden among lush trees. Demolished in June of 2016, this 5,000-square-foot structure was the old Fantasyland station of the extinct Skyway to Fantasyland/Skyway to Tomorrowland attraction.

Guests who never got to experience the Skyway may find it hard to appreciate its greatness—but great it was, especially back in the 1950s and '60s, when cable-suspended gondolas were still a decade away from becoming ubiquitous transit systems at ski resorts. Old **souvenir books** claim that the Skyway was "the first aerial tramway of its kind in the United States" ("of its kind" refers to the gondola-style ski lifts already starting to appear in Europe). In the 1950s and '60s, most guests at Disneyland had nothing to compare the Skyway to, so it really did seem special.

Like the **Monorail** (which wouldn't open until 1959) and the **PeopleMover** (1967), the Skyway was an ambitious attempt to introduce efficient public transportation into Disneyland. The Skyway's efficiency wasn't its hallmark, however; other transit systems could easily carry more passengers at higher speeds for longer distances. But the Skyway offered something no other Disneyland attraction could: by adding height to sights, it gave guests a lingering view of the park from high above.

The hyperbolic **attraction poster** certainly emphasizes the ride's panoramic views, making it look as if guests were *hundreds* of feet aloft and rising on steeply pitched cables. While the trip was not quite that dramatic, the views from almost six stories up in the air were more breathtaking than any other sight that Disneyland could offer. Riding on a thin steel thread, with their gondolas open to the air and offering a full 360-degree view, guests might have felt more connected to the sky than to the park below.

The Skyway to Fantasyland and the Skyway to Tomorrowland were really the same attraction, operating in opposite directions and built for $300,000 total. Both Skyways ran on the same cable, both shared the same support towers, and both connected the same two stations in Fantasyland and **Tomorrowland**. The Fantasyland station had a Swiss theme, though the inscription on the building came from *Alice in Wonderland*: "'Up above the World You fly, Like a Tea-Tray in the Sky,' said the Dormouse." The futuristic station near **Autopia** a quarter-mile away had a more spartan design.

Using their D tickets at either station, guests rode in small red, blue, yellow, and green gondolas with flat roofs and no windows. Over the years, the design changed: the 1956 originals were cylindrical and included only two individual, patio-style chairs, while 1965's new **Bob Gurr**-designed gondolas were rectangular and contained seating for four passengers. In the early years, the ride could be taken for either a one-way journey or a

MOUSCELLANY

In the U.S., several large aerial tramways operating at much higher altitudes predated Disneyland's small, "first of its kind" ski-lift gondolas. One of the most famous trams was the Sky Ride at the 1933 Century of Progress Exposition in Chicago; its two towers were 628-feet tall, and the thirty-six-passenger cars ran 215 feet above the fair.

seven-minute round-trip, but in later decades all trips were one-way only. The altitude varied depending on where the forty-four gondolas dangled along their route, but usually they averaged a height of between forty and sixty feet (the central suspension tower, standing tall on the hill where the Matterhorn would be built, topped out at eighty-five feet).

Along the way, guests got incredible views of Tomorrowland and Fantasyland. When it was erected in 1959, the **Matterhorn** was right in the Skyway's path, so an east–west passageway was opened up that enabled guests to make an exciting trip through the mountain's interior. Inside the Matterhorn, guests witnessed bobsleds hurtling through the mountain on their angled tracks. Also on view below the Skyway were the **Submarine Voyage**, **Alice in Wonderland**, the **Pirate Ship Restaurant**, and the **Casey Jr. Circus Train**.

Fallacious stories of severe accidents and even deaths have long swirled around the Skyway. None of these exaggerated rumors pertains to the Skyway's closure after thirty-eight years. There was certainly the possibility of an eventual calamity, but a more common problem was the irresistible temptation for some riders to spit, litter, or pour beverages onto the guests below. Additionally, the incongruous steel towers and cables seemed out of place when Fantasyland got a charming remodel in 1983. Imagineers considered modifying and updating the Skyway, but ultimately the buckets were grounded permanently in late 1994.

The Skyway took one last celebratory run with Mickey and Minnie aboard. Afterwards, the Matterhorn's holes were sealed up, the Skyway towers eventually came down, and the Tomorrowland station disappeared into memory.

Sleeping Beauty Castle

MAP: Fantasyland, Fa-2

DATES: July 17, 1955–ongoing

If Disneyland has a soul, it probably resides within the walls of Sleeping Beauty Castle. On the *Disney Parks: Disneyland Resort Behind the Scenes* DVD, longtime Imagineer **Tony Baxter** calls it "the symbol of the park." Even without seeing the castle in person, people everywhere recognize it as an iconic image representing not only Disneyland but the entire Walt Disney Company.

This was probably true even before the castle was built. Back in 1954, a year before Disneyland opened, viewers saw an animated castle in the opening titles of the popular ***Disneyland TV series*** and thus could have easily equated the castle with Disneyland and Disney entertainment. Later, a castle—not Disneyland's castle, but a castle nonetheless—became the center-piece of the corporate logo that prefaces Disney movies, as well as a prominent feature of countless commercials and print ads.

Pre-construction, the early concept illustrations of Disneyland usually place some variation of a castle at the park's center. **Herb Ryman's landmark 1953 illustration depicts a dominating fortress towering hundreds of feet in the air and surrounded by tall, battle-worthy ramparts. What finally arose, of course, was much smaller. The** 2000 **souvenir book** explains why **Disneyland's** "regal sentinel" was scaled down: "**Walt Disney** recalled that European castles of old were often built to intimidate the peasants. He believed a less imposing castle would appear friendlier and more inviting to Disneyland guests."

Indeed, the castle stands only seventy-seven feet high, making it half as tall as the **Matterhorn**, two-thirds as tall as **Space Mountain**, and one basketball player taller than the **Swiss Family Treehouse**. However, its position at the northern end of the **Hub**, where it can be seen from **Town Square**, makes the castle Disneyland's ultimate visual enticement—what Walt Disney called a "wienie." Another alluring wienie, one that attracts guests to the castle's courtyard, is the twirling, gilded **King Arthur Carrousel**, visible through the castle's entranceway. A photo in the August 15, 1955, issue of *Life* magazine reveals that guests also used to be able to see right through the castle's *clear* windows to the sky beyond.

During the actual design phase in 1954, architects briefly considered using the Snow White story as the castle's theme (early on, Walt Disney even called it Snow White Castle). Everyone soon settled on the Disney movie *Sleeping Beauty* instead. Nobody knew at the time exactly what the finalized castle should look like, since *Sleeping Beauty* was still early in production and wouldn't be released for five more years. Without a precise movie design to follow, Imagineers used several European castles as inspiration, especially Neuschwanstein, a notable sky-reaching Bavarian castle that predated Disneyland by only about seventy years. After reducing that fantastical, 213-foot-tall structure down to a more intimate size, Disneyland designers implemented the same forced perspective techniques they had applied to **Main Street** buildings. For the castle, the optical trick of using bigger blocks of cement at the bottom than at the top makes the walls and fiberglass towers appear to be stretching higher than they really are.

Sleeping Beauty Castle's façade is broad, yet intimate. At moat level, the majestic front facing the Hub spans about thirty-five feet across the first pair of cylindrical turrets, with the second pair set about fifteen feet back toward **Fantasyland**. A thirty-five-foot-wide circular courtyard in front of the castle offers paths to the **Plaza Gardens** and the **Snow White Wishing Well and Grotto**, plus a famous song lyric

MOUSCELLANY

The castle in the film *Sleeping Beauty* turned out to be very different from Disneyland's version. When it's first seen in the movie's introductory fairytale book, the castle is much more vertical than Disneyland's, its towers are supported by large, conspicuous flying buttresses that don't exist at Disneyland's castle, and it features a bright yellow, green, and purple roof, while Disneyland's castle has a blue roof.

embedded in its pavers: "When you wish upon a star, your dreams come true." As seen in the 1955 souvenir book, the castle has always had a side entrance/exit that leads to a trail on the west side of the moat.

The drawbridge entrance is the main pathway through the castle. Within this entry are shops visible only upon crossing the moat—no distracting illuminated signage mars the exterior's integrity. The top portion of the castle, according to a legendary story, was turned around, either by design or by accident, so that what was intended to be the front is actually facing Fantasyland, not the Hub. Some experts claim that Walt Disney asked for this change because more spires would be visible from Main Street; others suggest that he wanted to differentiate his castle from Neuschwanstein; and still others say the reversal was a designer's mistake—or Herb Ryman's idea—that Disney later approved. Whatever the explanation, the castle's architectural details, from the bartizans and crenellations and balistrariae above to the spiraled columns and gothic arches on the courtyard side, all still ring true.

Sleeping Beauty Castle is full of Disney trivia: the spires feature twenty-two-karat gold leaf, and for years, one spire was made to look different from the rest; what's said to be the heraldic crest of the Disney family has adorned the entranceway since 1965 (some heraldry researchers denounce this claim as apocryphal); a "time castle" was buried in the forecourt on Disneyland's fortieth anniversary; a conspicuous bronze marker under the courtyard entrance possibly denotes Disneyland's original geographic center before **Mickey's Toontown** was added (some historians dispute the significance of this marker, and early maps place Disneyland's center in front of the castle, not behind it in the courtyard); the castle's downspouts are animal-shaped;

swans occasionally used to glide across the moat, while swan topiaries grow off to the side; and on and on and on.

The castle's drawbridge has officially been raised and lowered twice—once on **Opening Day**, and again for a rededication in late May of 1983 (*Disneyland: The Nickel Tour* notes many unofficial raisings and lowerings during that May week). Thick new railings and other safety improvements to the drawbridge mean that, as of September 2014, it can no longer be raised.

Other important modifications have been made to the castle since 1955. While guests today expect to see its familiar blue-and-pink coloring, the castle originally had gray stones at the bottom, and at one time, green ivy spread across its front walls. For some celebrations, the castle gets special decorations, such as "icicles" for the winter holidays, gold trim for Disneyland's fiftieth anniversary, and shimmering new decorations for the recent **Diamond Celebration**. Two enduring modifications came in 1957. First, the Sleeping Beauty Castle Walk-Through debuted. A few months later, the Fantasy in the Sky **fireworks** started exploding above the turrets nightly. Out front, two new fifteen-foot-tall, castle-themed towers (housing special effects for the fireworks shows) appeared in March of 2015.

Ultimately, there has been no building more indispensable to Disneyland's history and image than Sleeping Beauty Castle. Upon its completion, artists and writers immediately championed it as the building that best represented the park's truest self, which explains why the castle has been shown on more **souvenir book** covers than all other subjects combined. Guests also treat the castle differently—they don't usually linger at the entrance to any other land, but they do here. And if you ask anyone to think of Disneyland, there's a good chance that Sleeping Beauty Castle will immediately pop into that person's mind.

Along with the **Opera House**, the castle was one of the first Disneyland buildings to be finished. The Opera House was required for its initial functionality as a lumber mill. The castle, it's said, was required as an inspiration to the construction crews—to prove that dreams really could come true, to show them what make-believe looked like, and to remind them, finally, where Disneyland's soul resides.

> **MOUSCELLANY**
>
> One of the most delightful statues in the whole park is the small owl in front of the Sleeping Beauty Castle. Fashioned to look like the owl in Disney's *Sleeping Beauty*, this small statue presents a humorous photoop as it glares down at whatever subject is posed next to it.

Sleeping Beauty Castle Walk-Through

Map: Fantasyland, Fa-2

DATES: April 29, 1957–October 7, 2001; November 26, 2008–ongoing

The August 15, 1955, issue of *Life* magazine features a Disneyland pictorial that mentions a "model torture chamber" coming soon to **Sleeping Beauty Castle**. Two years after it opened, the castle did receive a significant enhancement that wasn't quite a torture chamber, though it did have some scary elements.

The entrance to the Sleeping Beauty Castle Walk-Through has never been overtly conspicuous—located in a western corner of the castle's inner courtyard, the doorway is so unobtrusive that unknowing guests have probably walked right past it. Inside, the Castle Walk-Through features narrow stairways that lead guests on a walk up into the castle's interior, eastward past imaginative dioramas, across what is called the "corridor of goons," and down to an eastern exit. One of the early Castle Walk-Through plans includes a route that would have taken guests outside to a second-floor balcony, where they would have seen sleeping guards still under Maleficent's spell.

While that dramatic option never materialized, the final results were still wonderful. Elaborate dioramas, designed primarily by Ken Anderson and echoed later by the Windows of Enchantment on Main Street, beautifully retold the story of Disney's

Sleeping Beauty movie. Large illustrated storybooks with ornate calligraphy, well-executed sets with dreamy colors and cinematic lighting effects, detailed figures with exquisite costumes and precise accessories, and delicate music from the Disney movie all combined to deliver artistic exposition. An update to the dioramas in 1977 changed the look somewhat (3D dolls replaced some of the cut-out figures in the scenes), but not the overall spirit, of the beautiful tableaux.

There were also some simpler effects that were surprisingly powerful, including a shadow of Maleficent (shown) that still lurks in one of the final corridors, making kids stop cold before proceeding (this effect was suspended for several years due to the bottle-neck it caused in the stairways). One effect that got a try-out but was permanently canceled was a "bottomless chamber" where guests' voices were picked up by a hidden microphone and echoed into the darkness (you can imagine how kids responded to that sonic temptation).

One of Hollywood's royals, Shirley Temple, and the Disneyland Band graced the Walk-Through's opening ceremonies in 1957. For the next forty-four years, millions of guests investigated the passageway into the castle. Many of those guests, it's safe to say, weren't so much fans of dioramas as they were fans of the famous castle itself, and they were curious to see what it was like inside. The cooling, calming effect of the dark interior was an additional draw on hot, busy days.

Though only an A-ticket attraction, the Castle Walk-Through was always a charmer, especially in its first years when its dazzling special effects were some of the best in Disneyland. As an extra bonus, in the 1950s, guests even received a lovely gift book at the exit. Unfortunately, a temporary closure in 2001 was quietly extended for several years because of accessibility issues and refurbishment costs. The loss was a disappointing development for anyone looking to recapture some Disneyland history or trying to find some shaded serenity in Fantasyland.

As Sleeping Beauty herself says in her movie, "They say if you dream a thing more than once, it's sure to come true." To the delight of fans who had been dreaming of a reawakened Castle Walk-Through, an upgraded version reopened in

MOUSCELLANY

Inside the ground-floor "accessible experience" viewing room in Sleeping Beauty Castle is an incredible triple-backed chair (shown) made of elaborately carved wood and upholstered with velvet.

late 2008. The well-received renovation introduced rejuvenated displays and a new ground-floor "accessible experience" viewing room for guests who couldn't negotiate the tight stairways. Veteran Imagineer **Tony Baxter**, who led the project, says on the *Disney Parks: Disneyland Resort Behind the Scenes* DVD that the refreshed Walk-Through is "a tribute to what Walt did at the dawn of Disneyland." After such a long absence, the Walk-Through's welcome return was a fairytale finish for a classic Disneyland attraction.

Snow White's Scary Adventures,
aka Snow White Adventures

Map: Fantasyland, Fa-8

DATES: July 17, 1955–ongoing

Seemingly innocent but deceptively sinister, Snow White Adventures has been charming adults and terrifying toddlers since **Opening Day**. Throughout its long history, the attraction has survived several name changes: the first **souvenir books** calls it the Snow White Adventures Ride; subsequent books amend that to Snow White Adventures; and later, the sign above the entrance read Snow White and Her Adventures.

The biggest name change, and an acknowledgement of the main issue some parents have always had with the attraction, came in 1983, when it was rechristened Snow White's Scary Adventures. Previously, the only warning about the ride's frightening nature was posted out front, on a small sign that also included a depiction of the ugly hag from the story. Consequently, parents often did not realize that this was not the gentle, child-friendly lark they expected.

Some happy elements have always existed inside. Even in its earliest days, guests were shown familiar scenes and characters from the classic 1937 Disney movie, including friendly animals and the dwarfs. However, as Grumpy says in the movie, "There's trouble a-brewin'"—in the middle of the ride, the tone of the scenes shifts from light to dark. In fact, for its first few decades, the attraction was more sinister than what we see today: there was no Snow White character, no prince, and at the end of the ride, the triumphant hag seemed to launch a boulder successfully at riders without being destroyed herself.

A major remodel in 1983 addressed some of the darkness by adding the bouncy "Silly Song" at the beginning, the handsome prince at the end, and the villainess's demise as she falls off a cliff. But still, the attraction's imaginative, detailed settings continue to range from the cozy and assuaging (the dwarfs' cottage and the glittering mine, for example) to the dark and menacing (the creepy forest and the castle dungeon). To this day, the evil queen (shown) still dominates the experience, and

her sudden transformation scene continues to traumatize kids as it has for decades.

Interestingly, like the nearby **Peter Pan** and **Mr. Toad** attractions, the ride's namesake star never appeared among the scenery until 1983's makeover. Early designers hoped guests would realize that *they* were embodying Snow White during the ride, experiencing her adventures the same way they experienced Peter's and Toad's. Few guests saw it that way, however, asking repeatedly where Snow White, Peter, and Toad were, so eventually all three stars were added to their respective attractions. Snow White arrived in 1983 on the cottage staircase (shown), with "lips reds as the rose, hair black as ebony, skin white as snow," as the Magic Mirror describes her in the movie. But even after she was introduced as a physical presence, her appearances were far outnumbered by the evil queen's repeated manifestations. When the souvenir books have featured photos of the ride's revamped interiors, they usually devote much less space to the young beauty than to Her Royal Ugliness. Scary adventures, indeed.

In addition to changing the name and adding Snow White, the 1983 remodel updated the woodland vehicles and extended the ride-time by about a minute. The most obvious change was to the building's exterior, where the simple medieval-tournament façade built in the 1950s was supplanted by a complex, well-detailed design that evoked the queen's stone castle, complete with skull decorations and a half-timbered tower over the entrance. Inside the **queue** area, guests are now braced for the frights to come by eerie voice effects and an ominous dungeon display (if children can handle the queue, supposedly, then they'll be fine for the actual ride). Within the attraction, the poisoned apple laced with "sleeping death" (which had formerly been a much-stolen prop) has been replaced by a hologram. A new 1983 **attraction poster** clearly depicts the ugly queen and warns guests to "Watch Out for the Wicked Witch," a straightforward attempt to prepare novice riders for what was to come.

MOUSCELLANY

One of the questions adults might ask about Snow White's Scary Adventures concerns the ending. After surviving a harrowing adventure, guests finally burst into the daylight, where they see a mural that reads, "And they lived happily ever after." On the mural is the handsome prince, finally making an appearance. Where has he been all this time? He wasn't around to romance Snow White at the beginning (as he was in the movie), and the dwarfs were the ones who eventually chased down the old hag, so what exactly did the prince do to earn Snow White's "ever after"?

Disney Legend **Ken Anderson**, whose career had already arced from the 1937 animated movie to the 1955 attraction, also steered the 1983 enhancement. To adults, Snow White's Scary Adventures is today more impressive than ever. To kids, it is still one of Disneyland's most affecting two-minute experiences. And to Walt Disney, the effective, delightful attraction just might draw the same feelings he had for the original story he'd heard as a boy: "Of all the characters and the fairy-tales," he writes in the April 1953 issue of *Brief Magazine*, "I loved Snow White the best."

> ## MOUSCELLANY
>
> In *Snow White and the Seven Dwarfs*, the wicked queen is seen standing at a castle window for five seconds, but outside Snow White's Scary Adventures, she appears at the tower window twice every minute to briefly scowl at the guests below.

Snow White Wishing Well and Grotto

MAP: Fantasyland, Fa-1

DATES: April 9, 1961–ongoing

Tucked into a quiet corner east of the **Sleeping Beauty Castle** moat, the Snow White Wishing Well and Grotto site has been a bucolic hideaway since 1961. A heart-adorned wooden bridge leads from the northeastern corner of the **Hub** to the old-fashioned, blue-roofed Wishing Well (which is a coin magnet—all the loose change tossed into the Wishing Well is given to charity). From the bridge and the well, guests get clear views of the placid garden Grotto, where a gentle waterfall trickles down among white marble statues of Snow White (detail shown), all seven dwarfs, and assorted woodland creatures.

Disney Legend **John Hench** was responsible for this tranquil spot. He also solved the predicament that arose during the statues' installation. In his book *Designing Disney*, Hench writes that the statues had been created as a gift for **Walt Disney** from an Italian sculptor. Intended to represent the characters as they appeared in Disney's 1937 movie, all the figures are about three feet tall—but Snow White, of course, should dwarf the dwarfs. To disguise the inaccuracy, Hench placed her at the back of the grotto, and the added distance and elevation give the illusion of proper height disparity.

Romance is in the air here—literally. The Snow White Wishing Well emits a soft, echoing rendition of the movie's "Some Day My Prince Will Come," as sung by the movie's vocalist, Adriana Caselotti (1916–1997). In 2012, enhanced lighting added new colors to the whole presentation of the well and statues. Inspired by the lovely sights and sounds of the garden environment, "numerous wedding proposals" are made here, according to a caption in the park's 2000 **souvenir book**. More fairytales come true when various Disney princesses make their rounds here to sign autographs and have their pictures taken.

From here, guests can walk a few steps north to **Sleeping Beauty Castle** and a side entrance that takes them through a cozy, twenty-five-foot-long passageway into the castle's courtyard.

South Seas Traders

MAP: Adventureland, A-2

DATES: June 30, 1984–ongoing

Though the **Adventureland** and **Jungle Cruise** themes suggest exotic jungles and dangerous rivers, guests are actually in the middle of sunny Southern California, one of the world's surfing capitals. Consequently, South Seas Traders started in 1984 as a beachy-keen shop offering practically everything aspiring surfers could need (except surfboards). The sun wear, flip-flops, and sunglasses sold here would have been appropriate inside a nearby Huntington Beach surf shop. This being Disneyland, the Hawaiian shirts boast Disney themes.

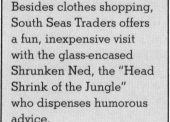

MOUSCELLANY

Besides clothes shopping, South Seas Traders offers a fun, inexpensive visit with the glass-encased Shrunken Ned, the "Head Shrink of the Jungle" who dispenses humorous advice.

In the past few years, South Seas Traders has been featuring more expensive items such as up-scale dresses and casual sweaters for around $60, plus sun hats, sandals, and the right jewelry for a tropical vacation. In 2015, a wall of Roxy beach clothes for women offered everything from T-shirts and hoodies to shorts and beach shoes. There's still plenty of gear for surfers, though, if they head to the racks of shirts, hats, and back-packs made by established surf companies like Vans, O'Neill, Billabong, and Quiksilver (the afore-mentioned Roxy and Quiksilver are the same company who share the same logo and, until July 2016, a store in Downtown Disney).

Souvenir Books, aka Souvenir Guide Books, aka Pictorial Souvenir Books

The souvenir books referenced throughout this encyclopedia are official publications of the Walt Disney Company. As such, they are valuable resources for anyone research-ing Disneyland history. Sold throughout the park at many stores and souvenir stands, the books have come out nearly every year since 1955, usually with updated photos and text, and frequently with a photo of **Sleeping Beauty Castle** on the front.

In early years the books cost only a quarter, a price so low that the profit on each sale was a single penny. Sometimes called souvenir guide books or pictorial souvenir books, most of the souvenir books are laid out horizontally and are approximately eleven and a half inches wide by eight inches tall. Typically they have soft covers, twenty-eight to thirty-eight photo-filled pages, and chapters dedicated to each of the park's lands.

For the Disney Company, souvenir books have served several purposes. First, they have been created as beautiful pictorial keepsakes to help guests remember their park visits. Armed with a book of photographs, a veteran guest is also better able to describe a visit to other potential guests. Imagineer **Tony Baxter** notes this theory in his foreword to *Poster Art of the Disney Parks*: "Walt knew that the feeling and stories sparked by the booklet would generate repeat visits far more valuable than any short-term revenue from its sale. Each visitor, in essence, became an emissary with a guidebook to introduce Disneyland to their friends. And the souvenir book also served to create an excitement for its owner's future visits."

The books have welcomed guests with warm words from an avuncular **Walt Disney**, introduced Disneyland's novel hub-and-spoke layout, and described the kind of thrills to expect from each major attraction. In the early decades, the souvenir books' large maps helped newbies envision Disneyland's unique geography. Also, back in an era when clunky, unreliable film-loaded cameras produced as many dark/blurry/misaimed discards as they did treasured photographs, the souvenir books offered perfectly positioned photos to guests who were unskilled with a camera or didn't even own one. Supplementing the lovely photos are imaginative drawings and evocative text that help capture the diverse environments of Disneyland. The simple illustrated maps were also useful, but only to a point: though they usually include a key with lists of attractions, stores, and restaurants, unfortunately the maps do not identify the location of every single item on the list, only a few landmarks. Souvenir books after the 1960s don't include any maps or lists at all, reducing their efficacy as research materials.

While the spirit of the books has been consistent over the decades, the format has changed substantially. The first souvenir book, called *The Story of Disneyland*, was finished before Disneyland was, so it was filled with artist renditions instead of actual photographs. A small, eight-by-five-inch photo-filled book came out later that year and includes a map of freeways that lead to Anaheim, showing how foreign the whole Disneyland concept was in 1955. The 1956 and '57 books, both tall verticals, are the first truly educational souvenir books and have on their back covers checklists of everything to see in Disneyland. The books from 1958 to 1964 all have the same eight-by-eleven-inch horizontal design, covers that blend photos with illustrations, and basically the same interior pages that are sporadically revised to accommodate important new attractions (the 1960 book even has a special wraparound cover devoted to the expensive new **Nature's Wonderland** area). These early books also incorporate preview pages that tantalize with concept illustrations of future developments such as the **Haunted Mansion**. At eleven by ten and a half inches, the 1965 souvenir book is almost square-shaped, adding heavy design elements and borders to the pages at the expense of large photos. The 1968 book (shown on page 445) returns to the format of the 1958–1964 books; and instead of the traditional castle portrait, this souvenir book features a rather informal photo of Walt Disney signing autographs on **Main Street** (the picture originally ran in *National Geographic* in 1963). In the 1970s, the books all take on the horizontal format and appear almost identical with their castle covers, save for the big photo on the back cover featuring that year's latest high-profile attraction—the **Country Bear Jamboree**, **Space Mountain**, etc.

The souvenir book's page count dramatically increased in the 1980s and '90s. While the covers boast creative designs that vary from year to year, the interior layouts during these years don't change much, and the center maps of the 1950s and '60s are sorely missed. The 2000 book is a small, squarish edition that is eight and a half by nine inches and dense with pages and photos. Later books return to the horizontal format but are no longer just about Disneyland—by covering Disney California Adventure as well, the books devote less space to the original park and thus are more functional as generic souvenirs than as detailed research tools. These more recent souvenir books still only cost about $10, and older collectible editions (priced from a few dollars for '90s books to over $100 for high-quality '50s books) are still abundantly available from dealers and online sellers.

Interestingly, **Walt Disney** himself became less of a presence in the books over the decades. He's been on many, but far from all, of the covers. Books of the 1950s and '60s include his portrait and a welcome letter, with four or five additional photos showing him laughing as a **Jungle Cruise** skipper, **Autopia** driver, or a participant in other Disneyland scenes. Fewer photos of him appear from the 1970s to the '90s, and the 2000 book doesn't include a single photo of the man Disneyland is named after.

Occasionally, the softcover books have been supplemented with special hardcover editions that are oriented vertically, are about nine by eleven and a half inches, contain over 100 pages, and commemorate special park anniversaries. Usually these hardcover editions re-tell the highlights of Disneyland's long history. While they always give some interesting historical perspective, often their text and photos are duplicated from book to book, limiting their usefulness. For the researcher, the annual softcover books are more informative because, when compared side-by-side, they provide a more comprehensive picture of Disneyland's year-to-year changes.

Recent souvenir books have come in both horizontal and vertical formats, but they're no longer updated annually. The softcover book for 2010, *Disneyland: From Once Upon a Time to Happily Ever After*, uses the nifty trick of pairing historic photos with new photos taken in the same locations. A more recent hardcover book, *Disneyland Resort: A Celebration of New Magic and Fond Memories*, came out in 2015 in time for the **Diamond Celebration** to give a general photo tour of Disneyland while also covering Downtown Disney, Disney California Adventure, and the Disneyland Hotel.

Space Bar

MAP: Tomorrowland, T-14, T-8

DATES: Summer 1955–September 1966

In Disneyland's first summer, a futuristic restaurant called the Space Bar opened on the eastern edge of **Tomorrowland**. The restaurant's name alluded to keyboards and outer space—two components of Space Age living—but it might also have been a description of the site itself, which did indeed take up a lot of space. So much space, in fact, that in 1961, a Space Bar Dance Area opened out front, and in 1967, the huge Carousel Theater took over the space.

Early in the planning stages, the Space Bar was going to be called the Stratos-nak, with an automatic vending service similar to New York's famed Automats. "You will enjoy a delicious dinner of the future delivered to you from an immaculate, ful-ly-automatic food service," according to a pre-**Opening Day** ad in the *Orange County Register*. "Just push a button of your selection—seconds later you will have a complete, piping hot meal." Unfortunately, the "fully automatic restaurant of tomorrow" actually debuted as a small fast food eatery of today. Guests ordered basic quick-serve items (burgers, chili dogs, sodas, etc.) at the counter, though a wall of vending machines did provide some self-service opportunities. The futuristic industrial design emphasized convenience over comfort.

A half-dozen years later, the whole enterprise was remade into a bigger, more inviting restaurant without vending machines. Rows of plastic chairs with little side tables provided functional seating on a covered patio with a Tomorrowland view. In 1967, the Space Bar became a displaced bar when the **Carousel of Progress** started spinning inside the Carousel Theater. A smaller Space Bar, reduced to a mere snack stand, reopened that year about 150 feet to the west underneath the loading area of the new **PeopleMover**. A decade later, the **Lunching Pad** replaced this Space Bar sequel.

Space Girl and Space Man

For a decade, Space Girl and Space Man roamed Tomorrowland. The Space Man role was inaugurated in August of 1955, soon after Disneyland opened. The character was so popular that crowds would trail along behind him as he walked. Later, Space Girl joined him for Tomorrowland treks. In 2007, **cast members** in the **Opera House** identified this pair as K7 (Space Girl) and K8 (Space Man), setting up a joke about a Space Dog named K9 that was never sprung.

Promoted as the "symbols of Tomorrowland" in Disneyland's 1959 **souvenir book**, the fit young space couple rode on attractions, talked with guests, posed for thousands of photos, and promoted a happy and energetic technological future. The pair wore big cartoonish outfits that were definitely futuristic but hardly realistic. The couple's varied wardrobe included clothing made of both white and foil-looking material, silver boots, huge glass helmets with antennae on top, thick padded rings for their forearms and shins, and little oxygen tanks to wear on their backs. Space Girl wore either a white pantsuit or

MOUSCELLANY

Today, there's a nifty tribute to the Space Girl character in the park: she's a Roastie Toastie turning the crank inside Tomorrowland's **popcorn cart** (shown on page 396).

a short white dress. Silliest of all was her cape—super-fashion taken right out of super-hero comic books. Like Space Man, she was tall, making her easier to spot but also conforming to the idea that people would be taller in the future.

Randy Bright, one of the **cast members** who donned the Space Man's silver space suit, later wrote a history book called *Disneyland: Inside Story* and eventually oversaw new attractions as vice president of concept development. Meanwhile, Terry Jo Steinberger, a strawberry-blonde Miss Universe contestant from nearby Garden Grove, was an eighteen-year-old Space Girl in 1964 and stood almost exactly six feet tall (shown). The costume, she told us, was "no problem to wear or to get on or off," and "it was easy to hear people" through the glass helmet. She also remembers pulling gentle pranks, such as posing stiffly inside the **House of the Future** like she was a statue, and then moving her eyes to surprise people. The job, she adds, was fun and a "once-in-a-lifetime experience I would not want to have traded for anything!"

Space Girl and Space Man stopped appearing in mid-1965, but real space men soon arrived. In 1969, the **Tomorrowland Stage** broadcast a live TV feed of Apollo astronauts Neil Armstrong and Buzz Aldrin walking on the moon. Eight years later, Scott Carpenter, Gordon Cooper, Wally Schirra, and Alan Shepard were among the astronauts on hand for **Space Mountain's** debut.

Space Mountain, aka Rockin' Space Mountain, aka Hyperspace Mountain

MAP: Tomorrowland, T-18

DATES: May 4, 1977–ongoing

Disneyland's second-tallest structure opened in 1977 at a cost of about $20 million. This dollar figure made Space Mountain the park's most expensive attraction and also the first to surpass the total cost to build all of Disneyland in 1955. For its money, the Disney Company got a futuristic cone in gleaming white that reached 118 feet high, housed a volume of 1.8 million cubic feet, and covered almost an acre of **Tomorrowland**. Space Mountain's crown of slender spires looms high above Disneyland's southeastern border, and the exterior beams that slope up the mountain's cone intensify its sense of majestic height.

The idea for a roller coaster attraction called the Space Port, which closely resembled Space Mountain but also included tracks spiraling down the *outside* of the structure, was drawn up by Disney Legend **John Hench** around 1964. The Space Port would have been a dramatic new highlight for the mid-decade redesign of Tomorrowland, but the high-priced attraction wasn't doable at the time, not with the nascent Walt Disney World project starting to eat up funds (in addition, computer technology still needed to catch up with the Imagineers' imaginations). The 1968 Fun Map shows an early version of Space Mountain in its proper Tomorrowland space; the caption calls it the "Spaceport & Rocket Flight Future Attraction," the drawing has swirling ramps around the exterior, and the tall slender spire on top rivals **Matterhorn Mountain** in height.

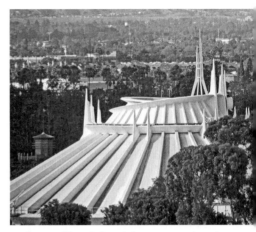

Space Mountain debuted in Orlando in early 1975, where it immediately drew raves from guests and roller coaster aficionados. Construction on Disneyland's Space Mountain began that same year on the land once used by the **Flying Saucers** (some observers see the profile of the old saucers echoed in Space Mountain's exterior). The Anaheim cone was about sixty feet shorter, and its 200-foot diameter about 100 feet smaller, than its older Orlando sibling. Plus, the Disneyland mountain had only one interior track instead of the two in Florida.

According to *Disneyland: The First Quarter Century*, over a million man-hours went into Space Mountain's design and construction in Anaheim. The finished product was shown off with a beautiful **attraction poster** of rockets streaking across a galactic background, and the **souvenir books** of the late 1970s present glorious evening photos of the glowing building on their back covers.

Opening in May 1977 to some of the longest lines in Disneyland's history, Space Mountain propelled the park to an **attendance** milestone: previously, 1970 had been the only time annual attendance had eclipsed the 10 million mark, but 1977 set a new record at just under 11 million. Guests were eager to see the second peak in Disneyland's "mountain range"—the first, the 147-foot-tall **Matterhorn**, had been erected in 1959, the 104-foot **Big Thunder Mountain** would follow in 1979, and the 87-foot **Splash Mountain** would arrive ten years after that. But Space Mountain wasn't really competing with the Matterhorn or anything else at Disneyland. Instead, it was contending with the dynamic new roller coasters luring teens to other Southern California theme parks in the 1970s. To zoom ahead of their rivals, Imagineers came up with a unique twist on the coaster concept that has now been validated with thirty years of success.

The Disney innovation of a roller coaster set in the darkness of space is simple in conception but sophisticated in execution. After waiting in a **queue** winding through long, narrow passageways, about 2,000 guests an hour can slip into sleek, open-cockpit rockets and hurtle for three minutes through two-thirds of a mile of unlit indoor track. The darkness makes the velocity seem much faster than the thirty-two miles per hour that is the rockets' maximum speed, and the banked curves and dips seem more thrilling because they're unseen and unanticipated. Air blasts from fans and the rushing sounds of the rockets themselves intensify the sensations. Enhancing the interstellar atmosphere are starry effects (created by floor-mounted disco balls), spinning galaxies, asteroids that have at times looked suspiciously like giant cookies, and a huge loading-area prop that echoes the *Discovery* spaceship from *2001: A Space Odyssey*. Adding heft to the building at its opening were nearby space-themed structures that also debuted in 1977, among them the **Space Place** and the **Space Stage**. Adding legitimacy to the whole enterprise were six of the original Mercury astronauts who attended the ride's opening day festivities.

In the 1990s, Space Mountain started to undergo changes. Beginning in 1995, Federal Express became the sponsor for a decade. Fast-paced music was added to the rockets in 1997. In 1998, the white exterior was painted in the same retro colors (bronzes and greens) that adorned other attractions in the remodeled Tomorrowland. In preparation for Disneyland's fiftieth anniversary, in 2003 the whole attraction closed for two years to replace the track, give the rockets a new look, update the queue area with a new silver spaceship, and restore the building's white exterior. The original entrance ramp is gone, replaced with a walkway that goes above the **Magic Eye Theater**. Souvenir photos are now snapped at the end of the trip à la the pre-splash photos at Splash Mountain, with Spaceport Document Control at the exit handling the transactions. More dramatically, in early 2014, the attraction reopened after construction work that remade the mountain's crown—instead of two slanting "rings" at the top, the mountain now has three, with new safety rails making it easier to clean the exterior.

Since 2007 a nighttime variation of the ride called Rockin' Space Mountain, which debuted as Rock-It Mountain in mid-2006, has brought new energy, new psychedelic lighting effects, new narration from a rock DJ, and new high-powered music to the space-y interior. Additionally, every September and October since 2009, special Ghost Galaxy effects have added Halloween chills to Space Mountain's thrills.

In November of 2015, *Star Wars* arrived in the form of Hyperspace Mountain, a new name accompanying an exciting update inspired by the famous film franchise. TIE fighters zoomed past guests as magnificent music thundered all around them, familiar sound effects blasted, and Admiral Ackbar emphatically declared, "It's a trap!" The hyperspace overlay lasted until Labor Day  2016, when it was replaced by the temporary Ghost Galaxy theme for **Halloween Time**. When Hyperspace Mountain returned in November, it was immediately greeted by long lines of guests, showing how new thrills can enliven an old favorite.

Space Place

MAP: Tomorrowland, T-16

DATES: Summer 1977–1996

When **Space Mountain** started drawing crowds into **Tomorrowland's** eastern corner, a new fast food restaurant opened up in the base of the mountain's complex to feed hungry space travelers. The Space Place was a large counter-service facility with seating for 676 guests. Pizza, hot dogs, salads, and ice cream were the main menu items. Special birthday celebrations and group parties were also available.

Despite having a busy attraction next door, the Space Place always seemed to have more space than patrons, and as its popularity gradually dwindled, its operating hours also shrank. Early in 1996, the Space Place was replaced by a temporary new attraction, the **Toy Story Funhouse**. Two years later, this area was subsumed within the spacious **Redd Rockett's Pizza Port**.

Space Station X-1,
aka Satellite View of America

MAP: Tomorrowland, T-5

DATES: July 17, 1955–February 17, 1960

> **MOUSCELLANY**
>
> Coke and Pepsi in one location? Although sponsorship arrangements in Disneyland eateries usually keep the rival beverages apart, the Space Place served them simultaneously. For decades, insiders informally divided Disneyland in two, with Pepsi generally being served in the western half and Coke in the eastern half. In 1990, Coca-Cola struck a deal to become Disneyland's sole soda.

With access to more artists than cash in 1955, **Walt Disney** decided to install an elaborate painting instead of an attraction in a central **Tomorrowland** building. In keeping with the land's Space Age theme, the exhibit room was called Space Station X-1, its position supposedly in orbit above the rotating Earth.

Bjorn Aronsen's lovely but dramatic 1955 **attraction poster** depicts guests thousands of miles above the planet; however, the "space platform" (as the **souvenir books** called it) presented a view from only ninety miles above the United States. For three minutes, the round room slowly revolved past a beautiful, detailed landscape painting that surrounded the perimeter. Created by two Disney Legends, **Claude Coats** and **Peter Ellenshaw**, the painting was necessary because photos from beyond Earth's atmosphere had not yet been taken (the first true satellite, *Sputnik 1*, wouldn't be launched until October of 1957, followed by America's *Explorer 1* three months later).

Inside Space Station X-1, guests had a broad view that began with the East Coast at sunrise, concluded with the West Coast at sunset, and showcased a daylight panorama of all the mountains and plains in the hours between. Since the entire country was shown in three minutes, this implied that guests were orbiting at about 60,000 miles per hour. Logically impressive, yes, but viscerally thrilling, no, which is why admission to this languid, sparsely attended viewing chamber cost only an A ticket from Disneyland's **ticket book**. To keep current with all the exciting satellite developments of the times, Space Station X-1 was renamed Satellite View of America in 1957.

Unfortunately, audiences still weren't boarding. Two years later, the lights went out on the space exhibit and went up on its **Art of Animation** exhibit replacement just in time to promote Disney Studios' latest animated movies.

Spirit of Refreshment

MAP: Tomorrowland, T-15

DATES: May 22, 1998–ongoing

The reintroduction of the red-and-white *Moonliner* rocket in 1998 brought with it a new beverage stand with a matching red-and-white logo. That logo, of course, belongs to Coca-Cola, and their **Tomorrowland** counter next to **Redd Rockett's Pizza Port** is called the Spirit of Refreshment. This is Coke's latest Disneyland establishment, the first being the venerable **Refreshment Corner** (aka Coke Corner) on **Main Street.**

If presentation is everything, the Spirit of Refreshment has the most appropriate presentation of any snack stand in Disneyland. Here, at the base of a towering rocket, **cast members** will sometimes launch plastic Coke bottles into the air and catch them again before serving. It's "hypercool," announces one sign; another says they're "Delivering refreshment to a thirsty galaxy." The most expensive thing here isn't a $3.25 Coke, though. It's "Honest Tea" for $4.

Splash Mountain

MAP: Bear Country/Critter Country, B/C-9

DATES: July 17, 1989–ongoing

In the 1980s, Imagineers were eager to put a high-profile thrill ride in **Bear Country**, which had become Bore Country for many guests. Something new and dramatic was needed to reinvigorate, and perhaps even redefine Disneyland's northwestern corner. That something turned out to be Splash Mountain.

The last and shortest of the four peaks in the Disneyland "mountain range" (including the **Matterhorn**, **Space Mountain**, and **Big Thunder Mountain**), the eighty-seven-foot-high Splash Mountain covers two acres of what was originally the **Indian Village** in **Frontierland**. Though it's in the same "thrill ride" category as the other Disneyland mountains, Splash Mountain is different from the rest in that its thrills aren't apparent until the very end. While the other mountain attractions are fast-moving roller coasters filled with rapid twists, turns, and dips, Splash Mountain is, for the first seventy-five percent of the experience, a gentle musical cruise more akin to **It's a Small World.**

Actually, Splash Mountain's heritage most likely dates back to the early 1900s, when the Old Mill water ride on Coney Island took visitors on a winding, scenic trip. On Splash Mountain, guests drift in hollow log boats for about a half-mile through amiable cavern settings reminiscent of the 1946 Disney film *Song of the South*, with the movie's Oscar-winning hit, "Zip-A-Dee-Doo-Dah," as one of the background songs (among the names originally considered for the attraction was Zip-A-Dee-Doo-Dah River Run). At one time, elements from the 1984 movie *Splash* (including a mermaid) were considered, but eventually the population was limited to cute critters, ranging from opossum families to croaking frogs, who sing the happy "How Do You Do" song while a simple plot unfolds about Brer Rabbit (shown) eluding the bumbling villains Brer Fox and Brer Bear.

About seven minutes into the ten-minute cruise, however, the mood begins to darken. The singing creatures' faces grow worrisome, ominous vultures appear, and the river leaves its cozy interior and seems to point upward to the distant **Fantasyland** sky. Only in the ride's last moments do guests fully understand what puts the splash in Splash Mountain—a thrilling water plunge reminiscent of another historic Coney Island favorite, the thrilling Shoot-the-Chutes. Diving down a fifty-two-foot slope at a forty-seven-degree angle, Splash Mountain's logs hit forty miles per hour as they zoom beneath an overhang of thorny briars and ram into a pool of water that sends waves splashing across the bow (and usually all over the guests). The logs travel so rapidly that few guests see the sign at the bottom that reads "Drop In Again Sometime."

The **souvenir books** from the late 1980s and early '90s proudly tout Splash Mountain as a record-setter, "the world's steepest, highest, scariest, wildest adventure." Signs along the **queue** warn guests that they "may get wet," understating the potential soak factor of a heavily front-loaded log nosediving hard into a splash pool. Inside the log, the thrill is perhaps the most intense at Disneyland; from the walkway out front, the screams, five-story plummet, explosion of water, and sudden disappearance of the guests and logs create as much concern as fascination. Fortunately, a happy ending built around a spectacular fifty-foot-wide set piece, the jubilant *Zip-A-Dee Lady* showboat, brings damp guests and a laughing Brer Rabbit home safely.

When it was first dedicated on Disneyland's thirty-fourth birthday after five years of planning and construction, Splash Mountain brought with it **Critter Country**, a successful update of the Bear Country theme that had existed since 1972. Lines for the new attraction immediately became some of the longest in Disneyland's history—but just as robust were the glowing reviews. Among the many satisfactual surprises along the way are the **Audio-Animatronic** characters themselves. Over 100 of them populate the caves, many of them recognizable as recycled entertainers from the **America Sings** attraction that once spun inside **Tomorrowland's** Carousel Theater from 1974 to 1988. Chickapin Hill is the name of the mountain's peak

MOUSCELLANY

Attentive guests might notice that some of Splash Mountain's splash isn't actually the result of the logs plummeting down the hill, but from water cannons shooting water up into the air.

(shown), and the Brer Bear is voiced by Nick Stewart, the same actor who vocalized the character in the 1946 movie. And just as guests begin their final drop down the mountain, a camera snaps a photo that is viewable at **Professor Barnaby Owl's Photographic Art Studio** just outside the exit. All this and more add up to an immensely popular attraction that at full capacity pumps about 2,000 guests through its caves per hour. Fortunately, **FASTPASS** tickets offer some line relief (for obvious water-related reasons, lines are longer in summer and during the day than they are in winter and at night).

Some estimate that Splash Mountain cost an extraordinary $75 million to build, but few guests would say it wasn't money well spent. There have been some modifications over the years. Originally the logs offered a single long bench with two backrests, with guests having to straddle the bench and basically sit in each other's laps. But in the 2000s, the logs were updated with individual backrests for support, and the whole cruise was upgraded with new safety features.

Terrifying to some, hilarious to others, and entertaining to all, Splash Mountain is a zip-a-dee-doo-dah-dazzler. The **attraction poster** gets it right, depicting the three Brers (Fox, Bear, and Rabbit) in a hollow log splashing down the mountain, and only one of the three is laughing.

Spring Fling

DATES: April 14, 1962–ca. 1972 (seasonal)

Hoping to generate some off-season excitement, in the early 1960s Disneyland executives created a special all-park event called the Spring Fling. It was first held on April 14, 1962, and was then repeated one weekend night every spring for about a decade. Though the name conjures images of bright sunshine and gambols among blooming flowers, the Spring Fling was a nighttime event that began at 8 PM and continued past midnight to as late as 1:30 AM.

> **MOUSCELLANY**
>
> The Spring Fling name was revived in March of 2013 for a week of **Limited Time Magic** activities that featured the Easter Bunny and an interactive "bunny hop" down **Main Street**.

Guests needed to buy a special ticket to attend the Spring Fling (in 1972, that ticket cost $6 per person), but admission included "unlimited use of all adventures and attractions." "Unlimited use" was a new concept at Disneyland in the 1960s, and it made the Spring Flings especially popular. Adding to the fun were special musical acts, dancing, and free prizes, which included trips, clothes, and cars. "Get into the Fling of Things," read the welcoming flyer—and guests certainly did, until the fling was finally flung in the early 1970s.

Stage Coach, aka Rainbow Mountain Stage Coaches

MAP: Frontierland, Fr-21

DATES: July 17, 1955–September 13, 1959

In the 1955 children's book *Little Man of Disneyland*, Disney characters introduce a few of Disneyland's upcoming attractions to an uninformed leprechaun. One of the few they mention is "a wonderful Wild West stagecoach ride." Though it must have seemed like a wonderful idea at the time, in practice the Stage Coach proved to be one of Disneyland's more problematic and dangerous attractions.

Also occasionally spelled as Stagecoach in the **souvenir books**, the three C-ticket coaches were beautiful wooden vehicles with large yellow wheels, bright yellow flourishes along the sides, the name Disneyland Stage Lines painted above the doors, and seating for about a dozen guests (half inside, half on the top, with even a "shotgun" space available next to the coachman). As mentioned in a photo caption in the 1957 souvenir book, these were Concord-style stagecoaches—that is, they echoed the luxurious design created for the famous overland stagecoaches of the mid-1800s by the Abbot Downing Company of Concord, New Hampshire. The accuracy extended to the ride experience, which was intentionally kept rough to maintain historical authenticity. When **Frontierland's** wilderness territory was re-modeled and the neighboring **Mule Pack** was rechristened the Rainbow Ridge Pack Mules, the stagecoach was also renamed in June of 1956 as the Rainbow Mountain Stage Coaches.

Teams of four horses from the **Pony Farm** pulled the stagecoaches through the same area traversed by the mules and the **Conestoga Wagons** (all three attractions loaded their passengers in the vicinity of today's **Big Thunder Mountain Railroad** boarding area). The operation was certainly photogenic—Disneyland's hardcover books include a picture of Vice President Nixon smiling from a window, and **Walt Disney** wears a cowboy hat in one of his poses next to the stagecoach.

The hyperbolic **attraction poster** includes an illustration of galloping horses, even though they rarely broke out of a trot—at least, they weren't supposed to. Unfortunately, startling noises from trains, ships, and other attractions caused the horses to spook and run occasionally. After several of the top-heavy coaches fell over and spilled guests into the Frontierland dust, the whole enterprise was shut down permanently in September of 1959, and the attraction was pulled from the 1960 souvenir book. The stagecoach's demise foreshadowed the abrupt end of another top-heavy Frontierland vehicle: the **Mike Fink Keel Boats**, which were quickly closed in 1997 after one of them capsized and dumped guests into the Rivers of America.

Stage Door Café

MAP: Frontierland, Fr-5

DATES: September 1, 1978–ongoing

The Stage Door Café is a counter-service option for a quick **Frontierland** meal. For years, the fast-food fare didn't stray far from the basic burgers-dogs-fries theme, but lately some more varied items have appeared on the menu, including fish and chips, chicken breast nuggets, a house-made funnel cake with toppings, and gourmet coffee drinks. On rare occasions (such as the special "Salute to the Golden Horseshoe Revue" show held in 2013), the café will present a special menu.

Formerly the **Oaks Tavern**, the Stage Door Café is adjacent to the **Golden Horseshoe** and its popular entertainment stage (hence the café's name). From the outdoor tables, guests have nice views of boat traffic along the **Rivers of America**.

Starcade

MAP: Tomorrowland, T-19

DATES: May 4, 1977–June 2015

Guests waiting on line for **Space Mountain** may not realize that the upstairs **queue** takes them past what used to be the upper floor of Disneyland's main video arcade. Called Starcade, in keeping with the rocket themes of **Star Tours** and other stellar establishments in the neighborhood, the illuminated complex once spread over two stories and housed dozens of games, making it one of the best arcades in the West. The upper story, however, has been closed for years. A thirty-foot-long X-Wing fighter from *Star Wars* used to be suspended above the escalator connecting the two floors, but since 2011, that ship's been hanging in the **Star Trader** store.

Even with only one floor of games, the Starcade has usually been a popular, noisy place, a perplexing fact to some guests who wonder why anyone would pay for Disneyland admission and then spend time playing indoor arcade games (they probably wondered the same thing about **Innoventions**, which for years offered the same video game consoles that guests could play at home). September 1985's *Mad* magazine parodies this same incongruity with a cartoon showing kids being bored inside a Disney park until they finally reach the arcade.

Drawing fans to the twenty-first century's one-story Starcade was a clever mix of the newest technology available and addictive faves from decades past (for $4 a pop), including simulated rides down ski slopes, on race tracks, or into space—"Something for every player," touted the Disneyland website. However, in 2012, the games got pushed aside so that more display space could be devoted to products from the Star Trader next door, making the room more "gift shop" than "arcade." That year also saw the late-October arrival of characters and video games from the film *Wreck-It Ralph*, which turned some of the Starcade into a meet-and-greet spot until mid-January 2013. Two months later, with *Ralph* gone, two-dozen arcade games (including fan-favorites like Missile Command, Pac-Man, and Space Invaders, plus a vintage air hockey table) returned to the ground floor. This space also promoted recent movies: a meet-and-greet area for the new *Big Hero 6* movie opened here in November of 2014, and a display of movie props, art, and costumes from *Tomorrowland* opened in mid-April 2015. However, in 2015, the Starcade was completely closed off to guests, its entrance blocked by an ATM machine.

Star Tours

MAP: Tomorrowland, T-24

DATES: January 9, 1987–ongoing

In the 1970s, Disney's own live-action adventure movies—especially *The Black Hole* and *Island at the Top of the World*—failed to draw the huge audiences of Universal's *Jaws* and 20th Century Fox's *Star Wars*. Because of this, when Disney designers considered replacing the decaying **Adventure Thru Inner Space** in **Tomorrowland** with a new attraction in the early 1980s, they had to look outside the company's own film oeuvre for successful movie tie-ins.

The result was a fruitful collaboration with writer/producer/director George Lucas that generated three separate Lucas-assisted attractions in a nine-year span—1986's *Captain EO*, 1987's Star Tours, and 1995's **Indiana Jones Adventure**. Lucas himself must have especially enjoyed his involvement with Disneyland; he had visited the park during its first week of operation (paying for his own ticket) and had been a dedicated visitor throughout the 1950s and '60s.

For the upcoming Star Tours, the curving exterior of the building was re-painted with zooming StarSpeeders to distance the new journey into outer space from the old journey into inner space. New as it was, Star Tours presented a high-energy amplification of what the old **Rocket to the Moon** attraction had done three decades before: put guests in a flight simulator that played movies of a space voyage. Rocket to the Moon, **Flight to the Moon**, and **Mission to Mars** in the 1970s all used primitive flexible-seat technology and small circular screens that paled in comparison to the intense, gut-wrenching effects possible in the mid-1980s.

In the original Star Tours, forty guests at a time were strapped into futuristic StarSpeeder 3000s with a first-person view of a wide movie screen in front of them. Ostensibly, guests were passengers on an uneventful jaunt to the forest moon of Endor, but unfortunately the novice pilot (voiced by Paul "Pee-Wee Herman" Reubens) quickly lost his way, turning the experience into action incarnate. Bursting through a glassy "iceteroid," passengers were flung into the middle of a battle scene straight out of the *Star Wars* trilogies: intimidating Imperial cruisers loomed, noisy explosions echoed, and enemy TIE fighters and friendly Rebel X-Wings darted nearby. Frantically maneuvering through a lethal dogfight, StarSpeeders negotiated the dreaded Death Star's claustrophobic trench, raced up to light speed, and thundered back to their hangars for a final crashing career.

Supplementing the vigorous visuals were the realistic effects delivered by the flight-simulation

MOUSCELLANY

Over the years, sharp-eyed and sharp-eared Disneyland fans have noticed historical park references within Star Tours. Among them: in the first version of Star Tours, the Mighty Microscope from Adventure Thru Inner Space was seen in the first hangar sequence; guests have heard an announcement asking for Tom Morrow from Flight to the Moon; and stripped-down robotic armatures from **America Sings** birds are in a droid-assembly room.

seats, which shook and shuddered in time with the effects onscreen. So intense was the heart-pounding, six-minute ordeal that **cast members** checked seatbelts as assiduously as if Star Tours were an inverted roller coaster, and the signs out front had some of Disneyland's longest health warnings.

Throughout the Star Tours experience, obvious and not-so-obvious references to the *Star Wars* movie universe added fascinating fun to the flight's thrills. The actual droids from the film, C-3PO (shown) and R2-D2, were on hand, with Anthony Daniels reprising his C-3PO vocals. Admiral Ackbar from *Return of the Jedi* supervised the **queue** area, an announcer paged a land speeder with the license plate THX1138 (the name of George Lucas's first feature film), and even Lucas himself made an appearance—his name was pronounced in reverse over the intercom and, in the film played inside the StarSpeeder, guests could glimpse him ducking down quickly as the ship hurtled toward him and came to a screeching halt (some experts disputed this last Lucas sighting and said it was an anonymous actor).

When it debuted in early 1987 at a cost estimated to be $30 million, Star Tours generated lines that extended all the way out to **Town Square**. In honor of its newest attraction, Disneyland even presented its inaugural guests with celebratory digital watches. Exactly ten years later, another special commemorative ceremony was held, this time with actress Carrie Fisher on hand.

Originally the Mars candy company sponsored Star Tours, but Energizer later took over, its presence acknowledged with a series of "Keeps On Going" posters near the exit. That exit still leads to an even more conspicuous commercial interest—dizzy with Star Tours visions, departing passengers lurch out of the ride and straight into the **Star Trader** store, a "duty free" shop with a galaxy of *Star Wars* merchandise.

On July 27, 2010, the first iteration of Star Tours departed for the last time. Officially reopened on June 3, 2011, Star Tours: The Adventures Continue is an acclaimed re-imagining that introduces a revised queue area, new film footage that visits different planets in the *Star Wars* universe, multiple paths through the plot, and the latest 3-D technology. Another change came in November of 2015, when some new footage related to *Star Wars: The Force Awakens* debuted. Now more than ever, Star Tours is a star attraction.

Star Trader

MAP: Tomorrowland, T-22

DATES: November 21, 1986–ongoing

What had been the Character Shop since 1967 became the Star Trader store in 1986. The new store's opening came six weeks before the neighboring **Star Tours** attraction started to take millions of guests into hyperspace. True to **Tomorrowland**, the colorful neon out front shows an astronaut Mickey tumbling through space.

Just like the old Character Shop, the Star Trader boasts one of Disneyland's biggest retail interiors, making it Tomorrowland's **Emporium**. At over 5,000 square feet, it's a space big and tall enough to comfortably suspend a thirty-foot-long replica of a *Star Wars* X-Wing from the ceiling. The Star Trader has space-themed murals on the walls, glowing twelve-foot saucers above the floor, and *Star Wars* clips running on monitors throughout the day. When *Toy Story* and *Toy Story 2* became blockbusters in 1995 and '99, merchandise for those films temporarily filled the displays, but since then the Force has arrived, in force.

That's because the Star Trader offers something that no other Disneyland store does—hundreds of different *Star Wars*-related items, everything from posters and toys to clothes and collectible models. One of the most popular activities here has been the "build your own light saber" kiosk for customized weaponry. Fans can also visit the Droid Factory, where they assemble the pieces "to build & name your own droid action figure." Once Disney bought Marvel's characters in 2009, lots of Marvel shirts, figures, and toys started to appear among the galactic gifts. And, appropriately enough for a big store in Tomorrowland, there was a wall of D-Tech gadgets, electronics, headphones, speakers, and cases. To help push the **Diamond Celebration**, in 2015's spring and summer the corner of the store closest to **Space Mountain** teemed with sixtieth anniversary merchandise.

As a new *Star Wars* movie approached that autumn, the Force became even stronger with this store. Marvel was pushed out and for months, *Star Wars* took over every shelf and display. Clever T-shirts and cool toys dominated, but some rare items soared with astronomical prices ($595 for a numbered painting called *Battle of Hoth*). For anyone looking for Disneyland's *Star Wars* headquarters, well, may the Star Trader be with you.

Star Wars Land

MAP: Park, P-19

DATES: 2019

The single biggest expansion at Disneyland ever. The re-routing of the venerable **Disneyland Railroad**. An eighteen-month-long suspension of the **Rivers of America** attractions. The permanent closure of the two-decades-old **Big Thunder Ranch** area. It would take something awesome to accomplish all of this, and "awesome" is exactly what the upcoming Star Wars Land promises to be.

When Disney CEO Bob Iger made the surprise announcement at the D23 convention in Anaheim on August 15, 2015—news that has thrilled millions of *Star Wars* fans around the world—he assured the excited crowd that Star Wars Land would be "a jaw-dropping new world" that would deliver "an authentic *Star Wars* experience" with "environments on other planets entirely populated with aliens, droids, and humanoid characters from the franchise." Concept art shows a natural alien landscape similar to the mountainous Cars Land area over at Disney California Adventure, plus a huge replica of the *Millennium Falcon* that will house some kind of space-flight attraction straight out of the movie's mythology.

The site for this strange new world is on Disney property north of **Frontierland**, space that has been partially covered by the **Circle D Corral** and Big Thunder Ranch. Spanning fourteen acres, Star Wars Land will cover an area slightly larger than Tomorrowland and equal to about two-thirds of the mammoth Mickey and Friends parking structure nearby. Guests will enter from the southwest (**Critter Country**) and the south (Frontierland) and encounter buildings and mountains that might soar to **Matterhorn**-like heights. To make way for construction, one-seventh of Disneyland's total attractions—including the *Mark Twain* **Riverboat**, the **Sailing Ship** *Columbia*, the canoes, **Tom Sawyer Island**, **Fantasmic!**, and the Disneyland Railroad—were all closed indefinitely, and the Big Thunder Ranch attractions were all permanently eliminated.

Demolition on the future Star Wars Land site began in January of 2016; Star Wars characters were on hand when ground was broken for actual construction on April 14, 2016. In February of 2017, Disney announced that Star Wars Land would open sometime in 2019. That three-year construction period approximates how long it took to complete a similarly ambitious development: the twelve-acre Cars Land in Disney California Adventure. Like Cars Land, the price to build Star Wars Land will be around $1 billion.

Disneyland has already produced several successful *Star Wars*-themed attractions and activities, including **Star Tours** and the *Jedi Training Academy* show at the Tomorrowland Terrace. But Star Wars Land is expected to take the phrase "immersive experience" to a whole new level. Fans are holding onto a new hope that the ambitious project will bring to Disneyland everything that Iger promised: "We knew it needed to be big," he told the D23 audience. "We knew it needed to be great. And we knew it needed to be every bit as thrilling as the films will be."

State Fair

DATES: Fall 1987–Fall 1988 (seasonal)

To boost off-season **attendance** in the 1980s, Disneyland staged several long-running special events. Between 1986's **Circus Fantasy** and 1988–1989's **Blast to the Past** was a celebration called State Fair. Held in the fall of 1987 and '88, the fair was a spirited simulation of the real thing held annually all across America.

Disneyland's State Fair filled **Main Street** and the **Hub** with traditional carnival attractions that ranged from ring-toss games to quilt displays. Guests were divided in their opinions about holding a fair—

a rather mundane type of event—at the one-of-a-kind Disneyland. While some visitors were amused by the old-fashioned midway booths and the pig races over at **Big Thunder Ranch**, purists couldn't believe that such ordinary attractions were being prominently showcased in a park famous for innovation. They also pointed out that **Walt Disney** himself had once declared that Disneyland would be a Ferris wheel-free zone—yet the State Fair Ferris Wheel stood right at Disneyland's main **entrance** (in the second year, the twelve-seat Ferris Wheel was moved to **Frontierland**).

Less popular in its second autumn than it was in its first, Disneyland's State Fair permanently closed with little fanfare, and the park quickly ramped up for its busy **holiday season**.

Storybook Land Canal Boats

MAP: Fantasyland, Fa-15

DATES: June 16, 1956–ongoing

In Disneyland's second summer, **Walt Disney** finally got the charming boat ride he'd wanted all along at the park. Limited on time and money in early 1955, he'd had to settle for the feeble **Canal Boats of the World** attraction that sputtered noisi-

ly across one undeveloped acre at the back of **Fantasyland**. However, even as that ignoble attraction was operating, plans were already underway for a huge remodel that began in the fall of 1955 and lasted into the following spring. Official dedication ceremonies were held on June 18, 1956, with some of TV's Mouseketeers on hand to celebrate.

When the seven-minute attraction restarted, it did so with verdant little knolls in place of the muddy slopes that had formerly rimmed the canals. A patchwork quilt made of plants lined one hill, and carefully manicured miniature trees and flowers (many planted in their original containers to stunt their growth) decorated the once-barren banks. Adorable villages and palaces from classic

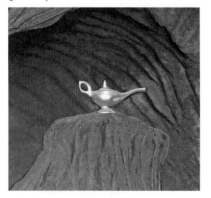

Disney animation now greeted guests. Among the meticulously detailed displays were windmills and houses from *The Old Mill* and *Three Little Pigs* cartoons (shown on page 461), gardens inspired by *Peter Pan*, Geppetto's village and toy shop from Pinocchio, the *Cinderella* castle and coach, and structures from *Snow White and the Seven Dwarfs, The Adventures of Ichabod and Mr. Toad*, and *Alice in Wonderland*. Constructed mainly from wood and fiberglass, all the buildings were built on a one-twelfth scale, reducing six-foot doorways to tiny six-inch versions. So well-crafted were the miniatures that the metal hinges on the tiny doors actually work (a necessity for changing interior light bulbs). To observe such intricate beauty cost only a C ticket from the Disneyland **ticket book** in the 1950s, and then a D in the 1960s and '70s.

Disney Legends **Morgan "Bill" Evans**, **Ken Anderson**, and **Fred Joerger** designed the new grounds and buildings of the attraction. A 1994 update added scenes from more recent Disney movies, including *Aladdin* (detail shown on page 460) and *The Little Mermaid*, all built with the same careful skill and gentle spirit. An addition in late 2014 brought in a detailed display of the village and snowy mountains from *Frozen*. There's plenty to see, however, before the cruise even begins, including Monstro the Whale at the entrance; guests who watch for a few seconds might see his eye blink

and his blowhole periodically emit steam. Veteran guests will also recognize the lighthouse in the walkway as the old ticket booth used in the days when riders had to pay their way onto each individual attraction; back then, the big flowery letters out front that spelled Storybook Land were spelled as three separate words (Story Book Land), not two.

Just as they did in the 1950s, guests today observe these scenes while sitting in low-slung bateaux similar to those in Northern European canals and rivers (though Storybook Land's upgraded boats are battery-powered). Costumed **cast members** drive the quiet boats along a track submerged in 465,000 gallons of water. These canal captains deliver live narration just like **Jungle Cruise** skippers do, though the Storybook script isn't fraught with the jungle's dangers and opportunities for puns. And unlike the Jungle Cruise boats, which are named after actual rivers, the canal boats are named after characters from Disney's own animated classics (*Alice*, *Ariel*, *Aurora*, *Belle*, *Cinderella*, *Daisy*, *Faline*, *Fauna*, *Flora*, *Flower*, *Katrina*, *Merryweather*, *Snow White*, *Tinker Bell*, and *Wendy*).

Because guests are required to climb in and out of the small, free-floating boats, over the years this attraction has unfortunately seen some bumps and bruises. Despite the occasional mishaps, the Storybook Land Canal Boats attraction has endeared itself to millions of visitors, and it's said to have been one of Walt Disney's personal favorites.

MOUSCELLANY

The acerbic British artist Ralph Steadman drew a comical sketch of a big-fanged Monstro about to devour a canal boat full of guests in his "Ralph Steadman's Disneyland" pictorial for the September 25, 1975, issue of *Rolling Stone*.

Story Book Shop, aka Western Printing Book Shop

MAP: Main Street, MS-3

DATES: July 17, 1955–April 1, 1995

One of the original investors in Disneyland was Western Printing and Lithographing, a Wisconsin company also known simply as Western Publishing. Among Western's imprints were two popular Disney lines that dated back to the 1930s: Little Golden Books and Big Golden Books. Western also created the wildly popular Disney comic books that were issued under the Dell Publishing name. With a back catalog of Disney comics and hundreds of other children's books (many featuring non-Disney characters, such as Tarzan and the Lone Ranger), Western Publishing was there on Disneyland's **Opening Day** with a children's bookstore on **Main Street**. The Story Book Shop's small site was off the street and behind the **Upjohn Pharmacy** in the **Crystal Arcade** building. The shop could be entered from inside the **Emporium** to the south or from the western end of **Center Street** just to the north.

> **MOUSCELLANY**
>
> A miniature train runs around a track up by the ceiling in the former Story Book Shop, circling past small village scenes, charming Disney displays, and a large book opened to pages that display the Story Book name, a nostalgic reminder of what used to be here.

Mattel bought Western Publishing in the 1980s, and a decade later the Story Book Shop came to the end of its last chapter. After surviving almost forty years of changes on Main Street, the shop disappeared during a 1995 remodel of the Crystal Arcade and has since been transformed into a room with Disney toys and merchandise. While the current room shows characters *from* storybooks, there are no actual storybooks for sale.

Strawhatters

The Strawhatters, a popular New Orleans-style jazz combo, started playing at Disneyland in 1956. Swingin' Dixieland tunes have always been their core repertoire (ask them and they'll proudly declare, "We play Dixieland jazz!"). In its early years, the group generally performed on a small gazebo stage in **Frontierland** several times a day; footage of the Strawhatters playing here while the *Mark Twain* **Riverboat** glides behind them is in the 1956 featurette *Disneyland, U.S.A.* (that gazebo was removed in the early 1960s). The Strawhatters have also performed at **Grad Nite** and other special events. Today, the straw-hatted musicians on **Main Street** often inspire nearby Disney characters to break out some dance moves. Guests have also been able to enjoy the group on board the *Mark Twain*: in 2016, while the **Rivers of America** were closed for **Star Wars Land** construction, the Strawhatters performed on the docked ship, an atmospheric location perfect for their nostalgic style.

> **MOUSCELLANY**
>
> The Strawhatters' name isn't unique; a non-Disney TV variety show called *The Strawhatters* aired in the summer of 1953 and '54. Additionally, other non-Disney music groups have used the same name and same hats while featuring different instruments.

Like the **Dapper Dans**, the Strawhatters have occasionally rotated in new members, but early incarnations of the group usually included a pianist, drummer, trumpeter, trombonist, and clarinetist. Five men are shown in Disneyland's 1965 **souvenir book** wearing gray plaid jackets, black pants, red bow ties, and the straw boater hats that lent them their name. Disneyland Records released a Strawhatters record called *Dixieland at Disneyland* in 1957; the group is also on that year's *Slue-Foot Sue's Golden Horseshoe Revue* record. The 2015–2016 ensemble had six members (a drum, banjo, three brass horns, and a clarinet), all belonging to the marching **Disneyland Band** and all wearing red, white, and blue outfits with white spats and the straw hats.

Stroller Shop

MAP: Park, P-6

DATES: July 17, 1955–ongoing

Since **Opening Day**, toddler-toting guests have made the handy Stroller Shop one of their first stops. A prominent location at the **entrance** has always handled the rentals. Originally, guests had to walk through the turnstiles to get a stroller, but as of January 2010, a new location outside and to the east of the turnstiles offers easy access before guests enter Disneyland. Renters who lose track of their strollers (but hopefully not the strollees) can get free replacements inside **Tomorrowland** at the **Star Trader**. Baby Jogger strollers with canopies rented for $15 per day in 2011. Also available at the Stroller Shop were wheelchairs for $32 and ECVs (electric convenience vehicles) for $70. Amazingly, five years later all of these vehicle rental costs were unchanged (can that be said about any other prices at Disneyland?).

Stromboli's Wagon

MAP: Fantasyland, Fa-10

DATES: Ca. 1983–ongoing

So the villainous puppet master in *Pinocchio* warrants his own **outdoor vending cart**, but the wise Jiminy Cricket doesn't? How does that work? Guests can puzzle over this conundrum while shopping at this elaborately decorated wagon parked near the **Village Haus** restaurant. Candy, sunglasses, postcards, and small souvenirs are the staples here, making this location (including the adjacent cart that's stocked with fresh fruit, frozen lemonade, and chips) a convenient, comprehensive pause from all the **Fantasyland** action.

Submarine Voyage,
aka Finding Nemo Submarine Voyage

MAP: Tomorrowland, T-10

DATES: June 14, 1959–September 8, 1998; June 11, 2007–ongoing

They aren't real submarines. Yes, they look like real subs, are named after real navy subs, are promoted as "the world's largest peacetime fleet" of subs, and were sponsored by a company, General Dynamics, that actually built subs. But if the true definition of a submarine is a vessel completely *submerged* beneath the water's surface, then what began circling in Disneyland's 9-million-gallon concrete lagoon in June of 1959 weren't *true* submarines. Technically, the eight aluminum vessels were more like fifty-two-foot-long sightseeing buses, each carrying thirty-eight passengers and running horizontally via wheels mounted on a rail, with the upper half of each ship always above the waterline. Even the caution sign out front says they're "semi-submerged."

None of this pedantry mattered, of course, because the original Submarine Voyage was a remarkable simulation of the undersea experience. Built in San Pedro, outfitted at the "Navy Yards" in Disneyland's northeast corner, and introduced simultaneously with the **Matterhorn Bobsleds** and the **Monorail**, the new submarines were part of the first big **Tomorrowland** makeover. Since the ships were based not on futuristic submarines but on existing navy vessels, they took the names of actual submarines (including the *Nautilus, Seawolf, Skate*, and *Skipjack*). A week after the subs began cruising, naval officials joined **Walt Disney** for the official June 14 dedication.

For decades, eager crowds swarmed the attraction that had cost $2.5 million to build and that even featured live **mermaids** in its lagoon for a few summers. Whether nosing out from under a waterfall or sliding gracefully through illuminated evening waters, the submarines made vivid postcard subjects. **Sam McKim** transformed the image of a sub streaking through the depths into one of Disneyland's most dramatic **attraction posters**.

The subs' **queue** ran underneath the Monorail station, making this a particularly bustling area. After paying with their E tickets from Disneyland's **ticket books**, guests boarded the submarines and descended through a hatch to sit in front of small portholes for a nine-minute voyage. Realistic ship-board sounds and bubbles streaming past the windows recreated a descent into "liquid space," and as each sub putted along at under two miles an hour, such memorable sights as exotic mechanical fish, the ruins of Atlantis, tethered artificial mermaids, sunken treasure, the polar ice cap, and a googly-eyed sea monster could soon be seen drifting past. Few guests recognized that some of what they saw wasn't in the open lagoon at all but was actually housed in a building underneath the **Autopia** roadway. The subs entered and exited  this building by going through cascading waterfalls (shown).

Seemingly nuclear but actually diesel-powered, the subs were a military gray color until 1986, when they were repainted in the yellow color scheme of oceanographic research vessels. They were given some less-martial names, too, including the *Explorer, Sea Star*, and *Seeker*. Then, deemed out of date in 1998, the long-running attraction finally closed, and in 2001, the **Autopia Winner's Circle** shop moved into the subs' queue area. However, the quarter-mile-long lagoon rail remained in place, suggesting that the missing subs would eventually resurface.

Finally, after a nine-year closure and an upgrade rumored to cost over $70 million, the much-missed subs returned on June 11, 2007, as the Finding Nemo Submarine Voyage (the *Finding Nemo* characters were chosen over a theme based on the 2001 Disney movie *Atlantis: The Lost Empire*). The fleet now runs on electricity, not diesel fuel, and the speed stays around 1.4 miles per hour for up to fourteen minutes of ride time. The volume of water in the lagoon has dropped by almost 4 million gallons. Also, a few new names have been added to the subs: the *Mariner*, *Seafarer*, *Scout*, and *Voyager*. The attraction's new story involves little Nemo, Dory, Crush, 126 sea creatures, 10,000 artificial plants, a dazzling erupting volcano, a beautiful coral reef made of thirty tons of recycled glass, and an Australian narrator who mentions the old attraction's mermaids and sea serpent. Ralph Eggleston's 2007 **attraction poster** highlights the changes: the sub is far in the background, while the *Nemo* characters are all in the foreground. The satisfying voyage immediately drew colossal crowds, proving that yesterday can thrive today in Tomorrowland.

On January 5, 2014, the submarines were pulled from the lagoon for a nine-month refurbishment. Many fans worried that the subs were being permanently mothballed, since this attraction is one of the most expensive to maintain and has a low ridership capacity. While the subs are back for now, it's possible that their days are numbered; if they were to disappear permanently, many guests would remember them fondly as one of Disneyland's signature experiences.

Sunkist Citrus House

MAP: Main Street, MS-6

DATES: July 31, 1960–January 3, 1989

For many years, a bakery sat in a prime **Main Street** location near the **Penny Arcade**. In the 1950s, that bakery was called **Puffin**, and in the 1990s, it was called **Blue Ribbon**. In between the bakery years, the Sunkist Citrus House used this spot to pour glasses filled with sunshine.

The Citrus House was the first of two Sunkist eateries in Disneyland—the other, **Sunkist, I Presume**, operated almost concurrently in **Adventureland**. When Sunkist came to Main Street in 1960, Puffin's ex-dining room was enlarged to include an adjacent space that had once belonged to the **Sunny-View Farms Jams & Jellies** shop. Despite these interior changes that recast the two rooms as one business, from the outside the Citrus House still looked like two separate establishments with two different paint jobs.

Fresh-squeezed OJ and from-concentrate lemonade were Sunkist's specialties. The refreshing juice bars were frozen favorites, and the short menu was rounded out with coffee and baked goods. Everything was served up by **cast members** in colorful striped costumes that included bow ties and green pants for the men and aprons for the women. The Citrus House cooled off hot guests for almost three decades until the Blue Ribbon Bakery took over in 1989.

Sunkist, I Presume

MAP: Adventureland, A-3

DATES: 1962–1992

Two years after the **Sunkist Citrus House** opened on **Main Street**, a nifty outdoor snack shack called Sunkist, I Presume debuted in **Adventureland**. The name, of course, was appropriated from Henry Stanley's famous 1871 meeting with David Livingstone in deepest, darkest Africa. Stanley's first words to the reclusive missionary were "Dr. Livingstone, I presume."

In deepest, darkest Adventureland, Sunkist's location was across from the **Jungle Cruise**; previously the **Tropical Cantina** had occupied the spot. Appropriately enough for the jungle theme, the little structure featured a thatched roof, its male **cast members** wore Hawaiian shirts and Bermuda shorts, and females wore long floral dresses. Sunkist juices, especially the Jungle Julep medley, were the beverages of choice to accompany the hot dogs served here. Behind the scenes, Sunkist, I Presume also made the mint juleps that were served on the *Mark Twain*. Above the scenes, the upstairs balcony was used as an employee break area. The **Bengal Barbecue** replaced Sunkist, I Presume in 1992.

Sunny-View Farms Jams & Jellies

MAP: Main Street, MS-7

DATES: 1955–1957

This small **Main Street** business is listed in the 1956 and '57 **souvenir books**, but it finished out the 1950s as an unnamed candy shop. From its location next to the corner **Carnation Ice Cream Parlor**, Sunny-View sold jams, jellies, and candied fruit. A small brochure distributed in the shop describes Sunny-View's goods as "delicious gifts," while a sign out front announced "preserves of distinction." Jams and candies gave way to juices and juice bars in 1960, when the **Sunkist Citrus House** expanded into this space.

Swiss Family Treehouse

MAP: Adventureland, A-5

DATES: November 18, 1962–March 8, 1999

What had been a landmark Johann Wyss novel in 1812 and a block-bustin' Disney adventure film in 1960 became the world's most elaborate tree house in 1962. At the time, Disneyland needed something to complement the **Jungle Cruise**, which had been operating as **Adventureland's** only high-profile attraction since 1955. The delightful Swiss Family Treehouse was a clever addition to the northern corner where Adventureland rounds to **Frontierland**.

The tree house took its design and décor from the *Swiss Family Robinson* movie sets and props, which included items salvaged from the sinking ship *Titus* and homemade creations fashioned from jungle materials. Initially a C-ticket and then (as of 1966) a B-ticket walk-through attraction, the tree house included a library, kitchen, private rooms, and viewing platforms, all of it furnished and functional, and all of it toured via 139 steps on the wooden stairways. Most memorable was an ingenious water-delivery system that lifted hundreds of gallons of water per hour to the upper levels using pulleys, bamboo dippers, and bamboo chutes. Throughout the tour, a lively **Buddy Baker** composition from the movie, "The Swisskapolka," was the buoyant theme song.

> **MOUSCELLANY**
>
> Many of the 300,000 artificial leaves that originally adorned the tree were reddish in color, but when they faded in the harsh sun they were replaced by green leaves.

Almost as impressive as the tree house was the tree it sprawled across. Playfully named by its designers as a *Disneyodendron semperflorens grandis* ("big ever-blooming Disney tree," according to Randy Bright's *Disneyland Inside Story*), the massive steel-and-concrete structure rose "seventy feet over the jungle" and spread "brilliant colored branches eighty feet in width," according to Disneyland's 1964 **souvenir book**. These stats revealed that the tree's width was greater than its above-ground height—but unmentioned was the depth of the foundation "roots," which drove another forty-two feet downward and helped give the whole structure a total weight of 150 tons. True to the Robinson's heritage, a Swiss flag flew from the top of the tree.

Seven stories up in the Jungle Lookout, a welcoming, hand-painted sign mentioned that here "adventure beckons . . . with every view & every sound, the jungle & its river call out their mystery." That "jungle & river" were indeed visible from the treetops, which afforded spectacular views of Adventureland and the **Rivers of America**.

Though the tree house was cherished for almost four decades, it got a dramatic makeover in 1999 and reopened as **Tarzan's Treehouse**. A few souvenirs have been retained in Tarzan's new domicile in tribute to the departed Robinsons.

Sword in the Stone Ceremony

MAP: Fantasyland, Fa-5

DATES: May 25, 1983–ongoing

Along with the much-ballyhooed 1983 redesign of **Fantasyland** came a modest ritual held several times a day ten feet south of the **King Arthur Carrousel**. The Sword in the Stone Ceremony derives from the 1963 Disney animated movie of the same name. As in the movie and T. H. White's 1938 novel, the fabled sword Excalibur is buried in a stone (at Disneyland, a golden anvil) and can only be extracted by "the true-born king of England."

For Disneyland's ceremony, a **cast member** dressed as Merlin the Magician auditions crowd members for the regal role of Wart, the story's youthful sword-puller.

Most are unsuccessful (as the movie's narrator describes, "Though many tried for the sword with all their strength, none could move the sword, nor stir it"). Occasionally, however, a nearby cast member taps a button to temporarily release the sword from the anvil. Immediately a sword-pulling boy or girl is heralded as royalty, and a royal fuss ensues ("It's a miracle, ordained by heaven" is the movie's declaration). Afterward, the replaced sword remains immovable until the next ceremony.

A free "Disneyland Today" brochure from 1986 lists three daily performances, a number that had doubled by the mid-2000s but that seems to have diminished drastically in recent years (though the anvil and its sword are still in place). That 1986 brochure also names the Make Believe Brass as the musical accompaniment helping to "manufacture merriment."

Tahitian Terrace,
aka Stouffer's in Disneyland Tahitian Terrace

MAP: Adventureland, A-12

DATES: June 1962–April 17, 1993

In June of 1962, Disneyland opened a new South Seas restaurant. The Tahitian Terrace, also briefly called Stouffer's in Disneyland Tahitian Terrace, was located just inside the **Adventureland** gates on the left-hand side. The building had existed since 1955 and been filled by the **Plaza Pavilion**. Though that restaurant had faced east toward the **Hub**, it had used the west-facing Adventureland side for a back patio overlooking the **Jungle Cruise**. This back half became the Tahitian Terrace. The unusual roofing revealed the building's dual function: half the roof was designed in the old-fashioned **Main Street** style, and half was made of tropical thatch.

Until the **Blue Bayou** debuted in 1967, the Tahitian Terrace was the fanciest restaurant on this side of Disneyland. Guests sat at outdoor tables, were served by waiters and waitresses, and dined on exotic Polynesian cuisine under the spreading branches of a three-story artificial tree. Cooked in the same kitchen used by the Plaza Pavilion, the Tahitian Terrace menu included island favorites like teriyaki steak, marinated chicken skewers, shrimp tempura, and tropical fruit salad with pineapple ice cream. The famous beverage was the juicy, non-alcoholic Planter's Punch. Back then, a full dinner, including a drink and dessert, cost under $4.

Live entertainment was included in that price, too. While dining, guests could watch the *Polynesian Revue*, a long-running music-and-dance spectacular featuring hip-swinging hula girls in grass skirts, male dancers dressed like island chiefs, a thrilling walk-on-fire display, and complimentary leis. Old **souvenir books** show colorful photos promoting the restaurant and the show, identifying the entertainers as the "exotic Royal Tahitians dance troupe."

Since it was held outdoors, the *Polynesian Revue* couldn't adhere to a steady year-round schedule, but it remained popular for over three decades. The show and the restaurant finally closed on April 17, 1993, to be replaced three months later by **Aladdin's Oasis**. Guests can still find a Tahitian Terrace, however—in Hong Kong Disneyland.

Tangled

MAP: Fantasyland, Fa-9

DATES: October 15, 2010–October 27, 2013

A month before *Tangled* opened in theaters, Disneyland's Tangled attraction opened in **Fantasyland**. Replacing the toy and candy businesses run by Geppetto, Tangled was a cottage where guests could get their photos taken with Rapunzel and Flynn Rider. Until early 2012, Rapunzel's famously long hair poured from the top of a tower and looped across Tangled's roof. In 2013, Rapunzel joined the Disney princesses in the **Fantasy Faire** village and, later that year, Tangled's cottage was transformed into a new meet-and-greet called the **Frozen Royal Reception**.

Tarzan's Treehouse

MAP: Adventureland, A-5

DATES: June 23, 1999–ongoing

Just as the **Swiss Family Treehouse** was based on a Disney movie that in turn had originated from a classic book, so too was its replacement, Tarzan's Treehouse, inspired by Disney's cinematic retelling of a popular story. In this case, the movie was *Tarzan* and the book was Edgar Rice Burroughs' 1912 adventure novel *Tarzan of the Apes*.

The Swiss Family Treehouse and Tarzan's Treehouse debuted under very different circumstances. When the original attraction opened in 1962, Disney's *Swiss Family Robinson* movie had already been a huge box-office sensation two years earlier; in contrast, when Tarzan's Treehouse opened on June 23, 1999, Disney's animated *Tarzan* had been in theaters for less than a week, which meant that the attraction had been planned and built long before anybody really knew if the movie would be a success. Fortunately for Disneyland and the movie studio, the new film and the new tree house were both instant hits.

Since the Tarzan and Robinson story locations are an ocean apart, and since each plot has its own distinct characters, Tarzan's Treehouse is a radical reimagining of the thirty-seven-year-old Swiss Family lodgings. Serving as a fun new "foyer," a thin, two-story tree now stands in the **Adventureland** walkway, with a rickety suspension bridge leading guests to the main tree. This immense artificial structure, already seventy feet tall, eighty feet wide, and 150 tons heavy, was modified to stand a little taller and broader. To make the tree appear more African and less Caribbean, it has been adorned with new leaves and hanging moss (it also flies Great Britain's flag now instead of Switzerland's). As always, views from the top can be spectacular for guests who make the seventy-two-step climb.

The tree house itself mirrors the maritime features detailed in the *Tarzan* film, including the ship's bow and the hanging dory. Also new is the presence of the movie's main characters. None of the Robinsons were shown in their tree house, but Jane, Tarzan, and other characters appear in this one, with Jane's drawings imparting the tale. For younger explorers, the coolest enhancement is the hands-on interactivity of the new base camp area, where musical pots and pans are set up as a primitive but enlivening drum kit (*Beauty and the Beast* fans have spotted some recognizable ceramics, too).

MOUSCELLANY

Lead an unsuspecting friend up to the top of Tarzan's Treehouse, where Sabor's lair (shown) awaits, and encourage him or her to pet the ferocious leopard. Watch your friend's reaction as Sabor senses the approaching hand.

As with everything else at Disneyland, the clever details of this attraction delight guests, especially those with emotional attachments to the Swiss Family Treehouse. The Johann Wyss novel sits on a table; some of the old hand-painted signs still hang on the walls; and several of the Robinson's furnishings remain in the tree house. Especially meaningful is the record playing softly on the ground-level gramophone—it's the familiar "Swisskapolka" song from the 1962 movie.

Taylor, Betty
(1919–2011)

Prior to becoming one of the most beloved entertainers in Disneyland history, Betty Taylor was a singin', dancin' dynamo on nightclub stages. Born in Seattle in 1919, Taylor had her own professional band while she was still a teen, landed bit parts in several 1940s movies, and played Vegas with Frank Sinatra in the early 1950s.

After auditioning at Disneyland in 1956, Taylor quickly landed a lead role in **Frontierland's** popular **Golden Horseshoe Revue**. She played the saloon's vivacious proprietor, Slue-Foot Sue, alongside co-stars **Wally Boag** and **Fulton Burley**. Taylor's vocal talents and spunky enthusiasm helped make the *Revue* a record-setting favorite, with Taylor putting in almost 45,000 performances total. She performed for a national TV audience on *Walt Disney's Wonderful World of Color*, and in the 1970s, park guests heard her pre-recorded vocals belting out "Bill Bailey, Won't You Please Come Home" in **America Sings**.

After some thirty-one years of delighting Disneyland audiences, Taylor formally retired in 1987, though she continued to make special appearances. Taylor, Boag, and Burley were all inducted as Disney Legends in 1995. Taylor died in 2011 in Washington at age ninety-one, one day after Boag passed away.

Teddi Barra's Swingin' Arcade

MAP: Bear Country/Critter Country, B/C-6

DATES: March 24, 1972–2002

Teddi Barra, her name a play on the legendary silent-screen actress Theda Bara, was one of the **Audio-Animatronic** singing bears in the **Country Bear Jamboree**. Nearby was Teddi Barra's Swingin' Arcade, so named because Teddi swayed on a big swing during her Jamboree song. Inside the arcade's small room, the "games of chance" (as the sign out front announced) included both Disney and frontier themes. Charming as they were, the selection was so limited (just nine machines) that most gamers sprinted to **Tomorrowland's** bigger **Starcade** once it opened in 1977.

Like the **Brer Bar** next door, the arcade was overrun by the twenty-first-century Winnie the Pooh invasion; **Pooh Corner** now spills into what was formerly Teddi's swingin' space. Observant guests can still see Teddi's name up on Pooh's building, however—a modest tribute to a pioneering bear.

Tencennial

DATES: 1965

To celebrate its tenth birthday, Disneyland threw itself a year-long party in 1965. The first-ever **Miss Disneyland** helped kick off the Tencennial events with a January appearance on *Walt Disney's Wonderful World of Color*. That episode, called "Disneyland's Tenth Anniversary," features a birthday party with a dancing cake and previews of upcoming park attractions. The year welcomed the debut of one landmark attraction, **Great Moments with Mr. Lincoln**, a new **parade** specially designed for the Tencennial, and a new anniversary song composed by the **Sherman Brothers**. Just over the horizon was another major addition: 1966's **It's a Small World**.

Three Fairies Magic Crystals

MAP: Fantasyland, Fa-4

DATES: November 2006–2008

In 2006, Three Fairies Magic Crystals opened along the walkway through **Sleeping Beauty Castle**. The first part of the shop's name, of course, alluded to Flora, Fauna, and Merryweather, the fairy trio from *Sleeping Beauty*; "magic" referred to the images lasered inside of small, clear-glass sculptures. Shaped like cubes, spheres, and even **mouse ears**, the sculptures made pretty gifts. When the **Sleeping Beauty Castle Walk-Through** reopened in 2008, the tiny Three Fairies shop became a small, ground-floor viewing area for guests unable to negotiate the castle's narrow stairways. Inside the 150-square-foot space are display cases and a mini-theater showing the Walk-Through's dioramas.

Three Kings Day

MAP: Frontierland, Fr-23, Fa-19

DATES: January 6, 2012–January 8, 2012; January 4, 2013–January 6, 2013

Disneyland has a long history of devoting weekends to various countries and cultures. Special music and dance groups, colorful costumes and arts, and themed foods and parade floats all arrived in the 1970s and '80s for international festivals (1982's Festival Japan was one of the most elaborate and popular). More recently, "Opa! A Celebration of Greece" brought Greek culture and food to the **It's a Small World** walkway in May of 2013.

Three Kings Day introduced the Latin American celebration of Christmas and the three magi (or three wise men) to Disneyland. The event was held for the first time on one January weekend in early 2012. **El Zocalo Park** in **Frontierland** was the center of all the action, which included special food, festive décor, bilingual art activities, and mariachi music. Characters such as the Three Caballeros joined the fun. The success of the first Three Kings Day was one of the factors that prompted the launch of the seventeen-day **New Orleans Bayou Bash** a month later. When Three Kings Day returned in January of 2013, it moved to the **Big Thunder Ranch** area; in 2014, 2015, and 2016, the event relocated to Disney California Adventure.

Ticket Books

According to *Window on Main Street* by Disney Legend **Van Arsdale France**, when **Walt Disney** was planning Disneyland in the early 1950s, "the idea was to have free admission"; but soon, says France, a modest admission price was added "to keep the un-

☾ Disneyland	EXCHANGE FOR CHOICE of ONE	30¢ "C"	ADULT ADMISSION
MAIN STREET	SHOOTING GALLERY		
TOMORROWLAND	CIRCARAMA		
FANTASYLAND	MAD TEA PARTY DUMBO FLYING ELEPHANT		
FRONTIERLAND	SHOOTING GALLERY RAINBOW CAVERNS MINE TRAIN MIKE FINK KEEL BOATS CONESTOGA WAGONS } CLOSED INDIAN WAR CANOES } AT DUSK		**C**
F000001	or any other "C" attraction		COUPON

desirables out." Thus, during Disneyland's first summer, adult admission was $1 for a ticket that, according to a July 15, 1955, guide in the *Los Angeles Times*, "entitles you to roam all the lands of Disneyland and view the many exhibits and free shows without any further charge." Attractions "and other unique amusements" were all "popularly priced" for an additional ten to thirty-five cents. This pricing scheme meant that attraction expenses were optional; guests could simply visit Disneyland without paying extra for any attractions. However, this also meant that guests had to wait to buy a separate ticket any time they wanted to ride something, and **cast members** had to perform time-consuming ticket-selling and change-counting duties within the tiny ticket booths stationed outside the attractions.

To make things easier for everyone, on October 11, 1955, Disneyland introduced its first ticket books (sometimes called coupon books). Van France credits public relations chief Ed Ettinger with suggesting the idea so he could dispel rumors that a day at Disneyland was extravagantly expensive. Ettinger eagerly promoted the new concept: a total of eight A, B, and C tickets (or coupons) could be bought for only

TICKETED ATTRACTIONS, 1955–1982

Ticket prices changed often (Alice in Wonderland, for instance, has been everything from a B to a D). This list gives the prices charged most frequently for attractions:

A Ticket
King Arthur Carrousel, Main Street Vehicles, Satellite View of America, Sleeping Beauty Castle Walk-Through, Space Station X-1, and 20,000 Leagues Under the Sea Exhibit.

B Ticket
Alice in Wonderland, Art of Animation, Big Game Safari Shooting Gallery, Casey Jr. Circus Train, Conestoga Wagons, Main Street Cinema, Main Street Shooting Gallery, Mickey Mouse Club Theater, Midget Autopia, Motor Boat Cruise, Phantom Boats, Swiss Family Treehouse, and Viewliner.

C Ticket
Adventure Thru Inner Space, Astro-Jets, Dumbo the Flying Elephant, Fantasyland Autopia, Frontierland Shooting Gallery, Junior Autopia, Mad Hatter's Mad Tea Party, Mike Fink Keel Boats, Mr. Toad's Wild Ride, Peter Pan Flight, Rocket to the Moon, Snow White Adventures, Stage Coach, and Tomorrowland Autopia.

D Ticket
Flying Saucers, Indian War/Davy Crockett's Explorer Canoes, *Mark Twain* Riverboat, Mission to Mars, PeopleMover, Flight to the Moon, Rafts to Tom Sawyer Island, Mine Train, Rainbow Ridge Pack Mules, Rocket Jets, Sailing Ship *Columbia*, Santa Fe & Disneyland Railroad, Skyway to Fantasyland/Tomorrowland, and Storybook Land Canal Boats.

E Ticket
America Sings, Big Thunder Mountain Railroad, Country Bear Jamboree, Enchanted Tiki Room, Great Moments with Mr. Lincoln, Haunted Mansion, It's a Small World, Jungle Cruise, Matterhorn Bobsleds, Monorail, Pirates of the Caribbean, Pack Mules Through Nature's Wonderland, Space Mountain, and Submarine Voyage.

$2.50. Nine months later, with **Tom Sawyer Island**, the Indian War Canoes, and other new attractions opening in **Frontierland**, the ticket books were expanded to include D tickets. Simultaneously, several existing attractions that had previously cost a C ticket, including the **Jungle Cruise**, were reclassified as D-ticket attractions.

The famous, high-demand E ticket joined the ticket books in June of 1959 to co-incide with the debuts of three big additions—the **Matterhorn Bobsleds**, **Monorail**, and **Submarine Voyage**. As before, several existing top-tier attractions, including the Jungle Cruise once again, were reclassified for the new higher ticket. For the next twenty-three years, no further tickets were added to the ticket books. However, new attractions were steadily added to the A–E lineup, and some existing attractions con-tinued to shift around, sometimes going up in cost (such as the **Main Street Cinema**, which climbed from an A to a B ticket), sometimes going down (**Sleeping Beauty Castle Walk-Through**, from C to B to A), and sometimes doing both (Snow White Adventures, from C to D to C again). Only a few attractions, notably the A-ticket **King Arthur Carrousel** and **Main Street Vehicles**, never changed their prices.

In 1957, the ticket books briefly included a small Special Bonus Ticket good for one free ride on any attraction. In the 1960s and '70s, guests could choose between "Big 10" books with ten tickets (one A, one B, two Cs, three Ds, and three Es) or, for a dollar more, "Deluxe 15" books (one A, two Bs, three Cs, four Ds, and five Es). If guests left with unused tickets, the tickets could be used later but couldn't be refunded for cash.

Over the years, several attractions never required tickets at all because either Disneyland or a sponsor picked up the operating costs. These free attractions included **Adventure Thru Inner Space**, the *Golden Horseshoe Revue*, the **Carousel of Prog-ress**, and child admission to **Great Moments with Mr. Lincoln**. Conversely, some at-tractions still charged a separate cash-only fee, even while the lettered-ticket system was in place. For example, the Mickey Mouse Club Circus cost an additional fifty cents during its brief run in late 1955; **Tom Sawyer Island**, an extra fifty cents in 1956 (a single D ticket thereafter); and the **Enchanted Tiki Room**, seventy-five cents in 1963 (before graduating to an E ticket).

The ticket book system ended in June of 1982 as Disneyland shifted to all-en-compassing **Passports** that offered unlimited use of all attractions. Meanwhile, guests holding old tickets from the pre-1982 ticket books can still apply them toward the cost of admission. Since these individual A–E tickets usually have printed values of less than $1, they're usually more valuable as nostalgic collectibles.

Tiki Juice Bar

MAP: Adventureland, A-11

DATES: Ca. 1976–ongoing

Talk about a match made in Disneyland—right outside the entrance to the **Enchanted Tiki Room** is the equally tropical Tiki Juice Bar. The Juice Bar's been serving a variety of juices and island-themed refreshments from under its little thatched roof since 1976, the year Dole began sponsoring both the snack stand and the Tiki Room. Over the decades, this juice spot has become so popular that in March of 2014, the Tiki Juice Bar was voted #65 on Yelp's official list of the "Top 100 Places to Eat in the U.S."

Unlike many of Disneyland's other quick-stop eateries, this one serves healthy treats like cold pineapple juice and pineapple spears. Its reputation, however, is based on the Dole Whip beverage introduced in 1986. Today's overheated guests will find two ways to chill, each for around $5: the tall, frosty Dole Whip Float, splashed with pineapple juice and accompanied by a little umbrella and a cherry, and the famous Pineapple Dole Whip Soft-Serve, which is piled into a low cup and somehow includes no ice cream or dairy products. These are indulgences everyone needs to enjoy at least once.

A refurbishment in 2014 made the service here more efficient than ever to accommodate all the eager explorers who line up to get properly fortified before heading into thrilling **Adventureland**.

Tinker Bell

The fact that a real live Tinker Bell was added to Disneyland in 1961 should come as no surprise. A lively animated version of the beautiful blonde fairy with an endless supply of pixie dust had already graced *Peter Pan* in 1953 (in the movie, Peter himself underscores her importance: "Don't you understand, Tink? You mean more to me than anything in this whole world"). With her scene-stealing looks and feisty personality, Tinker Bell became the energetic mascot for the new ***Disneyland* TV series** in 1954. That show's sustained success, and the popular re-release of *Peter Pan* in 1958, accelerated her rise as a vital Disney symbol. So once **Matterhorn Mountain** went up in 1959, **Walt Disney** knew it was time to bring in Tink.

A real Tink, that is. Walt Disney wanted an actual flying fairy brought from animated image to vivid life. To make this happen, the plan was to have someone in costume take the interior elevator up through the Matterhorn, strap on a harness, step on a platform at the mountain's peak, and slide 784 feet on a sloping wire to a mattress-padded platform in **Fantasyland**—a dramatic stunt that would last twenty-five seconds and would be witnessed by tens of thousands of dazzled Disneyland viewers night after night.

It was no job for a novice. Consequently, the person hired for the first flight was a veteran performer who had already performed as Tinker Bell. At the Hollywood Bowl in 1958, a four-foot-ten-inch circus aerialist named Tiny Kline had made a spectacular 1,000-foot glide from the hills to the stage while dressed as Tink for a special "Disney Night" concert. Kline, a Hungarian who was born Helen Deutsch, was sixty-eight years old. Her long career had included stints with the circus and stunts with airplanes that had her dangling in the air by her teeth.

Kline began performing at Disneyland in mid-1961. Every summer night, just before the **fireworks**, she leaped from the mountain and glided into the Fantasyland sky. Kline continued to perform until she passed away in 1964. A series of circus veterans then took up the wand. These later Tinker Bells continued the nighttime performances until 1977 and then have worn the wings from 1983 onward (speculation persists that, at times, the person performing as Tinker Bell has been a man—a rumor that park officials haven't confirmed either way).

Over the years, the shows have been similar to Kline's original performances, but there have been a few changes. For instance, in 2000's Believe . . . There's Magic in the Stars, Tinker Bell made her descent *during* the fireworks, not before. And Tink doesn't travel in one direction anymore; as of 2004, she's been gliding back and forth across the sky.

One thing that hasn't changed is her undiminished popularity. Tinker Bell is a featured player in modern **parades** (often getting her own float), and she has her own large, well-themed meet-and-greet area, **Pixie Hollow** (shown). She even got her own movie, 2008's *Tinker Bell*. Today, Tink is as well-known, beloved, and important as ever.

Tinker Bell & Friends

MAP: Fantasyland, Fa-3

DATES: November 2006–2008

The space within the **Sleeping Beauty Castle** entrance where the **50th Anniversary Shop** had been located became a new Tinker Bell gift shop in late 2006. The small, L-shaped room had three doorways—one leading to the castle's main walkway and two toward the castle's courtyard (usually only one of the latter two was open). Although it was called Tinker Bell & Friends, Tink dominated the shop without many friends in sight (maybe that was the joke—perhaps she doesn't have many friends). Tink costumes, toys, jewelry, bags, blonde wigs, wands, and more helped girls evoke their inner fairies. The shop took on a new name and new merchandise in 2008, when it became the **Enchanted Chamber**.

Tinker Bell Toy Shoppe,
aka Once Upon a Time . . . the Disney Princess Shoppe

MAP: Fantasyland, Fa-7

DATES: 1957–April 2009

For over fifty years, a charming toy and costume store thrived next to the **Snow White** attraction. Originally it was called the Tinker Bell Toy Shoppe—an appropriate name for a cute castle store, considering that Tink was sort of a cute castle mascot, thanks to her animated appearances at the opening of the *Disneyland* TV series. The largest store in **Fantasyland,** this was the area's main headquarters for enchanting gifts.

In 2002, the name changed to Once Upon a Time . . . The Disney Princess Shoppe, reinforcing the castle connection. The first half of the new name alluded to the love song "Once Upon a Dream" from the 1959 film *Sleeping Beauty*, while the Princess ending appealed directly to the store's target patrons. Little princesses and their parents could find much more merchandise here than in the smaller **Princess Boutique** nearby. Regal dresses, gilded crowns, magic wands, sparkly jewelry and tiaras, detailed dolls and statues, illustrated books, and Disney DVDs filled this store with the stuff dreams are made of. What's more, classic Disney movie princesses would stop by to meet, greet, and tell fairytales. The picture window out front, with its displays of royal wardrobes and accessories, was an irresistible magnet to young girls. A 2009 remodeling and renaming transformed the Disney Princess Shoppe into a salon called the **Bibbidi Bobbidi Boutique**.

Tomorrowland

MAP: Park, P-18

DATES: July 17, 1955–ongoing

Ad astra per aspera—Roman philosopher Seneca's call to reach the stars despite difficulties might have applied to Tomorrowland. No Disneyland area was as problematical in the mid-1950s as Tomorrowland, and no area has undergone as many revisions since then. The main challenge for Imagineers is easy to grasp but difficult and expensive to resolve: create a futuristic, guest-friendly land that continually stays ahead of ever-advancing real-world technological achievements.

Unlike the rest of Disneyland, which is set in the present (**Mickey's Toontown**) or the recent/distant/fabled past (all the other lands), Tomorrowland is set in the future. When the land was first being designed and built, that future was pegged as 1986, the year Halley's Comet would return. The target year was later pushed into the twenty-first century. Consequently, with Tomorrowland mandated to stay fresh and innovative—"a daring world of hopes and dreams," according to the 1956 **souvenir book**—many more new attractions have been introduced here than anywhere else in Disneyland. **Walt Disney** acknowledged this challenge, commenting that "tomorrow is a heck of a thing to keep up with."

Tomorrowland almost didn't debut on time. Concentrated work on the land didn't begin until there were only six months left before **Opening Day**, making it Disneyland's last area to be started and the last to be completed. Lacking adequate funds and time, in July of 1955, Tomorrowland had some empty buildings, a for-display-purposes-only *Moonliner* rocket, the **Circarama** theater, Monsanto's **Hall of Chemistry**, a barely finished **Autopia**, and not much else.

These attractions would be acceptable for a typical amusement park or state fair, but not for the exciting Tomorrowland Walt Disney had imagined, especially when compared to the ambitious descriptions Disney had pitched to potential investors two years before. According to the pitch, this "World of Tomorrow" would preview "some of the wonderful developments the future holds in store," including "a moving sidewalk, industrial exhibits, a diving bell, a monorail, a freeway children could drive, shops for scientific toys, and a Rocket Space Ship to the Moon." Artist **Herb Ryman** had drawn a conceptual Land of Tomorrow entrance that includes futuristic

architecture and the suspended pods of a new transportation system, as well as some kind of "interplanetary circus." Unfortunately, few of the things originally described and sketched were ready when Tomorrowland opened.

Late in 1954, with park construction underway, Walt Disney resigned himself to opening Disneyland the following July with "coming soon" signs in front of a closed-off Tomorrowland. Then, early in 1955, he decided to push Tomorrowland to the Opening Day finish line. The desired outcome wasn't completely possible, so the public's first glimpses of Tomorrowland were of festive banners and balloons that camouflaged the embarrassing absence of high-profile, high-tech attractions.

As guests streamed into Disneyland that first summer, Walt Disney continued to fill the land's approximately thirty acres with more to see and do. Within a month of Disneyland's debut, **Rocket to the Moon** was flying, the **20,000 Leagues Under the Sea Exhibit** was on display, and the **Phantom Boats** were sputtering around the Tomorrowland lagoon. By fall, **Hobbyland** and the **Flight Circle**, two underwhelming exhibits grounded in the present, were operating. Behind the scenes, Disney had solicited more corporate sponsors, and within six months he had brought in Kaiser Aluminum for the **Hall of Aluminum Fame**, the American Dairy Association for their eponymous exhibit space, and the Crane Plumbing Company for the **Bathroom of Tomorrow**. All the exhibits were functional, but hardly inspiring. "Todayland" was Walt Disney's own frustrated nickname for what he was presenting.

Inspirational attractions were on the horizon, however. The spring of 1956 brought the **Astro-Jets** and the **Skyway** to Tomorrowland; 1957 opened the doors of the **House of the Future**. Also debuting in 1957 was the song "Tomorrowland," written by Harry Warren, Harold Adamson, and Leo McCarey for McCarey's Cary Grant/Deborah Kerr film, *An Affair to Remember*: "There's a wonderful place called Tomorrowland, and it's only a dream away, and the moment you get to Tomorrowland, you'll forget about today." Anaheim's Tomorrowland was gaining momentum on its way to becoming that "wonderful place."

The next year brought an attempt at mass transit in the form of the gas-powered **Viewliner** train. A more audacious mass transit system arrived in 1959 with the first well-coordinated, large-scale surge in Tomorrowland development. Debuting in June along with the **Matterhorn Bobsleds** (labeled a Tomorrowland attraction at the time) and the **Submarine Voyage** was the **Monorail**. The first two were visually stunning, but the Monorail was the most significant addition, representing a determined attempt to make Tomorrowland a testing ground for serious experiments in futuristic public transportation.

With this trio of attractions in place simultaneously, in one fell swoop Tomorrowland had electrifying E-ticket options to brag about. And brag the marketing department did, filling Disneyland's **souvenir books** with ebullient text and enticing photos. Additionally, this latest and greatest expansion was showcased in much-seen promotional films and TV specials. The Tomorrowland that Walt Disney wanted, one that would be a "living blueprint of our future," was finally here.

Eight years later, with Disneyland turning twelve years old, a dedication ceremony attended by 1,500 invited guests and celebrities introduced 1967's "new Tomorrowland." This remarkable update, still one of the favorite moments in Disneyland history for many guests, re-branded the entire land as a shiny "world on the move," as it's called in the old souvenir books. Inside a dramatic new pair of angular, aluminum entrance gates, the creative **Adventure Thru Inner Space** attraction, restyled **Rocket Jets**, inviting **Tomorrowland Terrace** and **Tomorrowland Stage**, immense Carousel Theater with its **Carousel of Progress**, and **PeopleMover** (yet one more serious contribution to urban planning) all replaced familiar landmarks like the *Moonliner*, **Flying Saucers**, Flight Circle, and several long-running exhibits. New Tomorrowland's $20 million price tag (according to the book *Walt Disney's Disneyland*) was about $3 million more than what Disneyland itself had cost to build a decade before, but Imagineers got the impressive results they wanted. Dazzled guests felt like they had suddenly time-warped from 1967 to the twenty-first century. Ten years later, **Space Mountain** made them feel like they'd time-warped again into the mind-blowing "star gate" sequence of *2001: A Space Odyssey*. Ten years after that, **Star Tours** sent guests light-speeding into *Star Wars* territory. Who knew the future would be so fun?

On May 22, 1998, an even newer "new Tomorrowland" debuted, but this one was as controversial as it was exciting. Rather than continually chase an ever-elusive future, Imagineers decided to reinvent a "retro-future"—that is, a future as it might have been imagined a century before. Gone were the Skyway buckets, the Submarine Voyage, the PeopleMover, and the **Mission to Mars** flight (even the Matterhorn was missing, since the souvenir books had started listing it as a Fantasyland attraction). Jules Verne now seemed to be the main designer of sci-fi attractions like the **Astro-Orbitor**, **Rocket Rods**, and **Observatron**, their warm bronzes and coppers the colors of the Industrial Revolution instead of the stark whites, blacks, and chromes of the Space Age. And with edible plants filling the flower beds, the future at hand was as healthy and harmonious as it was scientific and gadgety.

Despite all the effort, somehow this future didn't work as well as it could have, and within ten years the disappointing Rocket Rods were being Toy Storied out of existence by the fanciful **Buzz Lightyear Astro Blasters**, the long-absent submarines were returning to the lagoon, and Space Mountain and other buildings were being re-painted white (some of them got futuristic murals, as exemplified by one on the **Magic Eye Theater**, detail shown). Despite rumors that the PeopleMover may eventually be resurrected, Tomorrowland's future, it seemed, was rooted in its past.

By November of 2015, however, it became clear that Tomorrowland's future (at least, its immediate future) is actually rooted in a galaxy far, far away. A new *Star Wars*-themed **Season of the Force** overlay landed in nearly every corner of Tomorrowland, bringing significant changes to Space Mountain, Star Tours, the Tomorrowland Terrace, and more. For the foreseeable future, the Force will be strong with Tomorrowland.

Tomorrowland Expo Center

MAP: Tomorrowland, T-14

DATES: November 16, 2015–ongoing

After spending over sixteen years as **Innoventions**, in late 2015 the big round exhibit building at the back of **Tomorrowland** was redubbed the Tomorrowland Expo Center. Instead of focusing on future innovations, the building looked to current Disney movie franchises for inspiration.

With the tidal wave known as *Star Wars: The Force Awakens* about to swamp theaters in December of 2015, the Expo Center's bottom floor was transformed into the Star Wars Launch Bay, a museum of archival exhibits spanning the whole history of the *Star Wars* movies. Costumes, props, models of various spacecraft, a meet-and-greet area with movie characters, a room of video game consoles, a short documentary about the new movie, and even a minor tribute to the Mos Eisley Cantina started drawing in fans from across the galaxy. The obligatory gift shop began selling expensive merchandise with out-of-this-world prices, including a $4,000 Darth Vader costume and a $9,000 Stormtrooper statue.

The building's upper level was given to another Disney-owned franchise, Marvel. However, the upstairs exhibits, Xbox games, character appearances, and gift shop in the Marvel Super Hero HQ got less fanfare, drew smaller crowds, and finally closed on April 2, 2016.

Tomorrowlanding

MAP: Tomorrowland, T-8

DATES: 2006–ongoing

What had been the **Radio Disney** booth under the **Observatron** became a new retailer called Tomorrowlanding in 2006. According to the sign outside, this small shop sold "gifts from outer and liquid space" (referencing the nearby **Star Tours** and **Submarine Voyage** attractions). However, by 2011, Tomorrowlanding seemed to be more of a generic Disney store offering hats, **mouse ears**, princess dresses from **Fantasyland,** and more items from areas outside **Tomorrowland**.

A big change came in June of 2015, when Tomorrowlanding got Marvel-ous. With a temporary meet-and-greet outside for Marvel characters like Thor and Captain America, the store loaded up on shirts, hats, toys, and figures designed with themes from the Marvel comics and movies. In a sense, Tomorrowlanding became a smaller version of what the nearby **Star Trader** store is for *Star Wars*, a Disneyland headquarters for famous movie properties that weren't originally created (but are now owned) by Disney.

By November of 2015, Tomorrowlanding had changed again. With a new *Star Wars* film about to hit theaters, the Empire struck back and new *Star Wars* items appeared on the shelves. Gone was the Marvel merchandise, and in its place were *Star Wars* weapons, figures, hats, shirts, and even personalized name tags spelling out in the film's alien language, Aurebesh. More popular than ever, Tomorrowlanding has successfully learned the ways of the Force.

Tomorrowland Stage, aka Space Stage

MAP: Tomorrowland, T-19

DATES: 1967–1986

The "new **Tomorrowland**" of 1967 introduced a showy new venue for theatrical extravaganzas and nationally known musical groups. The expansive Tomorrowland Stage filled Tomorrowland's eastern corner, where the **Flying Saucers** had hovered in the early 1960s. The stage itself was about thirty feet across and festooned with the same kind of arcs and abstractions that adorned the Tomorrowland Terrace.

The Tomorrowland Stage was a big setting for big shows in front of over a thousand guests. Among the large-scale musical spectaculars presented here in the early 1970s were *Show Me America* and *Country Music Jubilee*. Music stars who performed on the stage included Pat Boone, José Feliciano, Herman's Hermits, Linda Ronstadt (on July 15, 1971, backed by the newly formed Eagles), and Disneyland's **Kids of the Kingdom**. One high point was the live, big-screen broadcast of the Apollo 11 moonwalk on July 20, 1969. Not only was the event historic, but for many people it was the first time they'd seen a large-scale TV broadcast.

As **Space Mountain** was being constructed in 1977, the Tomorrowland Stage was rebuilt as part of that attraction's sleek new architectural complex. That year the stage also got a new name—the

MOUSCELLANY

Disneyland: The First Quarter Century describes *Show Me America* as a "fast-paced musical comedy" with "more than 120 sparkling costumes" and "favorite American melodies sprinkled with a touch of old-fashioned humor." Not mentioned is the roller-skating Statue of Liberty, played by young Teri Garr.

Space Stage, just one of the space-related titles (**Space Place** and **Lunching Pad** were some others) that arrived with the mountain. The kingdom-themed musical *Disneyland is Your Land* began running here in 1985, but a year later the show and the outdoor stage were gone. Starting in 1986, outdoor shows moved to **Fantasyland's** new Videopolis stage, and the Space Stage space became the **Magic Eye Theater**.

Tom Sawyer Island,
aka Pirate's Lair on Tom Sawyer Island

MAP: Frontierland, Fr-16

DATES: June 16, 1956–ongoing

Walt Disney never produced a movie based on *The Adventures of Tom Sawyer*, but he certainly had an affinity for the novel and shared a Midwestern background with its author, Mark Twain. Both men were alive concurrently: Disney was eight when Twain died in 1910 at age seventy-four. Disney was born in Chicago, about 350 miles from Twain's Florida, Missouri, birthplace, and both men grew up in small Missouri towns (Marceline and Hannibal) that were only about ninety miles apart. Both men grew to be giants of American culture. And both men created an island in the middle of a river.

Twain's *Tom Sawyer* does not include a place called Tom Sawyer Island, but it does have a fictional Jackson's Island, "about three miles long and a quarter of a mile wide" in the middle of the Mississippi River. On the island, Tom, Huck, and pal Joe Harper cavort as pirates and escape "civilization." Reaching the island via log raft, the three boys roam the woods and find "plenty of things to be delighted with."

Once Disneyland was up and running, in early 1956 Walt Disney turned his attention to the incomplete, visible-but-unvisitable island out in the middle of the **Rivers of America**. Early ideas for the area included a Mickey Mouse Island or a Treasure Island, based on Disney's 1950 movie. Once the Tom Sawyer concept was settled on, Disney did what he typically did for new attractions: he turned over the actual creation to an individual designer, who used his boss's general suggestions to map out the details.

Tom Sawyer Island, however, got some extra attention. In *Walt Disney: An American Original*, Bob Thomas writes that the island was the only early Disneyland attraction personally designed by Walt Disney himself. Disney did let master planner **Marvin Davis** have the first crack at it, but the results weren't satisfactory. According to Thomas, Disney took Davis's drawings and worked on them "for hours in his red-barn workshop. The next morning, he laid tracing paper on Davis's desk and said, 'Now that's the way it should be.' The island was built according to his design." Disney's daughter, Diane Disney Miller, writes in *The Story of Walt Disney* that her father "kept on adding things until he felt that there weren't any missing parts." **Richard Irvine** concurs in the April 1960 issue of *Reader's Digest*: "That island is all his."

The result is something close to Twain's rough-hewn Jackson's Island. Just as Twain's island is twelve times longer than it is wide, so too is Disney's island long and narrow. The original Tom Sawyer Island stretched 800 feet from top to bottom and varied in width from a trim 50 feet in the middle to about 250 across the northern

end, totaling almost three acres. A walk along the trail that went around most of the island (the northern section couldn't be accessed by guests) covered approximately a fourth of a mile. Across the water, most of the shore belongs to **Frontierland** and is 80–100 feet away, with **Rafts to Tom Sawyer Island** conveying guests back and forth.

Walt Disney added his own flourishes to Twain's undeveloped island, of course. "I put in all the things I wanted to do as a kid—and couldn't," he told *Reader's Digest* in 1960. A play structure called Tom & Huck's Treehouse—free of charge, like all other island activities—stood on a hill at the southern tip. The old island maps handed out to guests declare this structure to be the "highest point in Disneyland," meaning it was the highest point guests could visit (closed in 2013 for safety concerns, the tree house still stands).

In the island's center is **Fort Wilderness**, a two-story log structure straight out of a Western movie. Long ago the fort included historical displays, a refreshment stand, lookout towers with air rifles, and a secret passageway down to the trails (demolished and rebuilt in the twenty-first century, the fort is now inaccessible to guests). Additional island features included Merry-Go-Round Rock, Pirate's Den, Castle Rock, Smuggler's Cove, Teeter-Totter Rock, shaky pontoon and swaying rope bridges, and a fake cemetery behind the fort. And then there was Injun Joe's Cave.

McDougal's Cave is the scene of the thrilling climax to Twain's *Tom Sawyer*. While writing the book in the 1870s, Twain recalled his childhood days when he'd played in a cave outside of Hannibal. Now a national landmark, this cave was his model for the cave where Tom, Becky Thatcher, and other revelers made a giddy procession into marvelous subterranean rooms with exotic names like the Cathedral and Aladdin's Palace. Twain's vivid descriptions create a "romantic and mysterious" world with "a vast labyrinth of crooked aisles," a "tangle of rifts and chasms," a "multitude of shining stalactites," "glittering crystals," and "fantastic pillars." The original Disneyland cave, while not quite as elaborate and stretching only about 120 feet long, captured the natural wonder and adventurous potential of Twain's creation. Guests ducked through dimly lit passageways, crept along a dirt floor, negotiated

slender side paths, and peered into a "bottomless pit" where somber susurrations echoed and the darkness was pierced by stalagmites and stalactites. A similar tunnel, much less dramatic and conspicuous, ran for about seventy-five feet near the rock-climbing structures to the north.

When the island finally opened in July of 1956, the two winners of Hannibal's "Most Typical Tom and Becky of the Year" contest attended the dedication ceremonies. That first year, guests couldn't use any of their A, B, or C tickets from Disneyland's **ticket book** to enter the island—they had to buy special fifty-cent tickets for admission. Once on the island, guests could pursue one additional adventure: fishing. **Sam McKim's** early concept sketches of the island include one that shows the "Pier Tackle Shack," and something similar really did exist. Using Disneyland's poles, hooks, and bait, guests actually fished off the Catfish Cove docks at the island's southern end. Because they dropped their lines into a penned area of water stocked with live catfish, everyone was pretty much guaranteed success. Unfortunately, that was the problem—anglers reeled fish in with ease, but nobody knew what to do with their catch after that (supposedly **Aunt Jemima's Pancake House** was going to keep fish on ice). After enough odoriferous carcasses were found abandoned in lockers and bushes, the fishing attraction was closed (when the Disneyland Hotel unveiled its own Fishing Pool in the early 1970s, management had learned to provide cleaning, packing, and shipping services for the guests' fish.).

For many guests, Tom Sawyer Island has remained one of Disneyland's most unique and entertaining locations, and not just because it offers an ideal place to relax on hot days under real trees near cool water. It's unusual because although the environment is controlled and defined, it *feels* wild and untamed. Without any big stores or restaurants on the island, nothing distracts guests from their fun or coaxes cash from their wallets. Also, since it borders on three different lands (**New Orleans Square**, **Critter Country**, and Frontierland), the island offers grand views of landmarks like the **Haunted Mansion** and **Splash Mountain**. Furthermore, unlike most other attractions, Tom Sawyer Island is not a three-minute experience—guests can linger as long as they want, with dusk as the only deadline. And while other attractions bring guests indoors and away from the California sunshine, this one encourages visitors to stay outside in a ludic paradise so low-tech that it's almost *no*-tech. Since there's no set path or pattern to the island adventure, guests get to invent the island experience themselves, with no "safety bar" to stifle imaginative impulses to explore the many hidden areas, secret passageways, and multiple trails. As its signs say, the island really is "a natural environment for children of all ages."

Not all of those imaginative impulses have ended happily, however. Numerous injuries have resulted from the unfettered play; according to *The People v. Disneyland*, David Koenig's 2015 analysis of park lawsuits, "inch for inch, more falls have occurred on Tom Sawyer Island than anywhere else in the park." As a result, several of the island's original features that were sites of accidents, such as Teeter-Totter Rock, have been removed, and the caves have been made safer. Far more dangerous than anything that happens during the day is what has happened when the island has closed after sunset--several guests have tried unsuccessfully to hide on the island overnight, and two even drowned when they attempted to make it back to shore after dark. In addition, Tom Sawyer Island was the site of one of Disneyland's strangest days, when chanting **Yippie Day** protesters unsuccessfully tried to take over the island in 1970.

One of the island's most distinguishing features is the frontier cabin at the northern tip. In 2001 the *L.A. Times* called this structure "perhaps the most altered attraction" in Disneyland. For decades it was a burning cabin with an arrow-pierced corpse out front, then in the 1980s that dead setter was replaced by a moonshiner collapsed on the porch, and later the cabin's fire was said to have been set by a reckless unseen inhabitant. The blaze was finally extinguished in 2007, and in 2010, the cabin was restored to look like Mike Fink actually lives there (one of his famed keel boats is tied up on the shore). No matter the changes, the cabin has never been open to guests.

At the island's other end, changes came in 1992 when the southern tip was remodeled to accommodate **Fantasmic!** (in the island's early days, this area had lots of tall plants). A brief name-change to Tom and Huck Island in 1996 promoted a recent *Tom and Huck* Disney movie. More dramatically, the entire island closed in 2007 for an extensive (and expensive, at over $25 million) piratical renovation that brought out the Bobcats (the earth-moving machines, that is). Reopened on May 25, 2007, Pirate's Lair on Tom Sawyer Island added wider paths, a sunken pirate ship, hidden treasure, ghostly apparitions, a scary pop-up pirate (shown), a new island map (shown on page 483), and other changes with themes from the *Pirates of the Caribbean* movies. Pirate Lair's new **attraction poster** replaces the sunny design of the 1956 Tom Sawyer Island

poster with dark colors and a menacing skeleton straight off the big screen (shown on page 484). Begun in early 2016, **Star Wars Land** construction has brought a long closure to the island and seems to have reshaped its northern area, but final results won't be clarified until mid-2017.

Purists may deride any tamperings with Walt Disney's original vision of his Twain-inspired island, but as long as the island still exists at all, it will always be one of Disneyland's best old-school attractions.

MOUSCELLANY

One persistent rumor about Tom Sawyer Island is that it somehow "belongs" to Missouri through some kind of official annexation, but Disney Chief Archivist Emeritus Dave Smith finally settled the matter in 2013. On the website D23.com he wrote that the rumor was based on a joking request from Missouri's governor to give his state the deed to the island.

Toontown Five & Dime

MAP: Mickey's Toontown, MT-10

DATES: January 24, 1993–ongoing

Sharing a bright yellow **Mickey's Toontown** building with the **Gag Factory** is the Toontown Five & Dime, a cheery retail operation within laughing distance of **Roger Rabbit's Car Toon Spin**. Outside the Five & Dime are some of Toontown's signature jokes and surprises, including talking mailboxes and wacky phones.

Unfortunately, nothing in the Five & Dime costs only five or ten cents, but there are lots of inexpensive pens, key chains, mugs, frames, and other small souvenirs. More expensive Toon-themed clothes, bags, and plush toys are also available.

Toon Up Treats

MAP: Mickey's Toontown, MT-7

DATES: December 13, 1997–ongoing

About four years after Goofy's Gas Station debuted in **Mickey's Toontown**, a small "snack stop" opened next door. Toon Up Treats is always there, but not always open (only the busy seasons seem to warrant regular hours). Basic sandwiches, pre-made salads, chips, desserts, candy, and sodas provide fast fuel for guests on the go, with outdoor seating available nearby.

Topiary Garden

MAP: Fantasyland, Fa-21

DATES: May 28, 1966–ongoing

A topiary is a bush or tree trimmed into some recognizable shape, usually a geometric figure or animal. An arrangement of many small plants into a single pattern is not considered a topiary, thus the floral quilt planted on the shore of the **Storybook Land Canal Boats** and Mickey's large flower-formed face at Disneyland's **entrance** don't qualify as topiaries. Disneyland has had topiaries since about 1963; today's **Fantasyland** boasts numerous examples, including the joyful pachyderms near **Dumbo the Flying Elephant** and the giant swans outside **Sleeping Beauty Castle**.

By far, the most famous topiaries are the twenty or so gathered in front of **It's a Small World**. So special was this array of plants when it opened in 1966 that the area came to be known as the Topiary Garden. The best views are from the It's a Small World boats, which still loop around the garden to show it off from different angles.

Three key factors make the Disneyland Topiary Garden memorable. First and foremost, the whimsical subjects perfectly suit the imaginatively designed building and "the happiest cruise that ever sailed 'round the world." The animals have included a towering giraffe, an elephant balancing on its front legs, a laughing hippo, a fuzzy-headed lion (shown), a prancing reindeer, a dancing bear, a seal balancing a ball, and a three-part sea serpent. There are also densely verdant trees cut into cones, domes, and corkscrews, plus decorative hedges trimmed into cubes and spheres. The

fanciful greenery makes the garden look like a child's play area filled with wonderful toys.

The second factor is the scale of the sculptures. So much work goes into the creation of topiaries that other parks often keep their topiaries small and simple. At Disneyland, the finely detailed sculptures in the Topiary Garden are almost all life-size, each one taking up to two years to grow into its shape.

The third and final factor is the painstaking effort that keeps the plants in immaculate condition every day of the year, no matter the weather conditions. Most of the plants are tight-growing, small-leaved shrubs that are meticulously pruned by hand every few weeks. Disney's own "topiary engineers" create, train, and maintain the topiaries, but a San Diego company called Coburn Topiary & Garden Art has also grown and shaped some of Disneyland's plants.

Tour Guides

MAP: TS-2

DATES: September 1958–ongoing

To help novice guests navigate the overwhelming park, a small team of tour guides was added as a Disneyland guest service in 1958. Early on, the tours began at **City Hall** as informal presentations by about a dozen **cast members** wearing their own casual clothes. But the tours were so popular that Disneyland soon had a large team of trained guides who wore official uniforms and gave formalized spiels about the park (in *Window on Main Street*, **Van France** credits **Tommy Walker** with the idea for official tour guides; Martin Sklar's *Dream It! Do It!* says Sklar himself wrote the first script and even led the first tour).

By 1962, the Tour Guide program, led by **Cicely Rigdon**, was operating from what was called the Guided Tour Garden (or just the Tour Garden), a small landscaped area south of the **Police Station** in **Town Square**. Conveniently, guests automatically walked right past this location upon entering Disneyland via the west tunnel. A tour in 1958 cost $3.25 and included several major attractions; five years later, the two-hour Happiness Trip (as a 1963 ad dubbed it) cost $5 and included park admission, plus admission to some attractions (and a free ticket to board any Disneyland attraction at the guest's discretion). A 1964 park flyer describes how the "enchanting" guided tours enable guests to "enjoy several exciting Disneyland rides" while getting "interesting information about Disneyland from your attractive Disneyland Tour Guide."

Tour guides were first presented in Disneyland **souvenir books** in 1962. That year's book includes a photo of a female tour guide wearing the official uniform: a red-and-black plaid skirt, a red double-breasted vest, a white short-sleeve blouse, red knee-high socks, and black flats; not shown was a cape, a cold weather option. In the photo, the guide's black riding hat and a riding crop in her upraised hand add an equestrian flair (Walt Disney implies an equestrian connection when he calls Tour Guides "guest jockeys" in a 1965 episode of *Wonderful World of Color*). Because of their signature clothing, the guides were sometimes nicknamed "plaids."

> **MOUSCELLANY**
>
> The tour guides became popular and recognizable enough for Disneyland to sell a Tour Guide doll, "a true reproduction of the popular Tour Guide Girls" in the traditional plaid skirt/red vest outfit.

The team of guides now includes men and is made up of more than seventy-five **cast members**, many of whom speak more than one language. Like Disneyland, the tours have become more complex, and they now have themes targeting specific interests. Tour options in the twenty-first century have included a VIP Tour (a customized tour booked at an hourly rate) and various tours that run two to three hours long: Welcome to the Disneyland Resort (a general walk through the park); Holiday Time (highlighting winter's holiday traditions); Discover the Magic (including an interactive treasure hunt), Disney's Myths, Mysteries and Legends (held at night), and Cultivating the Magic (focusing on horticulture).

Prices, of course, have escalated over the years. For instance, the three-and-a-half-hour tour called A Walk in Walt's Footsteps (the most popular current tour, a fact-filled walk-and-talk that includes a lunch, souvenir pin, headsets with music and recordings of Walt Disney's voice, and a peek inside his private **apartment**) cost $109 per person in 2016, a price that did not include park admission. While they don't automatically move their groups to the front of attraction lines, tours do usually include some priority seating for a **parade** or show.

Town Square

MAP: Park, P-8

DATES: July 17, 1955–ongoing

The early concept sketches of Disneyland are very consistent in their representations of Town Square; usually what those drawings depict closely resembles the Town Square that was finally built. The famous **Herb Ryman** illustration from 1953, showing a square-shaped, one-acre plaza, a triangular third-of-an-acre green in the center with a soaring flagpole, and a few landmark buildings around the perimeter, was practically a blueprint for Town Square.

As historians have noted, **Walt Disney** carefully crafted Disneyland as if he were a film director laying out movie shots. For example, guests can't see Town Square until it's revealed to them; they enter Disneyland through one of two dark tunnels and then emerge upon a wide, dramatic vista. The move from tight close-up to breathtaking panorama is a cinematic strategy that intensifies the surprise and fixes the sight in guests' memories.

It's no accident that the first view of Disneyland is of an open, relatively calm area. Back in the 1950s, the general public didn't know what Disneyland was or how it was organized, so Walt Disney gave guests a chance to acclimate gradually to his dramatically different park. Town Square, the first area guests entered, was something they were already used to—a small-town civic center (at one time, planners even considered calling Town Square the Civic Center). Mind-stretching areas like **Tomorrowland** could wait; here at the beginning of the Disneyland experience, it was important to get one's bearings while being surrounded by such stable institutions as the **Police Station**, **City Hall**, and **Fire Department** on the west side of the

square, Old Glory and inviting benches in the middle, and the **Opera House** and **Bank of America** to the east. Ahead of Town Square stretched an old-fashioned avenue that could have been a street in any American small town. On the horizon, about three full football fields north of the tunnels, was the first fabulous, yet safely distant attraction: **Sleeping Beauty Castle**. Karal Marling calls this kind of environment "the architecture of reassurance" in her book *Designing Disney's Theme Parks*. Novice guests entered Town Square feeling quizzical and left it comforted.

There's one other Town Square strategy worth mentioning. In addition to orienting his guests to their new surroundings, Walt Disney had to manage the crowds. By spreading guests out across a broad square, he nimbly averted the instant bottleneck that would have occurred every day if guests had walked straight from the tunnels into narrow **Main Street.**

In addition to the "civic" buildings, Town Square is also home to formal entertainment and ceremonies. The **Opening Day** dedication, daily flag-lowering ceremonies, and lighting of the annual Christmas tree have all been held in Town Square. At night, the dignified lighting that outlines the structures (detail shown) is more restrained than the flashier signs that illuminate Main Street's façades.

Because of the wide range of events and its prominent placement at the front of Disneyland, the Town Square buildings and ceremonies are seen in every annual **souvenir book**. Old photos reveal little change in the exterior architecture (though some of the interior functions have changed over the decades). Town Square, thankfully, is timeless.

Town Square Café

MAP: Town Square, TS-7

DATES: December 1976–Spring 1978; October 1, 1983–August 23, 1992

Making an **American Egg House** sandwich were two iterations of the Town Square Café, which existed before and after the Egg House in the same **Town Square** location. The Town Square Café opened in 1976 as a replacement for the **Hills Bros. Coffee House and Coffee Garden**. This choice site was seen by thousands of morning guests as they

headed past the **Opera House** toward **Main Street**. What those guests saw was a full-service, sit-down restaurant for breakfast and lunch, and the only place to eat in Town Square.

After two years, the American Egg House took over the location. Five years later, the eggs were out and the previous café was back in, this time for almost a decade. The Town Square Café redux closed in 1992, and four years later the **Dalmatian Celebration** store opened in its place for the **holiday season**. The site has been a character-greeting area in the twenty-first century.

Town Square Realty

MAP: Town Square, TS-10

DATES: 1955–1960

Listed in all of Disneyland's **souvenir books** through 1959 is a business called Town Square Realty (or simply Real Estate). Located to the right of the entrance to the **Opera House**, this was the actual office of an actual realtor who was selling actual land in Apple Valley, a largely undeveloped area some eighty miles northeast of Anaheim. According to the book *Disneyland: The Nickel Tour*, the office dispensed information, handed out free Disneyland maps, and gave away little pouches of authentic California dirt. With its novelty wearing off, the realtor departed in 1960; a year later, the space was absorbed into the *Babes in Toyland* **Exhibit**.

Toy Story Funhouse

MAP: Tomorrowland, T-16

DATES: January 27, 1996–May 27, 1996

With *Toy Story* a hit in theaters as of late 1995, a play area based on the movie opened in **Tomorrowland** in early 1996. The site was next to **Space Mountain** in the old **Mission to Mars** building, which had been closed since 1992. The Toy Story Funhouse was never meant to have a long run at Disneyland—and it didn't, closing exactly four months later.

Disneyland's version of the Funhouse was based on an interactive exhibit that had been set up at the Disney-owned El Capitan Theater in Hollywood, the glitzy movie palace where *Toy Story* was being shown. After seeing the movie, patrons there could explore an exhibit for more *Toy Story* fun. At Disneyland, the Funhouse was spread over several rooms where guests could play video games, negotiate clever obstacle courses, interact with different displays, and buy photos featuring the movie's characters. A *Toy Story*-themed gift shop added to the fun. Outside the Funhouse stood a temporary stage where a musical show called *Hamm's All-Doll Revue* was presented regularly to standing-room-only audiences (it wasn't standing-room-only because the show was popular, but because there weren't any seats).

With spring about to give way to summer and Toy Story gone from theaters, the Toy Story Funhouse complex was removed in favor of . . . nothing. Two years later, Redd **Rockett's Pizza Port** would start serving pizzas from the old Funhouse location.

Trash Cans

In his book *Designing Disney*, **John Hench** notes how Disneyland's original designers "wanted everything that guests experience . . . to be an entertaining part of the story." Thus Hench and his cohorts "took the most basic needs of guests and turned them into attractions." One of those "basic needs" is the urge to unload garbage, especially when guests already have their hands full with bags, strollers, excited children, FASTPASS tickets, and more.

Just as another essential component of the park, its **restrooms**, are enlivened with a theme appropriate to the area in which they're located, so too are trash cans given creative decorations that identify them with their respective Disneyland locations. This attention to detail even made the first page of the first edition (published in July of 1955) of *The Disneyland News*, Disneyland's official newspaper in its early days: "Even the waste receptacles have the Disney touch, each 'land' having containers designed for its theme and period." Consequently there have been many different styles of trash cans in Disneyland, including faux-bamboo cans for Adventureland, faux-wood for Frontierland, cans with a gothic theme for New Orleans Square, and one with a futuristic design for Tomorrowland.

The traditional metal cans themselves are generally of a uniform shape (vertical box) and size (forty-two inches tall, twenty inches wide), with hinged doors in the upper third. Most have a polite invitation for "Waste Please." A few identify individual locations by name, such as one at **Redd Rockett's Pizza Port**; a few others are shape-specific or color-specific for the immediate area, such as Frontierland's old tree-stump trash cans or the red-and-black-striped trash cans that used to be outside the red-and-black **Pirate Ship Restaurant**. Most of the approximately 1,250 trash cans in Disneyland are placed twenty to twenty-seven steps away from each other (**Walt Disney** himself reportedly paced this distance off). Trash cans are carefully positioned to be easily accessible without obstructing pedestrians. These days, matching recycling cans often accompany the trash cans.

So memorable are the trash cans that a special series of ten collectible pins was produced in 2001. Each pin replicated a different trash can and even had a small swinging door. In 2016, guests could

MOUSCELLANY

Guests may recall Push, a full-size, remote-controlled trash can that would periodically entertain and interact with guests in Tomorrowland about ten years ago.

buy $20 holiday ornaments shaped and painted like Disneyland's trash cans, each one representing a different land or attraction in the park.

Tropical Cantina,
aka Adventureland Cantina, aka Cantina

MAP: Adventureland, A-3

DATES: 1955–1992

Listed in Disneyland's **souvenir books** in the 1950s is an **Adventureland** spot that the books called either the Tropical Cantina, Adventureland Cantina, or simply the Cantina (the latter name was painted on the building). No matter the name, it was always situated across from the **Jungle Cruise**. The signage out front announced that the establishment served "ice cold tropical drinks." The thatched roof and outdoor tables stayed when the new **Sunkist, I Presume** took over this location in 1962.

Tropical Imports, aka Tiki Tropical Traders

MAP: Adventureland, A-9

DATES: 1955–ongoing

Tiki Tropical Traders, renamed Tropical Imports in the mid-1990s, has been serving up **Adventureland** "curios for the curious" for five decades. Located in an exotic hut near the **Jungle Cruise**, the store used to sell merchandise that was less "Disney generic" and more "jungle unusual," including bamboo chimes, shrunken heads, exotic shells, and more. In the 2000s, the store added various juices and snacks to its shelves, as well as plush animals, sunglasses, and other sundries. Near the end of their voyage, Jungle Cruisers drift past painted signs that declare, "all items guaranteed authentic" and "English spoken" inside Tropical Imports.

Troubadour Tavern,
aka Yumz, aka Louie's, aka Meeko's,
aka Fantasyland Theatre Snacks, aka Troubadour Treats,
aka Enchanted Cottage Sweets & Treats

MAP: Fantasyland, Fa-17

DATES: June 19, 1985–ongoing

The tradition of serving fast food next to the big outdoor theater at the north end of **Fantasyland** began in mid-1985. That's when Yumz, a small snack stand, opened at about the same time as Videopolis, a new dance and concert area. The food at Yumz, just like the music next door, was teen-friendly, including quick-serve nachos, pizza, etc.

Another tradition here was to match this eatery's name to whatever was happening on the adjacent stage. When Videopolis began presenting a live show called *Plane Crazy*, Yumz briefly changed its name to Louie's (connecting to Baloo, *Plane*

Crazy, and *The Jungle Book*). The Yumz name was soon restored, and then in 1995, everything in this area was revised as well. Videopolis became the **Fantasyland Theatre**, *The Spirit of Pocahontas* moved onto the stage, and the snack stand was renamed Meeko's, after the *Pocahontas* raccoon. Meeko's offered the same basic snack food as its predecessor. After a couple of years, the theater began showing *Animazement: The Mu-*

> ## MOUSCELLANY
>
> The Troubadour Tavern is the second tavern in Disneyland history; from the 1950s to the 1970s, the **Oaks Tavern** served up fast food in **Frontierland**.

sical and Meeko's got remodeled first into Fantasyland Theatre Snacks and then into Troubadour Treats.

In 2004, when *Snow White: An Enchanting Musical* took over the theater, Troubadour Treats got a new name, some new décor, and a new transformation into the Nestlé-sponsored Enchanted Cottage Sweets & Treats. It was not all that enchanted, nor was it really a cottage, but the Enchanted Cottage did last for five years. The new Bavarian menu included sausages, pretzels, German chocolate cake, and more. To match Snow White's story, items were given fanciful names, like Diamond Mine Delight and Magic Wishing Apple. Outdoor patio seating, specialty coffee drinks, and souvenir containers added to the enchantment.

Even though the **Princess Fantasy Faire** replaced the *Snow White* show in 2006, the cottage retained its name until it was re-troubadoured into the Troubadour Tavern in late 2009. With the new name came new medieval tent décor and new menu items, including stuffed baked potatoes and bratwurst; a 2013 menu revision added some lighter snack options. The most elaborate beverage here might be the Enchanted Cherry Apple Frozen Lemonade, a hot-weather favorite (as is the shaded patio area).

20th Century Music Company

MAP: Main Street, MS-19

DATES: June 20, 1999–ongoing

The cigar store Indian standing on the right-hand side of **Main Street** may seem out of place today, but it serves to remind guests of the **Fine Tobacco** shop that was here during Disneyland's first thirty-five years. After spending the 1990s hosting various collectible shops, at the end of the decade this space next to the **Main Street Cinema** became a fun and fascinating music store.

Offering "new sounds for a new century," the 20th Century Music Company was originally all about tunes (not to be confused with toons). Antique instruments are still displayed on its upper shelves, a century-old, fifty-five-inch-tall symphonion music box stands by the door, and portraits of classical composers hang on the walls.

For Disney aficionados, the music store was nirvana (though the band of the same name wasn't represented). The jam-packed room showcased Disney-related books, sheet music, soundtracks, and CDs by the **Dapper Dans** and other Disneyland entertainers. For a while, special kiosks enabled guests to burn their own customized discs of Disneyland sounds, speeches, and announcements.

Things really started changing in 2011, when the store got a wall of iPad accessories and video games. Three years later, with the musical instruments still on display, most of the actual music was supplanted by pins and lanyards, turning what was a unique Main Street location into another pin-trading venue (the 20th Century Pin Company?). By mid-2015, the only music in the Music Company was a back wall of ninety CDs, plus a small rack with vinyl records of Disney soundtracks. A year later, those $22 vinyl records were supplemented with $35 picture discs decorated with images from prominent Disney movies.

20,000 Leagues Under the Sea Exhibit

MAP: Tomorrowland, T-23

DATES: August 3, 1955–August 28, 1966

Possibly the very last attraction **Walt Disney** worked on before **Opening Day** was the 20,000 Leagues Under the Sea Exhibit. According to Neal Gabler's *Walt Disney* biography, Disney conceived of the exhibit the evening before Disneyland's televised opening and worked on it late into the night with Disney Legend **Ken Anderson**, both of them donning masks for a flurry of eleventh-hour spray-painting. They were desperately trying to get something into the **Tomorrowland** building that would one day house **Star Tours**. Unfortunately, in mid-July of 1955, this building was mostly empty and would remain so for the two weeks that followed.

When it finally opened in early August, the Leagues exhibit didn't have much to do with the future, which supposedly was Tomorrowland's domain. Instead, the exhibit offered a walk-through tour of the nineteenth-century-style sets and props used in Disney's *20,000 Leagues Under the Sea* movie. While a movie set exhibit might seem pretty routine today, it was unique for its time, and guests, able to walk through the sub's chart room, pump room, diving chamber, and more, were elated to be closer to movie-making magic than ever before. Adding to the excitement was the propitious timing. The immensely popular Disney movie had come out in December of 1954, and on March 30, 1955, it had won an Oscar for Best Art Direction—Set Decoration. Thus Jules Verne's tale was still hot in the summer of 1955.

The sets on display included some of the actual interiors from the *Nautilus*, and among the props was Captain Nemo's pipe organ in his lavishly appointed parlor. A large, detailed model of the submarine and Vulcania paintings by **Peter Ellenshaw** contributed cinematic special effects, and a view of the giant squid through the sub's circular viewing window contributed genuine thrills. **Harper Goff** designed the sub and some of the sets, while the golden-throated **Thurl Ravenscroft** provided the narration.

What was intended to be a temporary Tomorrowland placeholder, and never more than an A-ticket attraction, was ultimately so popular that it lasted until 1966 and generated a dynamic Bjorn Aronsen-designed **attraction poster**. Finally, after eleven years, the sets were struck down to make way for the huge remodel that was on Tomorrowland's near horizon. In Disneyland, a reminder of the exhibit now resides in the **Haunted Mansion**, where a ballroom ghost still plays Nemo's pipe organ.

Tyler, Ginny
(1925–2012)

Eventually known as the "Disneyland Storyteller," Ginny Tyler was born Merrie Virginia Erlandson in 1925 in Berkeley, California. She grew up near Seattle and developed talents for telling stories and simulating animal sounds. After landing radio jobs in the 1940s, Tyler began hosting a daily TV show for children (she was billed as Mother Goose) and contributing vocals to novelty records (by the 1950s, she was using the stage name "Ginny Tyler"). Working for Disneyland Records in the early 1960s, she narrated LPs that told the stories of *Bambi*, *Cinderella*, and others.

From January to December of 1963, Tyler began her memorable stint at Disneyland. Named Head Mouseketeer (possibly because she resembled another famous Mouseketeer, Annette Funicello), Tyler led a daily live TV broadcast from the new **Mickey Mouse Club Headquarters** inside the **Opera House**. Seen only on one Southern California station, her segments were paired with syndicated reruns of *The Mickey Mouse Club* TV show. During the show, she interviewed guests and **cast members** and took viewers on tours around Disneyland. Throughout the 1960s, Tyler also provided voices for various animal characters, including the cute squirrel in *The Sword in the Stone*, the lambs in *Mary Poppins*, and the talking parrot in *Doctor Dolittle*. And, according to the book *Mouse Tracks*, Tyler contributed vocals to Disneyland's **Pirates of the Caribbean** and provided the "chilling cackle" for the evil queen in **Snow White's Scary Adventures**.

Later, Tyler opened a Burbank studio named Whimsey Works, where she coached actors. When she was named a Disney Legend in 2006, she delivered some of her acceptance speech in the voices of different Disney characters. Tyler died in 2012 at age eighty-six.

Upjohn Pharmacy

MAP: Main Street, MS-4

DATES: July 17, 1955–September 1970

On **Opening Day**, **Main Street** had a bank, department store, candy shop, general store, and other businesses that would have appeared in an early-1900s downtown area. To add even more authenticity, it the street also included an apothecary. The Upjohn Pharmacy wasn't a joke—the Upjohn Company was a huge pharmaceutical manufacturer founded in 1886 (they're now part of Pfizer), and the Disneyland pharmacy they sponsored was a detailed recreation of what a pharmacy would have been like at the turn of the last century. Meanwhile, a side room displayed 1955's latest pharmaceutical technology.

The pharmacy's location was on the western corner of **Center** and Main, just north of the **Crystal Arcade**. Old-fashioned medicines lined the shelves and antique pharmaceutical equipment (old microscopes, syringes, mortars, and pestles) was on exhibit, but it was the jar teeming with leeches that riveted guests' attention. While nothing was for sale, small jars of orange-flavored multivitamin supplements were given away by the clerks and real pharmacists at the counter.

The Upjohn Pharmacy gets a mention and an illustration in the "Special Shows and Exhibits" section of Disneyland's 1958 **souvenir book**. When Upjohn ceased its park participation in 1970, its corner site was soon split up and transformed—the side room became the **Hurricane Lamp Shop** and the main pharmacy became **New Century Watches & Clocks**.

Ursus H. Bear's Wilderness Outpost

MAP: Bear Country/Critter Country, B/C-6

DATES: March 24, 1972–November 23, 1988

Disneyland has had three outposts in its history. Preceding the **Safari Outpost** and the **Indiana Jones Adventure Outpost** was Ursus H. Bear's Wilderness Outpost, a new store for the new **Bear Country** that opened in 1972. Its name honors the character who supposedly founded the nearby **Country Bear Jamboree**. *Ursus* is also the Latin word for "bear," and outpost is apparently the Disney word for "retail store."

The Wilderness Outpost shared the long wooden building in the back of Bear Country with the **Brer Bar** and **Teddi Barra's Swingin' Arcade** (Ursus's spot was in the southwestern corner). The wilderness merchandise available here included country-style gift items, hand-carved wood products, and the usual Disneyland souvenirs. In 1988, when Bear Country was transformed into Critter Country, the mammalian Outpost transformed into the reptilian **Crocodile Mercantile** (later becoming the Winnified **Pooh Corner**).

Viewliner

MAP: Tomorrowland, T-10

DATES: June 26, 1957–September 15, 1958

Not satisfied with the old-fashioned trains circling Disneyland, the miniature **Mine Train** chugging through **Frontierland**, and the charming **Casey Jr. Circus Train** winding through **Fantasyland**, in 1957 **Walt Disney** decided to add a modern train to **Tomorrowland**. What was modern then, though, hardly looks modern now, so the inelegant Viewliner is usually remembered as one of the oddest contraptions ever to run on Disneyland tracks.

The new **Bob Gurr**-designed train had lots of similarities to other vehicles. The not-quite-figure-eight track, for instance, was only thirty inches wide, the same as the tracks for Casey Jr. and the Mine Train. The Viewliner's sponsor was the Atchison, Topeka, and Santa Fe Railroad, as it was for Disneyland's main train. The cab on the front car was a cut-down version of a 1954 Oldsmobile 88, which meant it had a height of under six feet, two swinging car doors, a car-like windshield, and the semblance of a car's blunt nose and headlight assembly. Inside the Viewliner's cab, the engineer shifted gears with an automobile clutch and drove with a steering wheel. The gas-powered V-8 engine from a Chevy Corvette could accelerate the train to about thirty miles per hour and pull five cars behind the locomotive.

When the Viewliner debuted as a B-ticket attraction in Disneyland's third summer, it had two complete trains, one blue and one red, running on the same track. There were stations in Fantasyland and Tomorrowland, with each train operating from just one (blue in Fantasyland, red in Tomorrowland). Not only were the trains painted differently, but their thirty-two-passenger cars also had Disney-themed names—*Alice*, *Bambi*, *Cinderella*, *Pinocchio*, and *Tinker Bell* for the Fantasyland cars, and *Mars*, *Mercury*, *Jupiter*, *Saturn*, and *Venus* for the Tomorrowland cars (no *Pluto*, since that name applied both to a Disney character and a heavenly body). The trains looped through the two lands and around the sites of what would become important new attractions in 1959—the **Matterhorn Bobsleds** and **Submarine Voyage**.

Almost 1.5 million guests rode the Viewliner, but its days were numbered once Walt Disney began investigating an experimental monorail in Germany. Only fifteen months after opening, the Viewliner closed in mid-1958, and nine months later, Disneyland's **Monorail** was up and running (the Monorail's loading area is right where the Viewliner's Tomorrowland station had been). Attempts to recycle the Viewliner trains into other civic projects around Los Angeles fell through, and two decades later they were demolished.

Village Haus, aka Village Inn

MAP: Fantasyland, Fa-11

DATES: May 25, 1983–ongoing

Back when the Fantasyland Theatre was drawing guests to the northwest end of the **Sleeping Beauty Castle** courtyard, the closest eateries in the immediate area were the little **Welch's Grape Juice Stand** and the quick-serve **Character Foods** hut.

Everything changed in 1983 with the landmark remodel of **Fantasyland**. The theater became **Pinocchio's Daring Journey**, the Welch's and Character Foods eateries disappeared, and the area's main restaurant became the Village Inn. Attached to the back of Pinocchio's building, the Inn was re-styled with an alpine theme, a gabled roof, and eventually a name change to Village Haus.

Two food companies, Sun Giant for the first decade and Minute Maid thereafter, have been the restaurant's sponsors. Inside, wood carvings and toys punctuate the décor, while elaborate wall murals depict scenes from Disney's 1941 *Pinocchio* movie. The menu has grown increasingly well-rounded over the years, shifting from burgers and fries to pizzas, pastas, sandwiches, and salads. A 2011 menu update added some gourmet cheeseburger options along with other new items. In 2015, a dynamic animated menu showed off photos of a fancy pastrami cheeseburger, a BLT flatbread pizza, and more. Seating is available inside and out, the outdoor tables offering views of the **Casey Jr. Circus Train**. Guests dine unaware that below them is a subterranean maze of storerooms, offices, and food-prep areas.

Villains Lair

MAP: Fantasyland, Fa-30

DATES: October 2, 1998–July 1, 2004

For such a choice location—the first store on the right as guests walk north through **Sleeping Beauty Castle** and into the **Fantasyland** courtyard—this charming building sure has gone through lots of tenants. **Merlin's Magic Shop**, the **Briar Rose Cottage**, **Quasimodo's Attic**, and the **Knight Shop** all operated here with varying degrees of success and longevity.

Among the past occupants was **Disney Villains**, purveyor of villain-themed merchandise from 1991 to '96. After a two-year absence, the bad guys rebounded in 1998 with a new shop in the old location. This one, Villains Lair, reprised the dark themes from earlier in the decade. After four years of selling lots of scary costume accessories, apparel decorated with wicked queens, and creepy glow-in-the-dark gifts, Villains Lair began operating on an infrequent schedule and finally closed completely in 2004. Some of the villainous merchandise relocated to other Disneyland stores, among them **Le Bat en Rouge** in **New Orleans Square**.

Wagner, Jack
(1925–1995)

"The Voice of Disneyland" during the 1970s and '80s, Jack Wagner was born in California in 1925. Surrounded by a musical family, he started in show business at a young age and worked for MGM in his teens. As an adult, Wagner got many supporting parts on popular TV shows of the 1950s, among them *Dragnet* and *Sea Hunt*. Fluent in several languages and possessing a warm, resonant voice, Wagner was also a popular local radio personality, which brought him invitations to do some announcing work for Disneyland's **parades** and special events in the 1950s and '60s.

In mid-1970, Wagner replaced actor Rex Allen as Disneyland's official announcer. For the next two decades, Wagner's friendly voice politely requested that riders on the **Matterhorn Bobsleds** "remain seated please," gave cheerful safety spiels at numerous other attractions, delivered official loudspeaker announcements, and introduced the **Main Street Electrical Parade**. Most of these performances were recorded at Wagner's memorabilia-filled home studio a few miles from Disneyland.

Wagner also produced Disney-themed records, did voiceovers on TV commercials, and performed the announcements for other Disney theme parks. He retired in 1991 after undergoing vocal cord surgery and died from a heart attack four years later. Wagner was named a Disney Legend in 2005. Since 1991, Wagner's successor as "the Voice of Disneyland" has been Bill Rogers, whose wife, Camille Dixon, does the announcements for Disney California Adventure.

Walker, Tommy
(1923–1986)

The younger half of the father-and-son Walker team was Tommy, born in 1923. Hired as Disneyland's director of entertainment, one of his earliest assignments was to orchestrate the 1955 **Opening Day** festivities. Walker also helped invent the famous **fireworks**, **parades**, **Candlelight Procession**, and other crowd-pleasing events.

Prior to his Disneyland career, Tommy had been a decorated World War II vet, a USC drum major, and the kicker on the school's football team. He's credited as the composer of the familiar six-note "da-da-da-DUT-da-DUH . . . CHARGE!" fanfare that's still heard in stadiums everywhere. Walker is identified at the end of a 1965 *Walt Disney's Wonderful World of Color* episode as the "Disneyland Coordinator."

Two years later, after a dozen years with Disneyland, Walker left to form his own entertainment company. He went on to coordinate such events as the opening and closing ceremonies of three Olympic Games, Super Bowl half-time shows, the Rose Bowl's Independence Day fireworks, and special performances at Radio City Music Hall. Tommy Walker died in 1986 at age sixty-three while undergoing heart surgery.

Walker, Vesey
(1893–1977)

In July 1955, when he was looking for someone to organize and lead a marching band for **Opening Day**, Tommy Walker didn't have to look outside his own family. His father, Vesey (pronounced "VEE-see") Walker, an Englishman born in 1893, had already led dozens of marching bands, including the one for Marquette University. Vesey Walker's original Disneyland gig was supposed to end after two weeks, but it wound up lasting until 1970.

According to Bob Thomas's *Walt Disney* biography, **Walt Disney** instructed Walker about the band's repertoire: "I just want you to remember one thing: if the people can't go away whistling it, don't play it." Whistle they did, and Vesey Walker's **Disneyland Band** playing in their crisp uniforms is a fond memory for millions of guests.

He was also a familiar presence in Disneyland's **souvenir books**—he appears in every single one from 1955 to 1968, sometimes with two photos, and usually identified by name. Working while in pain in the late 1960s, Walker overcame a rare paralyzing disease to make some final park appearances before retiring in 1970. He died seven years later and was inducted as a Disney Legend in 2005.

The Walt Disney Story, aka The Walt Disney Story Featuring Great Moments with Mr. Lincoln

MAP: Town Square, TS-9

DATES: April 8, 1973–Spring 2005

Legacy of Walt Disney, a tribute to the great man's many accomplishments, ran on **Main Street** from 1970 to 1973. When that corner space became **Disneyland Presents a Preview of Coming Attractions**, the awards and biographical material inside moved to the **Opera House**. The new exhibit replaced the Opera House's previous show devoted to another legendary American, **Great Moments with Mr. Lincoln**, though the Great Emancipator wouldn't be gone for long.

Dedicated by Walt's wife, Lillian, The Walt Disney Story instantly became one of Disneyland's most absorbing exhibits. As the sign out front announced, The Walt Disney Story included everything "from Mickey Mouse to the Magic Kingdoms" and was "presented free by Gulf Oil." Expanding on the earlier Legacy of Walt Disney displays, the Opera House's lobby was filled with artifacts and awards that celebrated Disney's diverse roles as an artist, TV pioneer, filmmaker, and international ambassador of good will.

Original art from Disney's animated films, props from his TV shows, family photos, and early Mickey Mouse merchandise were all on view. Disneyland itself was included via a fascinating high-speed film that showed the park under construction. For many guests, the most compelling display was the accurate arrangement of Disney's actual furniture and decorations from his offices at Disney Studios.

The second part of the exhibit was presented in the 500-seat Opera House theater. There, a twenty-eight-minute film retold Walt Disney's life story. Rare film clips and Disney's own narration took guests from his Midwestern upbringing through the beginnings of Walt Disney World. As entertaining as the film was, guests expressed nostalgia for Mr. Lincoln. So, after closing in February of 1975 for a four-month remodel, the exhibit reopened on June 12, 1975, with Lincoln back onstage, making the attraction on long presentation with a long compound title: The Walt Disney Story Featuring Great Moments with Mr. Lincoln. **Souvenir books** from the 1970s proudly show off the entire exhibit with several photos and detailed text.

Modifications were made to the Lincoln and the Disney exhibit over the following decades, and eventually the Disney film stopped showing altogether. For 2005's **Happiest Homecoming on Earth**

MOUSCELLANY

One of the unique items in the Walt Disney exhibit was the old-fashioned horseless carriage he used in **parades**.

celebration of Disneyland's fiftieth anniversary, Lincoln was temporarily retired once again as the theater was given over to a well-received film called *Disneyland: The First 50 Magical Years*.

Watches & Clocks, aka Timex Shop

MAP: Main Street, MS-13

DATES: July 17, 1955–1972

In 1954, exactly 100 years after its founding, Connecticut's Waterbury Clock Company renamed itself U.S. Time. That was the company's name when its new Watches & Clocks business debuted on **Main Street** on **Opening Day** (old **souvenir books** label it Watches & Clocks, but informally it was called the Timex Shop). The location was a small room one doorway south of the **Silhouette Studio**. Timex watches, which U.S. Time had put on the market earlier in the decade, were the shop's timeliest attractions; already ads were touting them as an affordable timepiece that "takes a licking and keeps on ticking." Many of the timepieces on display had Mickey Mouse faces and are now considered valuable collectibles.

Time finally ran out on Watches & Clocks when **Crystal Arts** moved into this space in 1972. Elgin's **New Century Watches & Clocks** across the way would soon become Main Street's primary watch store.

Welch's Grape Juice Stand

MAP: Fantasyland, Fa-9

DATES: 1956–1981

In Disneyland's first three decades, **Fantasyland** had few eateries, even fewer with a name sponsor. One of the latter was the Welch's Grape Juice Stand (as old **souvenir books** usually label it). Welch's Foods, the juice company founded in the 1800s, also sponsored *The Mickey Mouse Club*, and thus the stand's location was especially appropriate—it shared the building with the **Mickey Mouse Club Theater**. Exclusively promoting the company's main product, the Welch's concession was painted with lavish grape-themed murals. The counter sold cold cups of purple, red, and white grape juice, with frozen grape juice bars an icy option.

In 1982, the massive remodel that overhauled Fantasyland finally ended the Juice Stand's twenty-six-year run. A year later, the beautifully styled **Pinocchio's Daring Journey** and **Geppetto's Arts & Crafts** opened where the theater and Welch's had been.

Westward Ho Conestoga Wagon Fries

MAP: Frontierland, Fr-18

DATES: November 16, 1998–September 2, 2008

This modest little eatery in an out-of-the-way spot alongside the **Rivers of America** actually had several connections to Disneyland's past. In the 1950s, the **Conestoga Wagons** operated near this part of **Frontierland**; some of the wagons even had the words Westward Ho! painted on them.

Westward Ho Conestoga Wagon Fries had another connection to something that still exists today—the similarly named **Westward Ho Trading Co.** Both Westward Ho spots echoed *Westward Ho the Wagons*, a 1956 Disney movie about pioneers on the move. The Conestoga Wagon Fries stand actually resembled one of those wooden plains-crossing vehicles from the 1800s.

There was yet one more connection between Conestoga Wagon Fries and something else in Disneyland. The stand's sponsor, McDonald's, occupied another space, the **Harbour Galley**, in front of **Splash Mountain** until 2008. Both places sold virtually the same thing—McDonald's fries and sodas—until the McSponsorship ended, resulting in the disappearance of Conestoga Wagon Fries (the Harbour Galley continues on but with a different menu).

Westward Ho Trading Co.

MAP: Frontierland, Fr-27

DATES: September 2, 1987–ongoing

After three decades near the **Frontierland** entrance, the old **Frontier Trading Post** was renamed in 1987. The rustic sign out front announced the new shop as the rhyming Westward Ho Trading Co. The first two words allude to *Westward Ho the Wagons*, a 1956 Disney movie starring Fess Parker. For years, a five-foot-tall cigar store Indian, a twin of the statue in front of the **20th Century Music Company** on **Main Street**, stood out front.

Inside, the merchandise used to feature frontier souvenirs and American Indian-themed gifts, but it then switched to gourmet chocolates, jelly beans, and cookies. In recent years the store has sold pins, pin-trading accessories, tin sheriff badges, and seasonal ornaments.

What Will You Celebrate?

DATES: January 1, 2009–December 31, 2010

When the **Year of a Million Dreams** promotion ended after twenty-seven months, Disneyland kicked off 2009 with What Will You Celebrate?, a new campaign that gave guests free admission on their birthdays. Since few guests celebrate Disneyland birthdays alone, the additional paid admissions for friends and family (and all that celebratory dining and shopping) undoubtedly compensated for the giveaway, which continued through 2010. A new promotional campaign called **Let the Memories Begin** followed in 2011 (however, signs for What Will You Celebrate? lingered in front of the **Plaza Inn** well into 2014).

Wheelhouse and Delta Banjo

MAP: Frontierland, Fr-6

DATES: 1974–ca. 1990

In the mid-1970s, these two fast-food eateries replaced **Frontierland's** tiny **Malt Shop and Cone Shop** next door to the **River Belle Terrace**. The Wheelhouse, its name alluding to the nearby *Mark Twain*, was mainly a weekend spot for burgers, sodas, and ice cream; the Delta Banjo, its name referencing a restaurant that had been in this location in the late 1950s (**Don DeFore's Silver Banjo**), sold sandwiches and shakes. By 1990, both spots had been lost to remodels.

Windows of Enchantment

MAP: Main Street, MS-2

DATES: 1969–ongoing

There's a long tradition of big department stores putting imaginative displays in their ground-floor windows to attract pedestrian traffic. Starting in 1969, Disneyland did the same thing with the windows of its own department store, the **Emporium**. The store's **Main Street** location is the perfect place to advertise or promote something: thanks to the Emporium's proximity to the turnstiles, tens of thousands of guests walk right past these windows every day, usually more than once, making the Emporium perpetually one of Disneyland's most-visited stores.

The first window display promoted *Peter Pan*, which was being re-released into theaters in 1969. Since then, scenes from dozens of movies have been recreated with detailed artwork, moving puppets, and "charming three-dimensional vignettes" that delight nostalgic guests and "enchant a new generation" (those quotes come from the display text mounted in one of the windows in 2014 to celebrate their forty-fifth anniversary). While not as intricate or lavish as the permanent dioramas inside the **Sleeping Beauty Castle Walk-Through**, the Emporium's temporary windows still impress guests. Installed after-hours by a team of artists and designers, each installation beautifully evokes the spirit of their respective movies by bringing together detailed backgrounds and moving, spinning, dancing, and flying characters. Not every movie being shown in the windows is a Disney classic from yesteryear: recently, guests have enjoyed a lively display from 2007's *Ratatouille*.

MOUSCELLANY

Timed with 2015's **Diamond Celebration** were the debuts of possibly the most spectacular Windows of Enchantment ever; these used theatrical effects, ascending and descending characters displaying various costumes, and wide turntables to transition between scenes from Disney masterpieces (for *Cinderella*, the scenes switched from a ragged Cinderella with her Fairy Godmother to a gowned Cinderella dancing with her prince—a wonderful effect).

Wonderland Music, aka Main Street Music

MAP: Main Street, MS-13; Town Square, TS-8

DATES: 1960–1972

After spending five years on **Main Street**, the Wonderland Music store settled into a **Town Square** room in 1960. This new location was just north of the entrance to the **Opera House**, a space formerly occupied by **Jimmy Starr's Show Business Souvenirs**. Wonderland sold Disney movie soundtracks and music by Disney entertainers on vinyl records, plus sheet music of Disney songs and rolls for player pianos. Old **souvenir books** label this shop Main Street Music, perhaps to keep guests from looking for it near **Alice in Wonderland**.

Wonderland wandered off in 1972, and eventually the **Mad Hatter of Main Street** filled the space. Today, Disney music can be found nearby in the **20th Century Music Company**.

Wood, C. V.
(1922–1992)

One of the almost-forgotten members of the core Disneyland planning team was Cornelius Vanderbilt Wood, a Texan born in 1922 (some profiles call him an Oklahoman). Wood's background was in industrial engineering. Prior to his Disneyland years, he'd been a manager at the Stanford Research Institute, the same firm where **Harrison Price** worked (Price scouted locations for Disneyland, and Wood helped persuade Anaheim landowners to sell their plots to Disney). Still in his early thirties, Wood was hired as Disneyland's first general manager to help get the park built. Wood brought **Joe Fowler** and **Van Arsdale France** onto the nascent Disneyland project; Fowler would become the construction supervisor, and France would eventually be in charge of training Disneyland's employees.

Harrison Price calls Wood one of the "boldest, smartest, most shameless and colorful characters ever to career through this business" in his book *Walt's Revolution!* In his memoir *Window on Main Street*, Van France describes Wood as a "masterful salesman" who "could easily compete with the legendary P. T. Barnum." France also credits Wood with bringing in corporate lessees like Swift and TWA to help loosen Disneyland's tight financial situation.

It was Wood who oversaw the park's daily logistics: pre-opening, these included such details as having the official **Opening Day** invitations printed up; post-opening, it meant that Wood and his team essentially ran Disneyland, setting everything from park policies to park hours. However, six months after Opening Day, **Walt Disney** suddenly relieved Wood of his duties so that Disney himself, plus a hand-picked committee, could supervise daily operations. Some stories suggest that they had a serious falling out, reportedly because the egocentric Wood may have been taking credit for designing Disneyland (Wood may have considered himself a star, but his boss was a galaxy). Harrison Price writes that a separation was inevitable because of Wood's and Disney's immiscible personalities (the scabrous Wood could easily offend with off-color jokes). According to the *New York Times*, the circumstances may also have involved embezzlement. Bob Thomas's *Building a Company* pinpoints a dummy company Wood set up, to which he signed over Disneyland's merchandising in hopes of quietly collecting on souvenir sales.

Wood responded to being fired by starting his own amusement parks in Colorado, Massachusetts, and New York. Of these, the Bronx site was the most famous. Called Freedomland U.S.A. and promoted as "the World's Largest Entertainment Center" because it opened on 205 acres (as compared to Disneyland's 160), the park operated from 1960 to 1964. Wood, dubbing himself "the Master Builder of Disneyland," was aided by former Disneyland employees. Freedomland was loosely shaped like a map of America, and its themes were taken from American history (one area, Satellite City, pointed to the future). Unfortunately, a fire that destroyed some of the buildings before the grand opening, a serious ride accident in the first month, and a robbery in the first summer all led to immediate financial problems. When the 1964–1965 New York World's Fair opened in Queens, Freedomland U.S.A. declared bankruptcy, and some of its rides were scattered to other parks. Today, the site is home to the Bay Plaza shopping center, billed as New York City's largest retail complex.

Wood later co-founded the International Chili Society, helped bring London Bridge to Lake Havasu in Arizona, co-designed Lake Havasu City, and even landed a small part in a B movie. Wood died of cancer in 1992. Despite his early contributions to Disneyland, all official references to Wood seem to have been purged from Disney's public literature.

World Beneath Us Exhibit

MAP: Tomorrowland, T-6

DATES: July 17, 1955–December 1959

In 1955, the Richfield Oil Corporation sponsored two different locations in Disneyland. One (the **Autopia**) used gas, while the other (the World Beneath Us Exhibit) promoted it.

The World Beneath Us was located in **Tomorrowland** where **Little Green Men Store Command** is today. Disneyland's 1956 **souvenir book** describes the exhibit as a "Cinemascope Technicolor Cartoon & Diorama" telling "the story of oil." That cartoon, titled *The World Beneath Us*, had prehistoric cavemen teaching modern audiences about oil formation, with dinosaurs helping to illustrate the process (the 1958 souvenir book emphasizes the connection between decaying dinos and plentiful petroleum by placing a drawing of a dinosaur in front of an oil rig). The exhibit ended with "the world's most unusual diorama," according to Richfield's ads, a reference to an 840-square-foot "gigantic section-model" of the Earth's crust that incorporated mechanical motion to show how subterranean oil is forced to the surface.

The Richfield exhibit ran out of gas at the end of 1959. In May of 1960, the **Art of Animation** exhibit filled the building with a display promoting Disney's animated movies.

Wurlitzer Music Hall

MAP: Main Street, MS-20

DATES: July 17, 1955–September 1968

In Disneyland's first decade, guests streaming northward from **Town Square** onto **Main Street** encountered the Wurlitzer Music Hall on the first right-hand corner. The Wurlitzer space was big, so that it could display big products—pianos and organs. The 1958 **souvenir book** lists it in the "Special Shows and Exhibits" category, with text describing "daily organ concerts and display of pianos and organs." Pianos and organs were indeed played in the shop (the music could be heard on Main Street), and mechanical player pianos rolled out traditional tunes. Guests were invited to sing along, though it's doubtful many stayed to buy pianos with Disneyland beckoning outside.

The Rudolf Wurlitzer Company withdrew its sponsorship and its instruments in 1968. About a year later, the prominent corner was refashioned as an awards-filled celebration called **Legacy of Walt Disney**.

Yacht Club, aka Yacht Bar

MAP: Tomorrowland, T-10, T-7

DATES: Summer 1955–September 6, 1966

For over a decade, Disneyland had its own Yacht Club, though it wasn't as exclusive as it sounds. Basically serving fast food, the Yacht Club was a freestanding counter-service eatery alongside the **Tomorrowland** lagoon (hence the "yacht" reference). The aquatic theme included an exterior display of nautical pennants; the rest of the building, with its angled roof extending out over its customers, resembled an old McDonald's franchise.

In 1957, the Yacht Club moved to a new site. With the **Viewliner** and its station about to be built, the Yacht Club was lifted and transported about seventy-five feet away from the lagoon (the **Monorail** station would later stand where the Yacht Club had been). The Yacht Club was renamed the Yacht Bar, though the burgers-and-fries menu stayed about the same.

The 1959 **souvenir book** lists a Yacht Bar Dance Area adjacent to the Yacht Bar, a foreshadowing of future developments. In 1966, a major Tomorrowland remodel sank the Yacht Bar for good; a year later, the Tomorrowland Terrace arose nearby with its own zesty dance area.

Yale & Towne Lock Shop

MAP: Main Street, MS-19

DATES: July 17, 1955–1964

Looking for sponsors to help launch Disneyland, **Walt Disney** enticed the Yale & Town Lock Company to set up shop on the eastern side of **Main Street**. Inventor Linus Yale had patented pin-tumbler locks in the mid-1800s and then partnered with Henry Towne to become America's premier lock manufacturer, successful enough to diversify into forklifts and industrial vehicles.

At Disneyland, the Yale & Towne Lock Shop was located just south of the prominent **Market House**. Y & T is in the "Special Shows and Exhibits" section of Disneyland's 1958 **souvenir book**; an illustration shows a lock and a key, with text describing "a complete display of the locksmith's art, from the oldest to the newest." Inside the room, one wall told "The Story of Locks," and another displayed hundreds of keys. This might sound unexciting, but the Lock Shop lasted for almost ten years. Eventually the **Jewelry Shop** took over this space.

Year of a Million Dreams

DATES: October 1, 2006–December 31, 2008

In 1971, Disneyland hosted the Year of a Hundred Million Smiles. Some special giveaways helped count down the wait for guest number 100 million to walk through the turnstiles, a moment that finally occurred on June 17 of that year. Thirty-five years later, as soon as the eighteen-month celebration of Disneyland's fiftieth anniversary concluded, Year of a Million Dreams began, undoubtedly generating a million smiles.

Among the million gifts and opportunities offered to guests as of October 1, 2006, were special pins and **mouse ears**, free meals, invitations to march in Disneyland **parades**, and instant **FASTPASS** badges for quick access to attractions. The biggest giveaways were overnight stays in the Mickey Mouse Penthouse at the Disneyland Hotel and trips to other Disney parks. No purchase was required, and no special qualifications or competitions helped guests anticipate the sudden, surprising appearance of wish-granting Dream Squad members who toted bags with special Year of a Million Dreams logos.

Originally the Year of a Million Dreams was scheduled to last fifteen months instead of twelve, targeting a December 31, 2007, conclusion. But halfway through 2007, the promotion's ongoing popularity prompted an extension to the end of 2008. Given a new name, the Disney Dreams Giveaway dangled a new dream in front of guests—the chance to stay overnight in the **New Orleans Square** rooms formerly occupied by the **Disney Gallery**. On September 18, 2008, hoping to encourage "celebration vacations," Disneyland introduced the promotion that would follow the twenty-three-month Year of a Million Dreams promotion: 2009's **What Will You Celebrate?**, which gave guests free birthday admission.

Yippie Day

DATE: August 6, 1970

One of the most infamous days in Disneyland's history occurred on August 6, 1970. The International Yippie Pow-Wow, more commonly referred to as Yippie Day, was intended to be a "convention" for members of the Youth International Party. Yippies were led by Abbie Hoffman and Jerry Rubin, outspoken activists who staged theatrical pranks and demonstrations to attract attention to their anti-establishment views. In 1969, Hoffman had written in the satirical magazine *The Realist* that "media is free. . . . don't pay for it. Don't buy ads. Make news." The news the Yippies hoped to make at Disneyland involved a lineup of bizarre activities to be staged by protesters on the twenty-fifth anniversary of the atomic bombing of Hiroshima.

Hoffman and Rubin didn't show up, and the farcical "planned" events didn't happen (Porky Pig, a Warner Bros. cartoon character, was not barbecued for an afternoon feast). But 300 Yippies did arrive and began vandalizing landscaping, buildings, and parked cars. They climbed into the rigging of the **Pirate Ship Restaurant** and took temporary control of **Tom Sawyer Island**; they marched while chanting and shouting obscenities; they engaged in shoving matches with security personnel; and they ruined the Disneyland experience for thousands of paying guests.

Disneyland officials, who had been forewarned and were expecting the worst, prepared the park with extra security precautions, including the presence of hundreds of local police officers in riot gear. **Jack Lindquist's** *In Service to the Mouse* details the strong response and the "protecting our own" attitude displayed by the united **cast members**. Disneyland closed about six hours early that day and offered free return admission to guests. Eighteen arrests were made (according to the next day's newspapers, though that number was later raised to twenty-three), and, as Hoffman and Rubin had hoped, the event drew national media attention. Since then, other unofficial "days" have been well-attended and happily celebrated at Disneyland; popular annual events now include Bats Day, Gay Days, and Dapper Day.

Zorro Days

DATES: April 26–27, May 30–June 1, and November 27–30, 1958; November 26–29, 1959; November 11–13, 1960.

To advertise his *Zorro* TV series, which had premiered in October of 1957, **Walt Disney** brought the cast to **Frontierland** for some personal appearances. Zorro Day activities were held on three different weekends in April, May, and November of 1958, plus a November weekend in both 1959 and 1960. The event featured a **parade** down **Main Street** that spotlighted Guy Williams, TV's Don Diego de la Vega (Zorro), on horseback. There was also some swordplay between Zorro and his nemesis, Captain Monastario, as they battled on the *Mark Twain* **Riverboat** and across Frontierland roofs. Williams, named a Disney Legend in 2011, usually followed these battles with afternoon appearances at **Magnolia Park**. Zorro continued as a Disney presence into the twenty-first century; the studio brought him back to TV with 1983's short-lived *Zorro and Son* series, and Disneyland still incorporates Zorro imagery (detail shown) in and around its **Rancho del Zocalo Restaurante**.

In its first decade, promotions for contemporary live-action Disney movies and TV shows weren't unusual at Disneyland; the Mouseketeers from *The Mickey Mouse Club*, Davy Crockett, and the sets from *20,000 Leagues Under the Sea* had all been showcased before Zorro. After Zorro Days, two more movie-related locations, the **Swiss Family Treehouse** and *Babes in Toyland* **Exhibit**, joined Disneyland in the early 1960s. And rooftop battles, it seems, never go out of style—in 2008, another rugged screen star, Indiana Jones, was embroiled in his own rooftop escapades in **Adventureland** to support the latest Indy movie.

"The end of all our exploring
Will be to arrive where we started
And know the place for the first time."
—**T. S. Eliot,** *The Four Quartets*

Select Bibliography

Anonymous. *Disneyland: The First Thirty Years*. Burbank, CA: Walt Disney Productions, 1985.

———. *The Walt Disney Traditions at Disneyland: A University of Disneyland Handbook*. Burbank, CA: Walt Disney Productions, 1967.

Barrier, Michael. *The Animated Man: A Life of Walt Disney*. Berkeley, CA: University of California Press, 2007.

Barron, Lynn, and Ken Pellman. *Cleaning the Kingdom*. St. George, Utah: Synergy Books Publishing, 2015.

Bedford, Annie North. *Little Man of Disneyland*. New York: Golden Books, 1955.

Bright, Randy. *Disneyland Inside Story*. New York: Harry N. Abrams, Inc., 1987.

Broggie, Michael. *Walt Disney's Railroad Story*. Pasadena, CA: Pentrex Media Group, 1997.

De Roos, Robert. "The Magic Worlds of Walt Disney." *National Geographic*, August 1963.

Disney Miller, Diane. *The Story of Walt Disney*. New York: Henry Holt and Company, 1957.

Dunlop, Beth. *Building a Dream: The Art of Disney Architecture*. New York: Harry N. Abrams, Inc., 1996.

Evans, Morgan. *Walt Disney Disneyland World of Flowers*. Burbank, CA: Walt Disney Productions, 1965.

Faessel, Stephen J. *Images of America: Anaheim 1940-2007*. Charleston, SC: Arcadia Publishing, 2007.

Finch, Christopher. *The Art of Walt Disney*. New York: Harry N. Abrams, Inc., 1975.

France, Van Arsdale. *Window on Main Street*. Nashua, NH: Laughter Publications Inc., 1991.

Gabler, Neal. *Walt Disney: The Triumph of the American Imagination*. New York: Alfred A. Knopf, 2006.

Gordon, Bruce, and David Mumford. *Disneyland: The Nickel Tour*. Santa Clarita, CA: Camphor Tree Publishers, 2000.

Gordon, Bruce, and Tim O'Day. *Disneyland: Then, Now, and Forever*. Santa Clarita, CA: Camphor Tree/Disney Editions, 2005.

Green, Amy Boothe, and Howard E. Green. *Remembering Walt: Favorite Memories of Walt Disney*. New York: Hyperion, 1999.

Greene, Richard and Katherine. *The Man Behind the Magic*. New York: Viking, 1998.

Handke, Danny and Vanessa Hunt. *Poster Art of the Disney Parks*. New York: Disney Editions, 2012.

Hench, John, and Peggy Van Pelt. *Designing Disney: Imagineering and the Art of the Show*. New York: Disney Editions, 2003.

The Imagineers (text by Kevin Rafferty and Bruce Gordon). *Walt Disney Imagineering: A Behind the Dreams Look at Making the Magic Real*. New York: Hyperion, 1996.

The Imagineers (text by Alex Wright). *The Imagineering Field Guide to Disneyland*. New York: Disney Editions, 2008.

Jackson, Kathy Merlock, ed. *Walt Disney Conversations*. Jackson, MS: University Press of Mississippi, 2006.

Koenig, David. *More Mouse Tales: A Closer Peek Backstage at Disneyland*. Irvine, CA: Bonaventure Press, 2002.

———. *Mouse Tales: A Behind-the-Ears Look at Disneyland*. Irvine, CA: Bonaventure Press, 1995.

———. *The People v. Disneyland: How Lawsuits & Lawyers Transformed the Magic*. Irvine, CA: Bonaventure Press, 2015.

Korkis, Jim. *The Vault of Walt*. USA: Ayefour Publishing, 2010.

Kurtti, Jeff. *Disneyland: From Once Upon a Time to Happily Ever After*. New York: Disney Editions, 2010.

———. *Disneyland Through the Decades: A Photographic Celebration*. New York: Disney Editions, 2010.

———. *Walt Disney's Imagineering Legends and the Genesis of the Disney Theme Park*. New York: Disney Editions, 2008.

Kurtti, Jeff, and Bruce Gordon. *The Art of Disneyland*. New York: Disney Editions, 2006.

Marling, Karal Ann. "Just Take the Santa Ana Freeway to the American Dream." *American Art* Vol. 5, No. 1/2 (Winter-Spring 1991).

Marling, Karal Ann, ed. *Designing Disney's Theme Parks: The Architecture of Reassurance*. New York: Flammarion, 1998.

Marling, Karal Ann, and Donna R. Braden. *Behind the Magic: 50 Years of Disneyland*. Oakland, CA: The Henry Ford, 2005.

Mosley, Leonard. *Disney's World: A Biography*. New York: Stein and Day/Publishers, 1985.

O'Day, Tim, and Kevin Kidney. *Disneyland Resort: A Celebration of New Magic and Fond Memories*. New York: Disney Editions, 2014.

Price, Harrison. *Walt's Revolution! By the Numbers*. Orlando, FL: Ripley Entertainment Inc., 2003.

Samuelson, Dale. *The American Amusement Park*. St. Paul, MN: MBI Publishing Company, 2001.

Schickel, Richard. *The Disney Version: The Life, Times, Art and Commerce of Walt Disney*, 3rd edition. Chicago, IL: Ivan R. Dee, Publishers, 1997.

Sklar, Martin. *Dream It! Do It! My Half-Century Creating Disney's Magic Kingdoms*. Glendale, CA: Disney Editions, 2013.

———. *Walt Disney's Disneyland*. Anaheim, CA: Walt Disney Productions, 1964.

———. *Walt Disney's Disneyland*. Anaheim, CA: Walt Disney Productions, 1969.

Smith, Dave. *Disney A to Z: The Official Encyclopedia*, 3rd edition. New York: Disney Editions, 2006.

———. *Disney Facts Revealed*. New York: Disney Editions, 2016.

———. *Disney Trivia from the Vault*. New York: Disney Editions, 2012.

———, ed. *The Quotable Walt Disney*. New York: Disney Editions, 2001.

Thomas, Bob. *Walt Disney: An American Original*. New York: Simon and Schuster, 1976.

Van Maanen, John. "The Smile Factory: Work at Disneyland." *Reframing Organizational Culture*. Thousand Oaks, CA: Sage Publications, Inc., 1990.

Watts, Steven. *The Magic Kingdom: Walt Disney and the American Way of Life*. Boston: Houghton Mifflin Company, 1997.

Index

About the Author

This third edition of *The Disneyland Encyclopedia* (named a "Best Reference Book" by *Library Journal*) is Chris Strodder's tenth book. Among his other works are *The Disneyland Book of Lists*, the children's book *A Sky for Henry*, an adventure story for young adults named *Lockerboy*, the comic novel *The Wish Book*, the *Stories Light and Dark* collection of short fiction, a pop culture compendium entitled *The Encyclopedia of Sixties Cool*, and *Swingin' Chicks of the '60s*, a popular .nonfiction volume of profiles that garnered international attention, coverage in dozens of magazines ranging from the *National Enquirer* to *Playboy*, and exposure on national TV and radio shows. Strodder's writing has also appeared in *Los Angeles* magazine, *The Hollywood Reporter*, *The Huffington Post*, *USA Today*, *California* magazine, *Movieline* magazine, and others. Since his first memorable Disneyland vacation in 1966 (before New Orleans Square was built), Strodder has been a perpetual Disneyland visitor and a lifelong Disneyland researcher. Now living by the beautiful Pacific Ocean in Pismo Beach, California, Strodder expresses his gratitude to publisher Jeffrey Goldman and his remarkable team at Santa Monica Press. He dedicates this book to his parents, brother, and sister, four loyal Disneyland fans.

About the Illustrator

Coming from a family of artists and scientists, Tristan Tang enjoyed a wonderfully creative childhood in which she was encouraged to have a strong sense of curiosity and to fully develop her artistic self. She was able to combine her interests in mixed media art forms with cultural anthropology while completing her Fine Art degree. After enjoying rewarding work experiences in photography and scientific illustration, Tang discovered a love for visual effects and has worked as an artist on many films, commercials, and games. Some of her past Disney projects include the film *Pirates of the Caribbean: The Curse of the Black Pearl* and commercials for Disney's Animal Kingdom and Cruise Line. Tang dedicates the illustrations in *The Disneyland Encyclopedia* to her children, Trey and Anya. She thanks her husband, Alex, for his artistic contributions and inspiration on this project and her extended family for their infinite support.